ENRICO CORTE

(+39)3496277829

www.enricocorte.net

917-254-9252

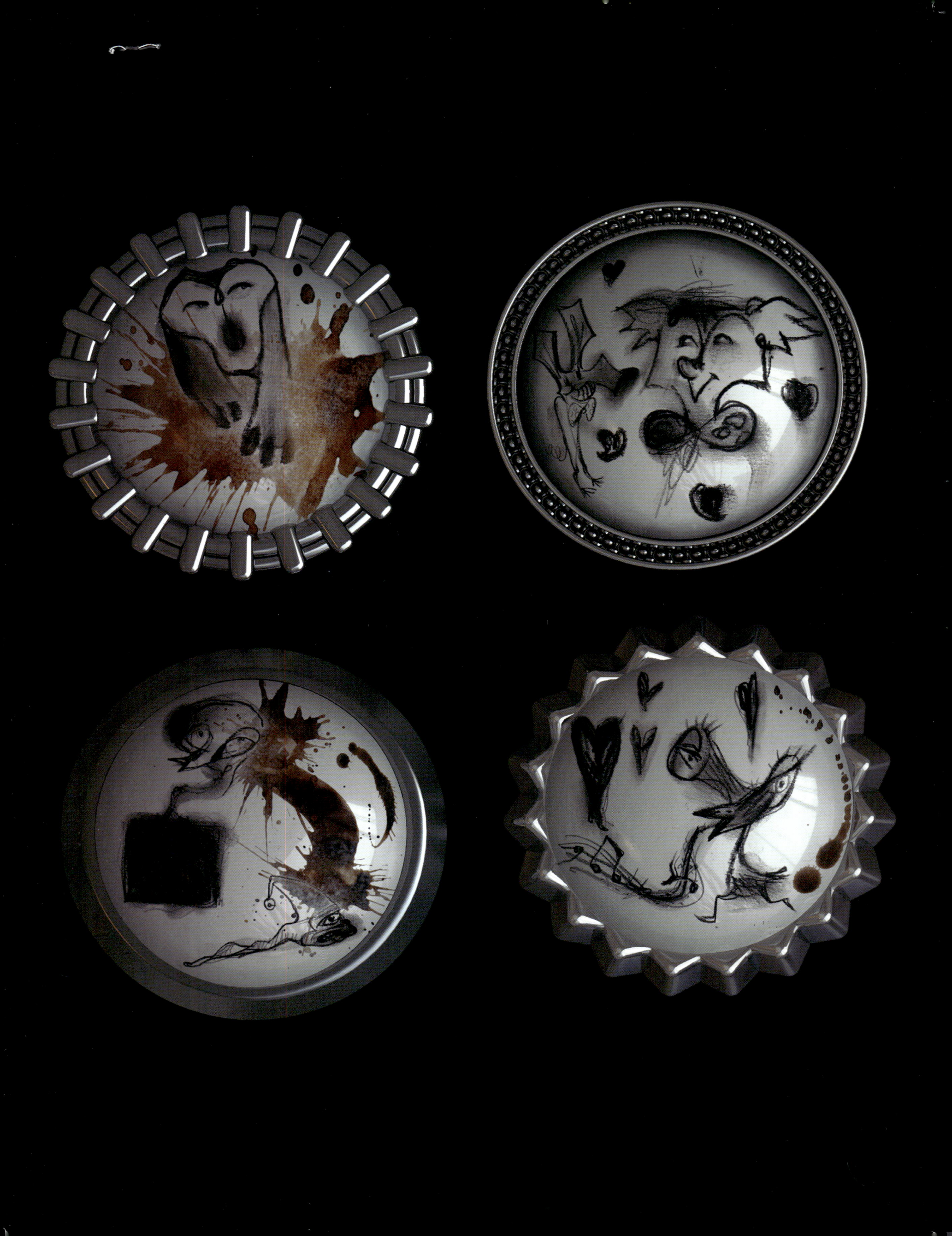

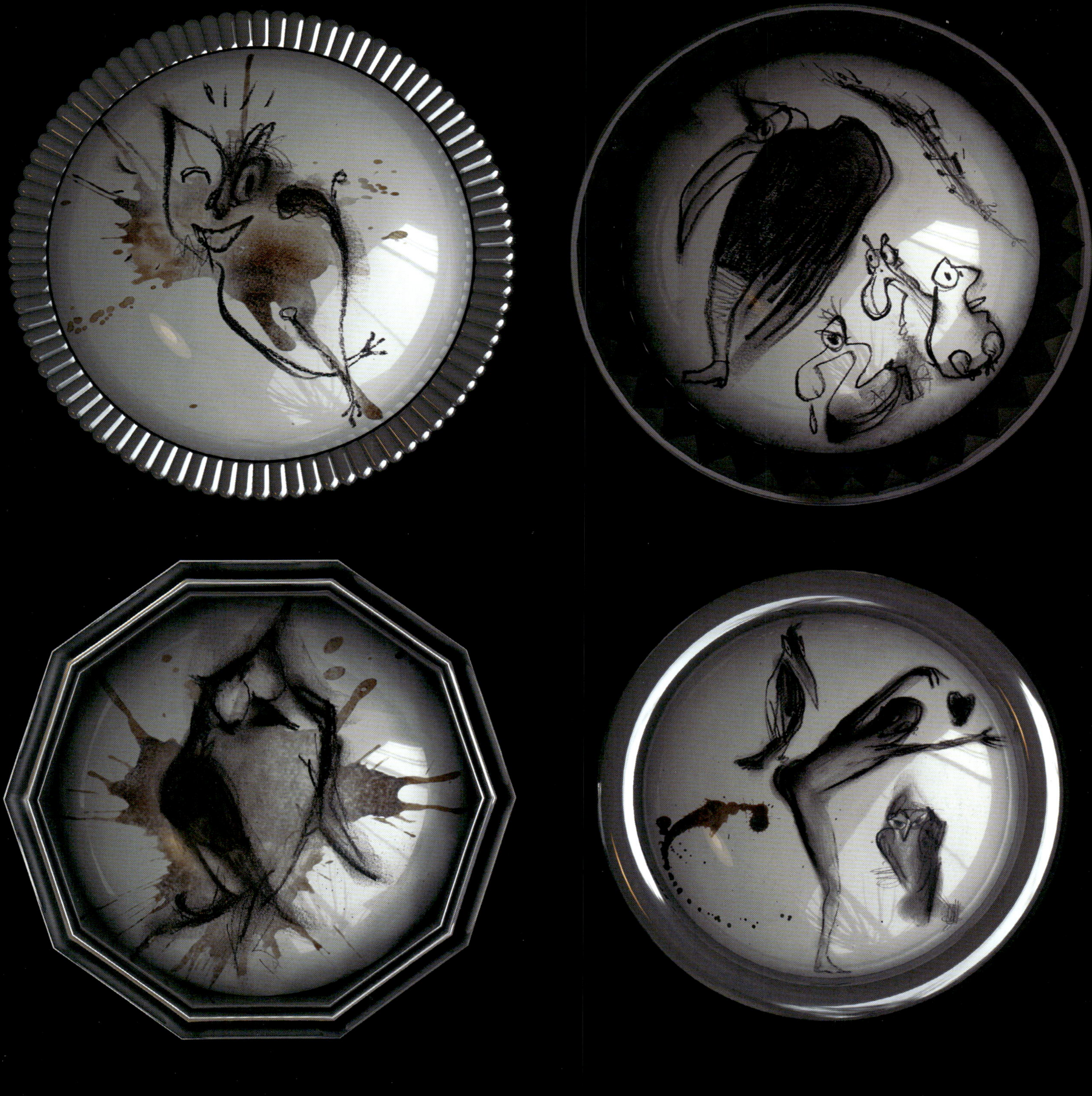

Four Settings at Dusk N°1 and *Four Settings at Dusk N° 2*, 2004. From the *Abstraction of the Void* series. Two lambda prints on cibachrome portraying 4+4 photo-ceramics from charcoal and ink drawings, with metal frames and natural light of sunset. Cibachrome dimension: 39½ x 27½" each (100 x 70 cm); original dimension of each setting: diam. circa 2¾" (7 cm). GC 1591, 1592.

[**Points** *of* **No Return**
in the **Contemporary**]

ENRICO CORTE - SPECTROSPECTIVE

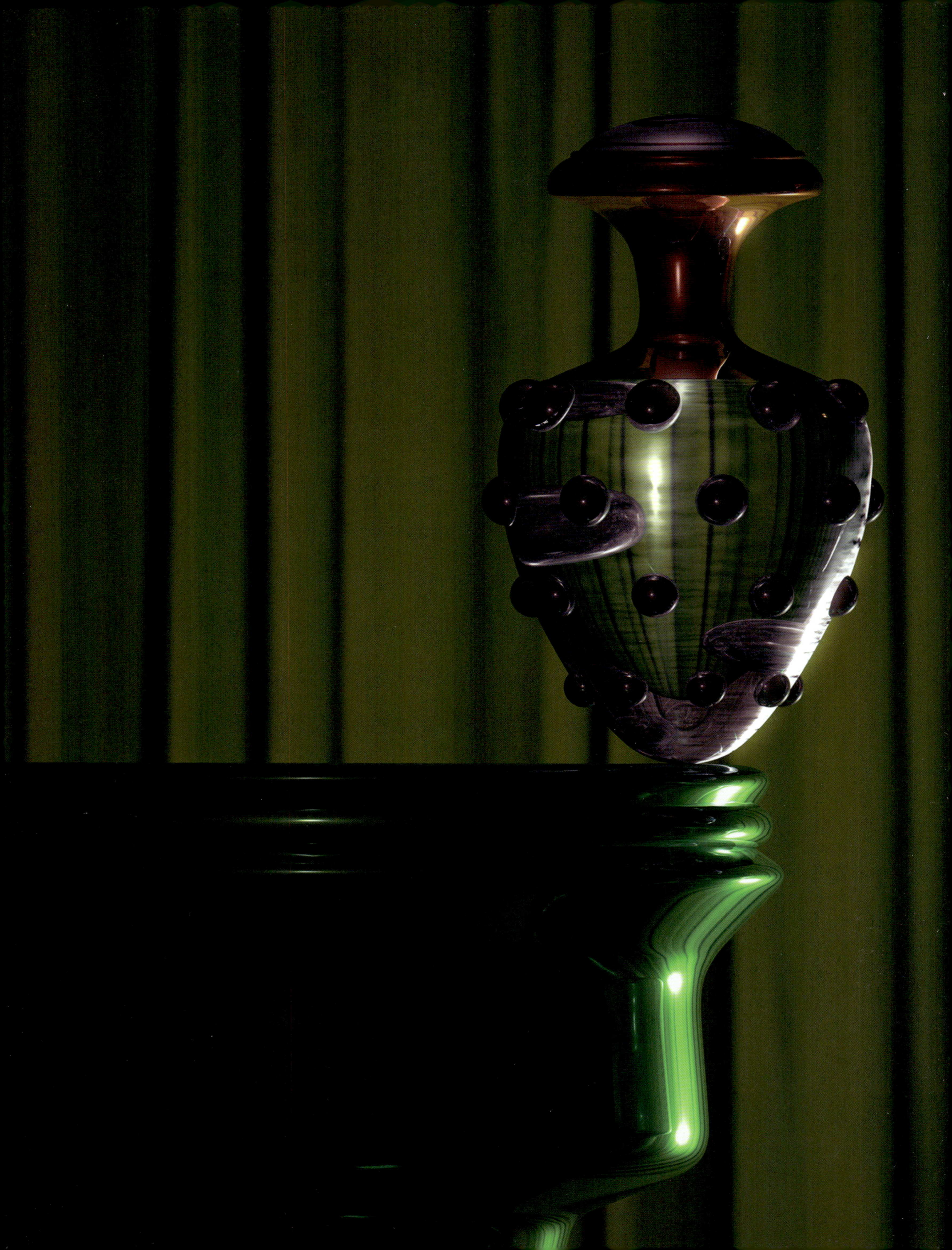

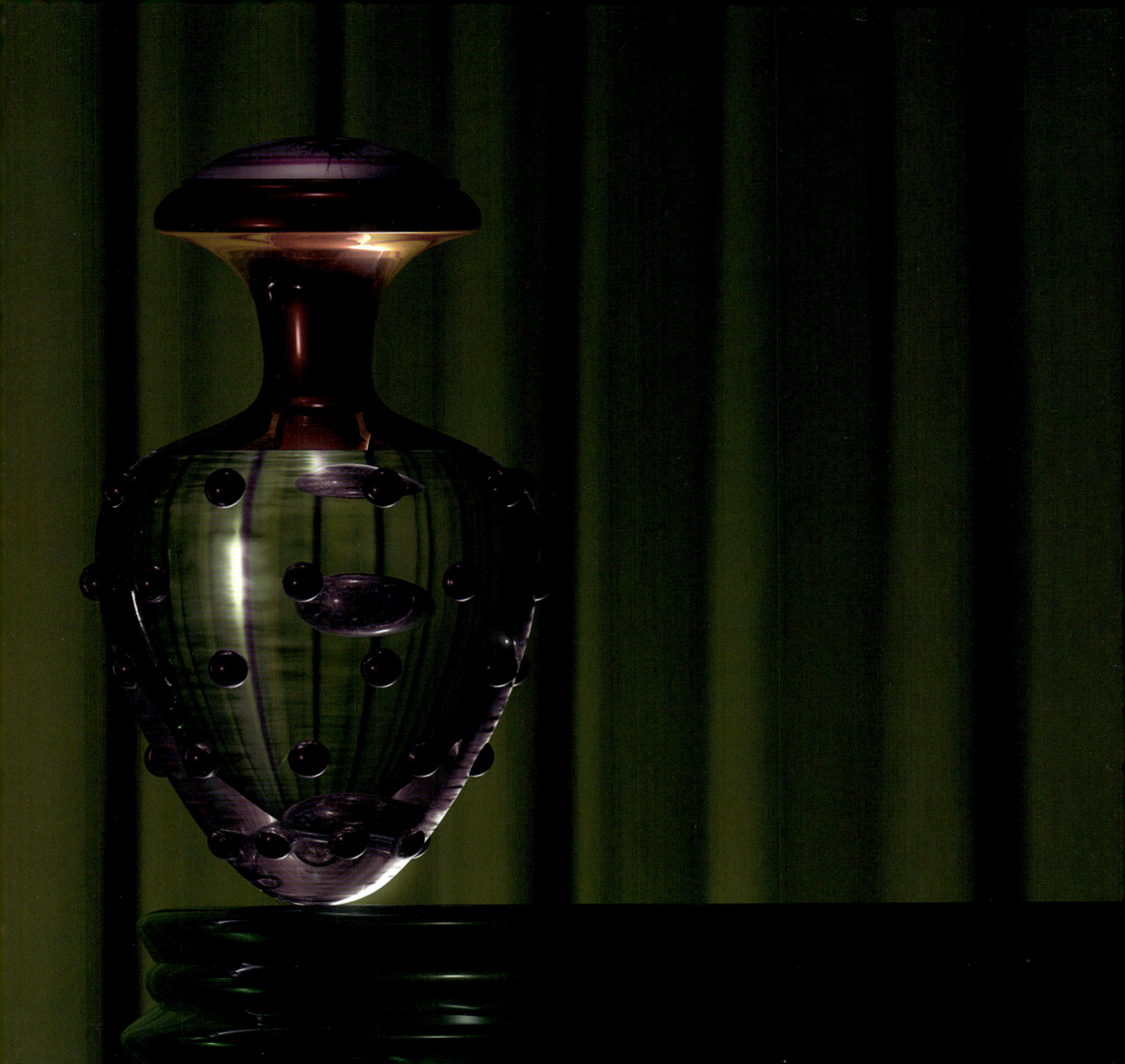

ENRICO CORTE

SPECTROSPECTIVE

ENGLISH / ITALIAN TEXT BY GIANLUCA MARZIANI

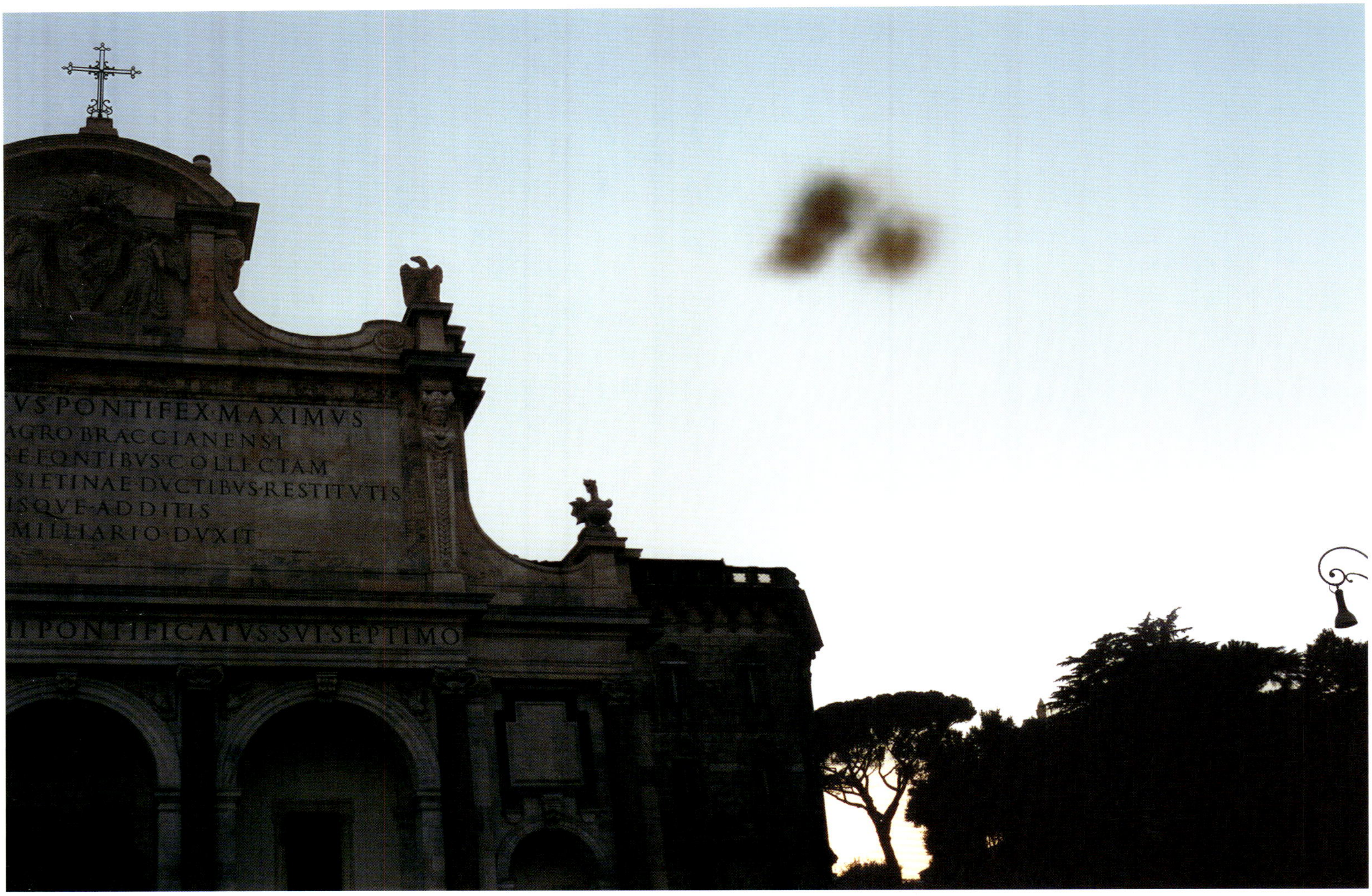

Day-rip Fireworks, 2002. Cibachrome print. 31½ x 42" (80 x 106,7 cm). GC 1452.

Enrico Corte – Spectrospective

translation
Alexandra Corradini, Bleu Harrison, Eleanor Paynter, Brian T. Williams

graphic design by *Nankino*, Rome

acknowledgements
Sean Alicante, Jimmy Bell, Paolo Cipollina, Bartolomeo Coccoli, Laura Colella, Claudio Composti, Mario Delli Colli, Valco De Nero, Alice De Sica, *Divine Photo Studio*, Diana Dubois, Corrado Fantini, Sandra Fedele, Mauro Foschini, Gismondo Gehenna, Syla Gong, Francesco Governanti, Gianni Grandi, Heike Curtze gallery, Orso Levante (r.i.p.), Fred Mascagni, D. Dee Masone, Lisa Norberg, Andrea Nurcis, Sofia Palladini, Gerardo Panico, Cristina Pattuelli, Silvia Pattuelli, Philippe, *Photokrisis SPA*, Alissia Reder, Tomaso Riposati, Paul Saint-Just, S.(o.B.), Max Solinas, Marcus Sonntag, Patricia Suggate, Toby Suran (r.i.p.), Annina Trusso, Giorgio Turboli, Willi Wassel, "Angel" Zard

The progressive numbering of the reproduced works refers to the General Catalogue N° 1 – 1978-2006 (GC), and to the Catalogue of Sketches and Preparatory Studies (SC) of The Enrico Corte Archives (TECA), Rome/Paris. TECA reasoned catalogue is edited by Annamarzia Todeschi

Damiani editore
via Zanardi, 376
t. +39.051.6350805
f. +39.051.6347188
40131 Bologna – Italy
www.damianieditore.com

Printed in Italy by Grafiche Damiani in June 2007
Printed on Magno Satin 150 gr.
distributed by
antalis

ISBN 978-88-6208-006-4

front cover: *Eyes* (detail), 1995-96.
Promo picture for *The Abstraction of the Void* series.

back cover: *Nightlife Butt Plug*, 1997.
Promo picture for *The Abstraction of the Void* series.

«... Don't have anything to do with Enrico Corte. Listen, my advice is to keep him out of the season. Not because he causes problems in the galleries, as far as I know, but because I don't understand the reason for all his... stridency, it makes you anxious. And that's all negative energy, too. It has nothing to do with what you see around you. Better to keep Corte out of the showing in the next exhibitions, believe me...»

Fragment of a message recorded by a critic on the answer-phone of an Italian art gallery.

If *Removal* becomes the subject of a work of art, the artist cannot help but become an *object* of Removal.

EC

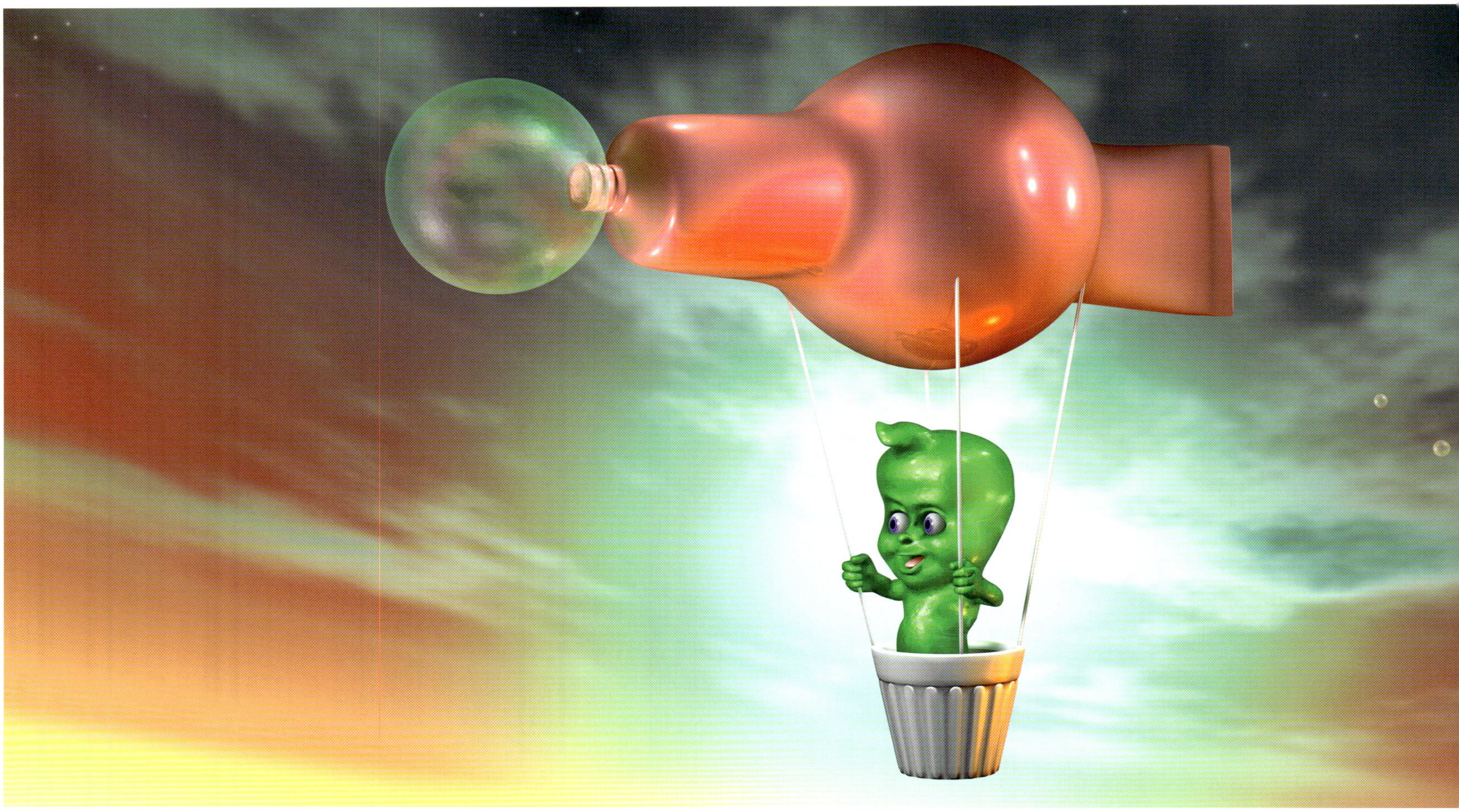

Duty is a game, from the *Fluororama* series, 1996.
Lambda print and cibachrome.
21¾ x 50" (55 x 127 cm).
GC 930.

I had *removed* the cornerstone.

EC

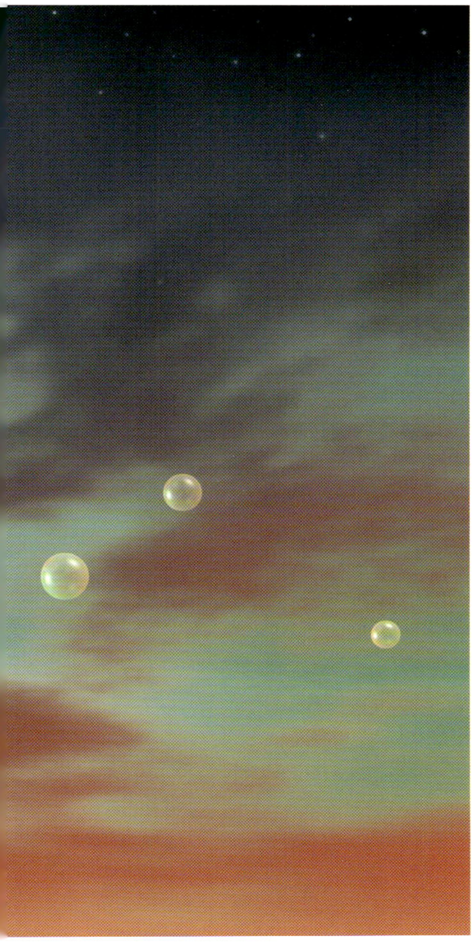

Never before have I experienced a period of such painstaking reflection when editing a text. I have always dedicated time to metabolize ideas, but never at such length as with Enrico Corte's work. We've been meeting for more than a year, during which I've observed his works in the flesh, let my objective perceptions ferment, taken notes, mulled over the works in photographs and digital files, kept my sensations simmering as I added pieces more or less abruptly, contemplated it all still further and eliminated burdensome memories. As I reflect on the more than twenty years of his creative journey, I have come to the conclusion that Corte is a perfect example of fragmentation, radical in its method but unitary in its aims and results. From this I deduce that, amid healthy excess and insane but stunning beauty, Corte's art conceals a clear perception of his deepest self, finely developed relationships between conscience and reality, rigorous connections with his own synapses. Quite simply: the self-portrait of a brain, an inner life which overflows…

The enormous mass of his works is tied to one basic principle: that of a gigantic *portrait of himself* in ways which differ in manner, style and external references. The body of the artist is represented again and again, but with alienating details; at other times we do not see it, but it is there, among figures that are real, absurd or barely plausible. Everything points to a ruthless sounding of his own inner universe, of the talons and tentacles that the mind extends into the outside world. Pragmatism of the western type crumbles, guilty of having produced self-portraits limited to the face and body, as though fantasy and lucid folly were not an active part in telling one's story through the external and the psyche. Differently, certain eastern or "alternative" models reinforce the power of the ductile imagination, of narrating liberating deformations, impossible structures, visions that lie between the absurd and the improbable. Thus, for the first time, the self-portrait becomes a subjective view starting from the artist's optic nerve and revolving around his own neural cells – their inner labyrinth – more than the outer, flat panorama.

In the following pages we will review his creative phases in a mixture of situations and themes, analyzing the membranes of a visual organism and its complicated inner mechanisms. I thought it would be right to alternate practical examples with the dominant themes. Faced with the aesthetic inhomogeneity and conceptual stratification of the works, the thread of clarity unwinds by means of synthesis and order, respect and empathy, passion and courage. Artists like Enrico Corte are a genuine rarity on the international scene: and I do not refer merely to his essential quality, but also to that deep bond with his works and their roots, the constant necessity to produce in order to breathe.

To cite one of Enrico Corte's all-embracing neologisms, I would consider the whole of this volume to be a *Spectrospective*. A strange word that travels through both past and future, taking in the widest possible spectrum of topics and aesthetic solutions. Enrico Corte's Spectrospective confounds all our unquestioned believes: about the relationship between old and new, youth and adulthood, content and container, the obvious and the hidden; it is a complexity that is both useful and necessary: that same complexity which is part of his profound vision of the world, the severe meaning in his way of observing, the unlimited borders of courageous thought. The Spectrospective is a kind of retrospective, and as such it embraces the whole *spectrum* of the artist's themes and techniques, thus providing a *spectral* panorama, because the subjects, references and suggestions which the works generate are often ghostly, too. The figure of the "Young Artist" is redefined (perhaps Corte never was truly young, at least as an artist): the Spectrospective is an elliptical parabola which sets the youthful works alongside those of the "established" artist, doing away with conventional notions such as "Time" and "Maturity" in art (as well as that of "Value", including financial value, which is closely connected to them).

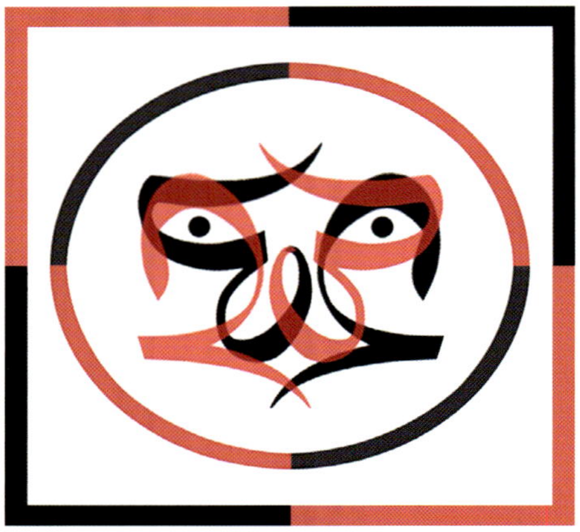

Artist's Logo 23, 1998.
Silkscreen on canvas.
Unnumbered edition.
Variable dimension.
GC 1261.

We should say at once that it is impossible to confine Corte within single categories. His autonomy from all the movements or groups that have arisen in Italy since the arrival of the Neo-expressionism on the international art scene is quite evident (although he began exhibiting in some of the best public spaces and private galleries at the age of eighteen). And yet it is extremely easy to allow oneself to become engrossed in his visual passages with their inhomogeneous grammar, the impressive, unbridled syntax. His ideas incorporate a myriad of extra-visions which are above all form: always a step beyond appearances, beyond the common morality, even beyond ourselves seen as univocal entities. Reflections follow one upon another, overlaying meaning upon meaning, urging one to create chains of questions. The Spectrospective is like that: it ensures the re-elaboration of form, shatters all methodological certainty, follows a meandering talent which repudiates the mannerism of method. Enrico Corte recounts his own inner processes, the cerebral codes, the serious laws of perversion, the geography of a radical outlook: and he does this by mingling excess and poetic gracefulness, Shakespearean might and formal irony. A project entailing spectral mirrors: where the past and future flow along a corridor of distorting surfaces, like a hall of mirrors in a Fun House, passing between necessary fetishes and contemporary references, countercultures which are new cultures, excesses that achieve their own catharsis.

The most obvious element by means of which the artist upsets the evidence of reality is that of the physical matter of things. What we get from the work is not limited to its appearance, to the first cognitive level of figuration. Every material simulates other materials; every play on irony hides paths of layered ethical density; every detail recalls its opposite or something far from its original use; every title circumnavigates the rhetoric of language so as to complete the meaning of the project. A linguistic model is molded on these upsettings, mingling cultural memory, individual themes and contemporaneity, using a power that has the ability to impress by using formidable archetypes of the present. Everything is relative, and much depends on the configurative frame of one's viewpoint: an hour-glass seems to be overturned and breaks the logic of time, just as a candle lying horizontally creates balance, but deviance, too; a hook is set in a position where it cannot support the weight of the picture; the mirror becomes concave, reflecting images upside down; some hinged paintings close the moment you come through the door. How can you get your bearings? Reason lies in the soil of doubt and anomaly, of difference which becomes normality. This theme of upsetting and overturning sums up the more than twenty years of Corte's creative flow. Upsetting form and substance, ideas and content, appearance and stratification. Turning every ingredient into its opposite, every simplification into complexity, every certainty into necessary doubt. The theme of "overturning" even takes us back to one of the first prehistoric representations of the World of the Dead, an archaic Spectrospective at the dawn of human iconography along a ramification where the memory of the artist runs free.

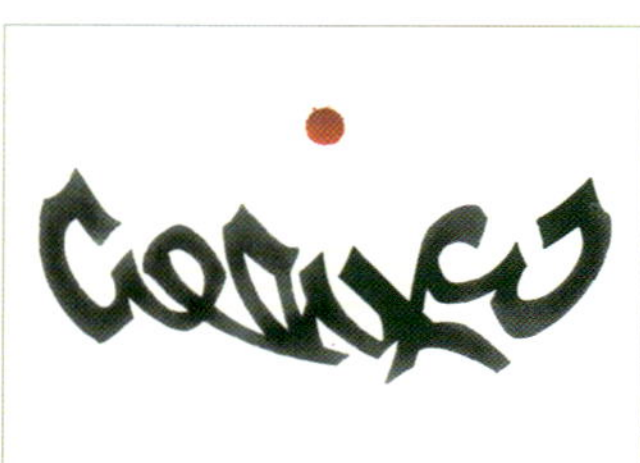

Artist's Tag (Sketch), 1987.
Ink on cardboard. Detail.
27½ x 19½" (70 x 50 cm).
SC 340.

The Spectrospective transforms this book into a mental space, a great opus made up of many works, a center of temporary gravity in which the evident and the hidden breathe the same air. Follow its ferociously mechanical rhythm that interweaves works and reflections. And remember: the flow of the text you are reading, closely traces the dynamism of a Spectrospective that is excitable, contaminated and never definitive, where the artist's life and words also have an important role. Check the data for logical documentation, but you should not think that the chronology points to specific sequential events, for in reality Corte's work represents one organic flow where there are vast numbers of ingredients and everything varies according to the combinations of the moment.

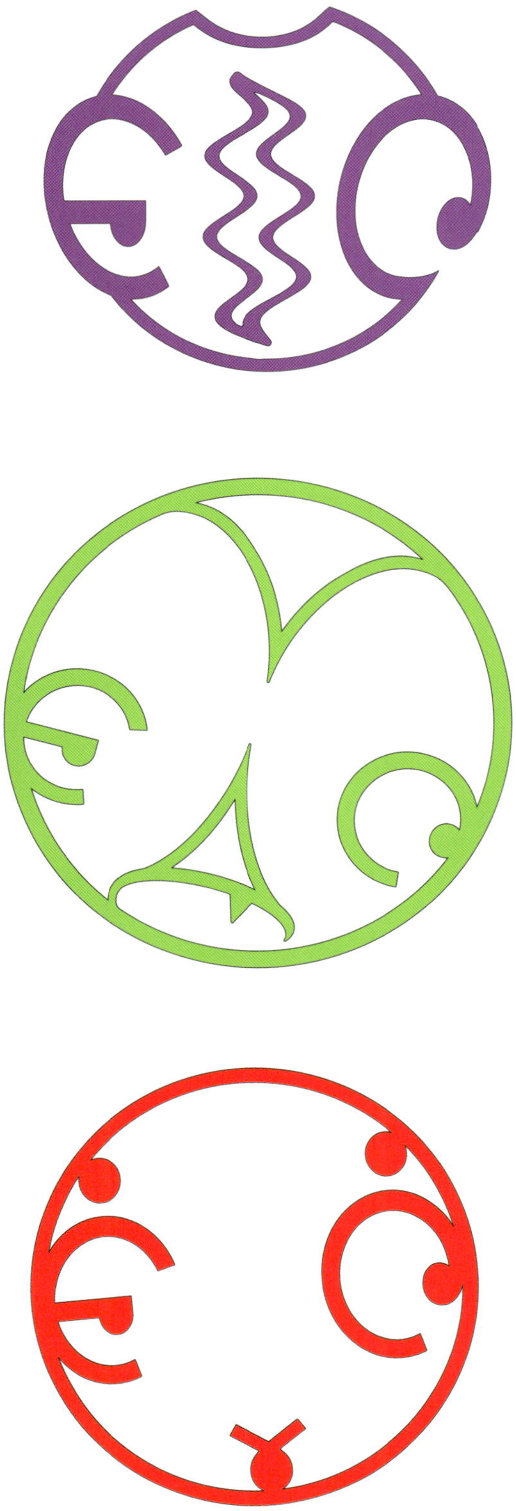

Branding Demoniettos (Artist's Monogram series), 1985.
Study for *The Access Keys* and *The Sacred Fire of Art* (cf. ill. pp. 122, 123).
Six silkscreens on paper (details).
Whole group: 19½ x 118" (50 x 300 cm).
GC 456.

The sequentiality of his journey never appears to show any sign of maturing with regard to the previous piece. On the contrary, every work has its own life, feeding on both the past and future, citation and archetype, details and totality, thus giving every single work an autonomy which frees it from deference to any particular situation, be it historical or spatial. Taking its cue from what life offers the artist, every project is always *here and now*: from birth onwards it constantly journeys through actuality with regard to the individual moment, just like every "classic" which is worthy of respect. Typically, in the classics, the passage of time does not alter the strength of the work, but modifies our interpretation of it. It is the external viewing that is molded in forms more and more elastic and tolerant as they adapt to the numerous hypotheses of the momentary appearance. And here we have hundreds of works that create one single, gigantic, inhomogeneous and tentacular digression with left over pieces that can be re-amalgamated again and again. Everything is recycled; nothing remains useless waste. Each work feeds on the past of the others, taking something of theirs to preserve the integrity of a coherent thought process and its extremely active tentacles.

Enrico Corte was born in 1963 at the very heart of the Mediterranean, in Cagliari, Sardinia, where he pursued his studies in art and literature, and held his first exhibitions. He later moved to Rome, the city where he still lives, thinks and operates. New York, Berlin and London, and to a lesser degree other European capitals, are places where he stays for brief periods but are, nonetheless, of fundamental significance to him. Other areas round off a personal history which shows us the psychically mature figure of Corte: the geographical places, whether chosen or casual, like the flow of life itself, are of great importance to the genesis of his works; they enter his projects, influencing and shaping them. But the works bear no sign of local allegiance and are transmuted into pure creative geography. In the photographic work *Spettrospettiva dell'Umano Destino* (*Spectrospective of Human Destiny*, ill. p. 110) the artist portrays himself as he observes a forest that has been devastated and reduced to skeletal forms by a recent fire, a frequent occurrence typical of certain areas in Sardinia, his land of origin. But, thanks to its title, the episode immediately assumes a more universal character of reflection. Cities themselves become a pretext for experience, just as Rome symbolizes a force which defines each of Corte's projects without ever completely unveiling itself before the eyes of the "average" tourist.

Rome, the epochal high peak of humanism in a centuries-long journey of iconography, stimulates Corte's disruptive impulse: an accumulation of supreme responsibility on the part of the past which, when it enters the works, avoids being specifically cited and survives only by watering down the powerful memory of a particular place. Rome, as a failed reconciliation between past and present... In the artist's work, as in the urban tissue of Rome, the slow practice of stratification ensures that in the end the various differing cultural contributions of the past, present and future generate not a simple sum of these factors but rather, by blending and ossifying, combine such specific weight that they produce a totally *new object*, which is waiting to be discovered, analyzed and classified.

Rome, then, seen as the definitive meaning of catastrophe in History: such a dispersion, pressure and stratification of history that its metabolism is dulled and it collapses into the black hole of contemporary culture, where the laws of creativity are overturned. This is why, in Corte's work, various artistic techniques (photography, painting, video, sculpture, and so on) are often placed alongside each other, if not totally distorted: but above all, in a more general sense, he brings together manual skill and industrial production, street-culture and academia, decadent vices and childhood enchantment, creation and self-destruction.

At the meeting point between lightness and immanent heaviness, thrust and force of gravity, one is always balanced on the edge of survival, one step from catastrophe, from the precipice, from psychic collapse. Now we shall see how all these elements take shape over the course of time and in individual works, since it is only on the material plane that we contemporaries can distinguish what is sterile from what is still fertile.

Among the first works that define the figure of Corte after his emergence from his student apprenticeship, when he was already well aware of the practice of contemporary art, we should mention the series of drawings entitled *250 Mele Marce* (*250 Rotten Apples*, ill. pp. 69-73), where we discover various elements which we will find again when analyzing his future works. It is a series of 250 self-portraits in chalk and charcoal on crudely cut rough paper, of the type butchers use to wrap raw meat. The artist, an adolescent at the time, chose to work almost entirely on the basis of an "office work" logic that demeaned the myth of "inspiration". Thus, by working in methodical fashion, he created one self-portrait every day over the period of a full year, beginning on May 10, 1978, and ending on May 9, 1979, but keeping the weekends, public holidays and his birthday free: in all, 250 "working days" for the same number of self-portraits. The artist did not always have at hand the rough paper, characteristic of this series of works, so on certain days he did the self-portraits on rusty iron objects, or aging wooden panels, found by chance on the street. At the end of the "working year," the final self-portrait shows us the artist with a "flat-top" haircut that he had cut that same day, whereas in the previous drawings he is seen with locks flowing down to his shoulders.

The *250 Rotten Apples* series is important because it contains several keys to understanding Corte's work: the perverse methodology, obsessive and sarcastic when faced with artistic creation, and the unripe sexuality of the adolescent who offers himself up to the public (immolating himself like many Punk rockstars at that time), whose feverishness is evident in the gestural-expressionist style, whose sense of guilt transpires in the way the stroke is smudged, and whose immature sexual ambiguity is emphasized by the presence in some drawings of scenes from latrines or public toilets. Even the length of his adolescent hair is an indication of the duplicity of the "gender" theme: the artist/youth with his long hair and indeterminate features is clearly very similar to a girl and has some lineaments that are almost interchangeable, yet the radical haircut in the last drawing may turn everything upside down, indicating both a maturing virility in the adolescent (more like a man), and also its opposite: the definitive loss of virile strength (cf. the myth of Samson and Delilah), or perhaps premature aging on the basis of "experience" gained.

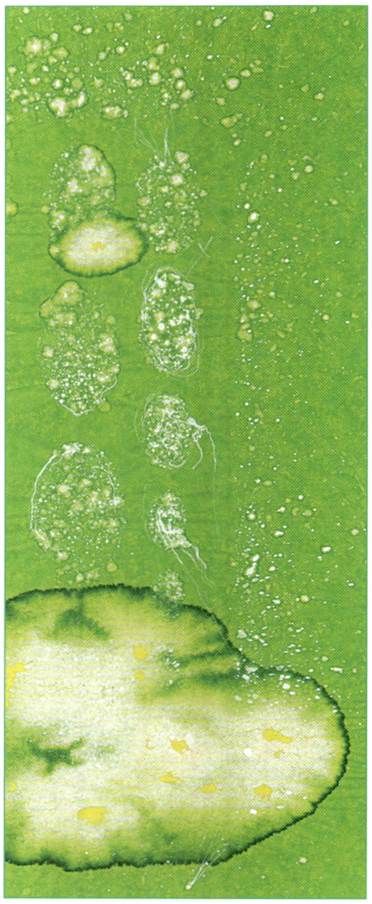

Detail of an "acid" drawing from the *Gastric Juices & Suctions* series, 1979. Creation here coincides with destruction.

The adolescent artist talks about what he knows best – the contradictions and tensions of his own age – and the physical materials that make up the works outline Corte's psychic self-portrayal. Every object, surface, patina, color, finish, outer coating or detail indicates a precise relationship between the idea and its formal practicability. The single piece always foresees a functional stratification that is directly connected to the inner vision. The butcher paper indicates a visceral quality, just as in other drawings tissue-paper is used to suggest the idea of fragility and evanescence. The work becomes an organic surface, a dense but rigorous fragment that mirrors the artist's thought as it is modulated. Each and every element is marked by meticulous, fanatical workmanship, but at times, as in a Yin/Yang symbol, it also contains a little of its opposite: the nervous gesture which "dirties" the result, or even destroys it.

This is what happens in the series of adolescent drawings from the same period, entitled *Flussi & Riflussi Stoici* and *Succhi & Risucchi Gastrici* (*Stoic Ebbs & Flows* and *Gastric Juices & Suctions*, ill. pp. 74-83). The first series is a group of drawings made by mixing sanguine pencil, human blood (the artist's) and animal blood (from the butcher's shop), as well as other colors in the red range obtained from edible, hence "visceral", materials (tomatoes, wine, etc.) that are used to draw images. In one drawing in particular, traces of the artist's sperm may, perhaps, be included in the "edible material" category. The other series of drawings, *Gastric Juices & Suctions*, also in pencil and tempera, is done on sheets of superimposed colored tissue-paper, which are then partially decomposed by using various types of corrosive acid spread with a brush (creation and destruction here coincide), together with a few drops of genuine human bile used as paint. To increase the "acidic ratio" of these paintings, he also added drops of lysergic acid (LSD) mixed with the tempera.

Corte uses the raw material of human waste and manipulates it as form and color, rehabilitating its original, liberating imprint. Liquids and substance melt like malleable material, by now a true abstraction in relation to the social status in which it was hoped to entrap them. The psychic self-portrait expresses its own structure by means of the materials which sustain the body and life itself. In both series of drawings, the themes suggested by the images – that emerge from these blends of organic material and scraps of pulpy paper – hint at nightmare childhood visions and kidnapping by aliens, in which barely defined figures appear, often in groups of four, and surround the child's bed or cradle at night, ready to steal him away. Geometrically-shaped masks, oversized mosquitoes, cats with gleaming eyes, hooded shadows, or even four of Snow White's dwarfs are the many visual substitutes for the removed image of the Alien, personification of the absolute menace. It should be said that in those years the subject of kidnapping by aliens and their psychic "removal" was not at all widespread in the visual arts: cinema and literature dealt with it in terms of science fiction, but the scientific analysis of the phenomenon (through regressive hypnosis of presumed victims, and so on) was only just beginning. Corte, in any case, seemed to be more interested in addressing the purely psychic phenomenon, limiting himself to a more general context of dreams or obsessive nightmares as a variant of an oppressive uneasiness which was to find other incarnations in subsequent works.

Other figures in Corte's work are the eyeballs in tuxedo, bow tie, top hat and indefinable facial features, arranged in a circle, which appear in the three identical sculptures of 1979-1980 entitled *Penta-Portraits* (ill. p. 84). They are the mysterious members of the Californian band The Residents, four (but are they actually four?) faceless, ageless brilliant experimenters with no name of their own: fore-runners of contemporary sounds, adored in those years by the young Enrico Corte, who came directly into contact with them and created various works referring to their obscure shock-image, which was established in a definitive form by the publication of the album *Eskimo,* a masterpiece of the year 1979. Corte was interested in the co-existence of visual forms and the methods of sound, but above and beyond the simple homage paid by a fan, which is beneath the artist, The Residents here assume a specific role. Corte maintains that this San Francisco band's particular approach to musical material, which is very difficult to categorize according to the canons of rock, electronic or "non-academic" music, is not so much a musical *style,* as is the case with many other bands, but represents its own musical *genre*, divided in turn into various sub-styles that spread through the band's different projects and records.

As well as the sense of mystery, it is the idea of absolute creative autonomy that fascinates Corte: the fact that one can work with coherence even though not identifying oneself with any one stylistic label (New Wave? Contamination? Contemporary music?) but experiencing them all and indeed anticipating them in a startling way – even managing, with extreme experimentalism, to appeal strongly to the broad rock-music public. It was the type of method that Corte had by now chosen for his own artistic activity, and this is why *Penta-Portraits* represents the band of four elements augmented by the inclusion of a fifth, indistinguishable member (a fifth eyeball in tuxedo), almost suggesting the artist's identifying himself as yet another member, or urging everyone else to identify with that member, and thus gradually swell the ranks of the mysterious masked group (abandoning any pre-established identity, be it geographic, social or sexual). Placed inside a tube of clear, swaying plexiglas that hangs from the ceiling, these five portraits of The Residents really seem to come from a "fifth dimension" tele-transported here by a luminous plasma ray.

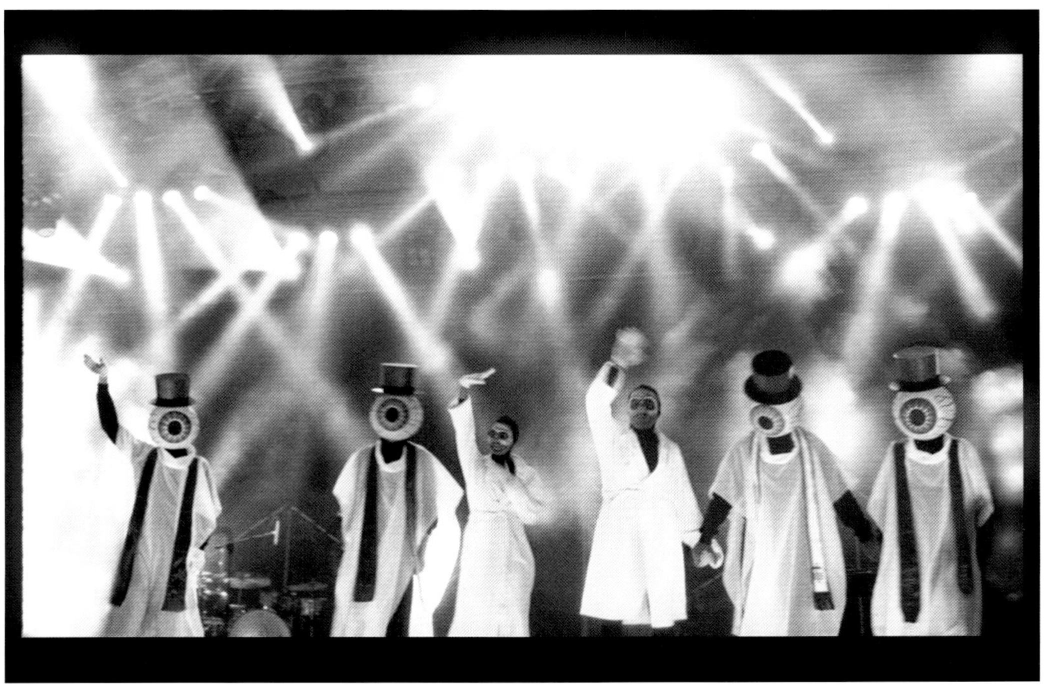

The Residents in concert, Arezzo, Italy, 1998. Photo by Corte.

In that same period, Enrico Corte – who was then, we should remember, between sixteen and seventeen years of age – also began to produce photographic works. The reason seemed to be the same as that given by other artists: «it didn't cost anything». If it is the artist himself who poses as a model, there are even fewer problems. In reality, Corte often chose to entrust others to take the actual picture – amateur photographers, for example – limiting himself to deciding the framing, pose and surroundings. Even when asked professional photographers to contribute, he told them to use an amateurish approach, and always avoided images that were too glossy. He only used the self-timer on a few occasions. *Pelle & Ossa* (*Skin & Bones*, ill. p. 85) dated 1980, is an example of the photographic re-use of the tubular sculptures *Penta-Portraits*, positioned as a background for a picture of the artist himself, in which Corte, after voluntarily rationing his food and reducing his weight to 40 kg, appears gaunt, as he performs a drum roll using two genuine human ribs as drumsticks. Quite literally: skin and bones.

The use of body manipulation and constriction recalls the Body Art tendencies of the previous decade, or perhaps anticipates those which would emerge in the 1990s. The reference to playing an instrument in a hallucinated or necrophiliac way is related to a branch of Rock music which was dissonant, abrasive and smugly degenerative (No Wave and such). It also seems that fasting to the point of wasting away was common then for boys of that age who wanted to dodge the draft. Rapid weight loss is also a common effect in young people who use substances like amphetamine or speed. In any case, the work should be viewed in the context of adolescence, seen as a symbolic moment of crisis and experimentation with various experiences, in which many social contradictions are mirrored.

Colored tissue paper cutout is the main feature in a series of works that Corte began to produce in 1980, sometimes including them in more complex mixed media works which he still continues to produce right up to this day. These are portraits of people – friends, acquaintances, or just occasional passing figures, all quite real and recognizable – created by cutting out the silhouette of their faces in profile on the tissue paper, which has been folded over several times. When it is unfolded, one sees the characteristic perforated arabesque, like a snowflake, but in this case made up of people's profiles. The figurative image thus exists in a formal *void*, and experiences a powerfully ambiguous condition, at the limit of the non-perceivable, ignis fatuus, phosphene, within the visual structure of the picture. The works of this type, hundreds over the years, appear set in a context of delicate decoration and childish play, whose visible result is similar to a hypnotic mandala. But this is one of Corte's first disguises, or pitfalls, which he uses as a tool to put across quite different intentions. What are the real psychological processes which lead a boy, a *painter*, to relate to the models that he portrays using this particular method? We asked the artist himself, and this was his reply:

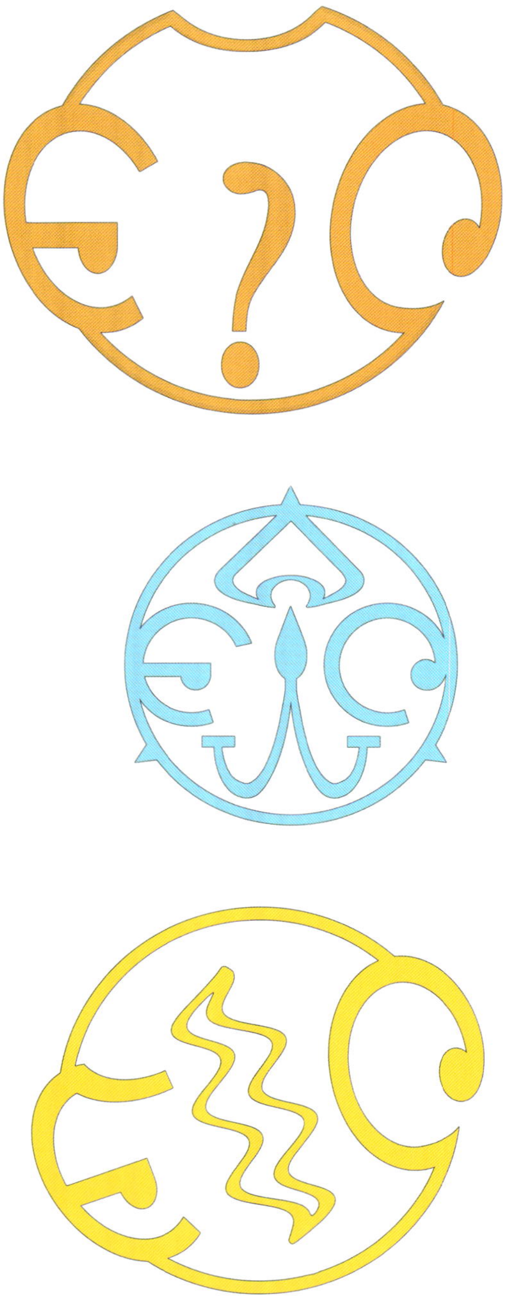

Branding Demoniettos
(Artist's Monogram series), 1985.
Study for *The Access Keys*
and *The Sacred Fire of Art*
(cf. ill. pp. 122, 123).
Six silkscreens on paper (details).
Whole group: 19½ x 118" (50 x 300 cm).
GC 456.

[Recording date: August 12, 2002 – excerpt]

In 1980 there I was, looking around and asking myself the usual adolescent questions, such as: how could I portray the total mental degradation, the disorientation in a life without reference-points, the dizzying effect of social hypocrisy, the annihilation of the dignity of man and the artist, the catastrophe of art, and the implosion of civilization that surrounded me? And how could I do so without falling into some figurative commonplace, into vain images of denunciation, or over-ambitious paintings of the wild or expressionist type that were so fashionable at the time? I had to be sharper and more subtle. First of all, I had to use *masks* to put people off the track and invent a visual paradox which was apparently quite distant from the nightmare that I wished to portray. I decided that I needed a mimetic figurative element that would camouflage, but at the same time concentrate everything into one single stylistic element, which would be fruitful and effective, just because of its concision, its absence of waste, visual overburdening, involvement and passion.

With all the grace and elegance of my youth and without the slightest effort, I immediately found what I was looking for. If I was interested in fragility, the inevitability of fracture, the crumbling of reality and psychic collapse, then I must use tissue-paper. And it must be in bright colors. If I was fascinated by the dizziness of the abyss, the thrill of disorientation, the lack of any foothold or reference point whatsoever, then I must create a whirling arabesque of holes and little bottomless ravines on paper; a decoration that would be neat and dainty. I observed people, as well: the flow, even more disorientating to my eyes, of masses of people, young and old.

Recognizing that there was a distance, perceiving them as elusive, I sought to decipher the reason for their presence, to find a collocation, a logic in the interchangeability of their roles. I had to sketch their features, fleetingly describe the profiles of each of these figures who were otherwise unfathomable, opaque, distant: the holes in the paper had to be cutouts of people's profiles. By folding tissue-paper over and over, a cutout profile would effortlessly become a thousand profiles; I didn't care if they were the same or different, as long as they were lost among the shards of life's mirror.

It was even possible that a kind of map of the human genetic code would emerge, manipulated by Aliens: an algebraic theorem of reproduction based on leveling-out and indifferentiation, on multiples, clones, biological robots... visions of this kind. All born from the simple line of a profile. People who were friends or just passers-by on the street – I used everybody's features. The first subjects of these cutout-portraits were the schoolmates of my adolescent years. More often, I used the profiles of those who helped me in producing a work – for example the photographer I used for a photographic work – or people who were around as I worked on it.

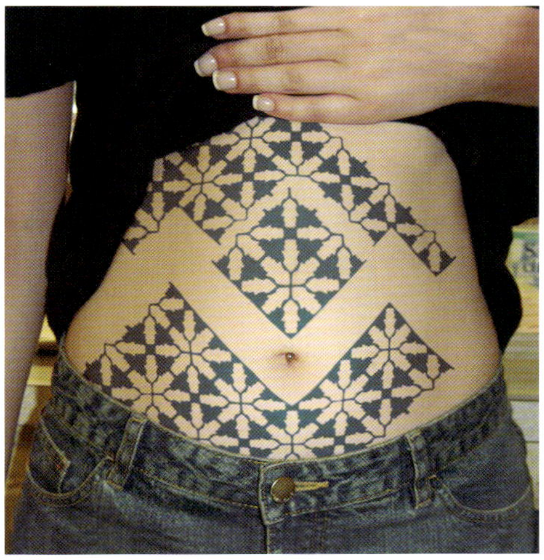

Tattoos inspired by Corte's *Cutout-Portraits*, 1988-89.

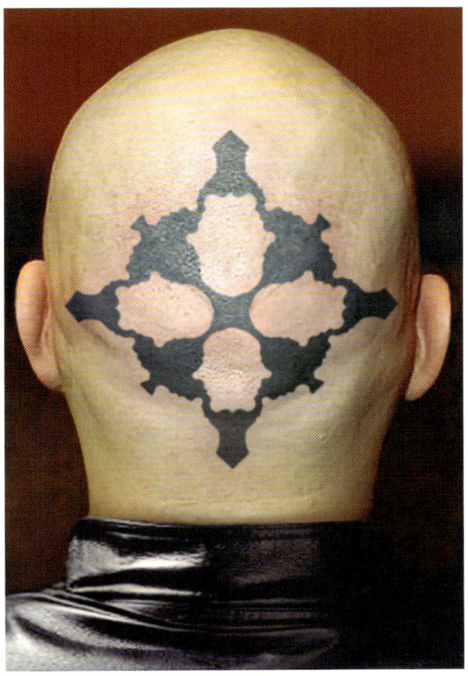

It was just one of the ways, basically, in which a painter creates his portraits and relates to the world around him. And by relating in that way, with such simple means, using a game of paper cuttings repeated ad infinitum which may be acceptable in a child but inappropriate and idiotic in an adult, in the long run I touched the true crux of the matter. Which was? Obviously to praise the multicolored elegy of childhood regression and the compulsion to repeat – repeated gestures that produce an even greater repetition of figures – like the unstoppable explosion of a grandiose death wish, of the deepest black. I find all this fantastic. Everything comes together, everything is therefore expressed with ease and expressive synthesis, masked to the right degree and ready to begin its game of hidden persuasion around the world. I was sixteen: I had *removed* the cornerstone.

Various considerations of a moral kind arose. For example, given that these pictures with their tissue-paper cutout-portraits had no inner figurative factor which could act as a point of reference, apart from minimal formal variations in their backgrounds, they could be hung indiscriminately, upright or upside down, without much changing the result. So that was one less worry... The next move was to further emphasize this characteristic by inserting little hooks at unlikely points on the frames, thereby also giving the future purchaser of the piece yet another possibility when choosing how to hang it. You get the best results when you manage to hang the picture upright on the wall, but with the hook and nail in the lower part of the frame, so that the work seems to defy the force of gravity, and appears to be about to fly away, held down by a mere nail in the wall.

I am told that I have a gloomy kind of sensitivity, and in fact I am at once attracted by the obscure side of a picture. In the sense that my eye always falls on the part in shadow, that shadow which the lighting in the gallery, museum or collector's house throws on the wall to the side of the frame. In my opinion, paintings *must* throw a shadow. When you are an object, a strong shadow is a sign of character. In this sense, I understand the critics and art connoisseurs who look for depth and substance in works. With greater "depth" you will have, of course, more shadow on the wall. Merely thinking of pictures which have the hook and nail at the bottom instead of the top, and thus tend to fly upwards, implies that the picture will come away from the wall and throw a beautiful clear shadow on it.

There are innumerable psychological processes that lead an artist to develop a particular way of structuring his own pictures. Apart from his own explicit declarations, we can add that the tissue-paper Cutout-Portrait model is an attempt, though not entirely successful, to maintain a *constant* in the infinite varying of forms from one work to another: a "center of gravity", a sort of "compass". These portraits of real people may likewise indicate a wish to maintain real contact with the world, even though from a regressive viewpoint, within a flow of works full of schizoid figurations. The very notion of Regression can be read using the old key of "classical" psychoanalysis (regression-denial), but more recent interpretations (Cooper, Deleuze-Guattari) reveal it, instead, as a powerful, revolutionary deflagration. In the end, as always, everyone is free to see whatever they wish in these *Cutout-Portraits* (ill. pp. 87-89 and 91).

Per Strada (*On the Street*) and *Youthanasia 1* are two photographic works which again portray the artist. The first (ill. p. 92) is a color photograph taken by a professional photographer following specific instructions from Corte, who then re-colored the image in watercolor because the photographer claimed artistic authorship. The young Corte appears here in a nocturnal city scene that is damp and menacing, seated in an ambiguous waiting posture on a bench flanked by two silk cushions stained with his own blood as if he were sitting in a grotesque kind of drawing room. It is the first work which suggests the theme of under-age deviance, prostitution, the agonizing encounter with the "Other", in darkness with only a few vague reference points. The alternative title of this work is *Quadrangoli Luminosi (Luminous Quadrangles)*, with reference both to the lighted windows in the background, and to the square silk cushions that reflect the light of a street lamp.

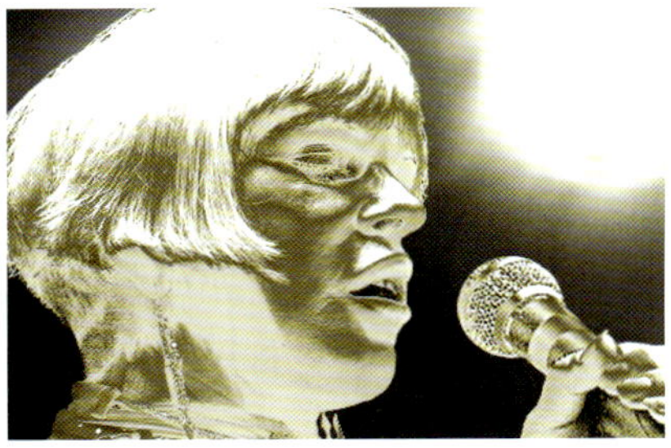

Throbbing Gristle reunion concert, Berlin, 2005. Photo by Corte (detail).

Youthanasia 1 (ill. p. 93) seems to be set in a disused public toilet, and perhaps alludes in a less oppressive way to the previous theme. Corte here portrays himself as a New Wave youth – as indeed he was – wearing a striped T-shirt (an item of clothing much favored by young people in Italy at that time) on which there are three badges of musical bands he had made by hand: the cloth is also torn at the level of the nipple (the nipple as a fourth badge). Behind him, a series of shapeless, lumpy little sculptures in wax, hair, thorns and various objects, like superstition fetishes (*Fatture*, in Italian), are mounted on pedestals fixed to the wall. If we look closely at the bands represented by the badges – specific references to generation, geography and personal taste – we see that nothing is casual, and everything contributes to revealing the artist's intentions and personality. Three seminal English bands like The Pop Group, Throbbing Gristle and Public Image Limited, are cases of an extreme approach to musical material, in which the search for a violent visual image is also relevant. Among other things, at least two of these bands confronted the theme of prostitution in physical and moral terms: the Pop Group with their well-known single *We Are All Prostitutes*, and the TG, still under the profile of the COUM-Transmission group of young artists, in their *Prostitution* exhibition at the ICA Gallery in London in 1976. PIL were *themselves* prostitutes, more or less. (I mention such small details to illustrate how, from his earliest pictures, Corte's work would always be saturated with hidden or semi-invisible references to the world which surrounded him at that precise cultural moment, with the reflections projected by that world onto his own personal passions or interests).

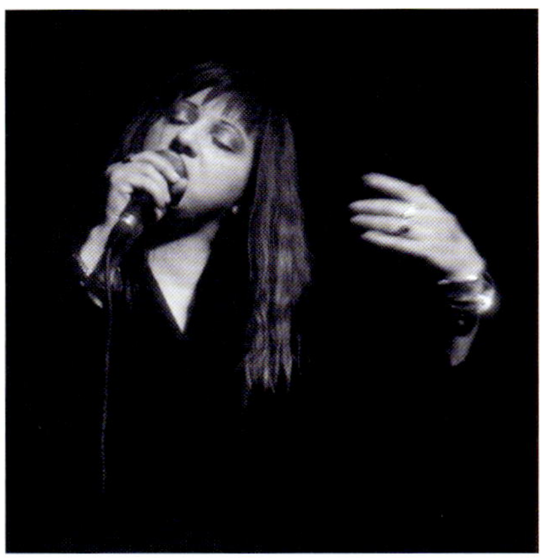

Lydia Lunch in concert, New York, 1999, photographed by Corte.

It should be said that, as his own sources of inspiration, Corte has almost never cited other visual artists of the past or present, as he has the representatives and albums of certain musical trends, for example the 1978 LP *No New York,* produced by Brian Eno as a collective instant-manifesto of New York's "No Wave", that featured four basic and frenetically self-destructive bands: James Chance's Contortions, Lydia Lunch's Teenage Jesus and Jerks, Mark Cunningham's Mars, and Arto Lindsay's DNA. The musical trends and projects which Corte witnessed as they were born and then grew up with (an appropriate example is *No New York*, but there were also bands of the late seventies that he listened to at the age of 15, such as Père Ubu and, obviously, Suicide) without doubt involved and influenced him as much as – if not more than – other visual artists from the past, or his own contemporaries (e.g. the Viennese Aktionists).

Music would always be the "sub-plot" on which the artist developed his visual projects. The badge, a characteristic object used by young people, which became widespread after the rise of Punk, is also the subject of other 1982 works, *Bad-ge* and *Nipping Nipple* (ill. pp. 100, 101): these are genuine badges with appropriate pins, in one case with malignant, bubonic and tumor-like growths in the place of the band's name (the pun in the title *Bad-ge* highlights the "wicked" roots of the object), and in the other, with a hyperrealistic nipple in wax which the artist sought to substitute for his own real nipple through the invention of a new type of piercing. Corte's aesthetic approach favors the contrast between formal appearance and content. A universe which speaks of color, music, figurative imagery, layered composition and popular culture in its less caption-like meandering. The result is like a little brooch, a badge: brilliant and ironic at a distance, wicked and deviant as soon as you approach, enthralling and painful when you touch it or put it on.

Courtesy: the artist.

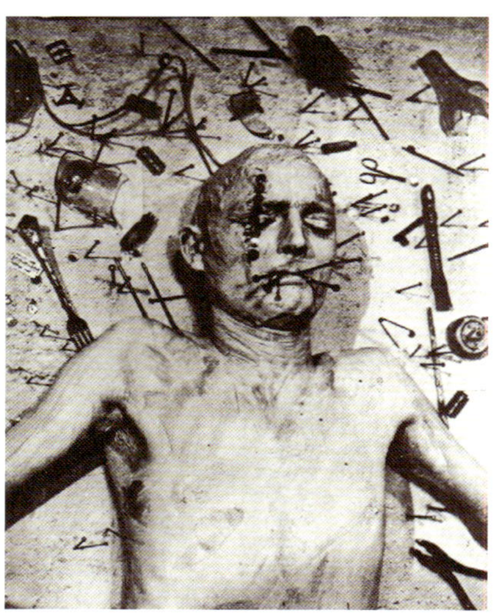

Günther Brus, Viennese Aktionist in the '60s. Corte wrote about him in a thesis published in 1988.

The main theme of the works produced by Corte in his passage from seventeen to eighteen years appears to be the extolling of the self-destructive impulse. Apart from the *Cutout-Portraits*, works like *Cheese*, *Youthanasia 2* and *3*, *Der Weg Zum Kubismus* and the various *Balconies* are infinite variations on this theme. Each one brings with it a complex history that reveals a great deal about Corte's particular operative method. I asked the artist to tell me in his own words about one of these, *Cheese* (ill. p. 94), and he showed me a newspaper article from his home city, which he considers to be the best possible descriptive comment on the provincial environment in which he was then working. With the precise intent of counter-attacking the social and cultural situation around him, Corte had already made certain choices, rather than others, in the artistic field, when he was very young. So, as not to be held hostage by his surrounding provincial reality, he exacerbates it, bringing it to a public crisis and destruction, and thus freeing himself of it. I entrust myself to his own direct and colorful words in explaining how. There, in a nutshell, can be found the various motives and attitudes which will return in his future works, in that so-called – presumed – maturity. Note how the artist, through his own eyes, starts from the present and voyages towards the past by means of a typical slowed-down, pythonesque tempo, with an exhaustive description of the most minute details, then suddenly makes a leap forward in years or even decades, but always maintains a detached position in the eternal present of his mind.

[Recording date: January 30, 2003]

A strange conception of art is the title of this little article which appeared in *Tutto*, a provincial daily paper published when I was a boy – in particular on page 3 in the issue of 4/2/1981. An ex-girlfriend of mine had saved this clip for twenty years; she recently sent it to me in Rome, thinking I'd enjoy it. The article is signed *C. De.* and I seem to remember that this corresponds to the name of a certain Carlo Devoto – or perhaps Corrado, and possibly Devoti – a freelance writer I met once and haven't seen since, and who even at that time didn't seem all that young to me. The text is embellished with a little photograph, grainy in its rough printed version which, after twenty years, has grown even paler. The caption states: «The student Enrico Corte». In that photograph, I appear in the foreground while a movement of my hand in part obscures my face. The photo was taken in haste, without me knowing it, and for that reason I don't remember the precise moment. I do, however, remember all too well the rest of the story described in this newspaper article, which I'll now re-read to you.

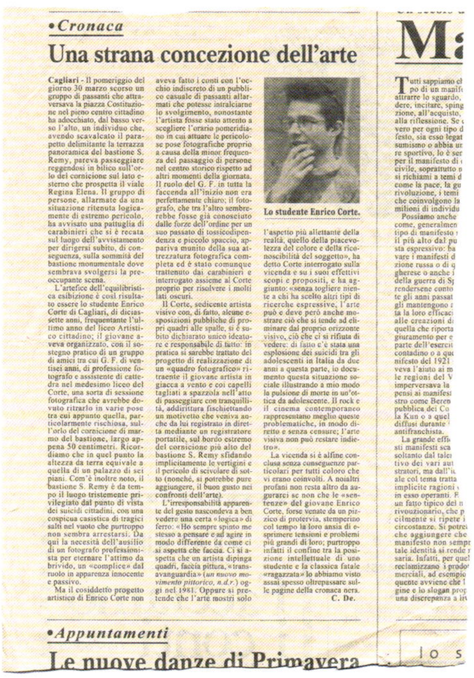

•Cronaca

Una strana concezione dell'arte

Cagliari - Il pomeriggio del giorno 30 marzo scorso un gruppo di passanti che attraversava la piazza Costituzione nel pieno centro cittadino ha adocchiato, dal basso verso l'alto, un individuo che, avendo scavalcato il parapetto delimitante la terrazza panoramica del bastione S. Remy, pareva passeggiare reggendosi in bilico sull'orlo del cornicione sul lato esterno che prospetta il viale Regina Elena. Il gruppo di persone, allarmate da una situazione ritenuta logicamente di estremo pericolo, ha avvisato una pattuglia di carabinieri che si è recata sul luogo dell'avvistamento per dirigersi subito, di conseguenza, sulla sommità del bastione monumentale dove sembrava svolgersi la preoccupante scena.

L'artefice dell'equilibristica esibizione è così risultato essere lo studente Enrico Corte di Cagliari, di diciassette anni, frequentante l'ultimo anno del liceo Artistico cittadino; il giovane aveva organizzato, con il sostegno pratico di un gruppo di amici tra cui G. F. di ventisei anni, di professione fotografo e assistente di cattedra nel medesimo liceo del Corte, una sorta di sessione fotografica che avrebbe dovuto ritrarlo in varie pose tra cui appunto quella, particolarmente rischiosa, sull'orlo del cornicione di marmo del bastione, largo appena 50 centimetri. Ricordiamo che in quel punto la altezza da terra equivale a quella di un palazzo di sei piani. Com'è inoltre noto, il bastione S. Remy è da tempo il luogo tristemente privilegiato dal punto di vista dei suicidi cittadini, con una cospicua casistica di tragici salti nel vuoto che purtroppo non sembra arrestarsi. Da qui la necesità dell'ausilio di un fotografo professionista per eternare l'attimo da brivido, un «complice» dal ruolo in apparenza innocente e passivo.

Ma il cosiddetto progetto artistico di Enrico Corte non aveva fatto i conti con l'occhio indiscreto di un pubblico casuale di passanti allarmati che potesse intralciarne lo svolgimento, nonostante l'artista fosse stato attento a scegliere l'orario pomeridiano in cui attuare le pericolose pose fotografiche proprio a causa della minor frequenza del passaggio di persone nel centro storico rispetto ad altri momenti della giornata. Il ruolo del G. F. in tutta la faccenda all'inizio non era perfettamente chiaro; il fotografo, che tra l'altro sembrerebbe fosse già conosciuto dalle forze dell'ordine per un suo passato di tossicodipendenza e piccolo spaccio, appariva munito della sua attrezzatura fotografica completa ed è stato comunque trattenuto dai carabinieri e interrogato assieme al Corte proprio per risolvere i molti lati oscuri.

Il Corte, sedicente artista visivo con, di fatto, alcune esposizioni pubbliche di propri quadri alle spalle, si è subito dichiarato unico ideatore e responsabile di tutto: in pratica si sarebbe trattato del progetto di realizzazione di un «quadro fotografico» ritraente il giovane artista in giacca a vento e coi capelli tagliati a spazzola nell'atto di passeggiare con tranquillità, addirittura fischiettando un motivetto che veniva anche da lui registrato in diretta mediante un registratore portatile, sul bordo estremo del cornicione più alto del bastione S. Remy sfidando implicitamente le vertigini e il pericolo di scivolare di sotto (nonché, si potrebbe pure aggiungere, il buon gusto nei confronti dell'arte).

L'irresponsabilità apparente del gesto nascondeva a ben vedere una certa «logica» di ferro: «Ho sempre spinto me stesso a pensare e ad agire in modo differente da come ci si aspetta che faccia. Ci si aspetta che un artista dipinga quadri, faccia pittura, «transavanguardia» (*un nuovo movimento pittorico, n.d.r.*) oggi nel 1981. Oppure si pretende che l'arte mostri solo

Lo studente Enrico Corte.

l'aspetto più allettante della realtà, quello della piacevolezza del colore e della riconoscibilità del soggetto», ha detto Corte interrogato sulla vicenda e su i suoi effettivi scopi e propositi, e ha aggiunto: «senza togliere niente a chi ha scelto altri tipi di ricerche espressive, l'arte può e deve però anche mostrare ciò che si tende ad eliminare dal proprio orizzonte visivo, ciò che ci si rifiuta di vedere: di fatto c'è stata una esplosione dei suicidi tra gli adolescenti in Italia da due anni a questa parte, io documento questa situazione sociale illustrando a mio modo la pulsione di morte in un'ottica da adolescente. Il rock e il cinema contemporaneo rappresentano meglio queste problematiche, in modo diretto e senza censure; l'arte visiva non può restare indietro».

La vicenda si è alfine conclusa senza conseguenze particolari per tutti coloro che vi erano coinvolti. A noialtri profani non resta altro da augurarci se non che le «sentenze» del giovane Enrico Corte, forse venate da un pizzico di protervia, stemperino col tempo la loro ansia di esprimere tensioni e problemi più grandi di loro; purtroppo infatti il confine tra la posizione intellettuale di uno studente e la classica fatale «ragazzata» lo abbiamo visto assai spesso oltrepassare sulle pagine della cronaca nera.

C. De.

•Appuntamenti

Le nuove danze di Primavera

Newspaper article concerning the creation of the work *Cheese*, 1981.

«Cagliari – In the afternoon of 30th March, a group of passers-by who were crossing Costituzione Square in the heart of the city stared from below at the figure of an individual who, having climbed the parapet along the edge of the panoramic terrace of the Saint Rémy bastion, seemed to be walking along, maintaining a precarious balance on the outside edge of the cornice which overlooks Queen Helen Boulevard. The group of people, alarmed by a situation which they, of course, considered to be extremely dangerous, notified the Carabinieri police who arrived on the scene and immediately raced to the top of the monumental bastion where this disturbing event was taking place. The perpetrator of this balancing act was thus discovered to be the student Enrico Corte of Cagliari, seventeen years old, who is in his last year at the Artistic High School in the city. With the help of a group of friends, among whom G.F. (26 years old), a professional photographer and assistant teacher at the same school, the youth had organized a sort of photographic session which was intended to portray him in various poses, including this very risky one on the edge of the bastion's marble cornice, a mere 50 centimeters wide».

It's so strange to have a "past" – it's like dreaming. There were eight of us that afternoon on the terrace. I and another seven willing friends whose aim was partly to stick their nose into this event – which I had proposed some days earlier – but also to keep numerous small details under control, one of which was to keep an eye on that wide open and crowded place so that we could shield the event from the indiscreet glances of inevitable shit-stirring passers-by.

Old schoolmates and friends from my adolescence seemed already *old*, as I observed them at twenty-four, twenty-five and twenty-six with the eyes of a seventeen-year-old who assumed that they had greater maturity and more life experience. Perhaps they really did have such experience: that of a generation totally adrift after having passed through the so-called '77 *Movement* in Italy, for whom any gesture or event whatsoever that had even the slightest hint of illegality / clandestinity / challenge / risk / alteration of consciousness / psychic perversion / necrophilia, gained their allegiance and enthusiasm, however weakened by heroin abuse. I just love that sort of thing... In their particular condition, in that brief season of theirs, in their own way I thought they were splendid.

In fact, one could do anything with those people. I, who was still a youngster, but well understood their "historical" weaknesses, could seduce them and manipulate them by playing on their worst frustrations, counting just on the fact that my rashness and delirious delight in deviance was, in their eyes, one of the very few alternatives to the monotony of provincial life. And *I did* manipulate them extremely well... at least for a couple of years, before their vague desire for revolt was swept away during the eighties. Some were lost in the hellish rounds of drug addiction, others – worse still – in those of matrimony; some took to reading the sporting newspapers, others became bald, and some – even worse – grew moustaches. And some even did all these things at once.

But on that day they were still a group of Stray Dogs, casually gathered together in an empty space in the damp breezes of March. On that afternoon, I was the glue that bound them together in their boredom, their uneasiness and their anguish. I'm not sure that there wasn't also a certain unconfessed attraction on the part of those lads towards me, an attraction of the most morbid type, even erotic one might say, which created a certain softness of character on their part, and a willingness towards me and my unfledged charms, that I might almost term servile. I can still see them buzzing around me and watching me as if to say "I mean, do you seriously want to do this? But what is it you want to do, exactly?"

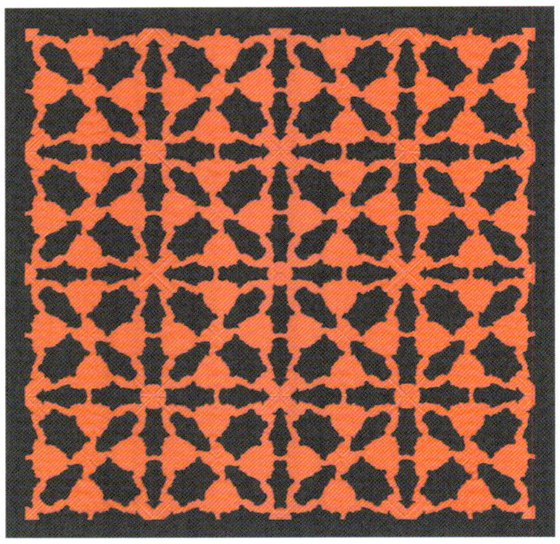

Multiple Death-wish Cutout-Portrait.
March 30, 1981,
day of the making of *Cheese*.
GC 319.

To do what I had to do, I needed to wait for the right moment: the time immediately after lunch when the number of people strolling along the streets was reduced to a minimum. «Hey, you lot – I said to my friends – as a true artist, while we're waiting I'll do your portraits: or rather, portraits of your profiles. The silhouettes of your faces will be the real profiles of your character which will appear as holes on paper multiplied into all the labyrinthine aspects of the mind».

I showed them the process, tracing a little schematic drawing in pencil of their profile on a square piece of tissue-paper which I then folded over several times. Next, with a small pair of nail-scissors I carefully cut out the outlines of the profile until I had made a hole in the paper, and when I unfolded it, there emerged a "snowflake" with a series of holes, of little empty chasms, whose arabesque was formed by the profile of the person portrayed, multiplied over the entire surface.

My friends stared at the brightly colored sheet of tissue-paper, mesmerized; they were at the height of compliance, drowning in an enchanted slow-wittedness. They certainly knew this trick from childhood, but I had touched the hidden chords of their regression, titillated their slumbering death-wish... Now it was time to get to work.

> *«... the bastion's marble cornice, a mere 50 centimeters wide. We should remember that the distance from the ground at that point is equivalent to that of a six-story building. The bastion of St. Rémy has long been known as a place which is sadly favored by those attempting suicide, with a notable case history of tragic leaps into the void, which show no sign of diminishing. Hence the need for a professional photographer to immortalize the terrifying moment: an "accomplice" in a seemingly innocent and passive role.*
>
> *But Enrico Corte's so-called "artistic project" had not counted on the indiscreet eye of a chance public of alarmed passers-by who would interrupt the event, even though the artist had been careful to choose the early afternoon in which to carry out his dangerous photographic poses, just because of the reduced number of strollers in the old town center compared to other times of the day. G.F.'s role in all this was not entirely clear at the outset: the photographer, who among other things was already known to the forces of law and order because of his past as a drug addict and small-time pusher, seemed to be carrying all his photographic equipment, and was anyway held by the Carabinieri and questioned together with Corte, with the precise aim of clearing up some of the more obscure points».*

Journalistic discretion and legal caution here make my friend, the photographer Gismondo, aka "Mondo Gehenna", appear with the mere initials GF. He was a talented visionary, then at least: very clever at masking his secret identity beneath the anonymous garb of an assistant at a high school, just as clever some years later at fleshing out in his own person the fact that he had no "second identity" at all... showing great mastery in producing a work which would magnify nothing other than his own unproductiveness. He was the true personification of what was known then in Italy as "going back to the Private", private, here, in the sense of privation, lacking, wanting, void.

Is he still mad at me, G.F., for the fact that he never made a cent out of the photos he took while I made millions? The money... I didn't go looking for it... nobody even thought about it. I was just a boy then, and not even all that ambitious. And after all, I had planned those photos in every detail, I posed for them, and afterwards I packaged them as artistic artifacts, and found a way to exhibit them. No small matter. He had just pressed a button, but then he sued me when I sold the photographs. However, by that time he'd changed his whole life-style, and already subscribed to a sports paper. (In fact, the pictures taken during that photographic session were exhibited in 1982 during my first solo exhibition and sold for a million lire: reprinted throughout the following twenty years, they were bought for much higher sums. The photographer was paid with only a Cutout-Portrait on tissue paper measuring 15 x 15 cm). But let's read on:

> *« ... more obscure points. Corte, a self-declared visual artist, with a few public exhibitions of his own paintings to his name, immediately proclaimed himself sole deviser of this scenario and responsible for everything: in practice the project involved the creation of a "photographic picture" portraying the young artist in wind-cheater and flat-top haircut, as he calmly walked along the outer edge of the highest cornice of the San Rémy bastion, even whistling a little tune which he also recorded live on a portable tape-recorder, challenging vertigo and the danger of sliding down (as well as good taste in art, one might add)».*

I like that reference to my wind-cheater (in reality, it was a heavy jacket), and above all to my haircut. After all, clothing had a specific role in the general economy of the photograph. I'd chosen to appear "nice" on purpose, even wearing trousers with a well-ironed crease: I did think, however, that a tie aged me too much, perhaps making me look like a *twenty-year-old* and no longer the budding adolescent that I was. I'd tried to put my hair in some sort of order, but an unexpected puff of wind at the moment the picture was taken, as well as adding to the rapid increase in my heartbeat, had totally ruined all attempts to smooth my abundant hair.

I was carrying the tape-recorder, even though you can't see it in the photo. While I was standing on the cornice, and as I moved about looking for the right place to pose for the shot, I actually recorded a meaningless little prattling and whistling tune on the tape, improvising there and then in the midst of the noise made by the traffic below, the crunching of syringes under the soles of my Clark's (typical casual shoes for a "young man" at that time), the chirruping of birds and the rustle of wind on the mike. By backing the visual image with this live soundtrack, I wanted to strengthen the impression of total mad irresponsibility and fascination with the abysses of the mind.

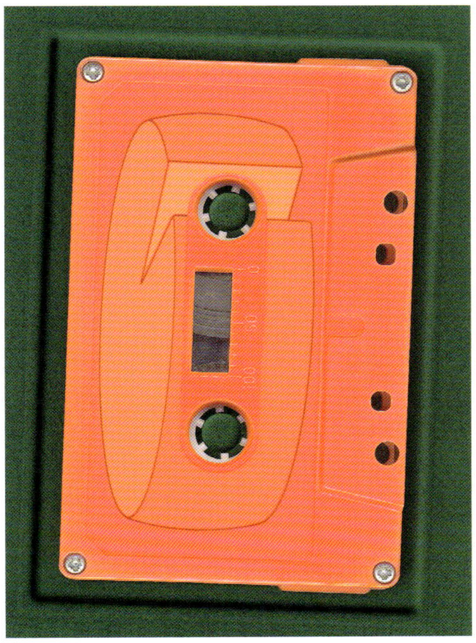

Cheese Symphony on cassette, 1981.
Edition of 50. GC 322.

Cheese is the title of the photographic image printed and then packaged as a picture, and *Cheese Symphony* will be the name of the recording, edited in a loop (7' for a total of 20' in all) and reproduced on an audiocassette in fifty copies which were put together by hand like little sculptures – numbered and signed – then exhibited and sold as multiples, separate from the photographic work. Three years later, in 1984, I managed to reprint the photograph *Cheese* in 36 x 36 cm format, covered with a vinyl film on which there was the clear face of a 45-rpm EP record, with the 7' of recorded sounds from the original tape. The object can be played on the turntable of a stereo like any normal vinyl record.

> *« ... good taste in art, one might add). It would appear that the apparent irresponsibility of the gesture hid a certain irrefutable "logic"».*

The work entitled *Cheese* – from the word that one says when posing for a photo, fixing the mouth in a smile which is supposedly unforced – all in all portrays a large corner section of the upper part of the so-called Saint Rémy bastion, a monumental marble commemorative complex, restructured over the years stretching from the 1800s to the fascist era, which was situated in the heart of the city where I was born and spent my adolescence: Cagliari.

In the beginning, the building was made up of concert halls, exhibition rooms, places for refreshment, terraces, underground crypts, gardens, finely staged stairways and, at the highest point, an elegant walkway with a panoramic view and benches shaded by palms. After the Second World War, this elephantiac complex suffered a rapid decline, despite occasional renovations and attempts to revive it, and is today remembered as being a favored place for loitering, drug dealing and committing suicide. I actually saw one of these not infrequent suicides when I was a boy.

The image in the photo is reproduced in slightly over-exposed black and white, cut into a square shape. Apart from the right hand side of the bastion, it also shows a view taken from above of the tree-lined avenues below, with a few parked cars and the façade of a 19th century building onto which the bastion throws a contrasting shadow. At the top of the photo there also is a large stretch of sky. In the center of the picture, at the point where the perspective frames the sharp edge of the bastion's façade with its flat cornice that juts out into the void, the eye falls on a small distant

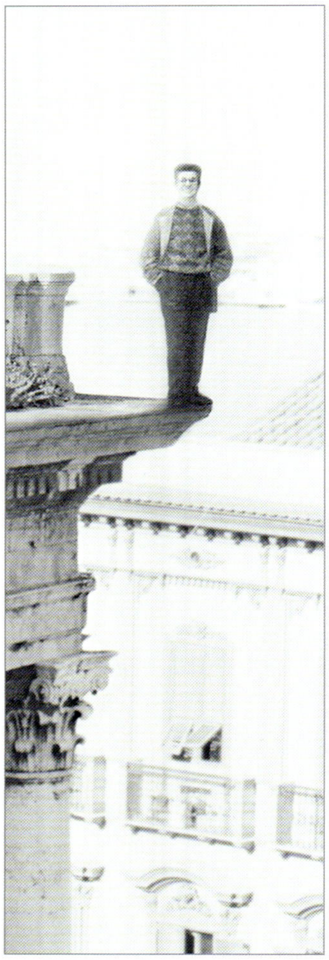

Cheese, 1981 (detail). Cf. ill. p. 94.

figure, a little out of focus because of the limited range of the camera. Smiling mischievously with hands in his pockets, that figure is me at seventeen: I'm standing upright on the extreme edge of the cornice overlooking the abyss, beyond the parapet that runs around the terrace, right on the brink. I'm not holding on to anything, and I wouldn't have been able to do so: I am surrounded by emptiness. Behind me, the view of roof tops fades into the spring haze. At the moment the picture was taken, by means of a vocal agreement with the far-off photographer, I was even trying to position my leg as though I were taking a step into space, though of course trying to keep my balance steady. But a sudden gust of wind took me by surprise at that precise instant, and I stiffened under the influence of a heavy rush of adrenaline.

A powerful and acidulous poison, adrenaline surges within you, feeding on you, strengthening your muscles, tempering your nerves, reviving your sense of balance, dilating the pupils, steadying dizziness, clearing the mind. And it creates dependence. My terror of the drop below little by little became more bearable, less paralyzing, while I wavered on the cornice, whistling hysterically and trying to find the right pose for the photo: and at the moment when the camera clicked, my fear grew fainter thanks yet again to the magic of adrenaline, making me at the same time evanescent and immovable. How strange. Only later, when I clambered back over the parapet and down to the solid ground of the terrace, did I feel as if I were going to swoon. Then, pulling myself together with style, I burst out into a great whoop of adolescent laughter before the wide-eyed faces of my group of friends. It was only when I once again set foot on "terra firma" and saw myself mirrored in their eyes that, for the first time, I clearly sensed the danger that I had escaped. Before that, my head had been in a fog. After, I realized that, from that moment on, all the time that I still had left to live would be a gift. And since it was a gift, I could waste it however I wanted, in total freedom, thoughtlessly and without worrying about consequences, as indeed I have, right up to the present. Even today, my idea of Success, in life and art, is still: managing to stop just one step short of the final smash.

One moment later, we noticed two Carabinieri policemen coming towards us on the terrace.

> *«... a certain irrefutable "logic". "I've always driven myself to think and act differently from what is expected of me. An artist is expected to make pictures, paint, "Trans-avantgarde" (a new movement in painting –* editor's note*) today in 1981. Or people demand that art show only the most attractive aspect of reality, that of the pleasantness of color and a subject that is recognizable", Corte said when he was questioned about the event and its real aims and propositions. And he added: "without in any way denigrating those who have chosen different positions, art can and must, however, also show what one tends to eliminate from one's own visual horizon, what one refuses to see. In fact there's been a boom in suicides among Italian adolescents for the past two years now: I'm documenting this social situation by illustrating the death-wish in my own way, from the viewpoint of an adolescent. Rock and contemporary cinema portray these problems better, in a direct fashion and without censorship: visual art cannot lag behind"».*

«The aim of my work is to destroy the family», stated the youthful Fassbinder, as he responded to a fake interview in his film "Deutschland im Herbst", which I saw when I was, I think, fifteen (if I remember well, I had gone to the cinema with some friends, but then we split up: they preferred "Grease"). «Great!», I thought, «if you want to reconstruct society, you obviously have to annihilate its first formative cell!» But how could I do that when my family had already been destroyed by destiny? But sure! The central point of the family is not the mother-father pole, as RWF seemed to believe, but rather the third pole: the child, the offspring. One can only really talk about a family when there is a child. So, the destruction of the *boy* had to be staged: my own self-destruction, adolescent suicide, the pulping of posterity. Well, one thing is sure: I was in good company in those years, with many of my contemporaries much more determined than me.

From that point onwards, my artistic activity has been the long, motionless funeral of the suicidal adolescent. Everyone grows older and passes on, I alone am still there on the brink, suspended over the emptiness below. The question is this: if an artist starts when he is very young to whistle as he walks along the precipice, and has someone piss in his face, and ends up by inserting a tube into his balls and blowing them up like a balloon, *has he gone forward*? No, of course not. There has never been any need to progress in the long motionless funeral of the suicidal adolescent. I live in an equilibrium without drastic fluctuations. For years I *have not aged*, which is why I'm fascinated and attracted by people who are representative of a certain sector – you know, like actors or musicians, writers, directors – who can say they are elderly, or at least in an advanced stage of their maturity. Who are clearly decaying, not only in their body, but also in their creative curve. They represent everything that I cannot be.

Over the years, I became so intoxicated with adrenaline, whose rushes I stimulated by seeking the most unlikely situations so as to immortalize them in photos, that a doctor who examined me when I was about twenty-one diagnosed me as having hypertrophy of the suprarenal glands, and an abnormal thickening of the cardiac muscles. He stated in no uncertain terms that a form of chemical dependence on adrenaline had set in, of the kind that usually occurs in those who practice extreme sports or who are subject to frequent physical or mental stress. This could cause me gastrointestinal or cardiac problems, blood platelet deficiency, damage to the central nervous system, and even glaucoma. Symptoms of premature aging and accelerated physical decay in the future.

That doctor really screwed up. In reality, from that moment onwards I've never aged physically. This could be my real contribution to Medicine... It's evident if you compare photographs of my features then and now. My hair is still black, I have no wrinkles on my face, and the structure of my body is almost identical to that of twenty years ago. And all this without gyms, dieting, face-lifting, hair dye or liposuction. I do think it's due to all those powerful doses of adrenaline that I absorbed in my youth, which have acted as a sort of homeopathic cure against aging. The brain is the source. Which is why I now advise all young people to follow this prescription of mine: begin as soon as you can to get yourselves into the most dangerous and complicated situations possible, invent new ones, look for trouble and shady sexual encounters, balance along the balcony railings outside your little room... and when you get the chance, smash lots of bank windows. Store up your adrenaline for the worst years of your life.

> *« The incident ended without particular consequences for all those involved. We, the uninitiated, can only hope that young Enrico Corte's "rulings", tinged as they are with a streak of pretentiousness, will moderate, in time, their eagerness to express tensions and problems greater than themselves. Unfortunately, as we have seen it too often in the sensational news pages, the fine line between an intellectual position of a student and a teenage "bravado" is quite blurry.*
>
> *C. De.»*

That is how the snapshot by Carlo, or Corrado, Devoto or Devoti, concludes. With a somewhat paternalistic observation by a gentleman who, in theory, might still be alive, though getting older. I'll probably never hear about him again; his newspaper folded shortly after the publication of this article, and all traces of him have been lost. With the confused but not unpleasant memory that I have of this man whom I knew only for a fleeting moment, I must say one thing in his favor: despite the sour final conclusions, his article is still, two decades later, the best thing written about my work. No critical art text about me has ever paid that same attention to detail, that loving description, step by step, of the chronological development of an action, that care in specifying the thought underlying the artistic gesture, and above all that deep respect for the words and declarations of an artist. The fact that I was a mere boy at the time, might perhaps have required a tone of greater condescension or reproof, less space, and greater rapidity in condemning and shelving the affair.

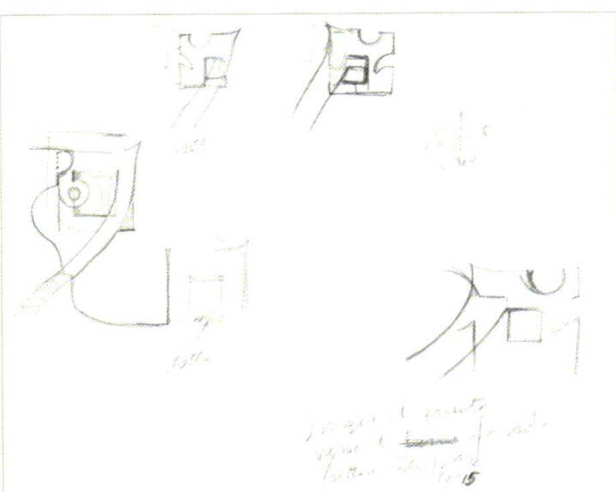

One of Corte's preparatory drawings for the unrealized work *1994*. Graphite on paper; 8¼ x 11¾" (21 x 29,7 cm). SC 660. This and other drawings, held together with two kilos of TNT in a red satchel seized by the Italian police in November 1994, were mistaken for the illustration for assembling a bomb.

No, none of the sensational news articles that C. De. predicted were ever dedicated to me, just a few in the rather less interesting culture pages. Apart from the one concerning the episode of a controversial exhibition that I had in 1987, entitled *Cleptoscopica*, which closed the day after it was inaugurated, and therefore led to my brief arrest and also the obligatory decision to abandon my city. It's true, too, that on 18th November 1994, who knows how, the police discovered a certain quantity of explosive material in the abandoned courtyard of a ruined building next door to my studio in via Bertola in Rome, together with sketches of graphic projects and the page of a newspaper with an article and photograph of Silvio Berlusconi, the then Italian Prime Minister, all in a red satchel with *1994* written on it in felt pen. It is just that courtyard, still abandoned, which you can see on the other side of my garden wall. All the findings were seized and taken away by a robot of the bomb disposal squad. Several articles were in fact written about this in the national press, but I am not named in any of them.

They were, in reality, sketches and materials for a sculpture on which I was working at the time, on the theme of state terrorism and the right wing's seizure of power in Italy, and it should in fact have been entitled *1994*. It all started with the interesting idea of modeling plastic explosive like a sculptor models clay, and so I had met some members of the emerging Black Block groups in

Rome, to see whether they could find some for me. Unfortunately, the only thing I could get was TNT, a fuse and some detonators, given that plastic explosive couldn't be found on the black market at that time. I bought the materials loose, so to say, intending to handle and set up the explosives myself in a somewhat intuitive, fanciful way, but also with the help of a military manual. I kept everything in my studio, and was working on this project in those days.

Then someone informed the police, who carried out a blitz on via Bertola, searching with great care my home too, as well as the studio adjacent to the courtyard where they had found the explosives. But you know... they have their own informers, of course – even though I'm not quite sure who tipped them off – but I also had mine, who were on the ball enough to allow me to take action at the last minute. Just that morning I had in fact received an unexpected phone-call from an acquaintance who, in an very roundabout way, warned me that the police knew of the contraband dealings in explosives and the involvement of some not more specifically identified resident in via Bertola in the Torpignattara area. This acquaintance advised me to move fast because the police were on their way. As soon as I put the phone down, I threw right away all the compromising material that I kept in a red satchel – the explosives, the detonators, the graphic designs of the work in progress, the page of the newspaper with Berlusconi's photo that I was using as reference for the sculpture – into that abandoned property on the other side of my garden wall, just a few seconds before the Forces of Law and Order burst into my studio. By doing this, I shook off all responsibility in the eyes of the law; there was no longer anything suspicious in my studio. The explosives landed without exploding on the rubbish and ruins of the abandoned courtyard which softened their fall: the idea of Success in life and art is, yet again, that of managing to stop just one step short of the final smash...

Law enforcement officers still have some doubts about me... in fact, given my difficult-to-classify status as an "artist", I was investigated for two whole years for suspected involvement in a plot against Berlusconi, and my studio was searched on numerous occasions over the following years with one excuse or another, by the regular and fiscal police forces. Then the inquiry was closed, without any outcome. Who knows where the remains of my unfinished sculpture now repose, in which police archive lie those sketches which were drawn by hand with so much care and then mistaken for plans to build a bomb... Of course, by losing a work I managed to save my ass from the police; unfortunately on that occasion there was no time to load a film and immortalize the lightning-quick toss over the wall in yet another photographic work of art, but... man, what a rush of adrenaline I had...

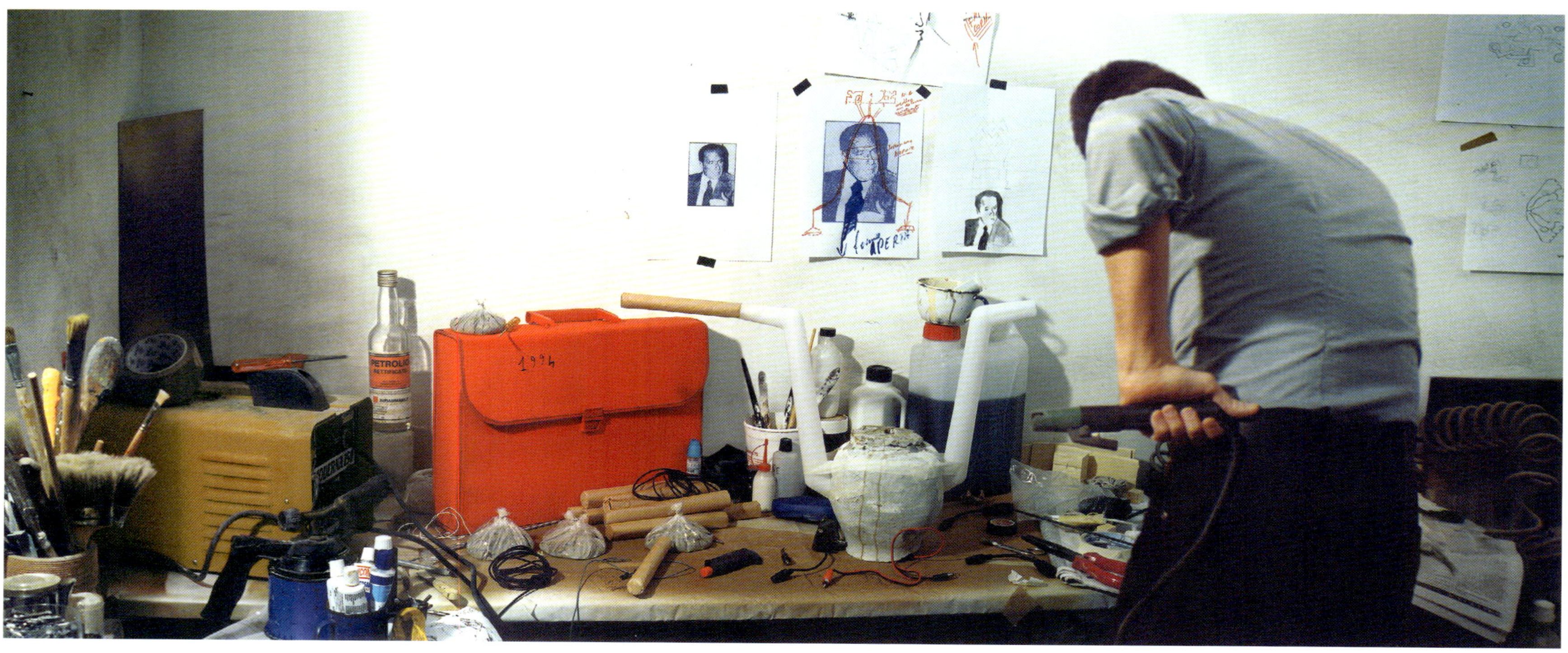

Corte at work with the explosives for *1994* in his Rome studio in via Bertola, November 1994.
Note the red satchel which would later be found in an adjacent courtyard and confiscated by the police with all its contents (photo © De Nero).

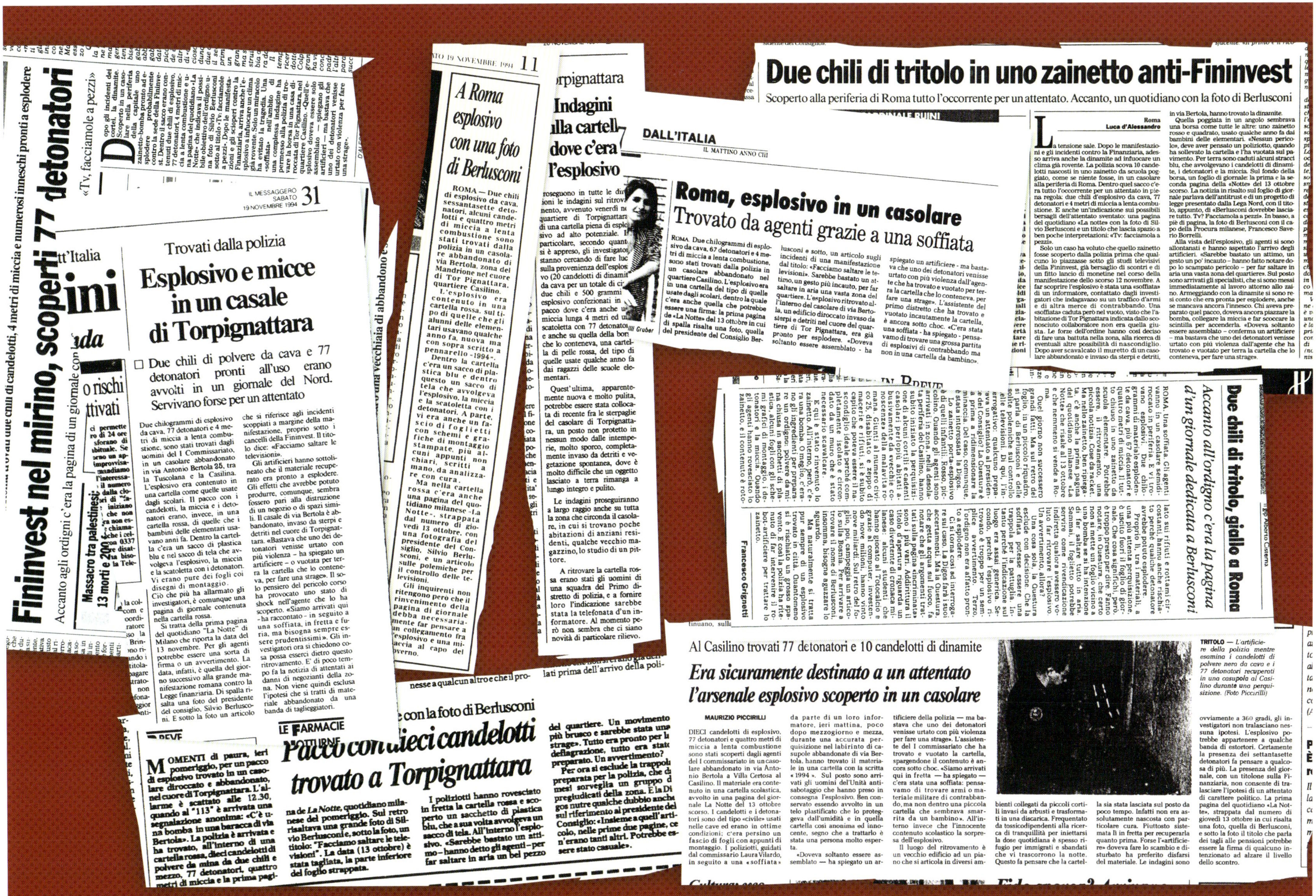

November 1994. Italian Press' reports on the explosives found in via Bertola in Rome, considered to be evidence of a future attempt on the life of the Italian Prime Minister.

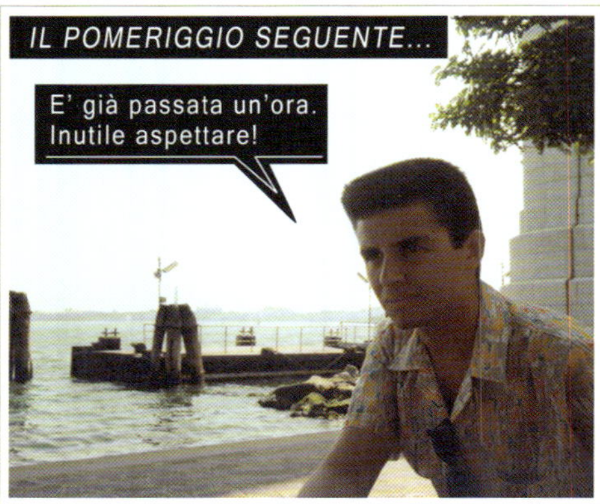

Always at work with photographers: Corte starring in the photonovel *Dilemma*, Venice, 1981-82 (© Geranio Publisher). The artist has invested his early earnings as a "pop" actor in his own art.

Here I take over again, to make the point that, over the course of time, Corte has had to resolve legal problems arising from the character of his works. But his project attacks conventional morality without any element of the gratuitous, the strident, the "juvenilistic". The echoes of generational rebellion cannot be found here and bear no relation to the rigorous silence of his expressive need. Here, there is no desperate search for "scandal", the type of scandal that is often sought for mere motives of publicity. For this artist, work passes through the cultural references of a given historical period, the areas of creative privilege, the poles of the best communicative evidence. So he could not but manipulate and filter the languages which influence our historical moment, like music, cinema, comics, industrial design, video-clips, advertising... worlds which are metabolized in his works in autonomous and unexpected forms, following the paths of a formidable disenchantment that is amalgamated with the cynicism of his genius.

Corte does not belong to groups or collective experiences. He does not express himself through any one single language, he journeys onwards using formulas of hard-won and honest originality. When he manipulates social customs, Catholic rhetoric, middle-class mush, he never makes any concession to second-hand populism or invalidating forms of communism. If there still exists an anarchist soil on which to build a structure somewhere between instinct and culture, Corte is one of its vital bulwarks. It is impossible to imprison or catalogue him in any one pigeon-hole, just as every single work demands an interpretation that opens out onto parallel planes: from a first level of evident formal impact, to the subsequent steps which climb down, layer after layer, into the hidden heart of innermost meanings. It is up to us to uncover them in time, absorbing the fluids of both individual and collective memory, fragments of removed nightmares, membranes of pagan freedom. We are free to choose the levels and order of interpretation, sacrificing or adulating what we perceive and feel. The zeal for the "destruction of the family", which the artist talked about in his adolescence, means this: Corte has never in fact "wedded" (until now) any single artistic style, but has instead chosen promiscuity in his interests.

Stratification, not simple contamination, is another significant aspect of this process. None of Corte's works follow a one-way street. On the contrary, each and every project acts on a multiple parallelism: that of a planning structure which goes beyond any superficial appearance and acts on manifold senses, and then that of an aesthetic model in which the work adds materials and details to an organized and complex organism. The planning structure implies a dialectic that is a mirror image of the brain's prismatic ramification. Corte represents a rare case where the work records and synthesizes the complex urges of the cerebral world, behaving as a brain with arms and creative hands might do. The formal model is born as a direct consequence of the project, stratifying the elements necessary for the defining of a way of observing that lies on the threshold between the psyche and the external reality.

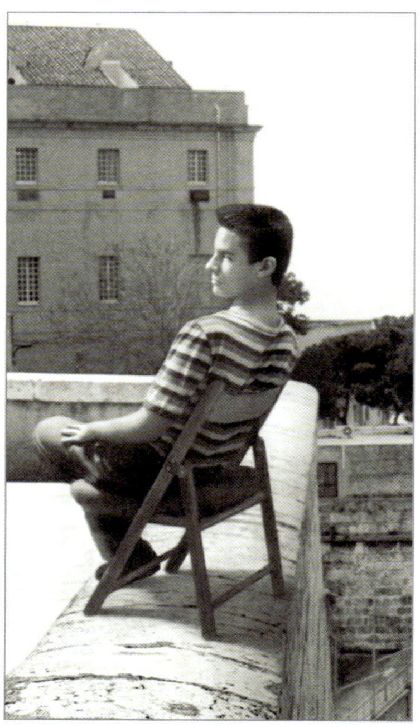

Youthanasia 3, 1981.
Left panel, detail.
Cf. ill. p. 98, 99.

Let's move on. *Youthanasia 2* and *Youthanasia 3* (ill. pp. 97-99), the latter in two panels, are variations, some months later, on the photo-piece *Cheese* (but without the recording of sounds). The city is the same, the location is different; the pose is seated, but the equilibrium is just as precarious. In the beginning, some not very observant critics mistakenly thought these images were clever photomontages. Some classified them as examples of Performance Art, another inaccurate description since they were created in secret, fleetingly and without the presence of the public, apart from the people involved in their practical execution. *Youthanasia 2* shows the artist seated on a chair, balanced on the parapet of a panoramic terrace, with a 25 meter drop below. Framed in long-shot, it could by far appear to be a mere postcard picture of a city "belvedere" if it were not for the small figure of the artist seated on the parapet, and the presence of a Cutout-Portrait superimposed on one side. *Youthanasia 3*, on the other hand, is a shot of the same pose taken from a closer angle, divided into two panoramic sections in which the thrilling action is almost diminished by the conventional postcard perspective.

Presuming absolute rigor in selecting his points of reference, here is someone who risks, both mentally and physically, submitting to the elastic contractions of the void, looking up and down, defining our fear through his own fears. On the other hand, only those who are really afraid can touch the peaks of courage and create visual signals with which to grasp and metabolize our underlying vertigo. Corte demonstrates the physical boundaries of courage, developing works which expand sensory perception and set the body face to face with the real danger of death. He develops the Situationist void of Yves Klein in an immobile and exclusively photographic dimension. But, unlike Klein, he chooses not to jump because that would too closely approach the definitive awareness of the end. Corte seeks his sculptural gesture in a hypnotic awareness of risk, and our mind goes back to the aerial poetry of Philippe Petit, the man in black tights who in 1974 walked for 45 minutes along a wire suspended between the Twin Towers of New York. An extreme and definitive gesture, immobile in the sky like the iconographic memory of utopia. Corte, too, walks along the tightrope of life, and chooses not to die, because the artist experiences death in his own work, using it within the symptomatic tensions of the most radical way of life.

The organic material and challenging of death are part of the volition of an artist who is lucidly hallucinated, rather than a "simple" visionary. An adult game with an immortal eye, logical and yet quite mad, like the divinatory nature of one who creates visual archetypes with the very ingredients of the body. Corte uses essential physicality, the link between mind and body, courage as an inner principle. Never forgetting the stylistic code of irony, the true balancing factor in a project that is serious and never facetious, universal in its grammar, unclassifiable in its expressive outcome.

At times, in the type of work we are examining, a paper Cutout-Portrait is superimposed on the photographic print, as in *Youthanasia 2* or in other works of the period such as the series *Der Weg Zum Kubismus*, or *Idolatrina*, in which the artist portrays himself while someone pisses on his face. These are profile portraits of the people who helped the artist technically in creating the works (for example, the photographer, or perhaps the unknown "pisser"...). *Idolatrina*, in particular (ill. p. 96), shows us an image of a powerful content, that is comparable to very few others in the art of that period at an international level, and none whatsoever in the Italian context. Vaguely asymmetrical and based on clever plays of light and shadow, in reality it reveals a rigorous structure which exploits the dynamism of the geometric module – triangular in this case – which we will find in many subsequent works. *Idolatrina* develops still further the visual obsession with the face as an empty space to be filled, to be dirtied: a metaphor for the unknown joys or sorrows that are experienced only through re-defining the conventional concepts of "identity" and even "dignity".

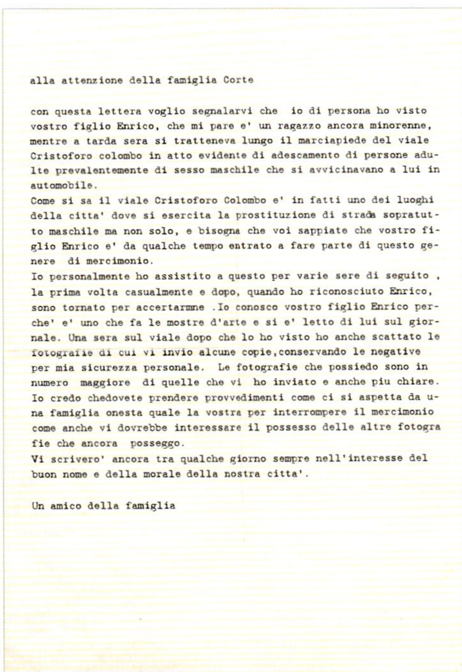

alla attenzione della famiglia Corte

con questa lettera voglio segnalarvi che io di persona ho visto vostro figlio Enrico, che mi pare e' un ragazzo ancora minorenne, mentre a tarda sera si tratteneva lungo il marciapiede del viale Cristoforo colombo in atto evidente di adescamento di persone adulte prevalentemente di sesso maschile che si avvicinavano a lui in automobile.
Come si sa il viale Cristoforo Colombo e' in fatti uno dei luoghi della citta' dove si esercita la prostituzione di strada sopratutto maschile ma non solo, e bisogna che voi sappiate che vostro figlio Enrico e' da qualche tempo entrato a fare parte di questo genere di mercimonio.
Io personalmente ho assistito a questo per varie sere di seguito , la prima volta casualmente e dopo, quando ho riconosciuto Enrico, sono tornato per accertarmne .Io conosco vostro figlio Enrico perche' e' uno che fa le mostre d'arte e si e' letto di lui sul giornale. Una sera sul viale dopo che lo ho visto ho anche scattato le fotografie di cui vi invio alcune copie,conservando le negative per mia sicurezza personale. Le fotografie che possiedo sono in numero maggiore di quelle che vi ho inviato e anche piu chiare.
Io credo chedovete prendere provvedimenti come ci si aspetta da una famiglia onesta quale la vostra per interrompere il mercimonio come anche vi dovrebbe interessare il possesso delle altre fotografie che ancora posseggo.
Vi scrivero' ancora tra qualche giorno sempre nell'interesse del buon nome e della morale della nostra citta'.

Un amico della famiglia

The blackmailing letter which included some of the photographs used by Corte for *Der Weg Zum Kubismus* series, 1981.

Der Weg Zum Kubismus (ill. pp. 102-104) is a series of photo-pieces that once again arose out of a strange and twisted story, and allows us to understand how the flow of life's happenings and on-the-spot invention are what mainly feed the development in Corte's work, rather than the elaboration of an artistic technique or recognizable style. An anonymous and vaguely blackmailing letter which arrived at Corte's home in 1981 indicated the presence of the young artist in city streets or avenues where juvenile prostitution took place. The letter, written in poor grammar, perhaps on purpose so that the author would be less recognizable, was signed "a family friend" and included photographs which supposedly showed Corte soliciting clients on the street, right in their cars. The author of the letter hinted that he was in possession of other photographs and said that he was ready to reach an "agreement" for them to be handed over.

Whether the act of prostitution was true or false («I was the kind of boy that daughters wouldn't want their parents to be seen with», Corte maliciously tells us), the artist's reaction was interesting. On his own, he took other photographs on the same theme, posing for them himself. He then presented them together with the other photos as if they were all his own work. In these images, one should note the use of the same striped T-shirt that had also appeared in previous photographic works, worn as a kind of "uniform" typical of the average teenager. Corte also had in mind certain TV broadcasts, in which people's faces were obscured because they needed to remain anonymous, for example during compromising interviews or scenes. The then-technology made it possible for the first time to use a kind of pixel squaring on the face or other parts of the televised image, so that the subject was unrecognizable. In previous years, they had usually superimposed a rough blurring of focus on the image, or a black blob in compromising moments. Corte grasped the visual analogy of this kind of pixelization with cubist painting, or with the simplified idea that one might have of Cubism. Using an airbrush and masks, he superimposed pixel grids on the faces of his presumed "clients", and over their car number-plates if they were in the photo, thus making it quite impossible to identify them, and then he entitled the whole series of photographs *Der Weg Zum Kubismus* (The Way of Cubism), borrowing the title from a book written in 1920 by Daniel-Henry Kahnweiler, Pablo Picasso's first art dealer.

Behind Corte's customary play on words (*The Way of Cubism / The Street of Cubism*: when translated into Italian, "weg" can mean street or way), the theme of putting the body at risk comes back again: a mad rhythm to expand the body and compress it, destroy it in order to retrieve it, change it, overturn it... and with this action, assume all the features that we have mentioned thus far. The body constructs the work in its individual, social and cultural liberating muddle. And through its relations with the outside, multiplies the ways of interpreting the world itself.

These works were proposed by Corte for a celebratory exhibition on the centenary of Picasso's birth (1981) organized by an Italian art review, but were refused. They were purchased *en bloc* the following year, at Corte's first solo exhibition in a museum, when he was nineteen. The "family friend" was not able to make any claims of artistic authorship in this case.

Although the element of the city garden and "urbanized nature" is already present in the photographs of the *Der Weg Zum Kubismus* series, with their scenes of dark alleys and parks in which dubious sexual activities take place, surrounded by buildings with a thousand eyes, it was to be better expressed in the multi-media installation that Corte set up in 1981 with Andrea Nurcis, the *Grande Esposizione di Rarità Botaniche* (*Great Exhibition of Botanical Rarities*). From that moment, the long-lasting sodality between EC and AN began. Nurcis, born in the same city as Corte, would never form an "artistic couple" with him but would nevertheless remain his preferred partner for the next twenty years in many important "projects for four hands" (or six, when the two decided to raise the stakes by including a third collaborator in their partnership). The idea which is at the basis of the sporadic but oft-repeated collaborations between Corte and Nurcis is that of creating a "third way" in an Art market which recognizes as canonical operators both the single, individualistic artist closed in his own world, and the artistic couple, often united in life as well as art. Over the years, Corte and Nurcis have exemplified a situation that eludes these conventions, by proposing an activity which is more open to collaboration and the varied encounters of life, but in which the relationship between these two is still favored from the outset.

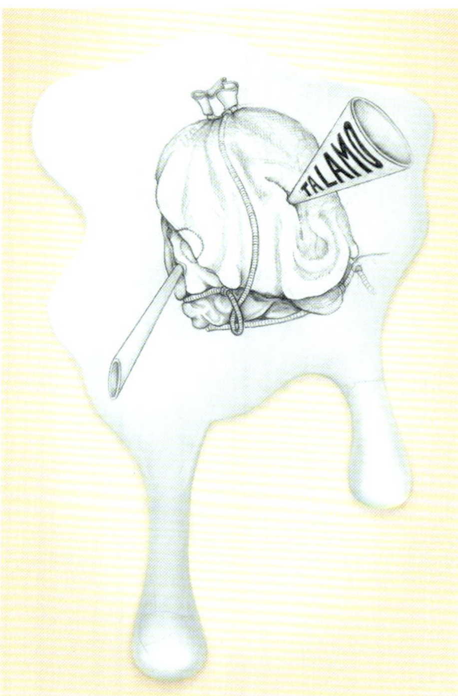

Andrea Nurcis: *Untitled*, 1996.
Graphite on enameled polyester.
Courtesy: the artist.

The *Botanical Rarities* by Corte and Nurcis (ill. pp. 105-109) were plants, shoots, mushrooms, rhizomes and inflorescences created in colored wax, paraffin, vaseline, vinyl and synthetic substances together with pieces from real plants such as thorns and dry leaves. They were created in an imaginative way, at the same time precise and accurate, almost illusionistic I should say, and it required months of work. Their appearance was abnormal, deformed, with burgeoning boils and malignant growths (with a veiled reference to the nineteenth-century anatomical ceroplastics of the Italian masters): slimy filaments entrapped (real) insects; aerial roots fed on blood-like fluids oozing inside test tubes like those of a mad scientist; mould and funguses corroded fleshy tree trunks; grafting as unlikely as deviant copulation exuded gastric juices. The various suppurating botanic examples were placed like aborted fetuses in specially designed glass cases, which in turn stood on fake marble laminate pedestals, with colored inlays that recalled the kitsch furnishings of the 1960s.

The showcases and pedestals were set in various strategic corners of an urban botanical garden and displayed to the public. Under the summer sun, the wax and various substances of which the plants were made slowly began to throb, melt and self-destruct, creating an effect of palpitating suffering that made the biological specimens seem even more alive. The installation was supplemented with a number of loudspeakers hidden among the foliage, which broadcast the recordings of tropical bird sounds, distorted by various electronic filters (echo, reverberation, tremolo, and so on) until they became unrecognizable. An explanatory text put up at the entrance to the botanical garden introduced the installation through a story which was pure fantasy, though credible and accurate right down to the historical details and references. The monstrous plants, said the text, had been created in a laboratory by some German botanists at the end of the 19th century, almost presaging Lombrosian theory or Nazi ravings about "degenerate races", and the few remaining specimens of this series of original experiments which had survived over the years, had been subsequently exhibited in a number of traveling exhibitions in various German cities. According to the calendar, these fictitious exhibitions of improbable plants had begun on 26th February 1962 in Munich, and ended on 21st June 1963 in Berlin (the respective birth-dates of Nurcis and Corte).

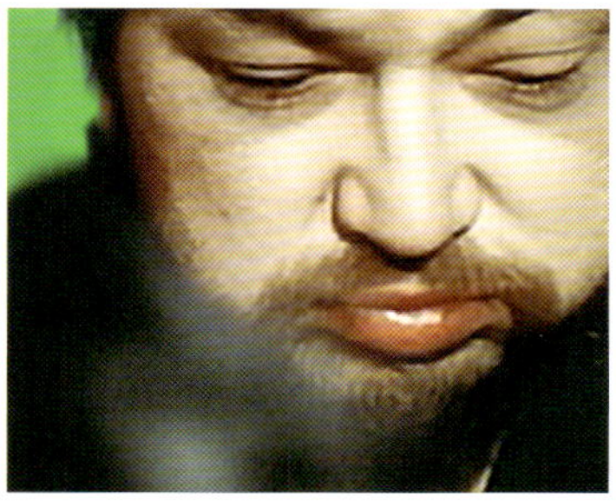

R.W. Fassbinder in Venice, 1980, photographed by Corte (detail).

And thus, just as the 1960s are evoked in the kitsch style of the pedestals, so also a series of paintings imitating posters, in a recognizable *Jugendstil* graphic style, were put up inside the botanical gardens like just so many equivalent relics of the false traveling exhibitions. It should be added that some sentences written in rather macaronic German would have revealed the parodic character of these posters to any careful observer. The blooming of a vaguely joking sensitivity helps to place the whole work within the "adolescent" context that had already been present in the previous works (the adolescent artist speaks about what he knows best).

This environmental work with its ephemeral and self-destructive aspect was created by Corte and Nurcis after a period of living in Germany, and was meant to be a homage to German culture in general, of which they were both enamored, and to the New German Cinema of the period (in particular to director Rainer Werner Fassbinder, whom they met in Venice in 1980, and who was duly destined to self-destruct just one year after the presentation of the *Rarità Botaniche*. Foresight? From a "spectrospective" point of view, Corte would speak of an "early commemorative celebration").

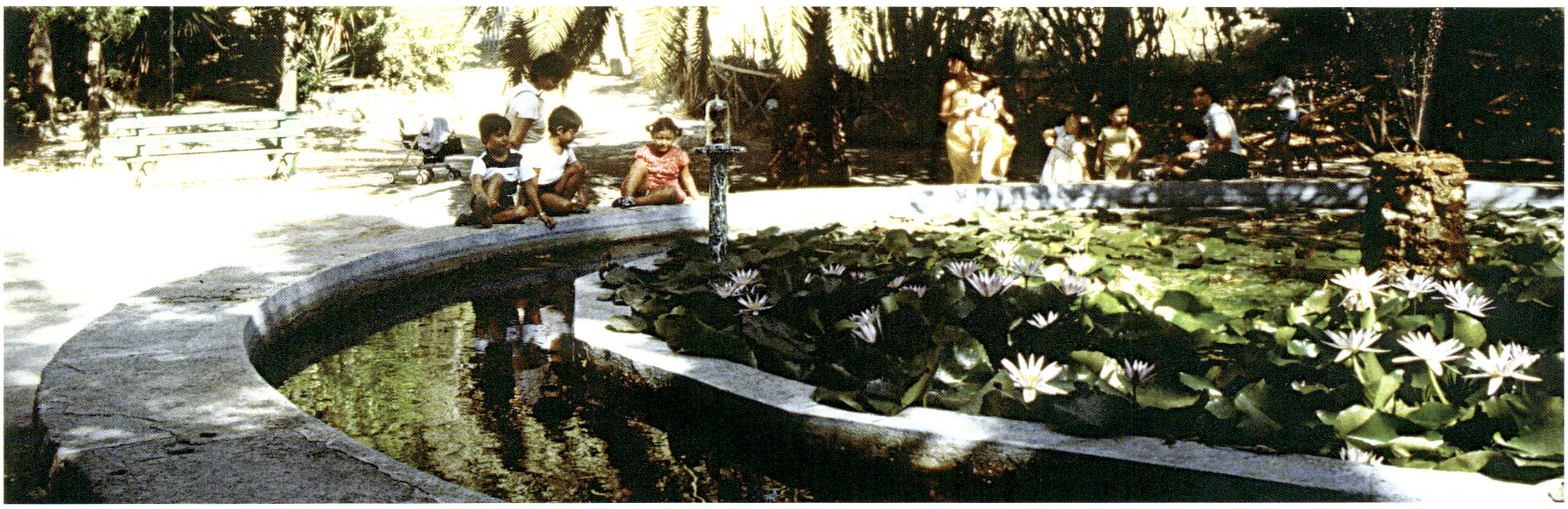

Botanical Rarities, 1981.
Detail of the installation.

In this Garden of Good and Evil, where unhealthiness grew naturally and nature logically developed through miscarriages, innocence and experience lived together in equilibrium (above the void?) like a tragicomedy of adolescent years. The installation as a whole lived in a dimension of its own, far from the widespread interest in neo-expressionist painting that characterized the early '80s in Italy and abroad. But it foresaw the '90s taste for genetic aberration, biological grafting, and the "Post-human" (or in this case *Post-vegetal*) prosthesis. Within the installation, the weird, contaminated and distorted laws of history and biology were in force: features of the labyrinthine universe of references and formal inventions on which all Enrico Corte's art would develop.

Another aspect should also be pointed out, one entirely "spectrospective", which appeared in *Rarità Botaniche* and then developed over time in other similar or different works: the parody-like taste for the *celebration*, *anniversary*, *commemoration.* This conceptual element could already be seen in the "working year" represented by the self-portraits of *250 Mele Marce* and also in *Der Weg Zum Kubismus* (Picasso's centenary), and would become more evident in the future works, both as a way of de-mystifying the *parade* of official culture, and as a possibility of reinterpreting the same work some time later from differing points of view. In fact, the waxen *Botanical Rarities*, which already contain the element of celebratory commemoration by using the fictitious calendar of the 1960s exhibitions, would later be in part resumed and re-used by Corte (thus contradicting their ephemeral character) in some commemorative works marking 15 years from its creation (1981-1996; ill. p. 109) and on their twentieth anniversary (1981-2001; ill. p. 267).

The reference to early 1960s' multicolored kitsch, and some characteristic types of interior decoration or architectonic buildings, recurs in many of Corte's works from the beginning of the 1980s, and this also signifies an ambiguous celebration of his birth, but in a hallucinatory and necrotic way. A work like *Il Balcone: è il mio strumento di suicidio preferito* (*The Balcony: is my favorite suicide tool*) and the series of *Balconies* which followed over a period of five years (ill. pp. 111-115) best explain this concept.

Fascinated from childhood by an Italian way of decorating houses which used mosaics in square multicolored tiles as decoration on the façades of buildings, around balconies or other similar parts of the structure, Corte recreated this same type of mosaic using original period materials and applying them to panels that were similar in size to the front of a balcony in a block of council apartments. This resulted in mosaic pictures of an abstract kind, with a range of colors on average brighter than the real mosaics of the 1960s, and juxtapositions that were more disturbing to the eye. Onto these mosaics, once again Corte glued some of his Cutout-Portraits of folded and cut up tissue paper. We don't know if there is a direct relation between the individual work and the person portrayed in the cutout stuck to it; they perhaps represent only passing encounters or acquaintances.

The balcony is still a place with a fine view, a Belvedere, but it is also a very suitable means of suicide. The '60s-style decoration tells us of the artist's birth, the Cutout-Portrait again suggests the inescapable co-presence of the death-wish. The manual work that lies behind the mosaics of these *Balconies* already requires such an effort for the hand and eye that it implies a sadomasochistic relationship with the body. Corte asserts that his eyesight began to fail as a result of having worked so long on the tiles with their hypnotic and strident contrasts of color, and we will see the development in several future works of the concept *perception of the image = pain*. From the chromatic point of view, the artist also extended the range of standard colors used for the little ceramic mosaic tiles, a range that was limited to the building requirements of that time. Using thin coats of enamel for glass spread over the tiles, he created a more multicolored work. Perfectionism.

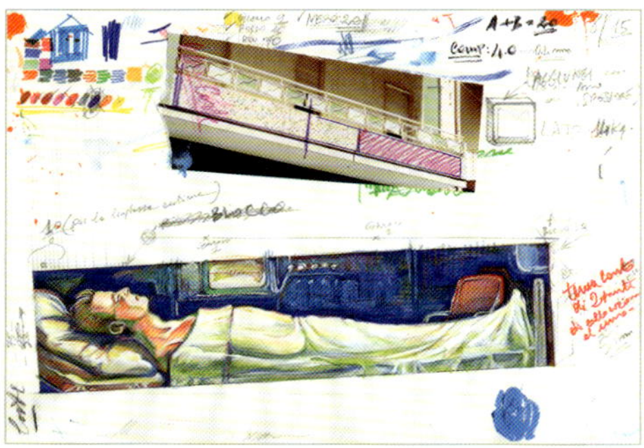

Study for *Bal-coma 1*, 1983.
Ink, tempera, pencil and photograph on paper. 8¼ x 11¾" (21 x 29,7 cm).
SC 203.

Because of the precision implicit in making them, the *Balconies* are also the works which required more preparation through sketches and color-tryouts than any of the others (in general, Corte does not make preliminary sketches for his works but passes straight from the idea to its realization without too much significant rethinking). The final *Balconies* are different in character from the first, and their mosaics show images of a figurative type: *Bal-coma 1* and *Bal-coma 2* (ill. pp. 113-115) already in the wordplay of the title make explicit reference to death by means of the theme of hospitalization and the graphic design of the encephalogram. The artist portrays his own features in mosaic while he lies, presumably poised between life and death, on a hospital bed.

The coexistence between image and sound or music, which is not to be found in the *Balcony* series, returns in a composite work with four photographs, encased in a plastic structure together with two fragments of magnetic tape, that portray the artist standing in front of one of his paintings. The title of this work, made in 1983 during a stay in London, is *Marble Fever, Marble Junkie, Marble Hustler, Marblefucker* (ill. p. 116). The picture that appears behind the artist in the four photographs is an enamel painting on glass, oriented and lighted in different ways, that imitates the veining of marble and is thus linked to the kitsch decoration of the pedestals in *Botanical Rarities,* and with other future works. The two pieces of magnetic tape, inserted into the structural support of the work, refer to the recording of a dialogue in English between Corte and a non-identified person, fragments of a negotiation over the price of something that could be the fake-marble painting, or even a sexual service provided by the artist. The work once again implies a dimension of ambiguous suspension somewhere between deviance and immolation, in an icy-cold context of paint and materials. The poor visual quality of the photographs and the facial expressions of the skinny twenty year old Corte relate a turbid opacity, a problematic choice of life, an obligatory rite of passage in the journey of experience.

A relation between image and sound is evident in the small 1984 work *Tra i Solchi* (*Amid the Grooves*, ill. p. 117), a reworking of a picture taken two years earlier, *Il Bacio* (*The Kiss*, ill. p. 116). *Tra i Solchi* is rather like a "postcard record", of the kind produced in the '50s and '60s and, in fact, in order to create it, Corte had referred to an old firm that specialized in souvenirs of this kind: postcards on whose surface, together with images of the city, there was a transparent vinyl coating with musical grooves cut into it, which could

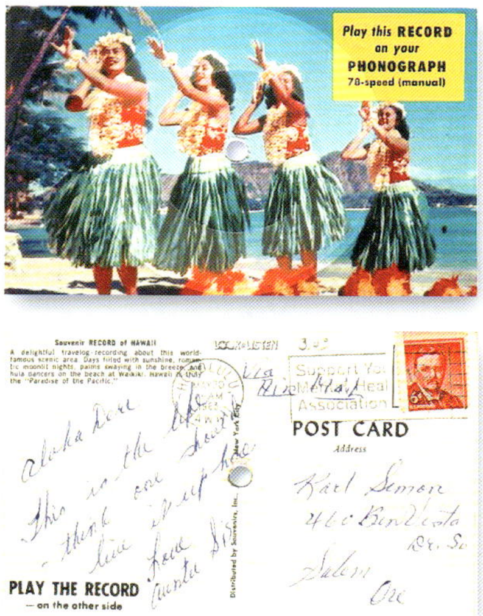

A typical postcard record, circa 1960.

be played on a record-player (it was often folk music or popular local songs). The image on *Tra i Solchi*, like that of *Il Bacio* from which it derived, is an anomalous embrace between distant parts of the body: the music recorded on the surface is an electronic piece by Corte, called *Rockets which don't bother to explode.*

Fake marble also plays a significant role in a 1982 work, *Marmo Malato* (*Sick Marble*), an enamel painting on red formica that does not imitate marble, but rather the laminates which imitate marble. It is the likeness of a likeness, and incorporates within it the signs of its own deception: two small broken loudspeakers, like black cancerous growths. Once again there is a relationship with the diffusion of sound, but from the viewpoint of ineffectiveness and impotence. The tomb-like coldness of the work, on the border of inexpressiveness, the duplicity of the portrayal, the technical handicap that it suggests – everything relates mistrust towards the rules of Art. But the outbursting flow of life's events yet again heats up the atmosphere. In fact, during his first solo exhibition in a museum of contemporary art, Corte "borrowed" a sizeable group of physically handicapped people from a nearby orthopedic clinic, and photographed them as they observed the work *Marmo Malato.* In this way he achieved a further work, composed of ten photographs of the same number of disabled people, entitling the series *Il Sistema dell'Arte* (*The Art System*, ill. p. 118), with which he illustrated his skepticism, detachment, critical attitude and equally aggressive contrast to those mechanisms in the artistic establishment which, in the early 1980s, were beginning to appear in all their ferocity.

A photographic work like *Disegno (Schizzo)* [*Drawing (Spurt/Sketch)* – in Italian "schizzo" means both spurt and sketch; ill. p. 119] also tells us about the first years of the 1980s. The image shows some affinity with the previous *Idolatrina*, but there are some significant differences. The face of the nineteen year old artist is spattered with traces of sperm which form a kind of abstract "drawing" on his features. The only other object in the picture is a hairy body part, presumably male, out of focus, that enters askew in the oblique setting. The spurt of sperm could be the product of the artist's self-masturbation, but the presence of another body which we intuitively sense looming outside the frame perhaps places the action in the sphere of a homoerotic encounter. Corte's intention was to create a work with the smallest possible number of elements, with only a *void* around his own face (he would say that his real aim was to be «the most handsome artist around»… implying that the 1980s showed a huge *void* in ideology. Form is always *precipitated* content). The hairstyle, the expression, the setting, the black and white and the slant of the lights, all point to a certain revivalist taste for the photographic poses of the '50s and '60s which we again find on many Techno-pop record covers in the '80s. But apart from the visual aspect, this work relates a period in the early '80s when sexual uninhibitedness triumphed, and AIDS had not yet become the nightmare of a generation (in fact, information about the disease was still limited).

Incredibly, this work more than any of the others was destined to create numerous problems for the artist in his relations with art galleries. Not only was it impossible to exhibit it, but at the time it provoked aggressive reactions from various art dealers in Italy (almost all of them, in fact), and the artist's youth disturbed them even more. This can be explained by the fact that, until that moment, there hadn't been any other work in Italian art – in a strict contemporary art context at least – which had dealt explicitly with homosexuality. On this theme, one can perhaps refer back to some drawings by De Pisis in the 1930s, produced, however, for an underground market and not for the official exhibiting circles. In the post-war period, Informal, Pop, Conceptual Art and the currents of Arte Povera and Neo-expressionism in Italy all avoided dealing with a theme which is evident, however, in other cultural fields such as the cinema, music and literature. Thus an artist shows us to what extent visual arts may sometimes lag behind their own times.

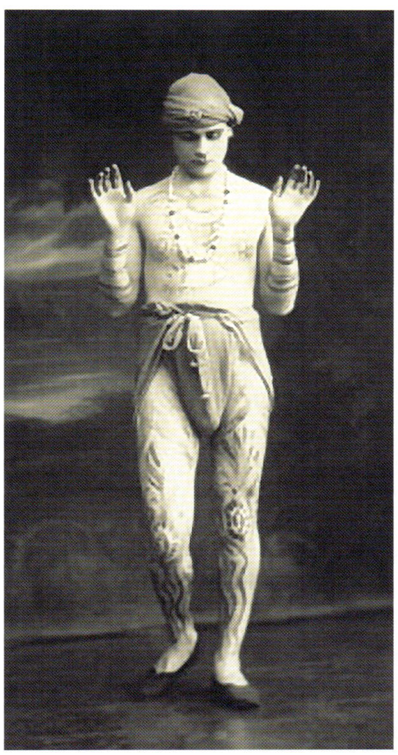

Filippo De Pisis, Paris, 1926.

Corte has never, however, intended to confine himself within a context of "homosexual art" as many other artists have done over the years. There are various works of his with heterosexual themes, even if marked with paranoia and necrophilia such as the double photographic portrait of himself and his young girlfriend made up by a professional in maquillage for corpses, meaningfully entitled *La mia metà, il suo doppio* (*My half, her double*, 1984). In the end, Corte can say of himself: «I have the type of body which may interest men, women and various in-between categories. And for a certain period I didn't

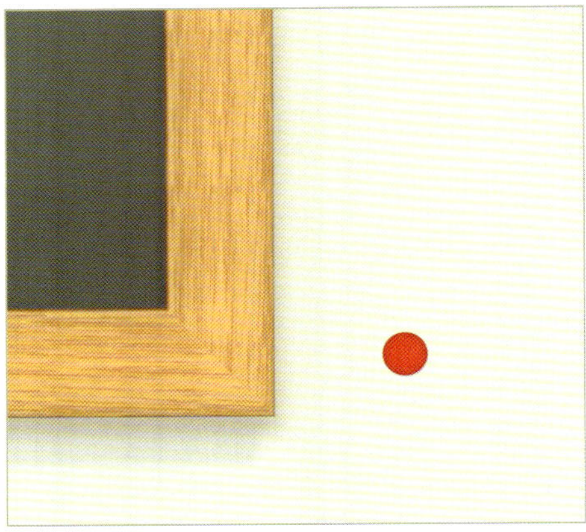

The red round sticker indicating the sale of a picture. Corte calls it «the very Personal Daemon of every artist».

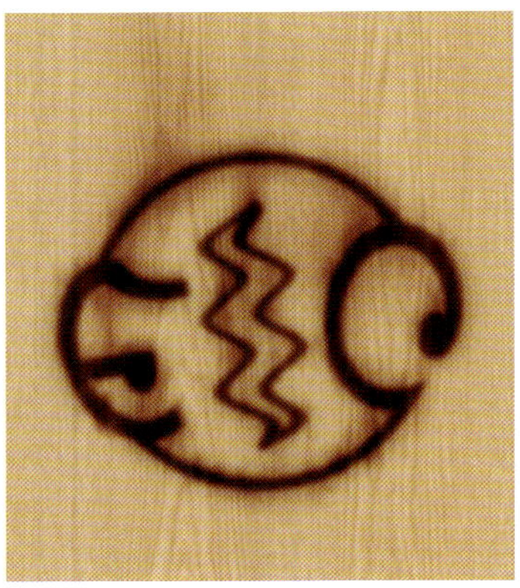

Burning Demonietto, 1985 (detail). From a series of 3 fire brands on wood. 9¼ x 6¼ x 1¼" (23,5 x 16 x 3 cm). GC 463.

think it necessary to say no to any of their advances». And in recent times he has been heard to state categorically: «I'm fucking sick of people who want to fuck».

In reality, few artists face the implications of sex in such a transversal refined way such as Corte. Here it is not a matter of joking about fetishism, the themes of dominance and submission, or the feasible limits of the body and pain. For Corte, sex and sexuality do not appear in easy or pornographically pedantic forms. Organic fluids, the cult of suffering, extreme relations, forms of courage return to the scene and become the unpredictable journey into sexuality, first psychic and then physical, of an artist with no inhibitions. Inhibition is the justifying sign of a self-inflicted limit. Liberation from limits marks a complete break with moralism in favor of subjective morality.

Corte's photographic works are interspersed with paintings and sculptures which live in the spectrospective dimension, taking up and developing previous themes, and creating new symbioses between materials, elements, characters, in a strategy of cohesion and not eclecticism. This is the 360° gaze of the artist as he stands on the edge of a cornice, on a high point in the center of the Mediterranean Sea. *I Demonietti Psichici* (*Little Psychic Daemons*, ill. p. 120), a sculpture from 1983, is related to the domestic monstrosities around beds and cradles that we first saw in *Risucchi Gastrici* and *Riflussi Stoici*. It recalls the eyeballs of *Penta-Portraits* and recycles one of the silk cushions, stained by the artist's blood, of *Per Strada*. But we see, for the first time, the recurring character called the *Demonietto Psichico*, shown here in one variant of a little Martian-atom: he will appear from time to time, included as an element in more complex works likewise the Cutout-Portraits, in various guises, disguises and metamorphoses. The Demonietto Psichico is the little doll – roly-poly – toy balloon – oddball – queer – alien – devil – gnome – fetus – mime – pimple – testicle – hernia – nodule – herpes – infected blood blot, etc. etc., but he may also show up as a branding iron (that marks the flesh with the anthropomorphic "EC monogram", ill. pp. 122, 123), or the red sticker that is put on the just sold painting (...«the real Personal Daemon of every artist», E.C. 1985), or as Magic 8 Ball (the cheap, popular American fortune teller), or a gambling chip, and so on. As the artist himself specifies:

[Recording date: February 7, 2000 – excerpt]
The *Demonietto Psichico* is also a symbolic reference to the urban legend of the "Red Moon" – or its variant, the "Red Eye" – which appears to artists lost in the Night of Doubt, in the most critical moment of their creative journey, when they must take a decision which will affect their chances of going down in History.

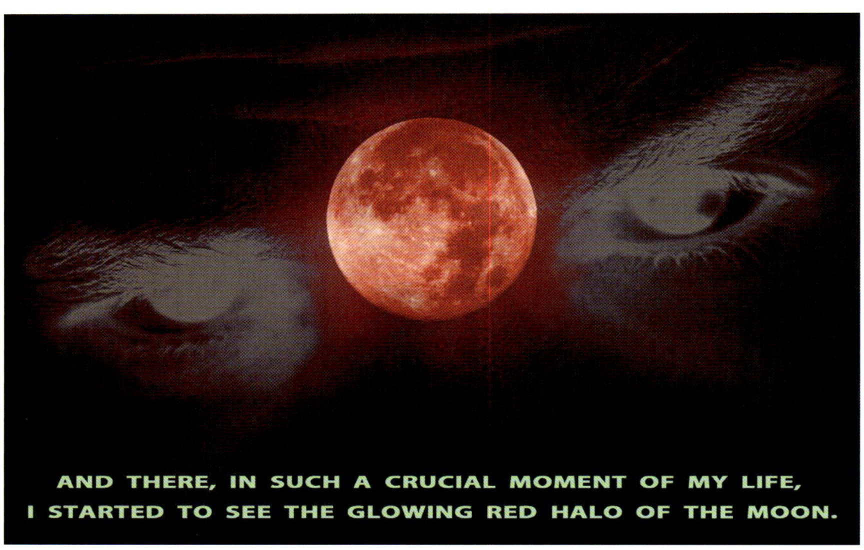

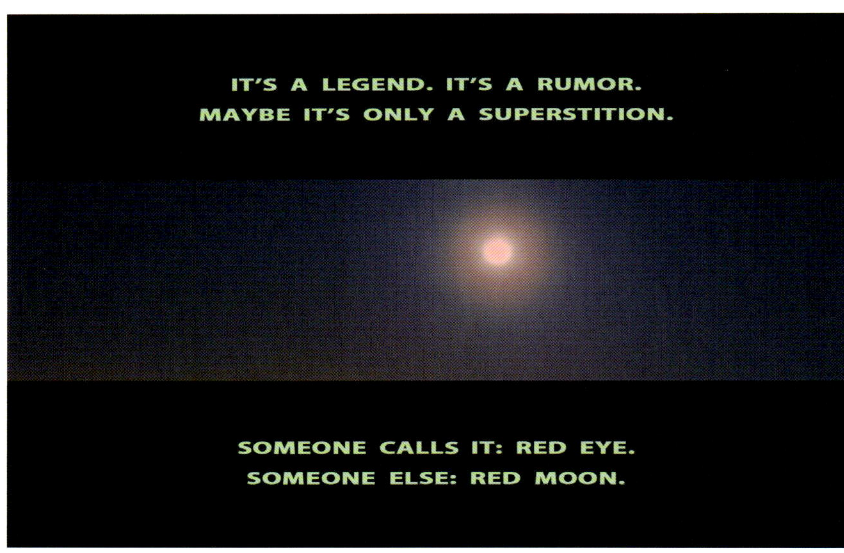

Video stills from *The Truth behind the Legend: the Red Moon Experience*, 1989-94. Cibachrome prints, variable dimensions. GC 817, 820.

Detail of a Little Psychic Daemon with overturned hourglass (from *N.E.O.*, 1995; see ill. p. 192) compared to the classic Magic Eight Ball: automatic and mechanical Fortune Tellers represent the embodiment of Evil in many popular traditions around the world.

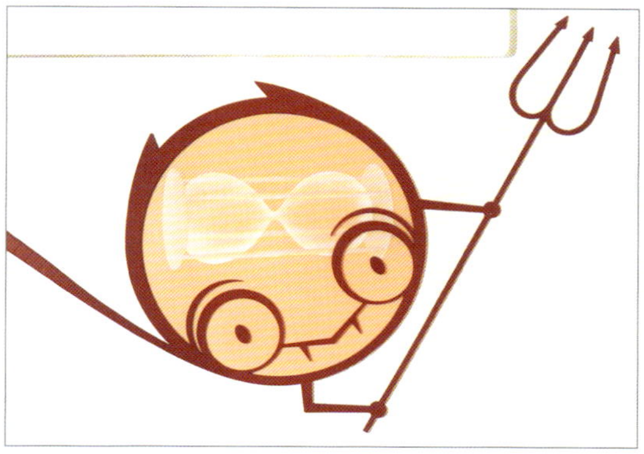

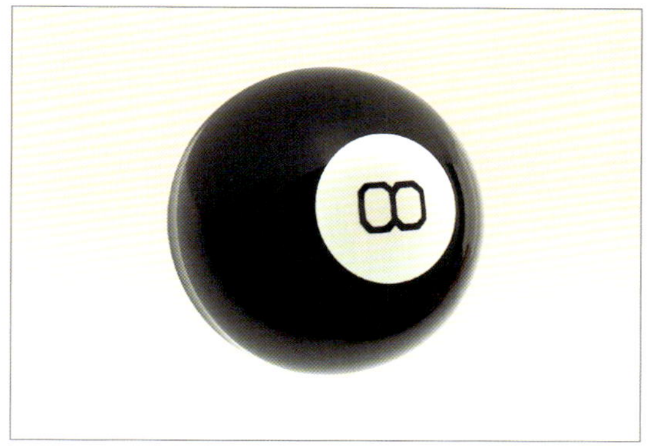

In short, the Demonietto is the corporeal synthesis of an entire creative tension, of the *gamble* of creation. He is a visual formula that returns over the years and in the works, certainly as an obsession and, thus, as a unified symbol of the Freudian *Unheimliche* (Uncanny) in its various incarnations through the ages of man. As an easily recognizable visual element that is even pleasant and "endearing", the Demonietto structurally fulfils, through a sort of "decoy tactic", the task of capturing the attention of even the most distracted spectators and guiding them, we might even say "initiating" them, in the perilous paths of a work of art: in part Psychopompous, in part Pied Piper.

Protagonists of a puerile-looking painting, in synthesized forms, they perform their ring o' roses inside the illustration for a children's textbook: they are *I Fantastici Demonietti Psichici* (*Fantastic Little Psychic Daemons*; cf. ill. below), suspended between microcosm and macrocosm so as to explain the laws of Life to us, like true otherworldly beings. But beware: as in many *Cutout-Portraits*, this picture is hung up by means of a weird system of little hooks that are not where they should be, and which place this naïve and childish painting in a context of total deviance. *Le Catastrofi ai Testicoli (Catastrophes to the Testicles)* is the second title of the work (the "double title", as well as the "double face", is a frequent feature of Corte's work), which plays on both the alliteration of sound, and the reference to spherical shapes and to the idea of infantile regression as a death wish. The work is a castration mask, another Supreme Menace. The child's picture painted by an adult tells of the impossibility of growing up, just as the Cutout-Portraits are infantile games that are inappropriate at a mature age.

Image of male genital nullification (left) used as reference for the work *The Fantastic Little Psychic Daemons* or *The Catastrophes to the Testicles*, 1983; enamel, pastel and collage on paper; enameled frame with lateral hooks and nails; 41 x 30½" (104 x 77,8 cm); GC 422 (right).

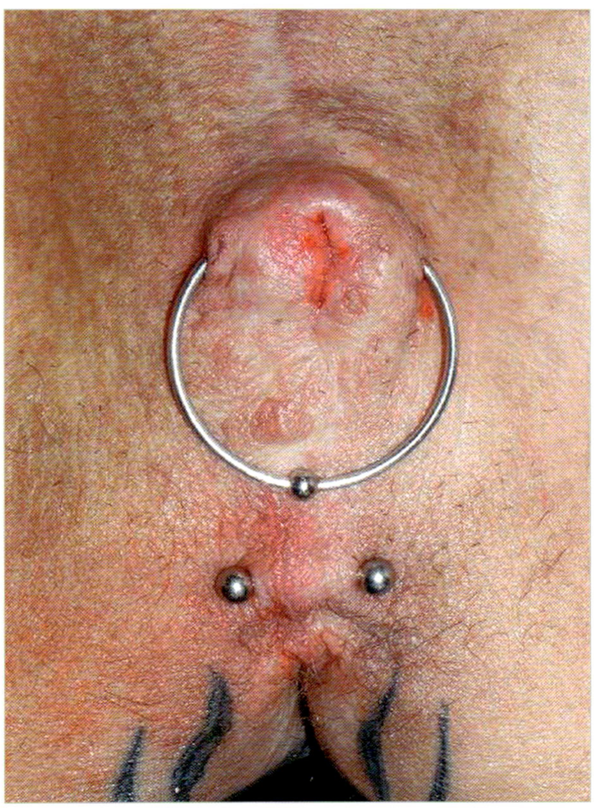

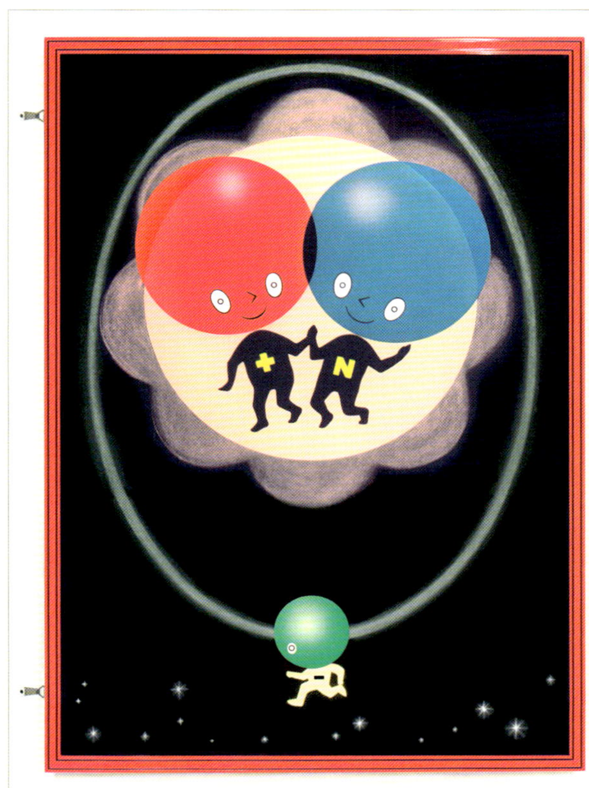

Meanwhile Corte continues to defy the laws of balancing above the void, in photo-pieces like *Abysspective* and, above all, *Il Faro*, which proves to be the last of this type. Compared to previous shots, *Il Faro* (*The Lighthouse*, ill. p. 121) uses not a public space but a private one for its setting: the terrace of an apartment block. The artist's intention was to have himself illuminated on the cornice by a wide beam of light like a police spotlight but then, once he was in place, he realized that the self-fuelled beam located on the terrace opposite was not powerful enough and barely managed to light up his figure. The photographer on the terrace opposite was responsible both for taking the photo and for the beam, and the posing artist placed so high up in front of him right near the harbor, himself became a lighthouse (a Lighthouse for Humanity?). All this unbeknownst to the inhabitants of the building, who were miraculously unaware that anything was going on, one of whom was at that moment tidying up his bedroom only a few feet from the happening (as can be seen in the lighted window). From a technical point of view, the photographic image of *Il Faro* is more professional than the others, and indeed the work as a whole seems to have been so successful that it is doubtful if it could have been done any better. For this reason Corte stopped producing similar pictures.

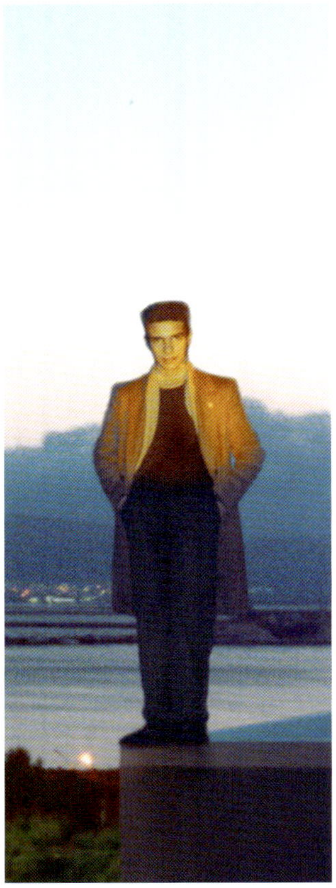

The Lighthouse, 1984.
Detail. Cf. ill. p. 121.

But for Corte, interests of a technical type almost never give rise to the project for a work of art. The work arises out of the unpredictable events that life offers day after day, from chance encounters which permit a vague and indefinable idea to take shape and form. And in this way, being open to life counterbalances the death wish that is so often proposed by Corte as an aesthetic model. A typical example is *Il Film Della Vita* (*The Film of Life*, ill. pp. 124-127), the first work that directly and constantly incorporates a human corpse. A real corpse which, with its slow decomposition, is an integral part of the work from its conception, even though hidden from sight by a marble tombstone. This is the result of a very strange story, developed over a long period of time, in which the principal, contrasting ingredients of art co-exist: lucidity and hallucination, cunning and devotion, as well as a good measure of "delirious" cynicism. The "dream of the 1980s", expressed in 1982 through *Disegno (Schizzo)* as an era of uninhibitedness, hedonism and pleasure, returns two years later in *The Film of Life* to show a different, icy face.

The artist himself explains this to us: through his words, his odd relationship with the condition of his time once again emerges – including certain aspects we would rather not see. A reality seized just a second or so before it vanishes beneath our feet, even if we are not balancing on a cornice, is then experienced by the artist in an intense, obsessive way, until he reaches the point where he can mold it like soft clay.

[Recording date: June 19, 2003]

Round about 1983, I began to ask myself whether the so-called "film of life" – as we like to term that rapid flow of images showing all the events of our existence condensed in one single instant, which apparently occurs at the final moment of death – unwound in a linear fashion following a chronological and narrative scheme of the "beginning-development-end" type, that ran with coherence from birth to death. Or if, as seems to me more likely, it went the other way, "rewinding", and started not from the first image of life, but rather from the moment of death experienced by the subject in that precise second, and then went bit by bit backwards, at supersonic speed, back to the very moment of birth, back to the darkness of pre-birth, the blank screen on which Life and Death come to terms.

It seemed to me that the problems connected to this matter were fascinating, and before dealing with the complicated possibility that a visual sequence broad enough to incorporate the time span of a human existence could be synthesized into one single moment (while maintaining a perceptive "legibility" without sinking into indeterminate chaos) I began to think of how I could somehow verify the sequential development of such a phenomenon, which was anyway considered by some to be nothing more than idle talk or legend. Of course, I could not undergo the experience, directly and by myself; I had to find at least one person who was on the point of experiencing the condition, both special and very common, of "being about to die". And above all, someone who would have the willingness of soul, as well as the remaining physical energy, to communicate to me before passing away, *in a flash*, the details about the clockwise or anti-clockwise direction of the images of his own past existence.

One might, for instance, consider a potential suicide victim: hear of the self-destructive aspirations of some acquaintance, or the friend of a friend. Talk about it, convince him, involve him in collaborating. Seduce him with the idea of the doubly useful aspect of his proposed final gesture:

should he support my fervent desire for knowledge, then his suicide would certainly become useful for Humanity, unveiling the mysteries of the Unfathomable, or those of physiological and neural chemistry, as well as that type of individual usefulness, conviction of which arises in the aspirant at the moment they decide to actually commit suicide, based on considerations that are variable, subjective, and therefore secondary in this context.

The fact is that, objectively, I didn't find it easy to meet people with those personality traits and plans of action. Not that there weren't people around with self-destructive urges, no: I've always met people who had *only and exclusively* self-destructive aspirations. And rightly so. What they lacked was a *method* which would lead to a practical and punctual organization of the extreme gesture: a praxis and even a choreography that could be established well beforehand, which I could take part in with my project of recording a testimony from the edge of the Abyss. The psychological marginalization of these *freaks* caused them to be just as isolated from others, so they faced this alienation in a naïve, amateurish and unreliable way.

Look, despite a certain unconscious humor in my telling you this "with hindsight", at twenty I handled the whole issue with the seriousness and commitment that a situation like this demanded. And it wasn't as if I had nothing else to do... Anyway, my curiosity wasn't merely idle: my real aim was to create a work of art, a painting, let's say, or a film or something similar, based on the order in which a series of images from the "film of life" proceeded. The idea was to have the largest possible number of images live together harmoniously – in the sense of a *fluid progression* which would amalgamate figures that were different from each other and not *necessarily* in harmony: images that would be the bearers of a meaning, and of their own intrinsic *inevitability,* in the least possible material space. But first I had to discover the temporal logic, the priority in the development of the sequences of the metaphysical "film of life"! Come to think of it, even today I don't believe I'm all that far from this kind of intention when I start a new painting... but now I no longer have that fervent desire, that frenzy for knowledge. Now I have Experience, the lack of which burned me up in those days.

In theory, it seems that the "film of life" appears more often to men and women who die a violent death, such as an accident or even suicide, or so it seems from the accounts of those who have miraculously escaped from such situations. Other rumors have it that it is not unusual for those who are dying of illness to experience this psycho-optical phenomenon. So I began to visit hospitals and the wards for the terminally ill. This is the period I remember with most difficulty, but it was completely useless and not only because I did not achieve my aims – due to the restrictions on visiting hours, the disapproving presence of relatives or nurses, and the contrast and obvious lack of dialogue between the apparent or real futility of my needs and the destiny of all those unknown faces: hordes, heaps of faces – but useless, above all, because I already had personal knowledge of that image of hospital grief: I had carried it with me since childhood, and to renew the experience – what can I say? – well, it certainly didn't broaden my vision of the world. However, time passed and I still hadn't managed to solve my problem. It was then that I discovered how little it pays to rely on others, even if only in part or for practical purposes, when creating your own works of art... I always paint my pictures by myself.

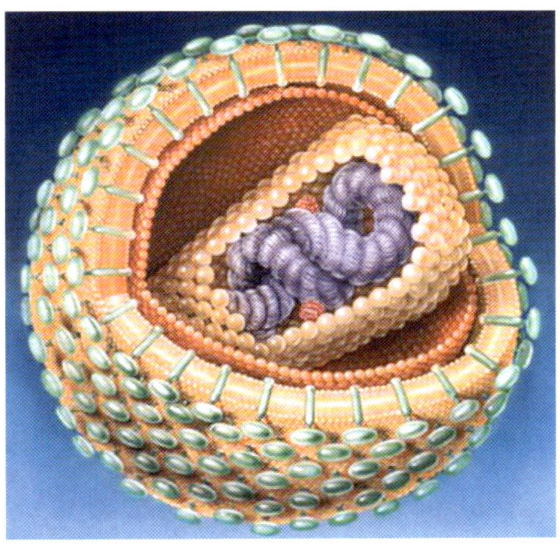

Structure of the Human Immunodeficency Virus.

Then, at a certain point, something happens. I find out that Roberto, an old school friend of mine who I hadn't seen for a while, is totally fucked. They tell me he'd caught the "plague of the 20th century" as it was called in the early 1980s. The news doesn't surprise me all that much, knowing as I did of his promiscuous sexual habits and abundant use of heroin: but since he is still quite young, I'm anyway struck by hearing this news.

Certainly, throughout my life I've had to find solutions to some very peculiar problems. How have I managed? I left home looking for them and... well, as you can see, in one way or another I've always managed to find them.

So I get in touch with Roberto. First of all, I talk to his family, who he still lived with, and they tell me at once that he is in a critical state. Then I meet him at his home. He is in bed, and clearly in very bad shape. His physical appearance had changed a great deal since the last time I'd chanced to meet him, about two years earlier: he is no longer handsome, his bones and skull now stick out, and he has almost no hair. His character, however, even though in the grip of that devastating disease, seems to have maintained certain aspects which I'm happy to rediscover during those first few moments in his company. It is as though we'd seen each other just the day before. He is pleased to see me, he treats me with affection but also with a certain nonchalance, revealing that

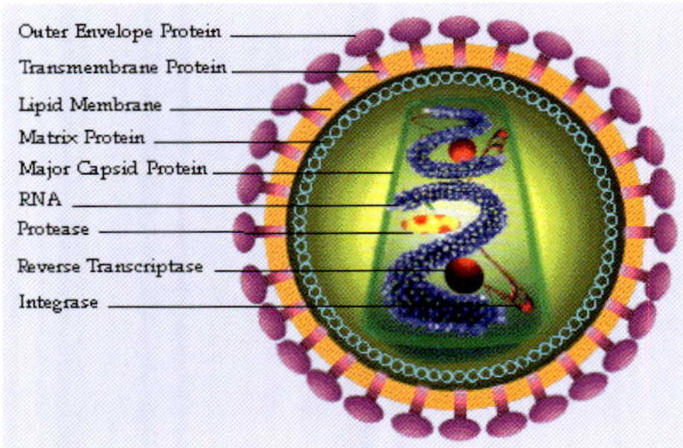

Components of the Human Immunodeficency Virus.

vague and distant coolness which was already one of his characteristics when I met him at the end of the '70s when he was 18 and I was just 15. In part he still has that attitude of affected cynicism common to the first New Wave generation. Understandably, there is a slight dimming of his aesthetically-inclined taste for the idea of decadence, now no longer merely hinted at but tragically experienced in the first person.

It doesn't take long to re-establish the former complicity between one-time adolescents. Even in this strange moment, desperate as it was for him, Roberto still remains attached enough to his one-time artistic aspiration as to understand the peculiar reasons for my research, and to support my aim. I explain to him in detail that I need him to give me a clear vision of how the sequence of images of his not very long life rolled past at the moment of death, if he were able to perceive them as, in a mix of legend and reality, it is said. We also need to organize things so that this would happen despite the many predictable obstacles: above all I would have to live by his bedside and look after him while awaiting the moment of his departure, rather like a vulture. And on his part, there must be a commitment to preserve sufficient energy and lucidity, even during the final spasm, to give me the response to my problem with his last surge of life. I also get a cassette tape recorder, since it was quite probable that I would need to re-hear or de-codify the words that he gasped out with his last breath.

The *beauty* of it is that the whole situation was not as melodramatic as it might seem. I settle down well enough in their big, rich people's house, with the sick man constantly under morphine in a state of stultified stupor in which, however, his detached New Wave dignity still managed to survive. Roberto's parents and brothers were almost always absent, busy with work, and perhaps exhausted and resigned after too many months of their loved one's illness. Actually I got the feeling that, since at that time it was not clear how the new virus was transmitted, his relatives and other friends preferred to keep as far away from him as possible.

I entertain Roberto during the day, putting on all his favorite records, and the rest of the time, since the musical therapy had a presumable psychological effect on the patient but could not slow his physical decline, I watch him deteriorate in his bed. Moreover, given the amount of morphine available in that household, I stealthily take advantage of it myself. In a moment of gratitude for my "affectionate company" Roberto give me the whole series of tapes with music that he had composed and performed on synth. I accept the gift out of formality, knowing full well that all that material would very soon find its way to the bottom of my trash can.

My condition was undoubtedly bizarre, and in my memory it seems to occupy an indefinite time: today I need to look up the exact dates on an old calendar in order to form a precise picture of those days. After all, I didn't even know this guy particularly well and all of a sudden I found myself in a situation of tragic intimacy, even further complicated by the possible contagiousness of a disease which no-one yet knew anything about. Roberto, as a serious New-waver, had always admired those who initiated new fashions and generational trends in clothing, music and social behavior, and now he found himself among the first to inaugurate one: the trend in dying of Aids.

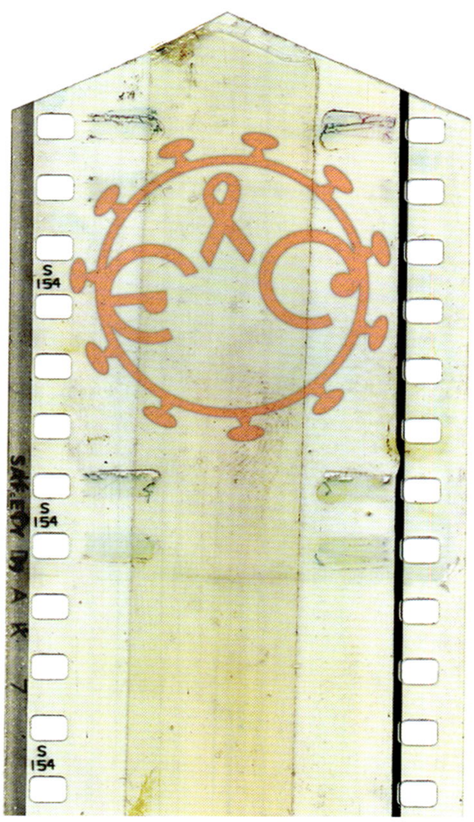

Branding Demonietto - Project for a Memorial Tombstone (dedicated to Kurt Raab), 1988. Emulsion on pvc. 48¾ x 31½" (123,6 x 80 cm). GC 574.

A few days pass and, just think, the situation come to a head. The illness worsens, he has a permanent temperature and constant pain, and the morphia is no longer effective. One morning, we are alone, Roberto, myself and a young nurse. It's clear to all three of us that the curtain is coming down... *right now*. Roberto, who is dripping wet, whispers to me: «I've never felt like this before. I'm on the brink, there's no turning back». OK, I get ready, pull a chair up close to his bed-side, switch on the recorder, and try to hold his attention with vague sentences and small talk so that his last glimmers of lucidity would not be blanked out, and he would not lose consciousness. He let out a rattle, a shudder, his eyelids closed over the dispirited orbits; I put the palms of my hands over his face to stop the trembling and, using both thumbs, delicately try to lift his eyelids so that I can check his glassy gaze and make sure he is still aware... Christ, it feels like I'm touching damp tissue-paper: his eyebrows slide away like the skin of boiled beans, and then my friend looks at me... he is still there, still lucid.

Watched with some disgust by the nurse I say, «Robbie, be careful. You know you've got to tell me what I asked. We're about to part and as you go you'll probably have a last vision when all your life passes before you in a flash». Roberto nods, with another rattle. «You've got to be ready like we agreed», I add, «and as soon as it happens try to tell me as clearly as you can, and quickly, because this will be the last moment of your life, the answer to what is indispensable for me to know». Everything that happened between Roberto and me from that moment on, as well as being true, can be directly verified by the personal testimony of Ms. Sandra Martino, a district nurse who is still working today. The sequence of events that I experienced as they occurred, second by second, is told just as it is impressed upon my indelible memory, lucid and clear, even if some have insinuated that there was a possible distortion in my perceptions owing to long term lack of sleep and the continual consumption of morphine – all of which has yet to be proved. But let's go on.

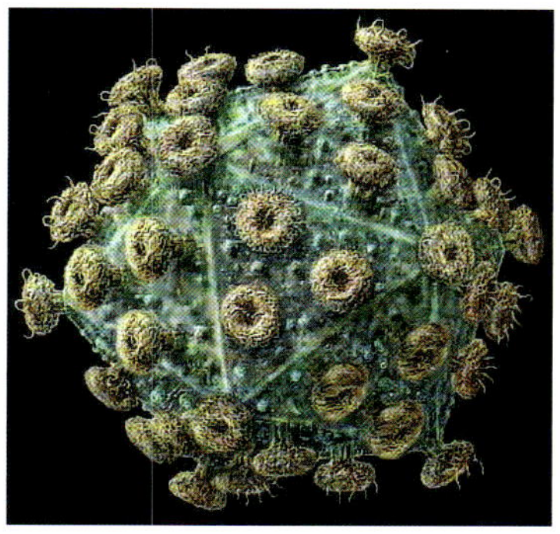

Scheme of the HIV envelope.

I keep holding my hands over his face. «Tell me, Roberto, my friend, is my hypothesis correct: that at the moment of death, the sequential images of one's life do not follow a linear pattern from beginning to end, like a real film, but go backwards like a tape as it mechanically rewinds, returning to the moment of birth and even beyond?» At this point, the temperature of Roberto's skull, which I held gently between the palms of my hands and could feel was burning with fever, drops by almost twenty degrees, while all the blood which filled the myriads of tiny veins in his eyeballs is instantaneously sucked away, and they now seem totally white, empty of traces... even his irises are affected by this rapid mutation, and from hazel become almost green; it's inexplicable: I'd never seen anything like it! But his pupils... God, his pupils!... In the space of a second I see them contract and dilate, contract and dilate at least a thousand times, like a crazy electric crackling. His pupils *are seeing something at extraordinary speed*... In a moment, his minute pupils rapidly change shape a thousand times, one after another: I see them become pinheads, then great black circles set to capture as much light as possible, then once again invisible pinheads, again and again, with hundreds of untidy intermediate variations in size, opening and contraction.... And all this *in a split second*! Well, in *that second*, Roberto's face no longer shivered with fever: as I said, I feel his skin suddenly freeze and then, *a second after*, his mouth opens to emit the most pestilential breath you can imagine, real fumes from hell, the like of which I've never smelt in all my life, together with the sound of a sentence which is his legacy to me, i.e. my *answer*. The recorder had already been on for several minutes, so I've been able to listen to that last sentence many times over the years, a phrase which was in any case quite clear to my ears from the outset, in its brevity and concision, despite Robbie's voice being broken by spasms, and my jumping backwards as I smelt that breath of mephitic wind.

«It's true – the opposite». That is the phrase. *It's true the opposite*, and Robbie pops off. It is definitely an answer, and the most one could offer at the point of death. But I still don't know how to interpret it. Whether the truth is *the opposite* of what I had been asking Roberto at that moment – i.e. if the sequence of images goes backwards, as I'd imagined – and that phrase then means that the images *do not run backwards* but instead go from birth to death just as life has been lived by the dying person. But «It's true: the opposite» could also mean that the images seen at the moment of death *really do* describe the story of one's life by rewinding, backwards, like a videocassette, just as I had cleverly intuited from the start... this, in the end, is my modest contribution to the Knowledge of Humanity.

The Film of Life, 1984 (detail).
Cf. ill. pp. 124-127.

Of course, I consider the second theory much more rewarding. In any case, I suggested to Roberto's family that they should carve his last words on a tombstone, since he would have been pleased with that (I lied): words that were rendered even more sibylline when taken out of context. I even offered to design the gravestone with a drawing of my own, and to carefully follow each stage of its creation in the stone-carver's workshop. His parents had no difficulty in accepting my proposal: I had been one of Roberto's best friends and I'd been with him right to the end, and moreover I was Enrico Corte, a young artist but already active and promising, with a lot of press coverage at local level. My offer seemed generous to them and, to their eyes, that tombstone might one day have had a certain value. And anyway, they were well-off, cultured and refined, and thus can "shell out" money without any problem. I watched them as I gave my spiel and grinned to myself, thinking: rich people… I've never felt so sorry for them.

So Roberto's parents bought a large piece of a newly constructed, evocative structure in the cemetery, designed to contain the new coffins of the future dearly departed of the city, in an infinite series of niches. The structure, six meters high and thirty meters long, in bricks and mortar covered with various rows of marble slabs which were little by little removed and replaced by proper tombstones, originally had an even more imposing and metaphysical aspect because it was completely new, virginal. Since it had only recently been finished, no other body before Roberto's had yet been put there, and there were no other tombstones apart from the one I had designed for him. We were, so to speak, the first on the scene. In the impenetrable glow of that enormous, immaculate magic wall lined with marble, the shiny reflecting black of "my" tombstone with a white inlay above and the ambiguous inscription, stood out, at least then in 1984, and attracted so much attention that it made the smallest commemorative flower superfluous. Even today Roberto's grave with its original 1984 tombstone can be seen, now surrounded and concealed among the others which have accumulated over time, in Area C / Lot 45 of the Saint Michael Cemetery in Castellani Square, Cagliari, Italy.

But there was yet another problem to solve, less pressing than the first, but that still intrigued me, mostly for creating a future work of art. How could all the images of a life exist in one second? A life, however brief, is nevertheless long. Perhaps it was possible to condense time through a system of double or triple exposures which overlaid several sequences together, like in the experimental films of the 1960s? Or eliminate dead time by selecting the less significant data and then canceling it, i.e. the *opposite* of the 1960s films? And if the latter, how could one establish the criteria by which the importance of one image was given priority over another? And who, indeed, was to establish it?

Throughout my life, I've had to find solutions to some very peculiar problems. How? I left home looking for them and… well, I've always managed to find them.

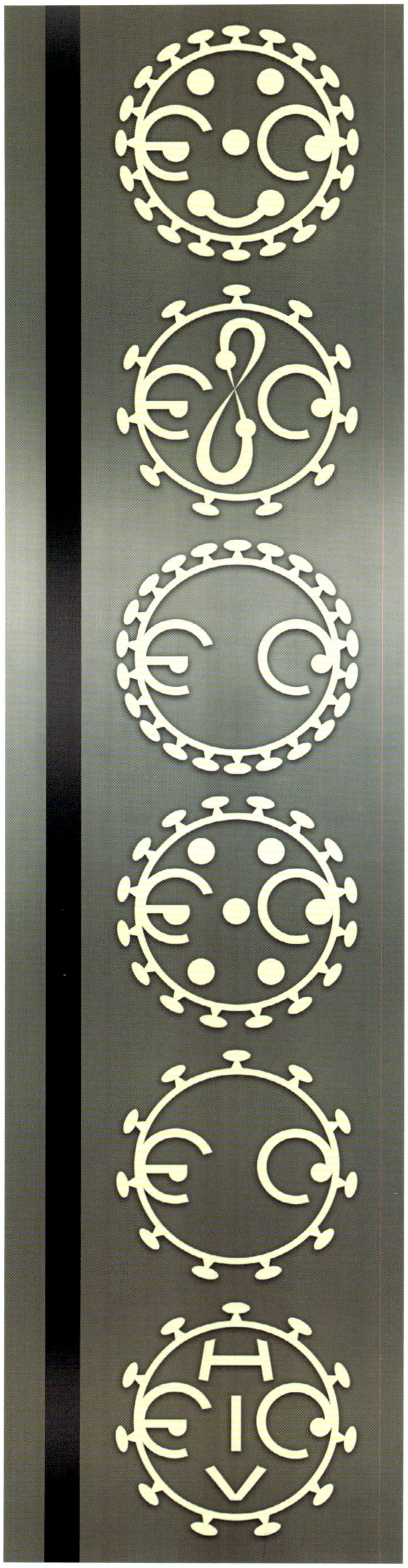

Branding Demoniettos for Bug Chasers, 2004.
Silkscreen on metal.
118 x 19¾" (300 x 50 cm). GC 1515.
(The so-called Bug Chaser is a gay man who deliberately attempts to contract HIV by having unprotected sex with a man or group of men who are known to have the virus.)

After having left behind him the experience of posing balanced above the void, and the macabre but unrepeatable adventure of incorporating a corpse into the work of art (a work which, rightly so, is not just "the tombstone"), the problem that the *painter* Enrico Corte faced at the age of twenty-one was how he could produce works which were more conventional but nevertheless not completely divorced from those premises. How could he bring the same sense of precarious balancing between two possibilities (leap into the void or stay put), between the alternating vision of front and back (abyss or terra firma; the decomposing corpse behind the unchanging stone). How could he once again portray that immobile point in space suspended between two contradictions, but in the form of a picture or a work of art which could be fitted into the commercial circuit, a *work like any other*.

This then was how the series of double-faced pictures came about: large panels that could be suspended from the ceiling or between two walls by means of steel cables, and painted on both sides. From 1984 to 1987 various works structured in this way followed one after another: *Demone Psichico*, *Tenie Psichiche*, *Larve Psichiche*, *Lemuri Psichici* (*Psychic Daemon*, *Psychic Tapeworms*, *Psychic Larvae*, *Psychic Lemurs*, ill. p. 136) and still more, which presume that the spectator will walk around the painting, and the painting will become a plastic element in space similar to a sculpture, sometimes incorporating three-dimensional elements on one or both faces.

The figurative themes were chosen on the basis of visual contrasts in form and color from one face to another. Here we find images that have appeared previously: the omnipresent Cutout-Portraits, the painted veins of fake marble (to which, however, almost indistinguishable upside down profiles of people have been added), the didactical representation of atomic structures (but modified, as in *Equi-lirium*, 1984, where the protons and neutrons of an atom are lined up in an impossible formal equilibrium; ill. p. 128).

We also encounter new forms: the overturned hourglasses (other "equilibria of temporal immobility" which we will find in other works, such as the hypnotic *C(L)ep(S)y(D)ra*, almost irritating to the eye – which recalls the face of an insect, the dragonfly called Aeshna Clepsydra; ill. p. 135) and the fable-like images taken from a book of children's fairytales (in this case, a disturbing image of deterioration taken from the "The Little Lead Soldier" by Hans Andersen: the little Soldier and the Ballerina as pathetic, sterile lovers who burn and melt in the same Inferno as that populated by the

Little Psychic Daemons… Another destruction of the Family?). In addition, in the background there are strange square structures, empty and askew, that define an ornamentalism which is almost its own cancer: the reference might be to the interior decoration of the '50s and '60s, i.e. the moment before Corte's birth, but also to a sort of DNA spiral, distorted and corrupted by alien manipulation. Or they might perhaps recall the rows of empty burial niches of *Il Film della Vita* in a multicolored interpretation altered by LSD, or the rows of scrutinizing windows in the work *Per Strada*… But perhaps the meaning of those structures lies in all these things put together.

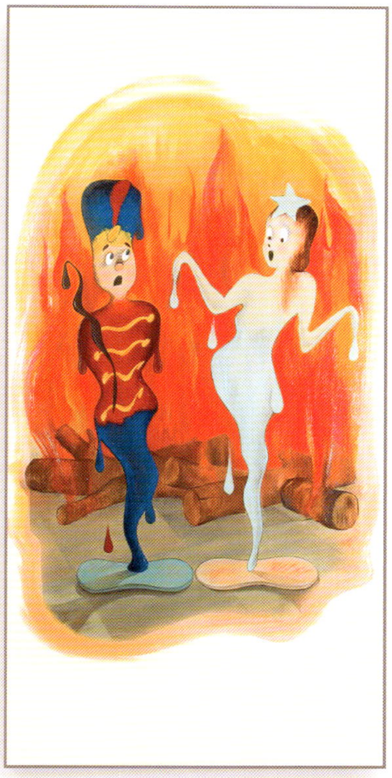

Era of Zero Births, 1985. Side A and B.
Double-face panel hung from the ceiling.
Oil and lacquer on wood.
38½ x 18½ x 0,8" (98 x 47 x 2 cm).
GC 468.

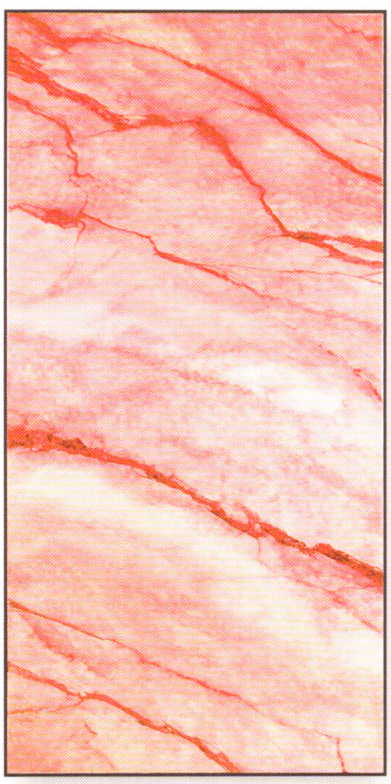

The use of a certain iconographic repertoire stresses some personal visual obsessions, recurrent phantoms of decay or displacement which have emerged from childhood, and which the artist finally succeeds in transforming into *social* obsessions, and not only in the sense of the collective unconscious. The 1985 work *Era della Natalità Zero* (*Era of Zero Births*) with its two sides on which two opposites confront each other (the heat of the fire which fuses the Soldier-Ballerina couple and, on the other side, the sterile, mortuary frigidity of the marbled surface with an upside-down profile hinted at between the veins) tells us of a crucial demographic problem in the year 1985, when in Italy, following a descending curve which had started in 1970, deaths outnumbered births for the first time. The problem of the low birthrate is still the subject of much debate in Italy even today.

Corte's stylistic approach in these works is almost always cold and detached, often achieved by means of the impeccable spray-painting on industrial materials, giving us a work on the Image in a frozen version, like that of the morgue, not unlike what the American graffiti artists, who were only a few years older than Corte, were doing at that time… but transposed into an operating theater for cerebral autopsy. In parallel with the realization of these paintings, which are to be hung from the ceiling, Corte began – not by coincidence – to collect used nooses (cf. ill. pp. 156, 157).

Shown in various exhibitions in Italy, the two-faced works reached the peak of their disorienting function in group installations. Either positioned as if they were walls of a labyrinth – through which visitors were forced to follow a multi-polar, obligatory path finding themselves at the starting point again having understood nothing – or otherwise grouped together almost in a single block in the middle of the room – with the spectators forced to scrape along the walls because of the lack of space – the double-faced works did not in any way try to appeal to the public, or attempt to enter the conventional structures of the art market. The limit was reached during a solo exhibition by Corte in Naples in 1986 (cf. ill. p. 129). The artist himself tells us:

[Recording date: June, 19, 2003 – excerpt]
The situation was this: a sizeable group of double-faced works, hanging from the ceiling at eye-level, almost entirely occupied the center of the exhibition room, like a multicolored fecaloma in the intestine. The spaces between the pictures were narrow and the public could at best peer into them, but couldn't get inside the block, the "labyrinth". Quite the reverse, in fact – people could barely move across the room because the space in the center was crammed with pictures hanging from the ceiling. They could just get in through the door and then slide along the walls, peeking with difficulty along the narrow passages in the mass of panels suspended in the void. Since I had been shrewd enough as to put a series of almost invisible little nails into the walls, as the people slid over them, in the limited space, they got hooked to the wall by their jackets, pullovers or silk blouses. And that was just what I wanted to achieve: the members of the public attached to the wall like objects, while the pictures in the center of the room observed them.

The double-faced pictures are not the only types of work that Corte developed around the mid-80s. *Resident in Venice* (ill. p. 131), created in collaboration with Andrea Nurcis, is a small, refined sculpture in Murano glass, made according to the artist's instructions by a glassmaker from the Venetian island of Murano, famous for its skilled foundries. Situated on the Venetian Lagoon, the work acquires a "psycho-geographical" character by playing on the fact that Venice is also a town in California, the American state The Residents come from. The viewer's gaze is confused by seeing the sculpture that appears in the foreground as tiny, whereas the monuments from the past tower in the background. The spectrospective becomes almost a "counterspective", or an *antipodespective*, muddying the waters, one could say, between the Lagoon and Venice Beach.

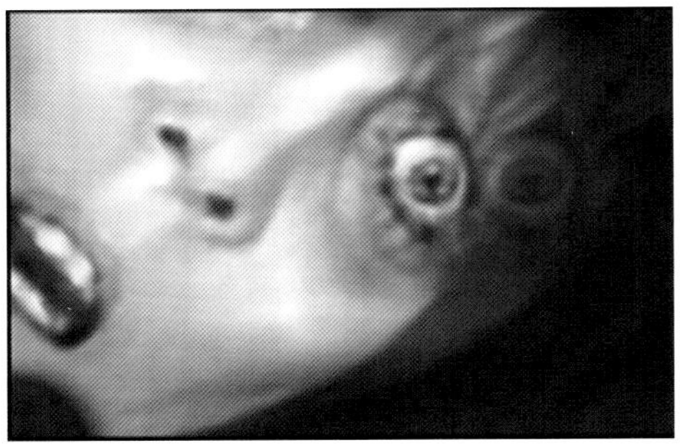

Nico Live, 1984. From *Portfolio*, a collection of ten photographs. Unnumbered edition. Variable dimension. GC 443.

Music is again the leitmotif of *N.I.C.O. Rejected Record Cover* (ill. p. 130), which was in fact an LP cover designed by Corte for the rock-star Nico, but refused by her record company. Corte met Nico, who had always been his musical idol, in 1984 during a concert, and he came to an agreement with her on the creation of a cover for her next LP. Once again, it wasn't just a matter of a fan paying homage: Nico, like The Residents, was the incarnation of a totally unique figure in the musical styles and genres of her time, and this was the action method with which Corte identified, too. The record company, however, demanded that a close-up of the singer's face be included, which Corte did using a photo he had taken of her. In Corte's interpretation, rather than looking like a "Star", Nico appeared to be a "Black Hole". And the graphic context of the cover stresses the more self-destructive aspect of Nico's figure, i.e. "shooting up" (= "bucare" in Italian: to make a hole) heroin, the substance that had dominated her life for years. All in all, the creation of a work about heroin was a duty for an artist belonging to a generation which was in its twenties in 1984, and Corte's objective was to give an interpretation of the problem through the attitude, approach and outlook of his generation: heroin as something with great *appeal*, whose omnipresent allure was hard to resist. On the front cover there is a photo of a giant syringe: the piston is shaped in cardboard and can be pushed with the finger into the body of the syringe. It is a consumer object, shown in an obscure light but not without playful meaning, charming. On the back, a black Cutout-Portrait with Nico's profile (and with a dose of heroin in the middle). After the singer's death in 1987 (not from heroin) Corte was however informed by the record company that his cover was not suitable.

This play on opposition/attraction with regard to the demands of the cultural market has permeated all Enrico Corte's activity. The double-faced works of the 1980s, for example, at the time represented a greater challenge to certain rules on the staging of an exhibition than might be thought today. At a certain point Corte was forced to "split" the two faces, i.e. create a series of paintings on more conventional backings, such as paper or canvas, in which the same visual themes as those of the double-faced pictures were developed in normal paintings to be hung on walls, which could at best be set one alongside the other (ill. p. 134). This was done to thwart certain unscrupulous dealers who wanted to cut the double-faced pictures in two, and sell both halves separately. For the artist this was a moment of intelligent concession to the demands of the market, and so these works acquired a specific cultural significance, due more to this aspect – the unveiling of a contradiction – than to the themes and images which appear in them. However, immediately afterwards, the artist took his revenge with works such as *Neural Marmo,* whose spiral-shaped installation prevented the public from even entering the room to see the work.

A compromise between the double-faced work and the picture hung on the wall is represented by the openable paintings produced from 1986 to 1988, generically called *Cross Fades*. The 1987 work *Tumulo Psichico – l'Astrazione del Petrolio* (*Psychic Tumulus – The Abstraction of Petroleum*, ill. p. 138) is a typical example of this: two square panels coated with shiny black formica are joined by invisible hinges and can be closed against each other or reopened at will. The back of the left panel is fixed to the wall; the right one is free moving and the action of opening or closing like a book is performed with this panel (or rather, the opposite of a book, which should be opened or closed from the left. This detail is not casual because the artist meant to stress the divergence between visual art and literary communication). Thus we have two shiny black "mirrors" on whose inside-faces the artist intervenes by using industrial enamels and various other materials: cut out tissue paper, sand, an inset concave mirror reflecting image upside down, and so on. When the two faces are closed one against the other, the only thing visible on the wall is a square of black laminate, empty, mirror-like, with an icy appearance. Then there is also a specific *Installation Project* for the so-called *Cross Fades* (ill. p. 140): it foresees a rudimentary system of pulleys which begin from the picture and end at the entrance door of the exhibition room, so that when a visitor opens the door, the picture on the wall opposite shuts in his face…

There are also many variations on the theme of the opening door, such as *Dismisurazione Dello Spazio* (*Dismeasurement of Space*, ill. p. 140)*,* in which a small door is incorporated into the body of a large painted panel, hung regularly on the wall. The artist's *idée fixe*, which he uses as an enigmatic psychological metaphor, is that the pictures must "cast

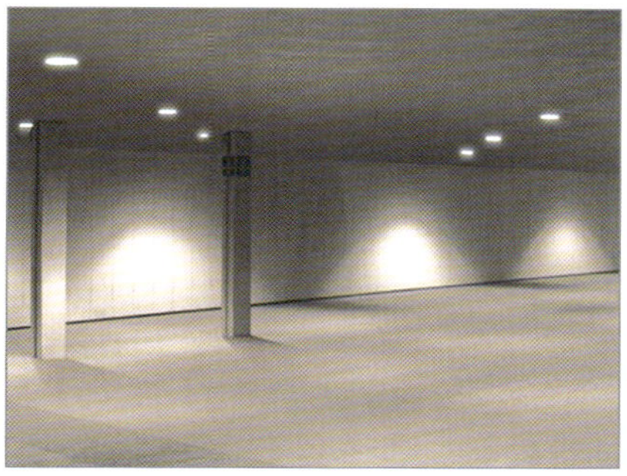

Corte's invisible pictures "buried" inside the art gallery walls. Piazza di Pietra, Rome, 1986.

a shadow", which is why they are suspended in space, or have movable or projecting parts: «to throw a fine clear-cut shadow on the walls». But the display of a state of conflict, vertigo, confusion or even castration of the visual gaze, would lead Corte to create not only works which closed in the face of the public, but even pictures which crashed down like drawbridges before the spectators (risking to crush their skulls) who, as they walked around, inadvertently activated a system of springs connected to the floor in front of them. When he was reproved for this habit of creating self-moving or projecting works "that cast a shadow", Corte conceded to the needs of the public by reaching extremes, like the time he set up an exhibition where the pictures were walled up inside the gallery walls. "Buried" inside deep niches covered with plaster, the pictures were not only immovable but also invisible… and without any shadow at all (years later they are still there, unbeknownst to the new proprietor of the premises). And more still: in 1986 he set up an installation consisting of a huge prefabricated room, in inflatable rubber like a dinghy, but perfectly inhabitable and fitted with "all mod cons", which collapsed on the floor after the attempt to hang a painting on its wall with a nail (*L'Errore nel Quadro – The Error in the Picture*).

All this, we should remember, paradoxically took place in the historical context of the 1980s painting boom. But in this phase of his activity the artist made no reference to the mainstream, to the strategies of the Art market, but rather to a more subterranean "wave", somewhat similar to that which from the early eighties onward was to be termed *Industrial Culture*. Or rather, he tried to "infect" the body of so-called contemporary art with some of the tendencies arising from the Underground.

In art, Corte uses *paradox* as a tool for cultural analysis, something similar to what was called, in the thinking of the Frankfurt School, the "Critique of Ideology". With the difference that the artist is now no longer fussy about cynically using for his own ends elements that derive from the culture industry and form part of the "mass culture". For the artist these elements are only devices to be dismantled and reassembled following a logic more sadistic than scornful or apocalyptic. Through the use of paradox he stops himself once more «just one step from the final crash», i.e. from Frankfurtian apocalypticism.
On the other hand, some subsequent fringes of contemporary Thought (such as the writings of Frederic Jameson in the USA or Stuart Hall in Great Britain, partly indebted to Antonio Gramsci, one of Corte's countrymen) give an interesting interpretation of mass-culture not in terms of ideological domination but as a field for the re-articulation of identities, roles and differences that are in constant mutation, in which utopian elements survive the "reality check" and hence elude the logic of power. Amid the mesh of converging notions from the two Schools, Corte puts his own idea of paradox into practice.

The work *Rimozione* (*Removal*, ill. p. 154), dated 1986, is an example of the anomalous positioning of the hook on a painting, which Corte uses as an expedient over time and in various works. In this particular case, the setting up of the drawing – a triple self-portrait in sequence of the 23-year-old artist, which is almost a rapid sketch – seems at first sight to indulge in a certain kind of figurative academicism, but only enough to highlight the contrast with the inappropriate position of the hook and the corresponding nail. Instead of hiding this anti-aesthetic element, the artist prefers to put it in evidence, giving it its own personal space in an unlikely point and integrating it in the structure of the work (its form even recalls the triangular module on which the drawing itself is based). And the picture becomes a tool that aims to deconstruct a cultural parameter: analyzing the "perimeter" of the work of art, its border-limit – like the cornice on which the young Corte balanced himself – rather than its figurative contents.

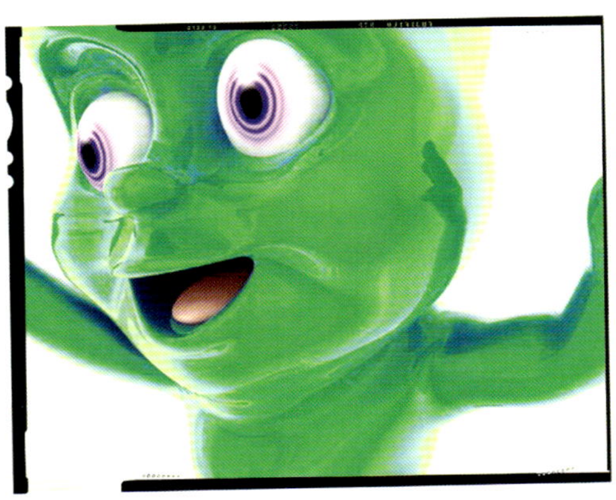

Working picture for the *Fluororama*. SC 362.

This is why shadows, psychisms, inversions and displacements do not distract Corte from observing the external reality around him. Whenever he can, the artist always seeks to avoid any form of escapism, of introspective self-indulgence. And often, behind the mask of the work, he unveils a social declaration. The 1988 *Fluororama*, is such an example (ill. pp. 141-149). It belongs to a type of work, repeated over time, which assigns a new role to popular consumer objects or those made for children. These objects – rethought and corrected – which usually date back to the '50s and '60s (the years of the artist's "pre-birth"), in particular refer to problems of sight (problems of visual perception as metaphors for artistic fruition – and here we are not far from the issues which obsessed the artist at the time of the *Film of Life*), and therefore involve the act of viewing in relation to situations of occult persuasion, hallucination, intoxication and pain.

The *Fluororama* is the reconstruction in the smallest detail of a visual diskette with a series of 3D slides to be viewed using a special binocular viewer. It comes complete with a logo, registered trade mark, stereoscopic viewer, graphics and suitable packaging, all assembled according to the artist's logic. The reference to reality which we mentioned is due to the fact that the work is inspired, though without declaring so, by the Australian journalist Ian E. Stephens' research on fluoridation as a system of mass brain control, which he puts forward in his 1987 book *The Dickinson Statement – A Mind-boggling Thesis*. Stephens' very detailed studies on the induced use of fluoride as an inhibitor of the will, and on the industrial/political network which lies behind it, caused a great deal of discussion towards the latter half of the 1980s and also when it was republished in the following decade. Corte took up these studies as the pretext for a work of "didactic" character, which was perversely directed at the younger generations in a suggestive, fascinating visual language that was intended to persuade them to take a daily dose of fluoride through their toothpaste.

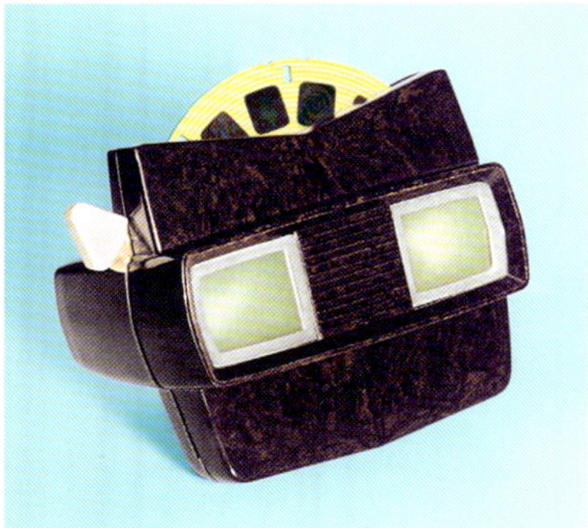

The binocular viewer for the stereoscopic slides of the *Fluororama*.

The seven photographic images created by a stereoscopic technique, and presented on the diskette as small slides, illustrate like dioramas the "educative" precepts of *Fluororama,* and are created by uniting painting, sculpture, small objects, superimpositions, photo-retouching and other "tricks", in an a very detailed work which required months of application. Each of the seven images should be considered as a single work of art which can be presented in the form of a large-sized print: in 1996 the artist also created a digital version of these pictures (ill. pp. 12 and 144-149). These are the only works in which Corte shows great respect for the quality of the photographic image. His approach to photography, in fact, almost always remains faithful not so much to amateurism (there is nothing casual in his work), as to the *improvisation* of the shot: whatever happens, happens. For this reason, he often uses cheap cameras, with standard 50 mm lenses, and film which is incapable of offering high image resolution. Corte even goes so far as to allow mold to form on the inside of the lens, to make the image even more "defective". But some photos demonstrate the great care he took in taking a exaggeratedly vertical or horizontal shot.

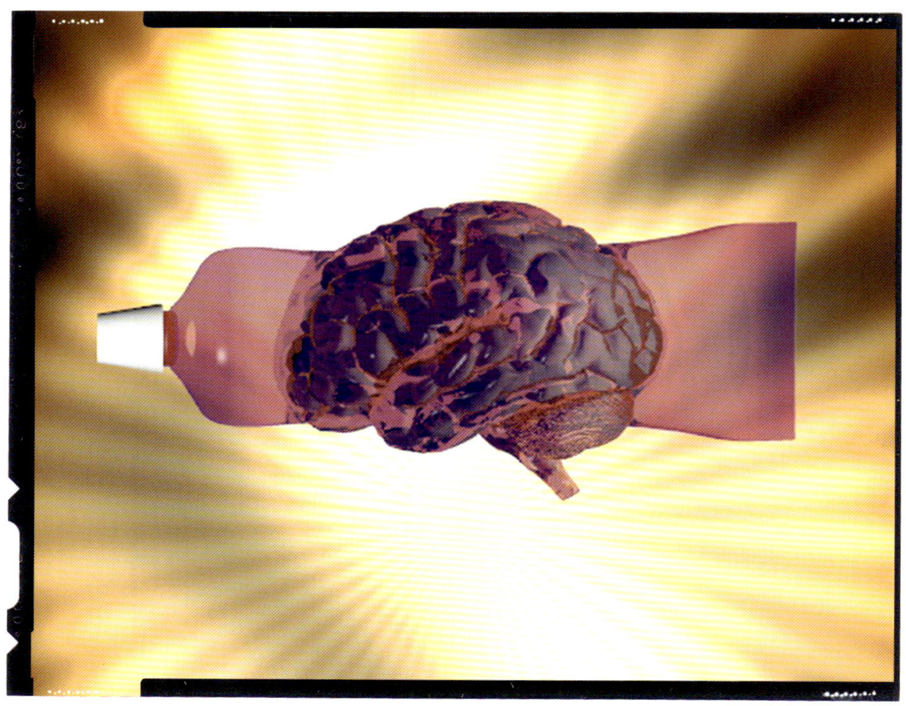

Working photograph
for the *Fluororama*.
SC 364.

For Corte, taking a photograph is a way of fixing a particular moment in the flow of life. He may assume the role of the voyeur, as in *Der Weg Zum Kubismus*, but more often than not he chooses the attitude of a "tourist of existence", whose *souvenirs* may be contaminated by elements of "distraction" such as mould or dust on the objective. (Note that, for Corte, taking on the role of "tourist" means a disenchanted denouncement of the impossibility of the "Tragic" and "Heroic" in the system of contemporary art. The impossibility of the Tragic is a theme which runs, semi-concealed, through a large part of his work, beginning with *Cheese*, right up to *Dolorama*). The photographs in three-dimensional

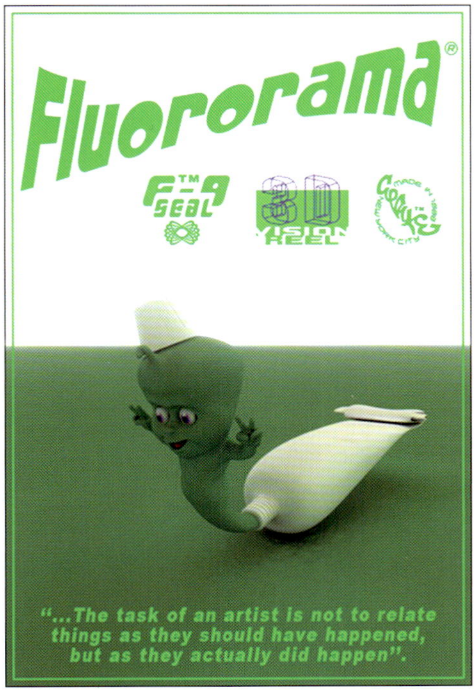

Promo Poster for the *Fluororama*, 1988. Print on paper. 47¼ x 31¼" (120 x 79,5 cm). CG 573.

style of *Fluororama* differ in the following way: they amalgamate with painting and sculpture in representing not a real world (which, however, they recall through Stephens' pamphlet), but a universe of pure intoxication, a kaleidoscopic Limbo populated by likeable toothpaste lemurs which wander among cerebral mucilage or in undersea ravines of an organic and viscous spatiality. It is interesting to note how Corte consolidates this hallucinatory scenario through a punctilious, hyperrealistic construction, with a fine "touch" and sensitivity towards plastic form that he has refined over the years. In *Fluororama*, Corte at last achieves a magic *equilibrium*: the maximum of complexity and stratification within extremely limited dimensions (the reel of *Fluororama* with its corresponding stereoscopic slides measures a mere 9 cm in diameter), in sharp contrast with the taste for the over-size in the art of the 1980s.

Linked to *Fluororama*, through its allusive theme of dental equipment and the oral cavity as a place of sinister bio-psychic processes, *Clean-o-rama* (1988-89) is a "sculpture" of paradoxical size – 10 meters high by 4 millimeters thick – made up of a long string of dental floss on which microscopic anthropomorphic remains cling, like winking new incarnations of the Demonietto. Observed through a magnifying glass, perfectly made, they look like balancing little psychic "snotballs", tightrope-walking "gnawings" that must be removed.

The interweaving of painting and sculpture in a hypnotic serial pattern enters Corte's work with an installation of pictures such as *25 Seconds*, *25¼ Seconds*, *25½ Seconds*, *25 ¾ Seconds* and *26 Seconds* (ill. pp. 150, 151). These are five almost identical pieces which contain casts of the artist's face, real twisted candles and Cutout-Portraits, while in the background three-dimensional landscapes and phosphenes fade into a hallucinatory backlighting. Time becomes distorted in this context of sensory deprivation where eyes, mouth and ears are blocked by the candles' waxy protuberances. Corte had to dedicate a whole year of work to create the entire series of five pictures (1989, when he passed from 25 to 26 years of age), but in their titles a year of work – his twenty-sixth – is equivalent to one second (i.e. the passage from 25 to 26 seconds, in five micro-fractions of time, or the same number of *micro-intervals in tone*: incidentally, we should remember that the use of micro-intervals is a crucial topic in the music of the 20th and 21st centuries).

At this point we may wonder: why does the artist focus on – and distort – this passing from 25 to 26 years of age? Because, as biologists have determined, the 25th year in one's life is, on average, the moment in which a human attains maximum efficiency, the highest rates of metabolism, of fertility, etc. From age 25 on, we could say that a person begins its long, imperceptible aging process.

By contrast, in the work *Sveltospettiva* (*Speedspective*, ill. p. 132) the execution of a small and simple pencil drawing may cover a sweep of twenty years with no visible distinction (note the intentional reference, in the drawing, to the game of "hopscotch": twenty years are contracted into a child's hop or the rapid gait of a man on stilts. Moreover, according to Mircea Eliade, hopscotch is a game which conceals the deepest archetypes of Life and Death, an allegory of the "labyrinth", an initiatory "descent into Hell", and subsequent return to earth, by the child).

The drawing *Bruciospettiva* (*Burnspective*, ill. p. 133) is coupled with *Sveltospettiva* and it also took twenty years to realize (1984-2004). Here, a series of small shaped masks were set over several points on a white paper sheet, allowing the daylight to yellow the uncovered spaces, thus, with the passage of time, producing a gradual, natural "drawing": removing the masks twenty years after, a self-portrait of the artist – of his smile – appears, whose adolescent physiognomy has remained unaltered for twenty years while the supporting paper structure deteriorates and ages. At that point, a few graphite strokes complete quickly the piece. *Sveltospettiva*, *Bruciospettiva* and the already-mentioned *Antipodispettiva* are works that upset the material, spatial and temporal coordinates of visual perception.

Coming back to works like *25 Seconds*, *25¼ Seconds*, *25½ Seconds*, *25¾ Seconds* and *26 Seconds*, we see that these kinds of pictures, somewhere between painting, sculpture and the insertion of "deviated" objects (above all candles lying horizontally, twisted or even knotted, which substitute the previous image of the overturned hour-glass), would acquire an increasing sense of heaviness and immanence over the years. The backgrounds with their loud colors, hypnotic phosphenes and Little Psychic Daemons dancing inside them, co-exist with complex and obscure symbioses, with mellow cross-breeding of everyday

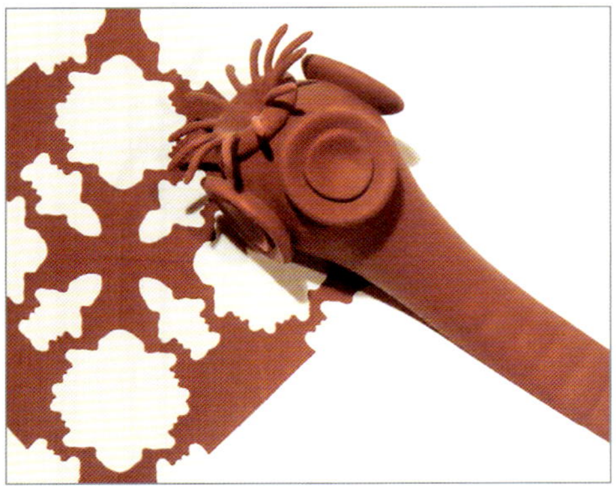

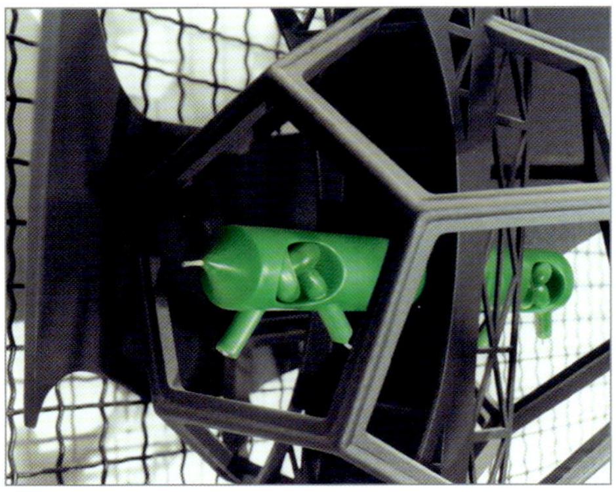

N.E.O. (Near Earth Objects), 1995.
Two details (see ill. p. 192).

objects whose form and function transmute into something else not easy to define: something *new*. The observer is forced to always change viewpoint, moving away and coming close again, sliding his head in between the perspective layers that are superimposed in the work, into the cannibalistic rite of the volumes, so as to discover hidden details.

The way in which the works are modeled is flawless: virtuoso manual skill to the point of obsession and industrial production not only co-exist, but create a visual paradox so that, in the cold perfection of form, one is indistinguishable from the other (as were the real vegetal parts and the fictitious ones in *Botanical Rarities* of 1981). At last, we reach the funereal monument of *Skullaby* (also called *Circonvolutarli & Circonvoltarme – Circumvolu-woodworms & Circumvolu-moths*, ill. p. 155) where the metaphor of *making a leap in the level of conscience* is expressed by the cast of the artist's body, sucked back into self-obscuration, plunging into the indefinable, into aphasia, *into his own shit.* Works like these, such as *Enuresi Psichica Notturna* (*Nocturnal Psychic Enuresis*, ill. p. 162), *N.E.O.* (ill. p. 192), *Radice Cubica* (*Cube Root*, ill. p. 164), *Cornucopia of Illusions* (ill. pp. 160, 161), *Screen Memories* (ill. p. 163), *Brainscan* (ill. p. 153) and still others, present very carefully calculated internal balances, relations between full/empty, urges and counter-urges, in a dialogue between form and content which almost imitates the neural network's labyrinth of mutual influences.

Already during the period of *The Film of Life* the artist was searching for a way to "compress" and balance the largest possible number of naturally incompatible elements. Perhaps not by chance, these are works that are contemporary to the discovery by a team of young neurobiologists in Milan of the role of individual synapses in cerebral communication, with the consequent identification, and even photo-reproduction, of the "elementary unit of activity" which develops from them. Indeed, in the artist's work, the balancing-act delirium of forms seems to be developed according to a logic which is more parascientific than esoteric. A parascientific and paratechnological logic, mind you, it defies the critique of many contemporary neo-positivisms, revealing gashes through which we perceive the dark areas of the mind, those ungovernable by the body. And thus many works of the 1980s even in their titles refer to medico-scientific terms like those relating, for example, to presumed physical and psychic damage due to the overproduction of adrenaline (mocking titles: these are forms of damage to which Corte, as we have seen, is immune).

Corte's works may often give the idea of mortuary heaviness, of a gravity in language that becomes the catacomb-like echo of indecipherable symbologies and, in fact, in a collection of interviews with about 80 Italian artists of three generations, published by the review Flash Art in 1988/89 (*La Parola agli artisti,* Flash Art Italia 147-150) Corte is the only one of his colleagues who connects art to a sense of guilt, expiation indeed, and above all to what would become one of the principal themes on the international art scene in the '90s: *Death*.

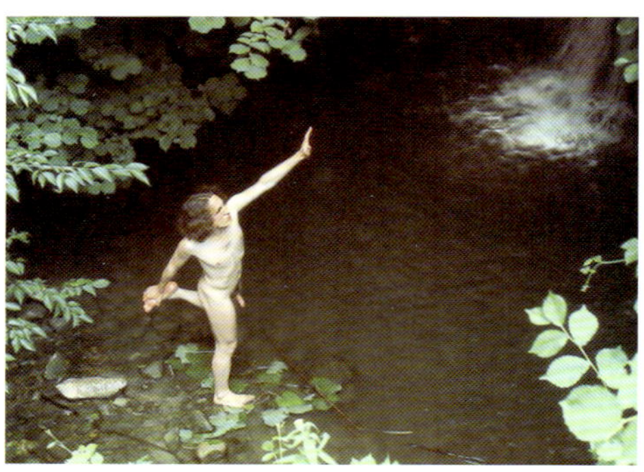

Luigi Ontani: *Alla Sorgente del Tutto e del Niente*; photo-piece.
Courtesy: the artist.

This idea of "heaviness" is however contradicted by a work like *RitagliOntani* (*OntaniCutouts*, ill. p. 152) in which Corte and Luigi Ontani, an established Italian artist of the previous generation, swap mutual portraits. We've seen how certain figures of contemporary culture enter into Corte's work; this always happens after long intellectual journeys, after a choice that favors the synergy between distant visions that fit together beyond paradox. This mutual homage occurred in the wake of a reciprocal respect. Ontani is an artist who has based his life-style and working pattern on a playful, lighthearted attitude: through his relationship with Ontani, Corte pointed out that in his own work heaviness and lightness co-exist (as in a 360° view from the top of the cornice).

But how do they manage to co-exist? From one point of view, the characteristic attitude of much of Corte's activity seems to be that of haunting the "dark side", that anxiousness one senses in youth to live all the most devastating experiences of life: a fascination with suicide, juvenile prostitution, the taste for intoxication, celebration of psychotic obsession, sexual drifts, anatomical modifications, vagabondage, contraband, accusation, prison. And last but not least, the most devastating experience of all: "getting by" for a full twenty years by producing works of art that make neither compromises nor concessions to easy understanding or commercialism. But like a fairytale hero, the artist lives through these experiences without being contaminated, an eternal, detached, icy adolescent in spirit and even, incredibly, *in body*.

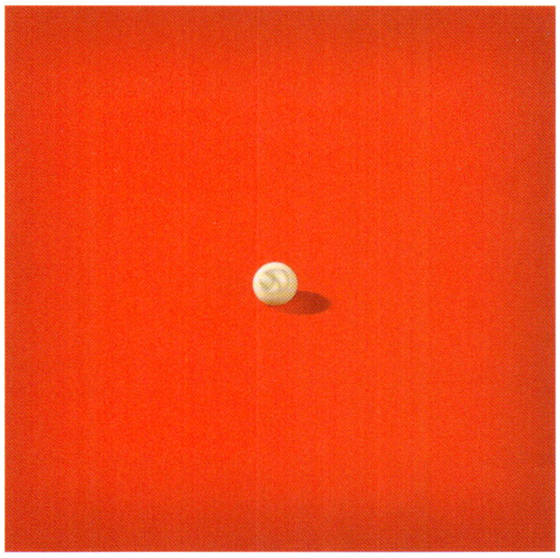

Psychic Moth Ball, 1991. Cibachrome from the photo-sessions for *Naftorama*. 39½ x 39½" (100 x 100 cm). GC 695.

On entering the '90s, the production of photographic works gave way to three-dimensionality, and in the few photos which the artist produced there is a spaciousness and formal synthesis free from the overloaded elements of the sculptural pictures, from which there is a deliberate differentiation. Examples of this are *Collezione dell'Artista* (*Collection of the Artist*, ill. pp. 156, 157), which reveals an irremissible necro-fetishistic aspect (with the artist posing in front of his own personal collection of rudimentary but genuine *second-hand* nooses, cords and hanging ropes – that have been *actually used* – collected over a number of years and supplemented with medical papers, police reports and newspaper articles), and *Abduction* (ill. p. 163), in which the latent obsession with kidnapping by aliens is once again taken up (and which Corte, who had already spoken about it in 1980, maintains to be the «fundamental psychological phenomenon of the 1990s»).

A totally separate issue, on the other hand, is *Naftorama*, with the corresponding *Sigh-seeing* (ill. p. 158), two images from 1991 which stemmed from a peculiar ephemeral "sculpture": moth-balls with tiny knots carved inside them. The naphtha balls are, in some way, new synthetic incarnations of the Little Psychic Daemons. Since the naphtha evaporates over time, what remains today is the cibachrome print *Naftorama,* where the entire group of balls appears, but installed by the artist inside a costly instrument for the spectrographic examination of olfactory particles given off by objects. This instrument is a container used in medicine to visualize the processes by which organic substances decompose, and the subsequent work *Sigh-seeing* is thus a similar cibachrome print obtained by means of the photographic processing produced by this spectrographic detector of olfactory particles (exposure time: about 48 hours). This is how Chemistry and Physics, as well as Botany, add necessary pieces to the psychic puzzle. They go into certain projects, act on sculptural volumes, leaving marks on the human body, and sometimes set off reactions with powerful conceptual consequences.

The self-destructive paradox of the naphthalene sculpture is made even more extreme by the accurate manual work necessary to carve those tiny, precise "knotted" shapes inside them. It should also be added that the artist, during the year 1991, *chose not to produce any other work of art* apart from *Naftorama/Sigh-Seeing.* Corte wanted to inaugurate the 1990s under the banner of *cupio dissolvi* with one single, self-destructive sculpture in which a considerable – and ill-considered – manual effort (the creation of the various "knots") is superimposed on an industrial product (naphthalene balls) which would leave behind nothing but the photographic simulacrum obtained by using a piece of hospital equipment. The true work of art is, therefore, the fact that *there is no longer any work of art in 1991.* Total emptying.

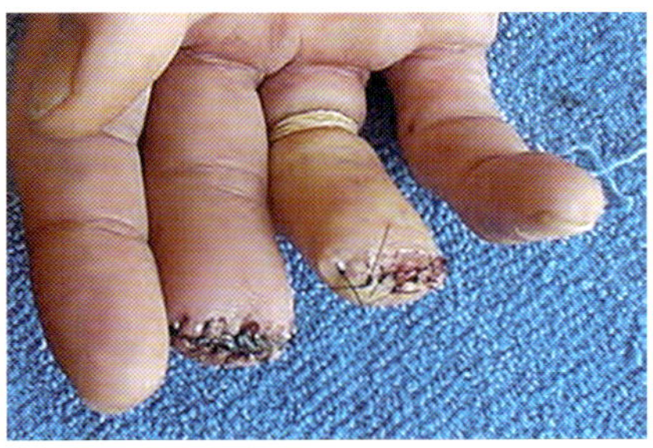

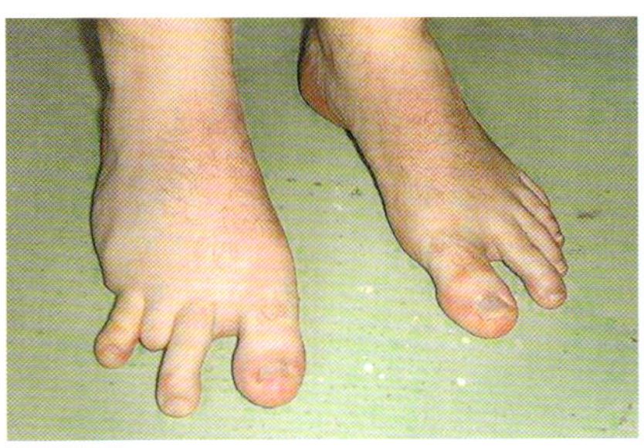

Hobbyism: voluntary self-mutilations.

The study of *emptiness* is one of the classic themes of sculptural art. Starting from the top of a cornice, Corte ended up extending his obsession with emptiness to a range of problems which invaded the psychological sphere and the social context on a global scale. This is the way one should interpret the ongoing "collaboration" with a group of young Roman thieves (in their own way "emptiness producers" in private dwellings), initiated by Corte in 2002 and which, due to the complex nature of its contents, I chose to leave out of this first monograph of the artist. I will instead discuss other examples of "emptiness" found in the pictorial and plastic works of the mid-1990s. These are dedicated to the *Hobbyists*, the *Devotees* and the *Wannabees*, i.e. groups of individuals who share the passion, erotic as well, for the practice of self-amputating parts of their bodies, such as fingers, hands, ears, limbs and, obviously, genital organs (medical definition of this passion: *Amelotatism*). The artist's sensitivity towards such phenomena is yet another example of a mature dialogue with real and realized counter-cultures.

I know of no projects by Corte which arise when fashions and tendencies "inflate" a phenomenon in the media. On the contrary, his psychic intuition plays a decisive – and never preclusive – role: a sort of emotional radar which perceives the most *honest* moment in a cultural trend.

The series of works *Hobbyists* (ill. pp. 164-170) consists of forty pictures created by combining drawing and pictorial techniques, from different visual references which always lead back to the world of self-amputation or to the related practices of piercing, branding and tattooing. Corte avoids dealing with these themes in an illustrative way, circling around and then "infesting" them with what springs to mind at that moment, letting himself be borne along by his own graphic skill. Their execution is cold and precise, and

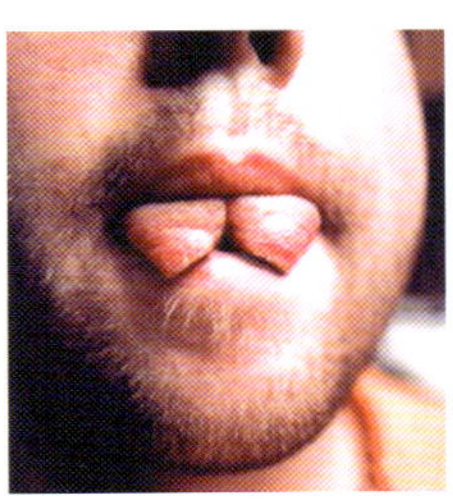

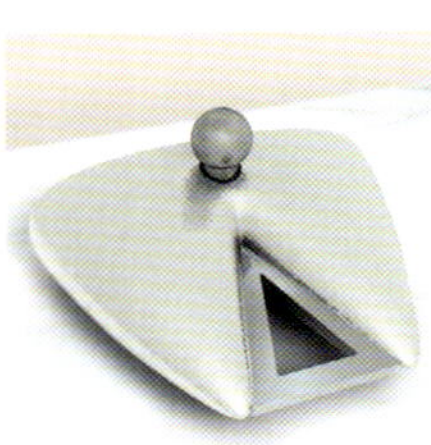

Artificial bisection of the tongue (left) and a piece of jewelry for bisected tongues (right; cf. ill. pp. 178, 179).

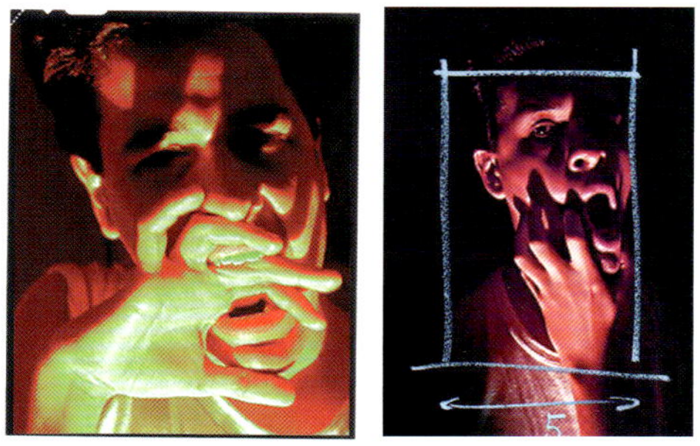

Working photographs for the *Hobbyists* series.
SC 650, 651.

the bright colors capture the viewer's attention like road signs. But, as usual, beneath all this the artist has hidden a substratum of occult references, a set of initiation symbols difficult to decode.

It is Corte's belief that, just as in the '80s and '90s certain "avant-garde" movements of body modification moved towards physical embellishment and decoration of an *augmentative* type (piercing and tattooing – but also scarifications, transdermal implants, etc. – as "additional" layers on one's body, by now mainstream in popular culture), so will we move towards a notion of radical *substraction* (amputation as "negative" decoration, and available to all). At present, the two possibilities still co-exist and affect one another.

To demonstrate this, Corte exhibited his *Hobbyists* pictures in Rome in 1997 together with a cumbersome sculpture in metal created in collaboration with Andrea Nurcis. The two artists planned that the sculpture would be "worn" by a third collaborator, "Piercing" Pino – a metropolitan fakir and professional piercer – who had various "new holes" in his body where he could insert his range of rings and jewels. Starting from a large central block, the multiple thread-like metallic protuberances of Corte and Nurcis' sculpture were inserted into Pino's numerous artificial holes, and then terminated in the classic pitchfork shapes, extensions of a similar number of little metallic Psychic Daemons. In reality, a few minutes before the inauguration of the Rome show, they realized that, despite the calculations made beforehand, the sculpture had one protuberance more than the corresponding number of holes in Pino's body. So the stoical "male model" at once pierced a new hole with a diameter of 5 mm, without anesthesia, by passing one of the metallic wires from the sculpture through the flesh at the level of his Adam's apple. The artists thus demonstrated that certain practices used in extreme Body Art have been surpassed by the behavioral reality of younger generations who are outside the Art world. The exhibition is documented in the video *Pino Piercing indossa una scultura di Enrico Corte e Andrea Nurcis (Pino Piercing wears a sculpture by Enrico Corte & Andrea Nurcis,* ill. p. 171).

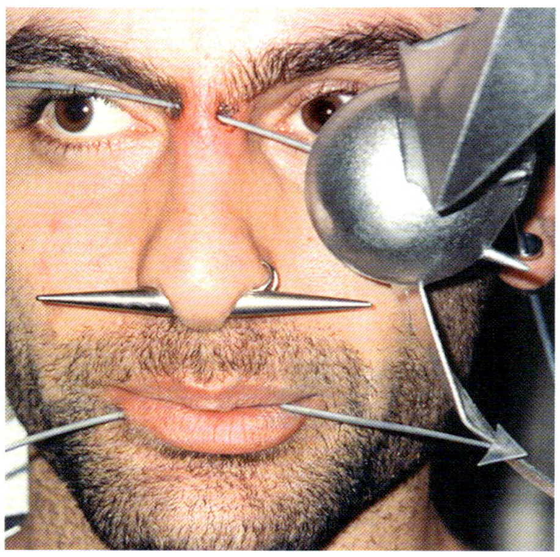

Pino Piercing wears a sculpture, 1997 (detail).

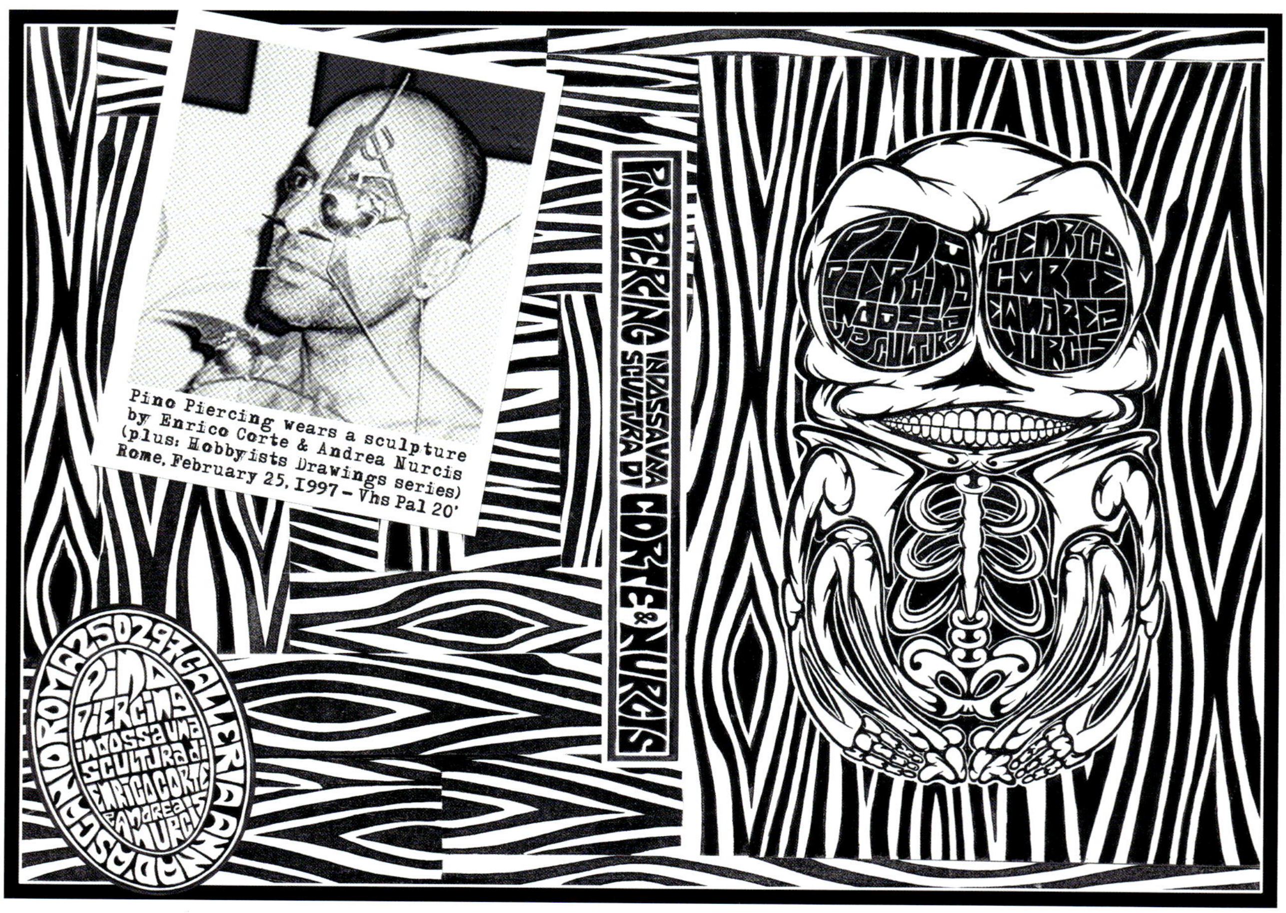

Pino Piercing wears a sculpture by Enrico Corte and Andrea Nurcis, 1997. Video sleeve and/or poster. Variable dimensions. GC 1099.

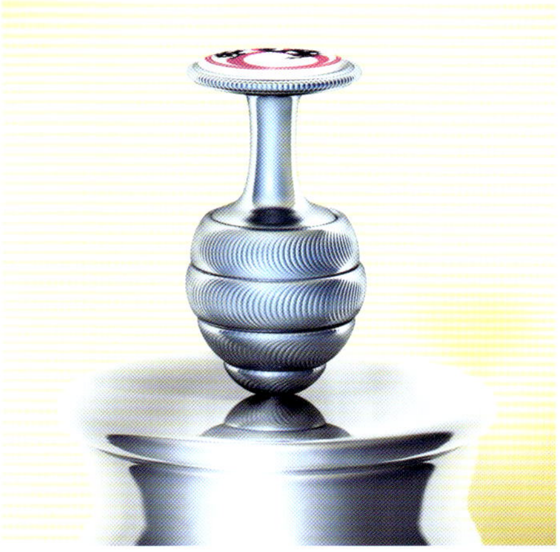

Daydream Butt Plug, 1997 (detail). Promo Picture for the *Abstraction of the Void* series. Lambda print. 39½ x 35¾" (100 x 91 cm). GC 963.

Corte also designed a notable series of "substitutive jewels" to replace mutilated parts of the body (the *Devotees and Wannabees* series; ill. pp. 172-179). Stumps, amputated fingers, bisected tongues and dissected genital organs were incorporated into small, richly decorated sculptural objects. At times these jewels, which celebrate emptiness and absence, have ceramic settings with the photo-reproduction of ink and charcoal drawings, whose nature contrasts with the metallic coldness of the objects. Conceived by following the logic of bad taste pushed to paradoxical levels, these jewels refer to the striking world of Rock, of Bikers, of all those counter-cultures which dramatize their difference to the point of excess. Another series of objects is conceived according to the same logic: comparable to the former in their search for a conceptual *abstraction of emptiness*, these are sculptures in surgical metal and glass, with ceramic settings, inspired by butt plugs, decorative "stoppers" to be inserted into the asshole especially during erotic games of a scatological kind (the *Abstraction of the Void* series; ill. pp. 177-191). Or rather, these sculptures by Corte *are* butt plugs, they have been conceived and created *to be introduced into that empty space*… even though one would imagine that their somewhat oversized dimension might create a certain difficulty in actually "positioning" them.

One could perhaps say, with a certain play on words, that Corte has passed from the *eschatology* of the big sculptures to the *scatology* of these little ones but, in reality, urine, sperm, blood, bile and various fluids had already existed in his work since 1979-80 («If Art can't change Society, it can at least change its diapers», E.C. 1983). But now bad taste reaches extreme levels of complacency, with "stoppers" which have a light-bulb and can therefore be used as anal electric torches in the gloom of dark-rooms, or also stoppers containing cremation ashes, or even stoppers in which mysterious "Sea-monkeys" really swim (these are suitable for "rubber" situations and outfits, which recall wetsuits and relative underwater paraphernalia), or else stoppers with reversible settings which contain a little vial of amyl nitrate, the so-called popper, a vasodilator that is well suited to the occasion.

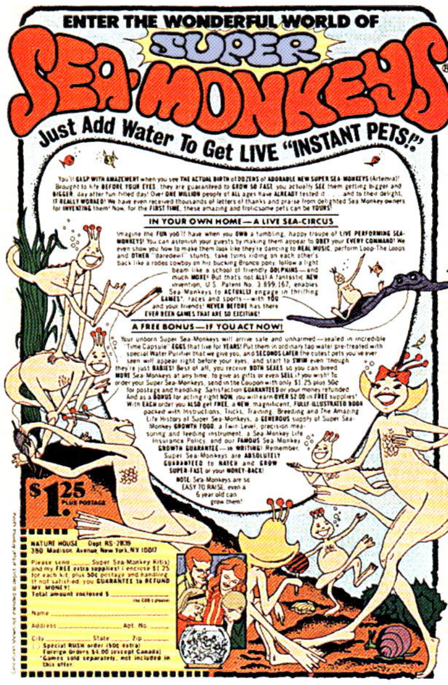

Sea Monkeys ad, circa 1970.

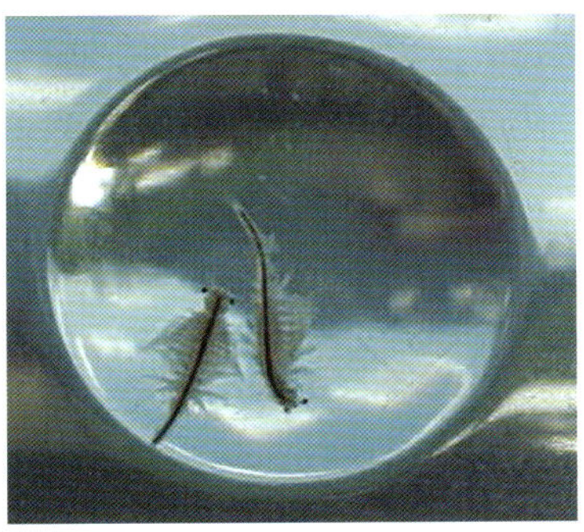

Freeze-dried mummies that come back to life: they're Sea Monkeys (cf. ill. pp. 188, 189).

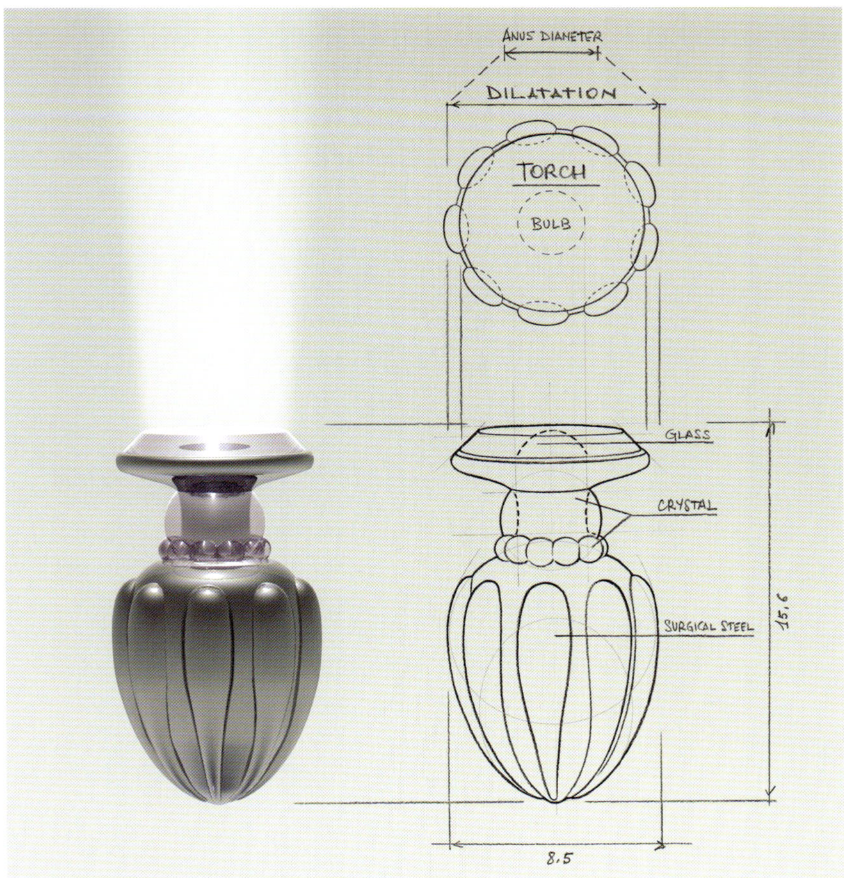

Project for a Torch Butt Plug, 1994.
Graphite and acrylic on cardboard. 17¾ x 16" (45 x 40,4 cm). SC 669.

On the whole, these butt plugs appear to be carefully planned in form, seductive in their sinuous shape, surprising in their formal crafting which combines chrome, glass, rubber, ceramic, printed pictorial images, engravings and vignettes. The promo-pictures and digital animations that Corte proposes as a publicity drive for their mass production show us these metallic and oval plugs placed in an "impossible" vertical equilibrium inside various environments, often in aseptic basins or among hygienic bathroom fixtures where there is, however, running water. In this way, with these vertical plugs, Corte goes as far as citing the practice of so-called "rock-balancing", the art of positioning little stones in equilibrium on riverbanks... a "discipline" warped by the caustic eye of the artist, who totally cancels the new age spirit of its Canadian origins.

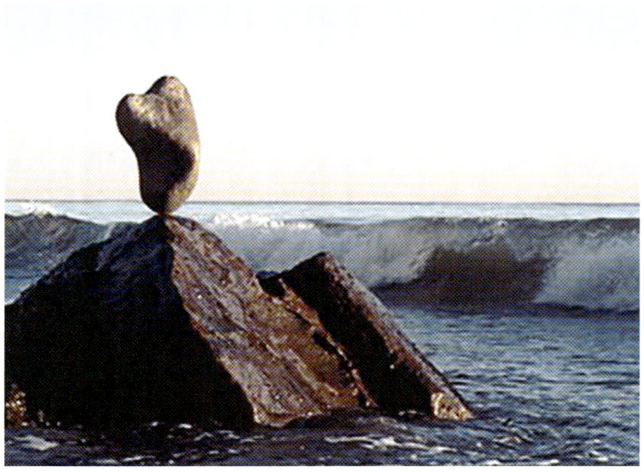

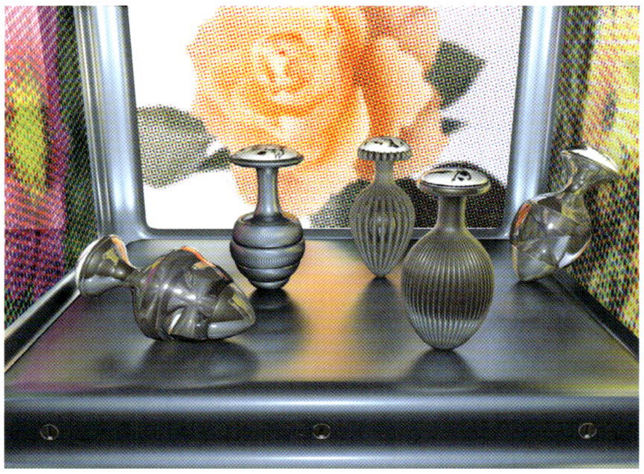

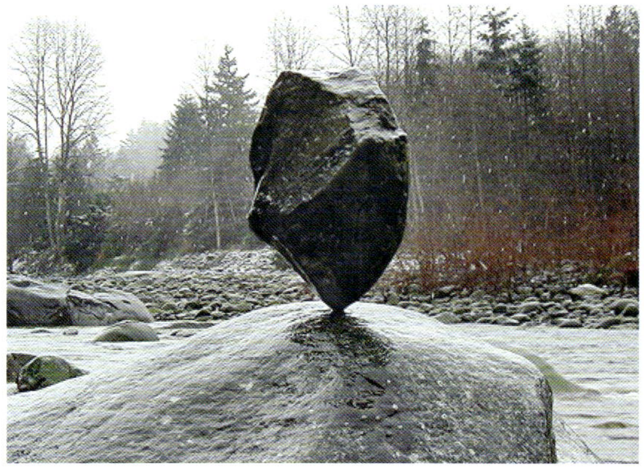

Rocks balanced on riverbanks (left and right) and Butt Plugs balanced on their pedestal (center).

The works of the cycle *Il Bordello dell'Arte* (*The Art Brothel*, ill. pp. 193-196) are also set in a licentious, dissolute, almost decadent context. They consist of 10 photographic prints – from a 35mm motion picture film – set on panels of fake-wood laminate which have been warped by heat. In 1995, Corte was thinking about creating a work to celebrate the centenary of the Venice Biennial (the theme of celebration, once again, but with an overtone of parody) and just the right moment arrived when a director asked Corte and Nurcis to build a screen-set and even recruit the actors and extras to be used in a scene of a film. Yet again, the real work of art involves the capacity to blend elements on the "palette of life". Corte's idea was to recruit a cast made up entirely of real-life whores, including himself with natural ease in the group (thanks to his stage presence, Corte has often been used by directors as an actor). In the film Corte spoke only a few lines on a seemingly luxurious stage setting with the aspect of a philosophical brothel, in which he had taken great care to leave many *empty spaces* – shelves without books, walls bare of pictures or with odd combinations of ancient tapestries placed alongside large reproductions of his own works – and a certain vague "cubist" incoherence in the subdivision of spaces (the furnishings and decoration of the set are an indirect reference to Cinema: Corte got them from the Italian interior designer of Sylvester Stallone's villas). During breaks in filming, he asked the Production to allow Nurcis, as a cameraman, to shoot several scenes backstage, using the leftover pieces of film in the tail-end of the spools. Later, Corte selected a series of frames from the footage shot by Nurcis and had them printed, even showing working writings, unwitting fingerprints and punch holes on the celluloid.

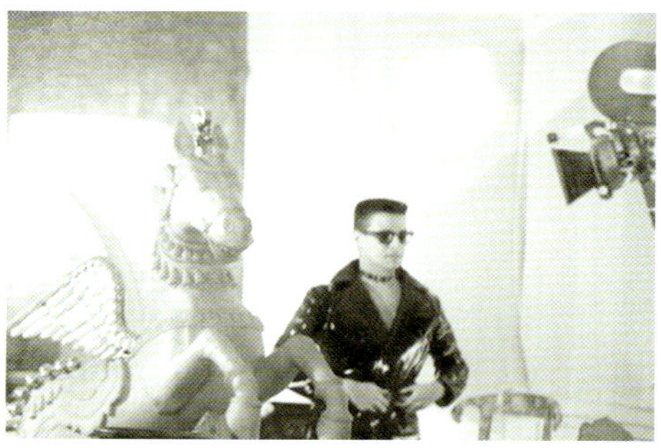

Detail from the *Art Brothel* series, 1995.

The photographic images which form the series portray the artist among an indolent group of prostitutes (males, females and transgenders) who are idling backstage in a film (we see the troupe and the equipment, but the "action" is deliberately out of sight). They do nothing but chatter and put on make-up, while on occasion some of them quite explicitly masturbate. The costumes of the actors and extras are somewhere between sadomasochistic outfits and Haute Couture, with physical "constrictions" such as metal collars, rubber suits and corsets. Almost revamping Baudelaire's notion of art as prostitution, each photograph carries a specific title which, in an allusive fashion, relates the image to the History of Art by paraphrasing the titles of famous paintings, names of art magazines, artistic techniques, and so on. One example is *Dripping*, which alludes to the pictorial technique of Jackson Pollock, recalling the detail of mascara dripping onto the face of an aging transsexual actress/prostitute with conjunctivitis. And again: *D'où Venons-nous?*

Que Sommes-nous? Où Allons-nous, Ce Soir?, where the cosmic interrogative of Paul Gauguin's famous painting is reappraised to fit in with the disguises and maquillage of characters of an uncertain identity, who are preparing for their usual licentious nightlife. These people, wishing to *lose* rather than find themselves, perhaps represent models to which Corte refers in this phase of his activity.

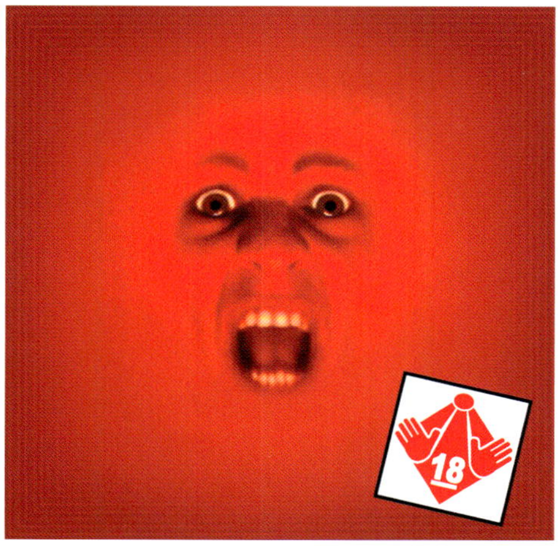

No Light Promo Poster, 1996. Lambda print. 59½ x 59" (150 x 149,7 cm). GC 1228.

The sterile *Art Brothel* has, in ideal terms, a certain affinity with the photographic series of 1982, *The Art System*, and may in effect be a brilliant commemorative comment on the centenary of an event such as the Biennial. (By the way, in 1990 Corte refused, despite many polemics, an official invite to exhibit his work at the Venice Biennale). The 10 photographic prints of the *Brothel* are placed on panels which give the illusion of being wooden, on which heat has created boils and scars that reveal the falsity of the synthetic material but, at the same time, ambiguously transform it into a fleshy substance that is almost palpitating and organic.

From 1996 Enrico Corte and Andrea Nurcis collaborated more closely with the shooting of their digital film *No Light*, and the subsequent *Homevideo*. And Nurcis proves to be a key figure in re-defining Italian art over the last twenty years in the sense of the "dark side". *No Light*, completed in 1997, sees the two artists adopting the features of the "characters" that recur in their reciprocal paintings, sculptures, and installations: for Corte, those of the Little Psychic Daemon, whereas Nurcis is a Hermit who lives in a sewer. Corte builds his alter-ego using computer graphics, with his own face and arms superimposed on a pulsating little red rubber balloon full of blood, while Nurcis plays the role of the Hermit in costume, wearing a habit of rough canvas which masks his facial features. During the 30 minutes film, composed of twelve scenes plus an epilogue, a narrative evolves through the long dialogue between the two characters, a sort of *Temptations of St. Anthony* with a dark and hopeless finale. So, characters get the upper hand of their creators.

The two artists develop their handling of the Italian language by means of the ironic imposition of an unusual manner of speaking, in rhymed quatrains, which resembles the nursery-rhymes of children's books. But at the level of imagery there is also a dialogue between visual languages (painting, sculpture, digital animation, expressionist cinema, cartoons, porno, video clips, and so on). Home-made "special effects" co-exist with most sophisticated technologies used in compositing, similar to the interchange seen in Corte's paintings and sculptures, somewhere between manual craft and industrial production.

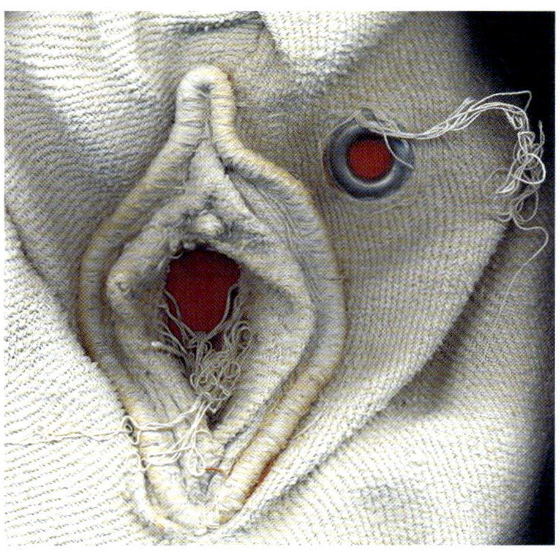

Sacco e Rosso (*Sack and Red*), 1997 (top), by Corte & Nurcis: detail of the Hermit's sack-habit, compared to Alberto Burri's *Sacco e Rosso*, 1954, jute, glue and acrylic on canvas, 33¾ x 39¼", Tate Gallery, London (bottom).

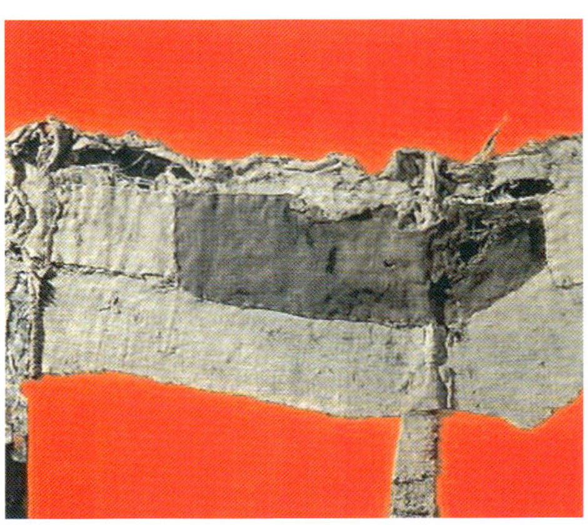

Music plays an important role, in the form of original compositions that allude to the pianolas used to provide music in the films of the silent era, whose sounds are then re-elaborated by digital instruments. But to an attuned ears it is evident that the artist has well assimilated John Cage's use of the prepared piano in the years 1942-54. From the technical point of view, the various pieces exist in an ambiguous situation somewhere between tonal music and atonality (a psychiatrist would define them as being reflections of the artist's sexual ambivalence), and use studied elements of cacophony. The compositional structure seems tonal, but lacks a *tonal center*, or if there is one, it proves to be a "promiscuous", wandering center, which moves in spastic jerks. The "sex" scenes in *No Light*, moreover, have no equal in the entire history of the Artists' Cinema.

No Light shows us an imagery which anticipates by many years the shocking photographs of segregation, scatology and humiliation taken at the American prison of Guantánamo, but in *No Light* these images look like they are filtered through the eyes of a child who happens to see them on TV by chance and, then, regurgitates them into colorful nightmares. Right from the title, the project proves "heavy", with the intention of making it difficult for the spectator to concentrate. The tragic narrative material is dealt with in a parodic fashion, following a precise axiom: in a cultural system that is dominated by market rules, "the impossibility of the *Tragic*" is evident. Any approach whatsoever to the *Tragic* is transformed into a parody of itself. Hence the only way to speak about the *Tragic* is to parody it from the outset. And this parody becomes the truly "tragic aspect" of the infinite system of signs we absorb every day. In various other works Corte makes us aware of the impossibility or non-attainability of this *Tragic*. In the case of *No Light*, the artist does not make a denunciation, but rather a disenchanted and cynical ascertainment.

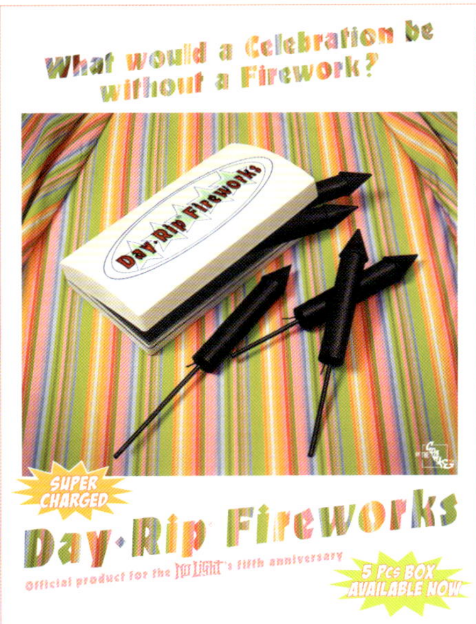

Day-rip Fireworks Promo Card, 2001.
Print on plasticized cardboard.
12½ x 9½" (32 x 23,9 cm). GC 1444.

No Light, one of the most complex multimedia projects ever created in Italy, develops in a composite, many-directional way, which has given rise to further *objets d'art*, cultural ideas, aesthetic proposals and different initiatives, such as:

A) gadgets and merchandise (*No Light Screensavers* for computers; the *Evil Tanks*, mini-tanks of sperm to be stuck with suckers on car windows, ill. p. 212);

B) pictures (the large *No Light's Storyboard* that recycles part of the scenery in pictorial form; a notable series of video stills on cibachrome, ill. pp. 198-211);

C) costume-sculptures (*Sacco e Rosso*, the grotesque sack-habit of the Hermit; ill. p. 51);

D) everyday objects (Demonietto and Hermit as Salt-cellar and Pepper-mill; Demonietto and Hermit as Inflatable Love Dolls);

E) board games (the *No Light Puzzle*, a frustrating double-sided metallic puzzle – one side for the Demonietto, and one for the Hermit – further complicated by the fact that some of the pieces that make up the images are magnetized in such a way as to repel each other and jump apart in all directions instead of staying together; ill. p. 212);

F) marketing strategies for the video that include the invention of new materials (e.g. *Mystiglaz*, a special method of advertising patented by Corte after working one year in a crystal factory, based on reflective light particles, invisibly fused within the glass windows of city buses to project writings and images in the form of sudden blinding flashes of light, exploiting direct sun rays when the buses are in motion; ill. p. 218);

G) public celebrations (with the shooting off of *Day-rip Fireworks*, patented "dark" fireworks, blasts of night in plain daylight that cost the artist six months of experimentation in a pyrotechnic articles shop; ill. pp. 10, 216 and 217);

H) "homages" from other artists (such as the concert given by American composer John Duncan *in total darkness* at the Aula Magna of the Architecture dept. of the Venice University, Italy, contemporaneous with a screening of *No Light* at the Italian Pavilion in Castello's Gardens, during the 48th Biennale, September '99).

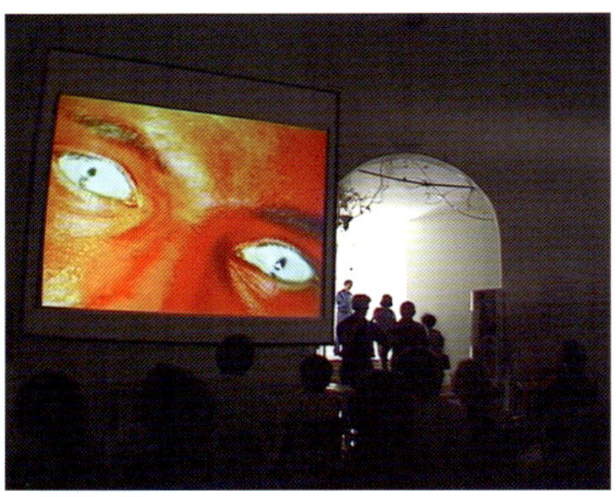

No Light shown on the big screen,
Italian Pavilion, Venice Biennial 1999.

...Note how the artist moves along the tracks of his activity following a tachycardiac rhythm, always chewing and burning ideas... So, he goes beyond his own productive capacity and beyond the absorption by the art scene and its public (yet another self-destructive strategy).

The work *Partouze's Sexy Vinyl Single* is derived largely from *No Light*. It is a faithful reproduction of a 78-rpm "movie record" produced for children in 1950s and early '60s (ill. pp. 214, 215). On its labels there are two sequences of stills from the film that, when seen through a multi-mirrored carousel placed on top of the spindle as the record spins on the turntable, form a brief animation in loop, like in an old praxinoscope. The two musical pieces on the record are taken from the soundtrack of *No Light* (composed and performed by *La Partouze,* and produced by Corte). It should be noted that in some sequences of *No Light* – which is marketed as a "propaedeutic project for childhood" – the authors show us those features and rapid flashes of light which have been scientifically established to cause epileptic attacks in children "with a low tolerance threshold". Well, we can see that the same sequences are found on the stills produced on the record label which, when animated in loop, should ideally create the infamous luminous flashes. In fact, as Corte discovered, their glittering flicker has an intermittent frequency similar to the speed of a 78-rpm record. And with this cynical reference to infantile epilepsy, the artist once again shows how attentive he is to the "neural" aspect of his work.

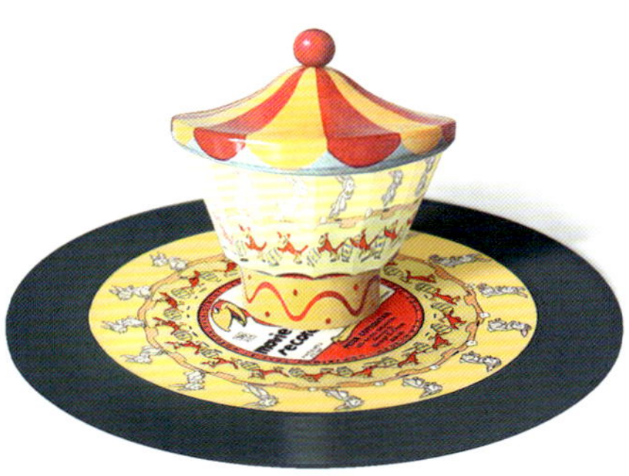

A movie record with its
faceted mirror. Late 1950s.

There is also a mini-video interpreted by Hermit and Demonietto, which is a genuine commercial short for the broadcasting station Mtv (*Drinkin' No Light*; ill. p. 198). Here, we see Corte's basic founding principle yet again: that of acting within widespread mechanisms through alternating layers of appearance and complex areas. We could say that Corte's approach to publicity for the video puts into play a specific *adbuster* strategy that we find every time the artist confronts his images with marketing techniques. A project for Mtv means, above all, rapid communication, a young public, reception lasting only a few seconds. And in fact this short film seems to be just that, a mini-clip full of irony. But, behind the surface, it is a stratagem for going into unexpected spheres. And everything turns to doubt: the woodworm busily burrows into the depths. Just like Philip Roth's masterly novel, "Sabbath's Theater" (1995), where the street puppeteer Mickey Sabbath pokes at the bigotry of New York by having his puppet erotically paw at the breast of a young

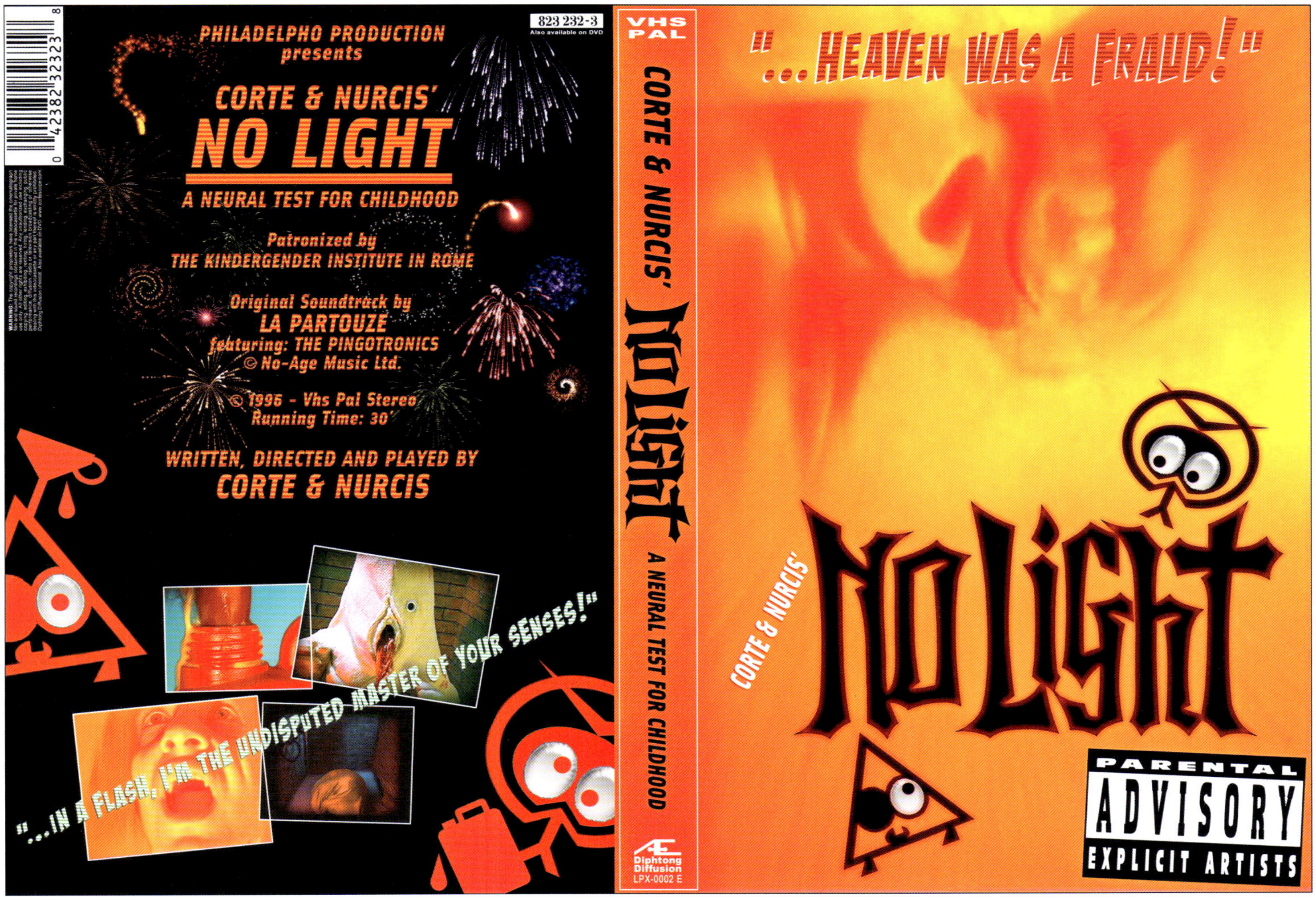

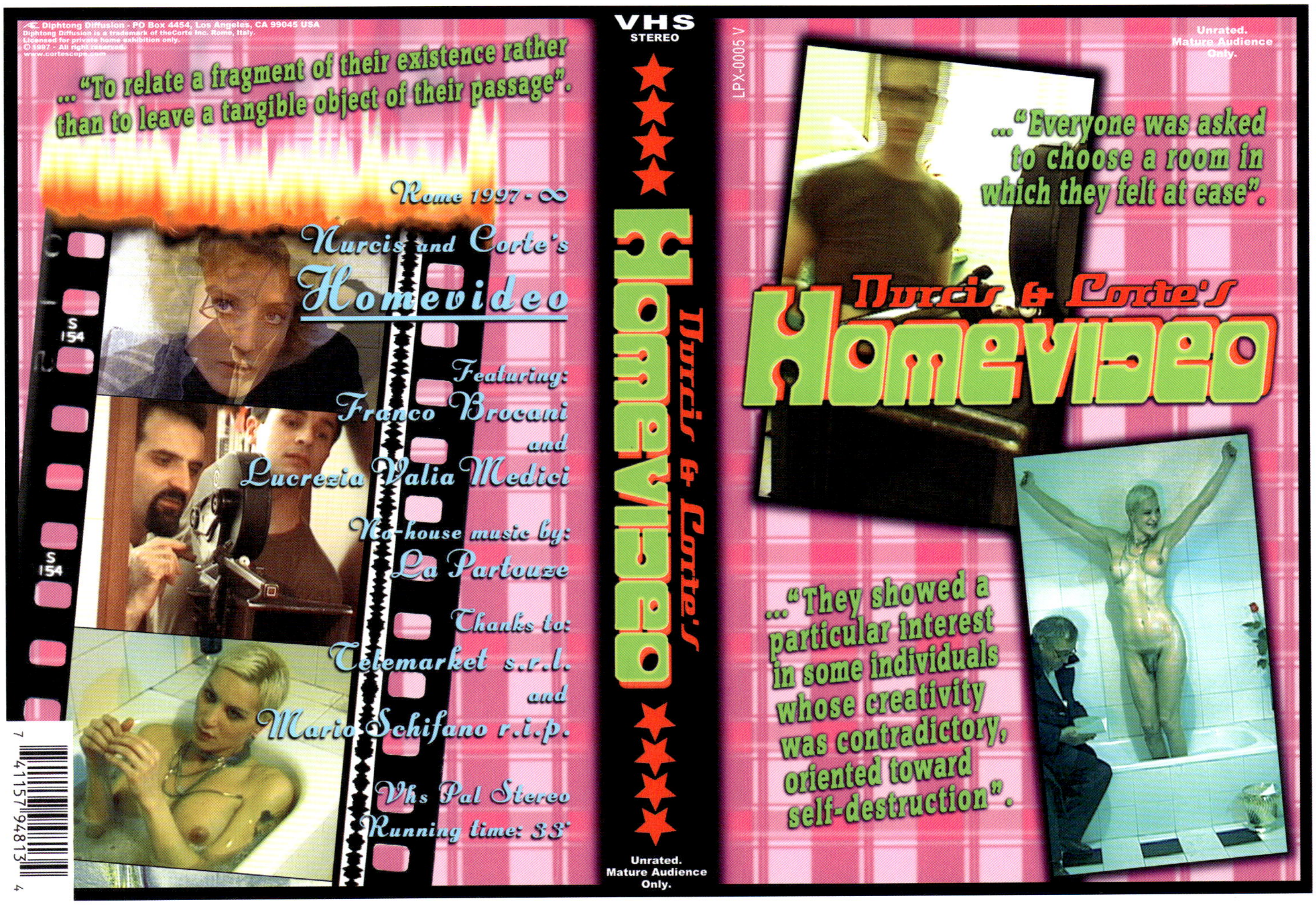

No Light and *Homevideo* videocassette sleeves and / or posters, 1996-97. Lambda prints, variable dimensions. GC 1227, 1229.

woman spectator. Here and elsewhere, the protagonist has a pretext for saying something different from what appears on the surface.

At last, *No Light* contradicts the by now codified structural "rules" of video-art itself, creating a stratification where the elements (costumes, photos, sculptures, installations, gadgets, shorts, soundtracks with corresponding "graphic" musical scores) seem to recreate the multi-signed geography of the mind. Starting with the multiple meaning of the title "No Light", there is a total antithesis to the infinite number of discourses on lightness, irony, play, decoration – those typical, malleable basic features of Italian art, recognizable to the point of being taken for granted, a sort of DNA which flows silently through social habits and cultural folds. Corte and Nurcis set themselves apart from this, and try to overturn those mannerist positions in an analytical way. *No Light* is a work that puts the spectator's patience, attention and exasperation to the test, right from their handling of narrative time, which is sometimes obsessively expanded and sometimes contracted, like epileptic spasms. In this way, their figurative signals conceal an anarchic distance from the localism of so much contemporary art. You cannot place EC/AN in one specific place since direct experience is filtered through their brain. The world passes into the brain; the brain rebuilds the work with the methods of instinct governed by specific reasons; the brain expels the subsequent form which becomes the final work, but is never definitive. The works as a whole make up a psychic self-portrait with its own variegated dynamics.

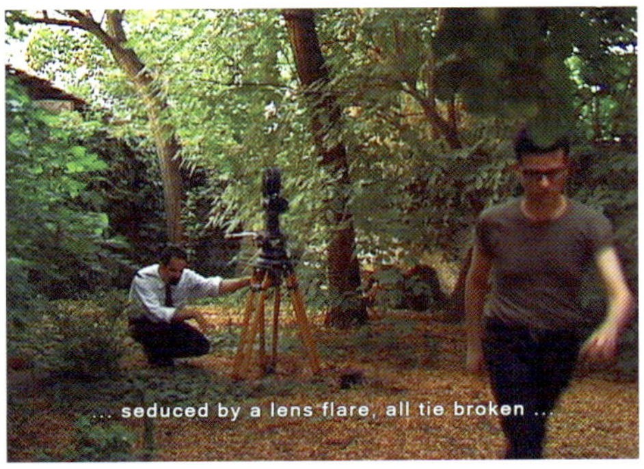

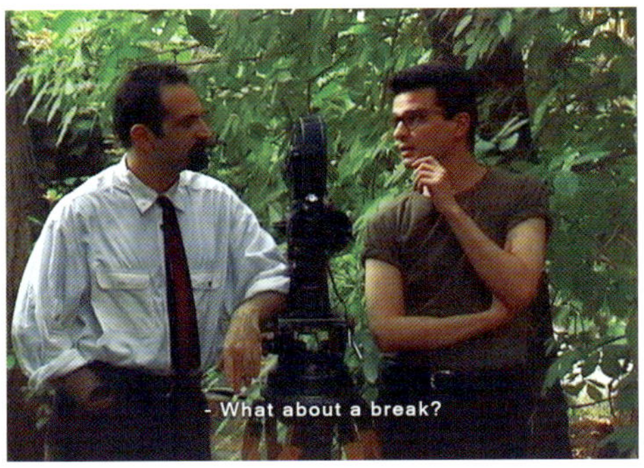

Ghost stills from *The Making of Homevideo*, 1997. Unedited.

The following project, *Homevideo* (ill. pp. 219-221), differs in setting and narrative organization, but not in its "cerebral" approach. It is an "open" work, incorporating many contributions and of an indefinite length which, up to now, the authors have preferred to leave in a stage of provisional editing lasting 33 minutes. The premise of this digital film, which is shown on the screen after the opening credits, is this: from 1997 onwards, Enrico Corte and Andrea Nurcis decided to open their joint house/studio in Rome to friends, acquaintances and occasional visitors, each of whom was asked to choose one room of the house in which to "put him/herself on show" through dialogues and story-telling, as well as other contributions such as letters, photos, music, and excerpts from videos or films.

These contributions, in particular, are inserted in the montage with a clever play on the narrative times by the two artists/directors, but otherwise the protagonists of *Homevideo* totally improvise and the filming reveals all their uncertainty, shyness and the inevitable "dead time", sometimes with exhilarating effect. Those who are invited are not "artists" but people working in other cultural sectors (cinema, music, etc.), or who experiment with their own creativity, day after day, in an independent way and outside the logic of any profession. In every room, Corte and Nurcis have placed various video-cameras, microphones and cine-cameras to film the action, leaving everything nonchalantly turned on around the guests, who go about their own business while the two artists continue to work on their own pieces. At the end of the project, when every room will have been occupied over time by various guests, the house-studio will be sold and Corte and Nurcis will move elsewhere.

(Some mention should be made of the place where Corte and Nurcis have installed their Headquarters. A mysterious architectural structure on the outskirts of Rome, it is an ancient farmhouse, semi-ruined and only in part renovated, rather isolated in those suburban surroundings, with a wild garden which hides it from view. It is made up of a group of rooms with living quarters that mingle with those used for work, as well as other structures such as a "crypt", and a turret that rises above the treetops... all encircled by a huddle of gloomy, wretched buildings, illuminated by dim lamps, to form the heart of the Torpignattara quarter, dating back to the early years of the 20th century – but look, this is yet another *spectrospective!* – it's now an almost legendary studio which the various guests of *Homevideo* have still not entirely succeeded in occupying).

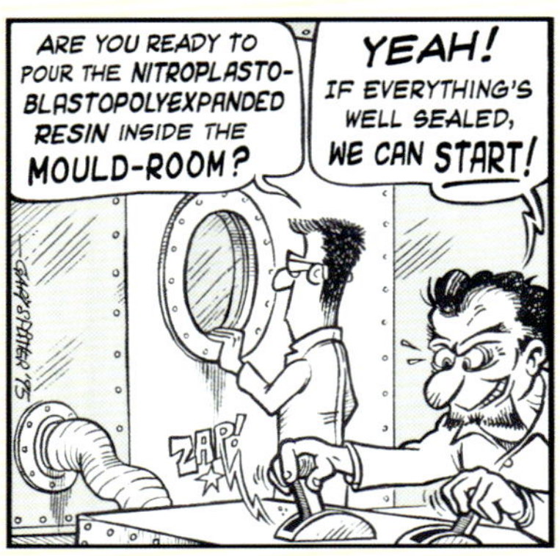

Corte & Nurcis as characters in a comic strip by Gary Splitter, 1995. Courtesy: the author and Kay Publ.

What Corte wants to show, through his guests, is the paradoxical aspect of creativity which may break through the boundaries into its opposite, or indeed, once again, into self-destruction. This is how we may explain the presence in the bathroom of a cinema director of the 1960s avant-garde (Franco Brocani) together with a transsexual model (Lucrezia Valia Medici): the former chose the dangerous path of "research", turning his back on a commercial kind of cinema which would have guaranteed him money and a better life; the latter had to destroy her male side so as to create a new personality. It seems that an erotic spark must erupt between the two at any moment, but in the end everything remains in a state of sterile suspension. Through fragments from films, letters and dialogues between the improvised "actors" of *Homevideo*, anecdotes and odd bits of information emerge, linked to facts and figures from the world of culture, cinema and art. The improvised lines revolve around the figure of Viva, Andy Warhol's superstar, and her working relationship with the director Brocani in Italy in 1970. The whole sequence seems to be a veiled reference to one of Warhol's "lost" films, *Tub Girls*, of 1967 (thirty years before *Homevideo*: yet another "anniversary"). There emerges a kind of portrait of an age through figures such as Sharon Tate, Mick Jagger, Louis Waldon, Kenneth Anger, Michel Auder, the Italian actor Carmelo Bene, and the Roman pop-painter Mario Schifano, who in those years was the epitome of the "underground" artist in Italy.

Through *Homevideo* Corte and Nurcis meant to create a *hypertextual* product that would not only entertain, like a normal art video, but also give strange and new cultural information: that would, in other words, have an *extra level of utility*.

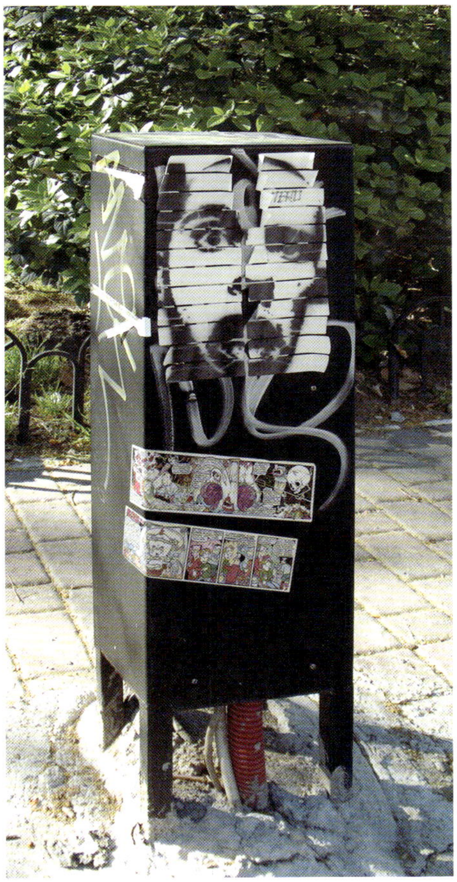

Another of Corte and Nurcis' common projects is that of the comic strips *Due o tre cose che so di loro* (*Two or three things I know about them*, ill. p. 197). Here the collaboration was widened to include a third contributor, the Anglo-Italian illustrator and graphic artist Gary Splitter, who is the material author of the strips. Through a series of 20 color plates, Gary describes his meeting with the two artists during a difficult visit to their "mythical" studio. With his fascinating graphic language which, to the expert eye, reveals a typical style of Italian comic strips, the illustrator describes in parody form the habitat of the artists, the studio furnishings, the people and habits that fill their day, their phobias and, above all, their works, reproduced with a "perverse" fantasy that exaggerates their formal characteristics to the point of absurdity.

After having himself assumed the cartoon role of one of his recurrent characters, the little Psychic Daemon, and having played himself as a prostitute in a film, the natural follow up for Corte was to have himself portrayed as the protagonist of a comic strip. The logic is yet again that of "bewilderment", a doubling up of roles in the eye of the Other, of a different angle in interpreting his own figure as an artist, through the filter of other cultural media. And under the pretext of an "amusing" comic strip, he succeeds in communicating, on the sly, some basic concepts of the work of both Nurcis and Corte, thereby reaching layers of society even outside the Art world better than many critical texts could do. *Two or three things I know about them* was also printed as stickers, and widely distributed for the entertainment of young and old alike. Several years on, it is still easy to find them stuck to the walls of the city.

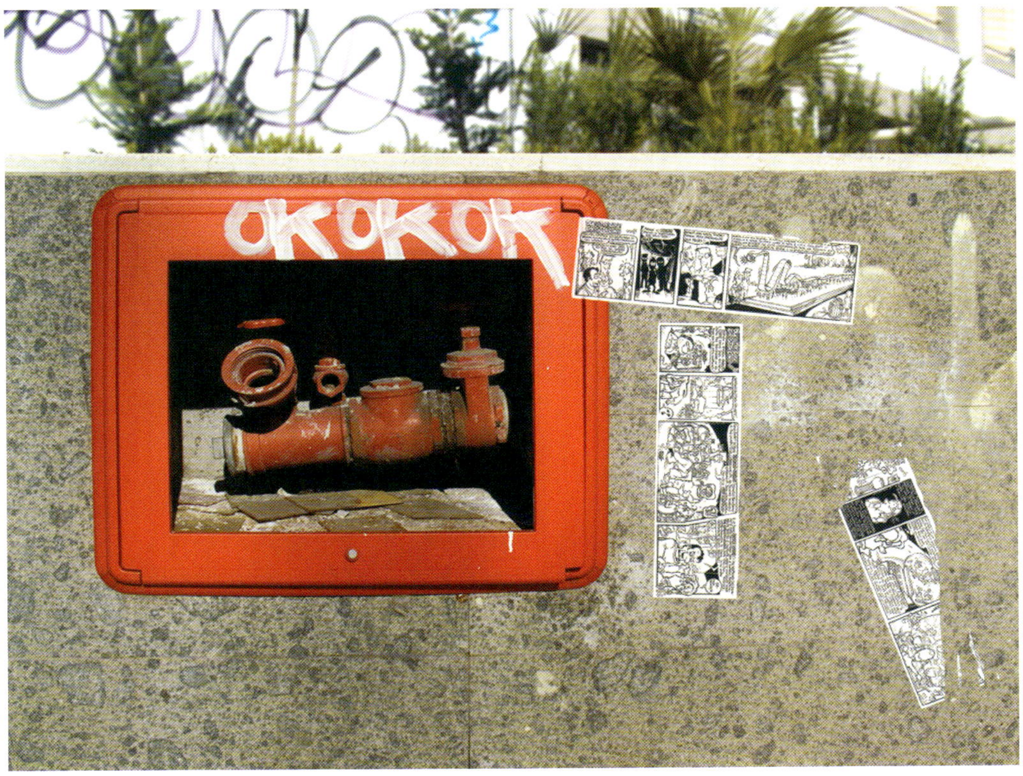

Top and right:
Two or three things I know about them,
printed as stickers.

A comic form portrait of Corte can also be seen in a funny "manga-kitsch" picture by another comic-artist, the Japanese Yapponaro Sato (*Enrico Corte European Painter*, cf. ill. below). These different, productive collaborations show Corte's desire to break away from

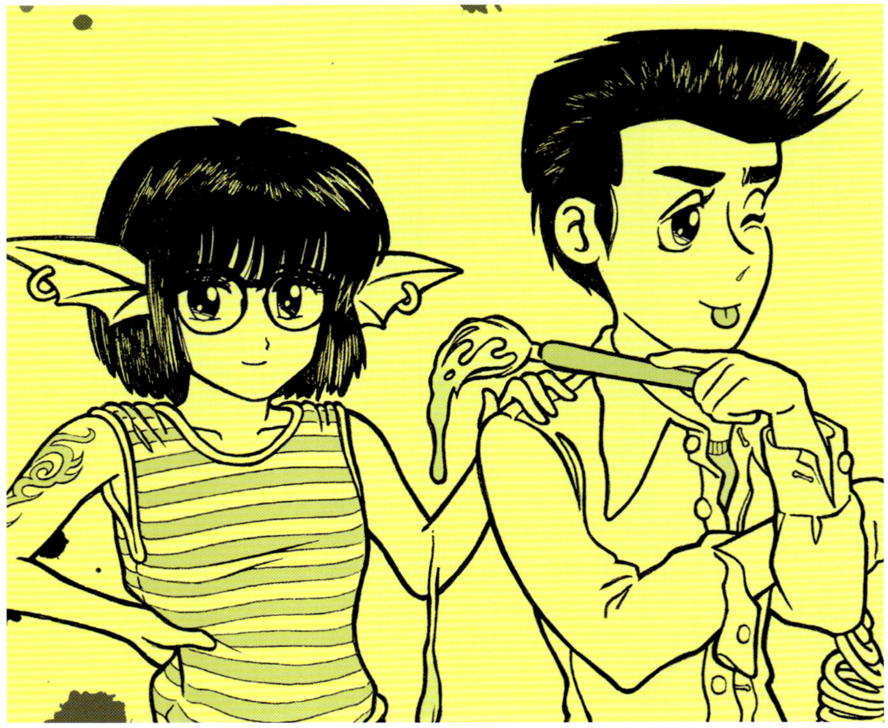

Yapponaro "Sarin" Sato: *Enrico Corte European Painter*, 1995. Ink on canvas. 19¾ x 27½" (50 x 70 cm). Detail. Courtesy of the author.

the self-indulgent individualism of the artist, in which one can easily become entrapped when making aesthetic choices like his. During the 1990s, he was always supported in his artistic and social activity by a small "entourage" of friends and faithful collaborators who someone, when commenting ironically on the often bizarre aspect of this company, defined with a play on words as a "Corte dei Miracoli" ("Court of Miracles").

Renowned for his willingness to poke his nose into marginal or even criminal environments, in 1996 we find Corte in the nocturnal underworld of Rome as he accompanies the photographer Joel-Peter Witkin, helping him to look for models to immortalize (freaks and assorted abnormalities, obviously). During one of these reconnaissances, trying to approach a hermaphrodite whore, he started a brawl and received a superficial wound to his hip made by a drunken pimp's knife (aimed at his chest).

The peak of this kind of behavior, which aimed at breaking away from individualism, would be reached when Corte put himself forward as the artist/curator of a series of cultural encounters in the Italian Pavilion at the 48th Venice Biennial in 1999, directed by Harald Szeemann (just as the Gramscian "intellectual" must be ready to "do" as well as think, so the intellectual figure of the artist must also "organize" as well as create). Here Corte cancelled his own artistic products, preferring to identify himself with the works of those operating in other sectors (cinema, music, theater, information and counter-information), that he himself chose on the international scene and invited to Venice. In the end, this ensemble forms a sort of ideal, multi-scopic self-portrait of the artist.

Courtesy: the artist.

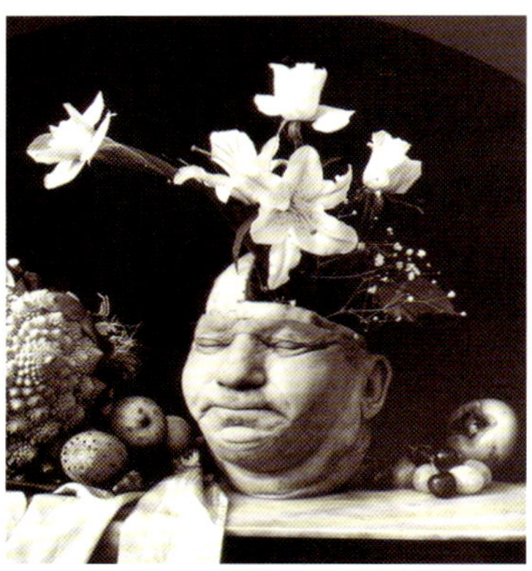

Joel-Peter Witkin, *Still-Life*, 1992, toned silver gelatine print, detail (top), compared to Corte's *My Son*, 1984, ink and charcoal on human skull-cap, 7 x 4¾ x 2¼" (18 x 12,3 x 6 cm), GC 454 (bottom).

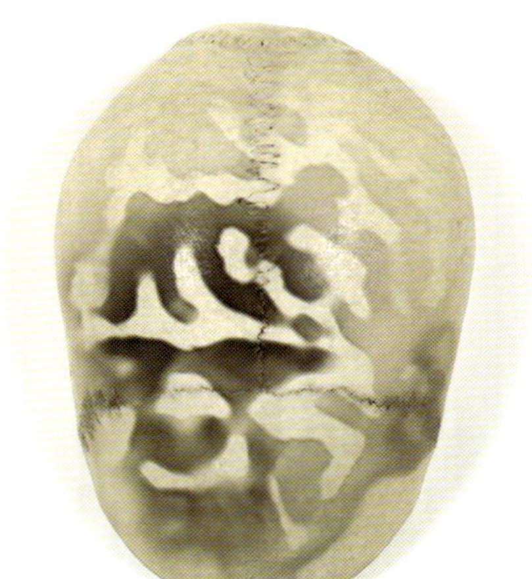

Among the many people selected and called by Corte to debate with the public at the Biennial, a great deal of interest was aroused by a group of film and radio directors from the then tormented ex-Yugoslavia, fundamental figures in the historic Radio B-92 which had been outlawed by the Milošević régime. Corte gets in contact with the directors in Belgrade, under the Nato bombing of Spring '99. The controversial, and almost impossible, arrival in Venice of these people at such a difficult moment should be considered one of the artist's masterpieces in diplomacy and shrewdness, which was effected through fanciful, semi-legal bureaucratic stratagems, with the support of the Italian ambassador in Belgrade and the Soros Foundation. Through this experience, Corte once again verified, but no longer under the mask of parody, the possibility or impossibility of the *Tragic* in the system of contemporary art, in this case regarding the *Tragic* experienced by an entire nation living only a few kilometers from the limelight of the Venice Biennial (Biennial defined by Corte, in an interview, as "escapist" ["Culture & Culture", RadioTre Rai, Italy, Sept. 1999]).

The intersecting of those encounters and the exchange of views enters deep into Corte's work, influencing the very structure of his thought and its subsequent material formulation. Another example occurred when a Chinese photographer asked him to choose a building in New York that could represent him (and our man opted for a street number, 666, the "Number of the Beast"; ill. p. 222). Years before, in 1988, a series of pieces made in collaboration with an illustrator – Diana Dubois – portrayed the artist during the trial that followed his controversial exhibit *Cleptoscopica* (closed the day after its inauguration) with clear reference to the classical and popular "courtroom drawings" done by commercial artists to document proceedings in the halls of Justice, where photography is prohibited (ill. p. 223). Here as elsewhere, the result is always the same: to speak of the body, even without the body and its protuberances, by seeking scattered signals that are the mental form of inner choices. Even external reality may formulate a segment of the gigantic psychic self-portrait.

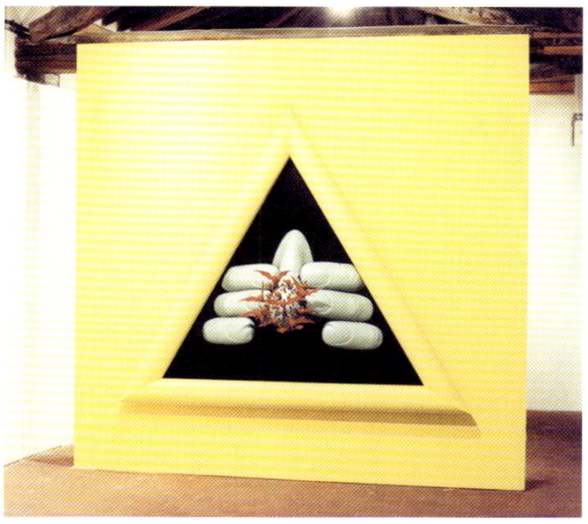

Three Cylinders, 1998, during its making.

For Corte, contemporary culture is a game of urges and counter-urges. Moving in and out of his role as artist, he nevertheless succeeds in producing a series of works with compact formal mechanisms. Bearing in mind the formalistic lessons of artists such as Cézanne and Picasso, or perhaps making a "tragic" parody of them, over the years Corte has created several sculptures based on modules like the cylinder, the cone, the sphere, the cube. These elements are, however, "drowned" in a context vibrating with different symbols and references, that are executed with maniacal attention to detail, arriving at the delirium of cruel bodily manipulations and distracting attention from the formalistic constructive premises.

In *Tre Cilindri* (*Three Cylinders*, ill. pp. 244-247) the module of the cylinder is used to build a large triangle which recalls the classic biblical image of the "Eye of God". But here, instead of the all-seeing eye, there is a huge suppurating nose squeezed by fingers, from which a crowd of Little Psychic Daemons spurts forth, like squirts of pus. It is a sort of Negative God, the Lord who governs the tormented universe in which Corte's creations roam. And the little daemons that cheerfully spring from its epidermis have bat wings and pointed forks. Each of them has its own physiognomy and an expression that is different, but always mocking, as if they were just so many perverted Pokemons.

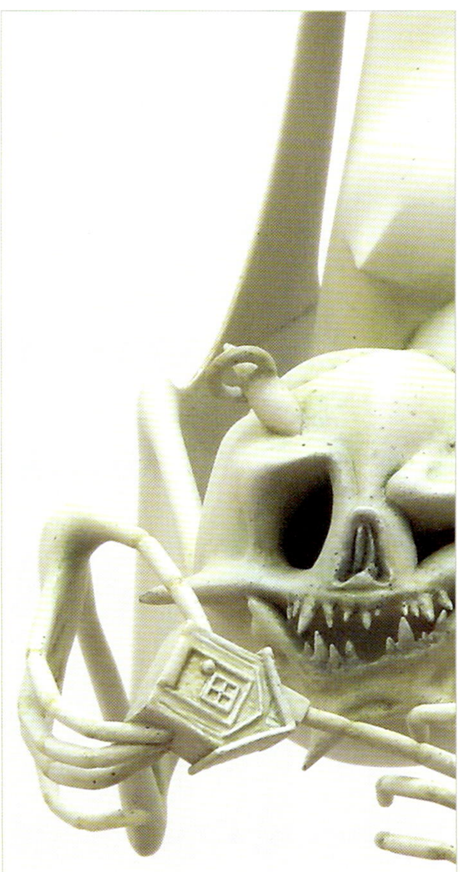

Three Little Cubes, 1999 (detail).

This kind of three-dimensional work is particularly flawless in its handling of plastic form and volumes: only the theoretic-formalistic presuppositions of the cylinder-cone-sphere become paradoxical. As in *Tre Cubetti* (*Three Little Cubes*, ill. p. 248), a superb sculpture suspended in precarious vertical equilibrium in the corner of the wall. Here we see a golden halo from which an elongated structure with a scrotum-like termination "drips", shaping itself as if by metamorphosis into a malevolent tapeworm/skull that has a piercing on one horn, which winks at us. This umpteenth daemon is making an obscene gesture at a little model house, inserting its middle finger into the narrow chimney, and he has two bat wings on its sides which, in turn, are transformed into two cubic, horned filaments of spermatozoa. These are, in fact, two more Little Psychic Daemons, but "cubicized" in form, i.e. rendered even more inhuman. Provided with a hole where the eye should be, and a cleanly cut mouth, these two little horned cubes assume a suffering expression, like two Greek masks of Tragedy and Comedy… but here Comedy is weeping too. The third little cube, mentioned in the title of the work, is the tiny house, symbol of the Domestic Hearth, manipulated and violated by the bony finger of the central daemon. In creating the work *Tre Cubetti*, Corte experimented, among other things, with the use of synthoceramic, a technique that he invented himself and cost him years of research and trials, but afterwards he took pleasure in dirtying and corrupting the smooth surfaces of the work with traces of grease, streaks of mould, and even clearly visible fly shit.

And in *Tre Sferette* (*Three Little Spheres*, ill. p. 249), we have yet another formalistic reference which is only a pretext, a way of evidencing the paradoxical attitude with which Corte upsets both form and matter. *Tre Sferette* is a photo-piece that includes the image of two sculptures, two marble Little Daemons that look very much like swollen spherical balloons, but with alien eyes, bat wings and spider legs. In their claws, both daemons hold strange devices that are somewhere between a dentist's drill and a scythe used for cutting hay. The Little Daemons are placed on a large marble pedestal, and between them the figure of the artist stands out in sharp relief, naked, revealing a strange modification of the scrotum.

It should be said that during the eighties, and even more so in the nineties, above all in North America, there was a growing interest among certain fringe groups in modifying their genital organs or other parts of their bodies, for erotic or ornamental purposes. The artist needs to feel in touch not only with the fashion trends, but also with the "avant-garde" movements of human behavior which will be the habits of the future. Growing groups of people, often but not exclusively in the gay world, like to modify their genitals using different methods – more or less definitive, more or less "heavy". For example, the size of the penis and testicles can be substantially increased by inserting silicone (permanent method) or saline solutions (temporary method). It is also possible to insert the genitals into special pneumatic containers, creating a vacuum inside by extracting the air with a pump (vacuum pumping), and thus causing an enlargement of the fleshy parts; or otherwise, air can be injected into a particular area of the scrotum at subcutaneous level by using a fine tube and slowly pumping it up as though it were a balloon. Corte uses this latter system: a temporary and less invasive modification than others, but not without serious risk (flash embolism, should air penetrate a vein). The operation is carried out after scrupulous tests and trials under the supervision of an expert in genital modification. In *Tre Sferette*, the scrotum thus becomes a spherical module, the third *little sphere* together with the other two Little Daemons, which stand on either side of it. Rather than being a work on solid form, this piece speaks of inflatable structures and is thus yet another variant on the theme of *emptiness.*

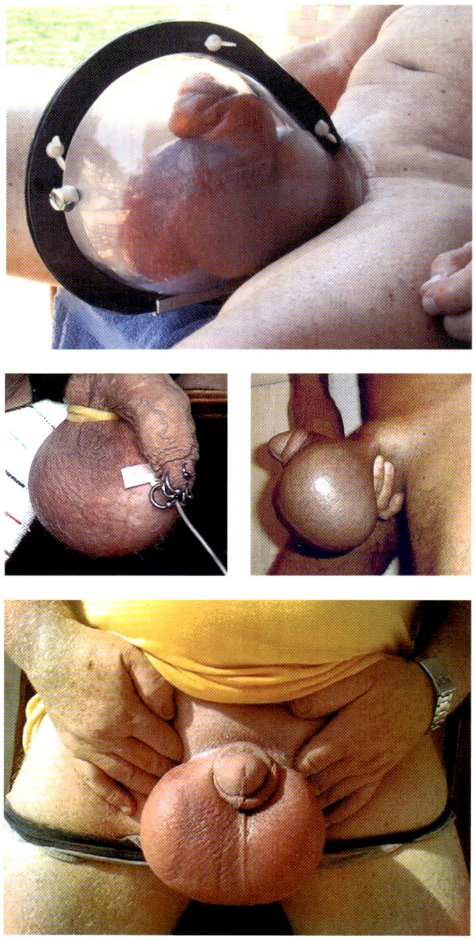

Various methods for artificially enlarging male genitals: by vacuum pumping, by air pumping and by injection of silicone.

The balloon full of air or blood, the inflatable object, the inflatable body (as well as the inflatable room/habitat already mentioned in *The Error in the Picture*): all of these are not without relation to the "rubber" scene, or that of the "balloon-fetish" – both of which the artist finds very attractive – populated by fetishists who like to sheathe themselves in clinging latex garments and wetsuits, sometimes inflated with air, or from which the air can be extracted, making them even more restricting. From here, after twenty years of frequenting settings of corporal/sensual experimentation, a piece was born that has little to do with more recent "body modification" art trends. Thanks to its characteristics, the work *Tre Sferette* is central to Corte's output, and there are several variations in which the photographic image is packaged in different ways, for instance "framed" in a life-belt apparently inflated and soft but is, in fact, made of hard *blastoplast* (see ill. p. 59). This emphasizes still further the theme of emptiness, one of the classic problems in sculpture, of which Corte gives his own particular interpretation. For the scrotal/genital theme, compare *Tre Sferette* with the 1982 work *Scrotospettiva* (*Scrotumspective*, ill. p. 110), far more synthetic and "impish", in which a simple crumpled piece of paper, ready to be thrown away, has become a work of art.

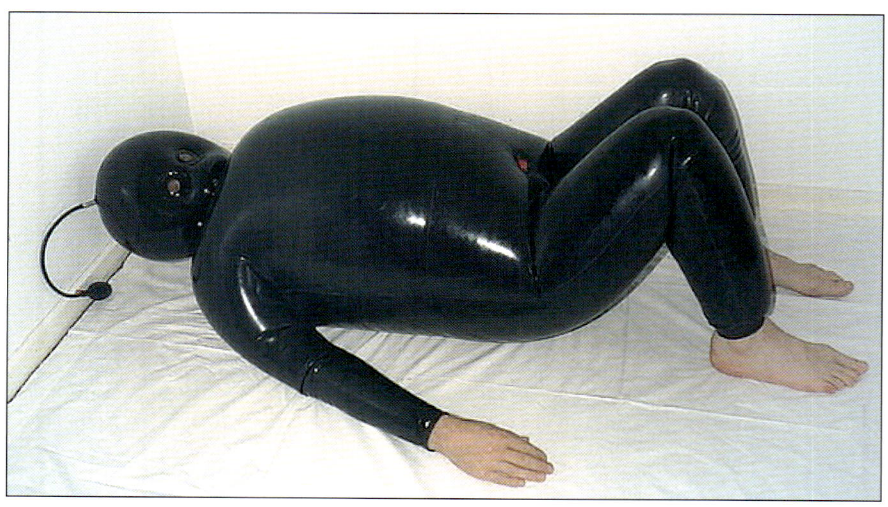

An inflatable black rubber suit.

Three Little Spheres (Life-belt Version), 2001.
Cibachrome print and blastoplast;
25 x 18 x 5¼" (63,5 x 46 x 13,5 cm).
GC 1404.

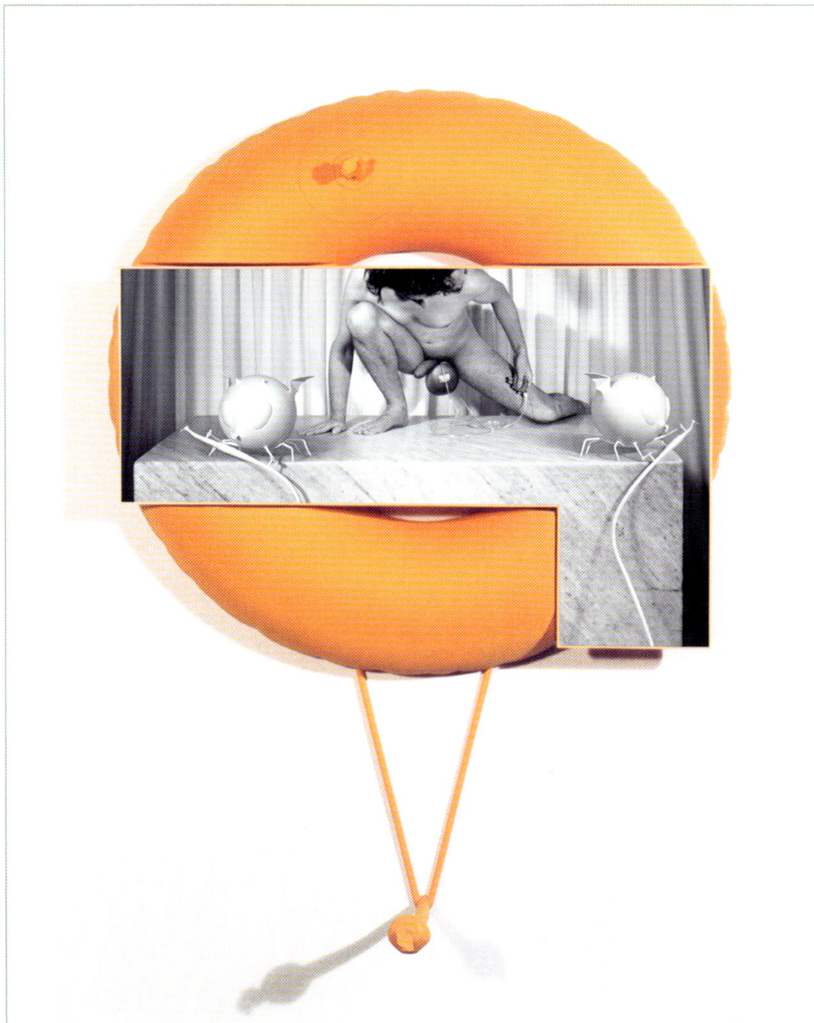

Several currents of contemporary Thought have analyzed and advocated the shattering of the Self, the manifold scattering of the conscience – from Lacan's "split subject" to its total dissolution with Deleuze. Of course, here we're talking about visual art, not philosophy, but these are the points that molded Corte. However, creative "schizophrenia" has become one of his habitual practices. Do you remember? Right from his début with the *250 Rotten Apples* series, he has acted out the parody of the painter as an "employee with a paint-brush", who never admits any self-doubt, specializing in only one recognizable type of painting with minimal variations for an art market which seeks reassurance. Corte doesn't give reassurance. But in his work, despite the multiplicity of the forms he employs, the inspiration that emanates from the "dark side" remains unvaried in time and so one cannot speak of simple eclecticism. It is not even true to suggest, as some critics have, that this characteristic origins in the generational factors, common to artists born in the 1960s and raised on TV channel zapping. In Corte's case, it is a matter of neural short-circuits produced by the flow of life which overwhelms the artist. There is, of course, the urge to experiment with everything, to risk everything; but that by no means implies the survival of the old-fashioned concept *Art = Life*.

If we admit, with a certain degree of simplification, that there is an analogy of function between brain cells and the chips of a computer, we might say that Corte already gave advance notice in the early 1980s of that type of tentacular, hyper-textual aesthetic culture (see *Homevideo*), based on rapid shifts in the ramified and unpredictable system of links: a culture that demands an interactive relationship with the public (many of Corte's works request their physical and mental participation) and not only the passive reception of programs "for a mass audience" (as occurs with TV exploitation). This culture is today the linguistic inheritance of the "Internet Generation".

In fact, Corte frenetically and omnivorously passes through different styles and techniques without lingering or repeating himself but, at the same time, he magically shows right from the start a perfect mastery of every means that he has used, reinvented and altered, whether it be old or new, handcrafted or technological. Corte considers this to be a vital strategy in a cultural society dominated by the constant bombardment of information, suggestions, stimuli, signals. And his refusal of all categorization, definition, conclusive classification, and any kind of "systematization" whatsoever, even economic («I bet you're going to ask me how I manage to get by», says the character Enrico Corte to a baffled Gary Splitter who is visiting his studio in the comic strips mentioned above), ensures that the artist always turns a critical eye towards such cultural systems. His works are never satisfied with merely existing, but emerge as the diagnosis of an illness («Every *filling up* of space by a work of art reveals a dizzying *emptiness* elsewhere, in some other area of Society», E.C. 1990).

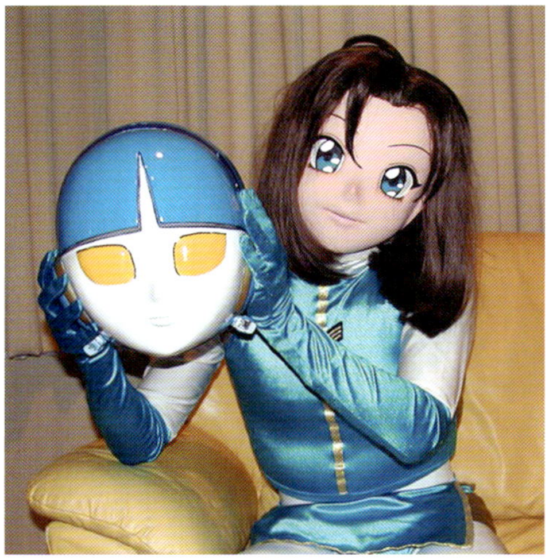

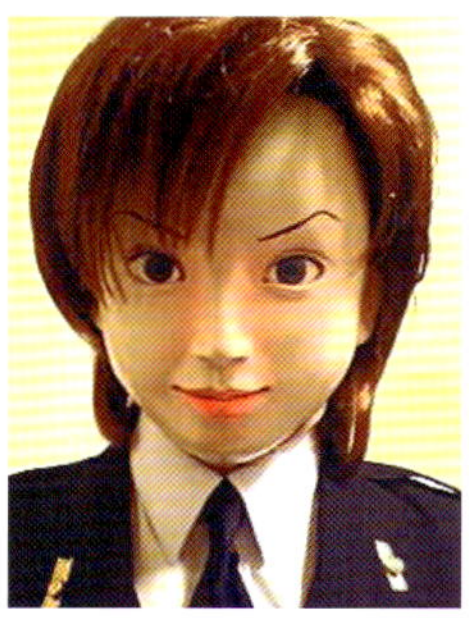

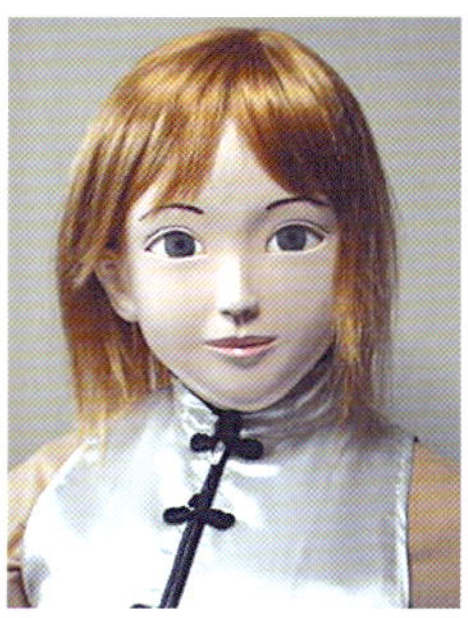

This page: Japanese *Maskon* people.

It is a short step from aesthetic schizophrenia to the metaphor of anthropological and communicative catastrophe, and it is in this light that we should consider the artist's interest, from 1996 onwards, in *Maskon* and *Anthrocon*, in which atomization of the personality, cultural conditioning, removal and masking go hand in hand. Over the years, this interest has been expressed through a conspicuous number of drawings. The word "Maskon" (from the union of Mask and Convention) describes the habit, that substantial groups of people have, of coming together and dressing up as the Lolitas of Japanese Manga comics, in even the smallest details. This "fashion" obviously came about and expanded in Japan, and is the culmination of a psychological situation in which the so-called *Otaku* also developed (young people "intoxicated" with one single consumer passion which rules their lives), leading to a total blending of reality with the illusory world of consumer goods.

The romantic or science-fiction Manga heroines take on a life of their own, driving their fans and followers, above all men, to impersonate them in body – by means of masks – and soul. These masks are costly fetishes, produced by specialist firms or made at home by the fans themselves, and supplemented with appropriate costumes, accurate down to the tiniest detail which do not leave any single part of the body uncovered. This is not a superficial phenomenon, or one that involves the simple sphere of idle games and pastimes, but conceals a more unwholesome aspect, a schizoid identification, a canceling of the person.

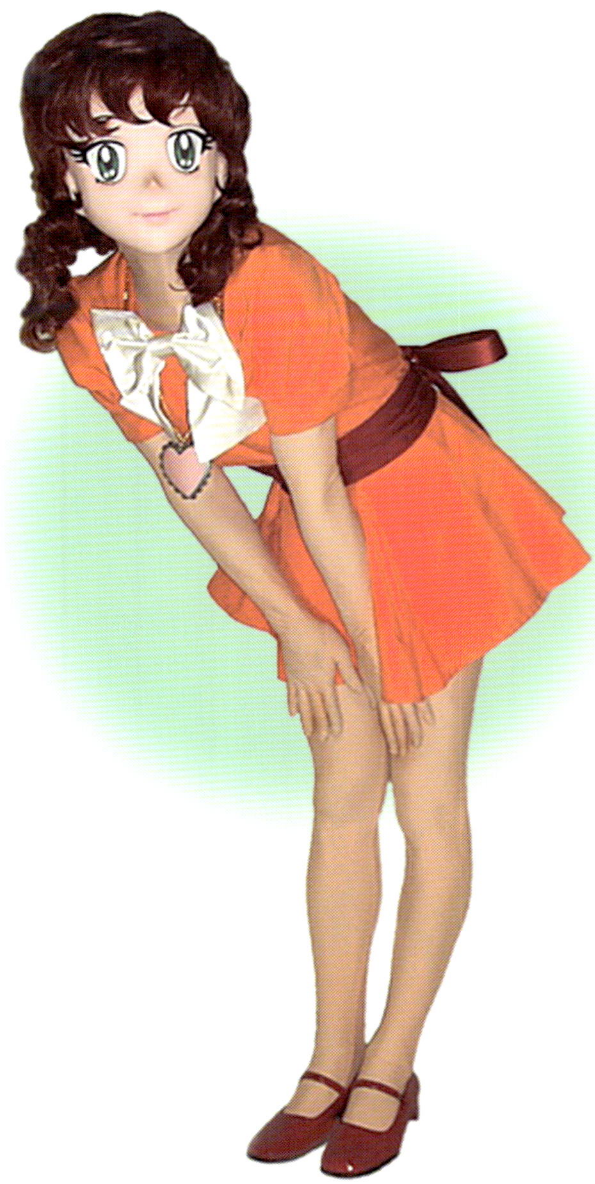

One could accuse the artist with his too "western" eye, of overloading it with sick elements which he, however, far from judging to be deleterious, considers useful for his own art. But it seems to me that Corte does not express drastic opinions, he only takes note of the phenomenon as it stands. The refusal to grow up, sublimated transsexuality, fetishism, the recovery of repressed eroticism… but the artist's interest, if well stimulated, always passes from the psychological phenomenon to the social one, never remaining tangled in the web of introspective self-satisfaction.

We should remember that, in the early nineties, Corte had already produced some series of paintings in medium-small dimensions, dedicated to some "obsessions" of the media that were characteristic of contemporary Japanese culture, which has always fascinated the artist, who is used to taking a 360° look at the aesthetic phenomena of his era. These three groups of paintings are entitled *Aidoru*, *Onapetto* and *Bishonen*, i.e. three character-types in the Mangas, responsible for the manifestations of a pathological split between concrete reality and adolescent fantasy. They foreshadow an anthropological and neural change in the youth generations of the 1990s, the so-called *Shinjinrui* ("New Human Race").

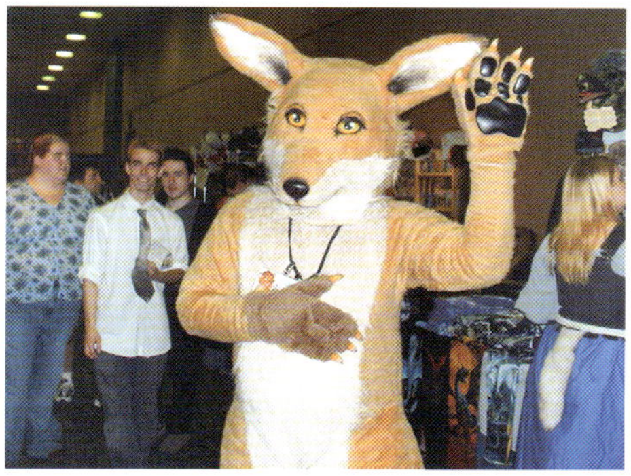

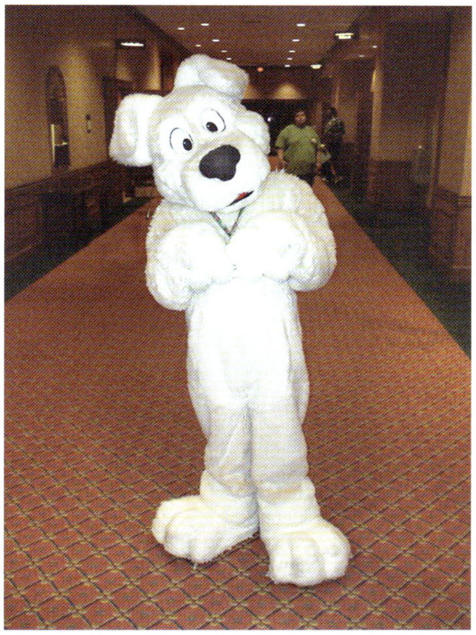

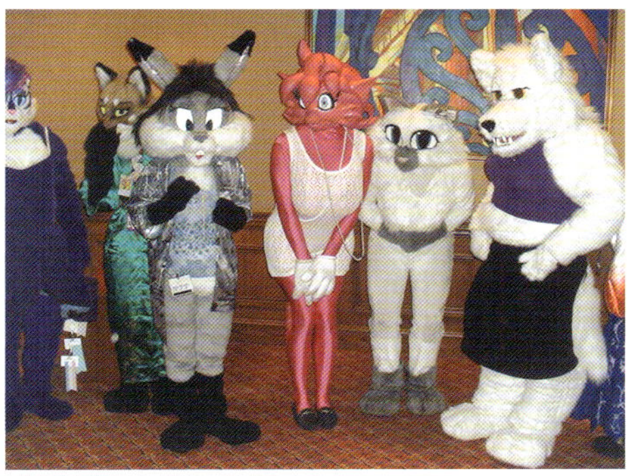

Anthrocon: Anthropomorphs Conventions.

"Anthrocon" (Anthropomorphs-Convention), on the other hand, is an annual fixture in certain American cities (Albany, Philadelphia, etc.) that has led to a situation and taste similar to Maskon, which has now spread throughout the world. It consists of encounters between individuals who share a passion, with latent erotic undertones, for dressing up as hairy anthropomorphic animals. Here, there is perhaps less transfer of personality than in Maskon, whereas there is a wider range of possible camouflages (various animal-types which can both hide/reveal as many aspects of the character as those who impersonate them). Corte interprets Anthrocon as being an initiatory sect with symbolic rites in which he inserts elements of his own visual universe.

So, Corte promptly produced a series of drawings and pictures dedicated to *Maskon* and *Anthrocon* (ill. pp. 230-233), and he did not stop there, then deciding to invent a new *social phenomenon* himself, a method of disguise seen as erotic sublimation to be promoted and heartily recommended. It was in this way that *Intericon* (Interiors + Convention) was born in 1998: the practice of dressing up as furniture and objects of interior decoration, and consuming one's sterile sensual encounters in total immobility. Extolled by Corte in various drawings (ill. pp. 234-239) and videos, and with many practitioners already, Rome is at the center of the Intericon movement. Finding oneself in the middle of an Intericon meeting means moving around in the half-light of what at first sight might appear to be anonymous furnished apartments, only to realize – with the upsetting of the "non-place" concept coined by Marc Augé – that the furnishings and ornaments are once again *masks*, sophisticated costumes which conceal the static and hidden participants, who can be recognized only by their rough breathing caused by the weariness of enforced immobility and growing excitement... here, then, is an interesting variation on Gramsci's theme of the artist who must "organize" as well as create.

The drawings created by Corte for the *Intericon* series stretch from 1998 to 2006 and are mostly executed in charcoal on paper, or on the cardboard of packing cases. Corte tends to avoid realism or the slavish illustration of reality, and his drawings often follow patterns that include figurative elements, even comic strips ones, but he contaminates them with abstract and informal graphic variations until, with time, he achieves a synthesis of representation not easy to classify, in which the eye anyway loses itself. Despite this, one can quite recognize all the figures who represent the *Intericon* series: anonymous bodies, immobile as though paralyzed by the effort of camouflaging themselves among the canonical furnishings of a house: tables, chairs, lamp-stands, electrical appliances, carpets, sofas, mirrors, pictures, musical instruments – even the most unlikely means are not disdained, such as the one that becomes the very symbol of the whole project: dressing up as the wall of a room by being covered in wallpaper and "mummified" against the bricks. By observing their features with care, it is even possible to identify the individual people who Corte portrays as they practice the motionless rites of Intericon: at times they are well-known faces in the world of Italian art and culture, regular visitors or supporters of the artist's work.

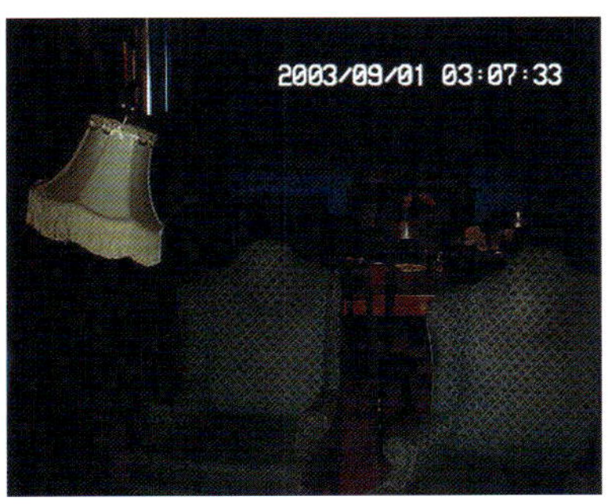

Still from *Beneath the Shades of Intericon*, ten hours videodocumentation of the fifth *Intericon* meeting, Rome, September 2003.

The packing-case cardboard on which the drawings are made is not brand new, and in many cases belonged to homeless people or tramps who used it to protect themselves from the cold; or else pieces of cardboard used by "guest workers", street vendors of trinkets, as mats for their merchandise (the homeless and the foreign worker, and thus stateless person, seen as living paradoxes who create a short-circuit – meaning that they prove a social *imbalance* – with the idea of dressing up as internal furnishings... on the other hand, the packing-case cardboard is also wandering and nomadic). This cardboard with its "lived-in" look, as well as being printed with technical information on its manufacture or covered in writing made by those who used it as a box, is obviously dirty and torn, with stains and traces of all sorts, and everything in the end is turned to expressive use and incorporated in the work. Thus the drawing becomes the favored battlefield of life and art.

On occasion the graphic virtuosity that has always been one of the "natural gifts" of Corte's work emerges, but it is a visual satisfaction contradicted by the deliberate peeling away of the image on the torn cardboard, or by the foul accumulation of filth. At times, the drawing appears not in charcoal or pencil, but by means of an eraser, "cleansing" the layer of dirt or grease on the cardboard.

Corte obtained this cardboard by explaining what he wanted to do with it to the owners, the homeless people or street-vendors, and buying it from them at an agreed price. The tramps of Rome are often artists themselves, so it was not difficult for him to make them understand his project, but the cardboard also comes from other European cities where he has stayed. In this case it is interesting to note how the appearance of the cardboard changes from one city to another, not only in the writings and technical information printed on it, but also in the type of dirt and grease that humanity has deposited on it over time. And these too are elements which determine the many variations in the drawings of the *Intericon* series.

Drawing, more than the act of painting, is here seen to be one of the guidelines of the artist's work, even though in a subdued and subterranean way. A further treatise would be necessary to discuss the continuous but "deviant" use that Corte makes of drawings on paper (cf. ill. pp. 90 and 240-243). But freehand drawing is still the most personal and immediate way in which the mind visualizes an idea of reality perceived through the eye.

The pleasure in paradox pushed to the point of aesthetic collapse is well represented by *Videoache*, a video project which is supposed to present a world parallel to our own but governed by one sole law, that of *suffering*. In the world of *Videoache* (the same one over which the suppurating Nasal Divinity of *Tre Cilindri* hovers) everything exudes suffering. We are born in pain, live in torment and die screaming. But this condition is represented not by human bodies – totally removed – but by objects: everyday objects brought "alive" and which, by means of visual manipulations, reveal expressive traits and anthropomorphic features. Here we are already beyond *Intericon*, in which bodies camouflage themselves as objects in their desire for pleasure, now reaching a dimension in which objects are camouflaged as bodies in the expression of pain. The human body is completely discarded because Corte is by now far from Post-human attitudes: he has always been interested in the *neural* dimension of art, and all his activities seem to be built on the model of the brain's labyrinthine circumvolutions. In *Videoache* the detailed description of pain even invades the *very act of mechanically recording the images of the various scenes* with a cine-camera (another object-person which populates this parallel world). In fact, the action of light as it makes its impression on the silver nitrate layers which cover the cine-camera's raw stock film, in defining the formation of the image produces corrosion, visible anguish, howling pain. Suffering characterizes the activity of a psyche that battles, creates, destroys, modifies, re-establishes. Dependent in a pathological fashion on the faculty of sight, on his own eyeball (remember *Penta-Portraits*?), with no possibility of escape, the visual artist provides us with a subtle key to the interpretation of *his* tragic destiny, using again the equation *perception of the image = pain*.

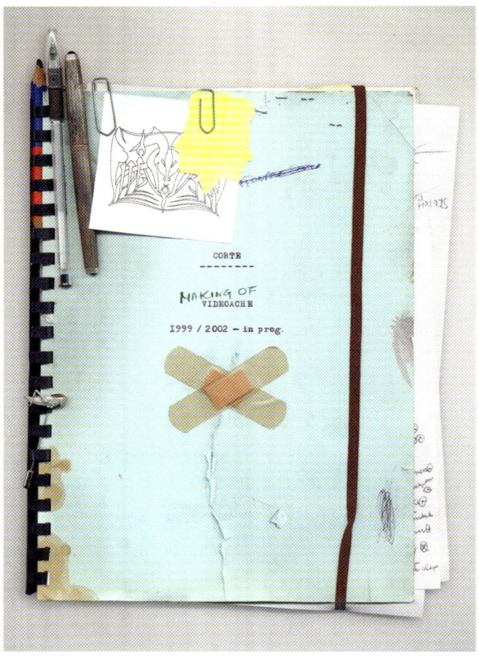

Script of *(The Making of) Videoache*.

Videoache is still today an incomplete project and, as such, a metaphor of creative tribulation. «I still have a concept of pain that is too symptomatic. I need time to let the case history of the counterpoints settle», stated Corte, whatever that may mean. But the real paradox is expressed in the fact that *Videoache* does not exist as a finished product, whereas a "Making of…" does, and through the latter we can reconstruct the original project in its entirety. The "market offer" process here is overturned (like the hourglass of the 1980s' paintings).

The Making of Videoache is a video that follows the artist as he wanders around America and Europe and, through sub-titles and editing expedients, illustrates the psychological processes behind the idea of the project. "Vacu-video" is the formula used by Corte to describe this sort of documentary in progress (ill. pp. 224-227), in which he manages to achieve, with acuteness and foresight, through images and words, the right unsettling feeling an impending sense of doom for the historic moment preceding the attack of September 11 on the Twin Towers (once again, it's his "anticipated commemorative celebration" concept). At 36 years of age, the artist faces his more introspective phase, and makes an attempt to project it on the surrounding social reality.

In addition to *The Making of...* we find the gadgets and the works of art derived from the unfinished *Videoache*. The work *Storyboard*, for example (ill. p. 229), first came about as a character in *Videoache* (a hyperrealistic trap-door located in a crypt, which "speaks" by opening and closing like a mouth, whose hinges and handles are just as many characters with a life of their own) and then became a picture in its own right, on which the artist has drawn sketches and notes about scenic sequences as though it were a provisional story-board of the video itself. *Storyboard* is a work that represents one of the two principal technical "orientations" of Corte's works, where he points out the aspect of impermanence and temporal deterioration of the component materials, which are even artificially aged by exaggerating some of their expressive features (including fake holes of woodworms). This type of work coexists with its opposite, i.e. those works characterized by maniacal formal cleanliness where the patina is perfect, the brushwork meticulous, the plastic volumes without imperfection. There is no contradiction between these two aspects, between the material that is uncontaminated and that which is ruined by time: the spectrospective eye mingles and confuses the two chronological moments.

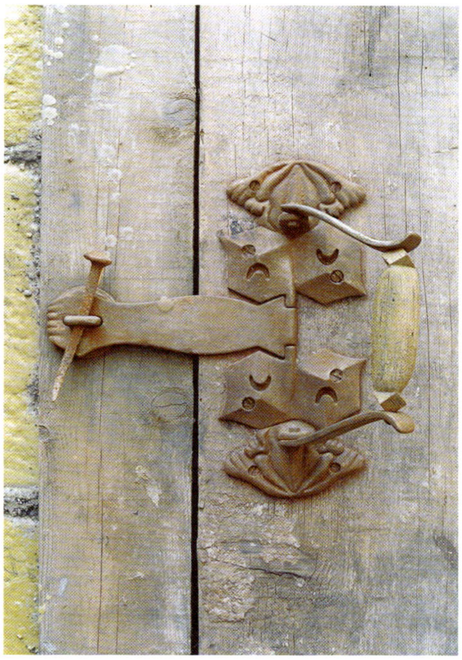

Detail of the handle and hinges of *Storyboard*, 2000 (cf. p. 229).

Then there is the *Dolorama*, a singular gadget patented by Corte, which allows the spectators to be more directly involved as they watch *Videoache* (ill. p. 228). It is a little rectangle of plastic, produced in series, with ten transparent blisters on one side and, inside, small sharp or pointed objects such as razorblades, nails, pins, thorns, fragments of glass or grains of salt. It works like this: the various Doloramas should be distributed to the public before they see *Videoache* (we have mentioned that *Videoache* is intended to show pain as it occurs). In practice, as it is projected, the most effective scenes should have a number from one to ten superimposed on the image and these numbers correspond to those on the blisters of the Dolorama. As a number appears on the screen, the spectator should open the Dolorama's blister with the same number and use the object inside it to gradually self-inflict little cuts and jabs (at the end, the work is completed by rubbing the grains of salt into the wounds). The different types of pain, self-inflicted "on command" as the numbers appear, correspond to the painful scenes in the video, and thus allow the spectator to totally identify with the fiction. And so we conclude this spectrospective voyage, with the image of the multicolored Dolorama, ready to invade the world, produced at industrial level as an infinite multiple of Enrico Corte's art and given as a present to his public.

One final thing. In this volume I have analyzed a hundred or so of Corte's works chosen at random from a production that numbers more than one thousand nine hundred. This means that one could write twenty more books like this, each containing a different selection of works, and thus give twenty further interpretations, all different, of the artist's work. These books could be shuffled together like a pack of cards, to start a game with History. But the time-span of the work runs simultaneously backwards and forwards, according to the propelling pattern of the mind. The future becomes memory, experience discovers its past. And the present is reborn in the perpetual actuality of the psyche. Once again, History is revealed as *the self-portrait of a brain*.

Logo for *(The Making of) Videoache*, 1999
SC 1130.

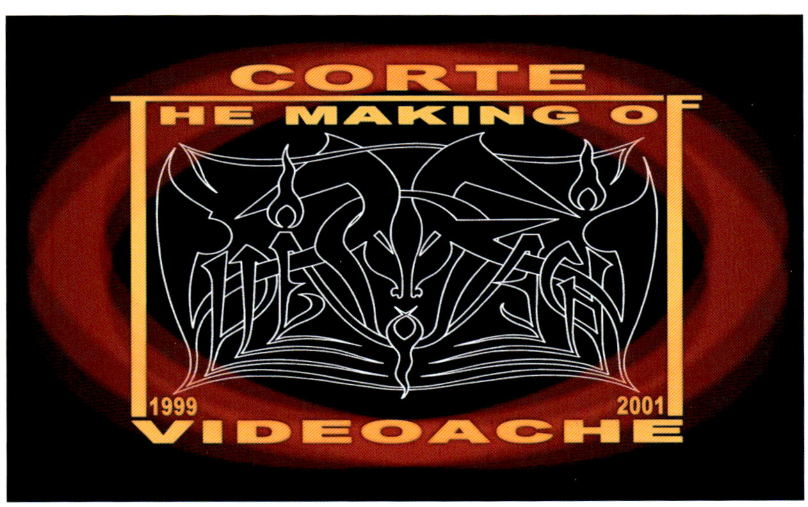

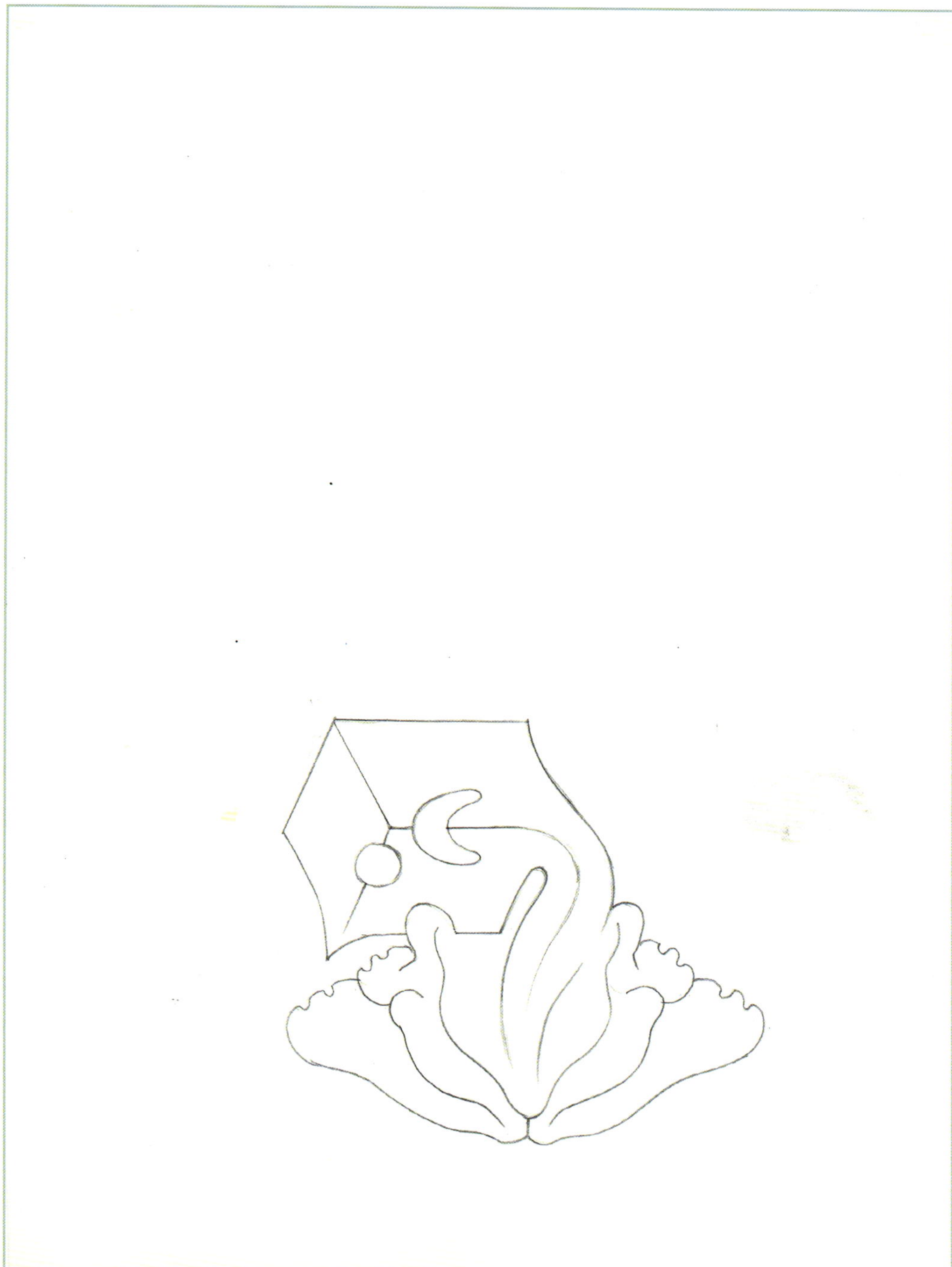

Study for the hinges of *Storyboard*, 2000.
Graphite on paper. 11¾ x 8¼" (29,7 x 21 cm).
SC 1054.

PLATES

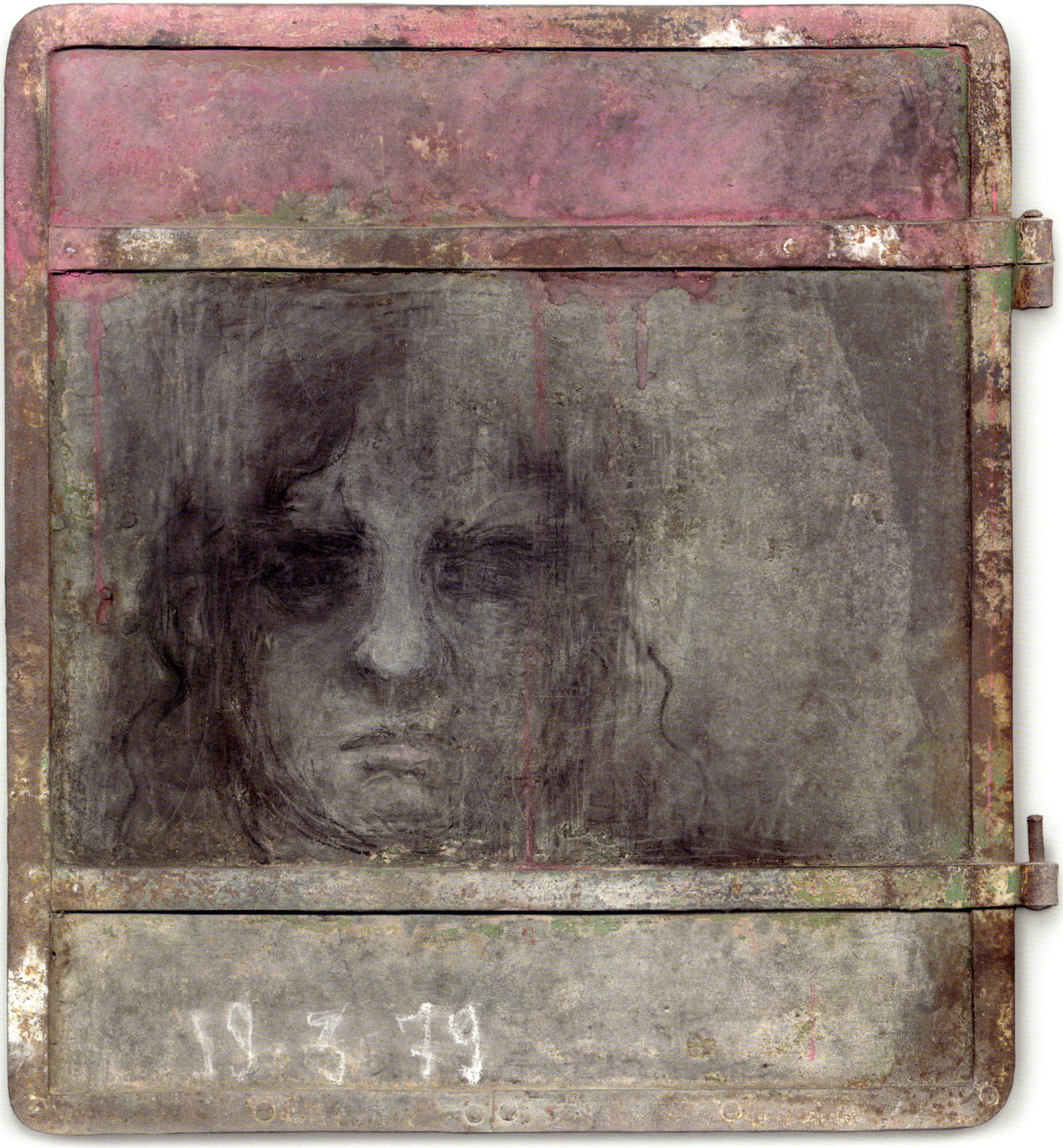

Drawing from the *250 Rotten Apples* series: *March 19, 1979.*
Chalk, charcoal, watercolor and rust on iron door.
20 x 18¼" (51 x 46,5 cm).
GC 218.

Drawings from the *250 Rotten Apples* series; clockwise from left:

Aug. 2, 1978; chalk, charcoal and watercolor on wood. 38¼ x 22½" (97 x 57 cm); GC 62.

July 31, 1978; chalk and charcoal on rusty iron gutter. 21 x 15¼ x 12¼" (53,5 x 39 x 31 cm); GC 60.

Feb. 15, 1979; chalk and charcoal on brown butcher paper. 21 x 14¾" (53,5 x 37,5 cm); GC 196.

July 20, 1978; chalk and charcoal on brown butcher paper. 21 x 14½" (53,5 x 37 cm); GC 53.

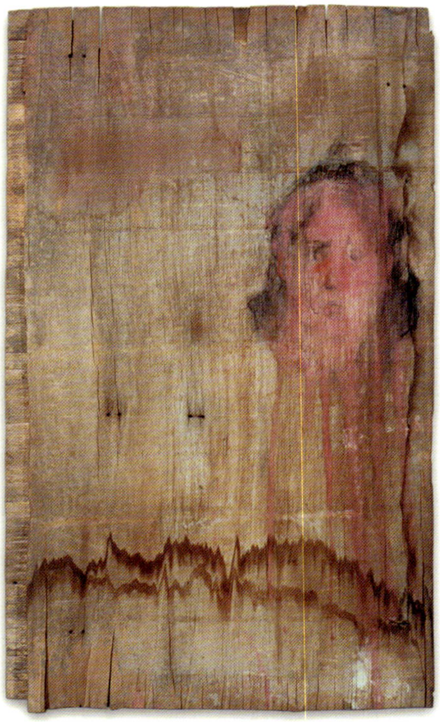

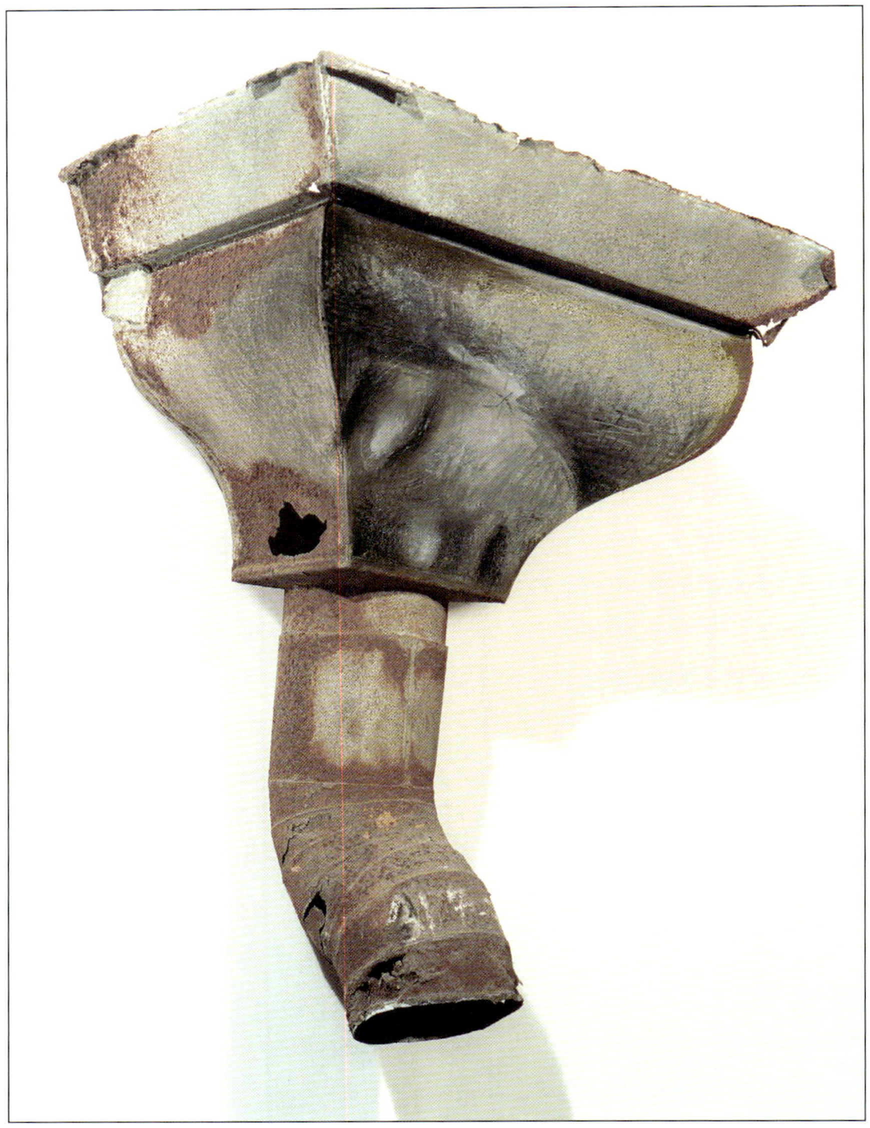

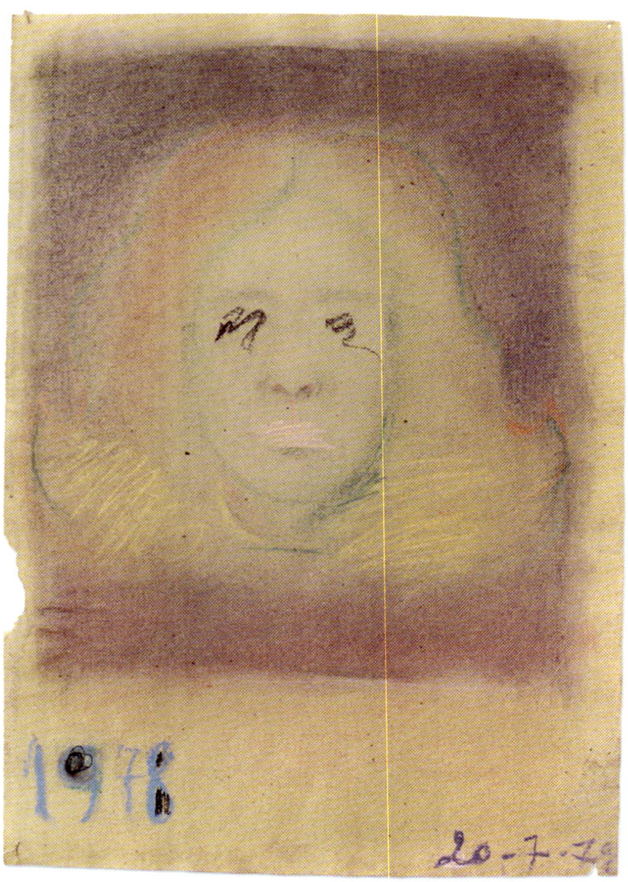

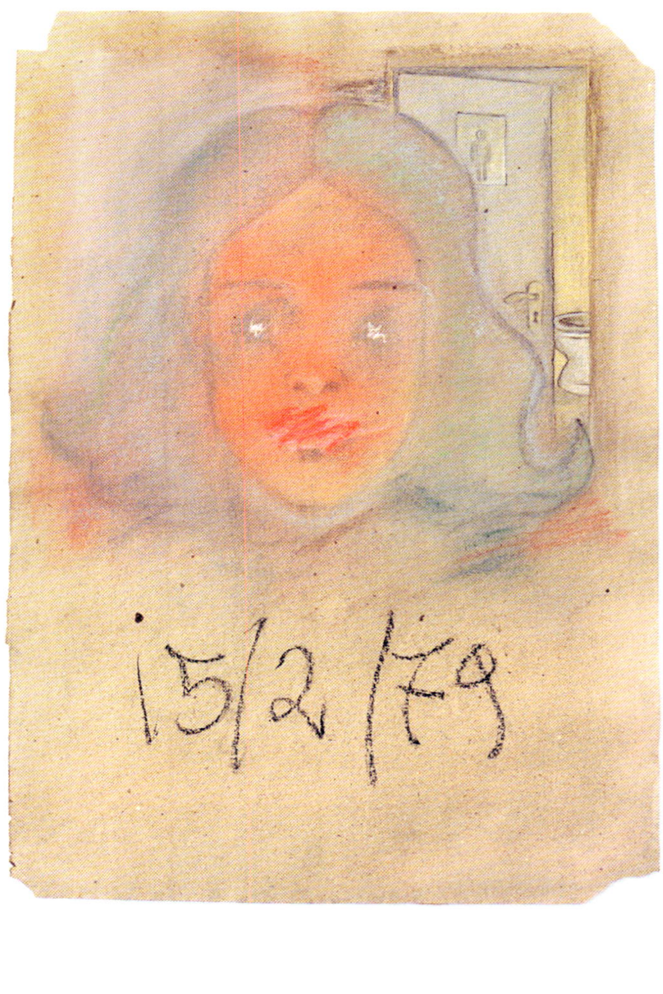

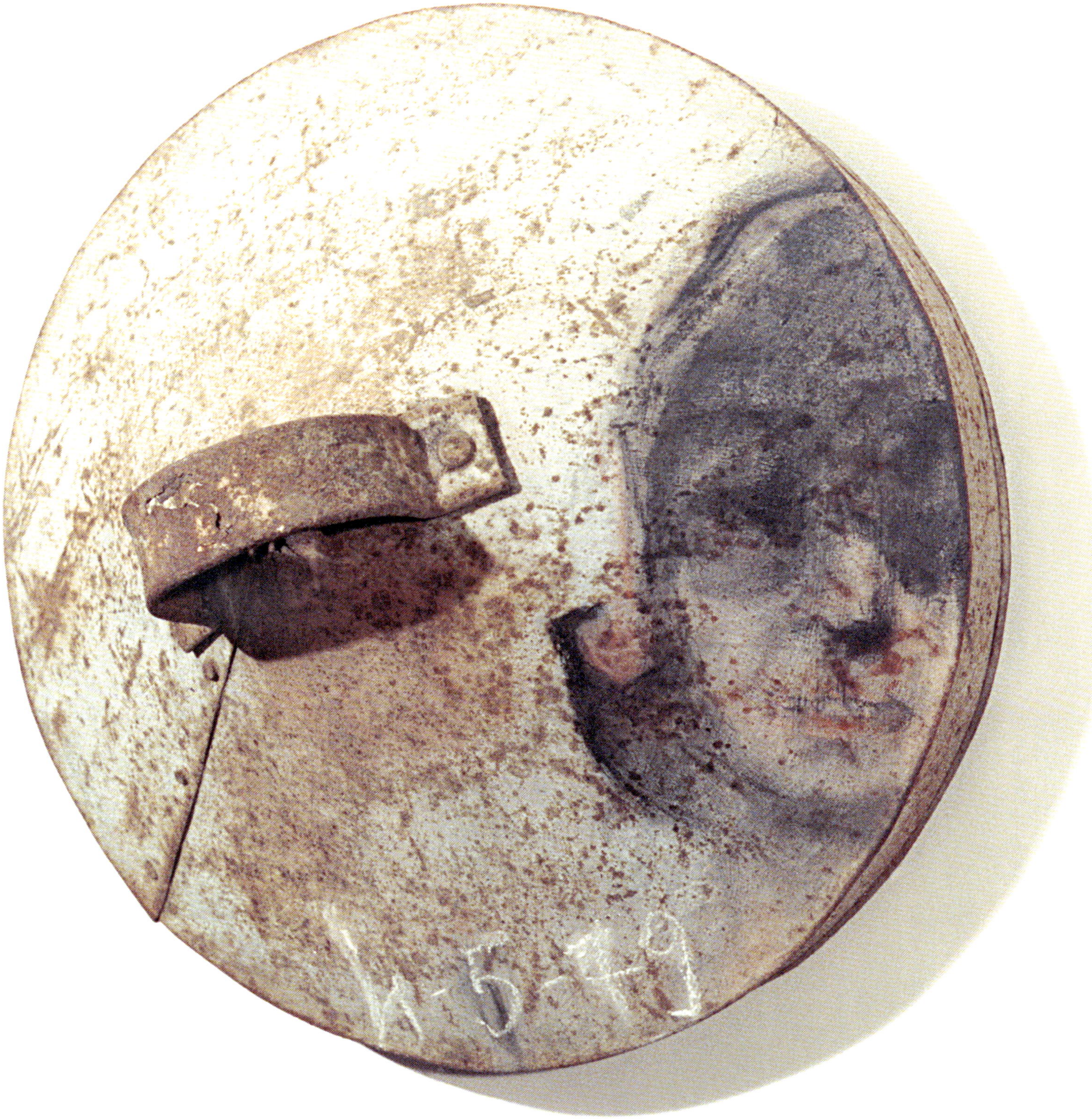

Drawing from the *250 Rotten Apples* series: *May 4, 1979.*
Pastel, chalk, charcoal and rust on iron cover.
15 x 15¾ x 7¾" (38 x 40 x 20 cm).
GC 249.

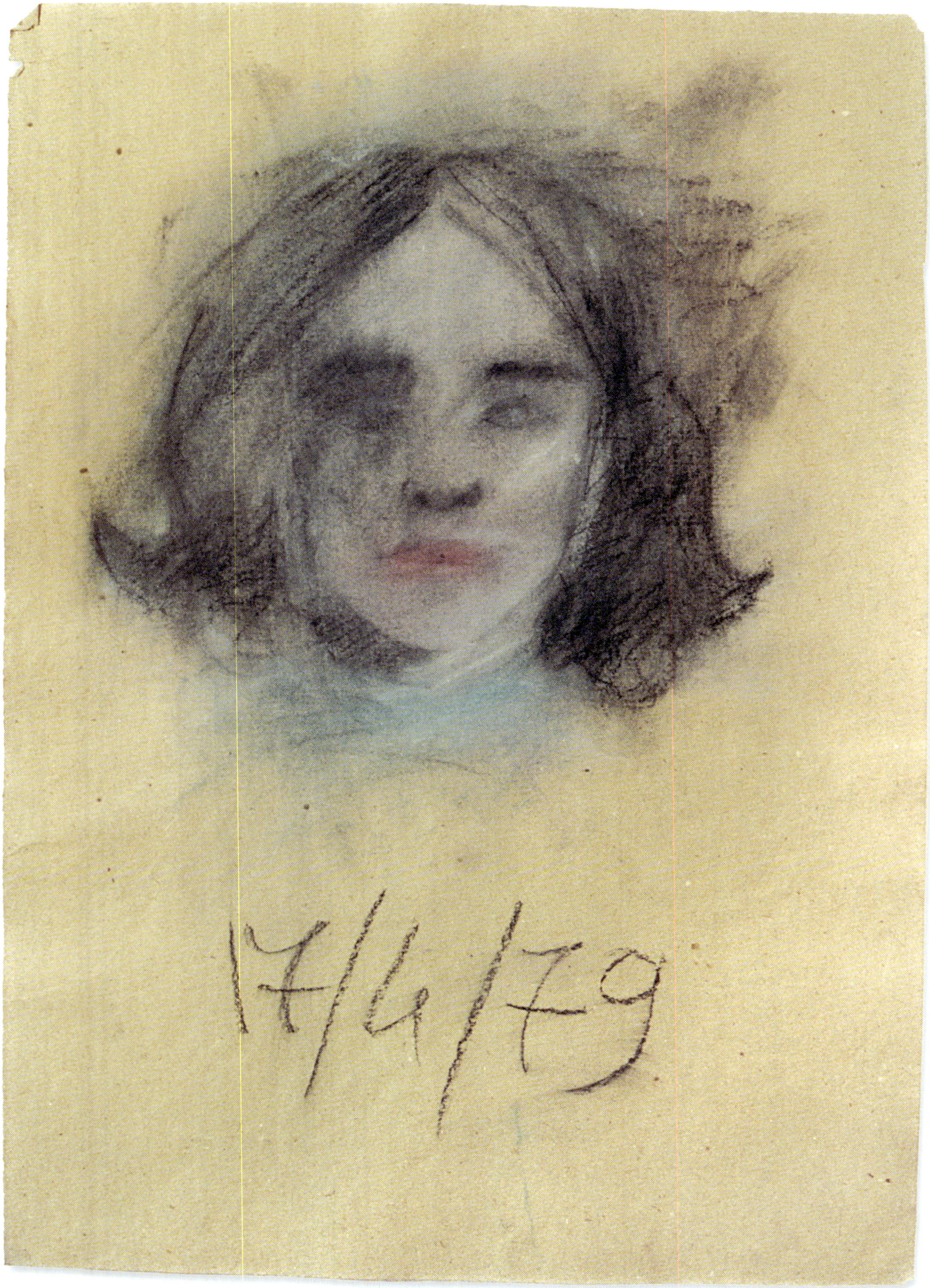

Drawing from the *250 Rotten Apples* series: *April 17, 1979.*
Pastel, chalk and charcoal on brown butcher paper.
21 x 14¾” (53,5 x 37,4 cm).
GC 238.

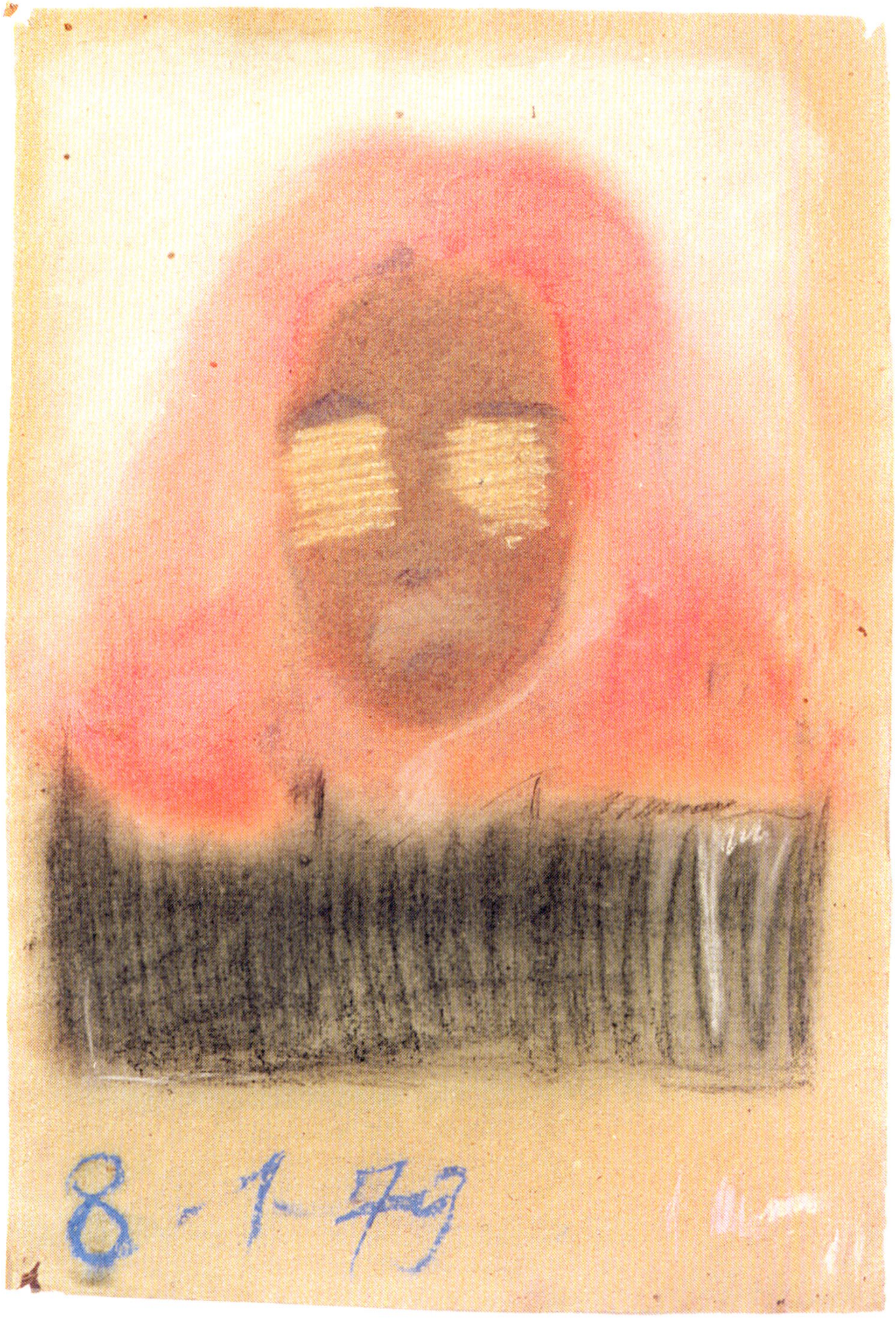

Drawing from the *250 Rotten Apples* series: *January 8, 1979.*
Pastel, chalk and charcoal on brown butcher paper.
21 x 14¾" (53,5 x 37,5 cm).
GC 168.

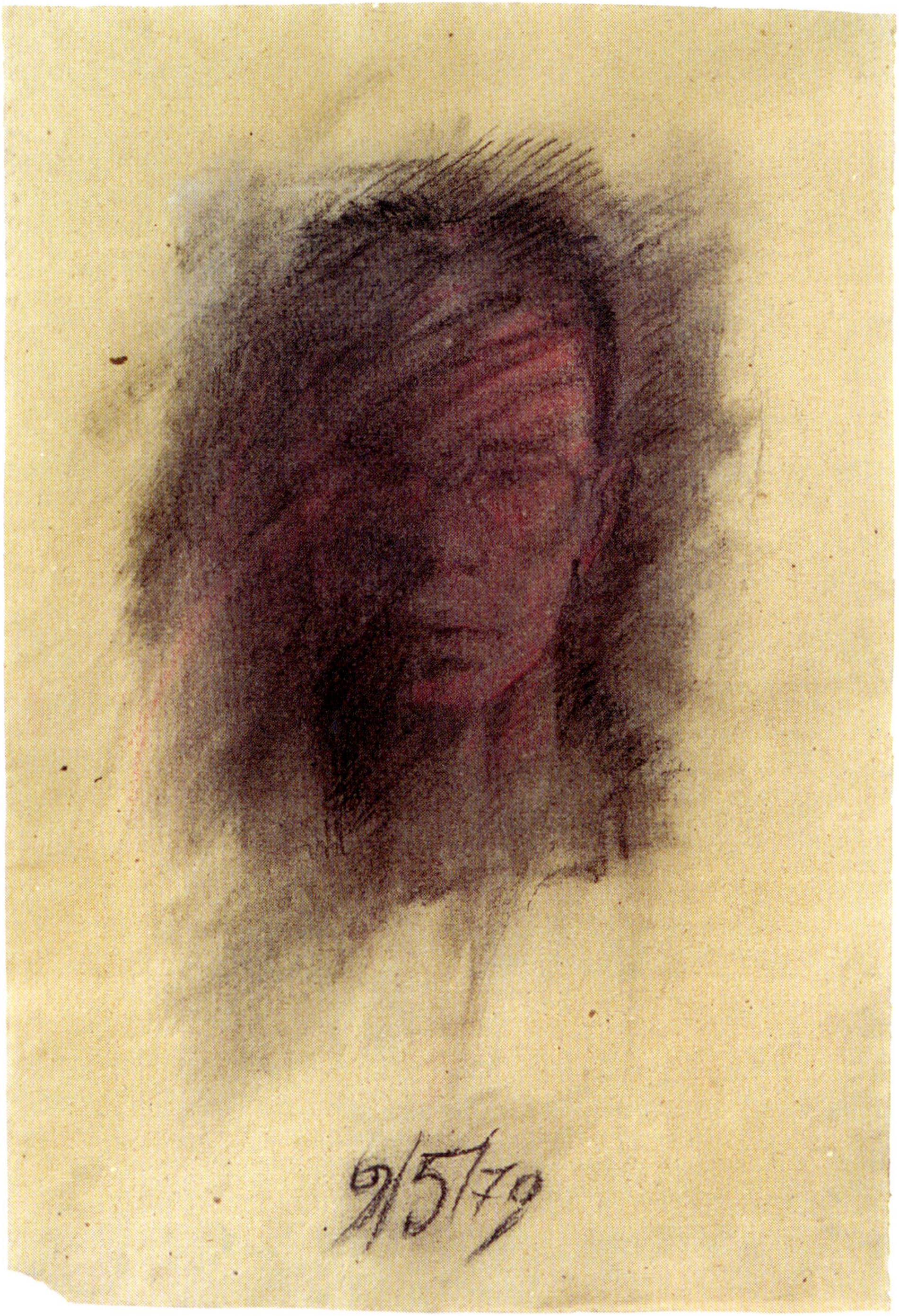

Drawing from the *250 Rotten Apples* series: *May 9, 1979.*
Pastel, chalk and charcoal on brown butcher paper.
21 x 15" (53,5 x 38 cm).
GC 252.

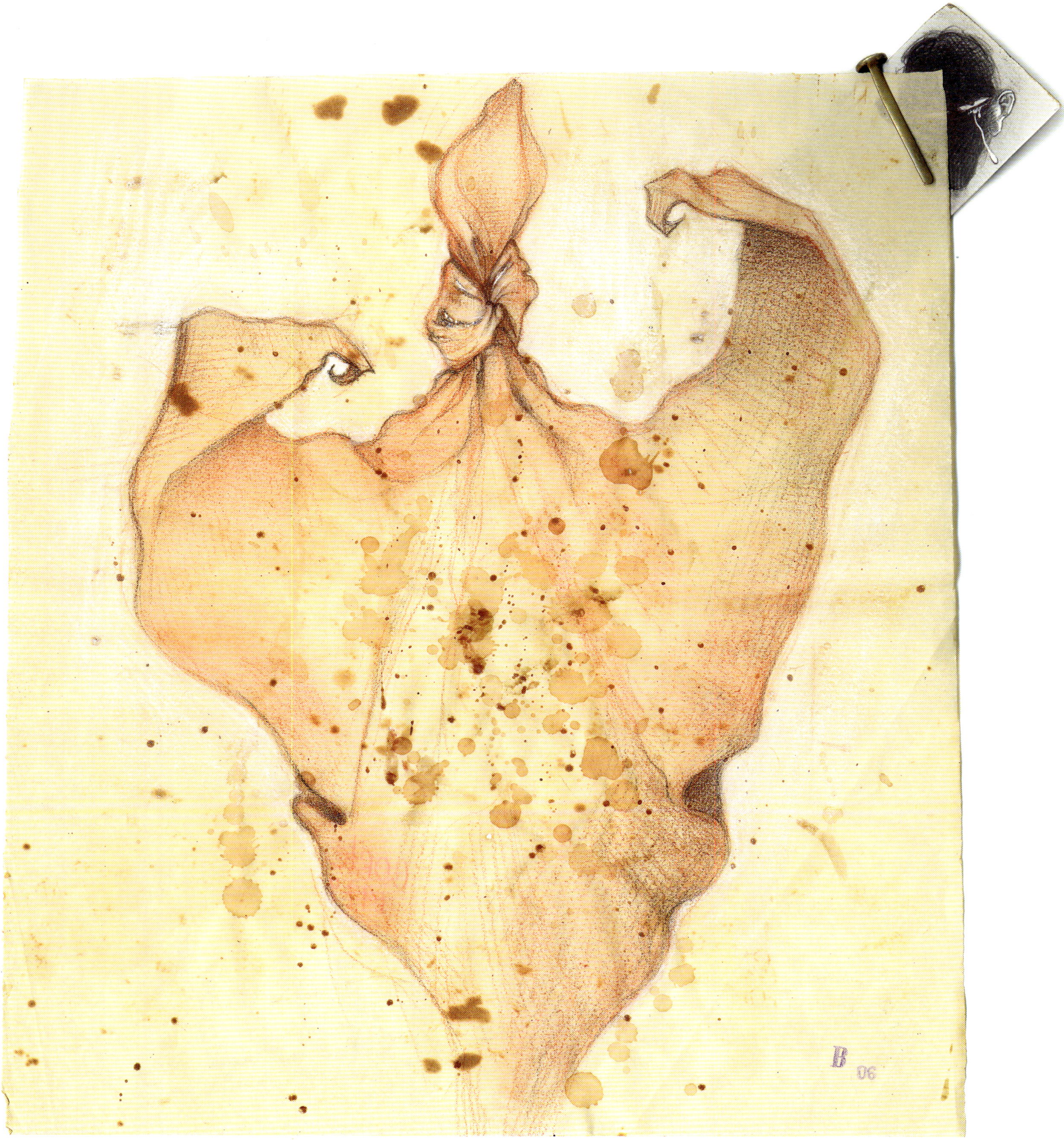

Drawing from the *Stoic Ebbs and Flows* series, 1979.
Graphite, tempera, sanguine pencil, human and animal blood, red wine, ink stamping on oil paper and fragment of grey paper, with metal clip.
11½ x 10½" (29,2 x 26,5 cm).
GC 269.

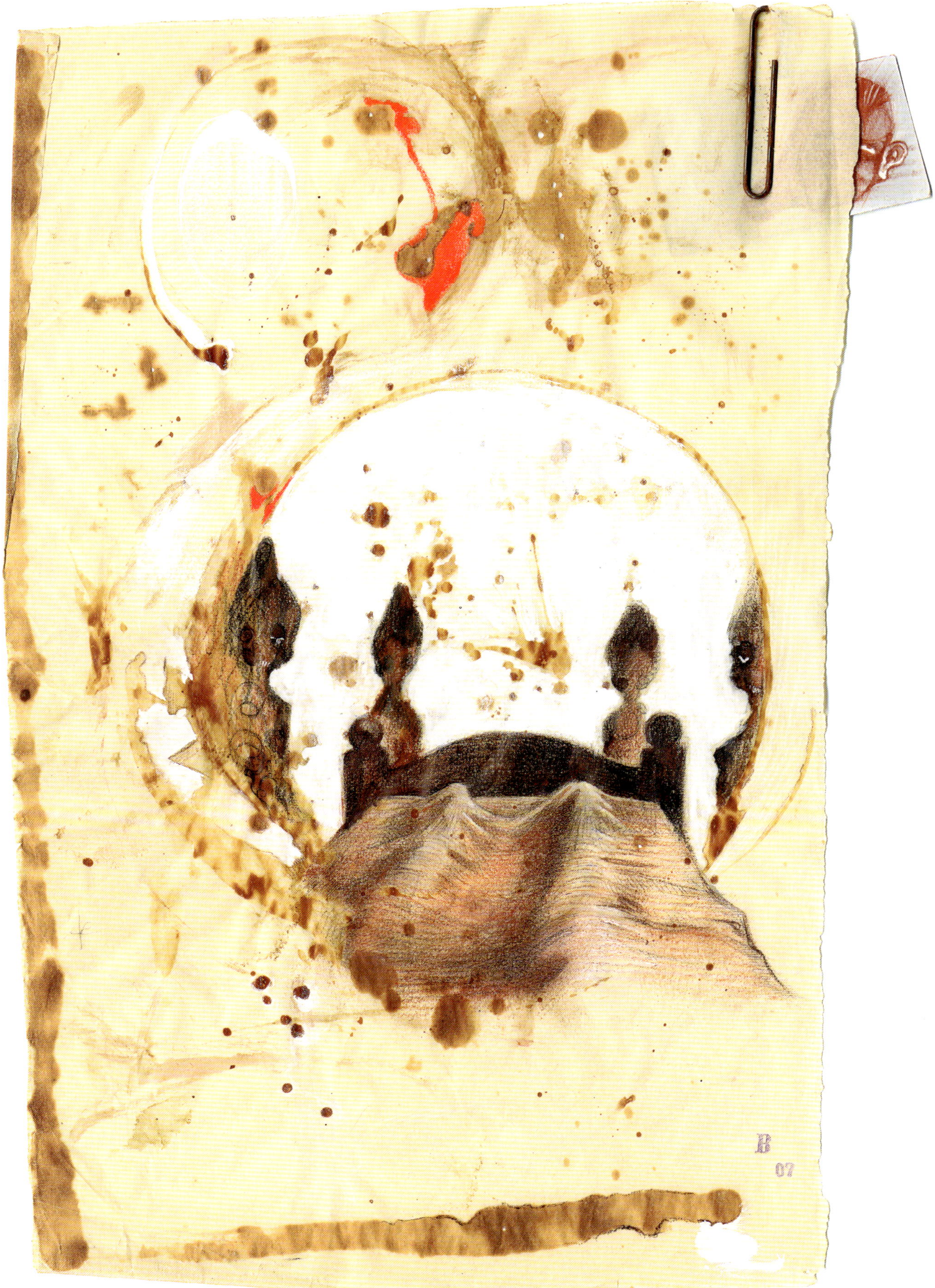

Drawing from the *Stoic Ebbs and Flows* series, 1979.
Charcoal, tempera, sanguine pencil, human and animal blood,
ink stamping on oil paper and fragment of grey paper, with rusty metal clip.
13¾ x 9½" (34,8 x 24,2 cm).
GC 260.

Top right: drawing from the *Stoic Ebbs and Flows* series, 1979.
Graphite, charcoal, tempera, sanguine pencil, ball pen,
human and animal blood, ink stamping on oil paper
and fragment of grey paper, with metal clip.
11½ x 9½" (29 x 24 cm); GC 261.

Left: drawing from the *Stoic Ebbs and Flows* series, 1979.
Graphite, charcoal, tempera, sanguine pencil,
human and animal blood, ink stamping on oil paper
and fragment of grey paper, with metal clip.
13¾ x 9" (35,3 x 23,3 cm); GC 263.

Bottom right: drawing from the *Stoic Ebbs and Flows* series, 1979.
Graphite, charcoal, tempera, sanguine pencil, human
and animal blood, blood-red orange juice, tomato juice,
garlic, toothpaste, sperm, ink stamping on oil paper
and fragment of grey paper, with metal clip.
11¾ x 10" (29,9 x 25,6 cm); GC 265.

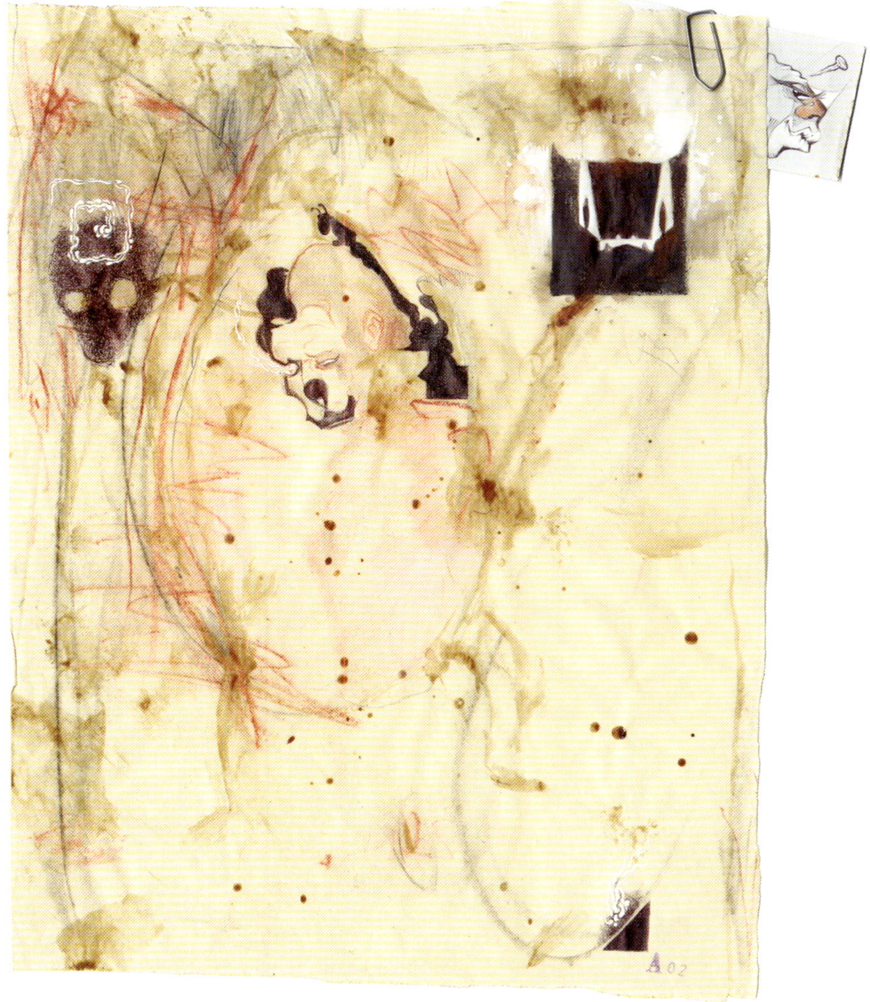

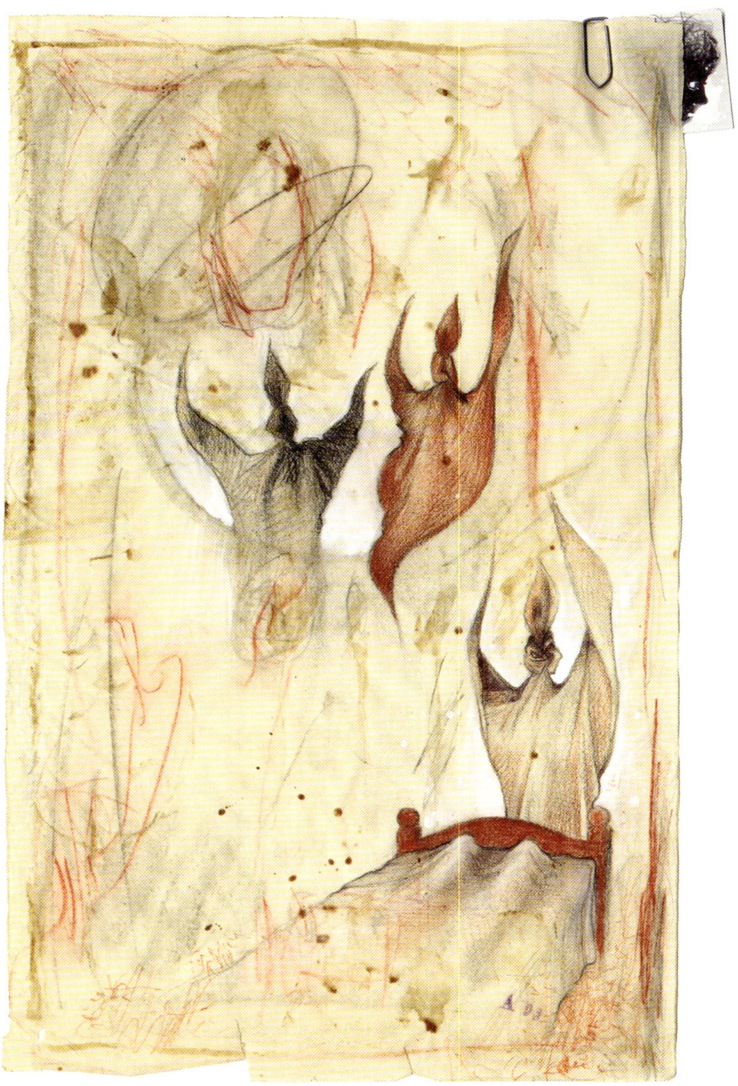

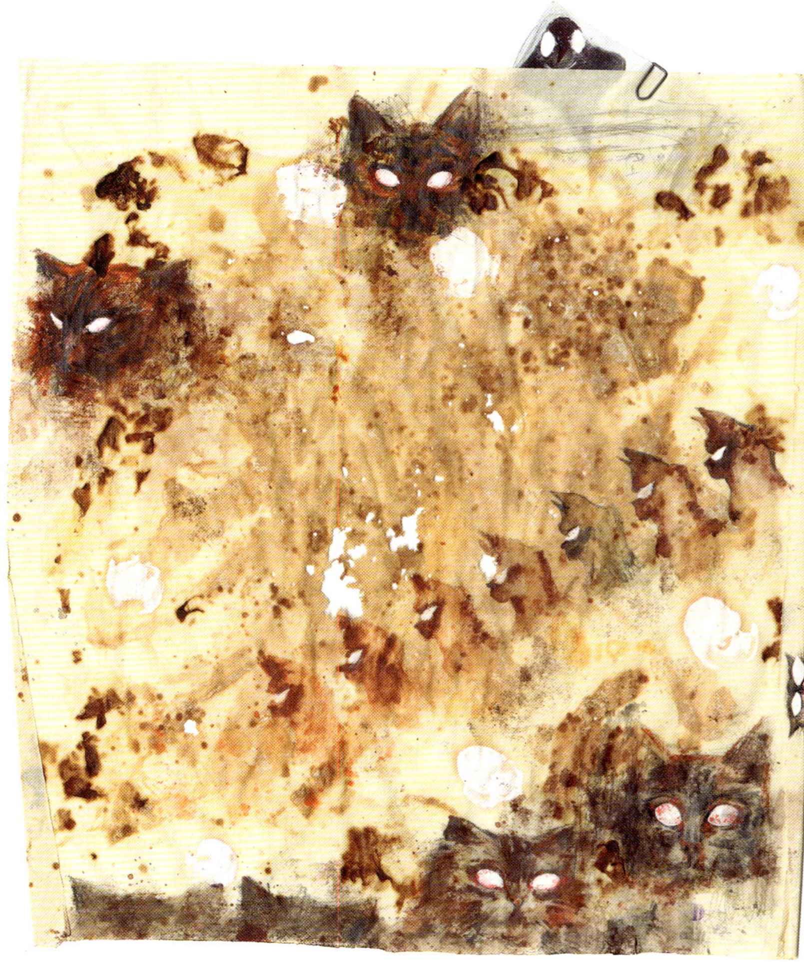

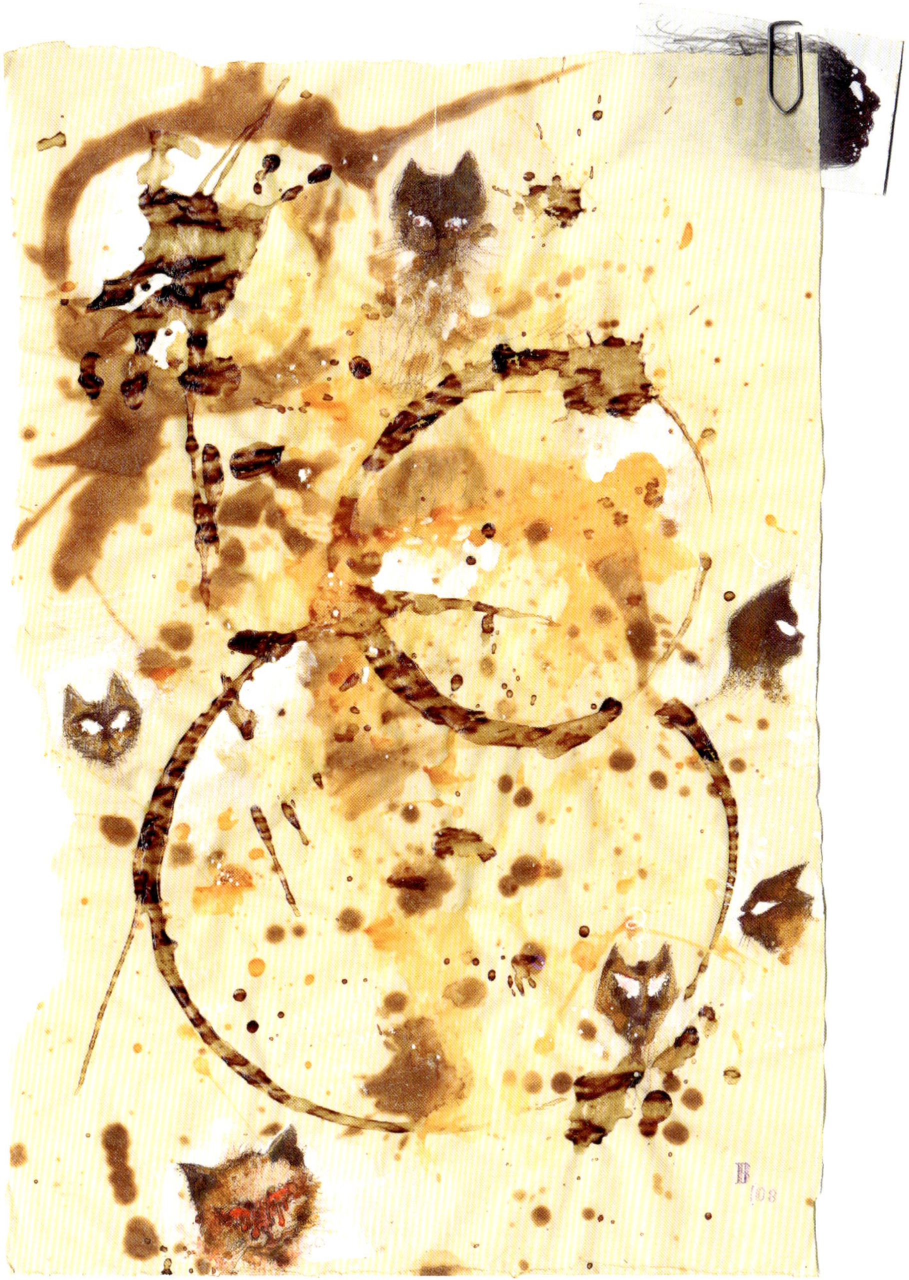

Drawing from the *Stoic Ebbs and Flows* series, 1979.
Graphite, charcoal, tempera, human and animal blood,
yolk, aubergine stains, ink stamping on oil paper
and fragment of grey paper, with metal clip.
12½ x 9" (32 x 23,3 cm).
GC 264.

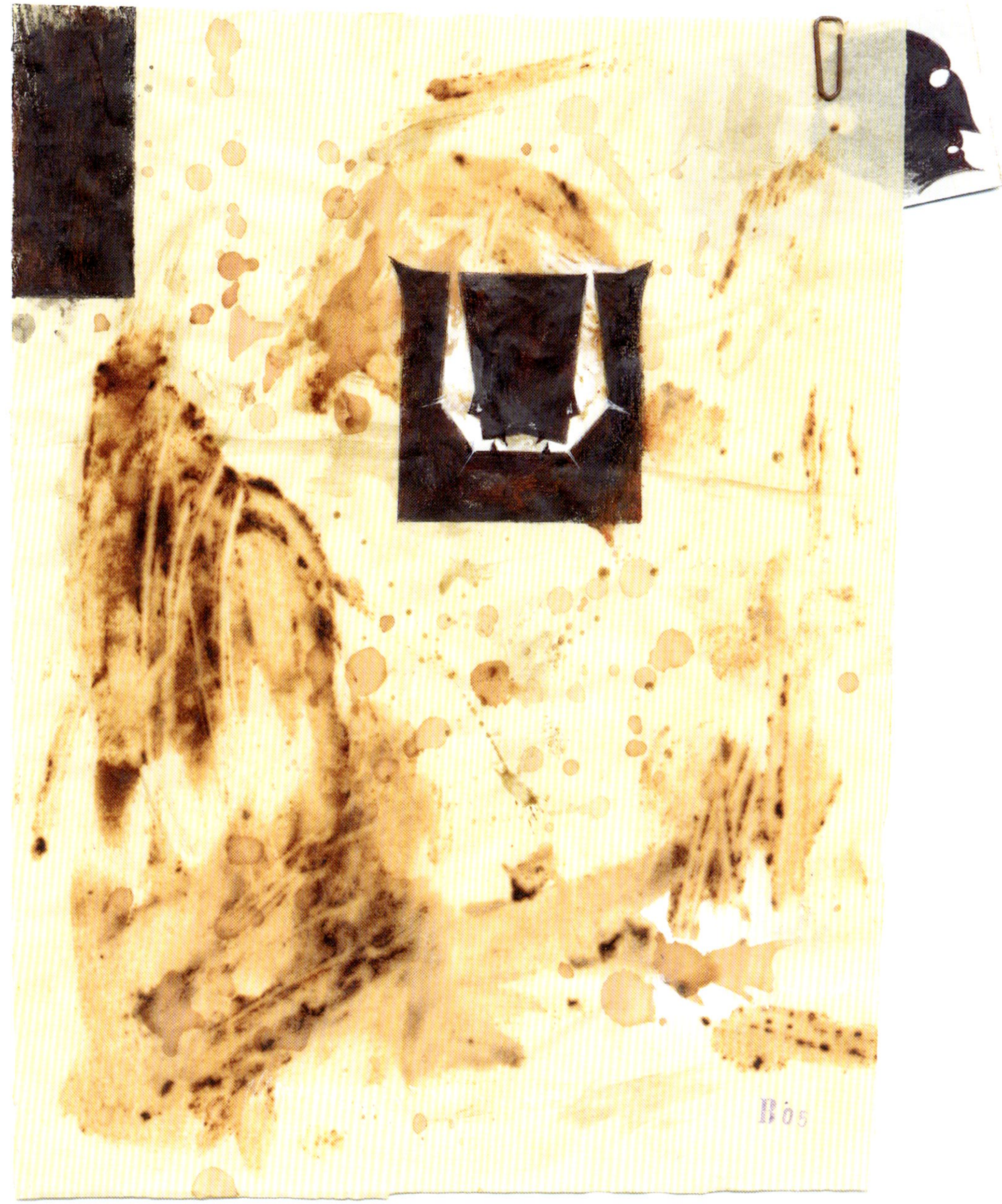

Drawing from the *Stoic Ebbs and Flows* series, 1979.
Graphite, charcoal, tempera, sanguine pencil, human blood,
red wine, tomato juice, ink stamping on oil paper
and fragment of grey paper, with rusty metal clip.
10 x 8½" (25,7 x 22 cm).
GC 262.

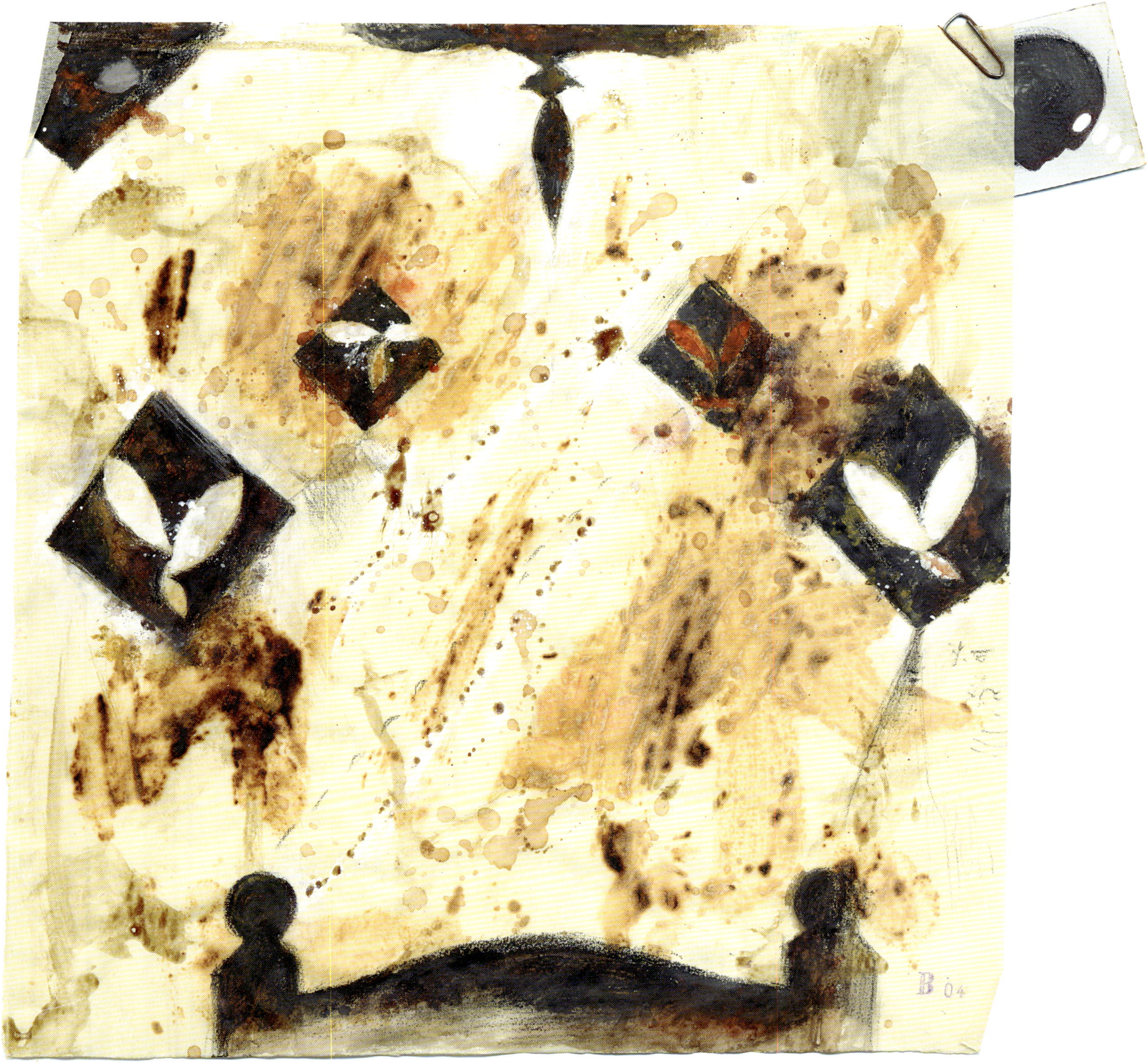

Drawing from the *Stoic Ebbs and Flows* series, 1979.
Graphite, charchoal, tempera, sanguine pencil, human and animal blood, tomato juice, red wine, ink stamping on oil paper and fragment of grey paper, with rusty metal clip.
10 x 10½" (25,3 x 26,6 cm).
GC 267.

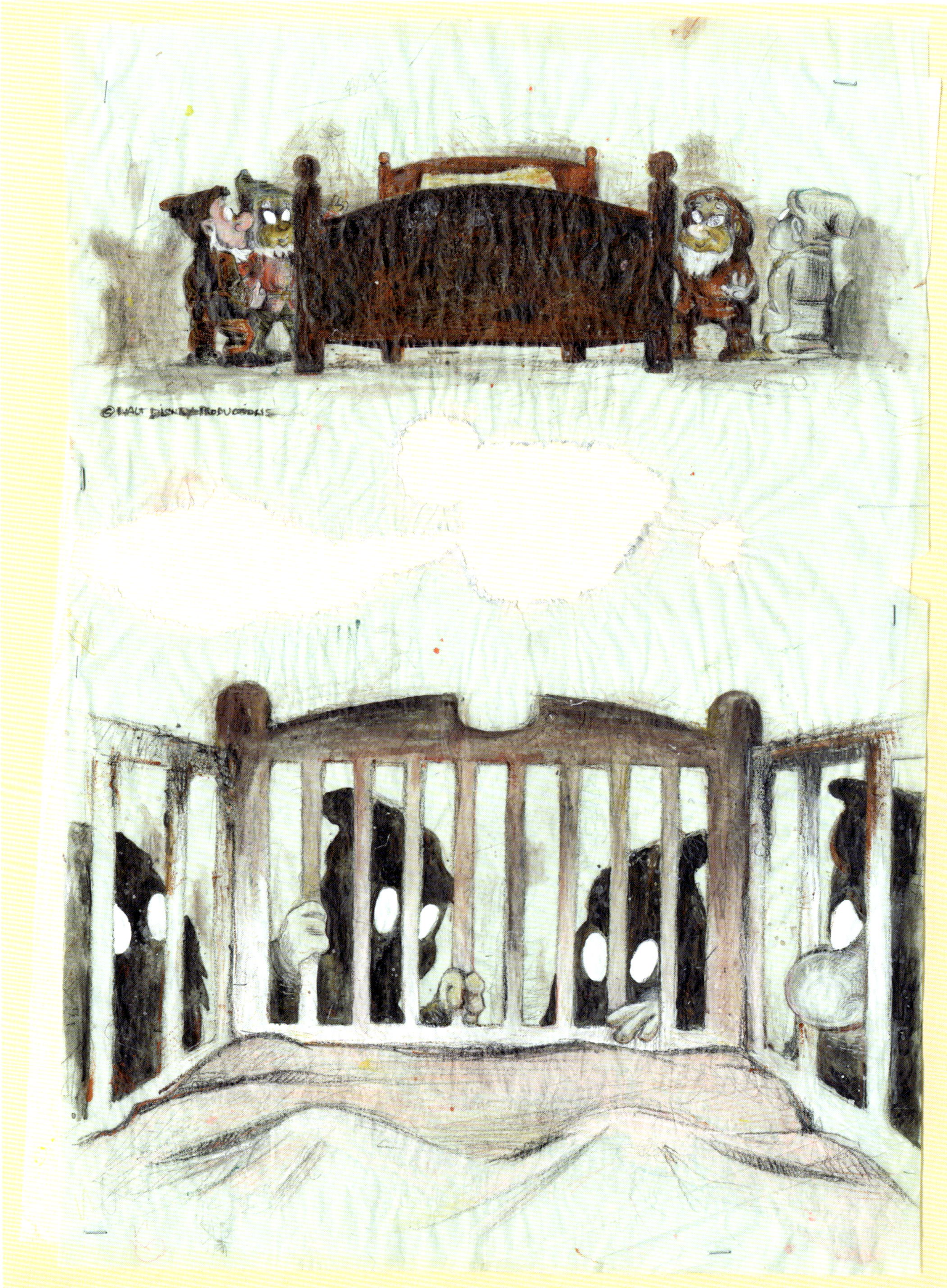

Drawing from the *Gastric Juices and Suctions* series, 1979.
Colored pencils, tempera, muriatic acid, drops of human bile on two layers of colored tissue paper, joined by metal staples.
14½ x 10¼" (37 x 26 cm).
GC 274.

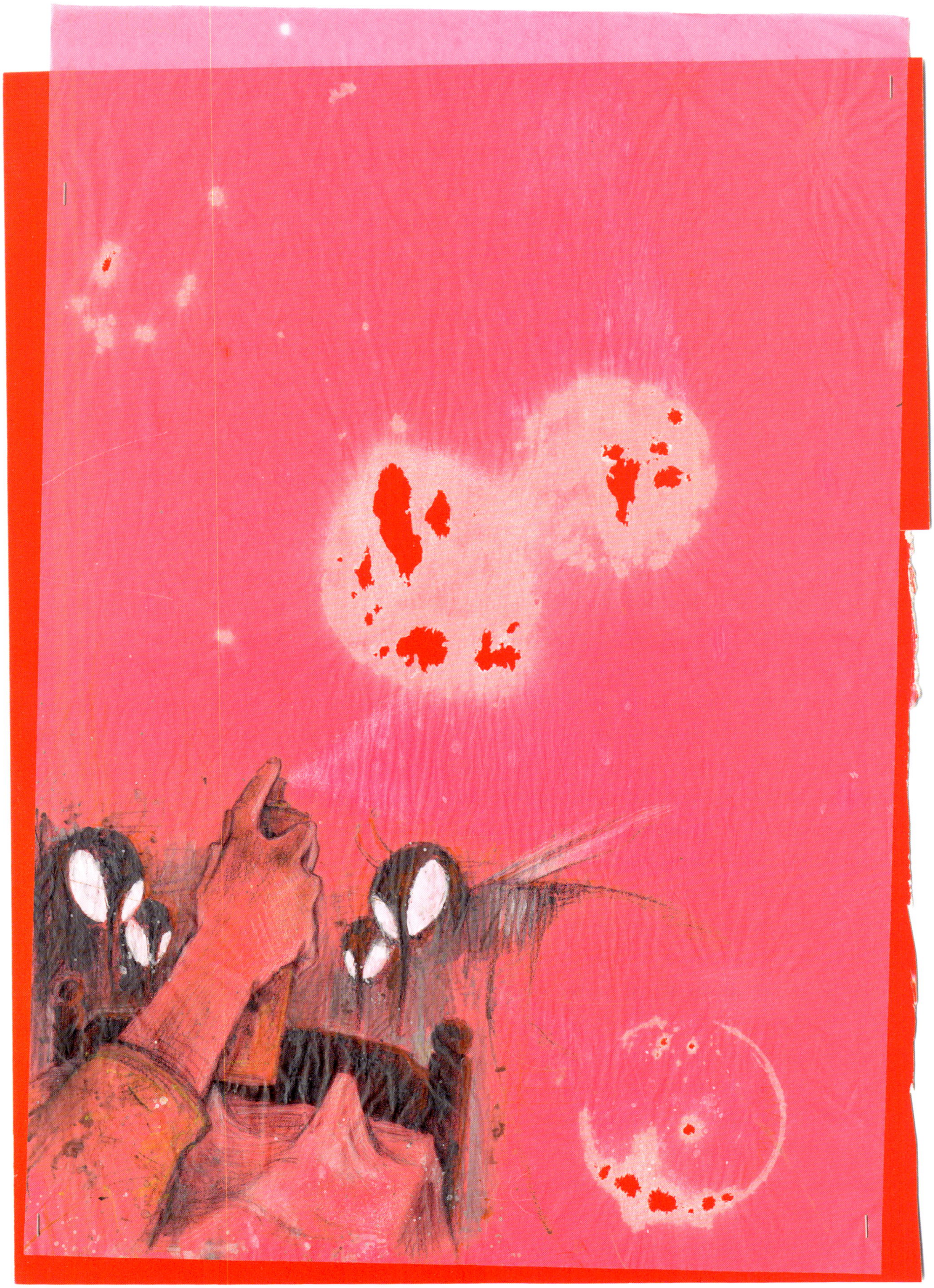

Drawing from the *Gastric Juices and Suctions* series, 1979.
Colored pencils, tempera, salycilic acid, sulfamic acid, drops of human bile on two layers of colored tissue paper and cardboard, joined by metal staples.
15¼ x 10½" (38,8 x 26,8 cm).
GC 277.

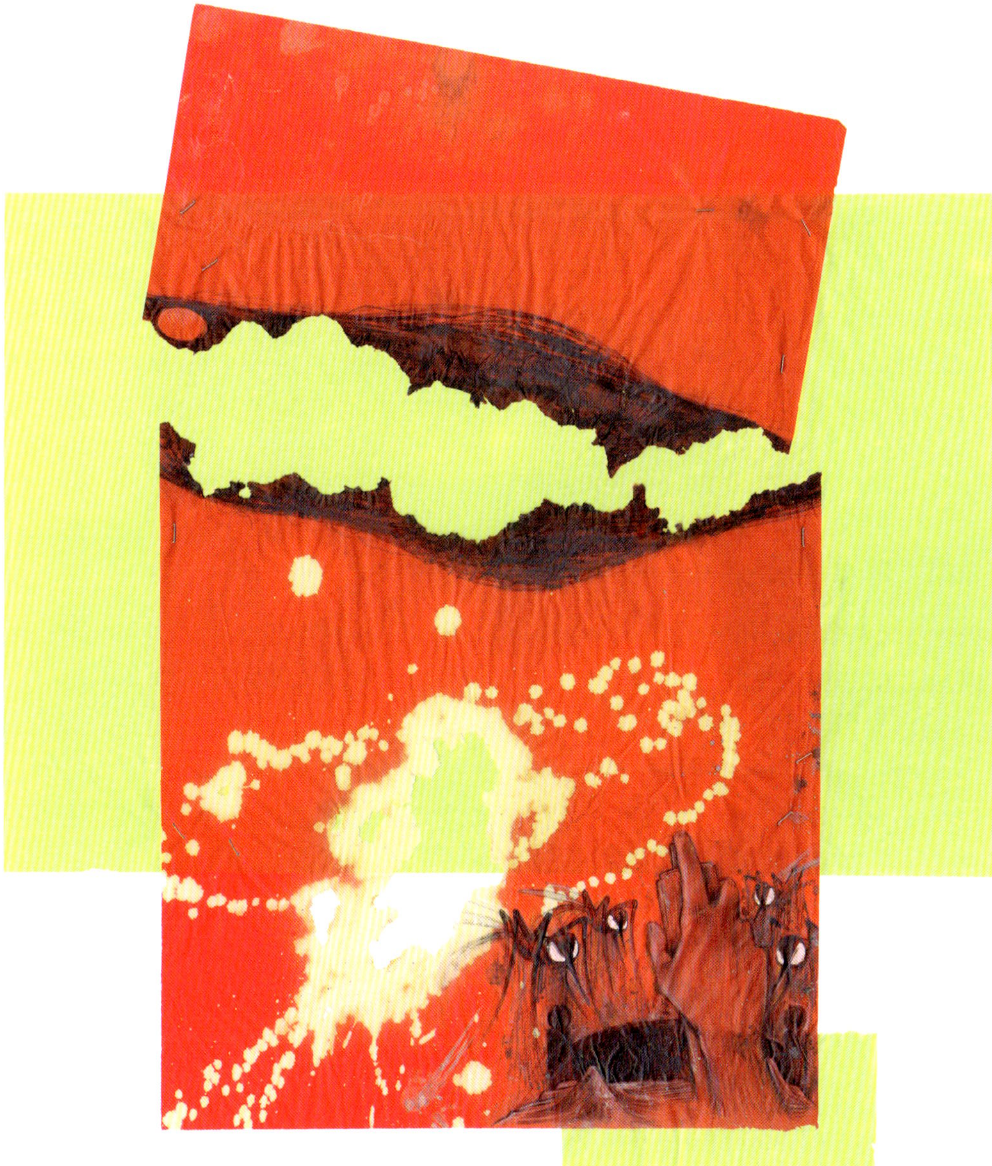

Drawing from the *Gastric Juices and Suctions* series, 1979.
Colored pencils, tempera, fluoridric acid, vitriol, drops of human bile on two layers of colored tissue paper, joined by metal staples.
17 x 14¾" (43,4 x 37,8 cm).
GC 278.

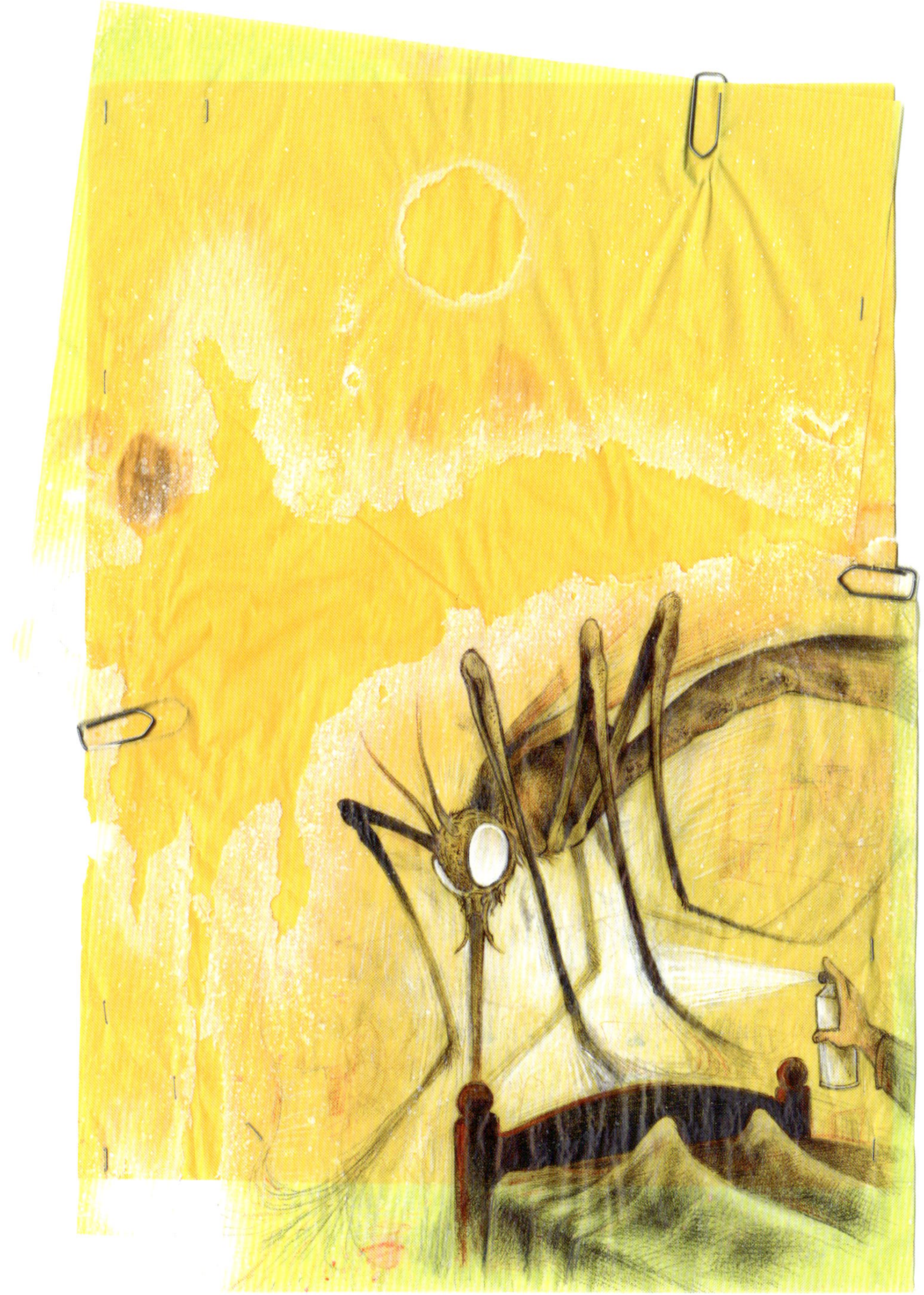

Drawing from the *Gastric Juices and Suctions* series, 1979.
Colored pencils, tempera, nitric acid, sulfuric acid, drops of human bile on two layers of colored tissue paper, joined by metal staples and clips.
15 x 11" (38,3 x 28 cm).
GC 276.

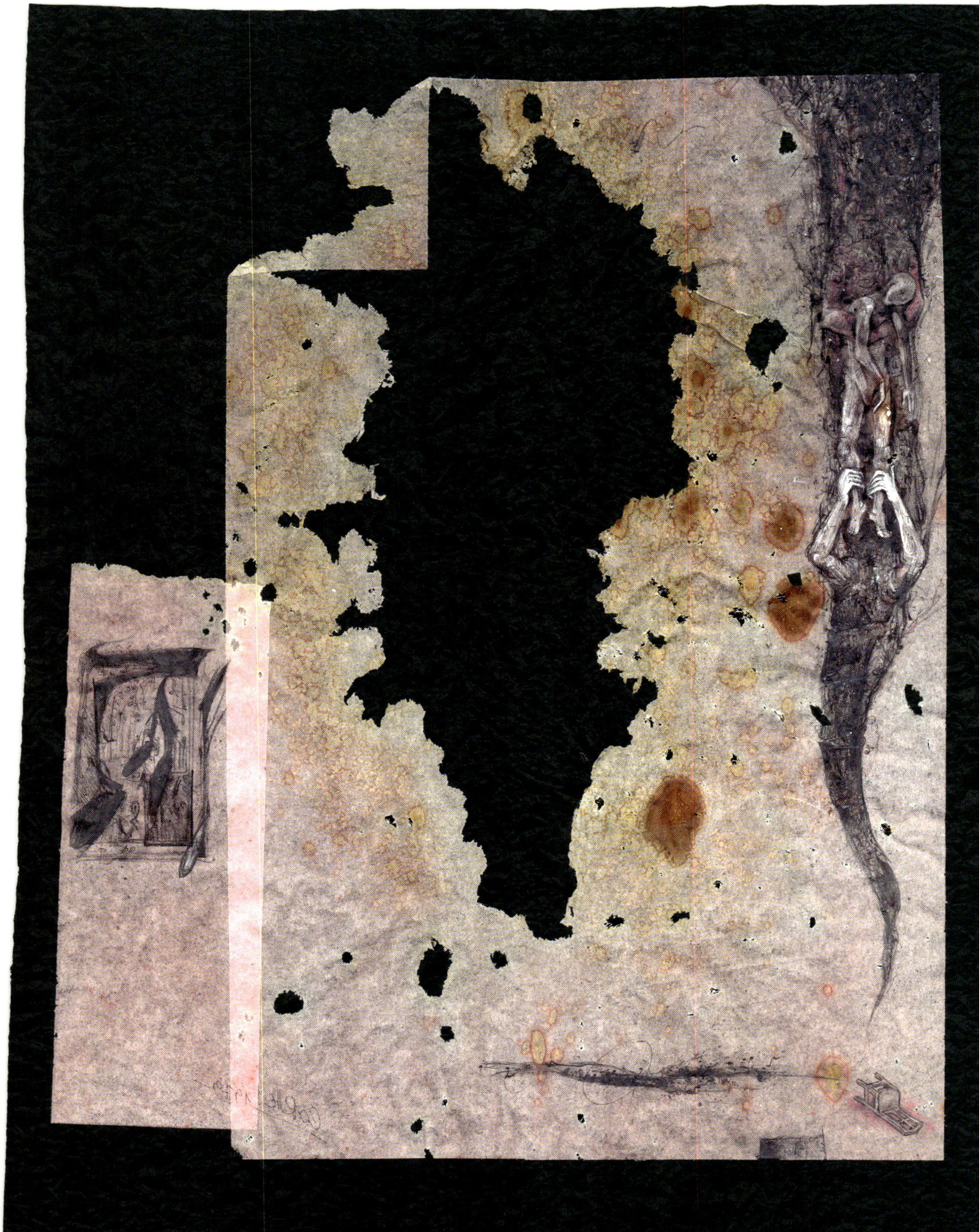

Drawing from the *Gastric Juices and Suctions* series, 1979.
Colored pencils, tempera, salycilic acid, nitric acid, drops of human bile
on three layers of colored tissue paper and tar paper.
17¼ x 13¼" (43,7 x 33,8 cm).
GC 272.

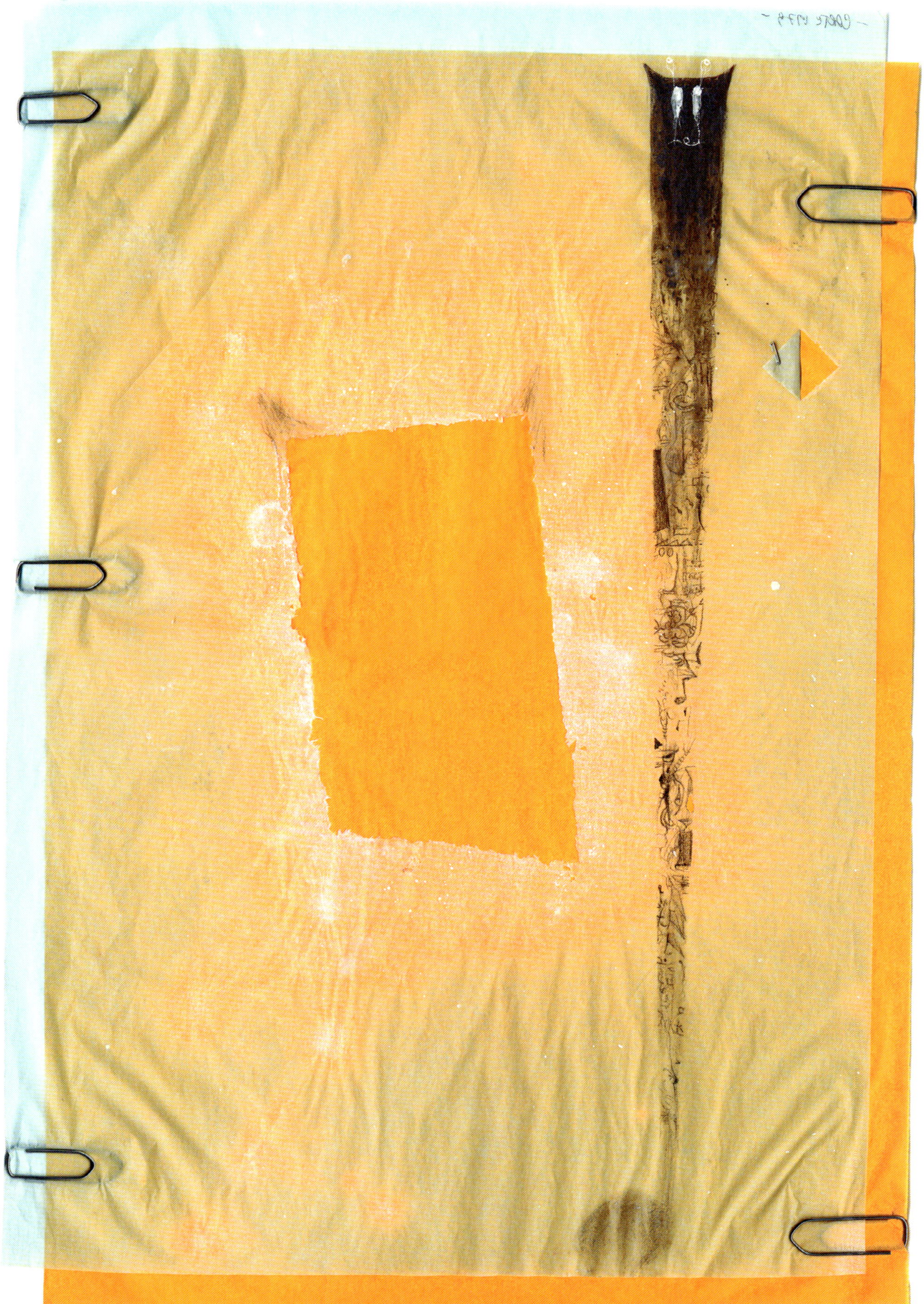

Drawing from the *Gastric Juices and Suctions* series, 1979.
Colored pencils, tempera, muriatic acid, sulfidric acid, drops of lysergic acid, drops of human bile on two layers of colored tissue paper, joined by metal staples and clips.
15¼ x 10¼" (39 x 26 cm).
GC 279.

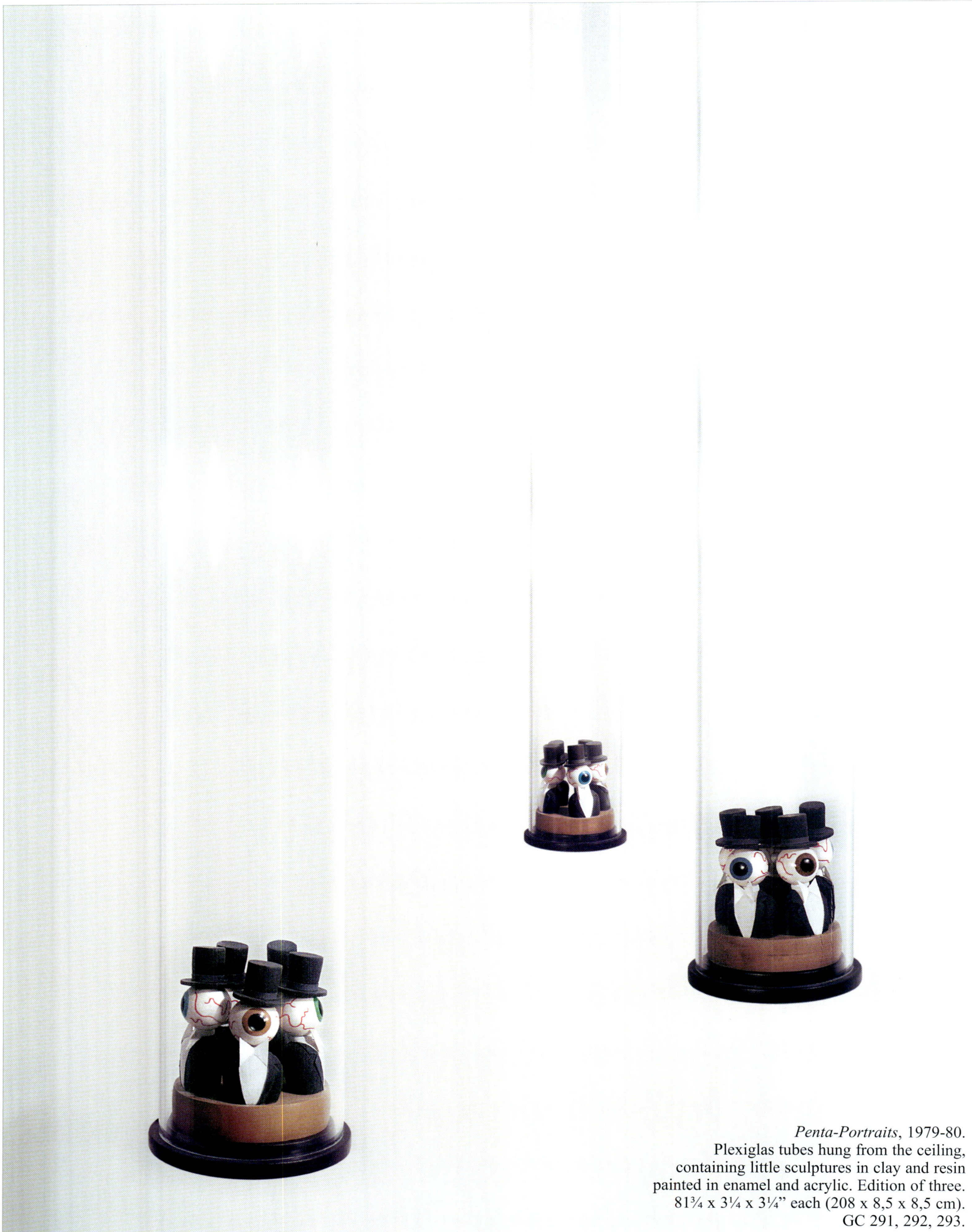

Penta-Portraits, 1979-80.
Plexiglas tubes hung from the ceiling, containing little sculptures in clay and resin painted in enamel and acrylic. Edition of three.
81¾ x 3¼ x 3¼" each (208 x 8,5 x 8,5 cm).
GC 291, 292, 293.

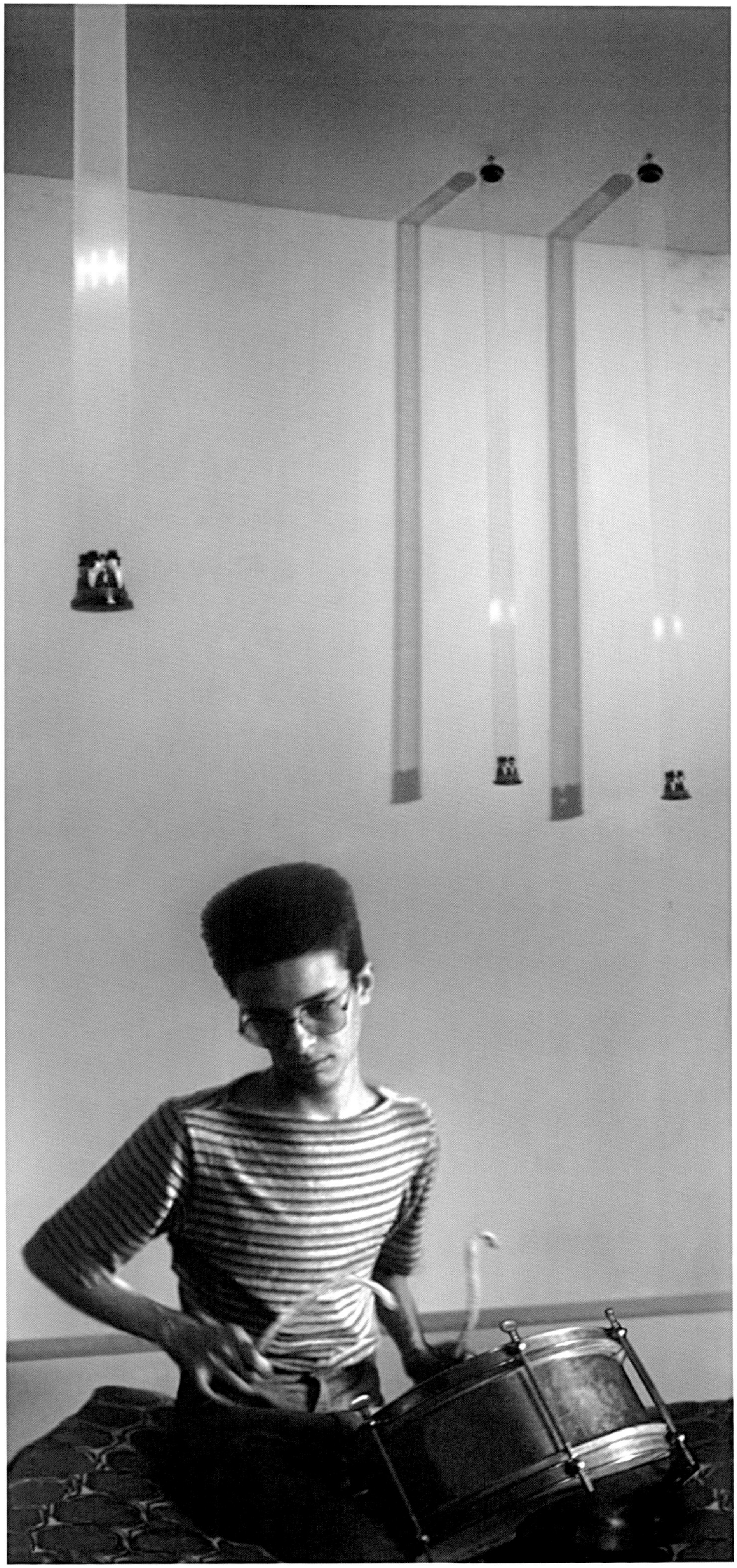

Skin & Bones, 1980.
Toned silver gelatine print
retouched with graphite.
25¼ x 11¾" (64,5 x 30 cm).
GC 294.

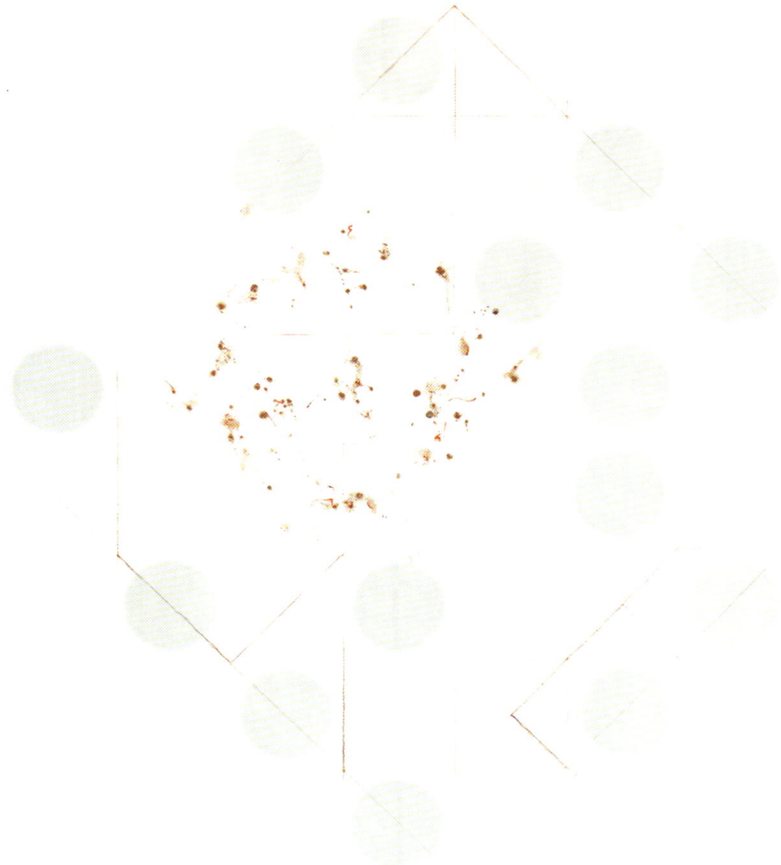

A.C.N.E., 1980 (detail).
From the *Cut-out Self-portraits* series.
Transition work between
the *Stoic Ebbs and Flows* series
and the *Cutout-Portraits*.
Blood stains from the artist's face,
previously cut with a razor blade,
and sanguine pencil on tissue paper sheet
applied on a white marble slab with holes.
43¼ x 31¾ x 2" (110 x 81 x 5 cm).
GC 295.

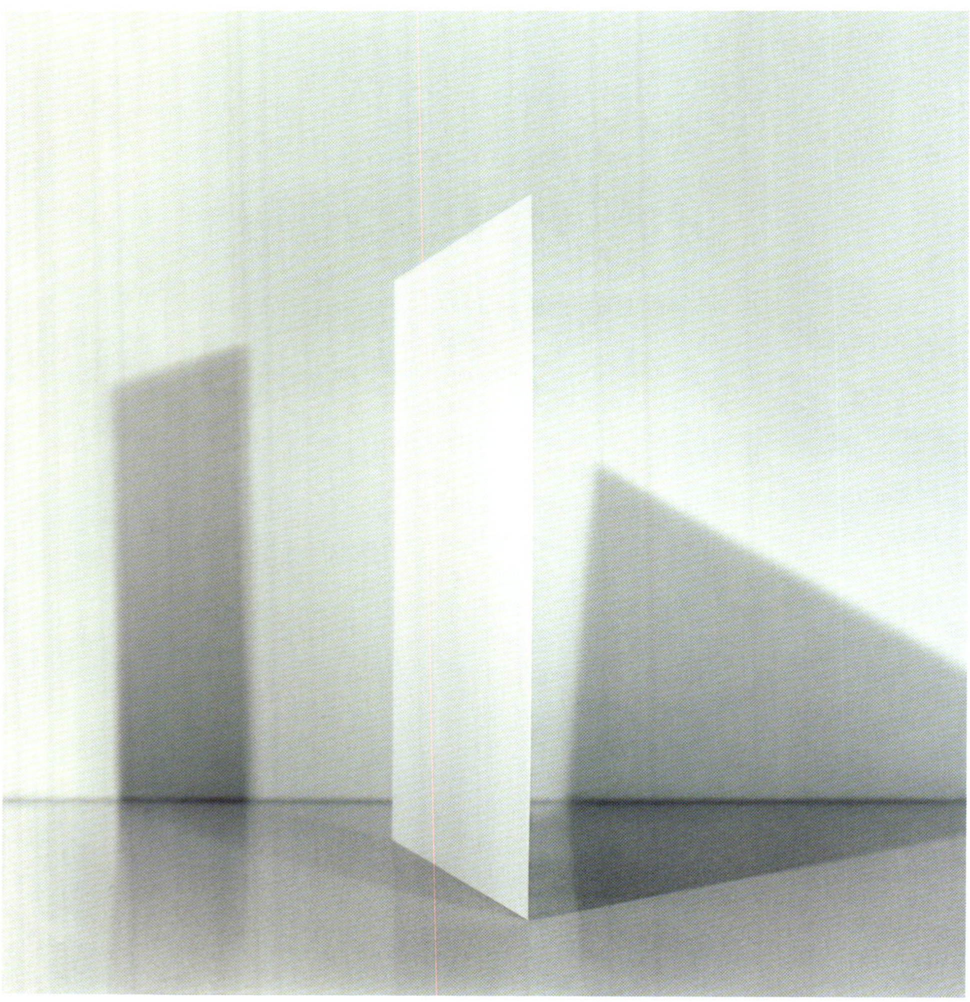

Sketch, 1980-82.
Blank sheet in vertical equilibrium.
11¾ x 8¼" (29,7 x 21 cm).
GC 315.

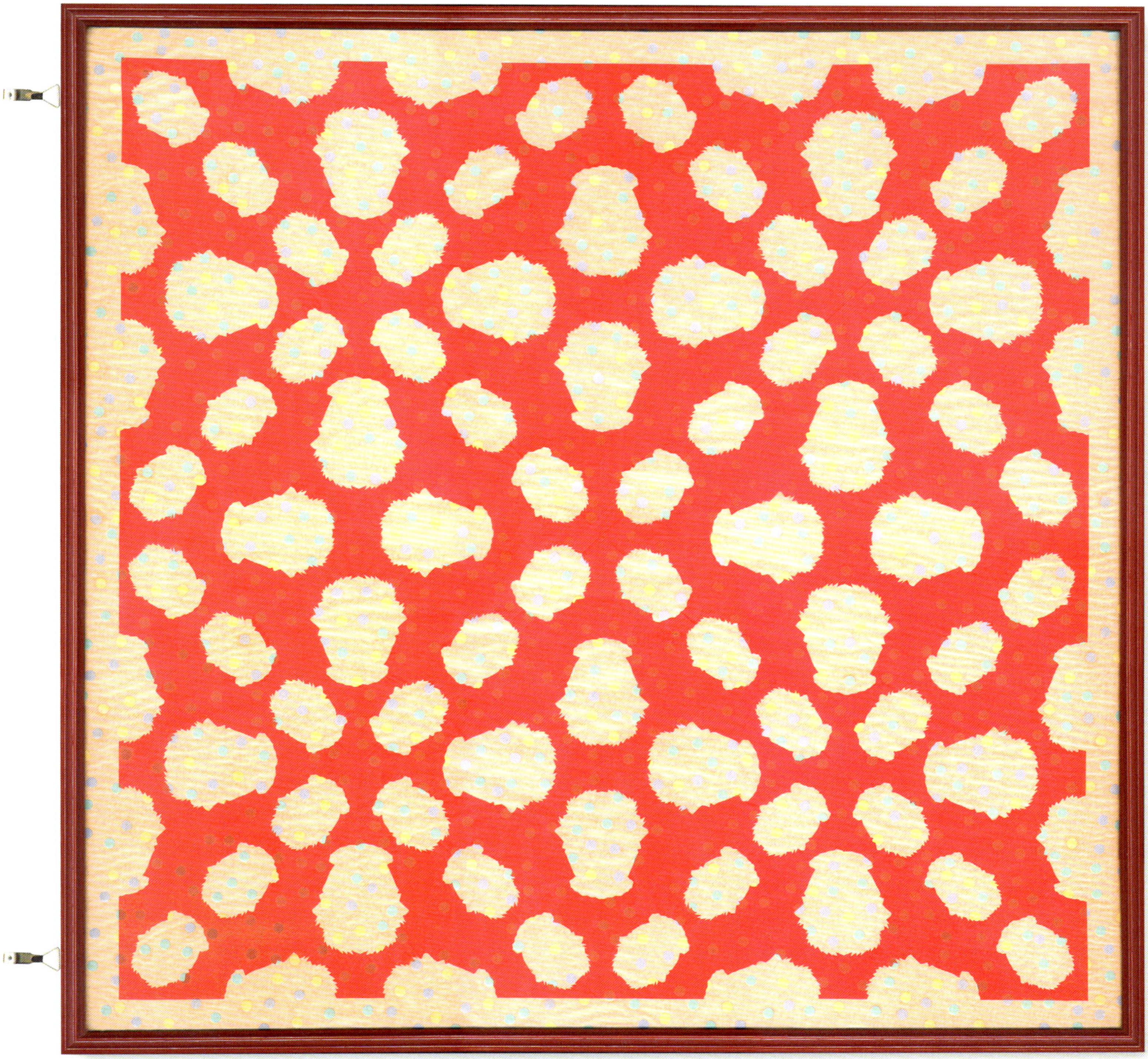

Cutout-Portrait, 1980.
Red tissue paper cutout; collage;
lacquer on wooden frame with metal hooks and nails in its left side.
22 x 22" (55,7 x 55,7 cm).
GC 297.

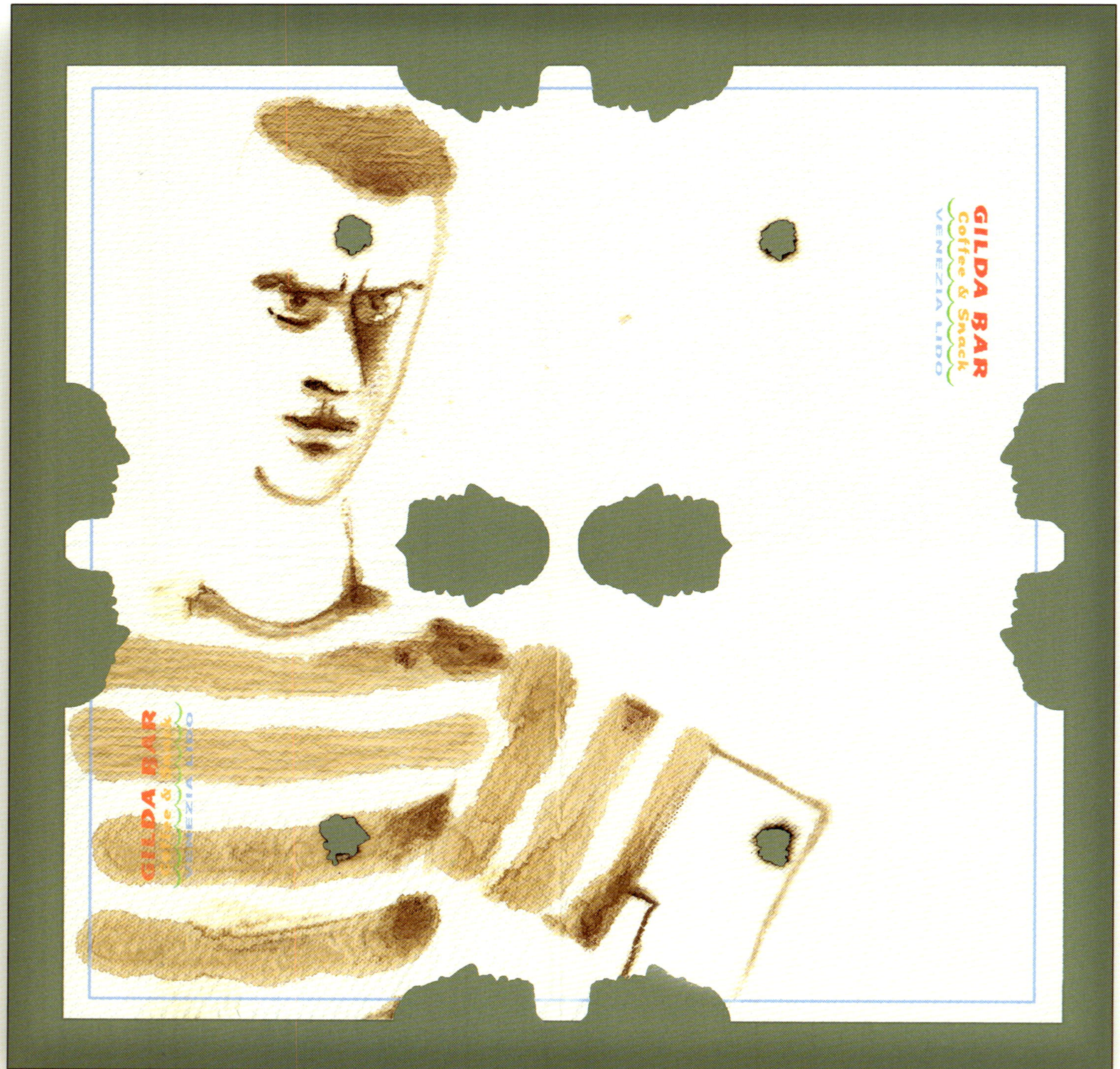

RWF Cutout-Portrait, 1980.
Self-portrait of the artist drawn with coffee on paper bar napkin with printed logo, cut by the artist in the profile of R.W. Fassbinder, and cigarette burn by R.W. Fassbinder.
12¾ x 12¾" (32,5 x 32,7 cm).
GC 309.

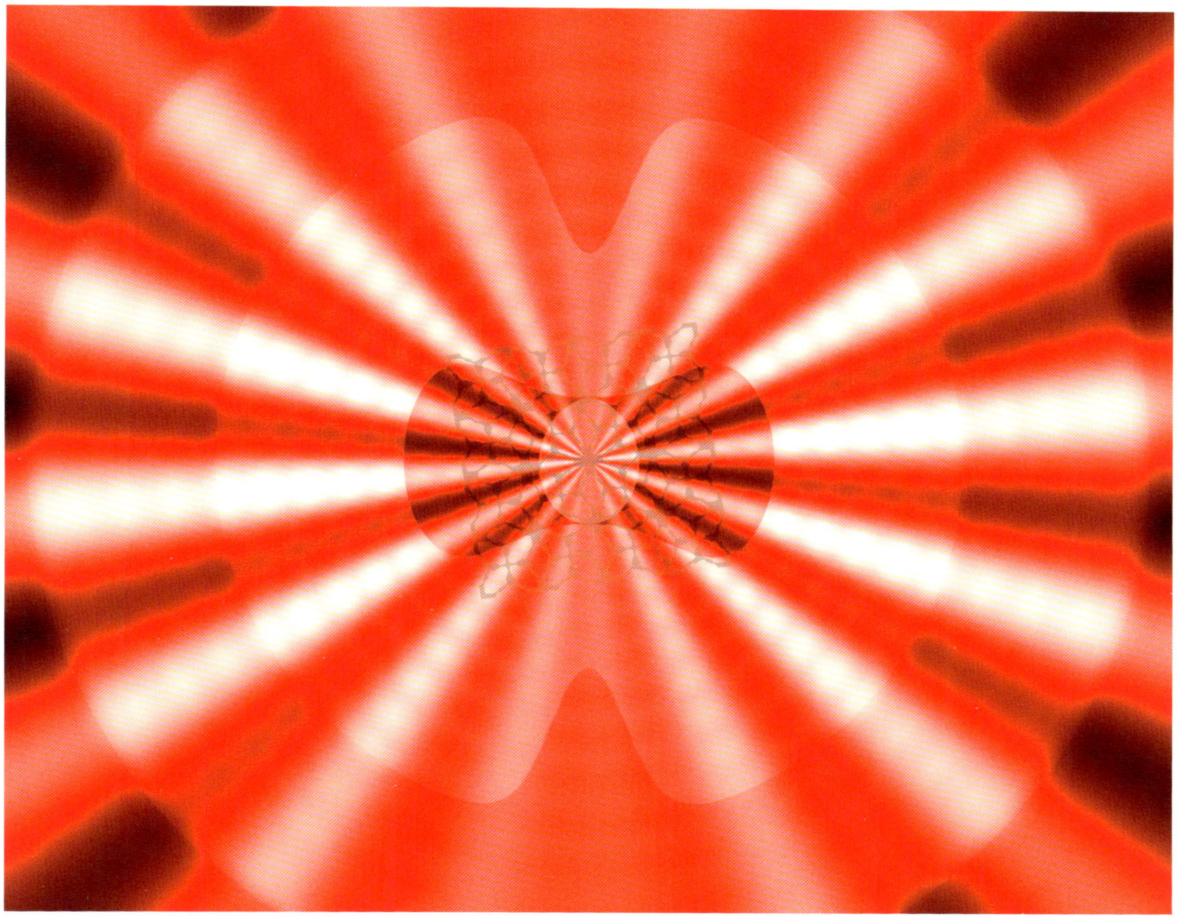

Cutout-Portrait (Vertigo), circa 1986. Detail.
Nitrocellulose lacquer on plastic laminate; tissue paper cutout;
metal hook and nail on lower side.
59 x 76¼" (150 x 193,8 cm).
GC 479.

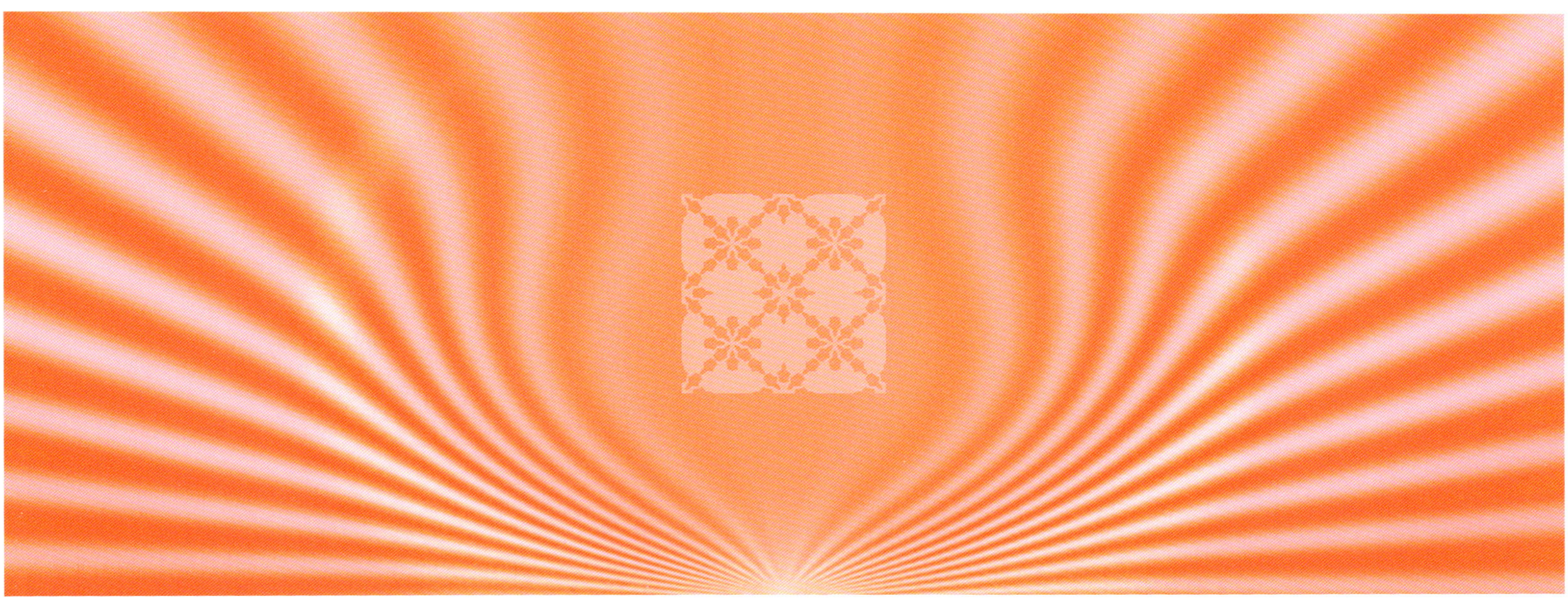

Cutout-Portrait (Lotus), circa 1986.
Nitrocellulose lacquer on formica; tissue paper cutout soaked in linseed oil.
118 x 43¼" (300 x 115,2 cm).
GC 481.

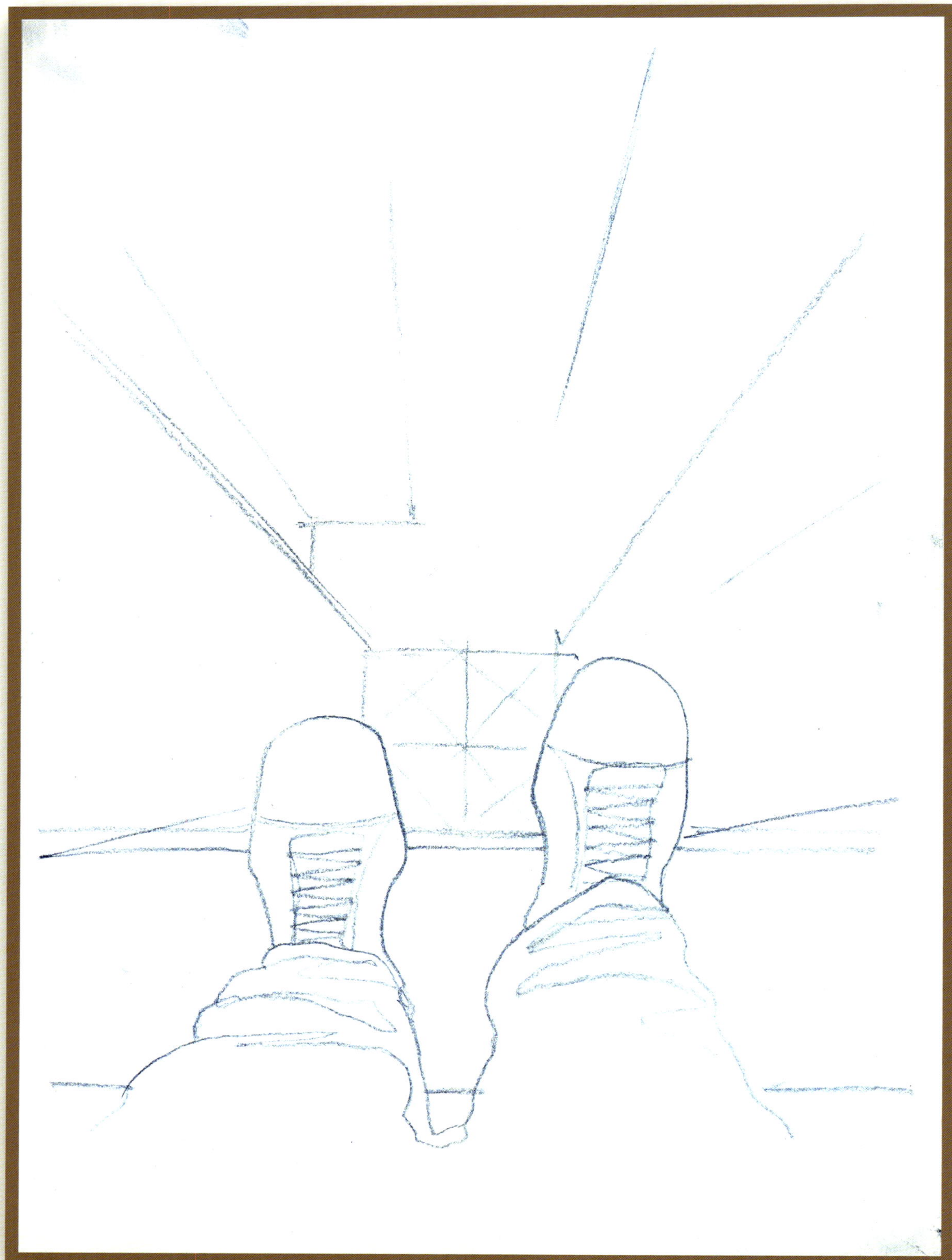

Vertigospective, 1986.
Drawing made standing on the roof edge of a five-story building.
Pastel on paper; cardboard backing.
18¾ x 13½" (47,8 x 34,5 cm).
GC 480.

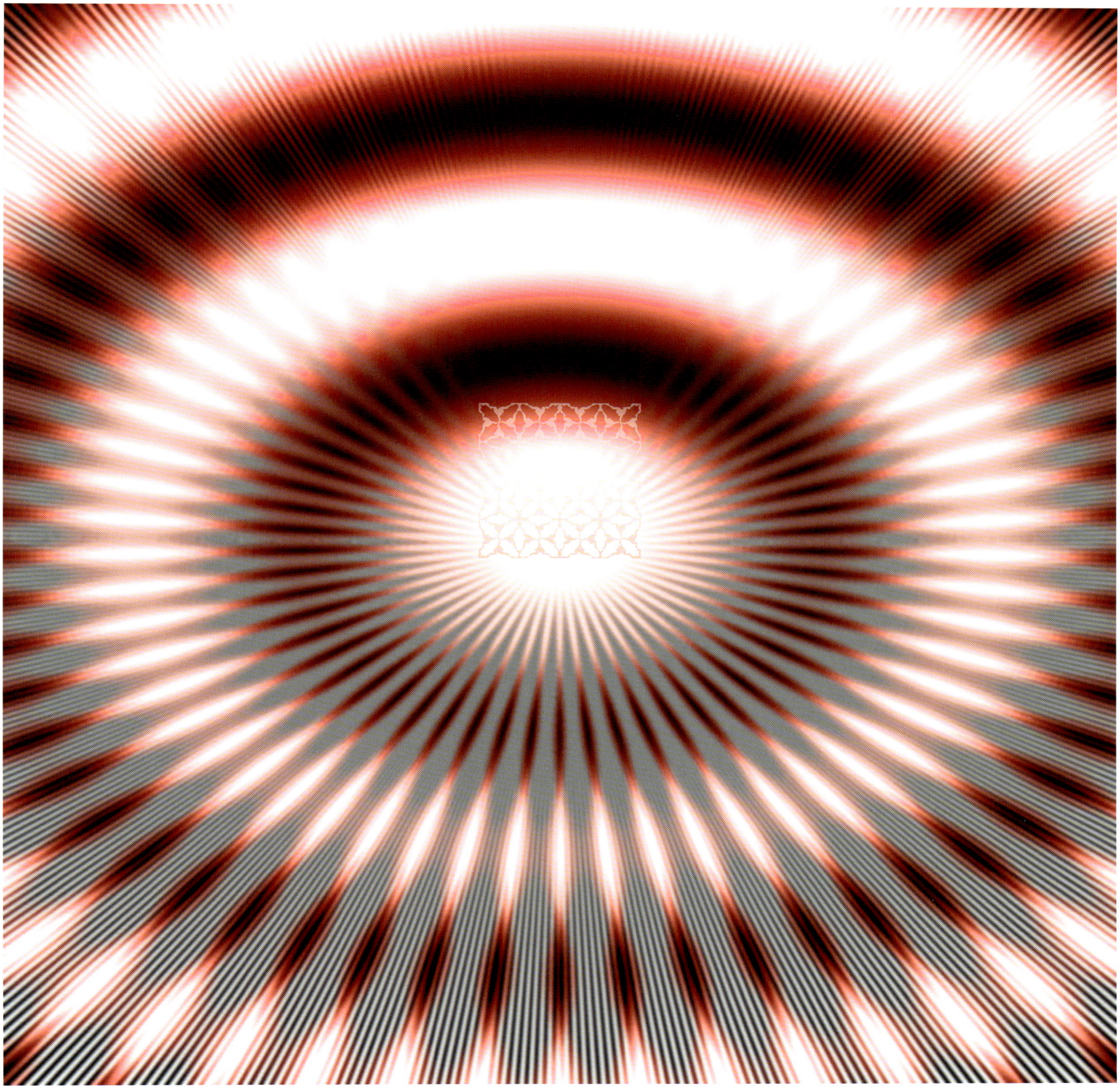

Cutout-Portrait (HalluKinetic), 1988-89.
Nitrocellulose lacquer on aluminum panel;
emulsion; tissue paper cutout.
63 x 63" (160 x 160 cm).
GC 602.

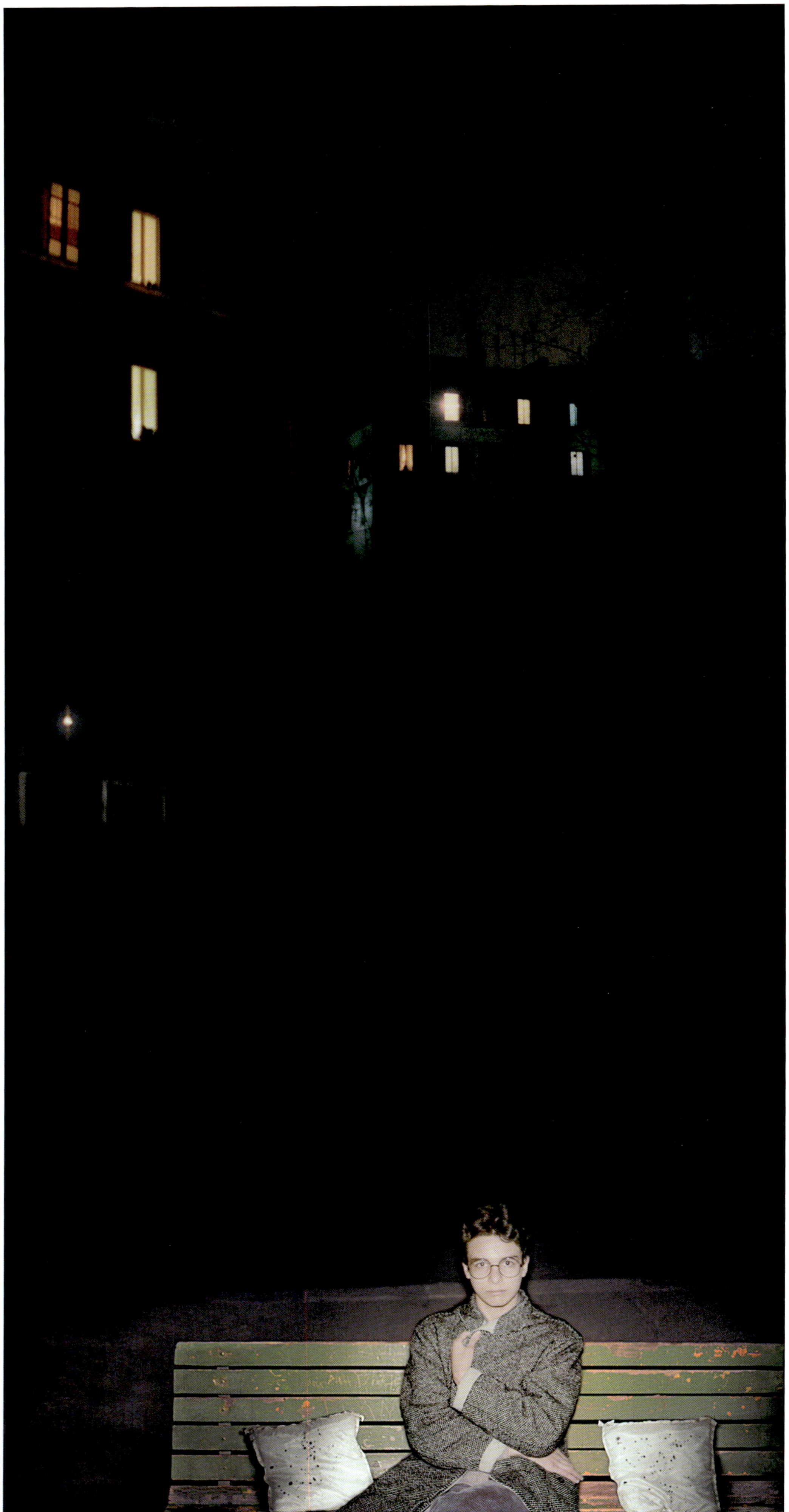

On the Street
or also *The Luminous Quadrangles*, 1980.
Watercolor on color photograph.
39¼ x 19¼” (100 x 49,8 cm).
GC 307.

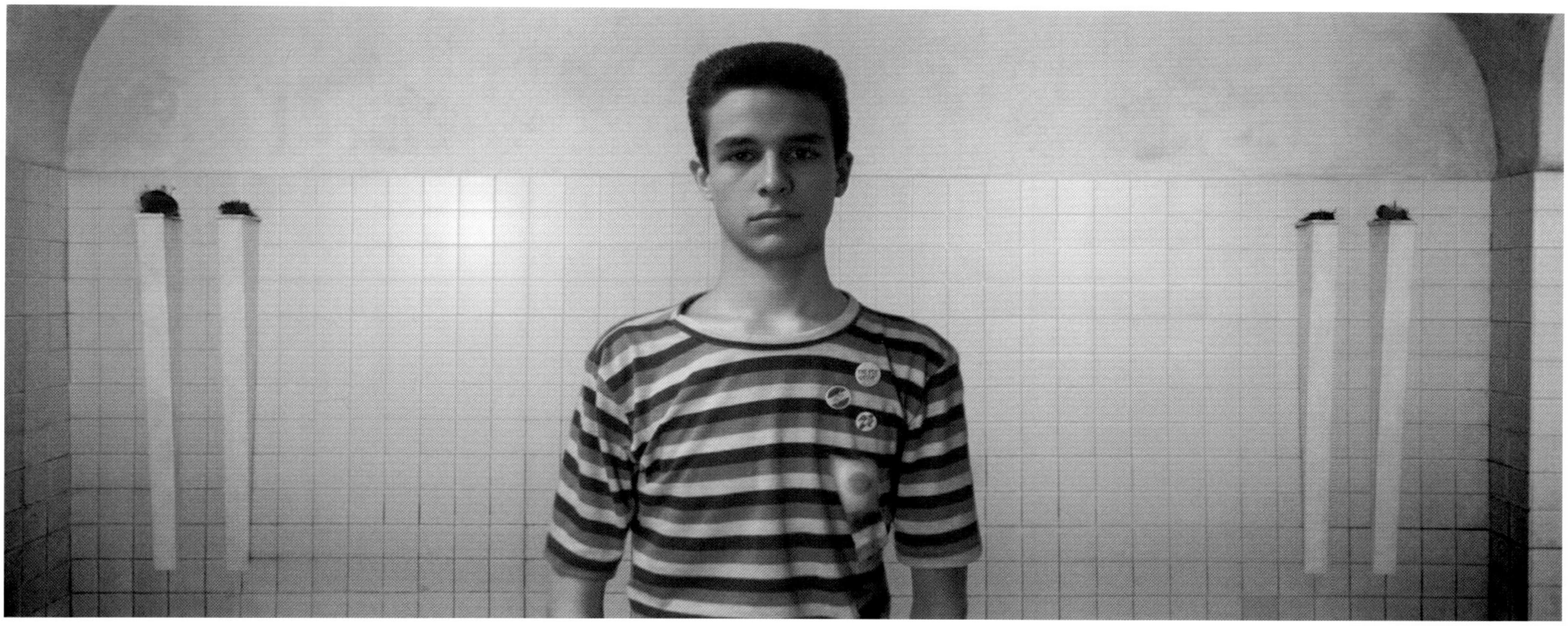

Youthanasia 1, 1981.
Silver gelatine print.
11¾ x 28¼" (30 x 71 cm).
GC 316.

Fatture - Evil Eye Fetishes, 1981.
From a series of 4 works in wax, pubic hair, silver jewels, thorns, tar, needles, mirrors and child glove; marble and plaster pedestals with pencil drawings.
Left: 41¼ x 3 x 6" (105,5 x 7,5 x 15 cm).
Right: 43¼ x 4 x 6" (110 x 10,5 x 15 cm).
GC 281, 283.

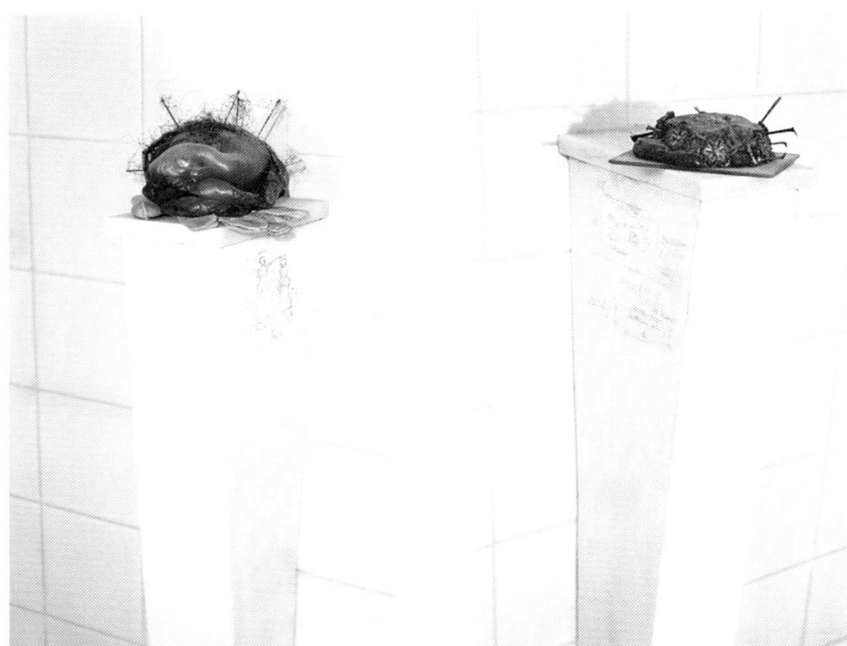

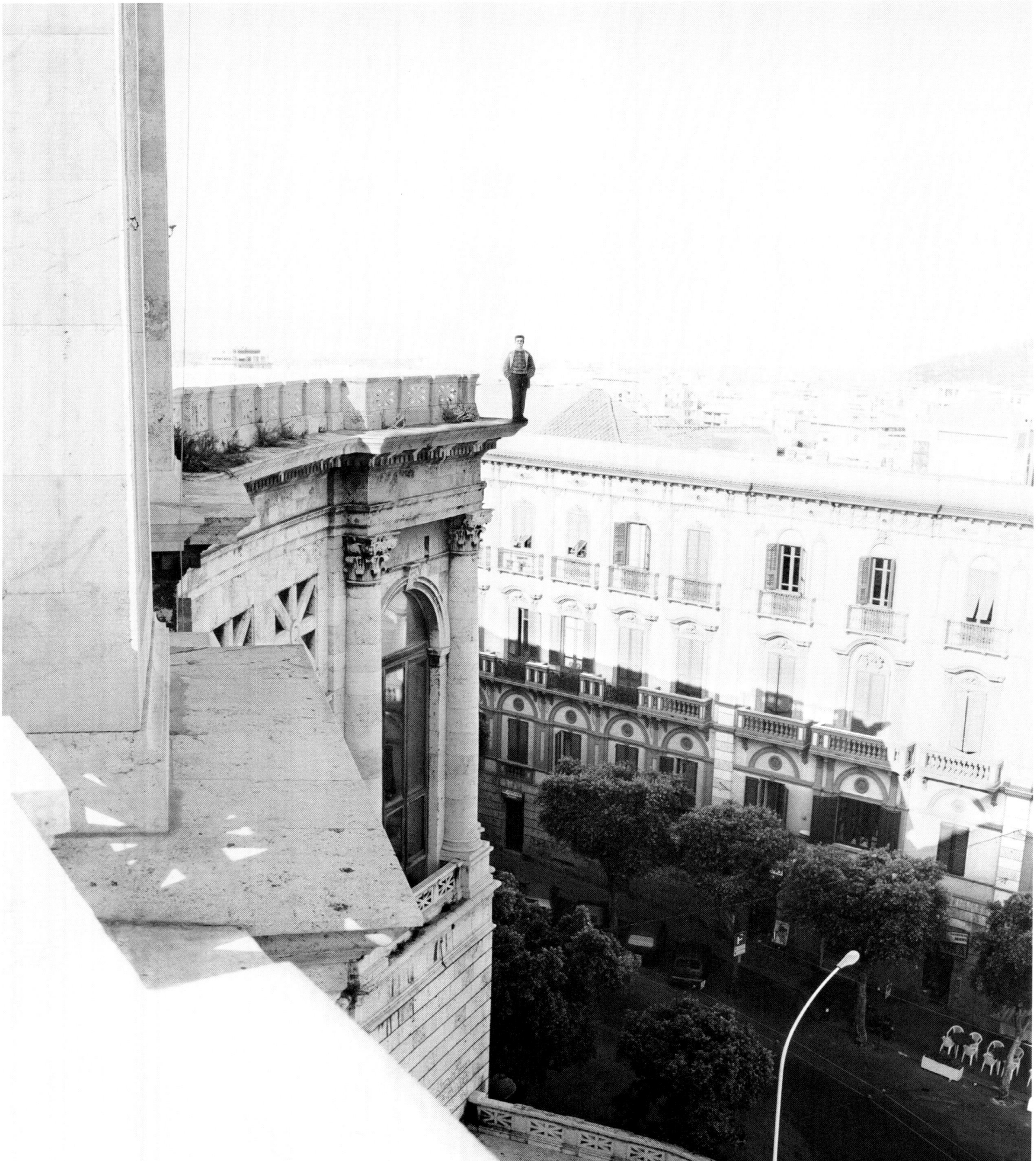

Cheese, 1981.
Silver gelatine print.
53¼ x 45½” (135 x 114,4 cm).
GC 320.

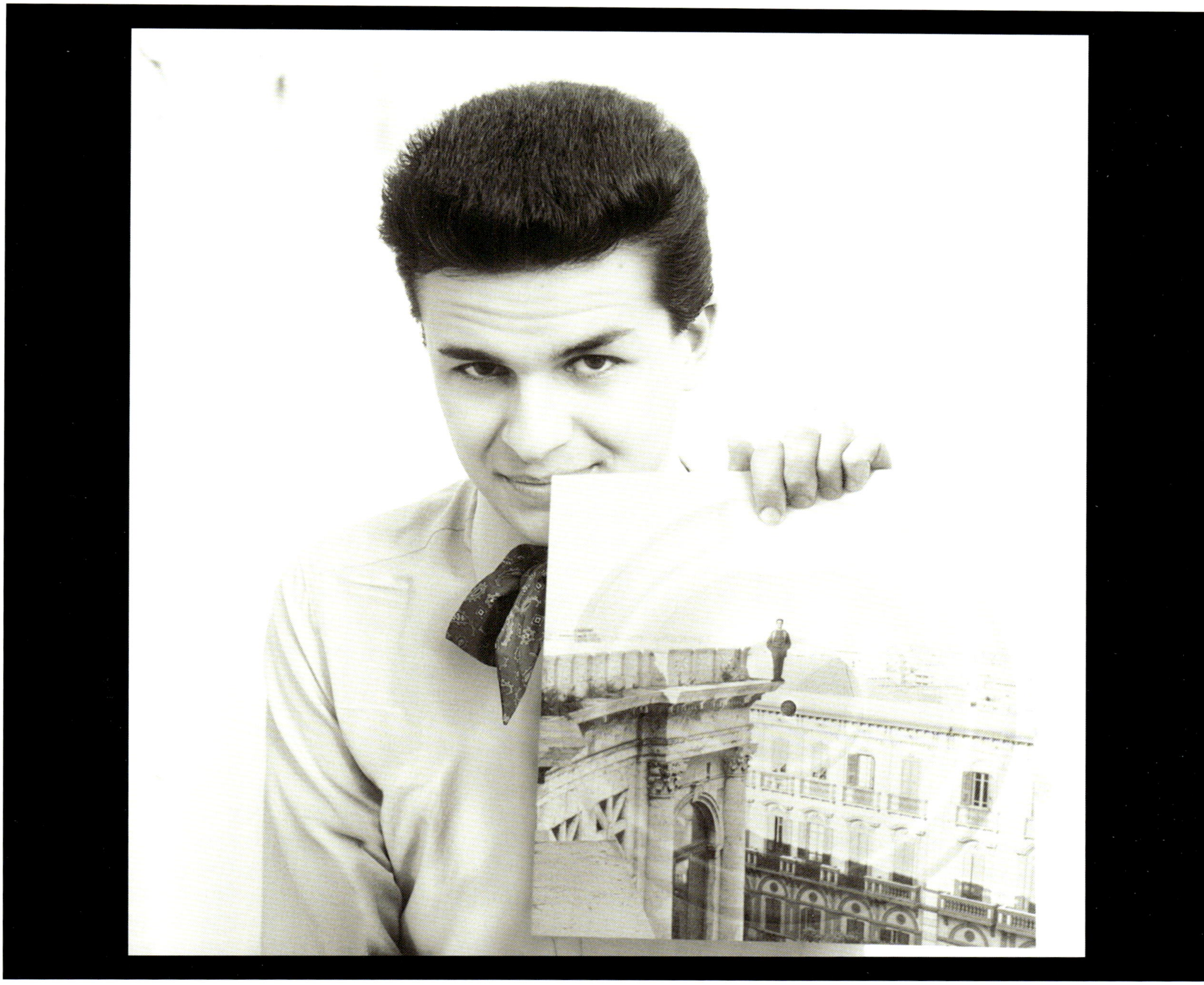

Cheese Symphony, 1984.
Black and white photographic print of the work *Cheese*
on plasticized medium-thickness cardboard,
with a 33rpm clear vinyl record embossed on one side.
14¼ x 14¼" (36 x 36 cm).
GC 438.

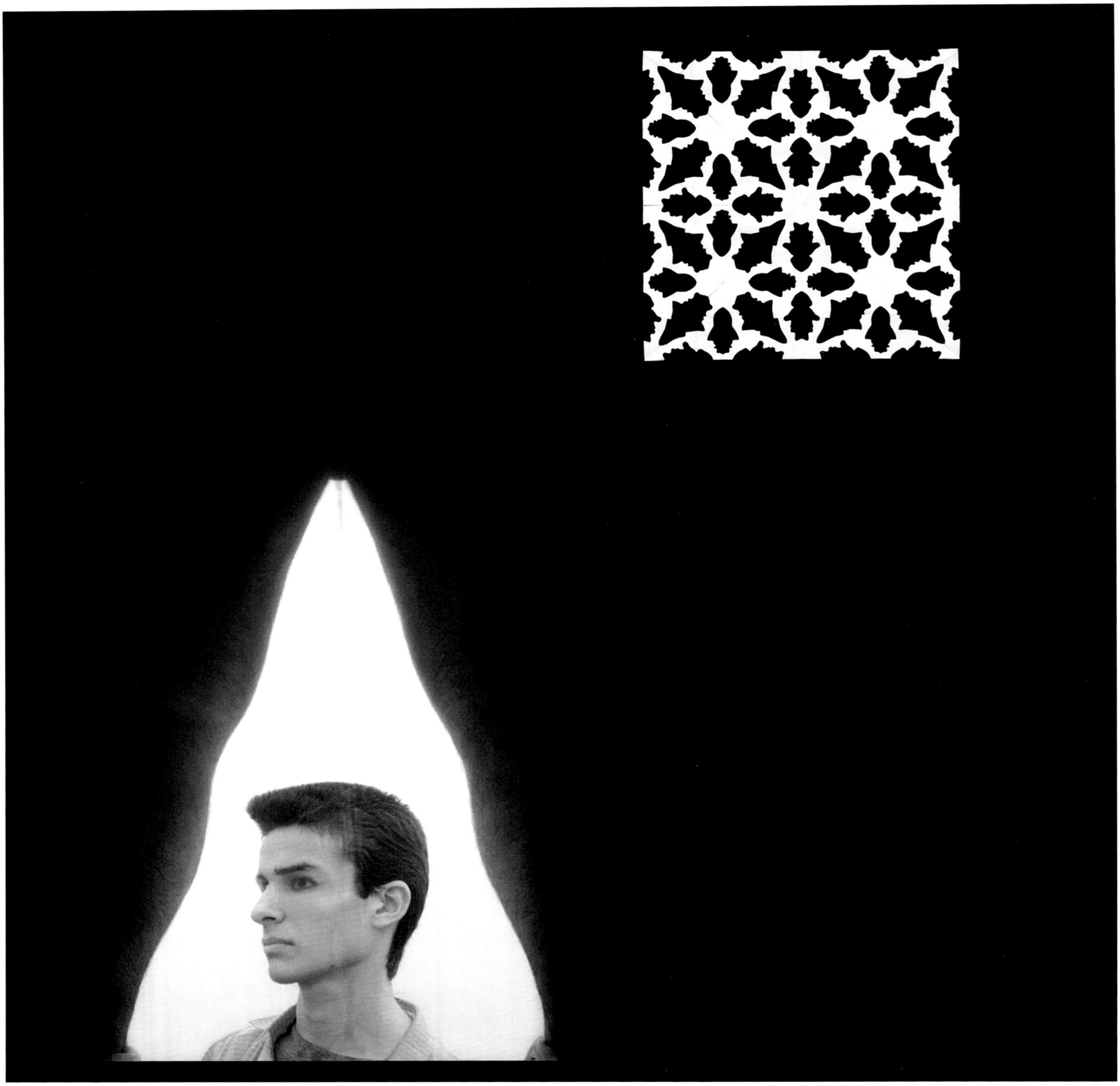

Idolatrine, 1981.
Silver gelatine print
with application of paper cutout.
43¼ x 43¼" (110 x 110 cm).
GC 332.

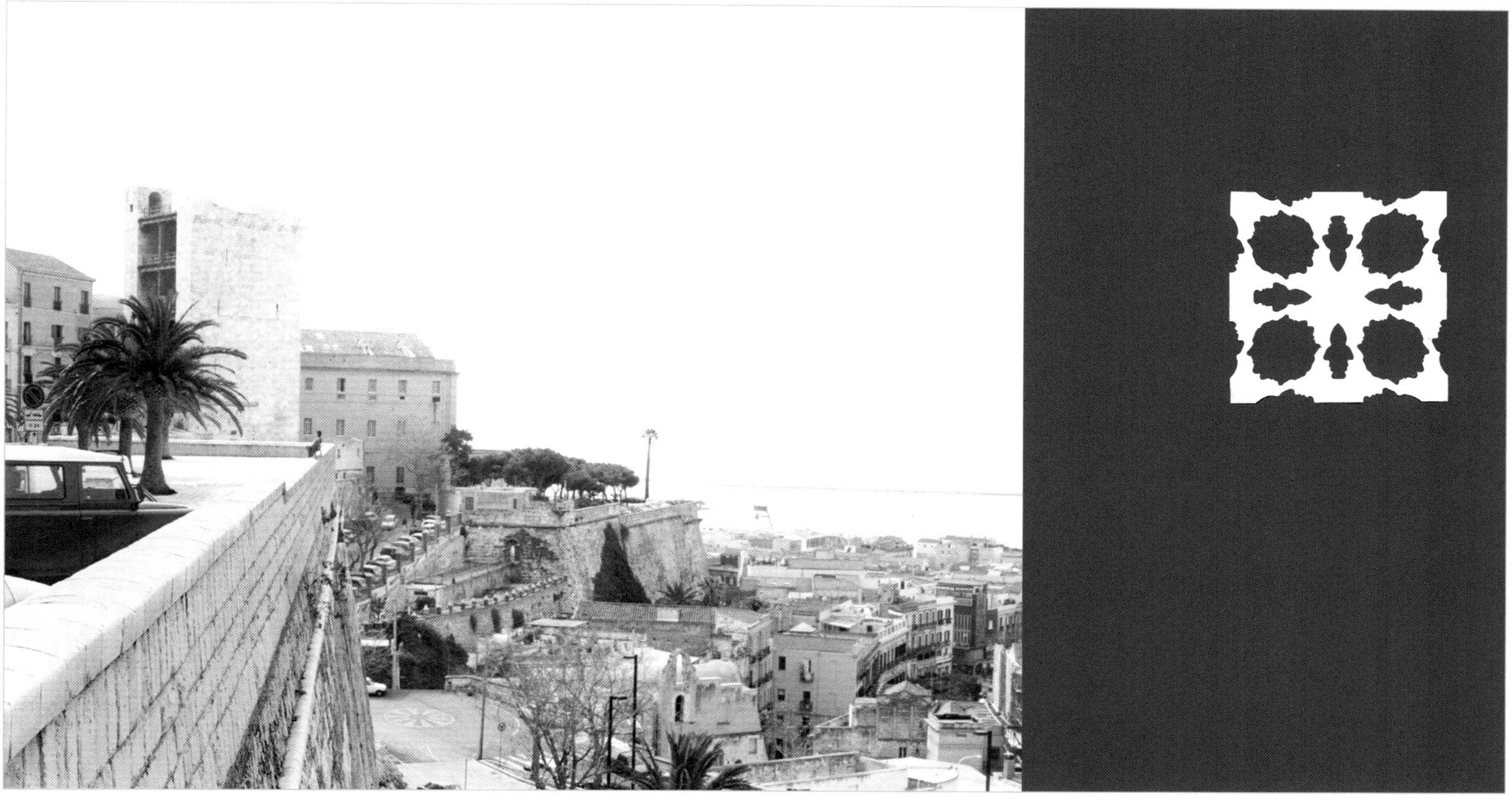

Youthanasia 2, 1981.
Silver gelatine print
with application of tissue paper cutout.
21¼ x 39½” (54 x 100 cm).
GC 330.

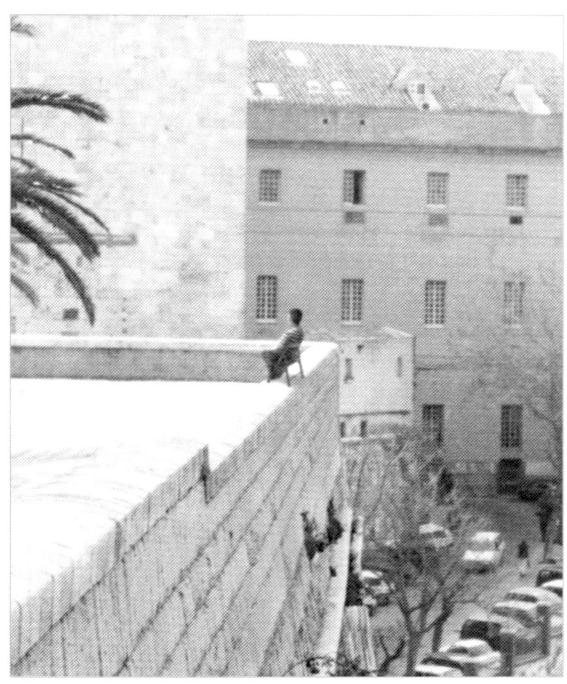

Youthanasia 2, detail.

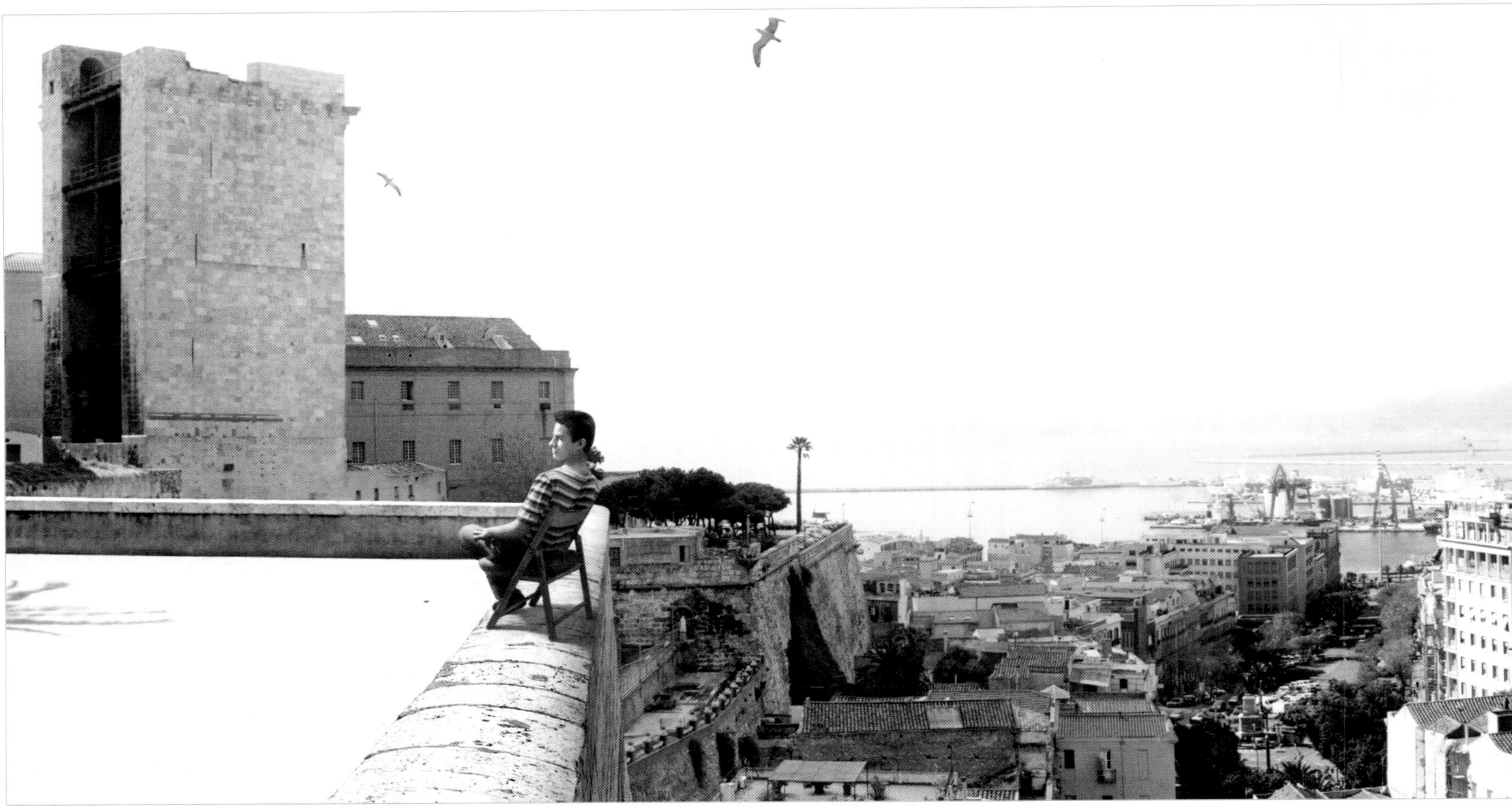

Youthanasia 3 - The future behind my back, 1981 (left panel).
Silver gelatine print on two separate panels.
Each panel: 21¼ x 39½" (54 x 100 cm).
GC 331.

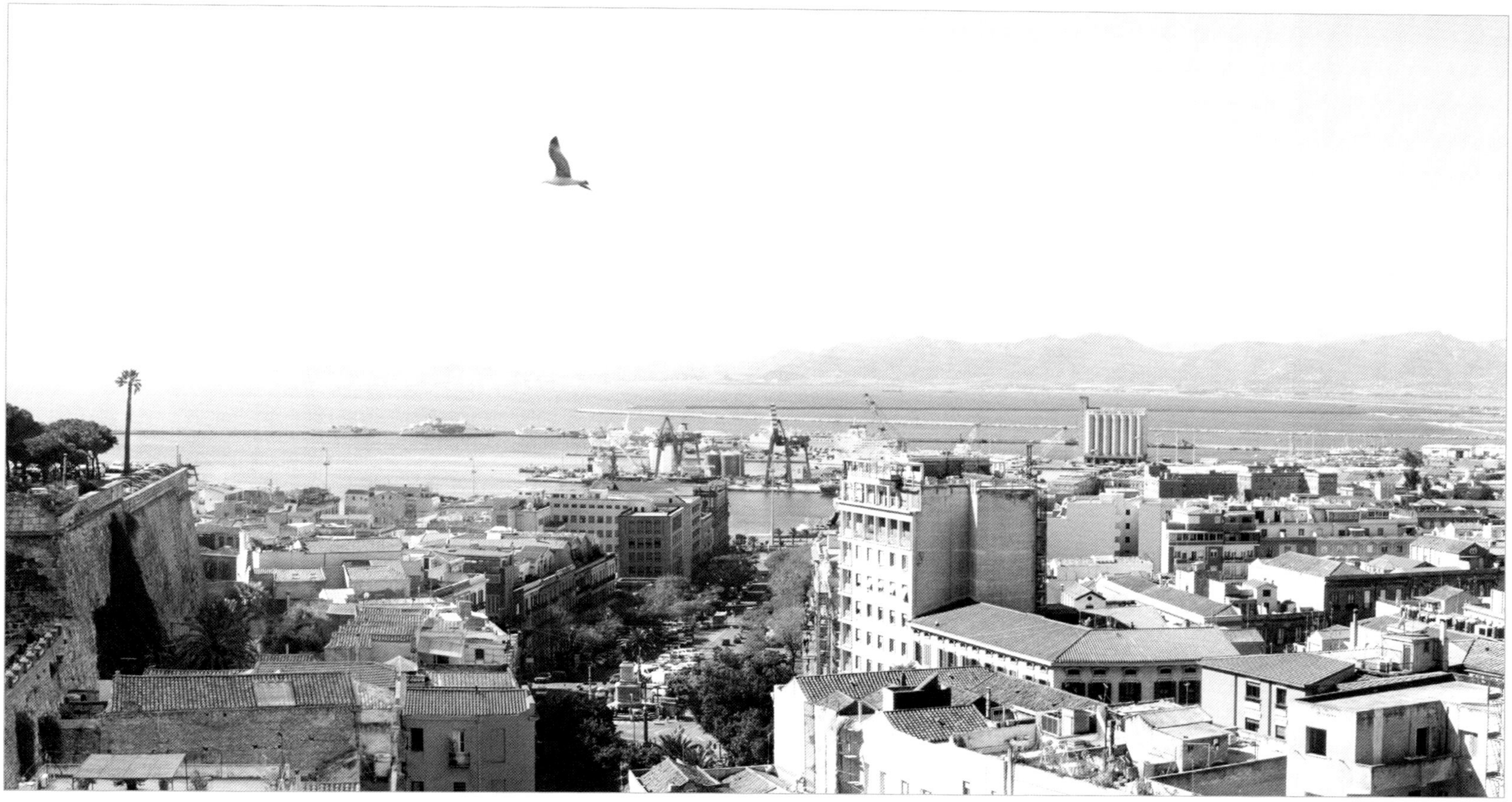

Youthanasia 3 - The future behind my back, 1981 (right panel).

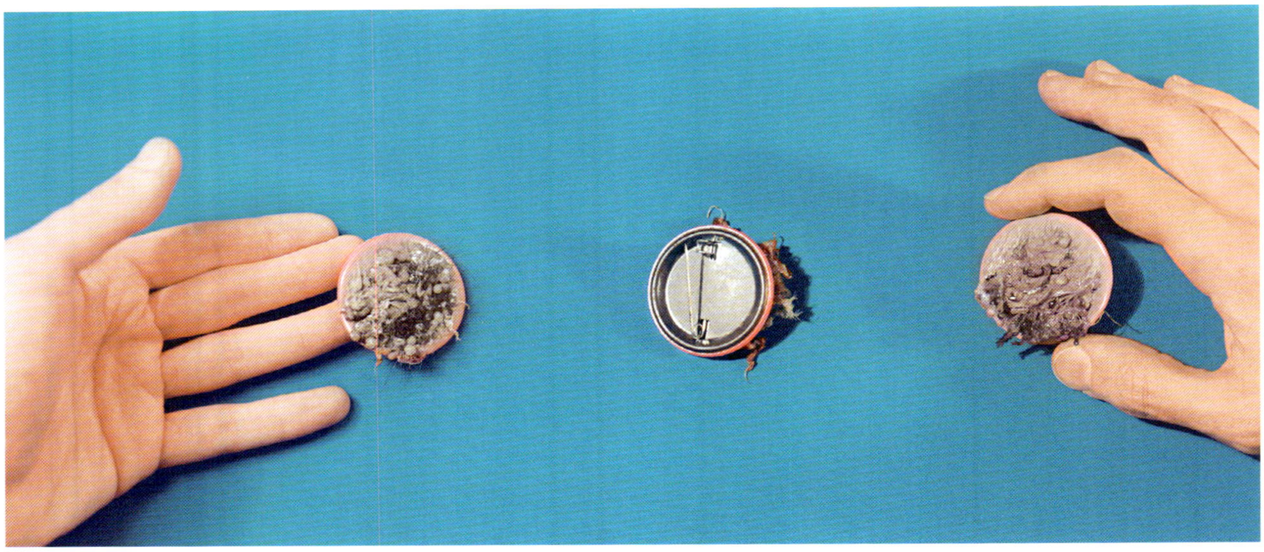

Bad-ge, 1982.
Metal badges with colored wax, tar, hair.
Diam. 1¾" each (4,5 cm).
GC 391, 392, 393.

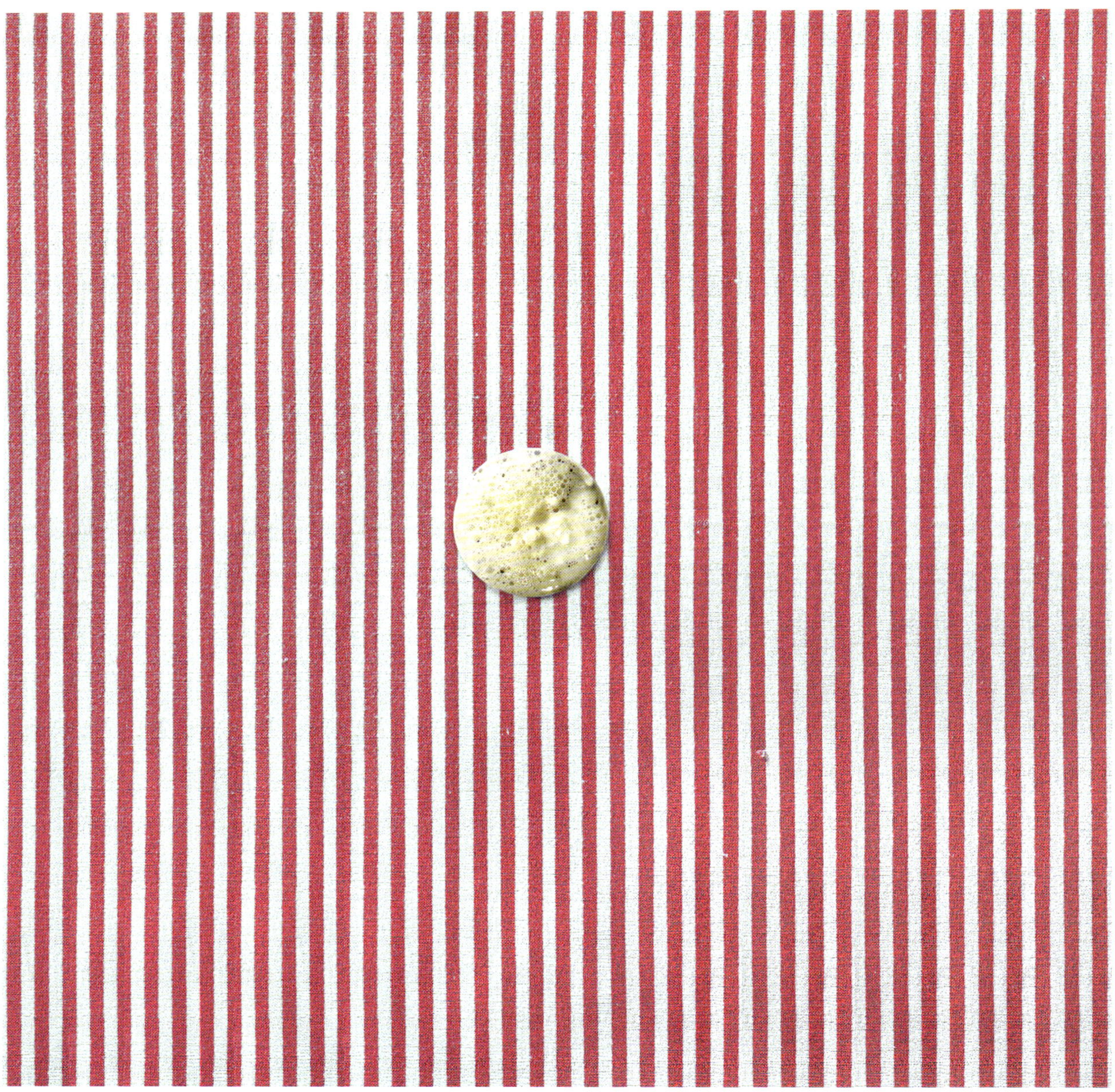

Spit Badge, 1983.
Spit-like badge in polyester and metal; edition of 50.
Diam. circa 1½" each piece (4 cm).
GC 407.

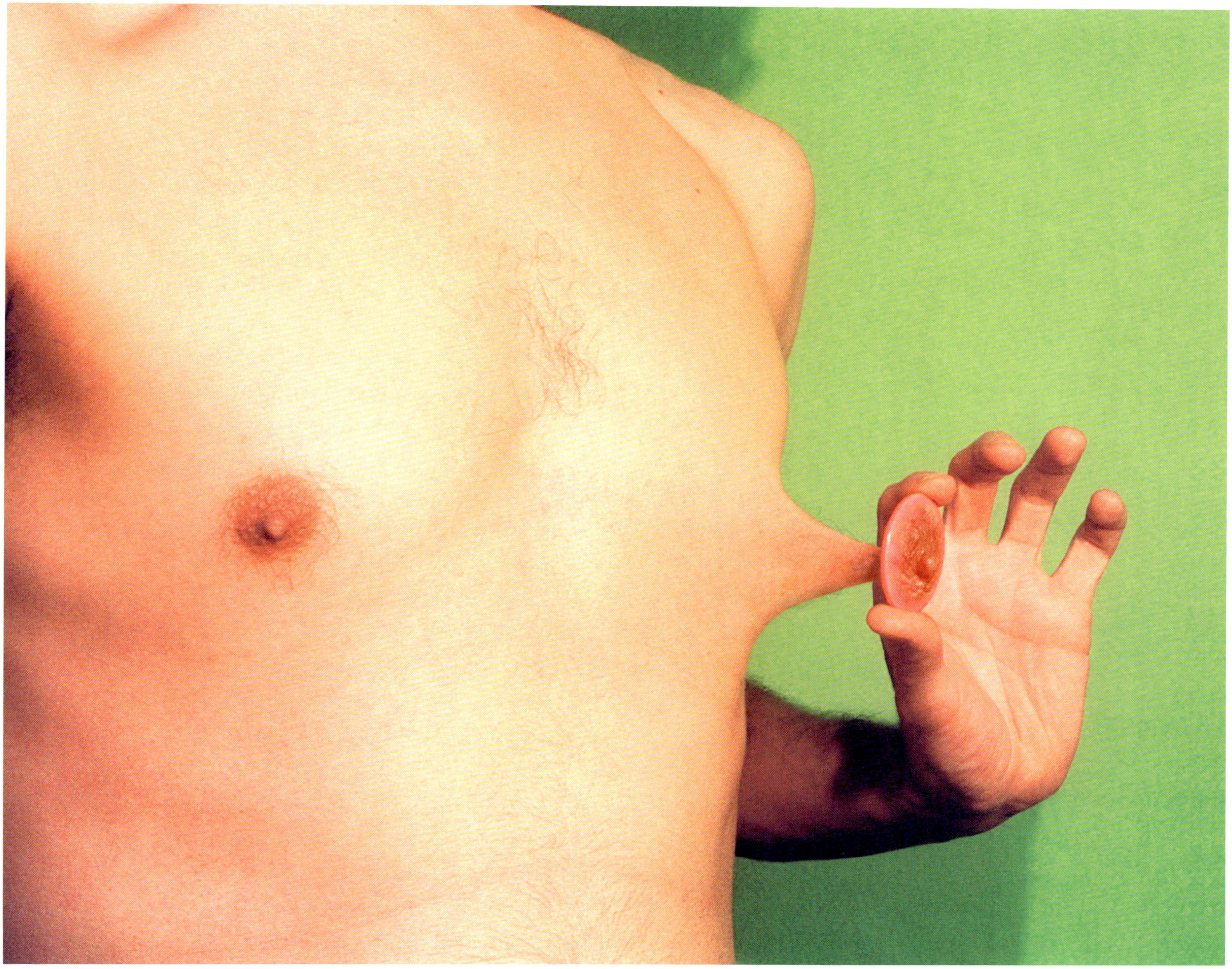

Nipping Nipple, 1982.
Colored wax nipple on metal badge.
Diam. 1¾" (4,5 cm).
GC 394.

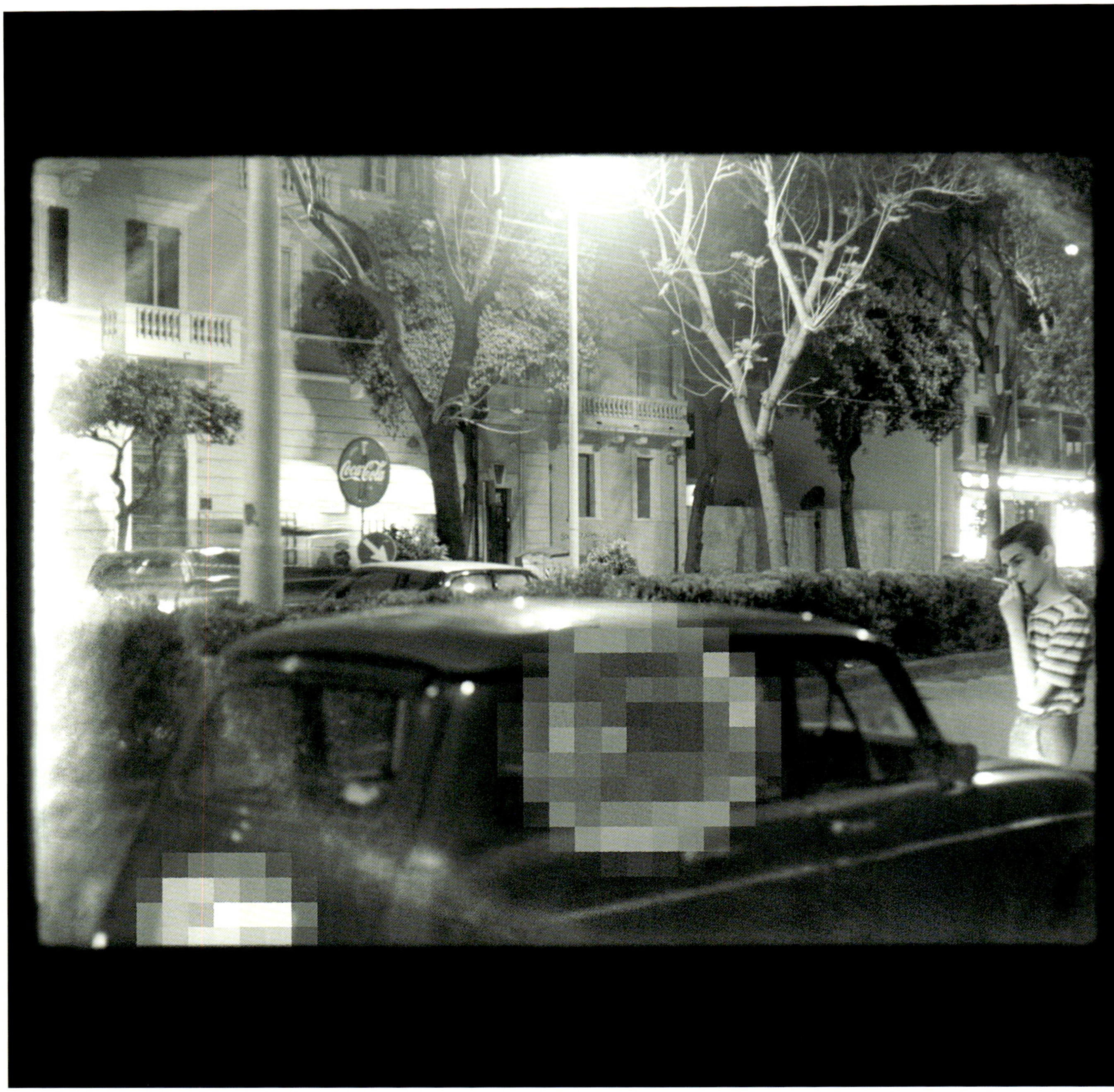

From *Der Weg Zum Kubismus* series, 1981.
Acrylic on silver gelatine print.
$23\frac{3}{4}$ x $23\frac{3}{4}$" (60 x 60 cm).
GC 323.

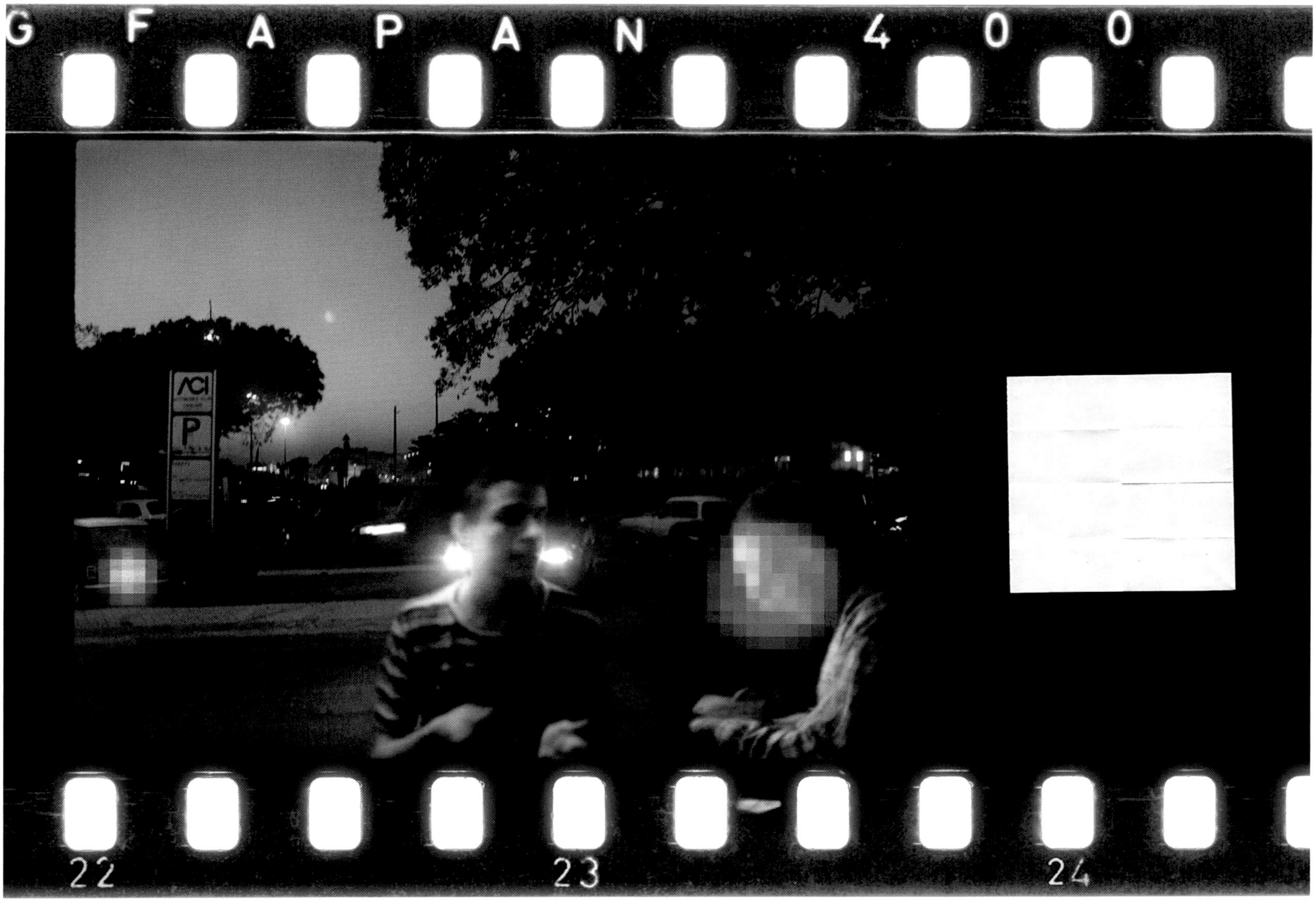

From *Der Weg Zum Kubismus* series, 1981.
Acrylic on silver gelatine print,
with application of a sheet of creased white paper.
23¾ x 31¾” (60 x 80,4 cm).
GC 324.

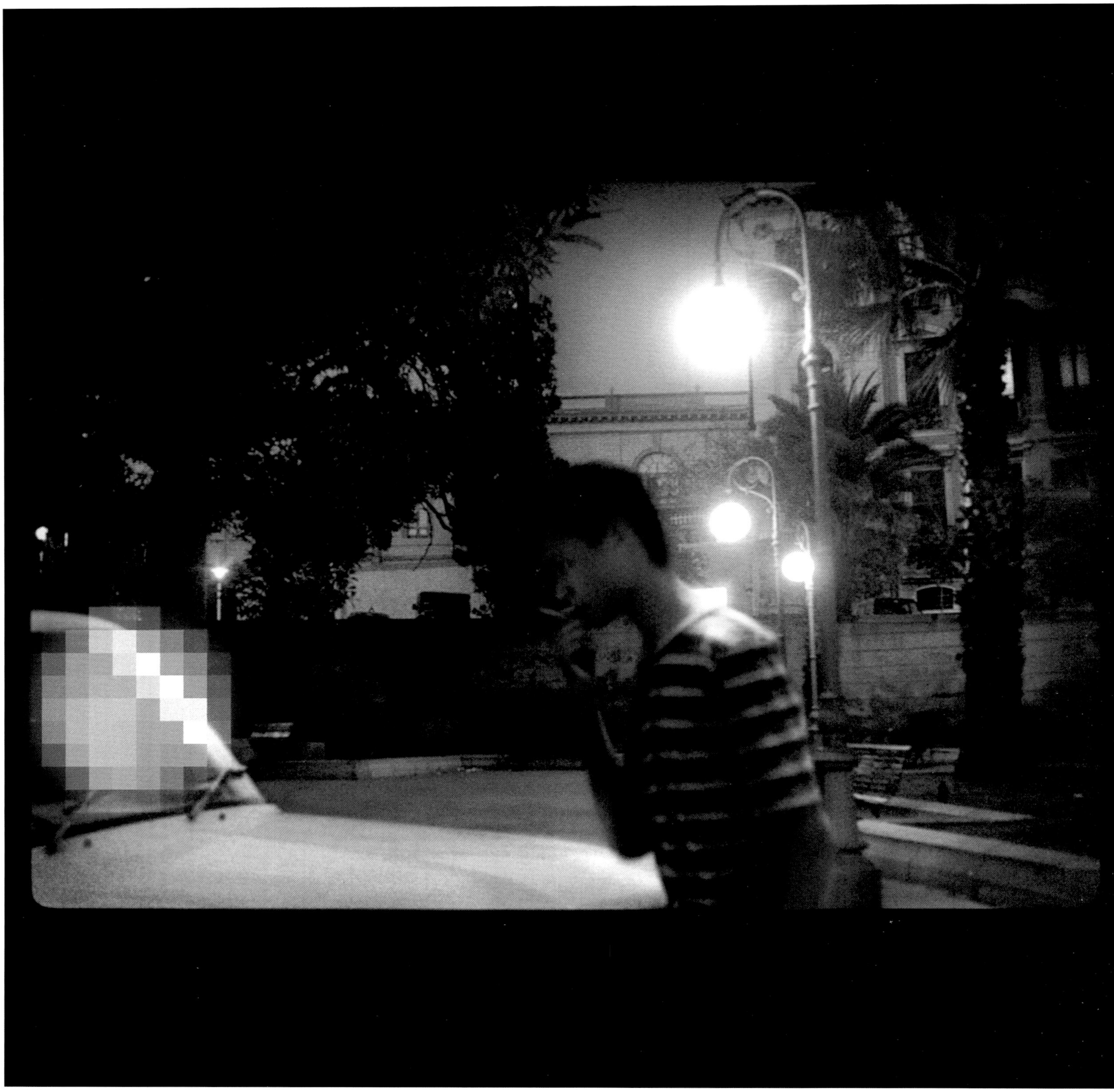

From *Der Weg Zum Kubismus* series, 1981.
Acrylic on silver gelatine print.
23¾ x 23¾" (60 x 60 cm).
GC 326.

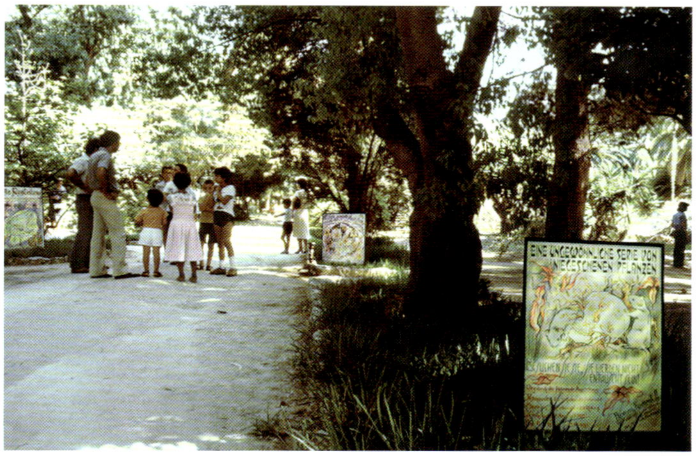

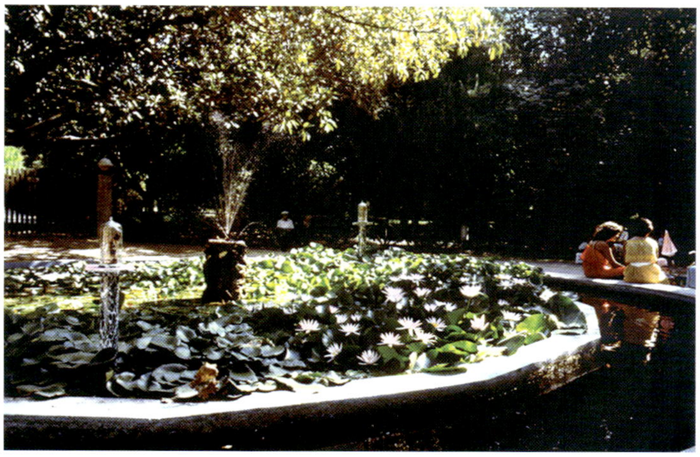

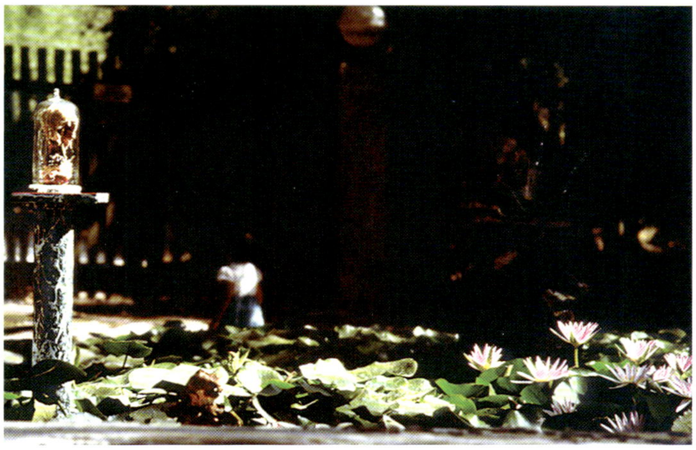

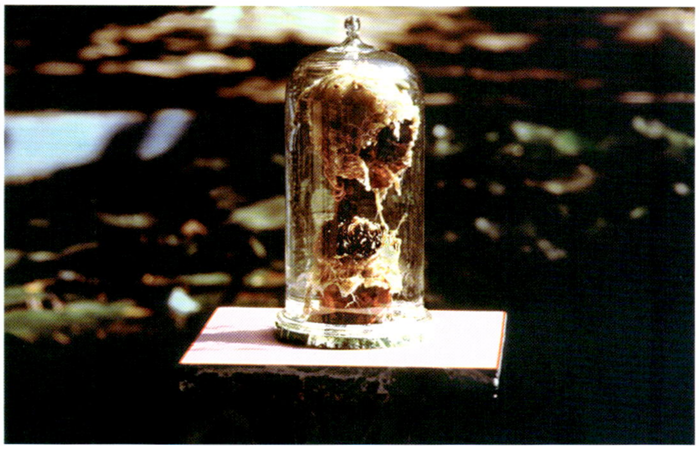

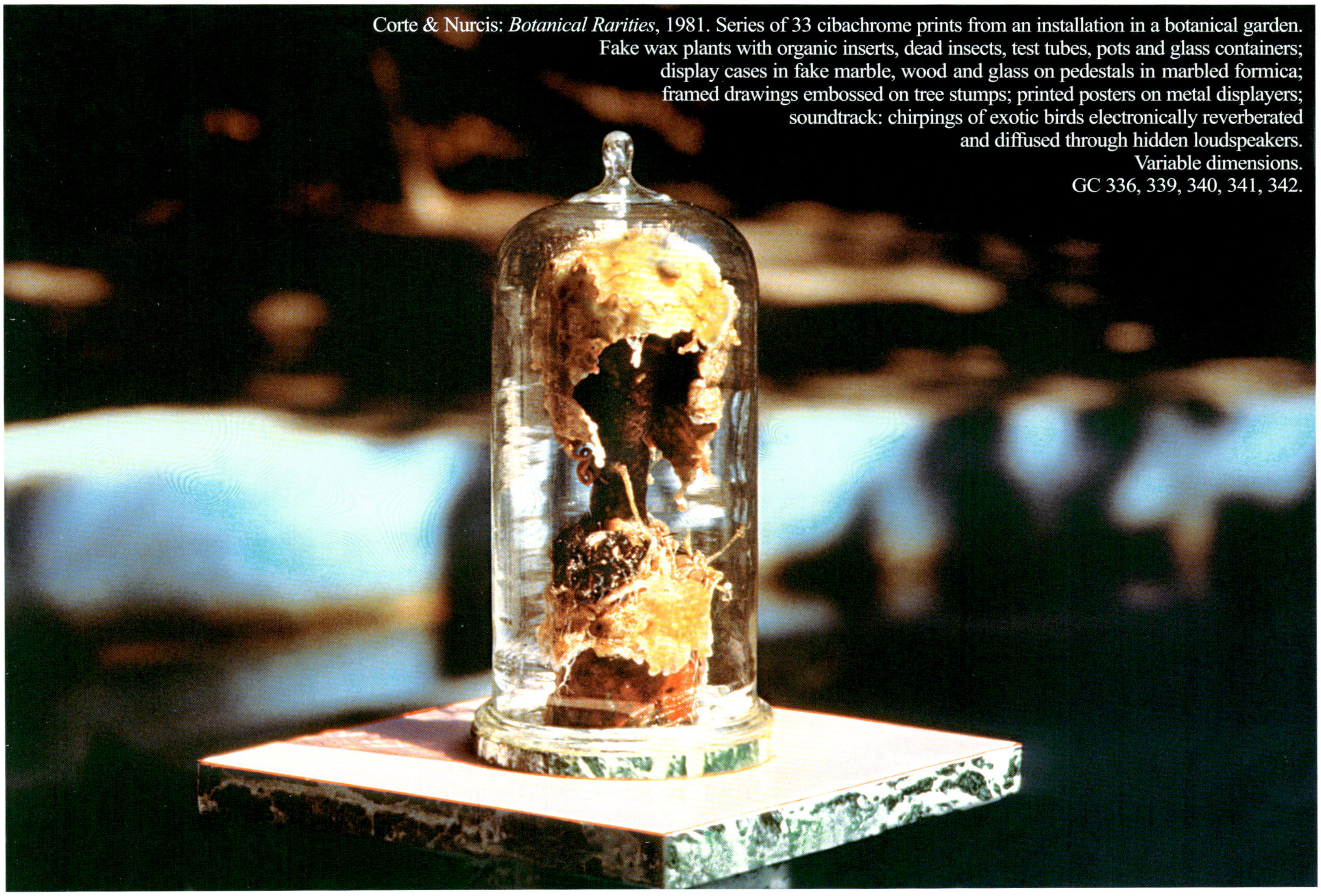

Corte & Nurcis: *Botanical Rarities*, 1981. Series of 33 cibachrome prints from an installation in a botanical garden. Fake wax plants with organic inserts, dead insects, test tubes, pots and glass containers; display cases in fake marble, wood and glass on pedestals in marbled formica; framed drawings embossed on tree stumps; printed posters on metal displayers; soundtrack: chirpings of exotic birds electronically reverberated and diffused through hidden loudspeakers.
Variable dimensions.
GC 336, 339, 340, 341, 342.

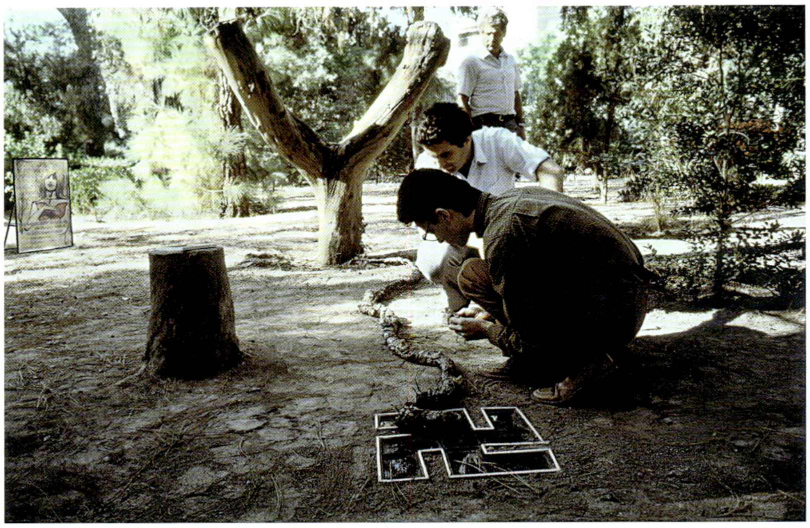
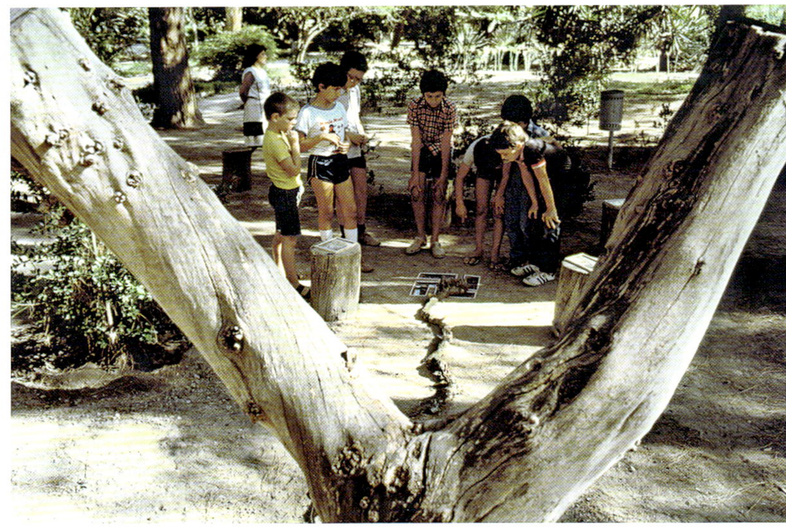
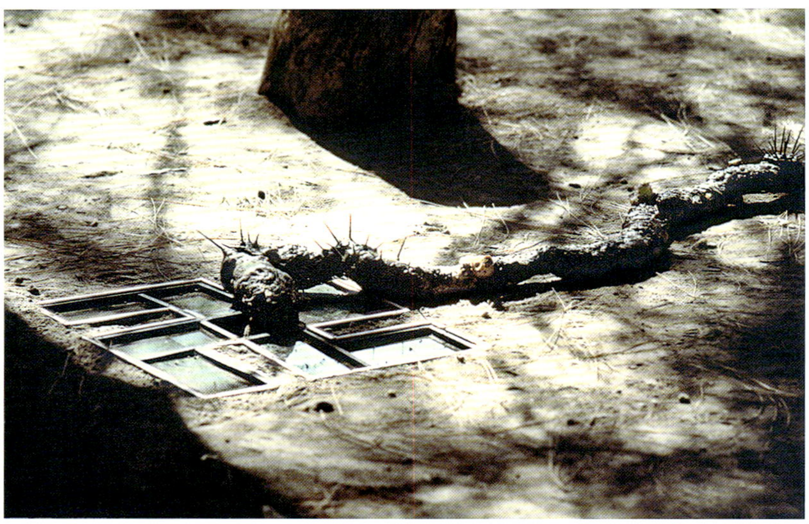
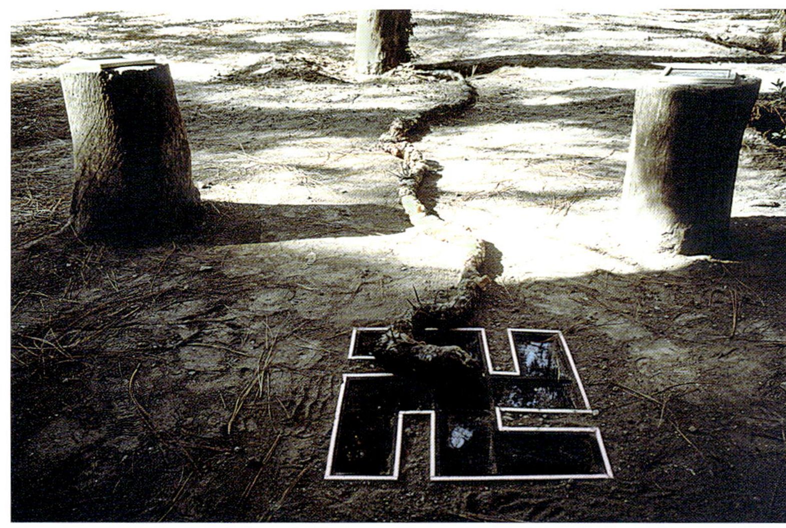
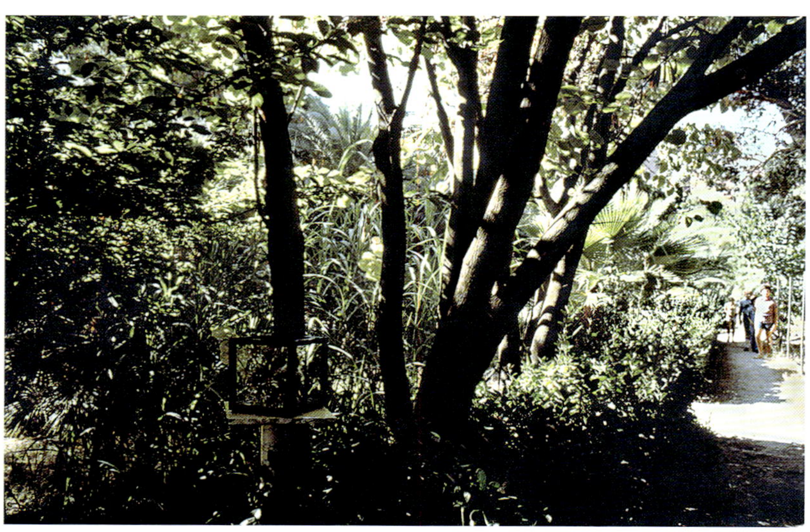
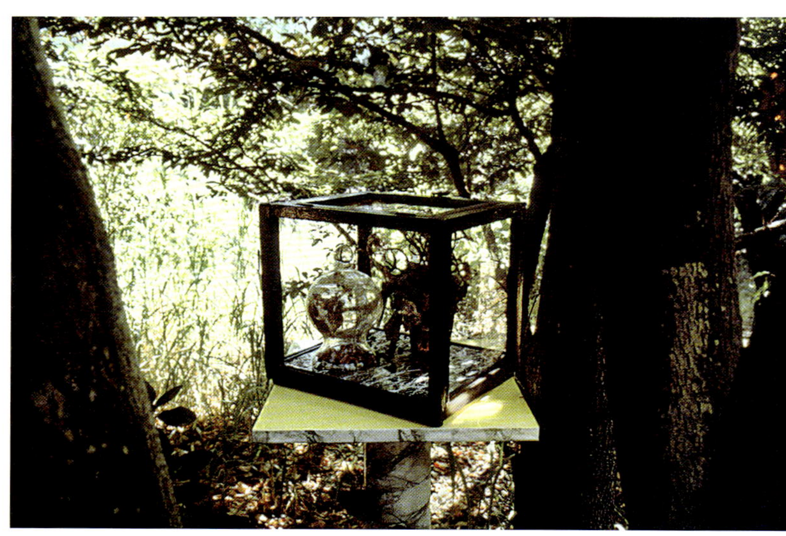

Corte & Nurcis: *Botanical Rarities*, 1981.
Cibachrome prints.
Variable dimensions.
GC 345, 347, 349, 351, 352, 353.

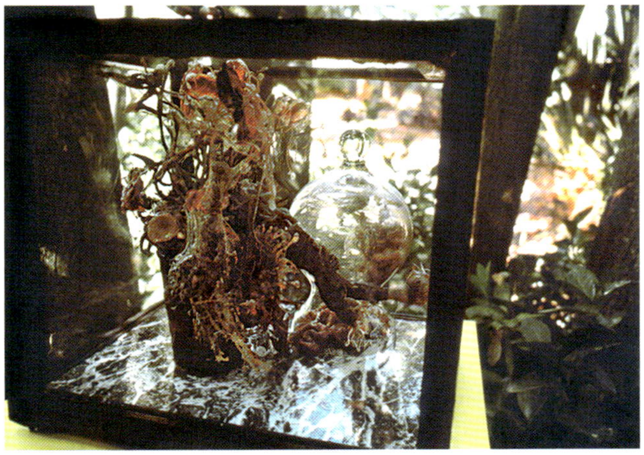

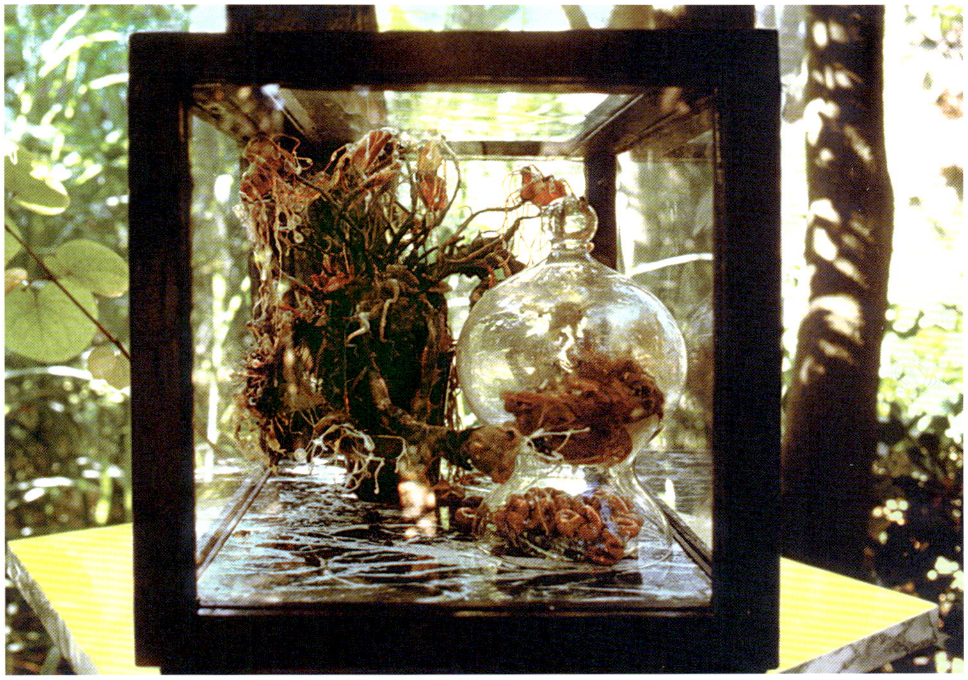

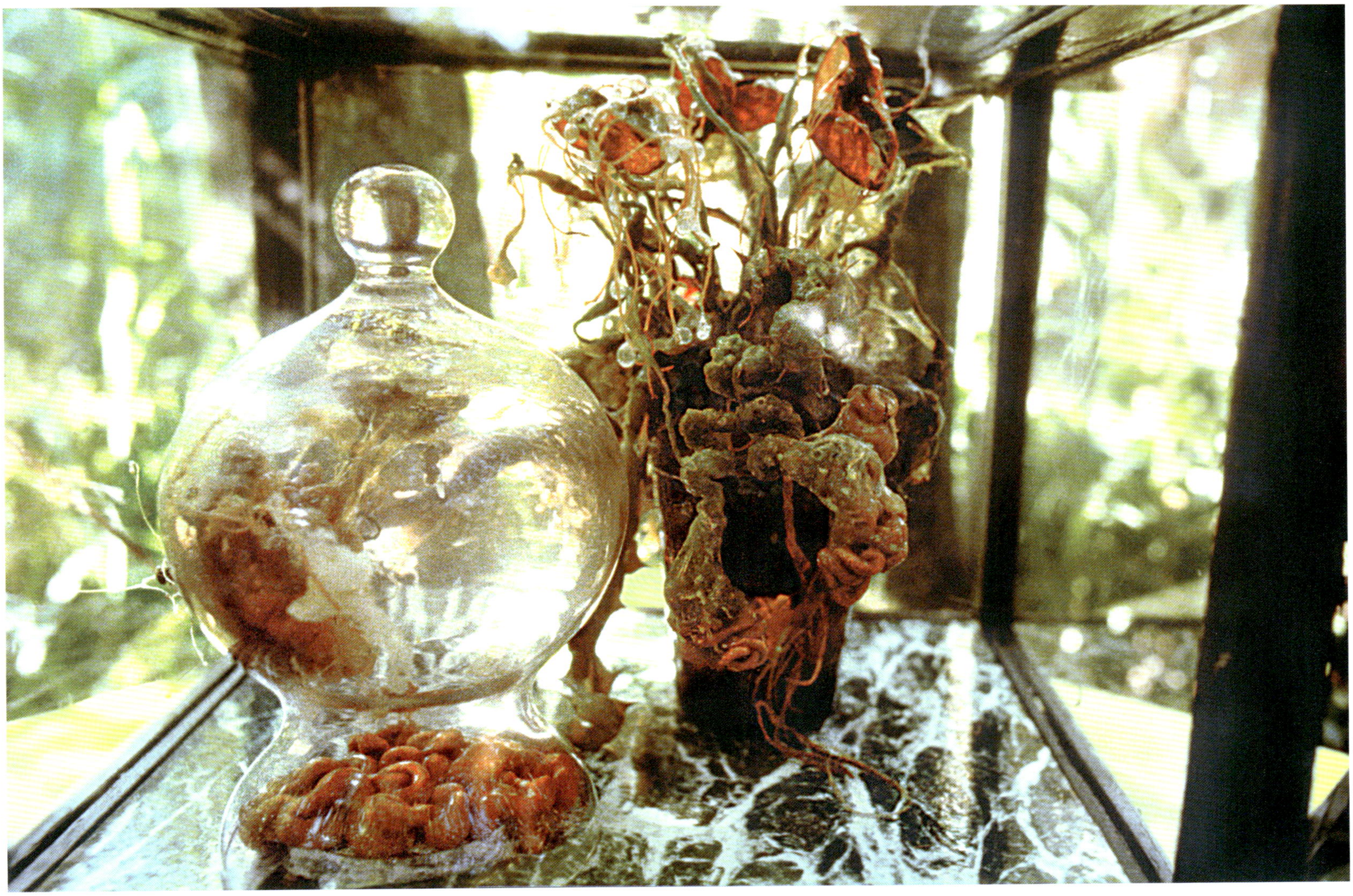

Corte & Nurcis: *Botanical Rarities*, 1981.
Cibachrome prints.
Variable dimensions.
GC 355, 356, 357.

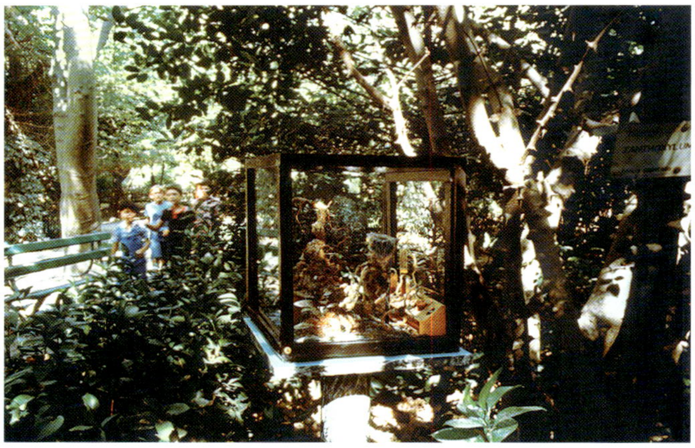
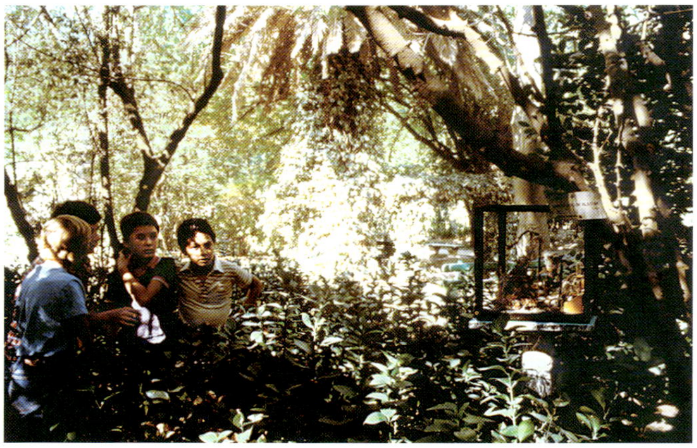
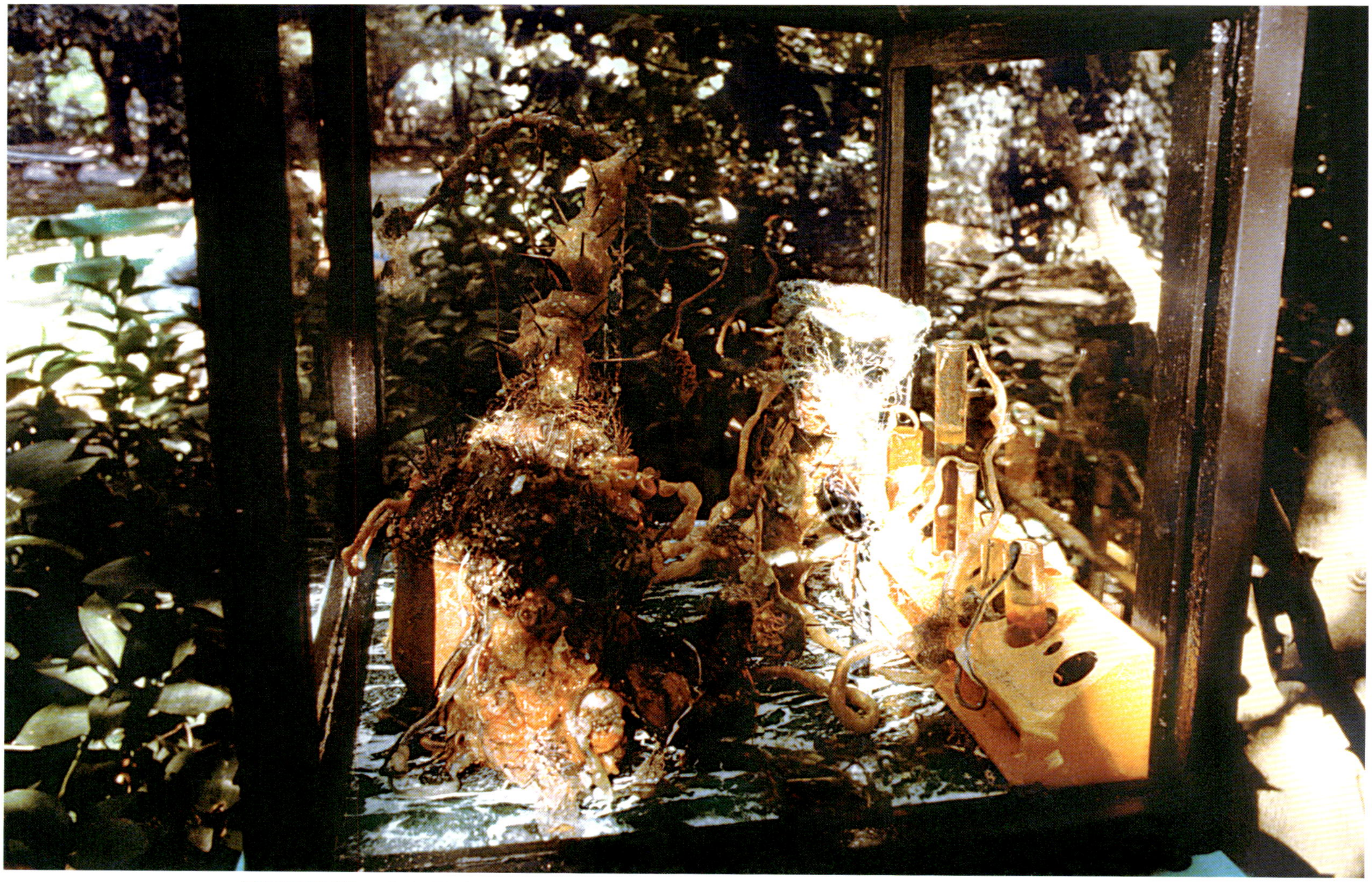
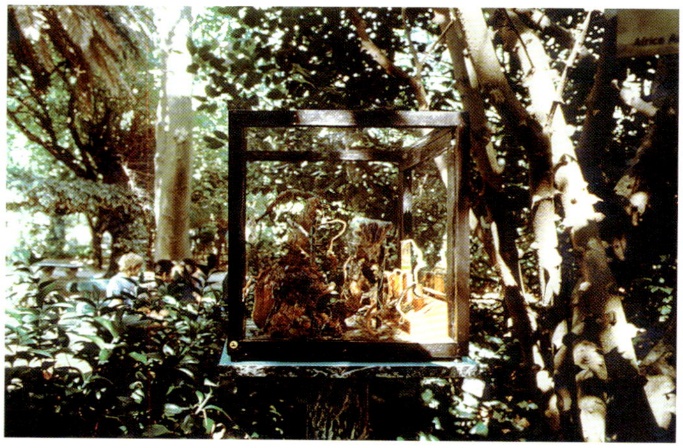
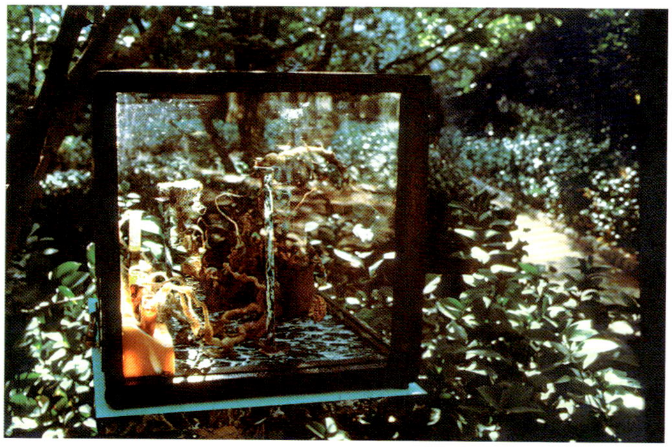

Corte & Nurcis: *Botanical Rarities*, 1981. Cibachrome prints. Variable dimensions. GC 360, 361, 362, 363, 364.

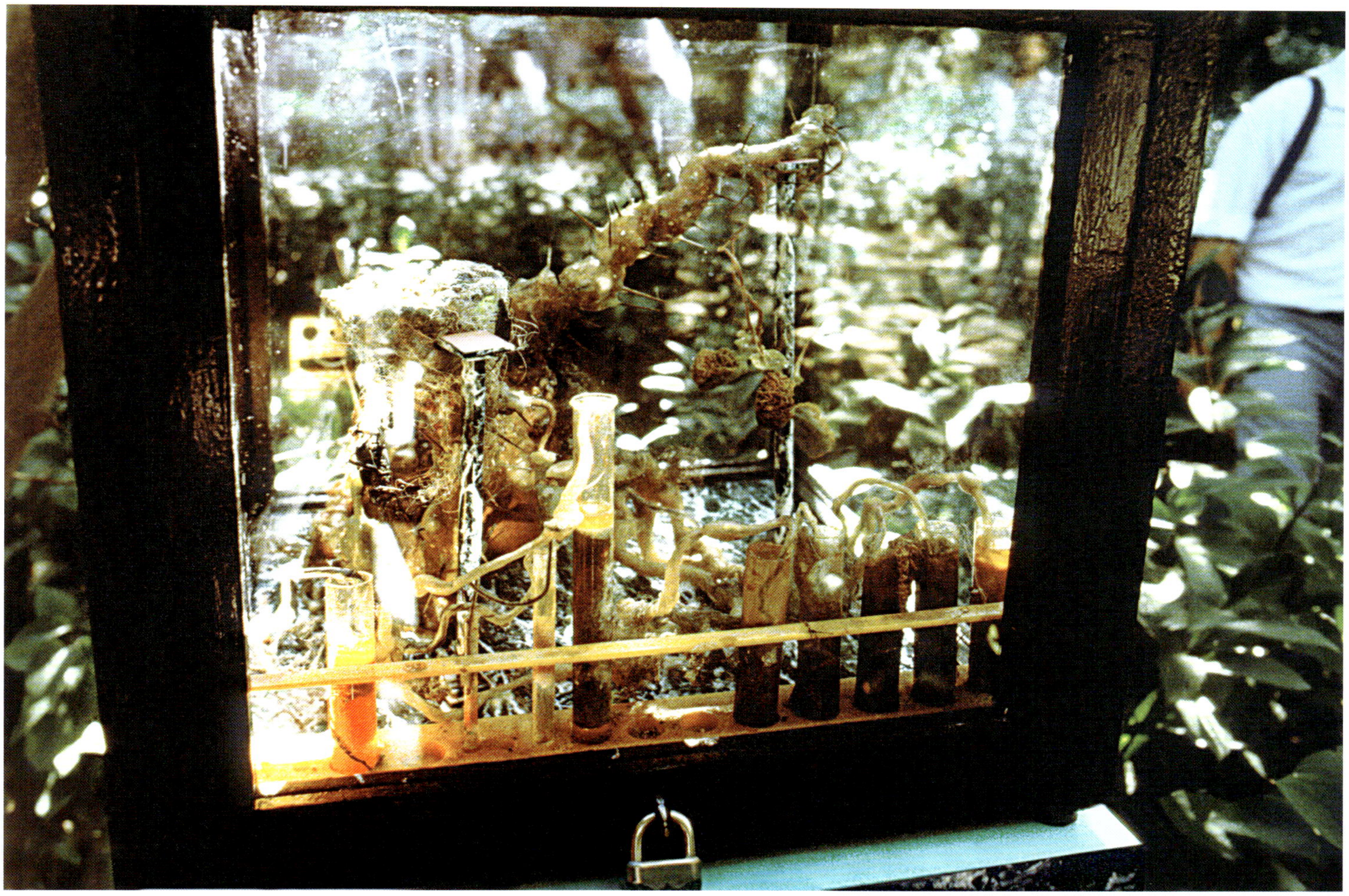

Corte & Nurcis: *Botanical Rarities*, 1981. Cibachrome print. GC 365.

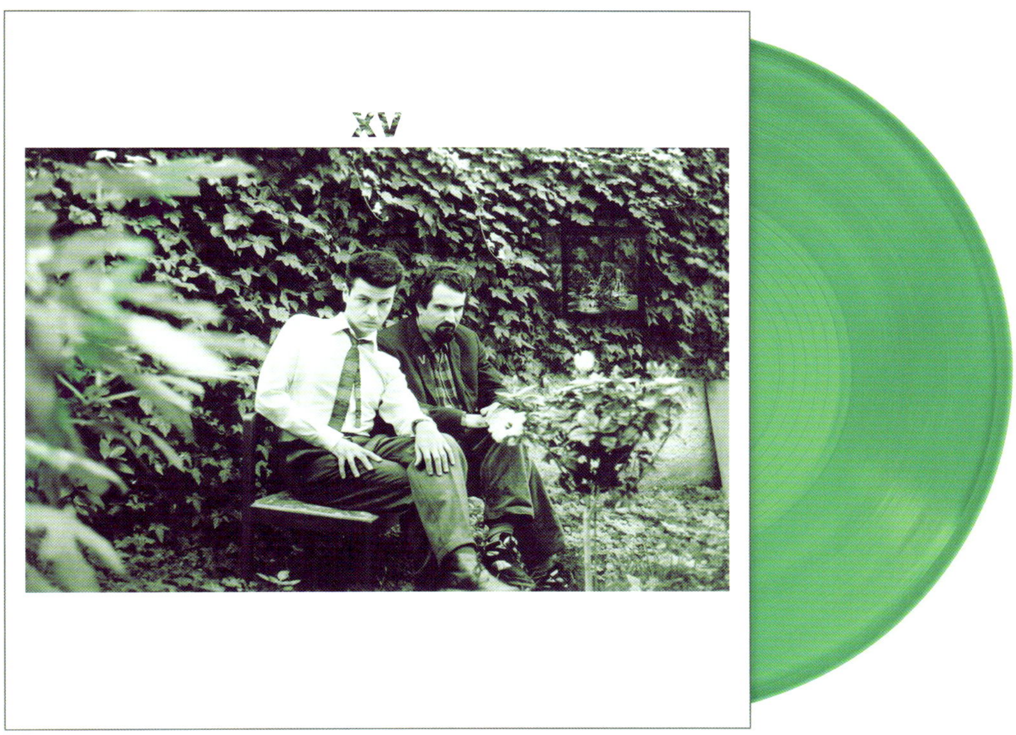

Botanical Rarities 15 Years After: Celebration Sad Party, 1996.
Toned photograph taken during the *Botanical Rarities* Commemoration in the garden of the artists' studio in Rome, used as a cover for a 33rpm green vinyl record containing the original soundtrack of the 1981 *Botanical Rarities* installation. Edition of three. 12½ x 12½" (31,8 x 31,8 cm). GC 976.

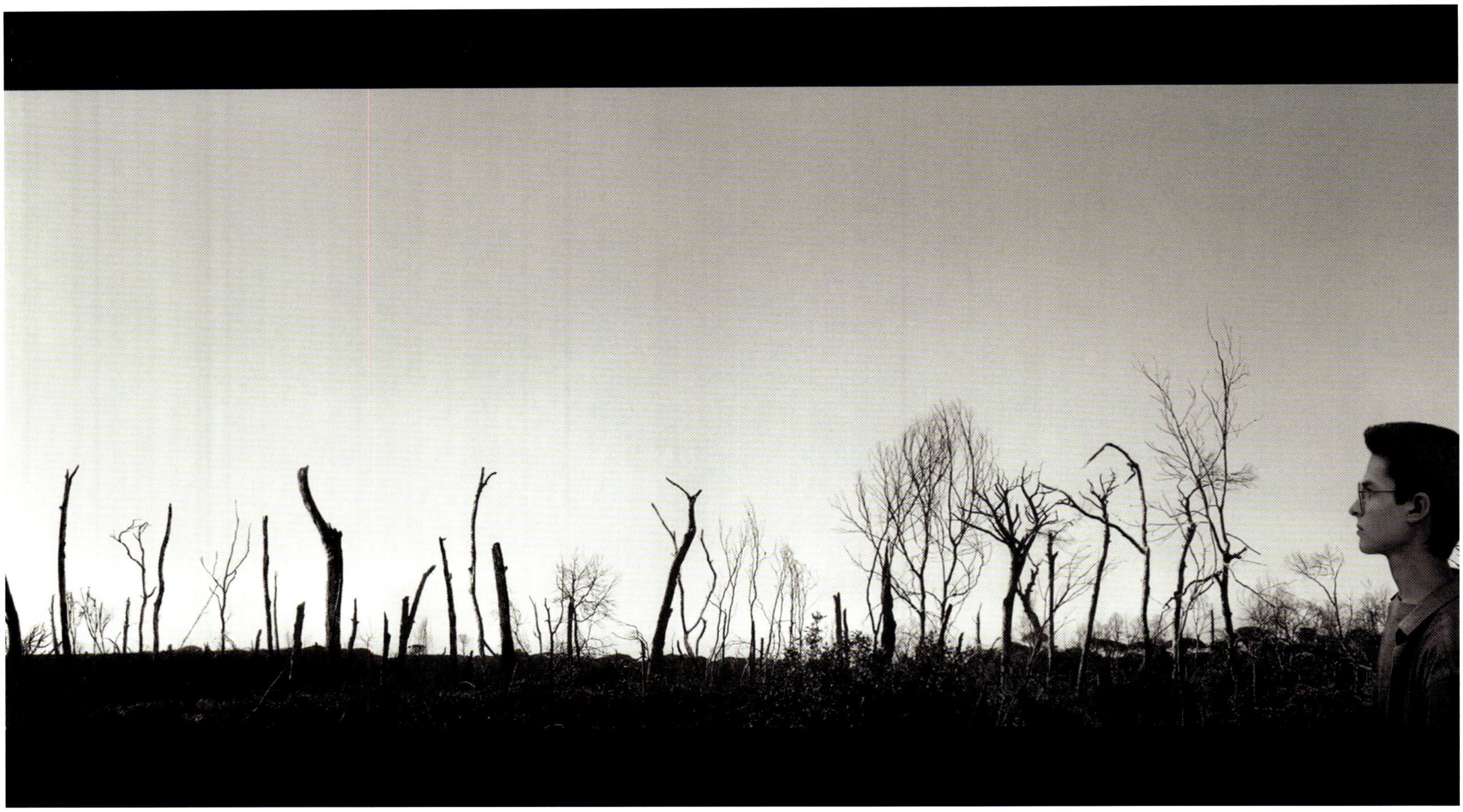

Spectrospective of Human Destiny, 1981.
Retouched silver gelatine print.
8½ x 31½" (21,8 x 80 cm).
GC 333.

Scrotumspective, 1982 (detail).
Clear resin cube containing a balled-up parchment-like paper with charcoal drawings of genital hair. Edition of 3.
10¼ x 10¼ x 10¼" (26 x 26 x 26 cm).
GC 397.

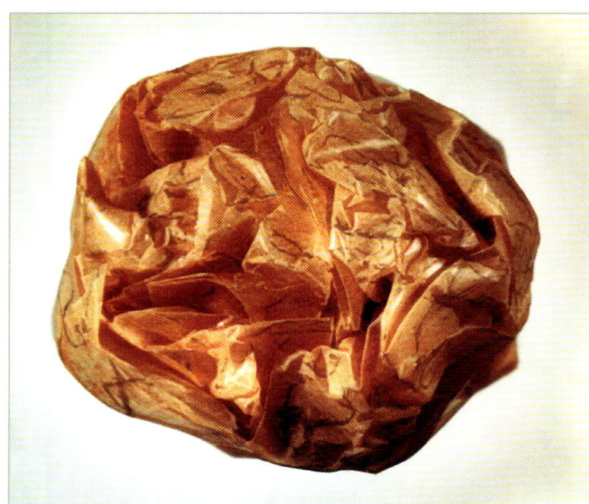

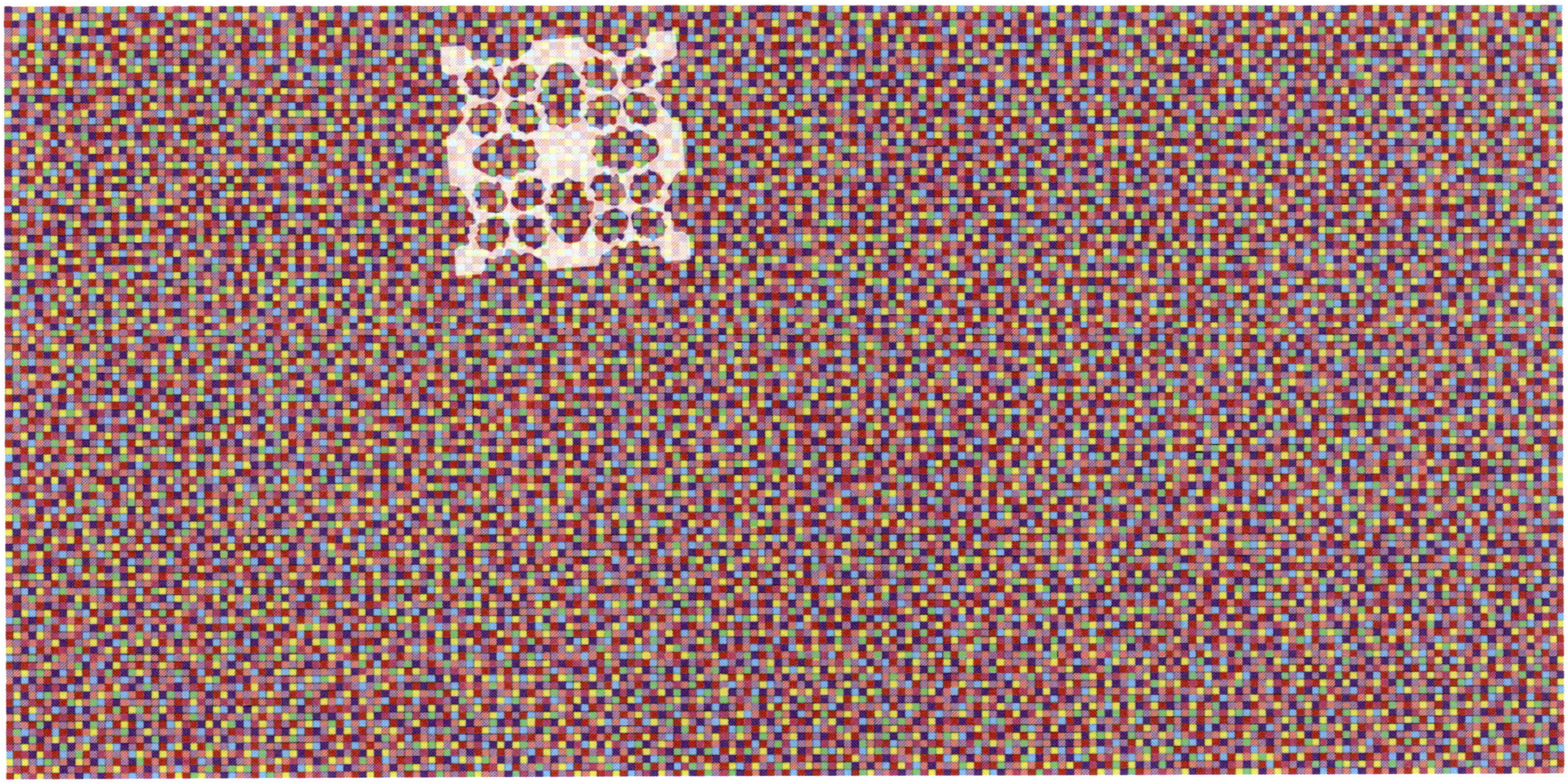

The Balcony: it's my favourite suicide tool, 1981.
Mosaic in small ceramic tiles retouched with enamel for glass,
with application of tissue paper cutout.
55¼ x 106¼" (140 x 270 cm).
GC 334.

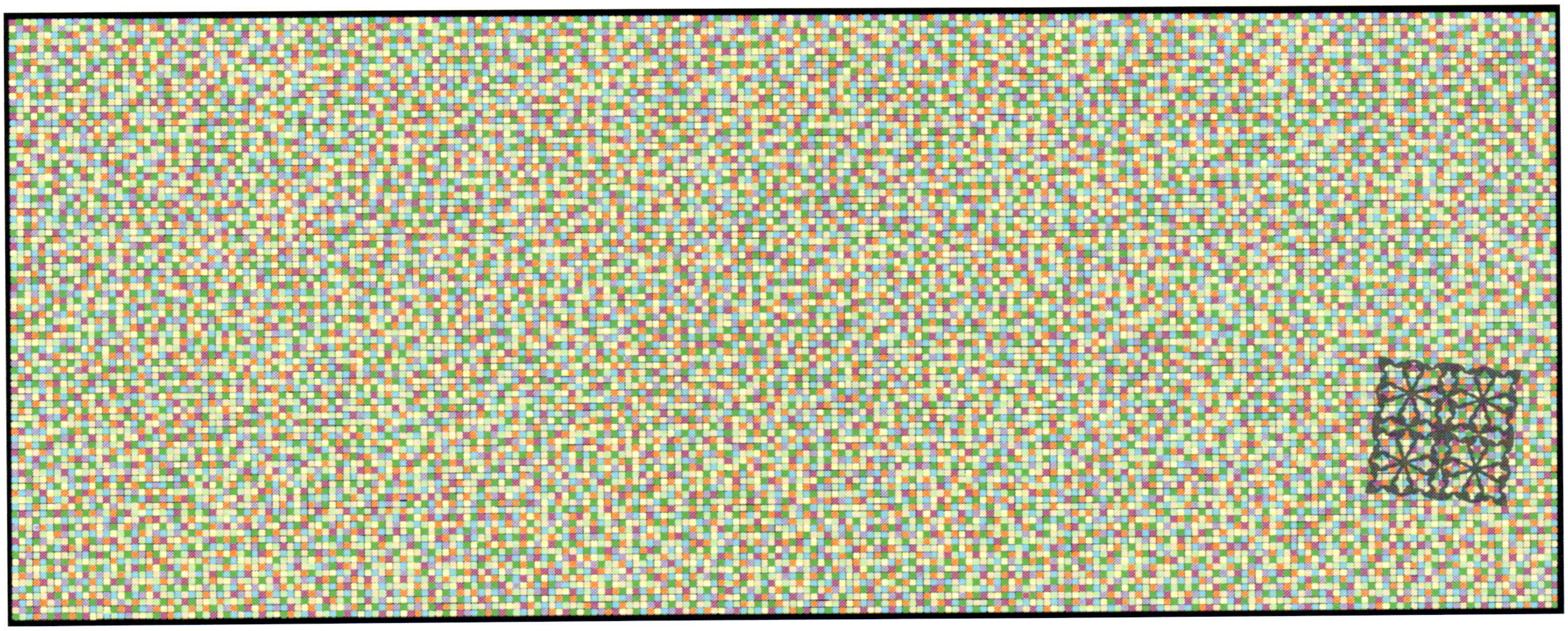

Balcony (Fade Out), 1981-82.
Mosaic in small ceramic tiles retouched with enamel for glass;
tempera on tissue paper cutout.
39¼ x 97½" (100 x 247,5 cm).
GC 370.

Balcony (Curtain Falls), 1983.
Mosaic; tempera on tissue paper cutout; fiberglass frame.
27¾ x 63" (70,5 x 160 cm). GC 408.

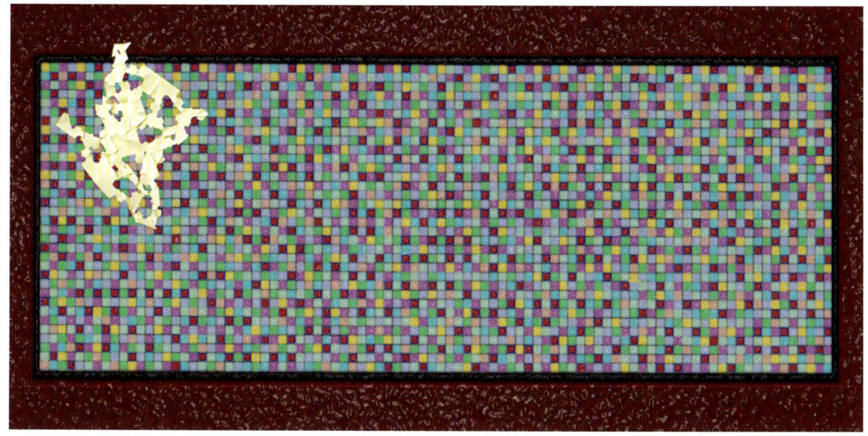

Balcony (Bones), 1982-83.
Mosaic; tempera on tissue paper cutout; fiberglass frame.
30¼ x 63" (77 x 160 cm). GC 400.

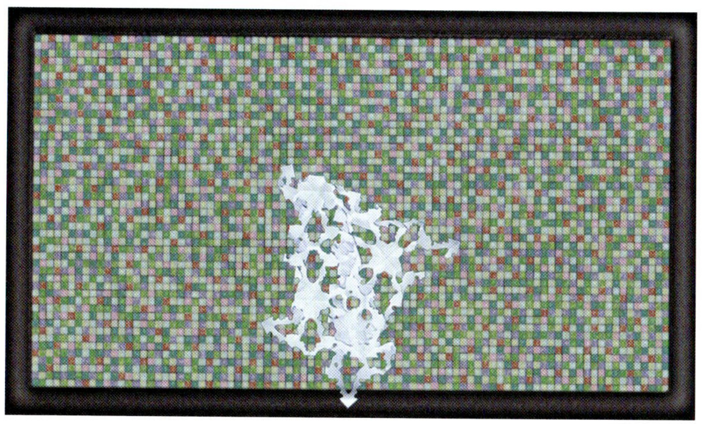

Balcony (Spooky), 1982.
Mosaic; tempera on tissue paper cutout; iron frame.
31¾ x 55¼" (80,6 x 140 cm). GC 371.

Skin and Bones Balcony, 1986.
White acrylic on mosaic; graphite on parchment-like paper; white lacquer on wood.
60¾ x 114¼" (154,6 x 290 cm). GC 489.

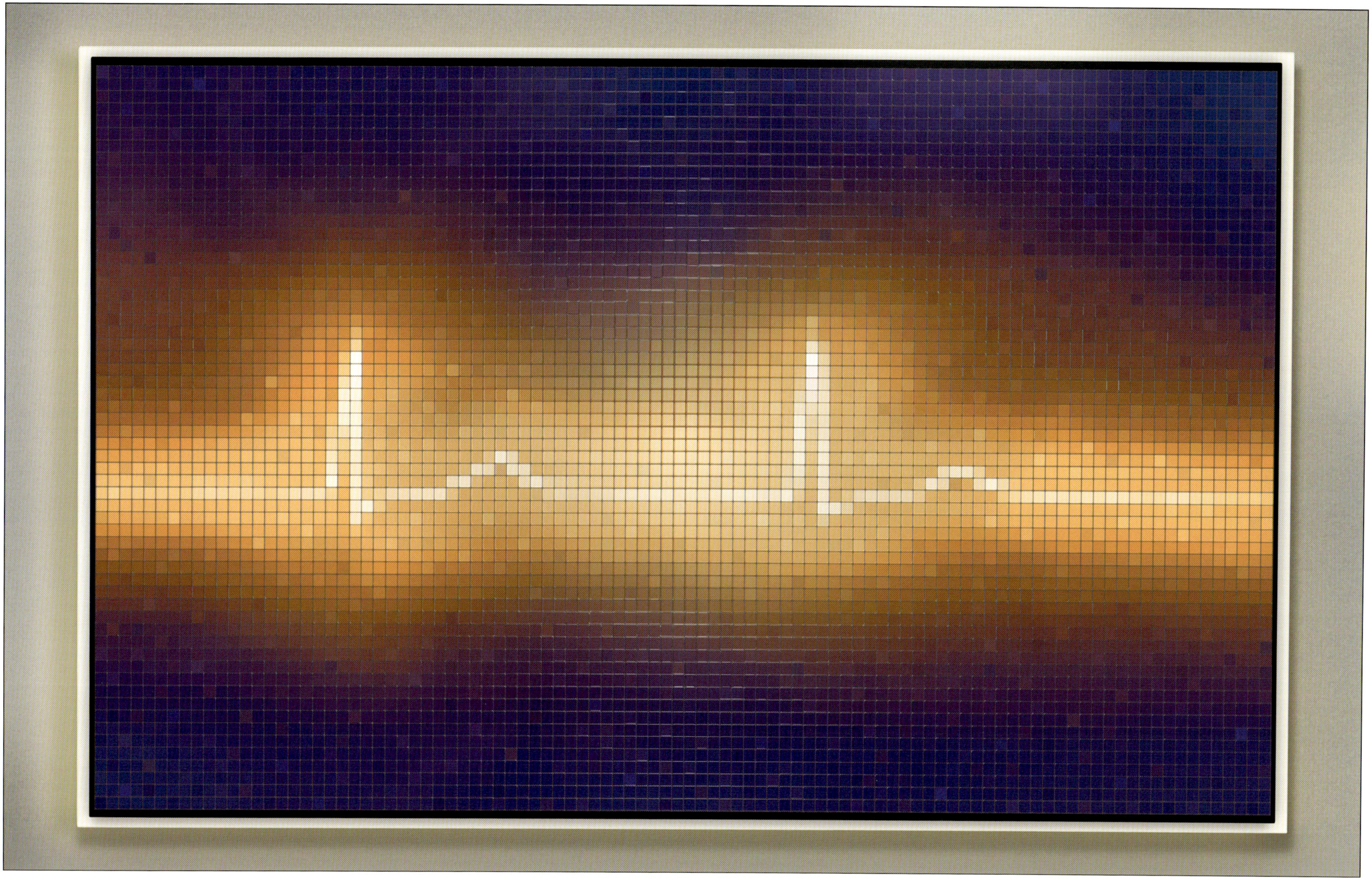

Bal-coma 2, 1983.
Enamel, ceramic, black and white marble.
43¾ x 78¾" (111,4 x 200 cm).
GC 412.

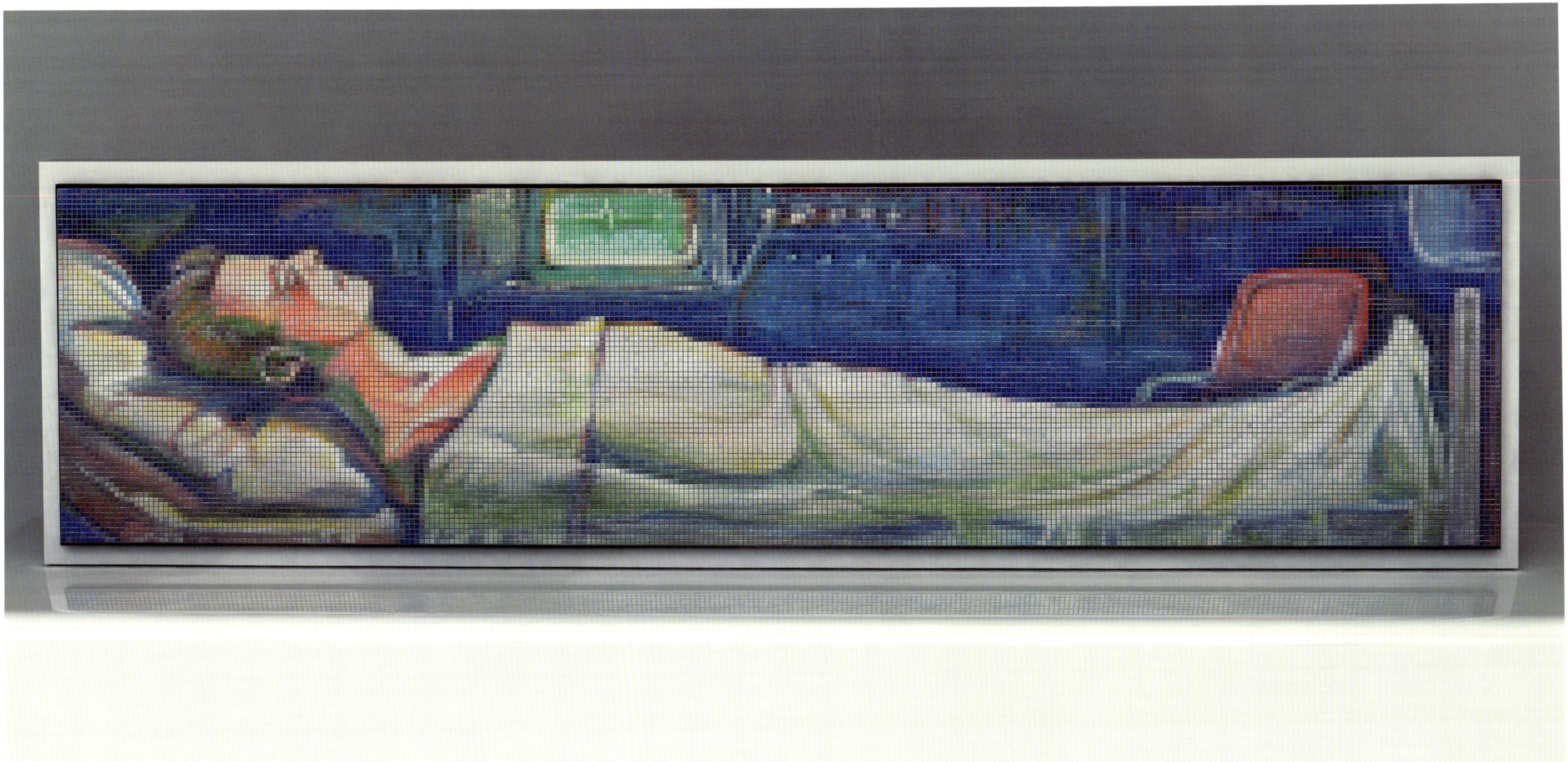

This page and opposite:
Bal-coma 1, 1983.
Enamel, ceramic, white marble.
25½ x 98½" (65 x 250 cm).
GC 409.

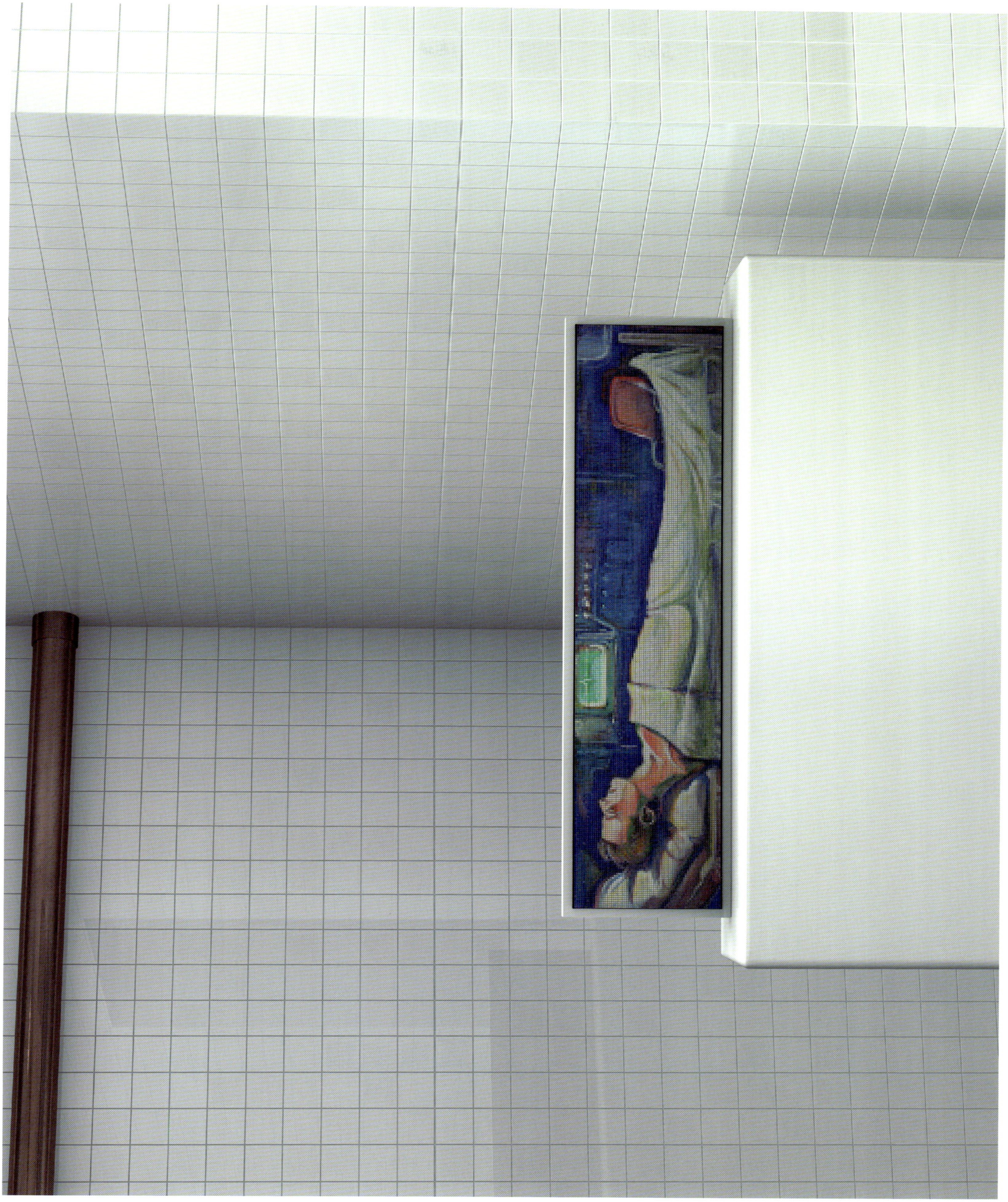

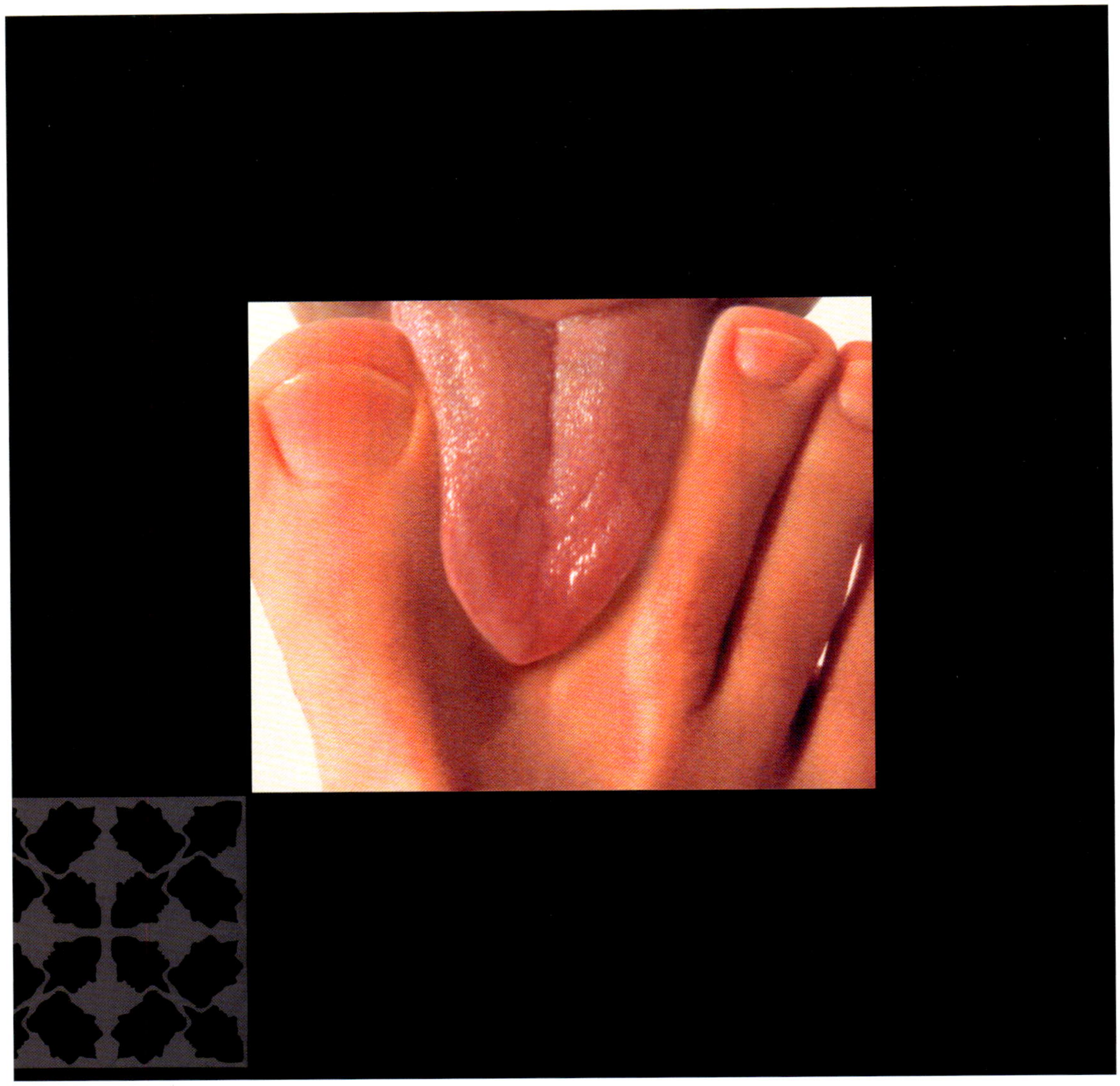

The Kiss, 1982.
Cibachrome print with application of black tissue paper cutout.
39¼ x 39¼" (101 x 101 cm).
GC 395.

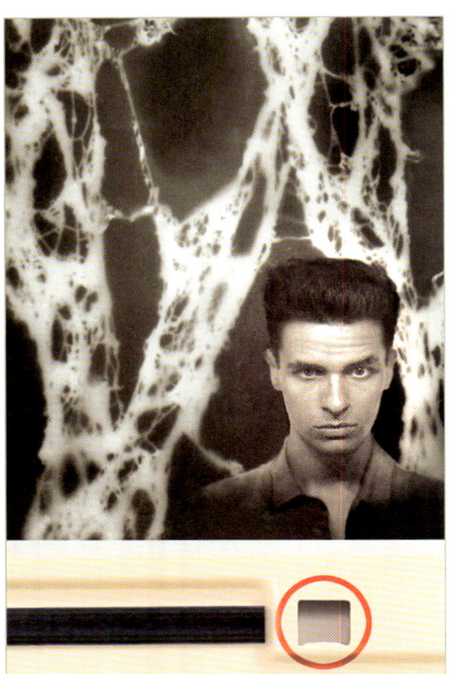

Marble Fever, Marble Junkie, Marble Hustler, Marblefucker, 1983 (detail).
Collection of 4 postcards in medium-tickness cardboard with retouched photographs, set in a molded fiberglass container with fragments of recording tape.
10¼ x 13½ x 1¼" (25,8 x 34,5 x 3 cm).
GC 417.

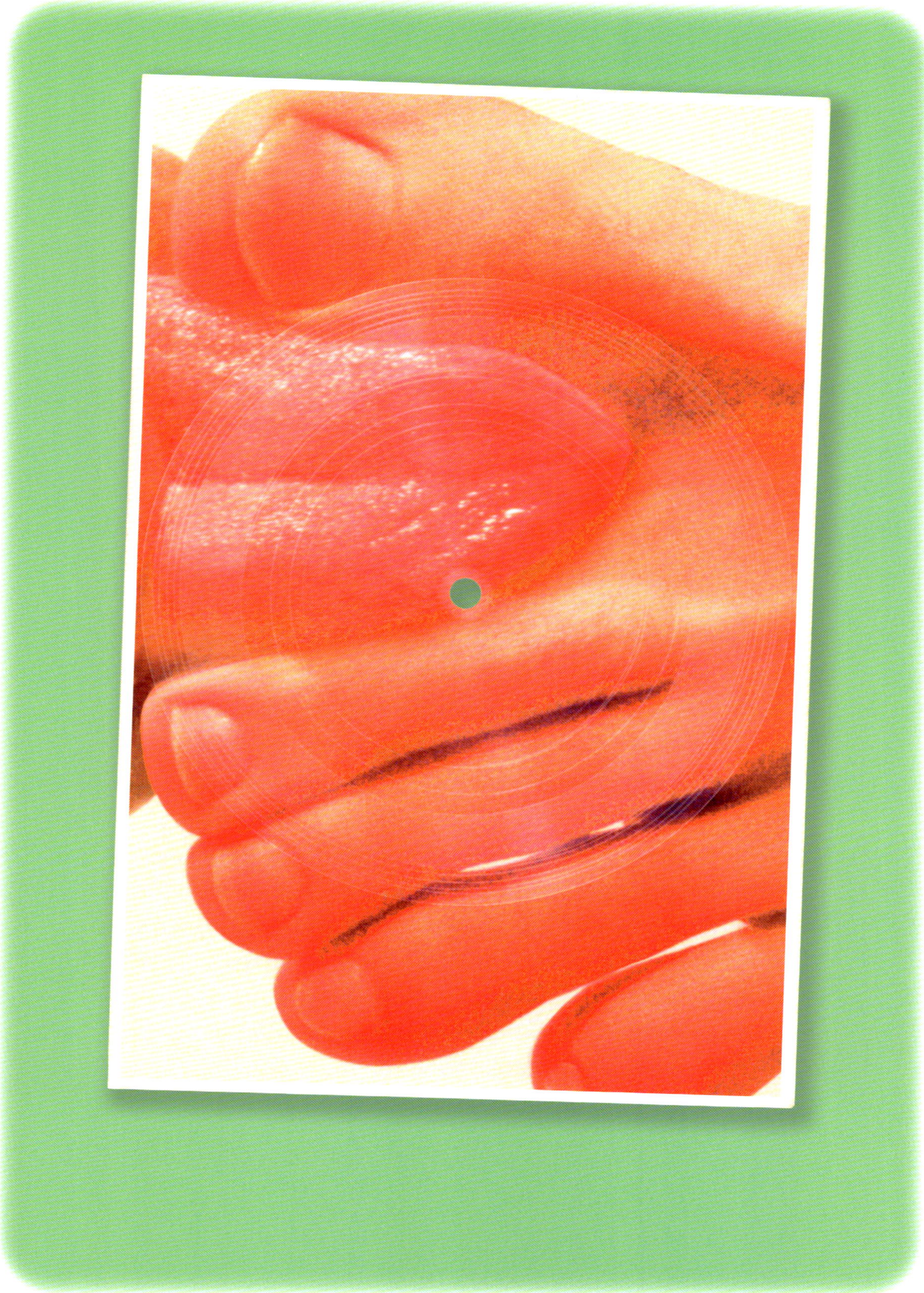

Amid the Grooves, 1984.
Photograph printed on medium-thickness plasticized cardboard,
with small 33rpm clear vinyl record embossed on one side.
11¾ x 7¾" (30 x 20 cm).
GC 439.

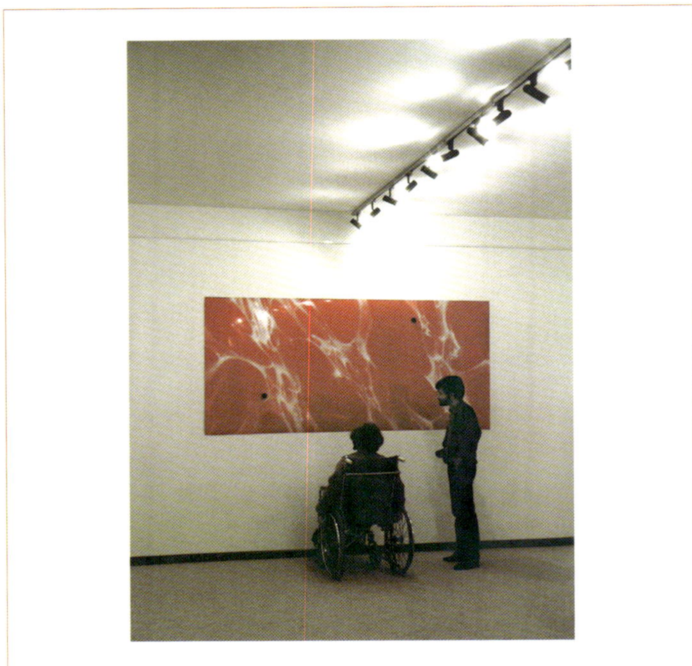
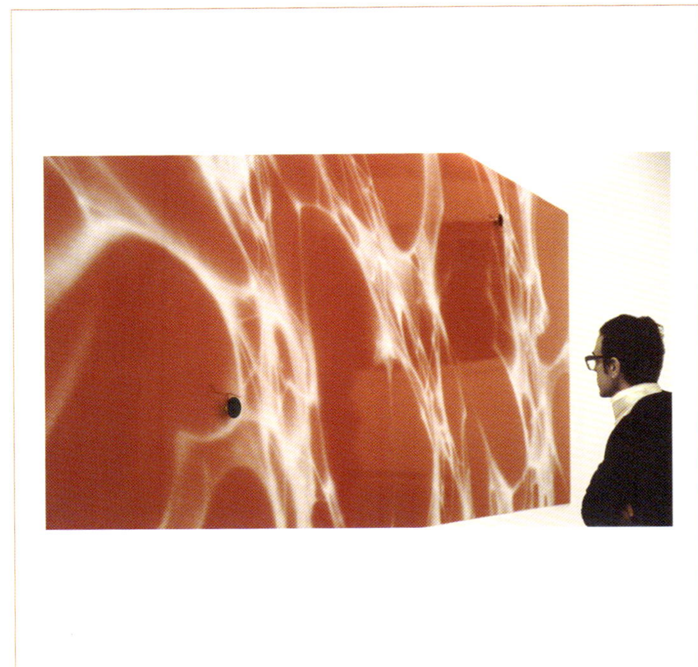
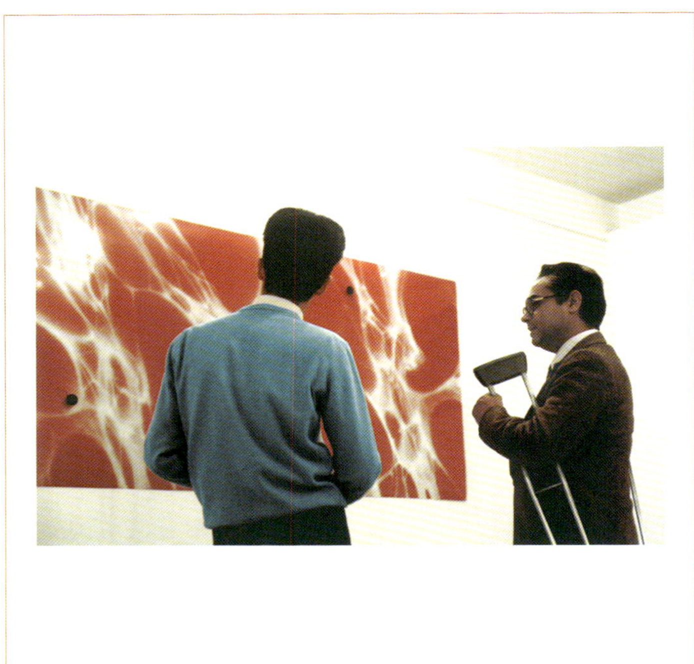
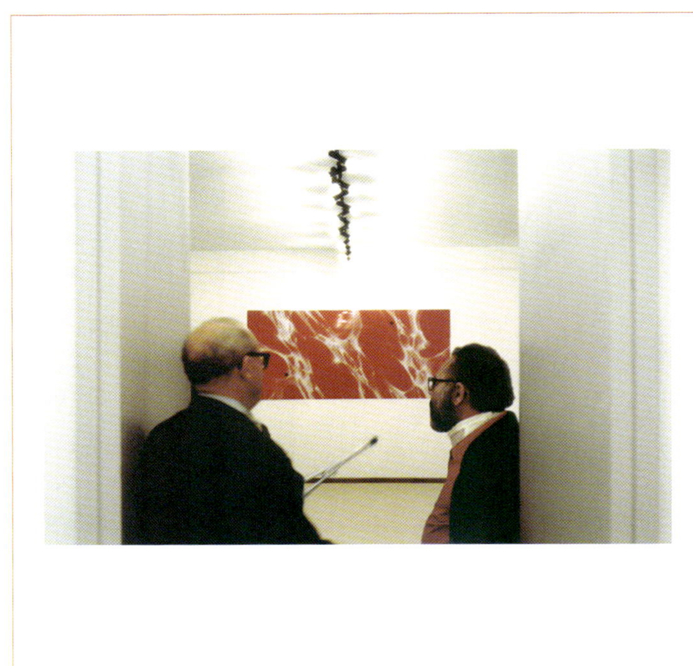

From the *Art System* series, 1982.
10 photographs portraying disabled people looking at the work *Sick Marble* on exhibit in an art museum.
Cibachrome prints; graphite. 19½ x 19½" each (50 x 50 cm).
GC 382, 386, 388, 389.

[*Sick Marble*, 1982. Nitrocellulose lacquer on formica, with two loudspeakers. 55¼ x 116¼ x 1¼" (140 x 295 x 3 cm). GC 375].

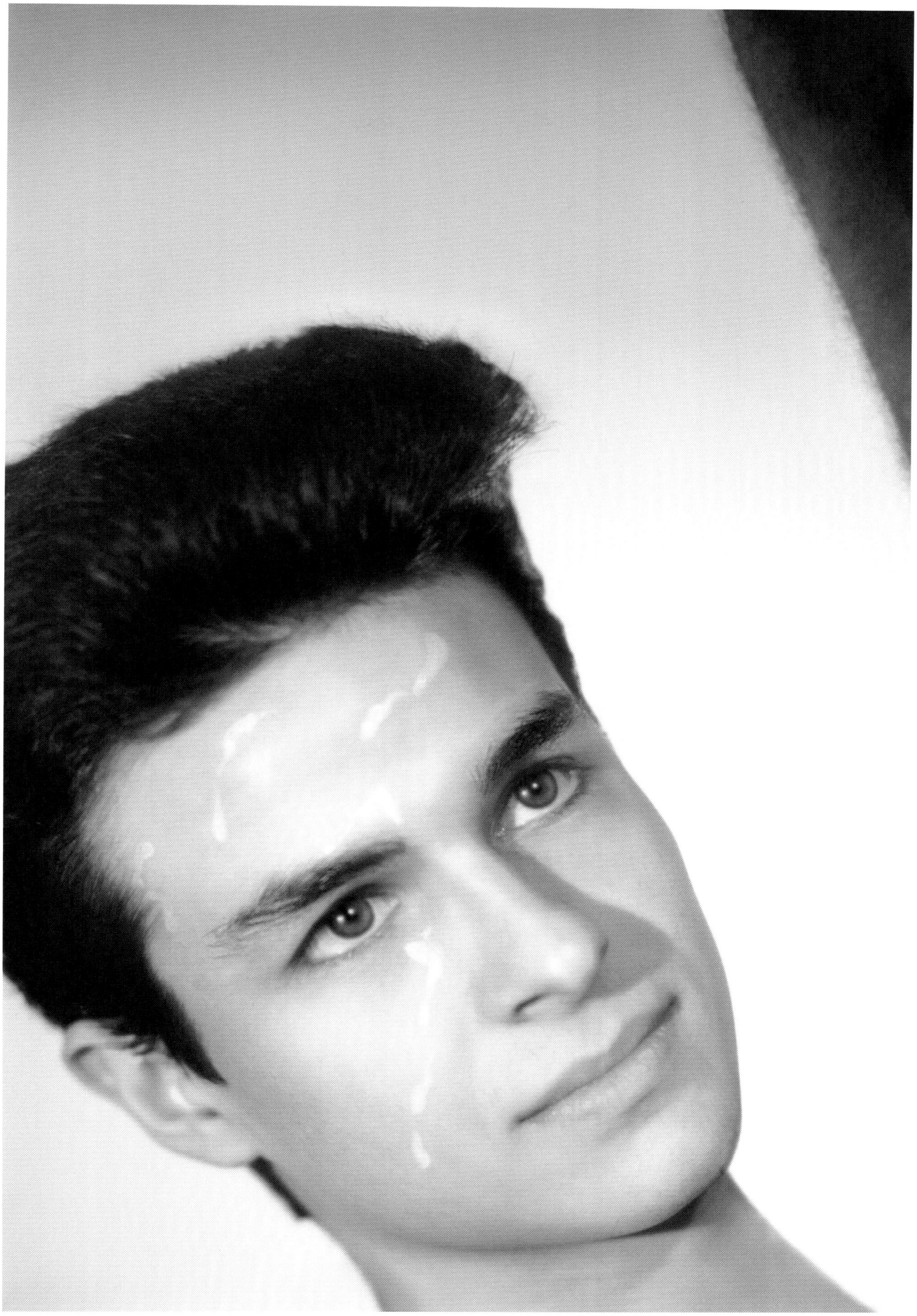

Drawing (Spurt), 1982.
Silver gelatine print.
27½ x 18½" (70 x 47 cm).
GC 390.

The Little Psychic Daemons
or also *The Artist's Bed*, 1983.
Enamel on fiberglass, pvc and metal;
silk pillow with blood stains produced by cuts on the artist's face;
plexiglas sphere.
Diam. 39½" (100 cm).
GC 421.

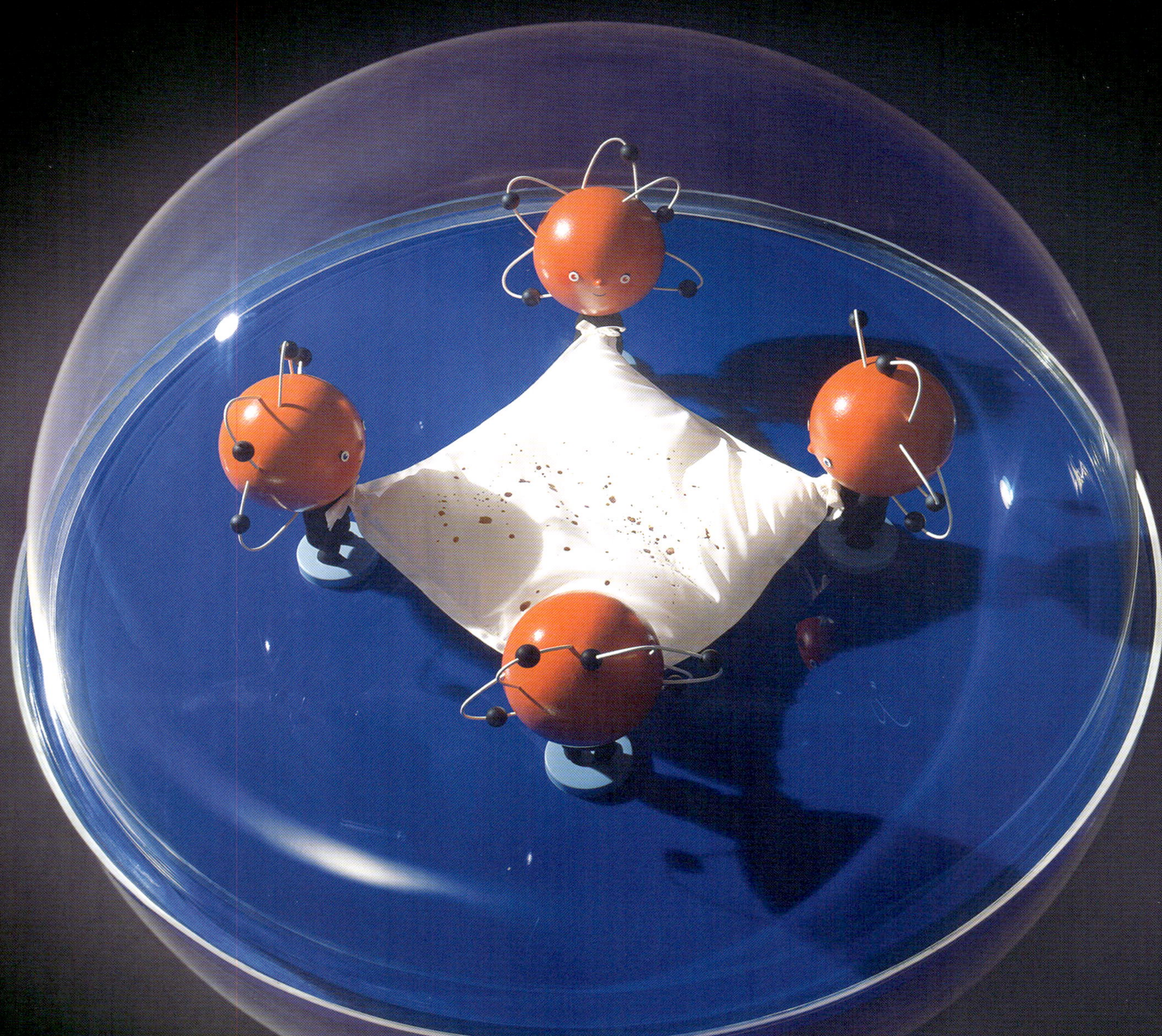

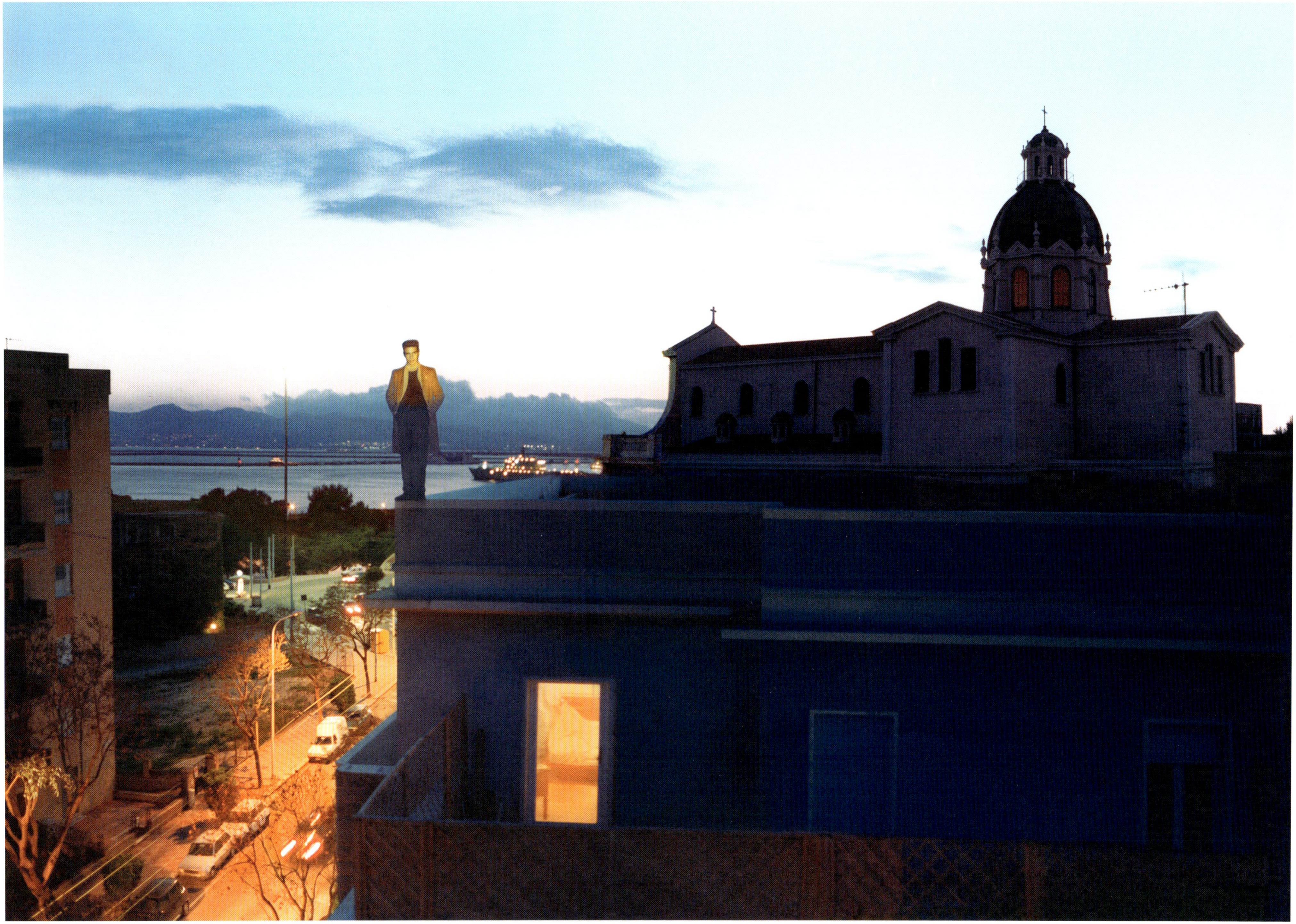

The Lighthouse, 1984.
Cibachrome print.
16¼ x 23½" (41,6 x 60 cm).
GC 430.

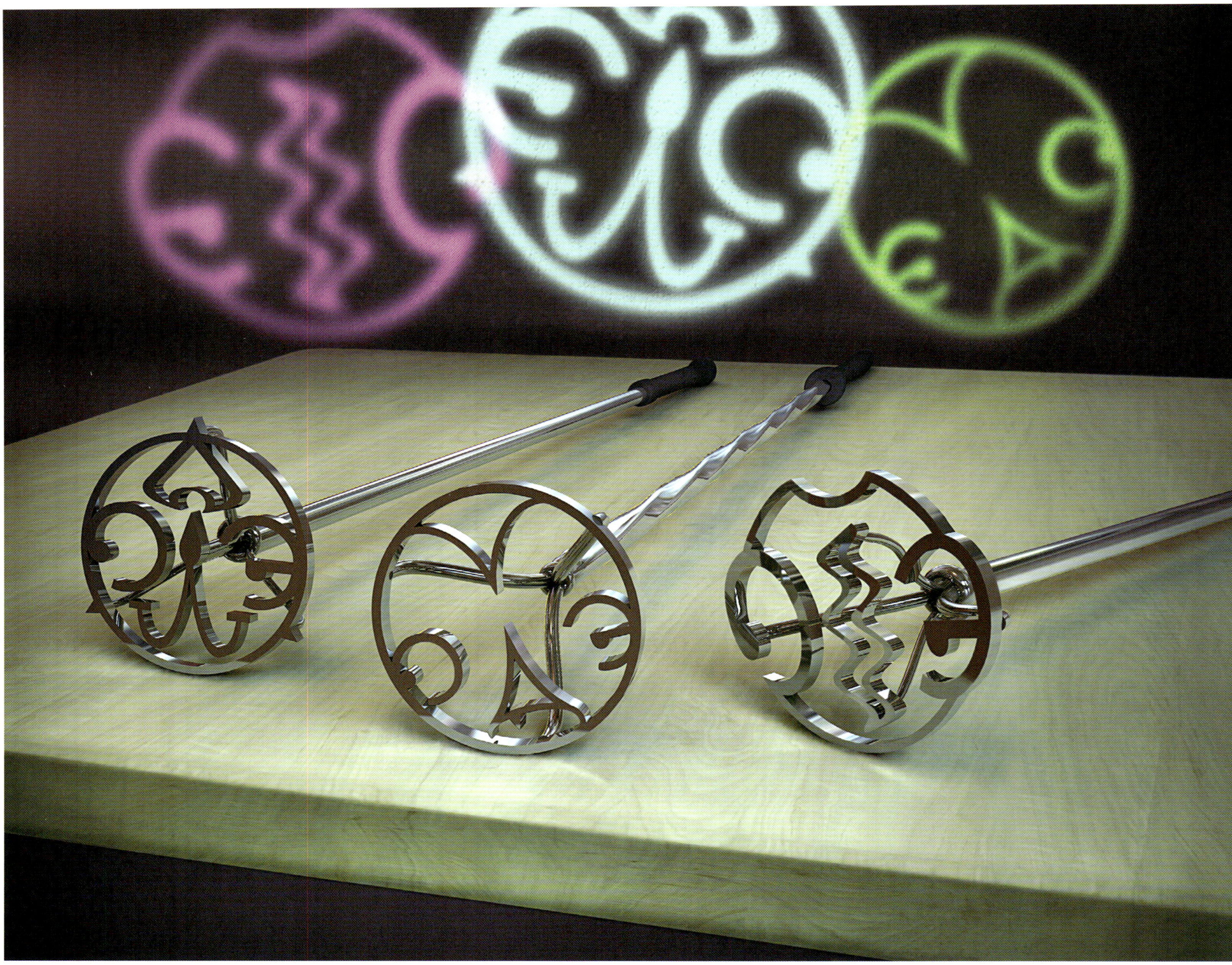

The Access Keys, 1985-86.
Promo Picture portraying a set of three tools for fire branding.
Original tools made of steel and iron, with plastic handles.
Left tool: 3½ x 3¼ x 17¾" (9 x 8,5 x 45 cm).
Center tool: 3¼ x 3¼ x 17¾" (8,5 x 8,5 x 45 cm).
Right tool: 2¾ x 3¾ x 17¾" (7,3 x 9,5 x 45 cm).
GC 457, 458, 459.

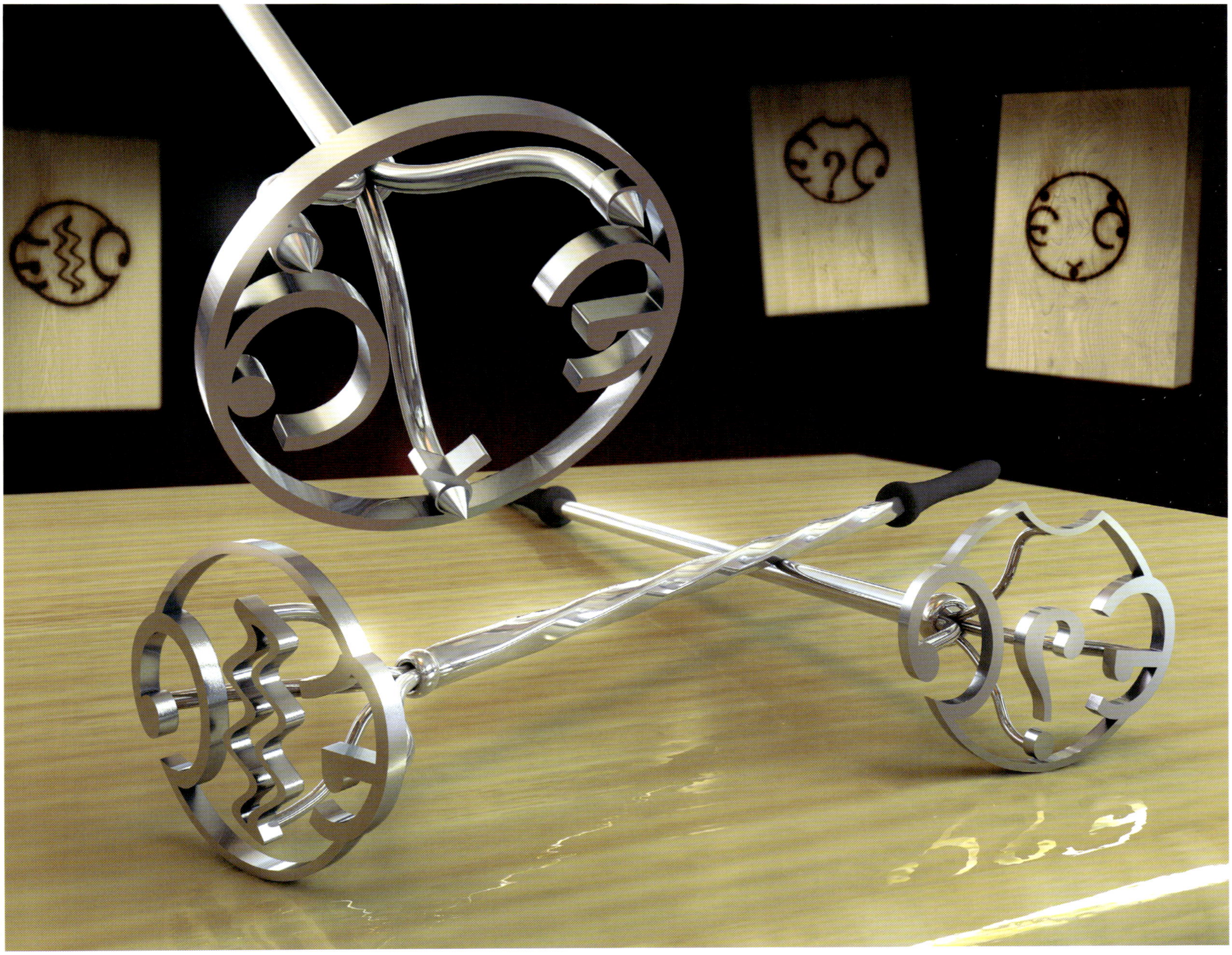

The Sacred Fire of Art, 1985-86.
Promo Picture portraying a set of three tools for fire branding.
Original tools made of steel and iron, with plastic handles.
Top tool: 3¼ x 3¼ x 18" (8,5 x 8,5 x 45,5 cm).
Left tool: 3¼ x 3¾ x 17¾" (8,5 x 9,5 x 45 cm).
Right tool: 2¾ x 3¾ x 17¾" (7,3 x 9,5 x 45 cm).
GC 460, 461, 462.

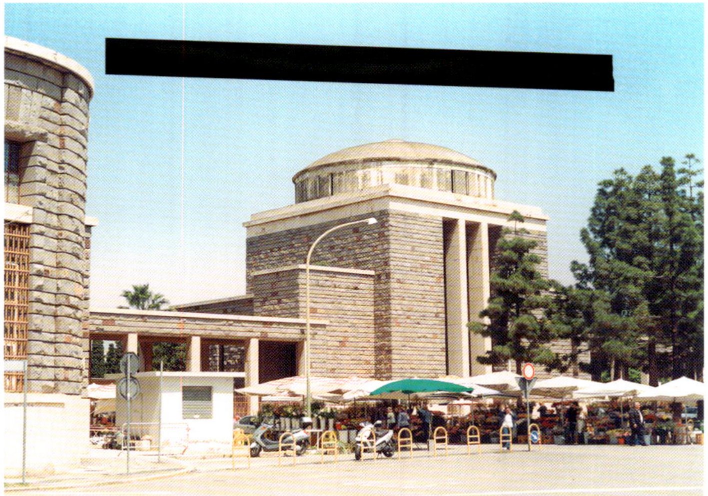

The Film of Life - Metal Postcard, 1984.
Photographic print on magnetic metal foil in postcard size,
portraying the cemetery in which the work *The Film of Life* is installed;
fragment of recording tape attached on front side;
writings, stamp and postmark on back. Unnumbered multiple.
5¼ x 8¼" each postcard (13 x 21 cm).
GC 432.

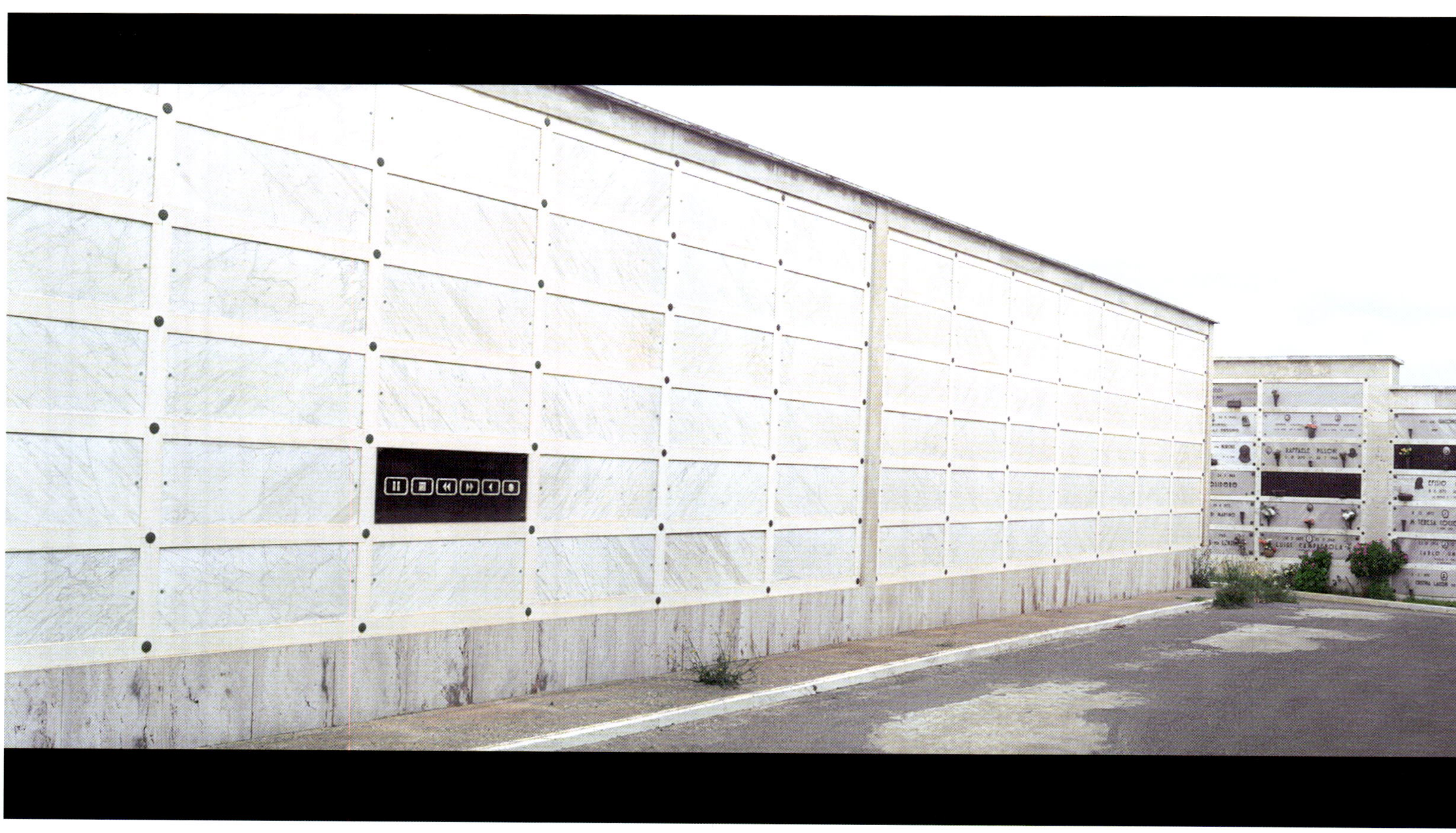

The Film of Life (left view), 1984.
Cibachrome print.
13½ x 23¾" (34,2 x 60 cm).
GC 434.

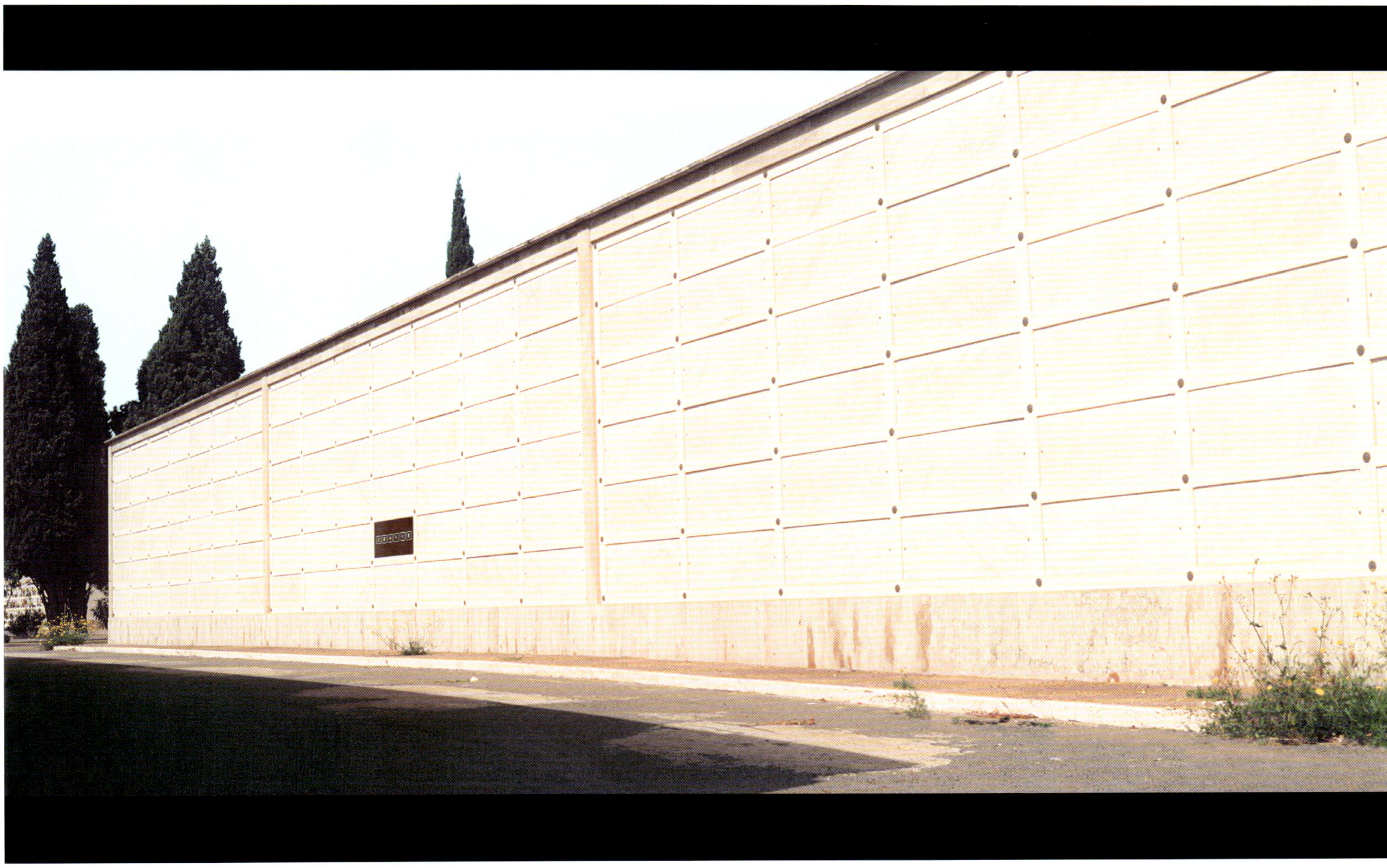

The Film of Life (right view), 1984.
Cibachrome print.
15 x 23¾” (38,2 x 60 cm).
GC 435.

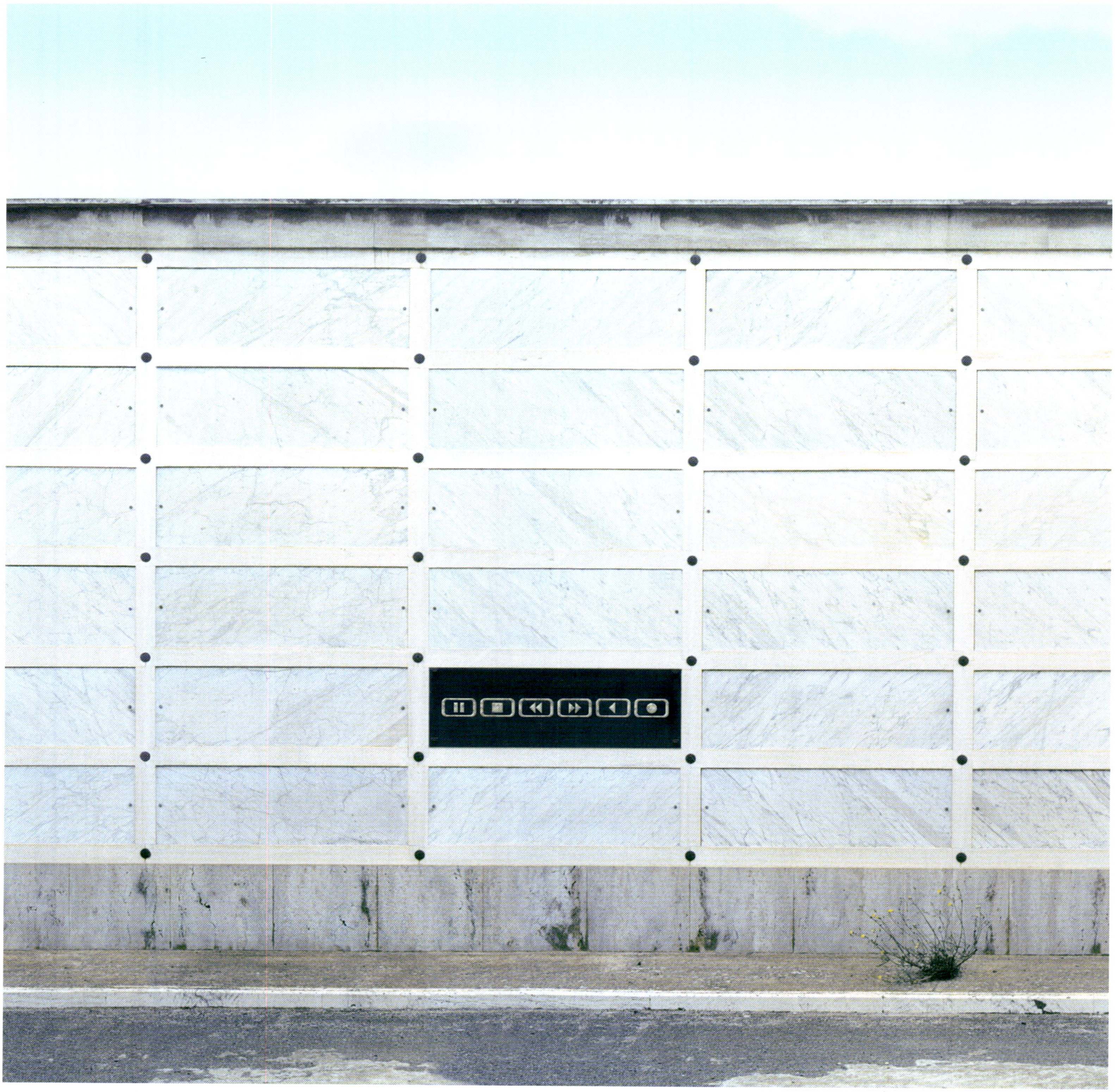

The Film of Life (front view), 1984.
Cibachrome print.
23¾ x 23½" (60 x 59,3 cm).
GC 433.

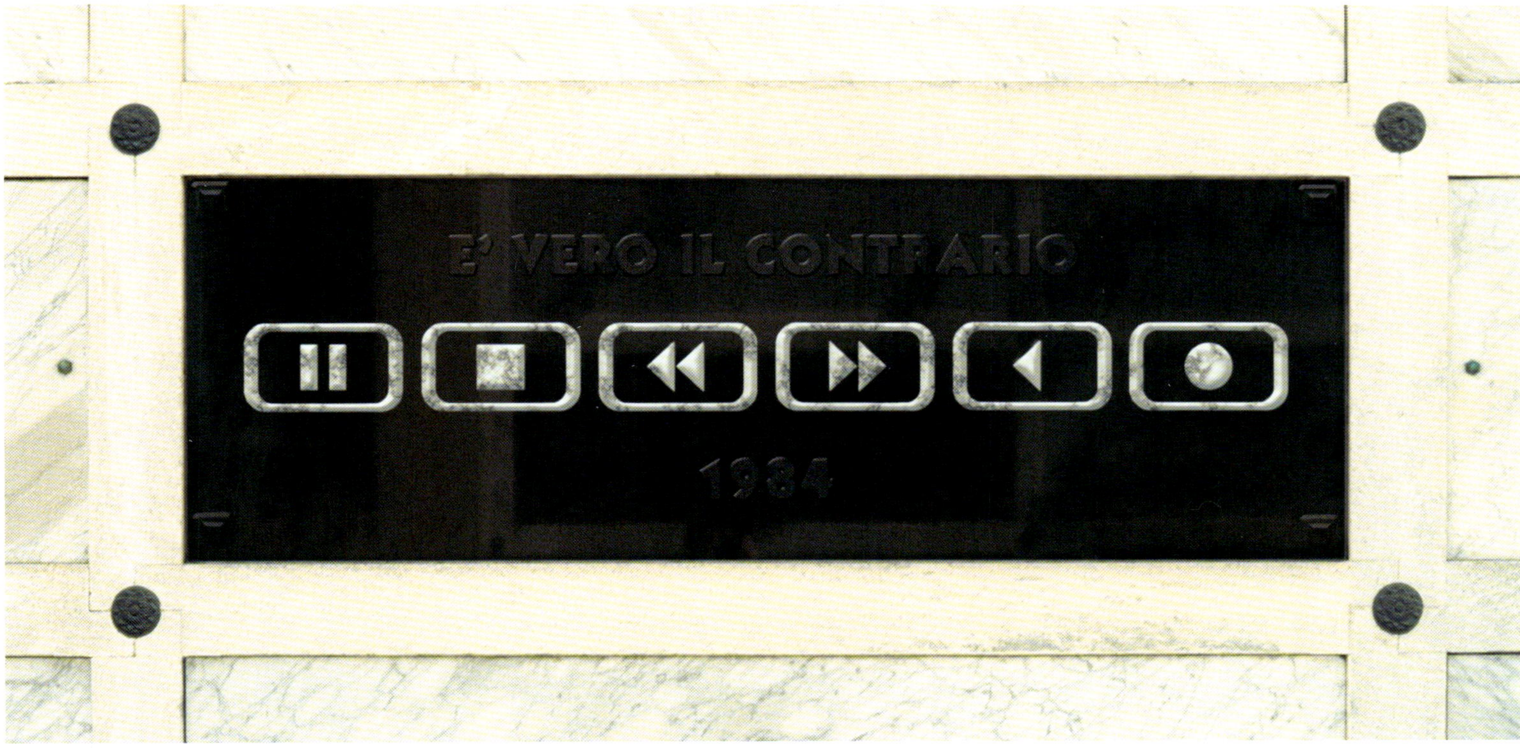

The Film of Life, 1984.
Black marble tombstone with black and white marble relieves;
hidden wooden coffin with human corpse.
29½ x 47¼ x 35½" (75 x 120 x 90 cm).
GC 431.

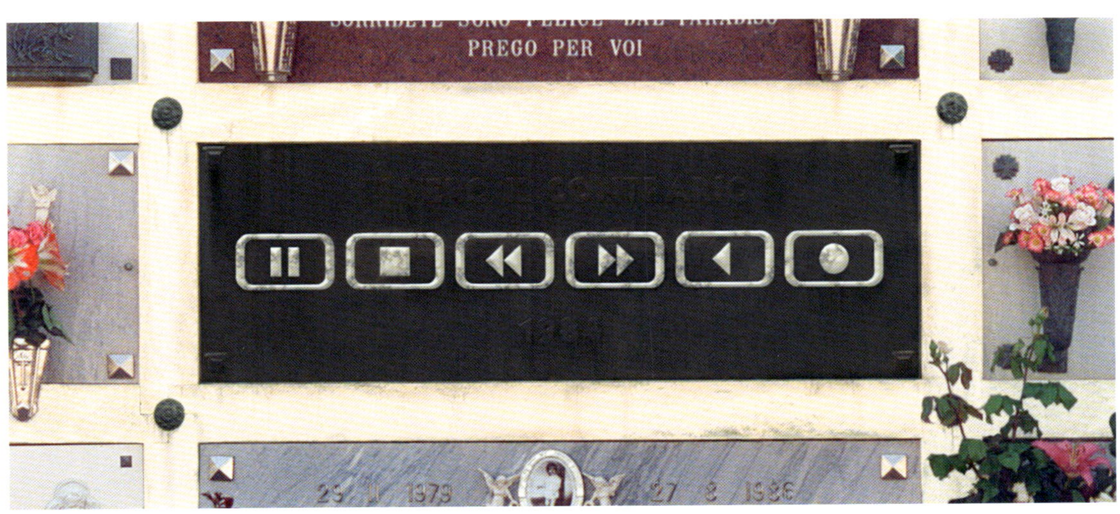

The Film of Life - 20 Years After, 2004.
Cibachrome print.
10¾ x 23¾" (27 x 60 cm).
GC 1579.

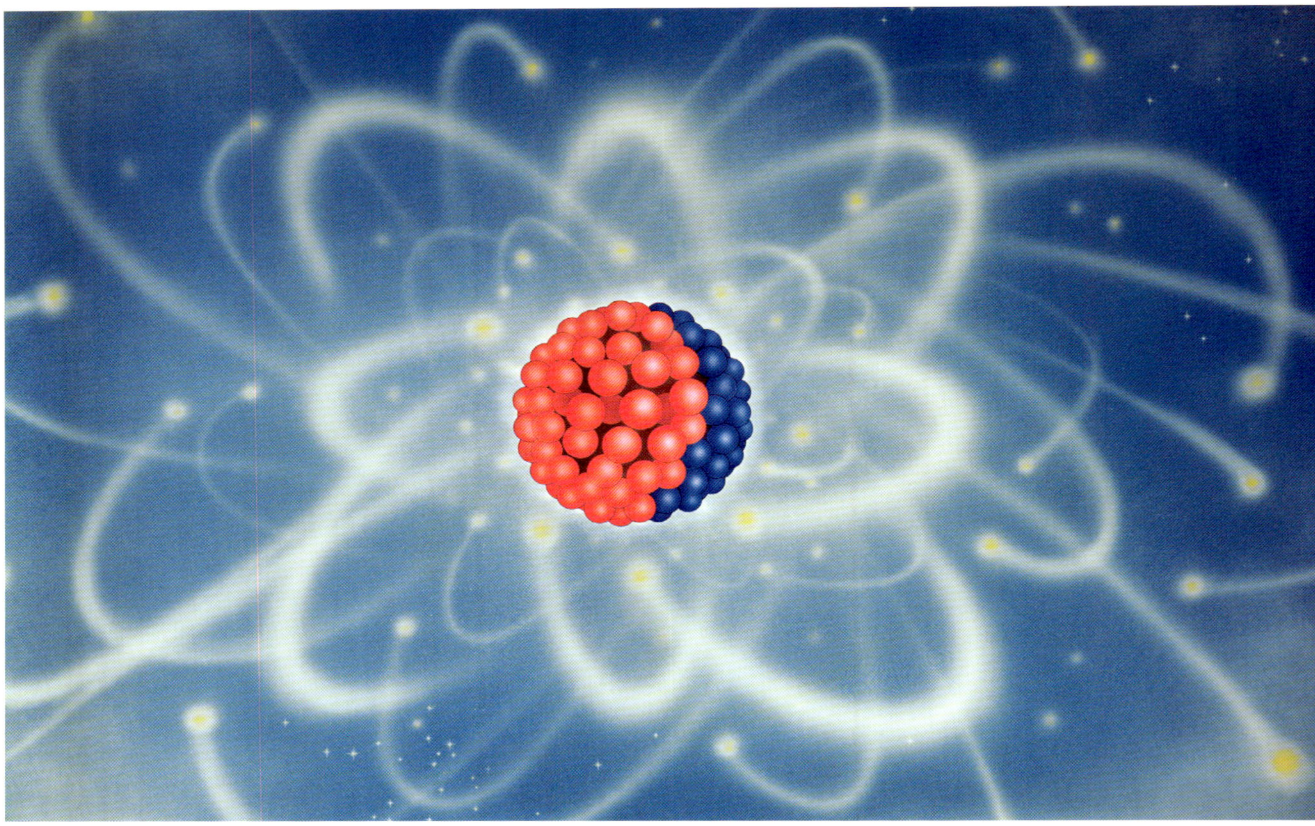

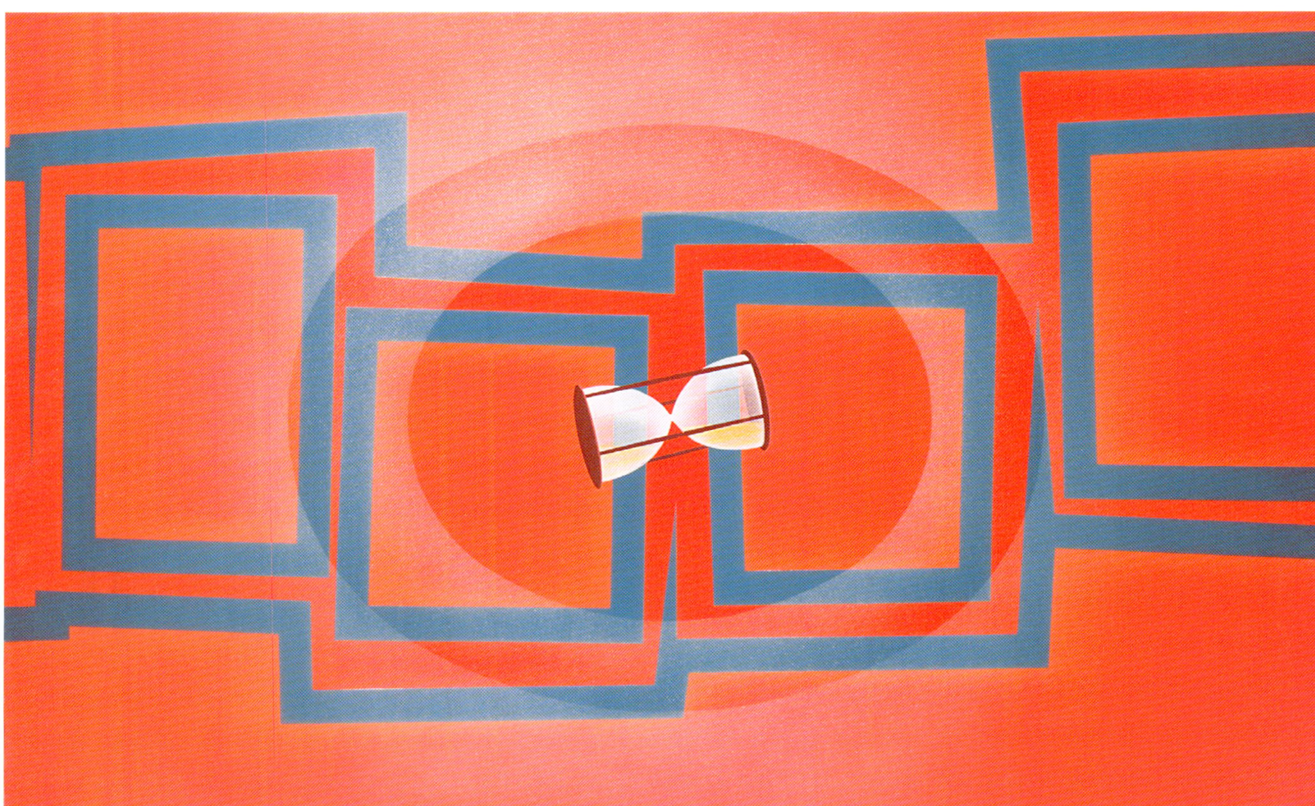

Equi-lirium, 1984.
Double-faced panel hung from the ceiling; side A and B.
Nitrocellulose lacquer on formica.
48 x 78 x 1¼" (122 x 203 x 3 cm).
GC 440.

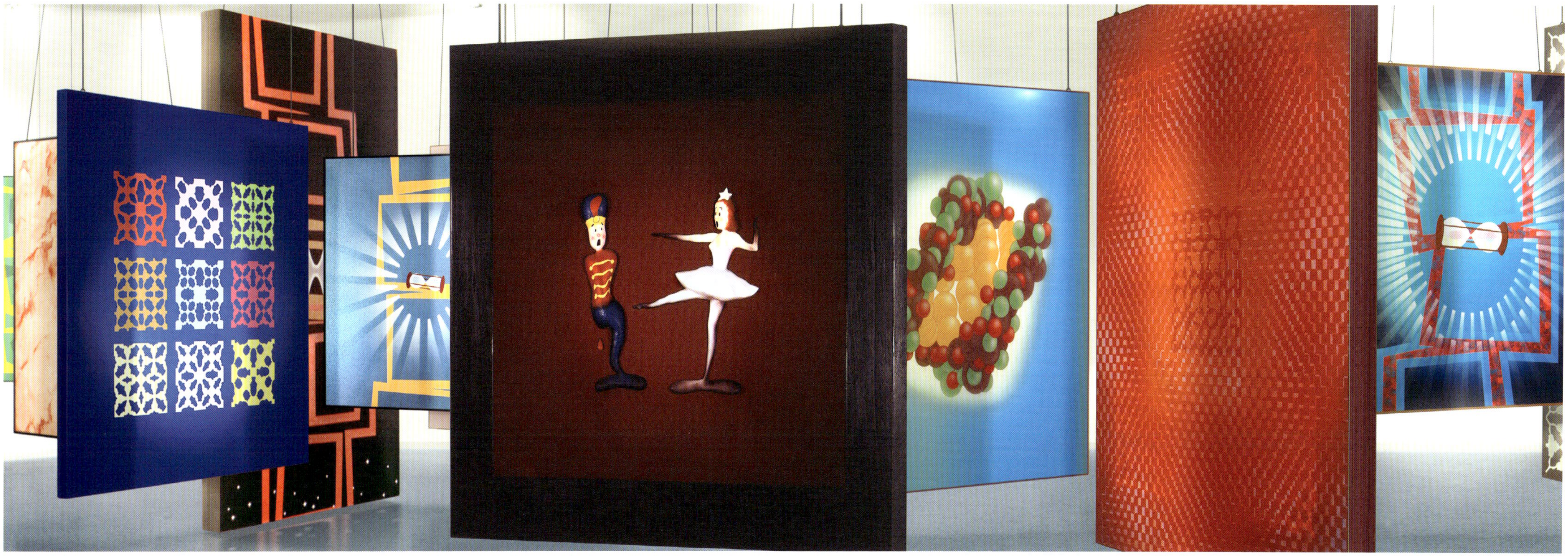

The *Destruction of a Home* exhibition (detail); Idra Duarte Gallery, Naples, 1986.
Double-faced works hung from the ceiling, 1984-86.
Mixed media, variable dimensions.

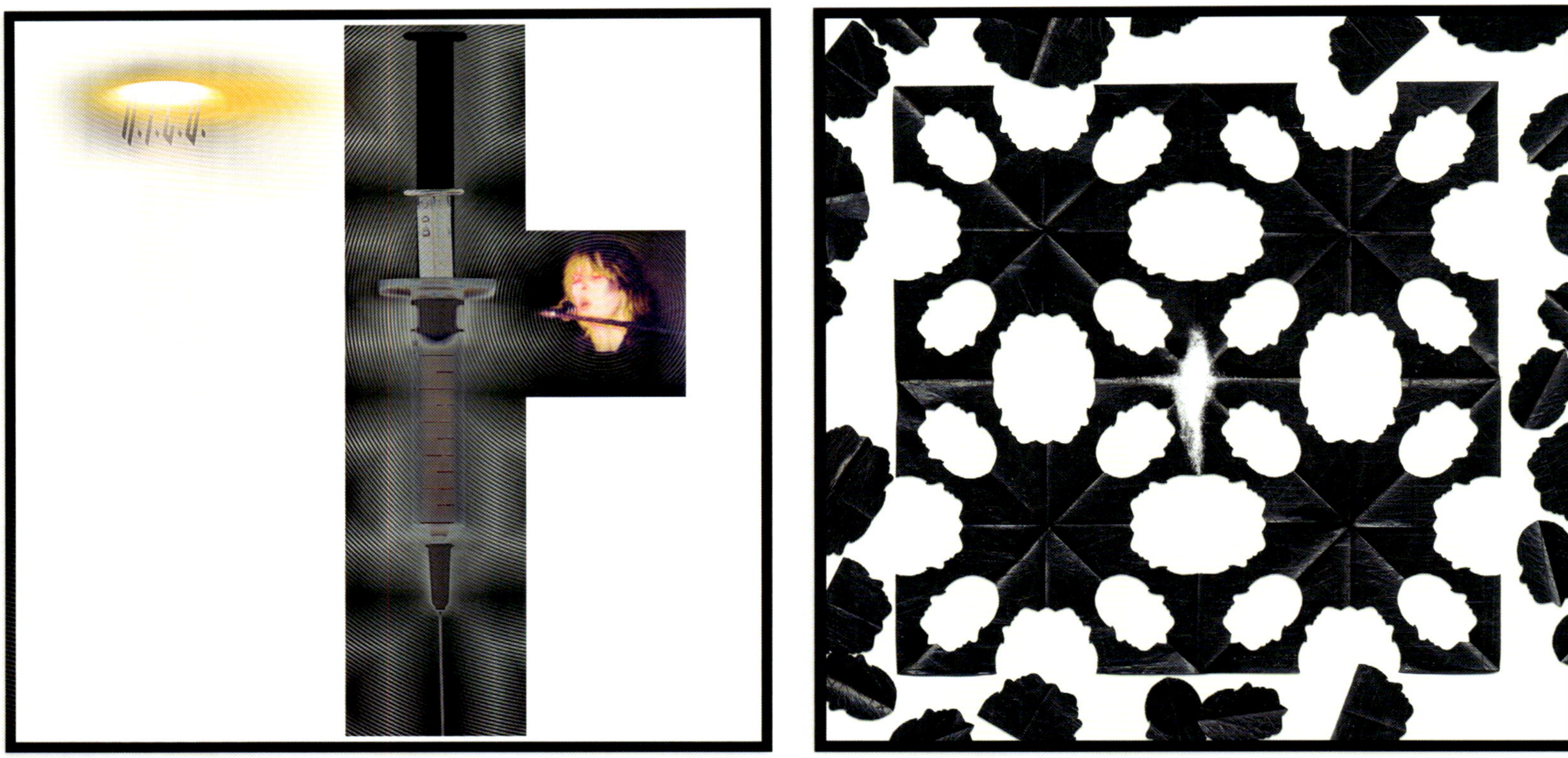

N.I.C.O. R.R.C., 1984-85.
Two separable sides, front and rear.
Acrylic and photo-elaborations on plasticized cardboard, with movable cardboard insert.
12½ x 12½" each side (31,8 x 31,8 cm).
GC 436, 437.

The Flash, 1984.
Photo of Nico just after she's shot heroin.
Toned silver gelatine print,
unnumbered edition,
variable dimension.
GC 444.

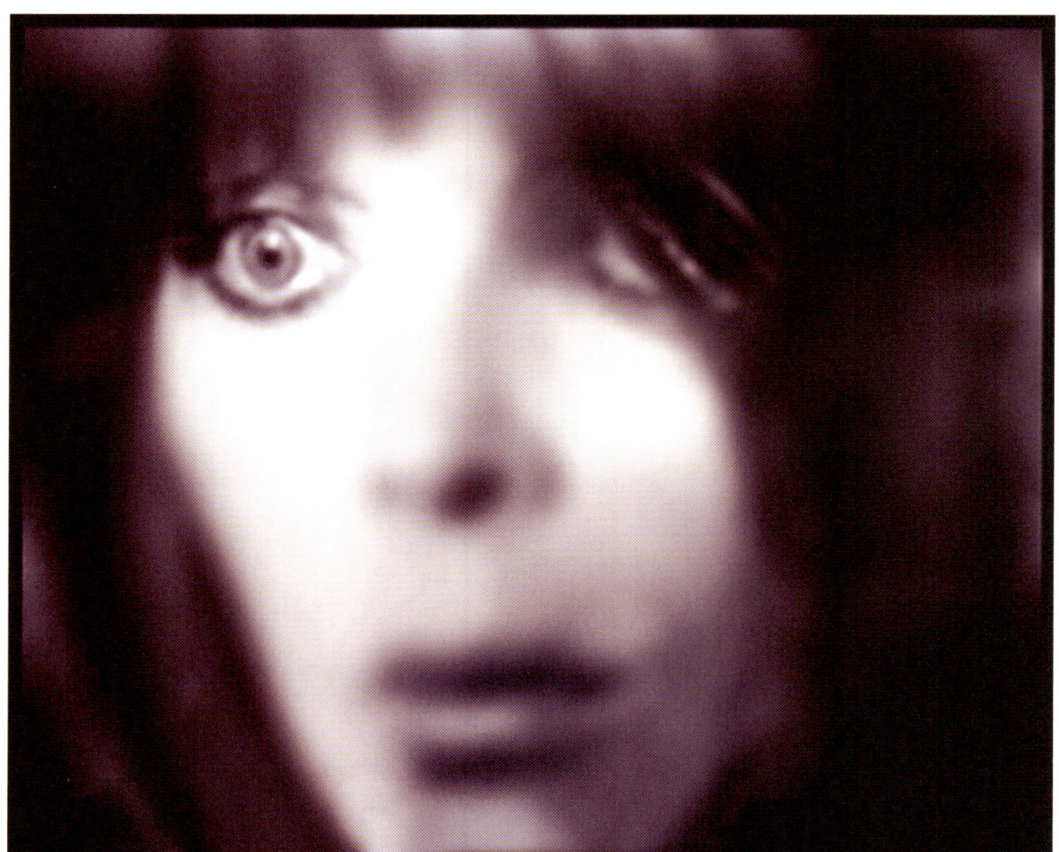

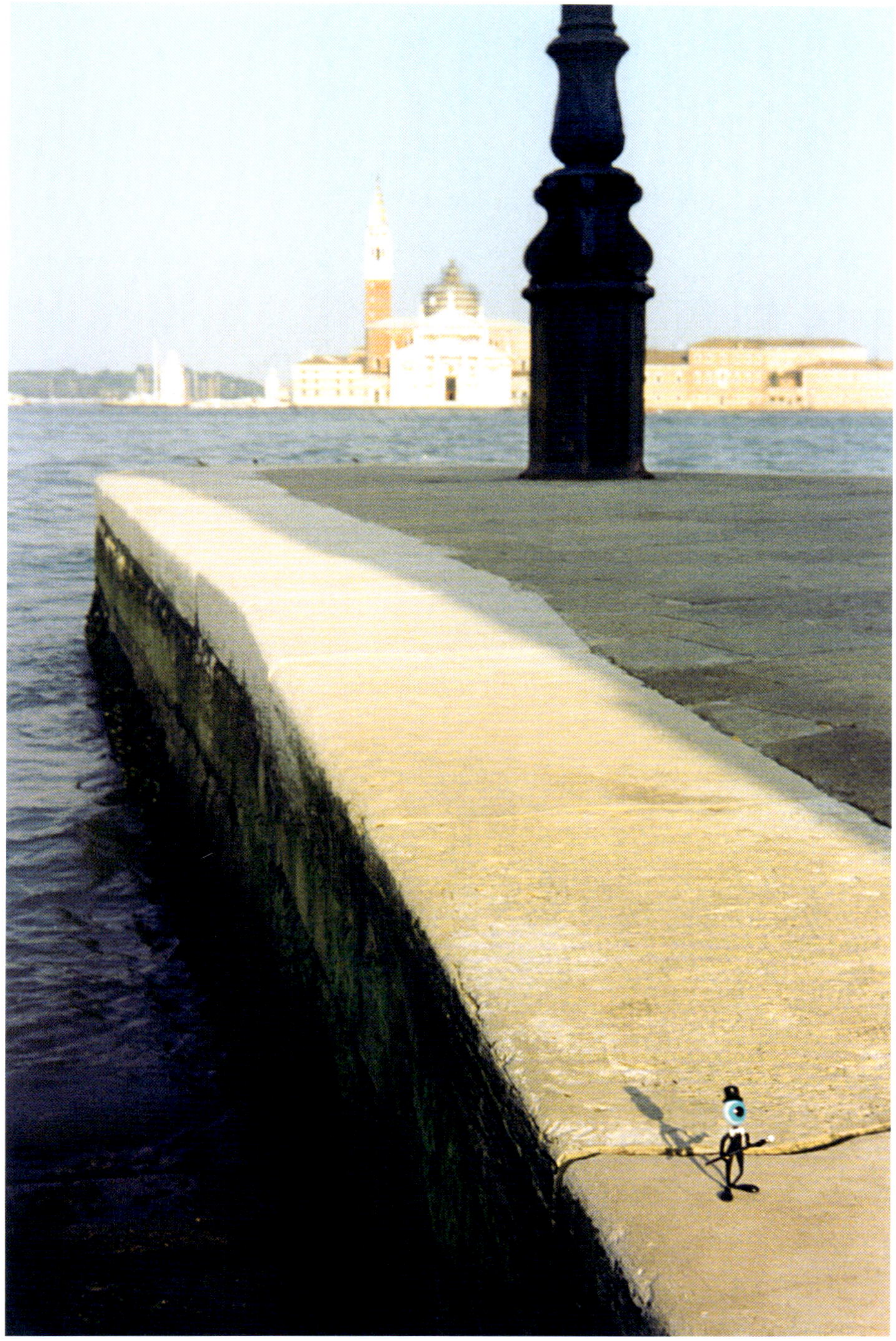

Corte & Nurcis: *Antipodespective: Resident in Venice*, 1984.
Little sculpture in Murano glass.
Ht. circa 3½" (9 cm).
GC 441.

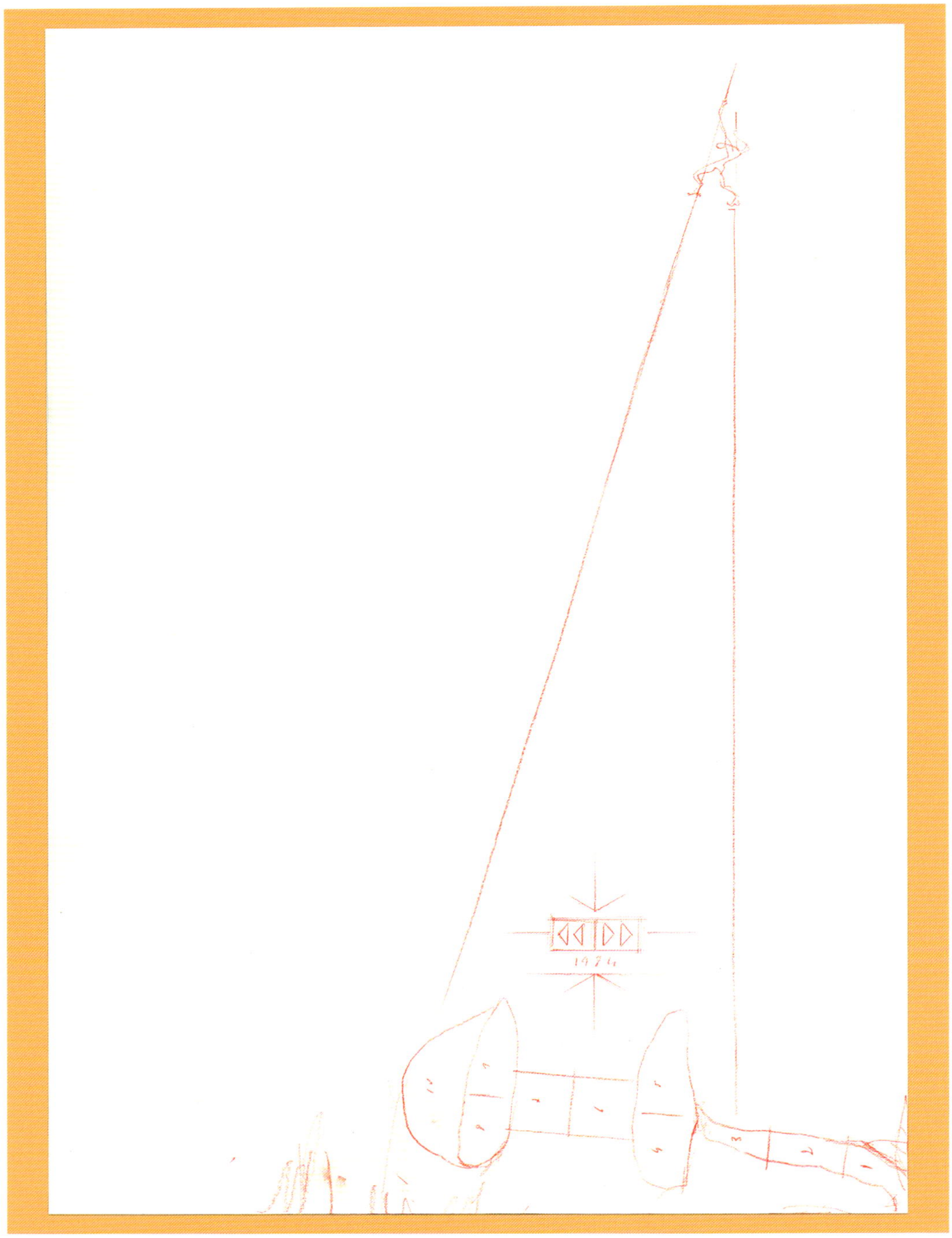

Speedspective, 1964-84.
Drawing begun at one year of age and completed at twenty-one with no visible distinction.
Colored pencil on paper.
19½ x 13¾" (49,5 x 34,7 cm).
GC 442.

Burnspective, 1984-2004.
Paper partially yellowed by sunlight over the course of twenty years; graphite strokes.
39½ x 39½" (100 x 100 cm).
GC 1580.

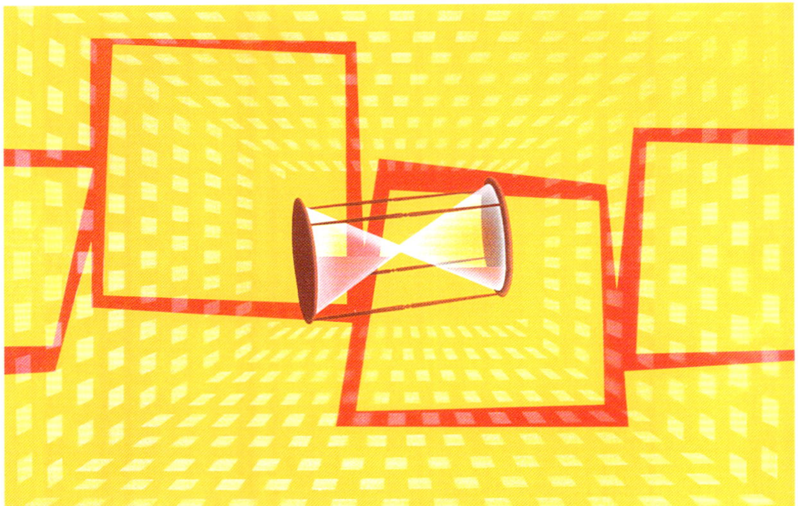

Pure Symbol, 1985. Enamel on bindakote.
27½ x 39½" (70 x 100 cm).
GC 470.

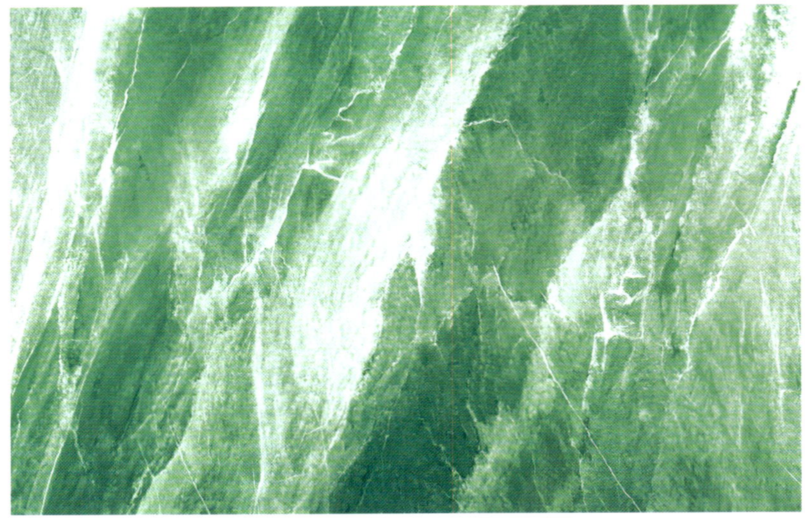

Green Marble, 1986. Enamel on bindakote.
27½ x 39½" (70 x 100 cm).
GC 476.

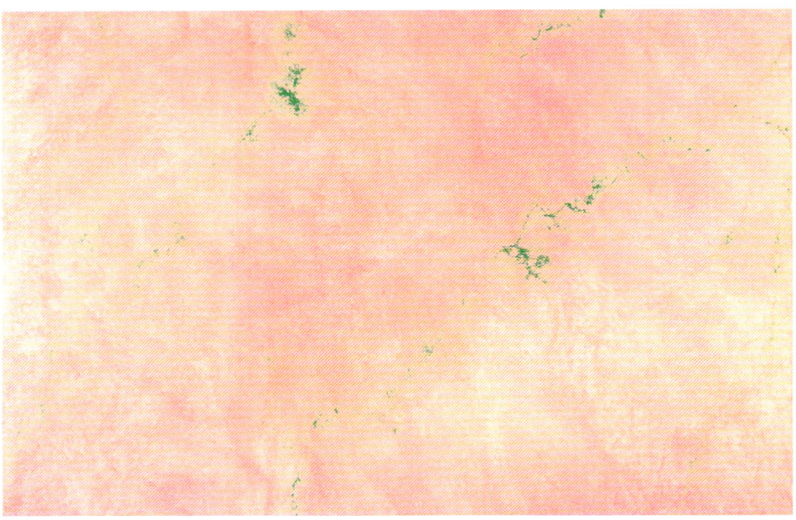

Pink Marble with Profile, 1986. Enamel on bindakote.
27½ x 39½" (70 x 100 cm).
GC 477.

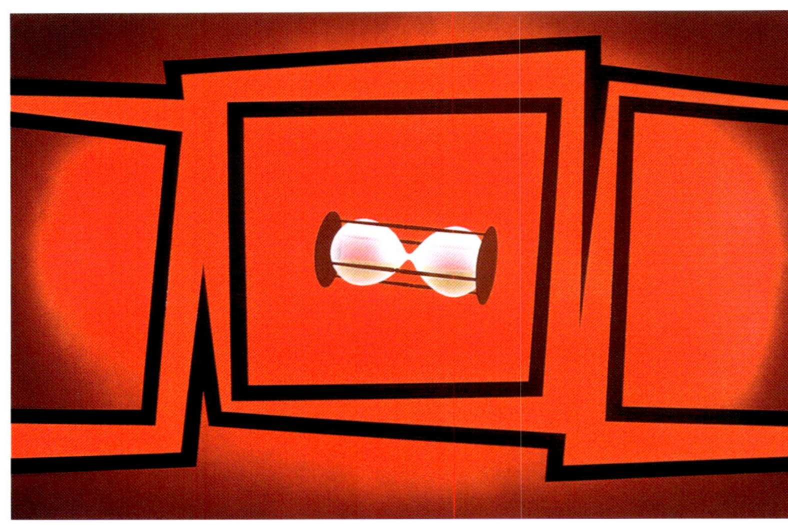

Brain, 1985. Enamel on bindakote.
27½ x 39½" (70 x 100 cm).
GC 471.

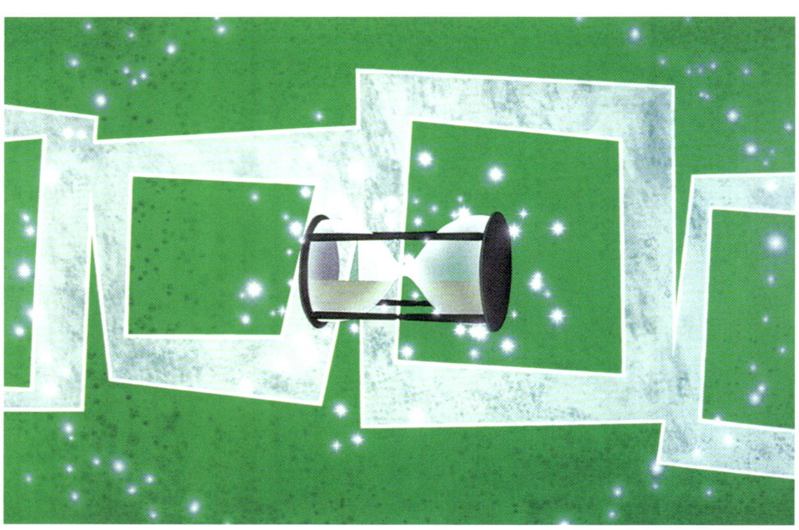

Hemispheres, 1985. Enamel on bindakote (detail).
19¾ x 39½" (50 x 100 cm).
GC 472.

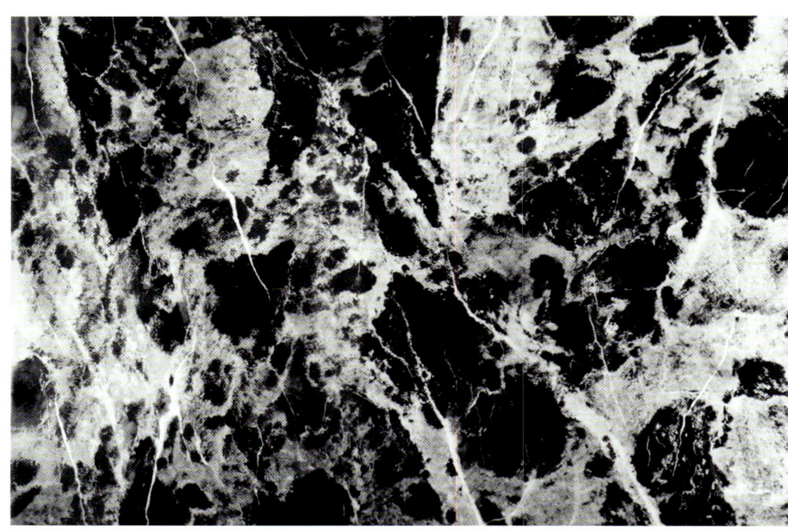

Obscure Marble, 1986. Enamel on bindakote.
27½ x 39½" (70 x 100 cm).
GC 475.

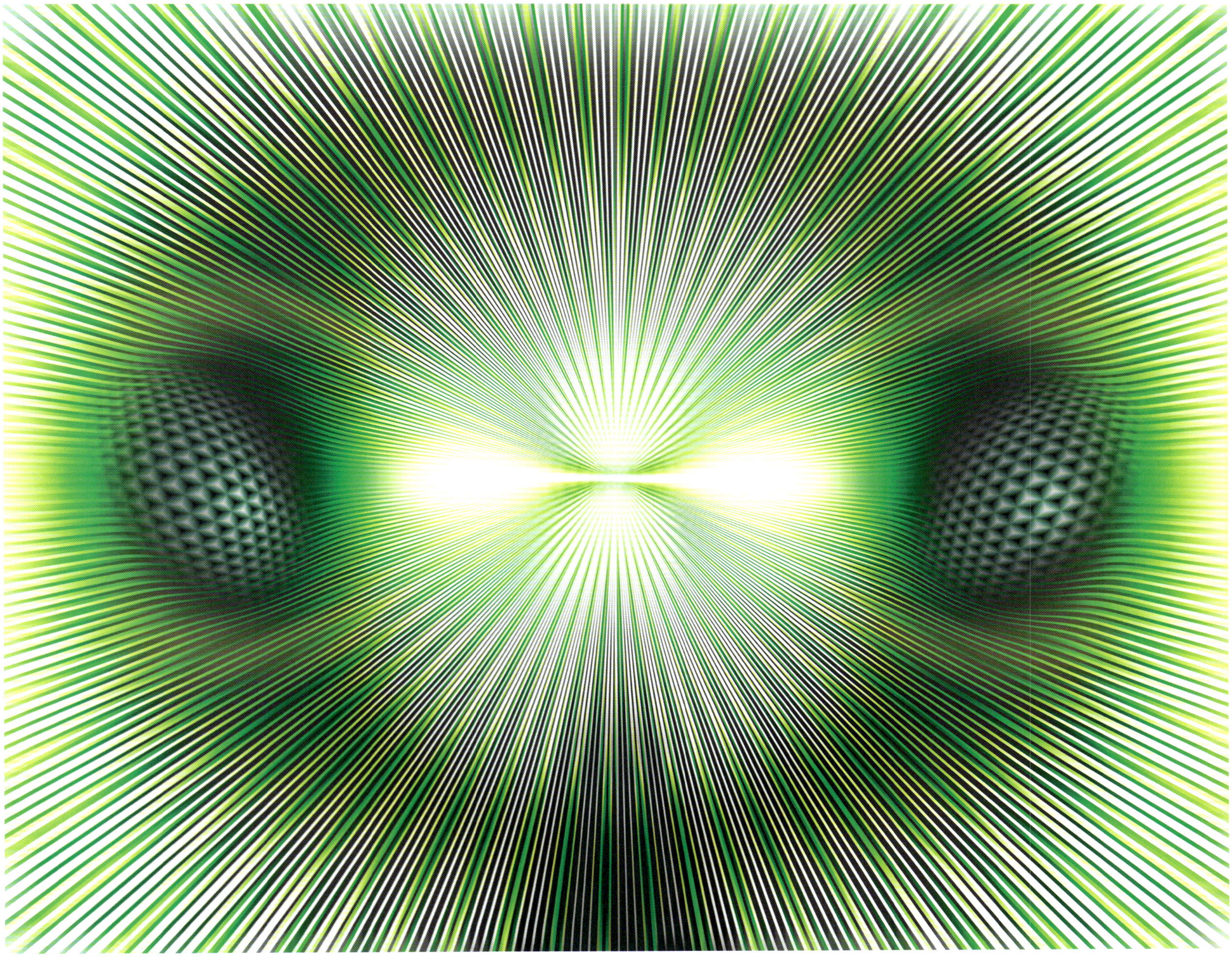

C(L)ep(S)y(D)ra, 1989.
Acrylic and silkscreen on formica.
55¼ x 68¾" (140 x 175 cm).
GC 625.

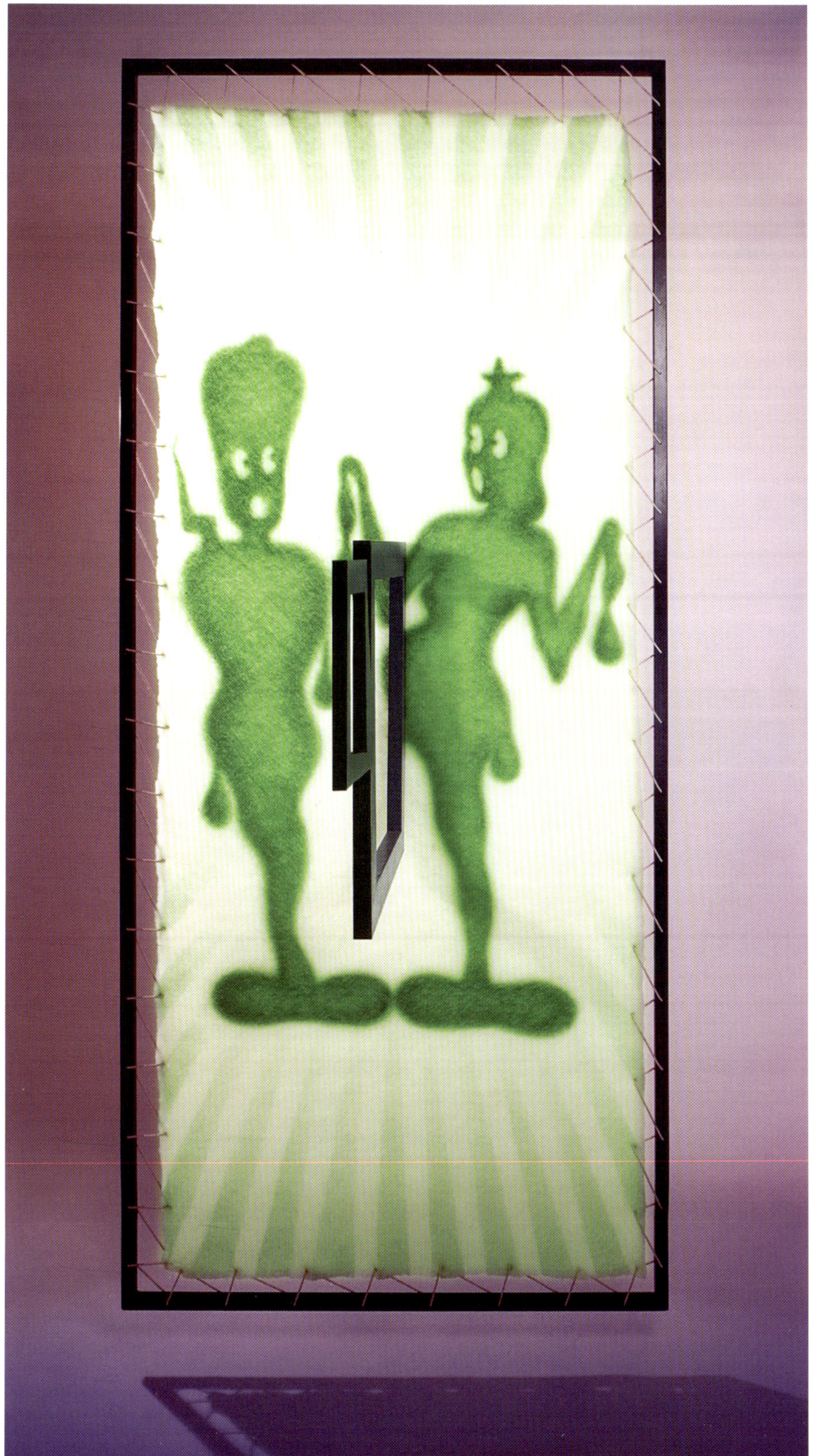

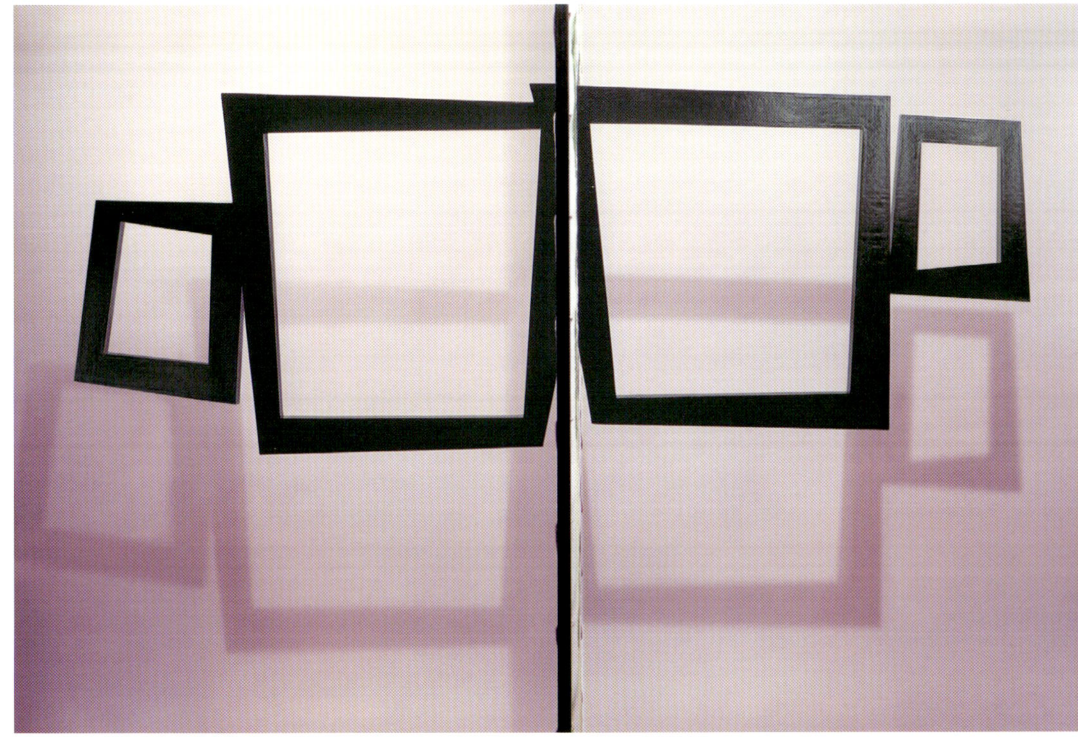

Psychic Lemurs, 1985. Front view (left) and detail of side view (top right).
Enamel on synthetic wool;
polycarbonate structure in snake-skin pattern;
rope; iron frame hung from the ceiling.
108¼ x 47¾ x 92¼" (275 x 121 x 234 cm).
GC 466.

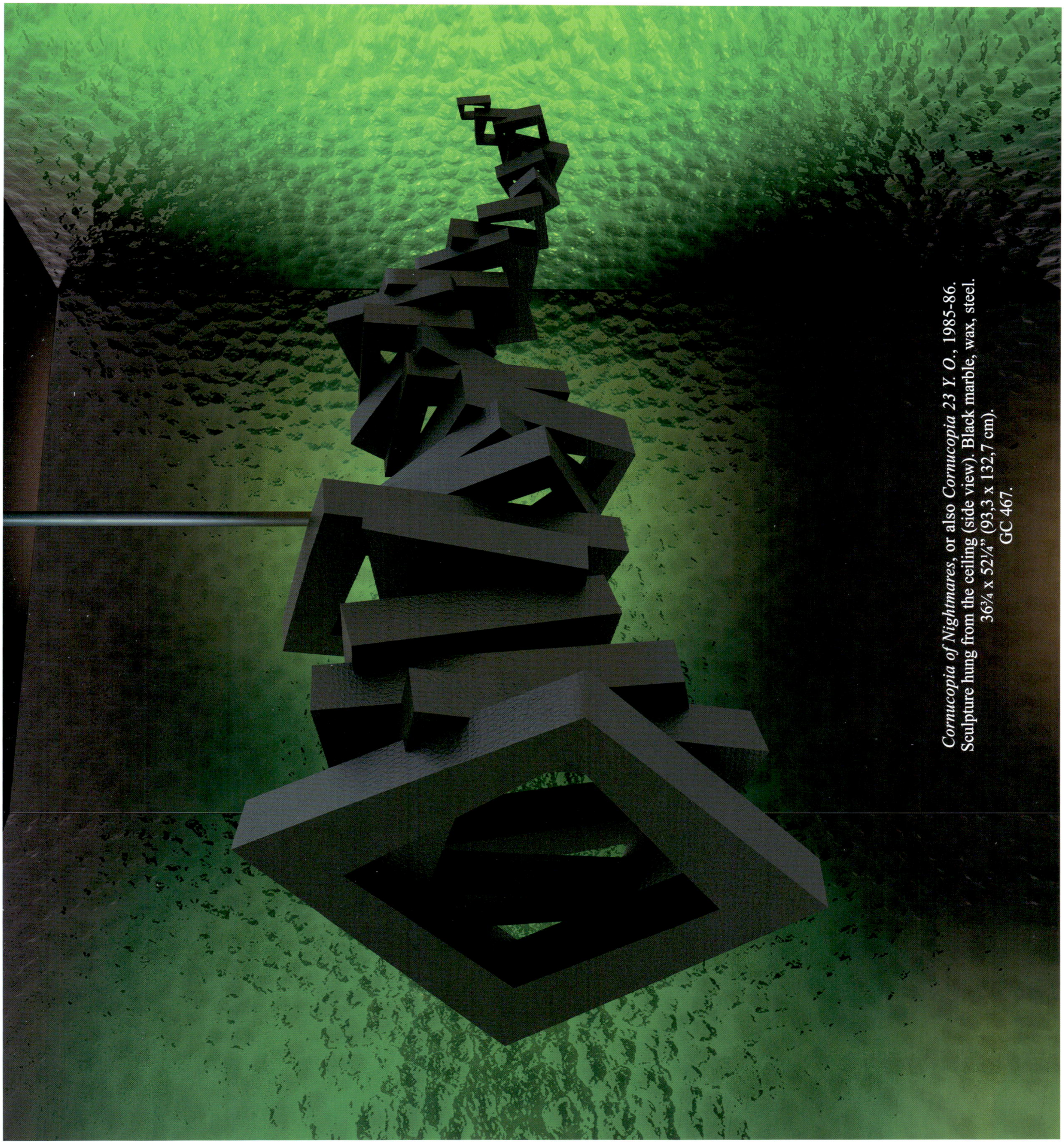

Cornucopia of Nightmares, or also *Cornucopia 23 Y. O.*, 1985-86.
Sculpture hung from the ceiling (side view). Black marble, wax, steel.
36¾ x 52¼" (93,3 x 132,7 cm).
GC 467.

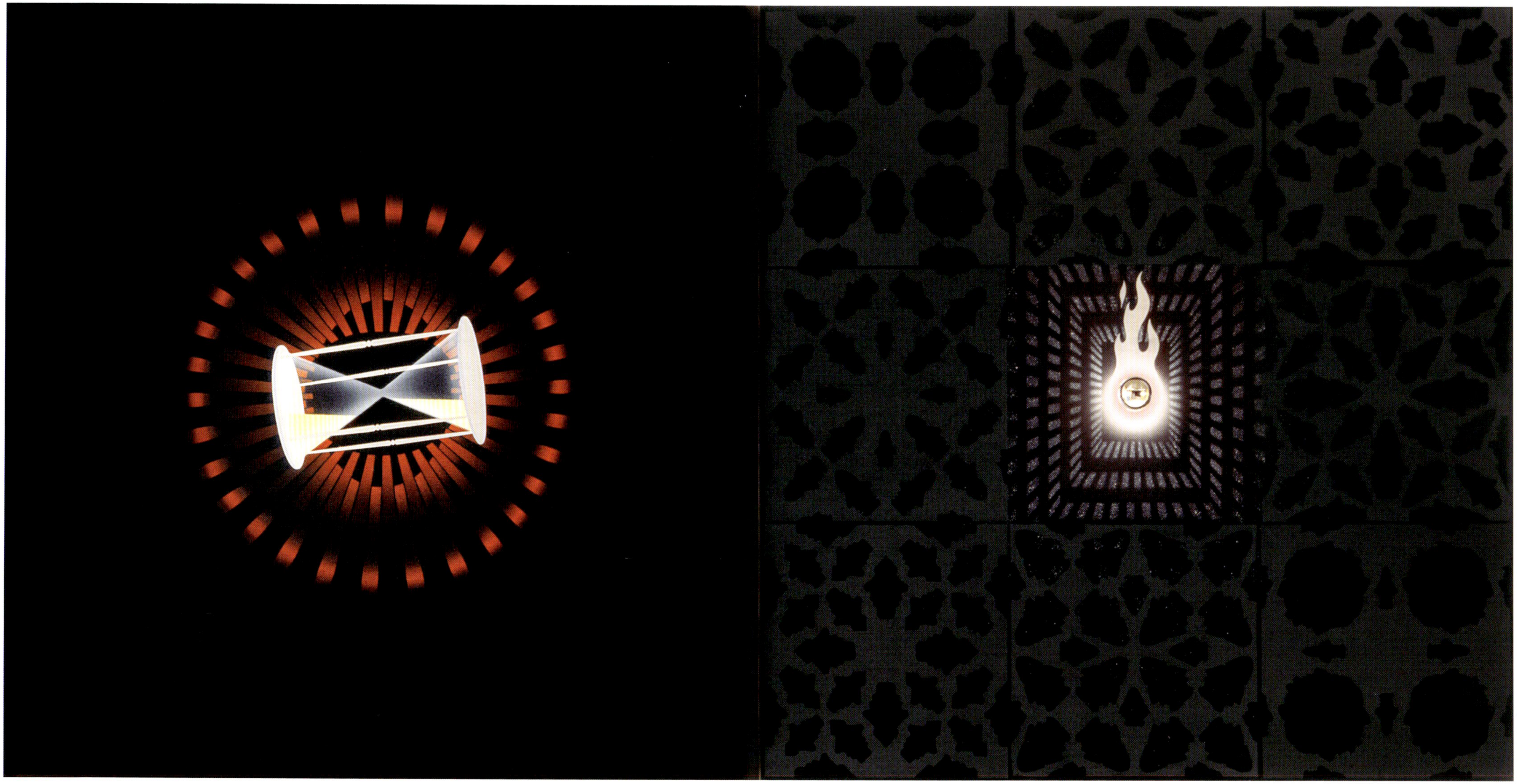

Cross Fade - The Abstraction of the Petroleum, 1987.
Nitrocellulose lacquer, silver enamel, black tissue paper cutouts and concave mirror on two openable panels in reflecting black formica, joined by hidden hinges.
Open: 39½ x 78¾ x 1” (100 x 200 x 2,5 cm). Closed: 39½ x 39½ x 2” (100 x 100 x 5 cm).
GC 530.

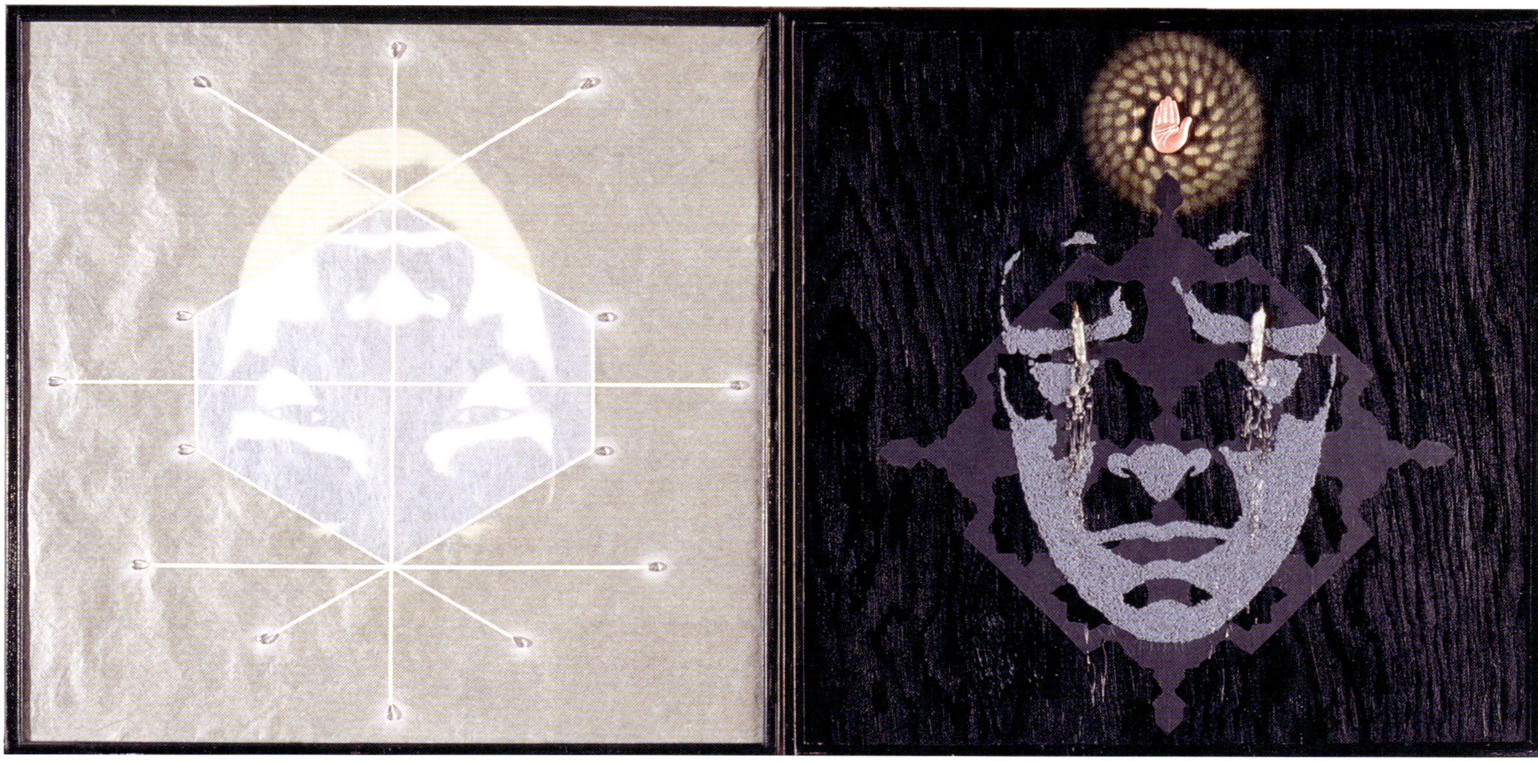

Directions, signals, headlights always out, 1987. Two openable panels joined by hidden hinges.
Enamel, acrylic with sand, glass drops, black tissue paper cutout
on wood, clay and parchment-like paper.
Open: 17¾ x 35½ x 1½” (45 x 90 x 3,6 cm). Closed: 17¾ x 17¾ x 3” (45 x 45 x 7,5 cm).
GC 532.

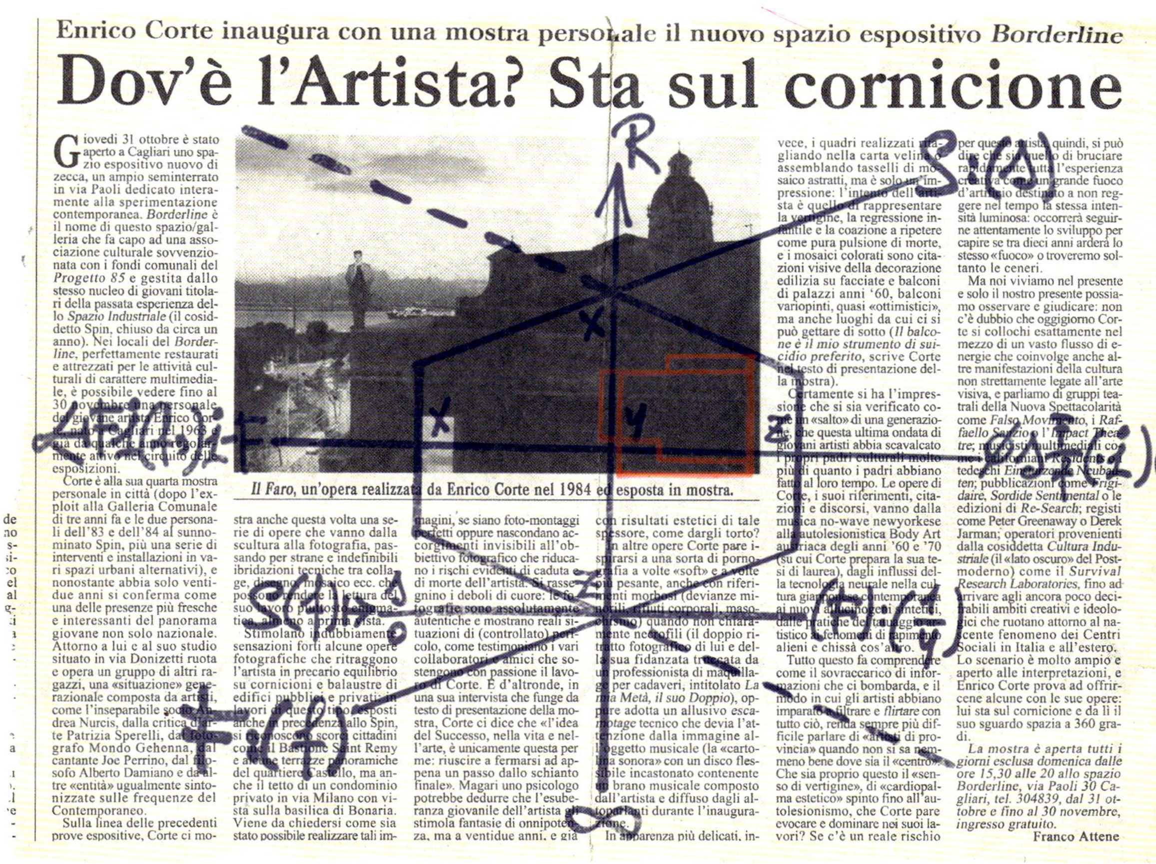

The Formula for Success, 1985.
Ink on newspaper cutting.
8¼ x 11¼” (21 x 28,5 cm).
SC 260.

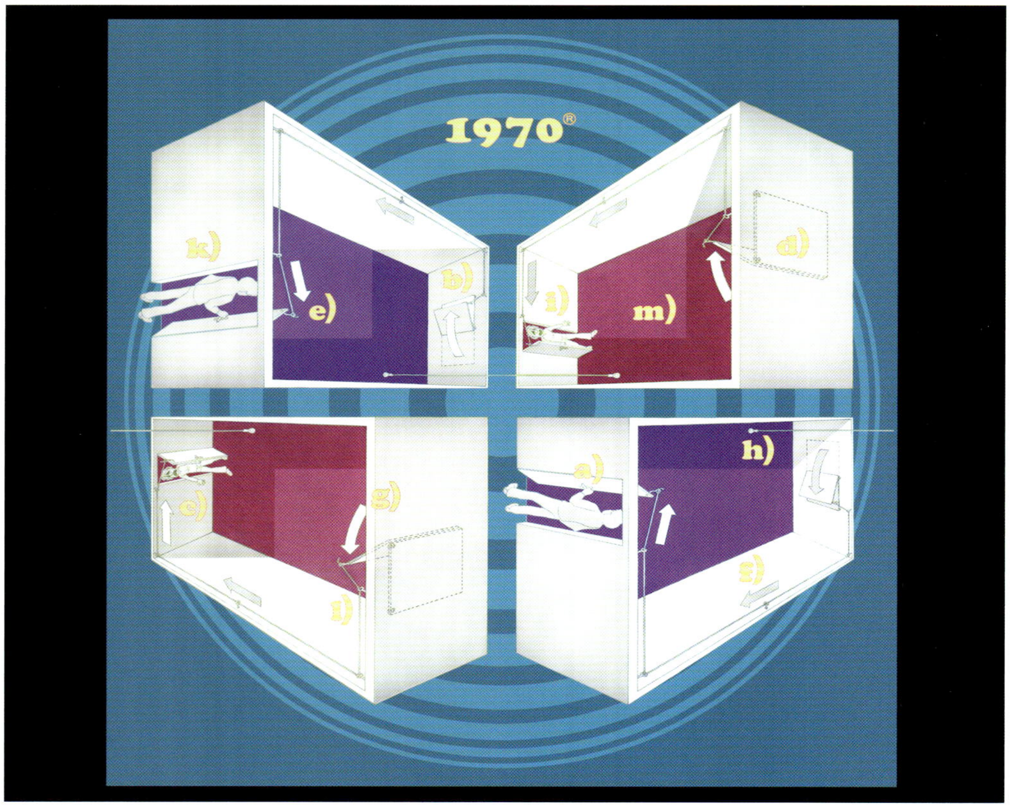

Installation Project of the Cross Fades as a Spectrospective of Human Destiny, 1987.
Silkscreen and enamel on paper; black formica.
39½ x 51½" (100 x 130 cm).
GC 528.

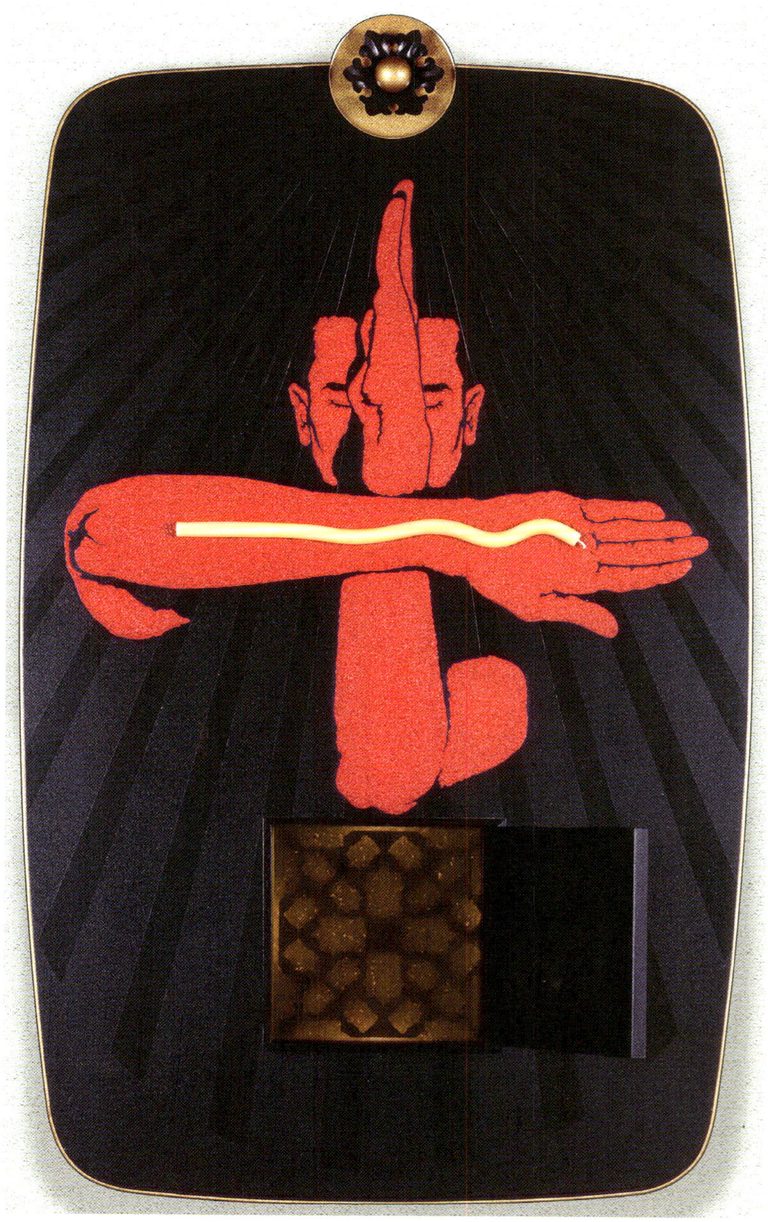

Dismeasurement of the Space, 1987.
Lacquer, flatting, acrylic with sand on formica, plexiglas, iron; warped wax candle; openable door with internal lighting.
50 x 30 x 3½" (127 x 76 x 9 cm).
GC 537.

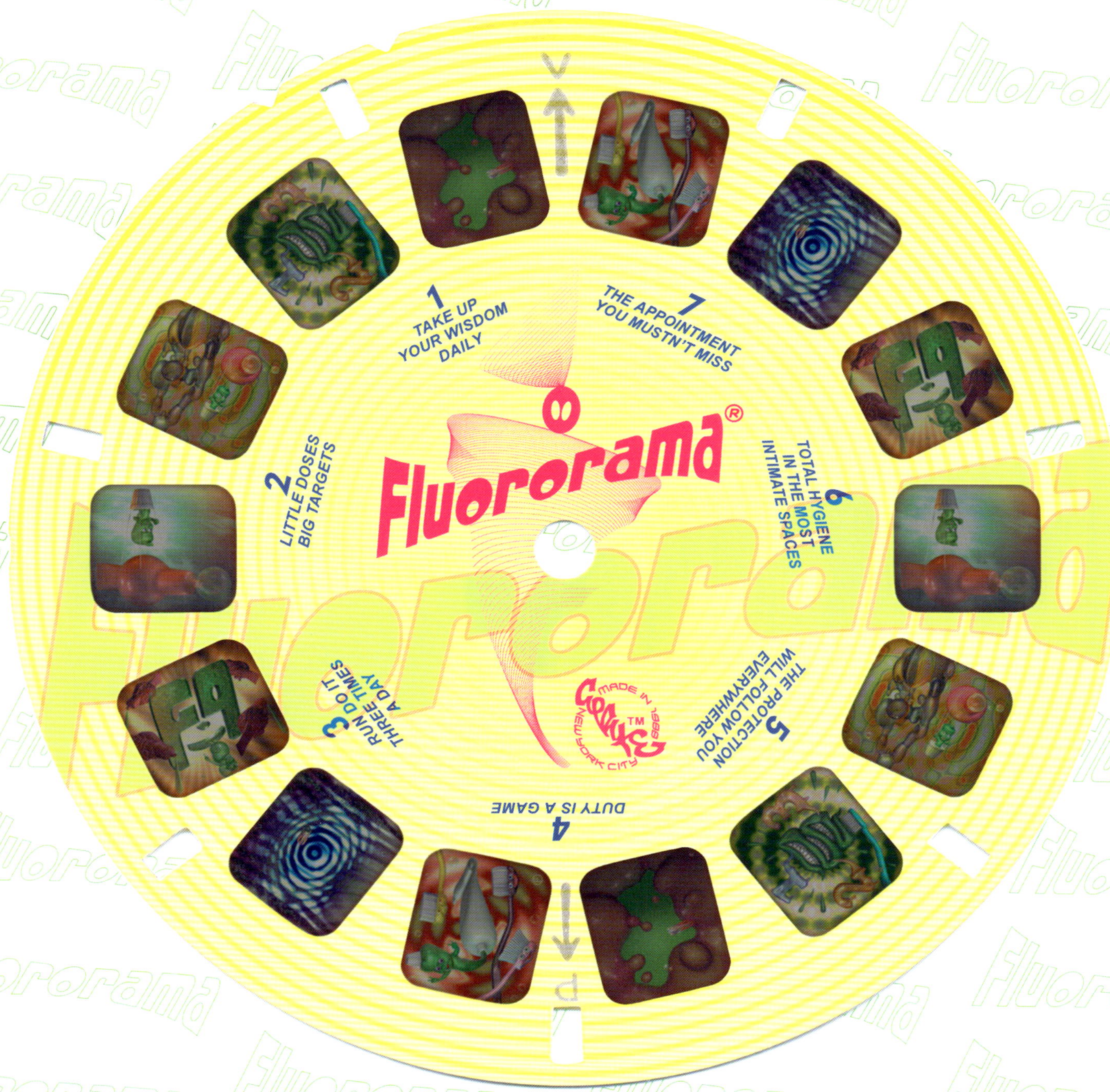

Fluororama Reel, 1988 (re-created in 1996).
Print on plasticated cardboard
with 7 pairs of stereoscopic color slides.
Diam. 3½" (9 cm).
GC 565.

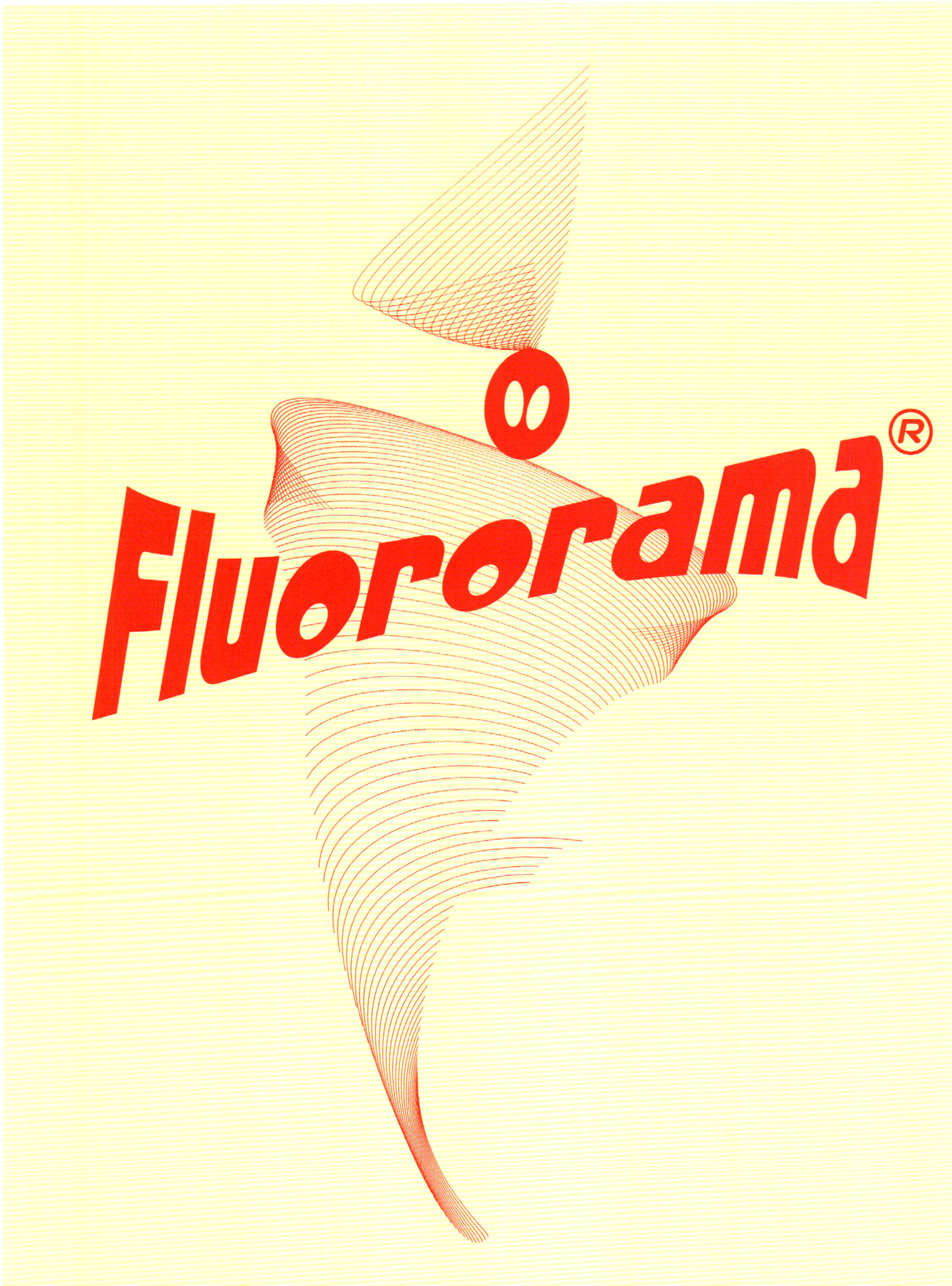

Fluororama Logo, 1988.
Silkscreen on pvc.
59 x 42½" (150 x 107,6 cm).
GC 564.

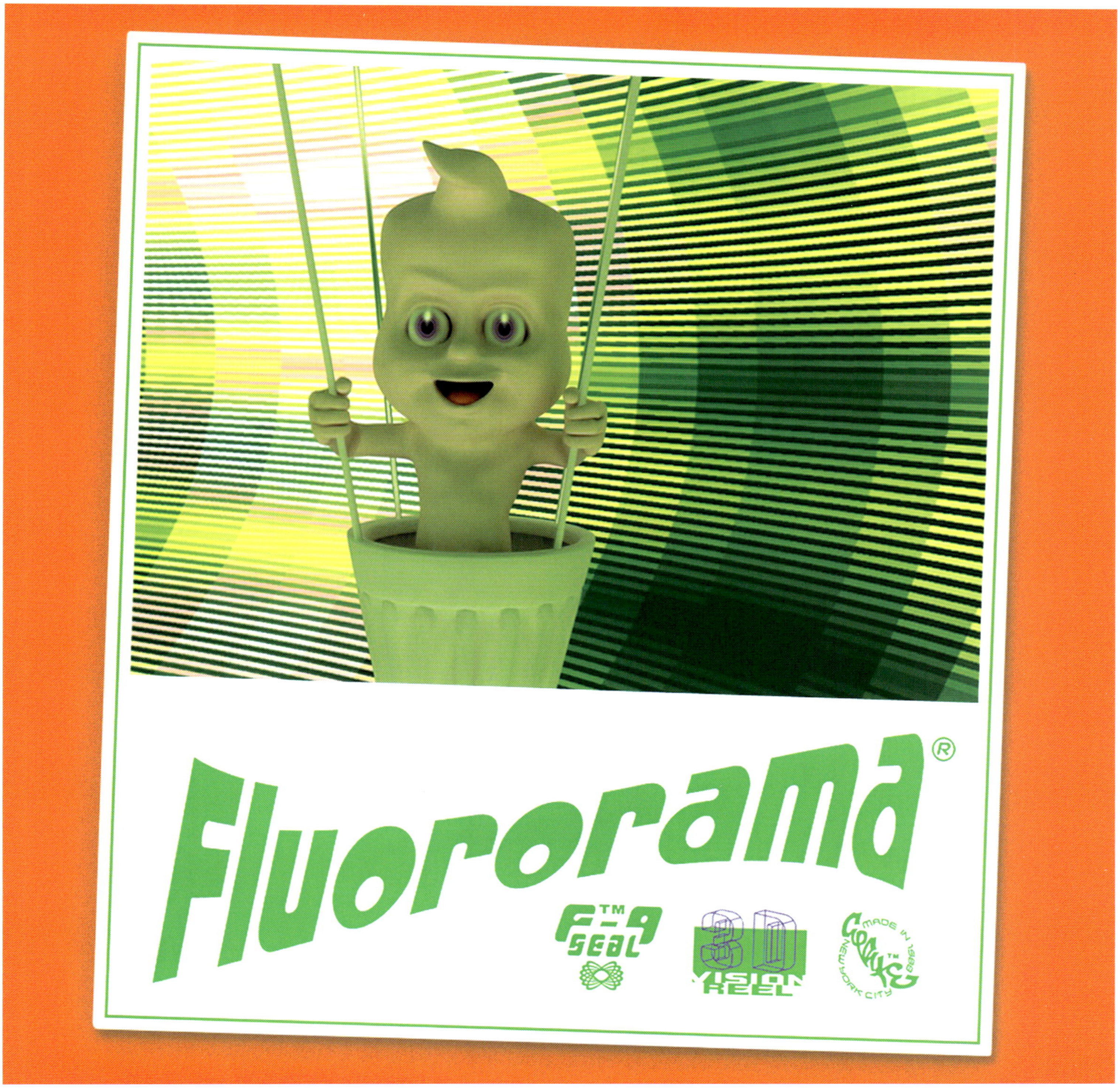

Fluororama Promo Card and/or *Promo Poster*, 1996.
Card: print on plasticized cardboard. Unnumbered edition. $11\frac{3}{4}$ x $10\frac{1}{4}$" (30 x 26,2 cm).
Poster: lambda print on paper. Unnumbered edition. $47\frac{1}{4}$ x $41\frac{1}{4}$" (120 x 105 cm).
GC 926.

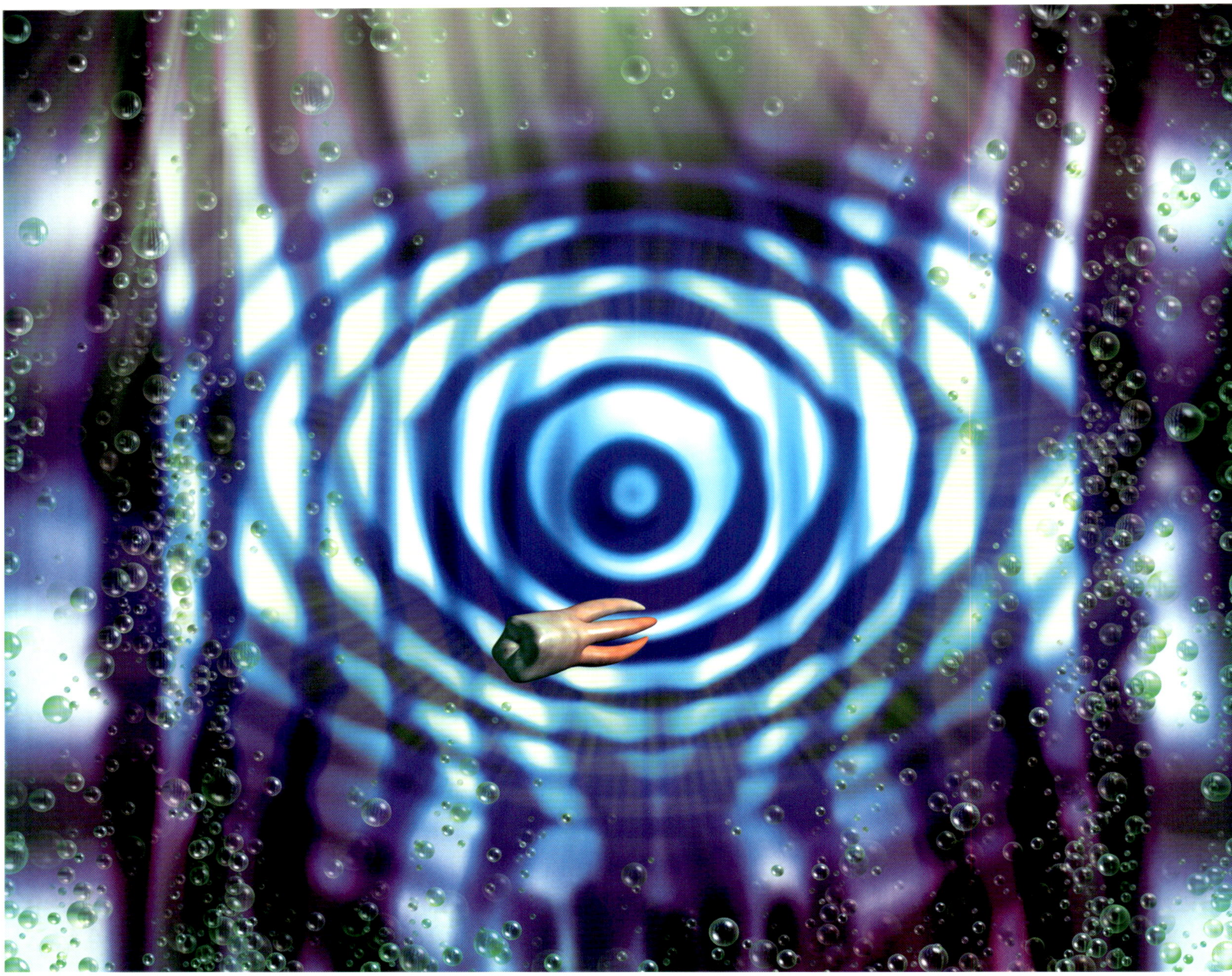

The protection will follow you everywhere, 1996
(digital version from the original 1988 *Fluororama* series).
Lambda print and cibachrome.
31¾ x 39½” (80,5 x 100 cm).
GC 931.

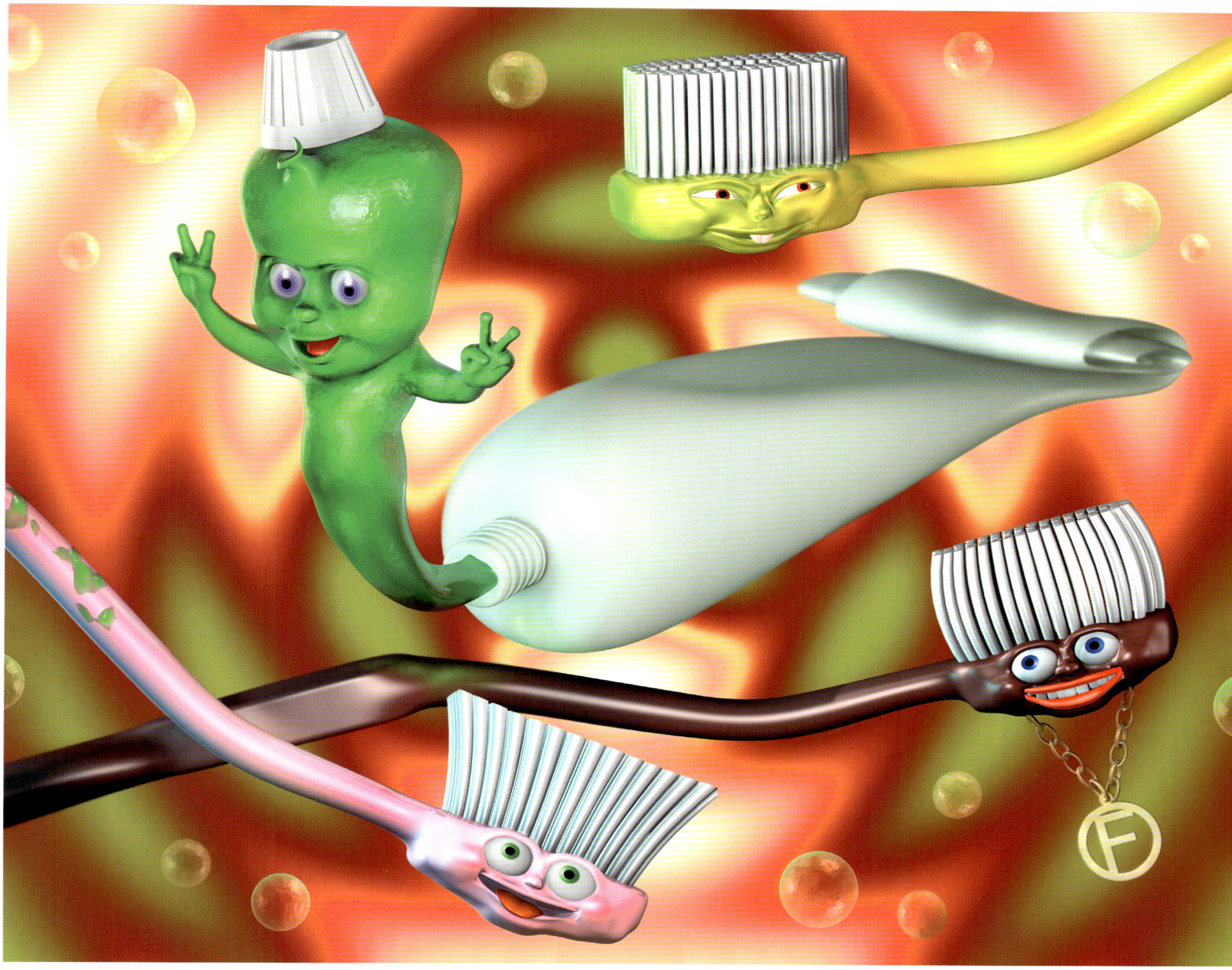

Little doses, big targets, 1996
(digital version from the original 1988 *Fluororama* series).
Lambda print and cibachrome.
31½ x 39½" (80 x 100 cm).
GC 928.

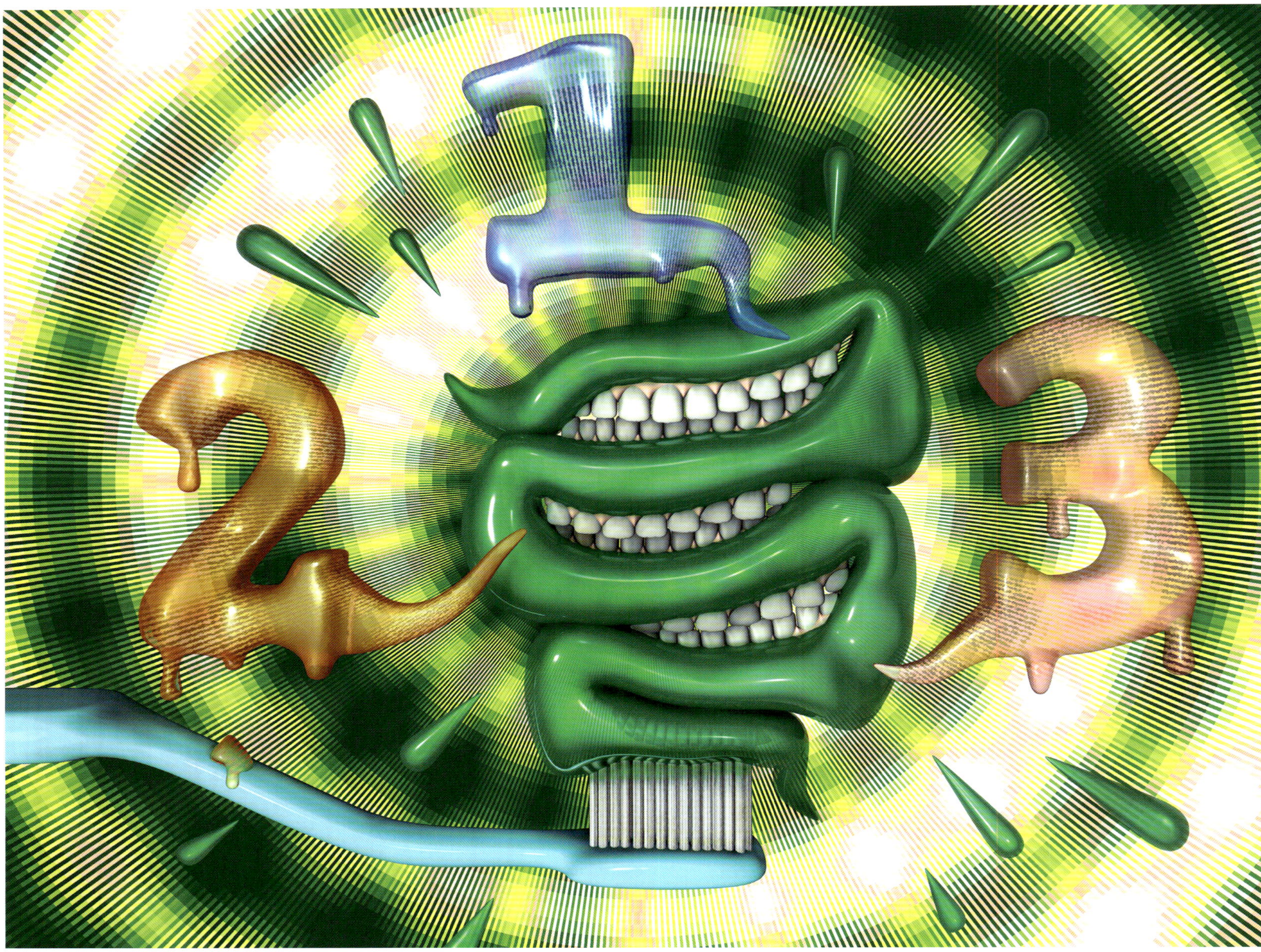

Run do it three times a day, 1996
(digital version from the original 1988 *Fluororama* series).
Lambda print and cibachrome.
30¼ x 39½" (76,6 x 100 cm).
GC 929.

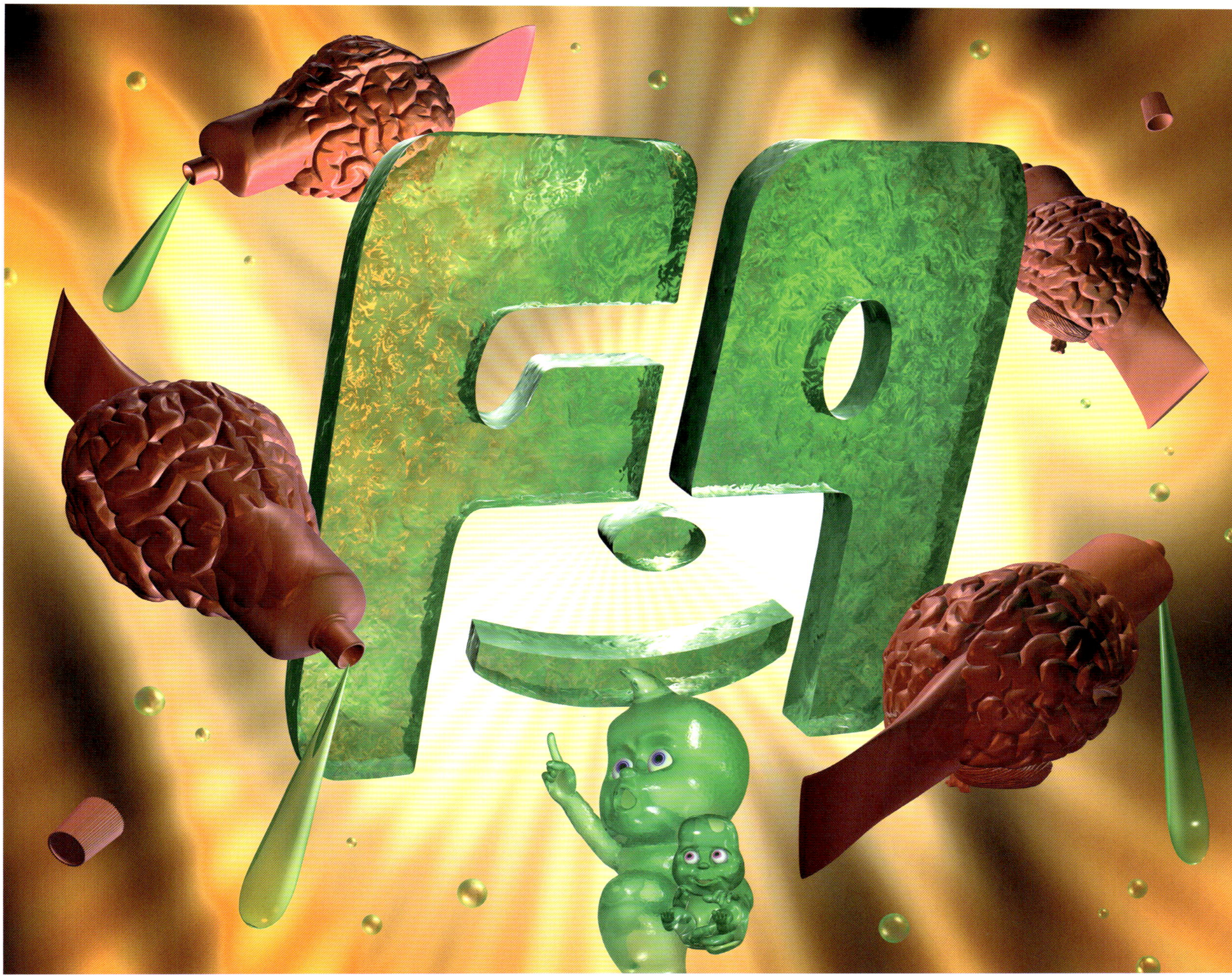

Take up your wisdom daily, 1996
(digital version from the original 1988 *Fluororama* series).
Lambda print and cibachrome.
31¾ x 39½" (80,8 x 100 cm).
GC 927.

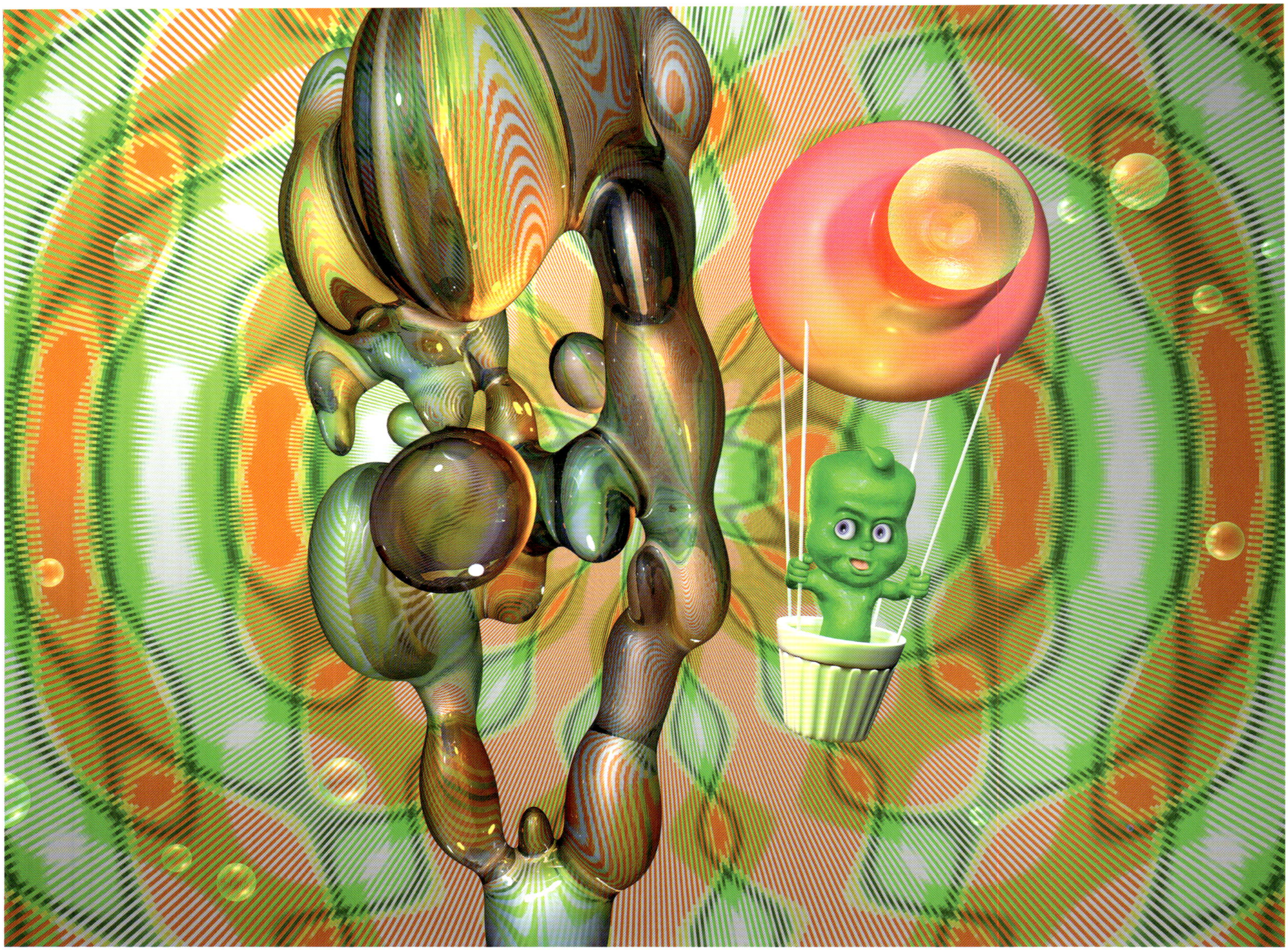

The appointment you mustn't miss, 1996
(digital version from the original 1988 *Fluororama* series).
Lambda print and cibachrome.
30 x 39½" (76 x 100 cm).
GC 933.

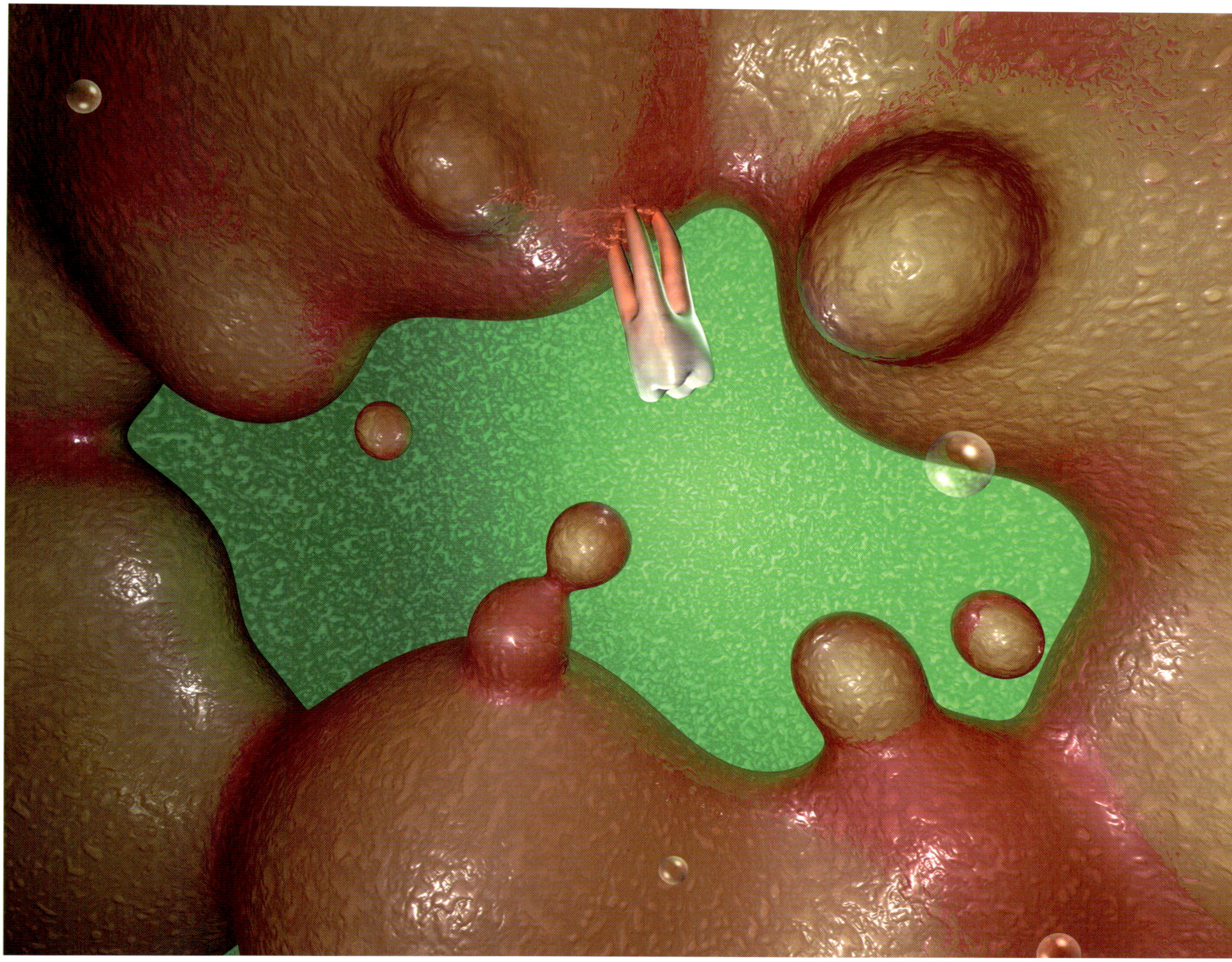

Total hygiene in the most intimate spaces, 1996
(digital version from the original 1988 *Fluororama* series).
Lambda print and cibachrome.
31¼ x 39½" (79,5 x 100 cm).
GC 932.

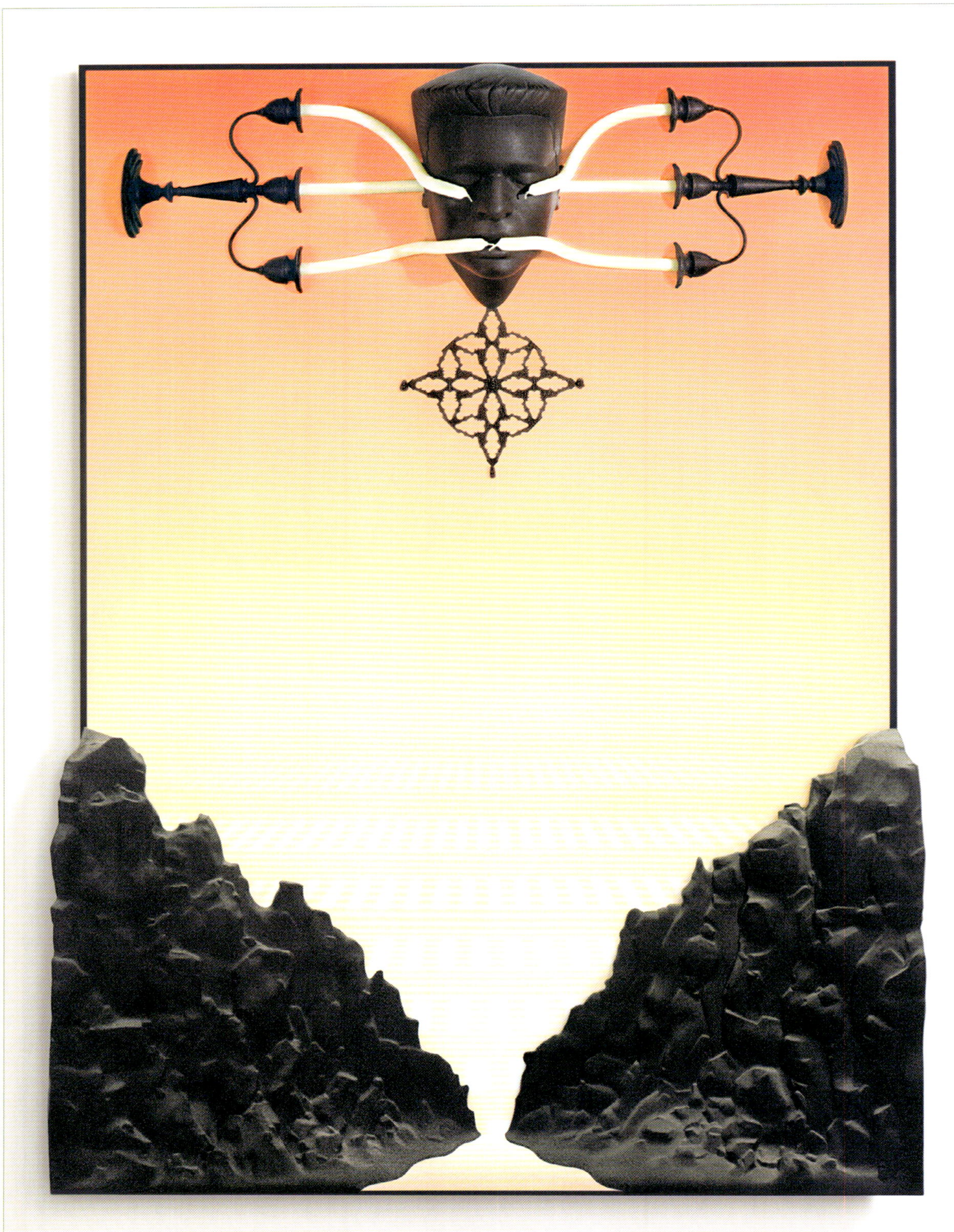

25 Seconds, 1989.
Nitrocellulose lacquer on plexiglas, fiberglass, pvc,
with paper cutout and warped wax candles.
54½ x 41½ x 6¾" (138 x 105 x 17 cm).
GC 617.

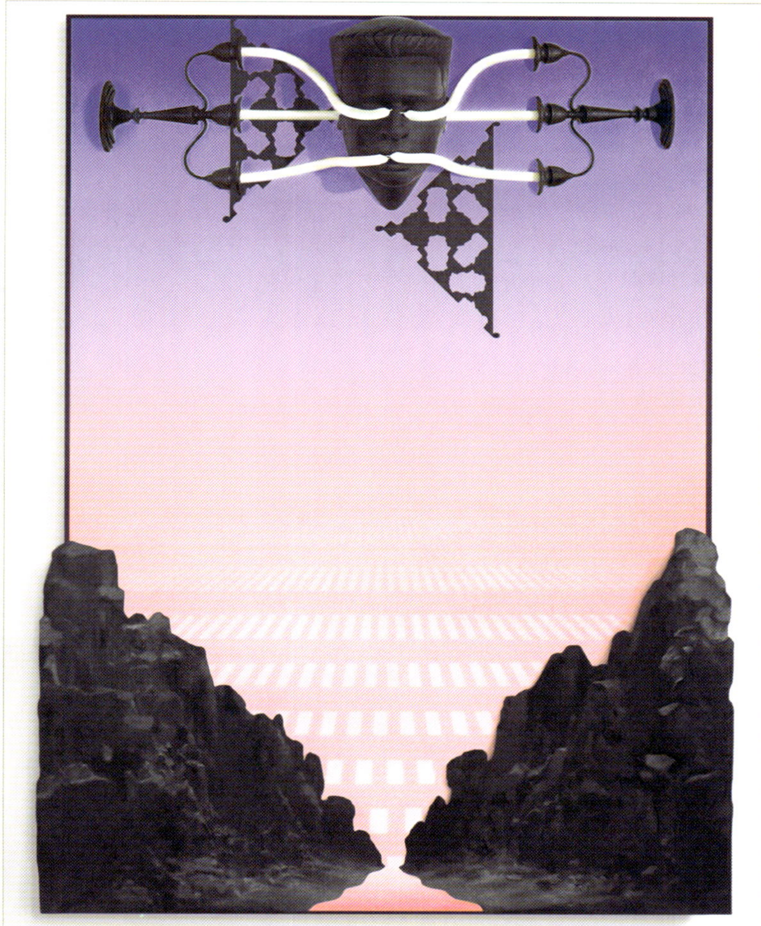

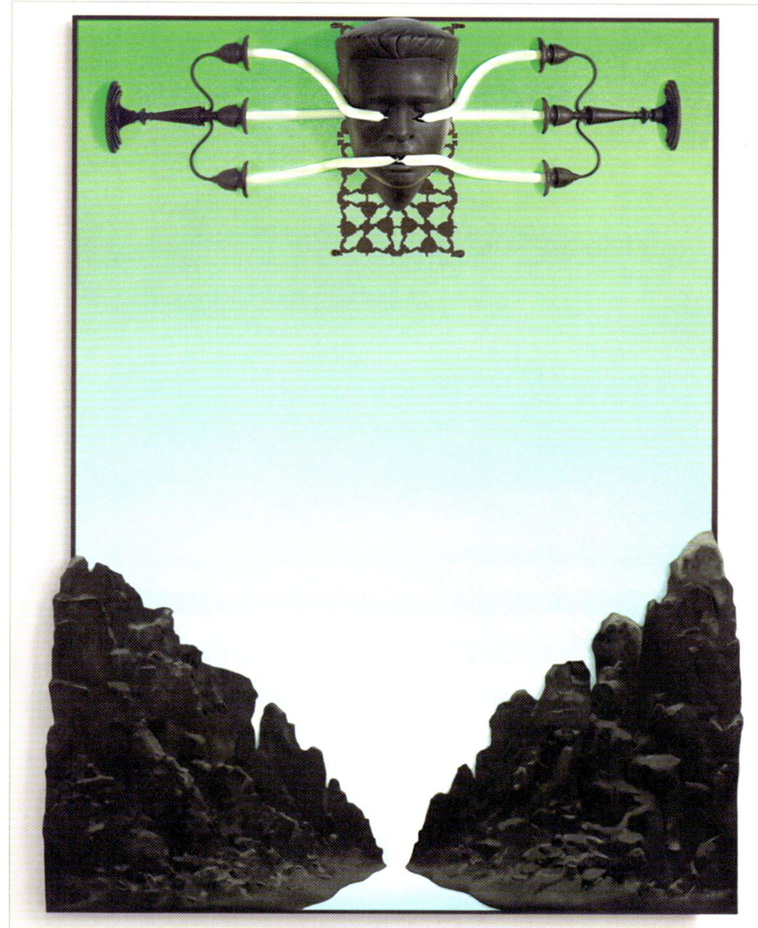

25¼ Seconds (left) and *25½ Seconds* (right), 1989.
Nitrocellulose lacquer on plexiglas, fiberglass, pvc,
with paper cutouts and warped wax candles.
54½ x 41½ x 6¾" each (138 x 105 x 17 cm).
GC 618, 619.

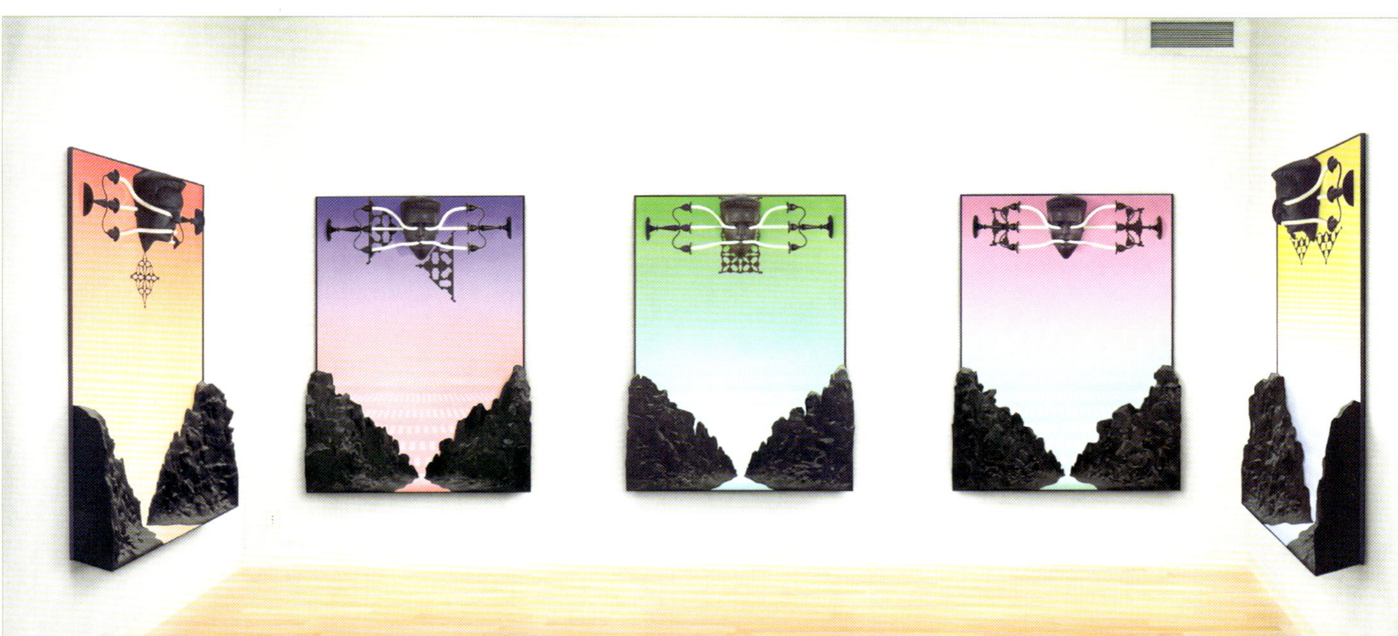

Left to right: *25 Seconds*, *25¼ Seconds*, *25½ Seconds*, *25¾ Seconds*, *26 Seconds*, 1989.
Nitrocellulose lacquer on plexiglas, fiberglass, pvc, with paper cutouts and warped wax candles.
54½ x 41½ x 6¾" each (138 x 105 x 17 cm).
GC 617, 618, 619, 620, 621.

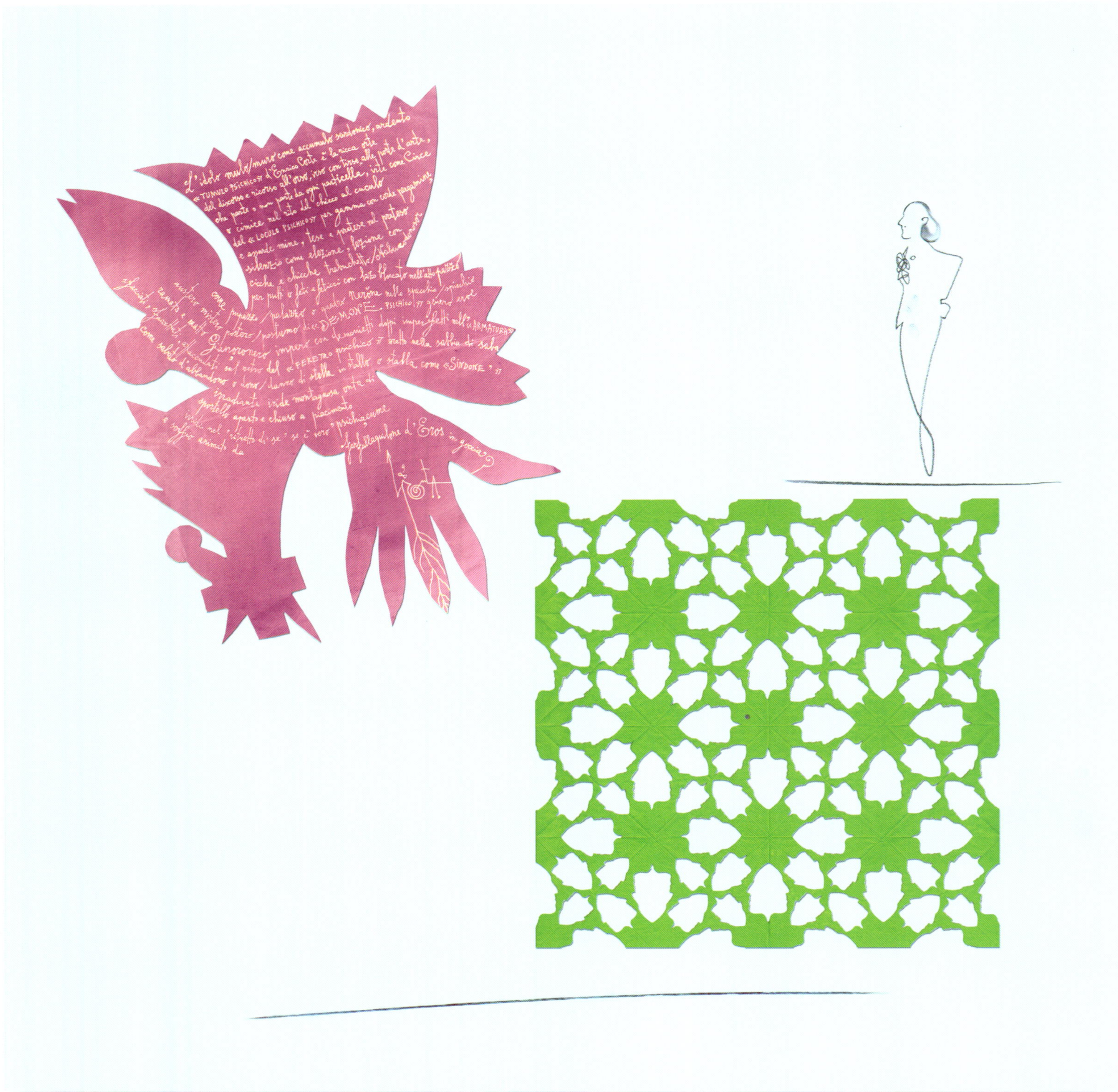

Corte & Ontani: *OntaniCutouts - Double Cut-out Portrait*, 1989.
Poem dedicated to Corte written by Luigi Ontani in golden ink on molded and watercolored cardboard (left);
cutout by Corte with Ontani's profile on green tissue paper with painted "mole",
plus charcoal drawing of Ontani's silhouette on watercolored cardboard (right).
39½ x 39½" (100 x 100 cm).
GC 603.

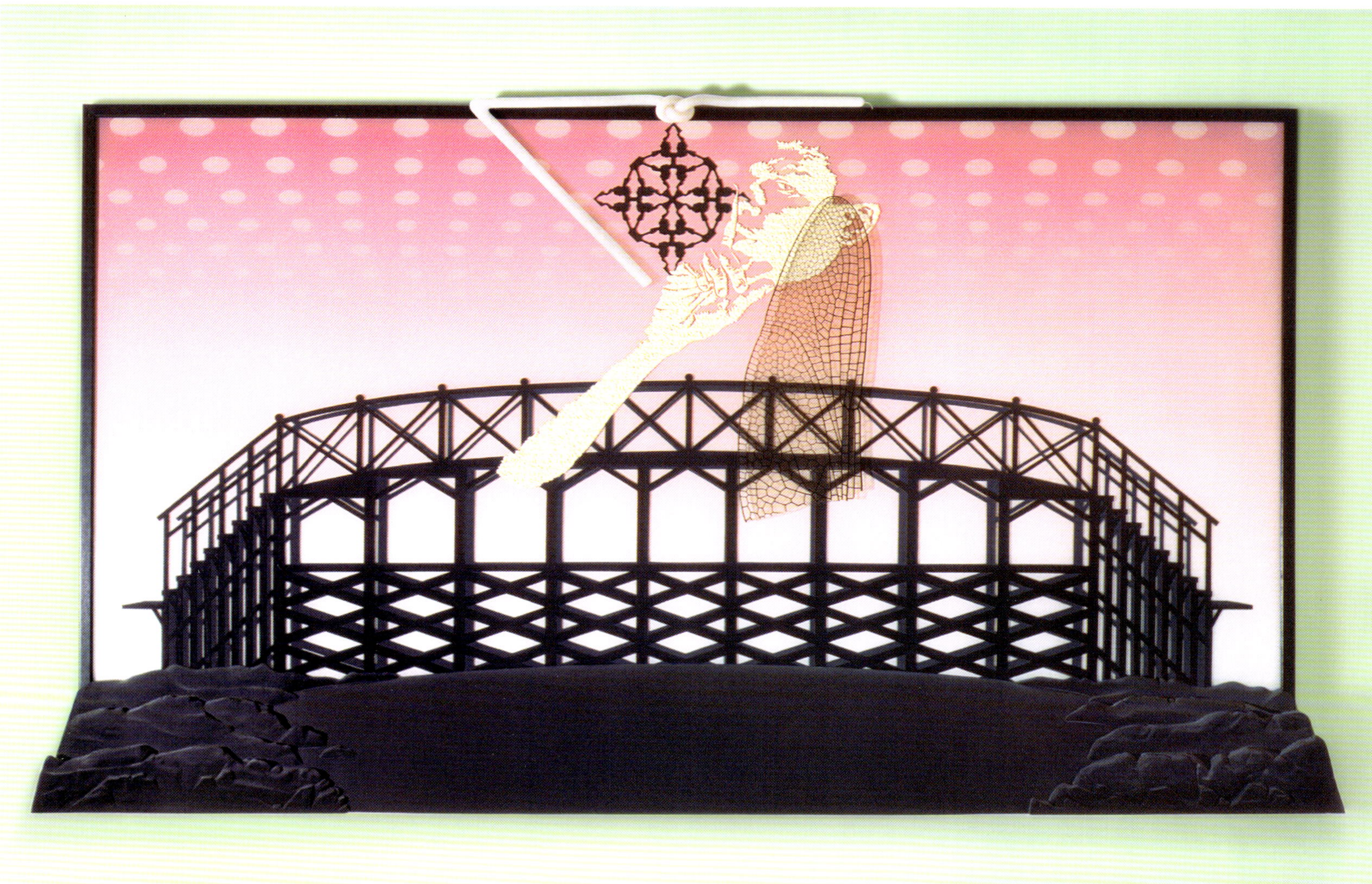

Brainscan, 1989-90.
Nitrocellulose lacquer on plexiglas, fiberglass, wood;
acrylic and sand on plexiglas;
acrylic on paper cutout;
bent wax candle.
40¼ x 67¾ x 2¾" (102 x 172 x 7 cm).
GC 651.

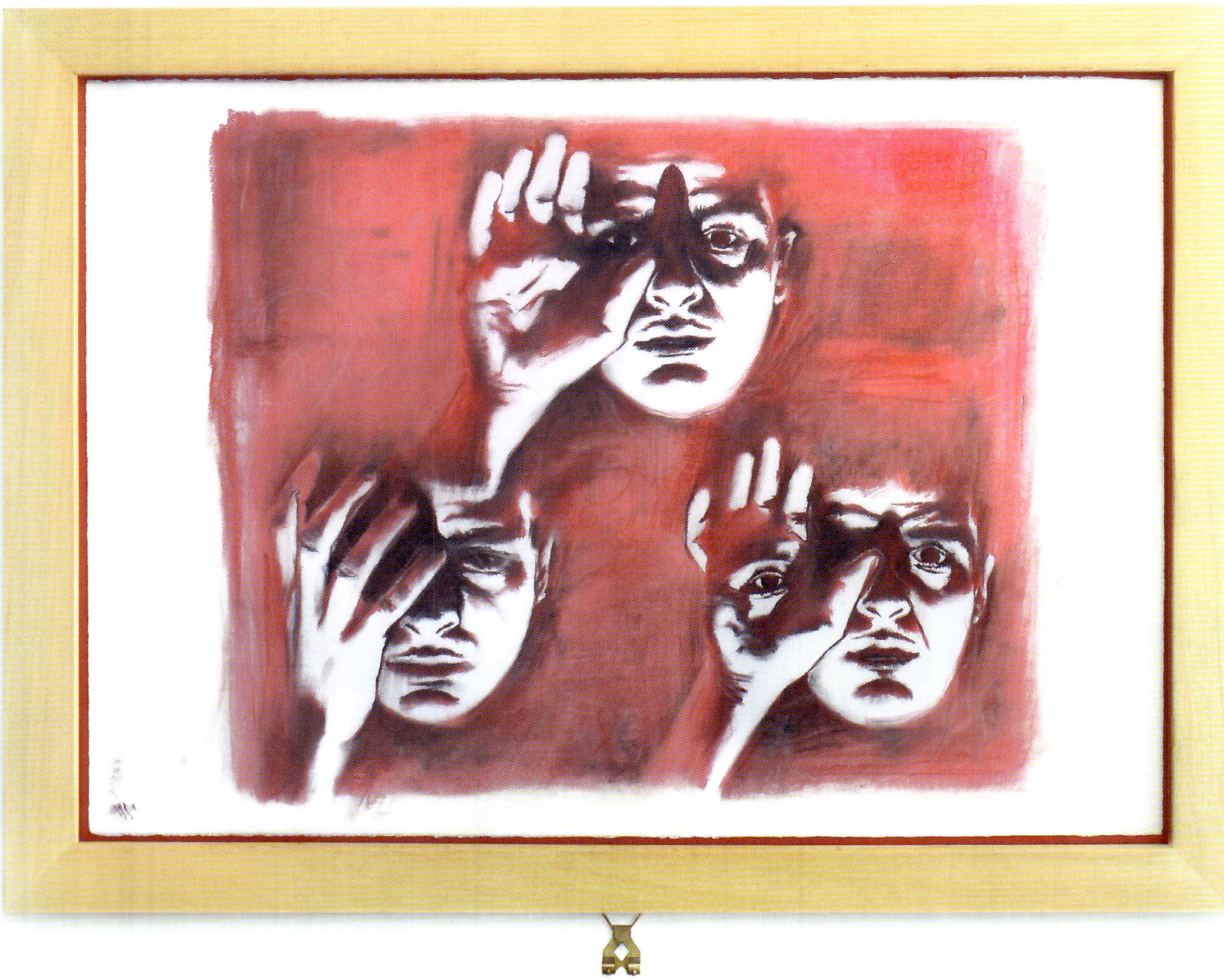

Removal, 1986.
Pastel and charcoal on paper;
wooden frame with metal hook and nails in its lower side.
34½ x 28½ x 1" (87,7 x 72,2 x 2,2 cm).
GC 497.

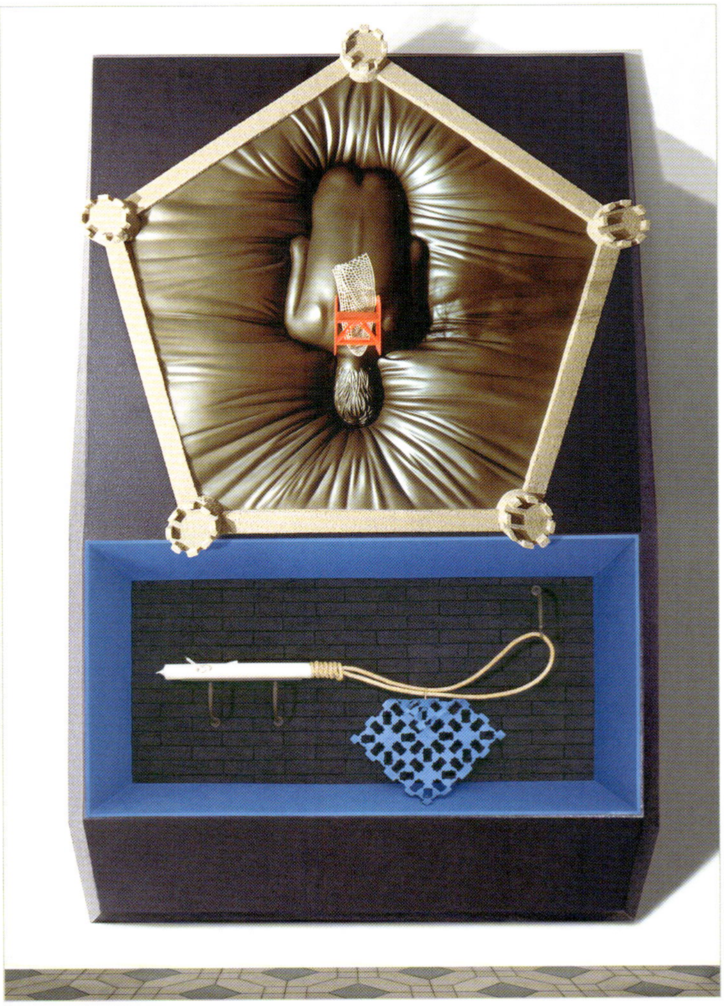

Skullaby
or also *Circumvolu-woodworms and Circumvolu-moths*, 1990.
Fiberglass, bronze, sand, bricks, rope;
enamel on glass;
tempera on paper cutout;
enamel and lacquer on wood;
carved votive wax candle;
moth-balls smell.
122 x 78¾ x 35½" (310 x 200 x 90 cm).
GC 652.

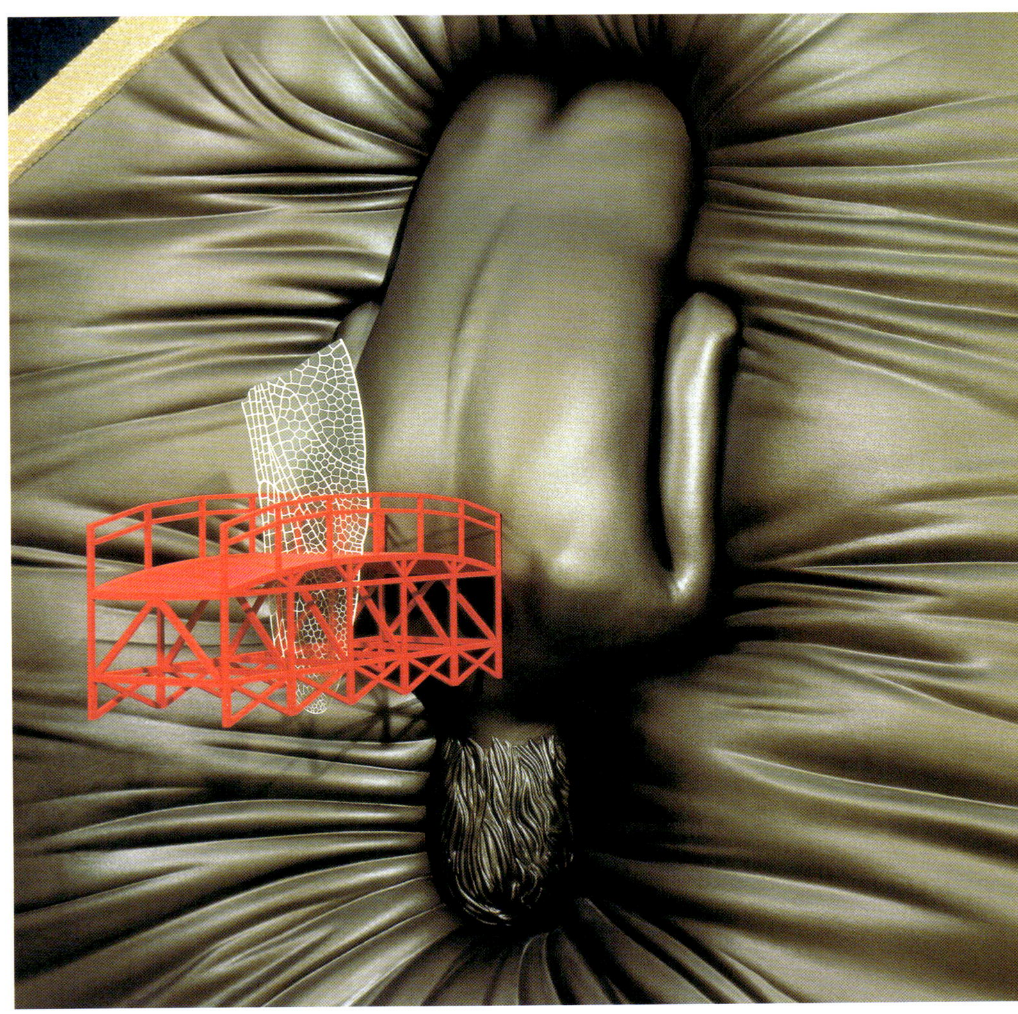

Skullaby, 1990. Detail.

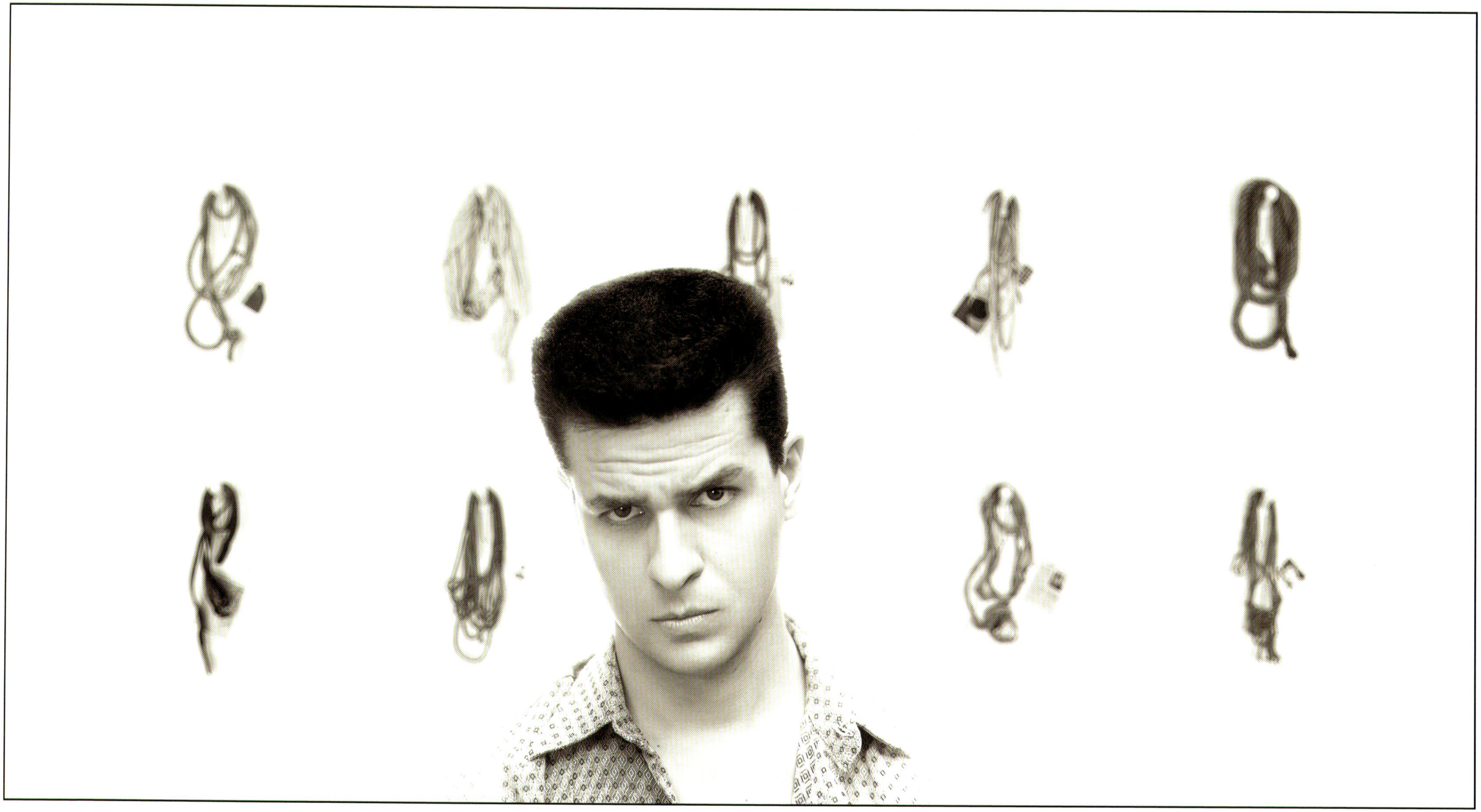

Collection of the Artist, or also *Schoinopentaxophilia*, 1990 (panel 1).
Silver gelatine prints on two panels.
41¼ x 78¾" each print (105 x 200 cm).
GC 655.

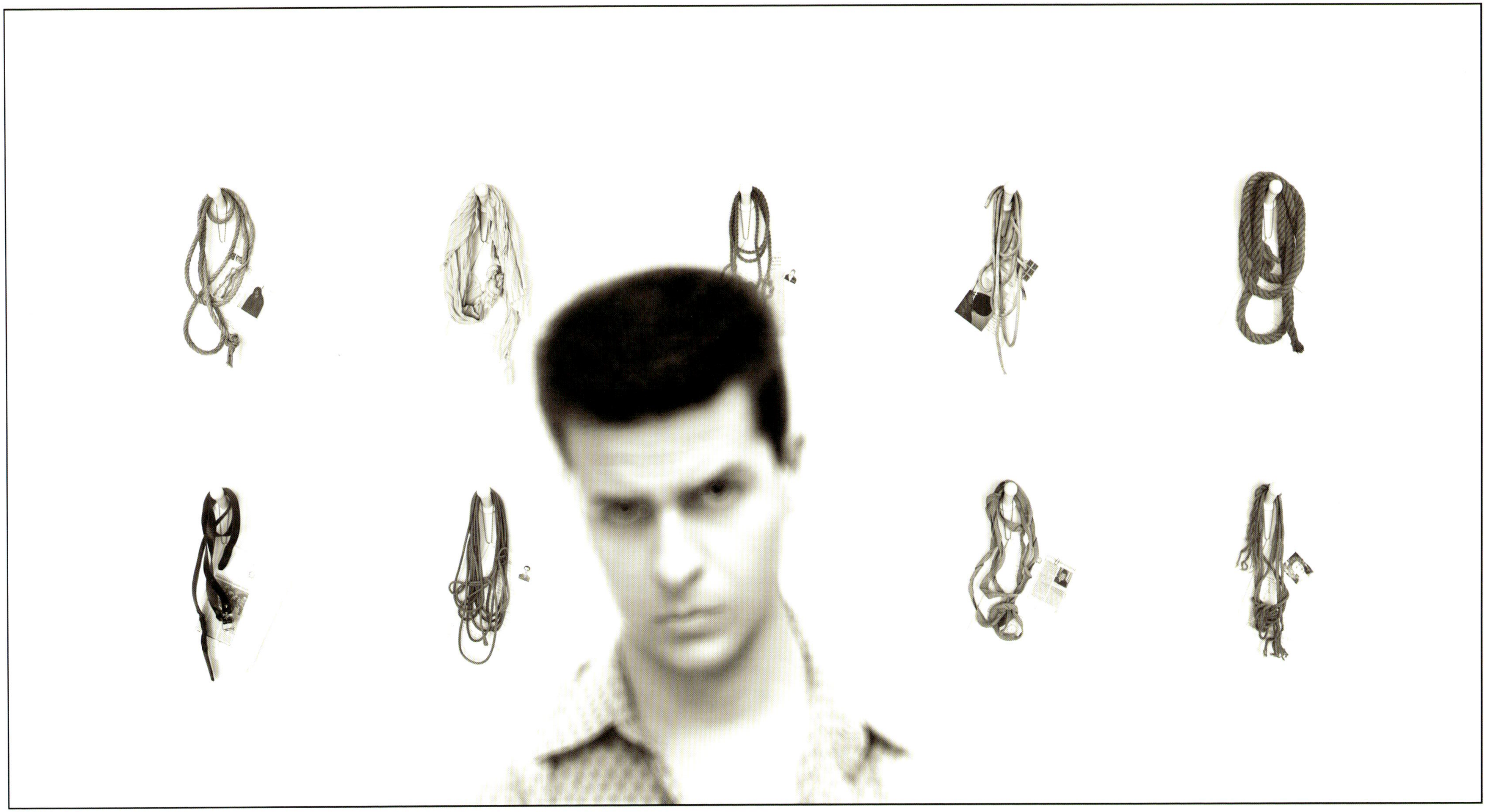

Collection of the Artist, or also *Schoinopentaxophilia*, 1990 (panel 2).

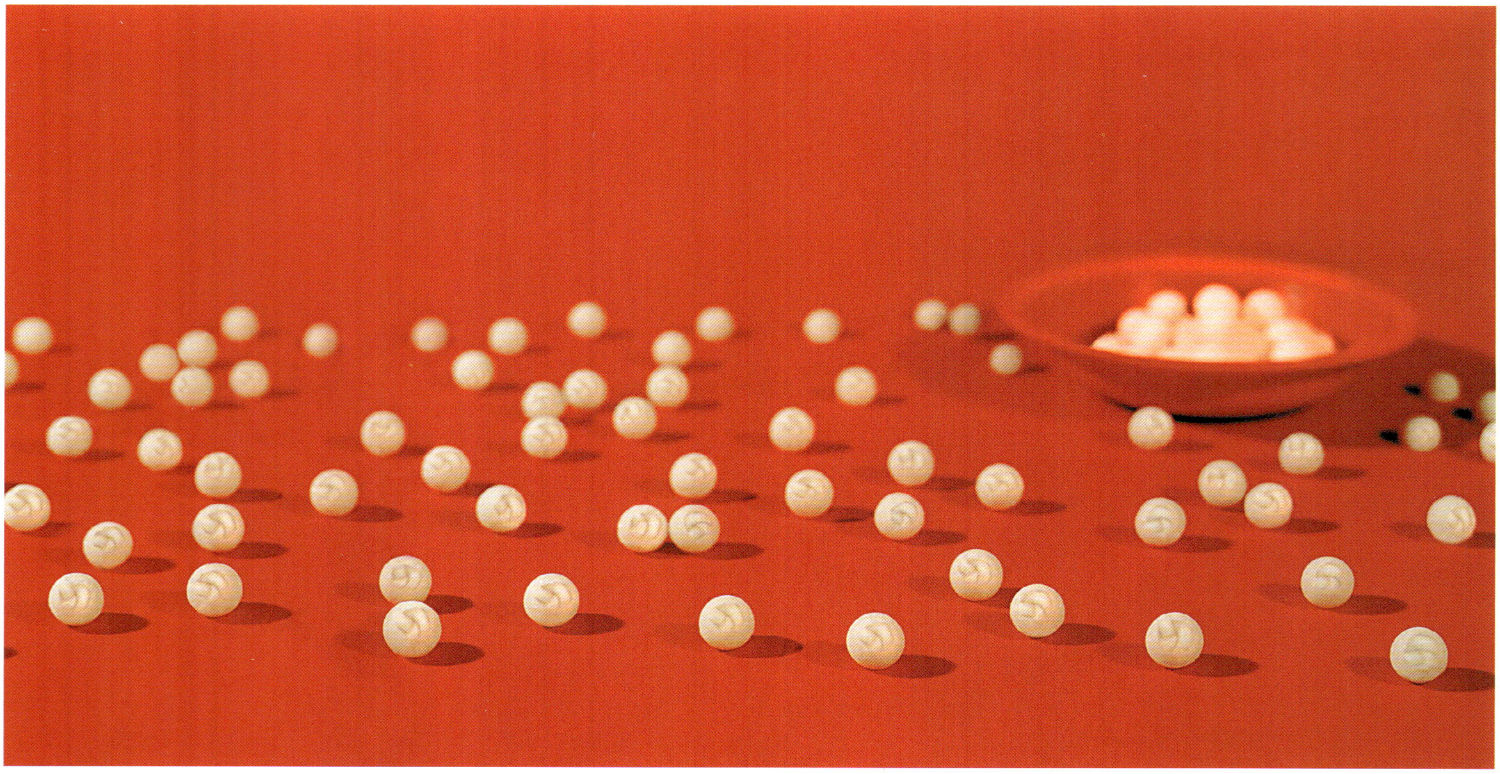

Naftorama, 1991.
Cibachrome print portraying a group of moth balls with tiny knots carved inside them.
39½ x 78¾" (100 x 200 cm).
GC 696.

Sigh-seeing, 1991.
Cibachrome print.
39½ x 78¾" (100 x 200 cm).
GC 697.

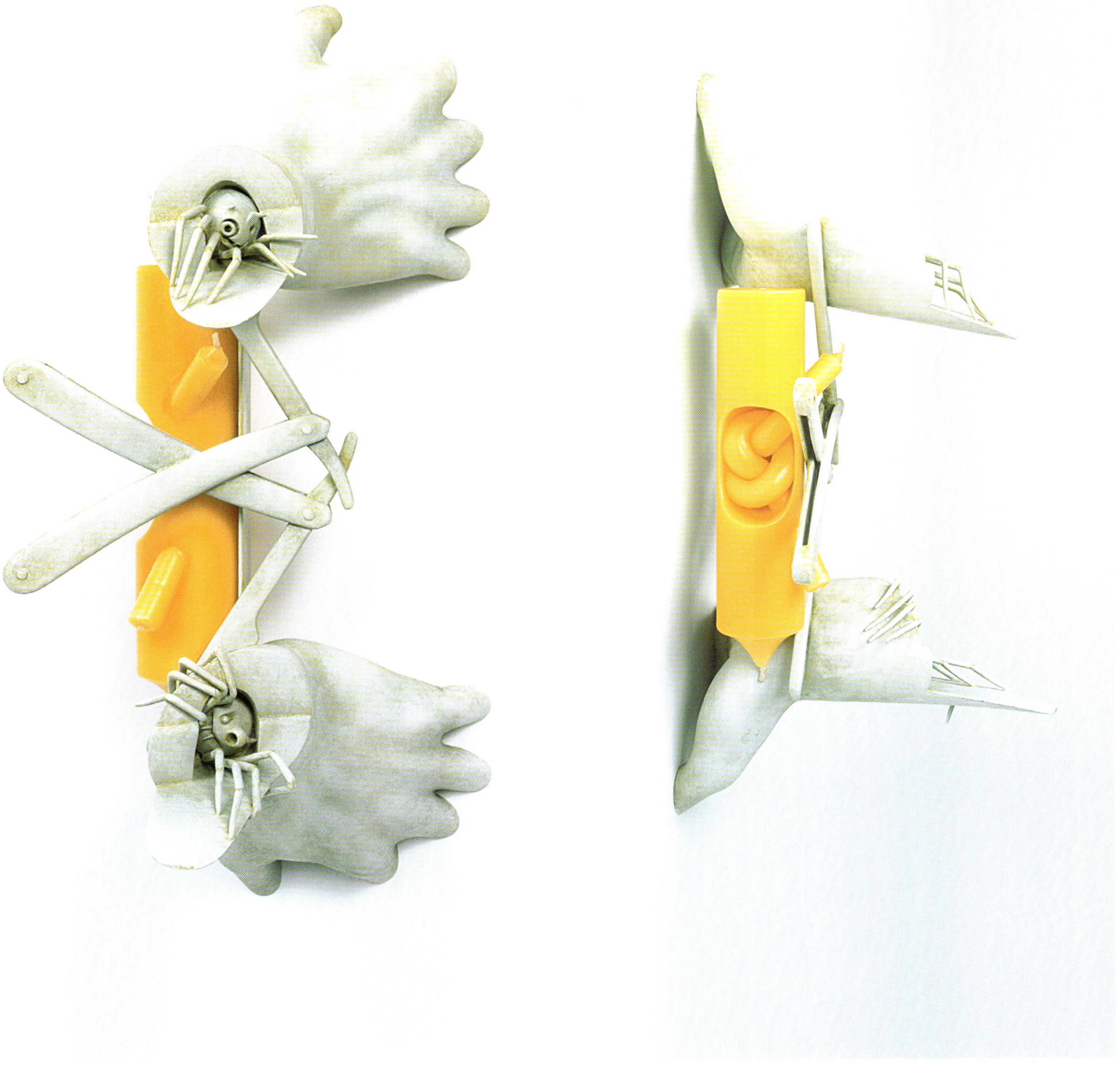

Pixie & Dixie, the Little Psychic Spiders, 1993-99. Front and side view.
Pigment, mould, grease and fly shit on synthoceramic;
carved yellow wax candle.
17½ x 13 x 8¾" (44 x 33 x 22 cm).
GC 1262.

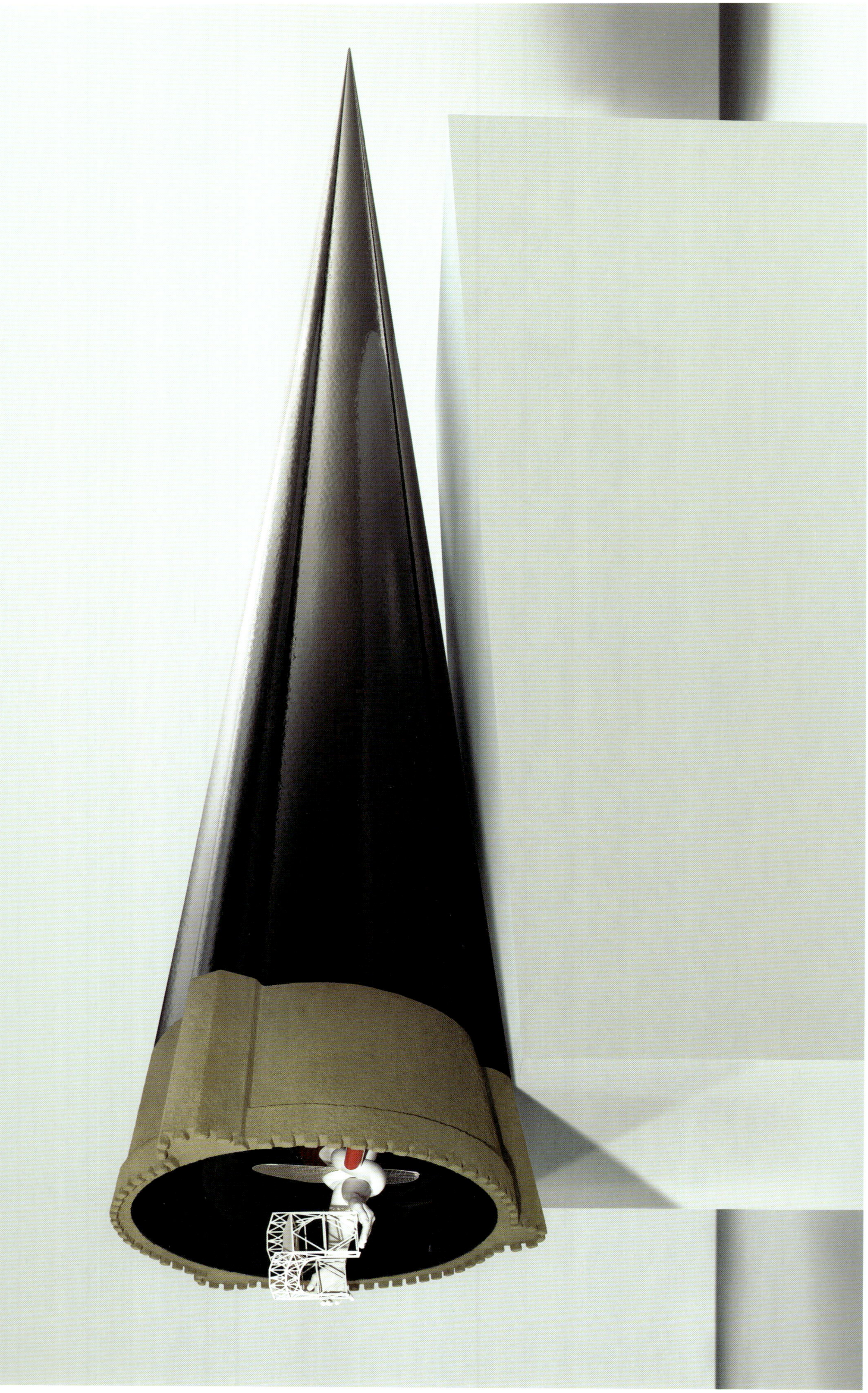

Cornucopia of Illusions, 1992-93. Side view.
Sculpture balanced on the edge of its pedestal.
Sand, fiberglass, lacquer, wood, carved red wax candle.
42½ x 45½ x 151½" (108 x 116 x 385 cm).
GC 780.

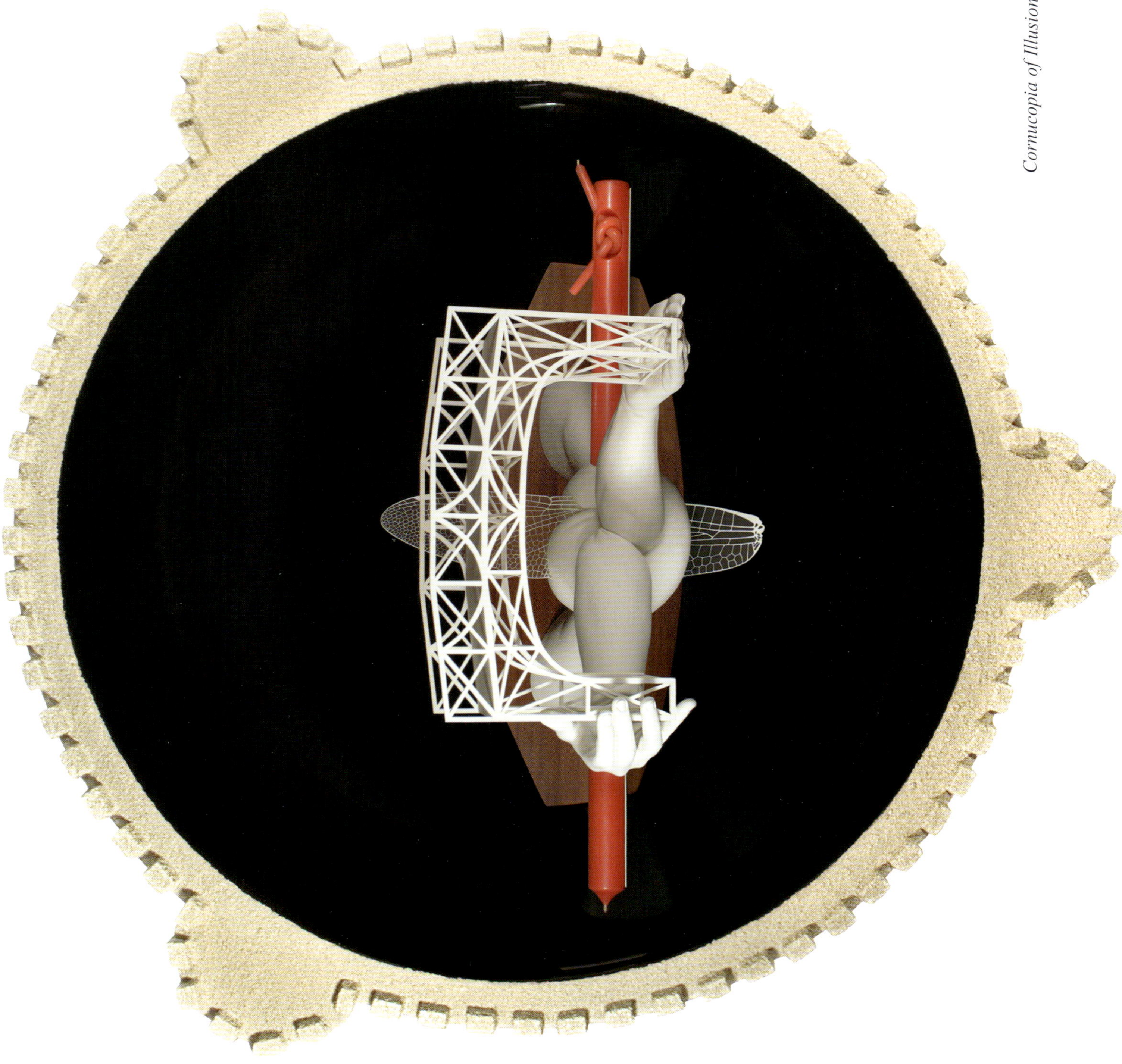

Cornucopia of Illusions, 1992-93. Front view.

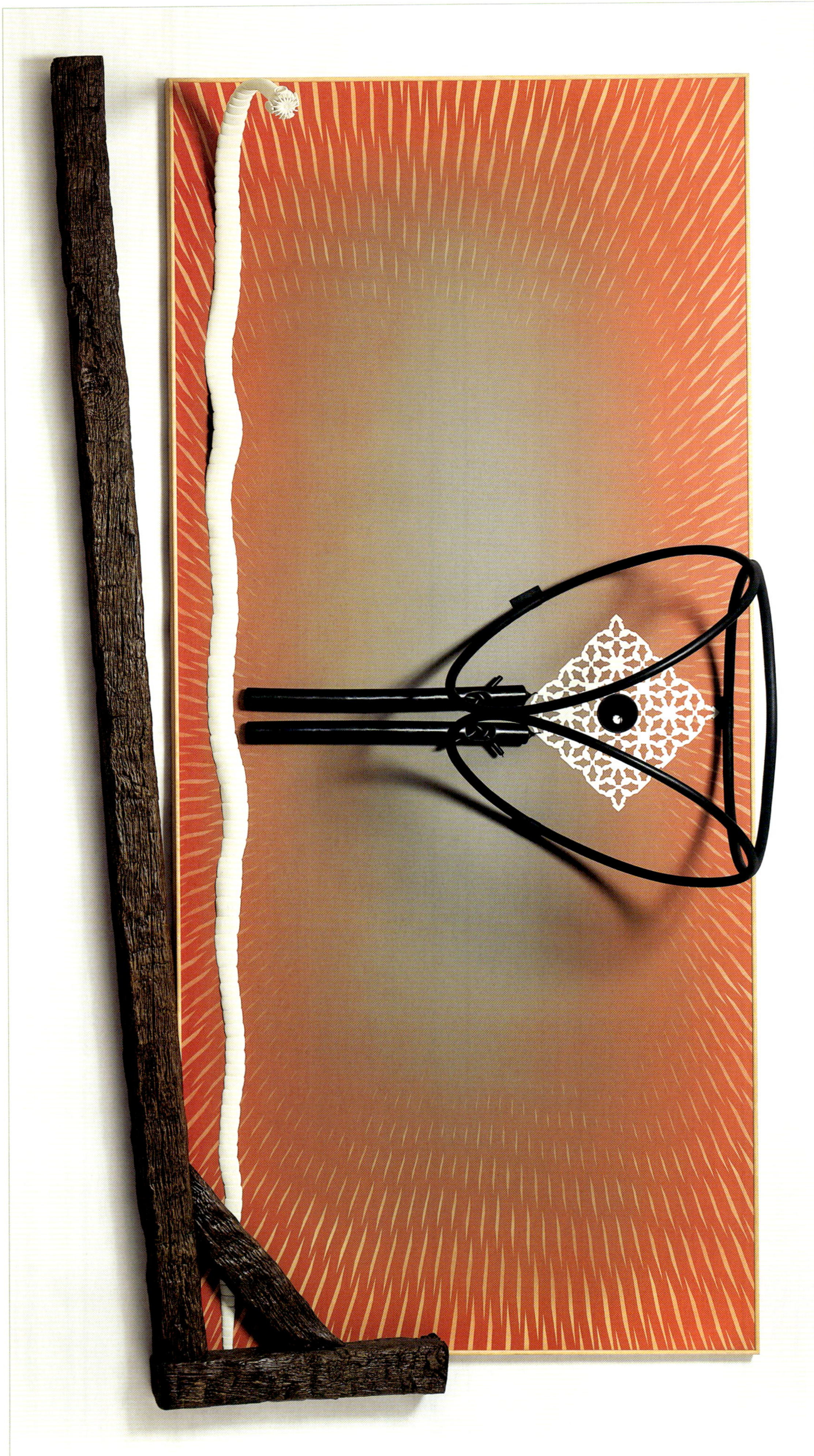

Nocturnal Psychic Enuresis
or also *Ring-a-ring-o'-ropes*, 1994.
Acrylic on wood, fiberglass, paper cutout;
carved black wax candle;
concave black mirror.
115½ x 59 x 26¾" (293 x 150 x 68 cm).
GC 810.

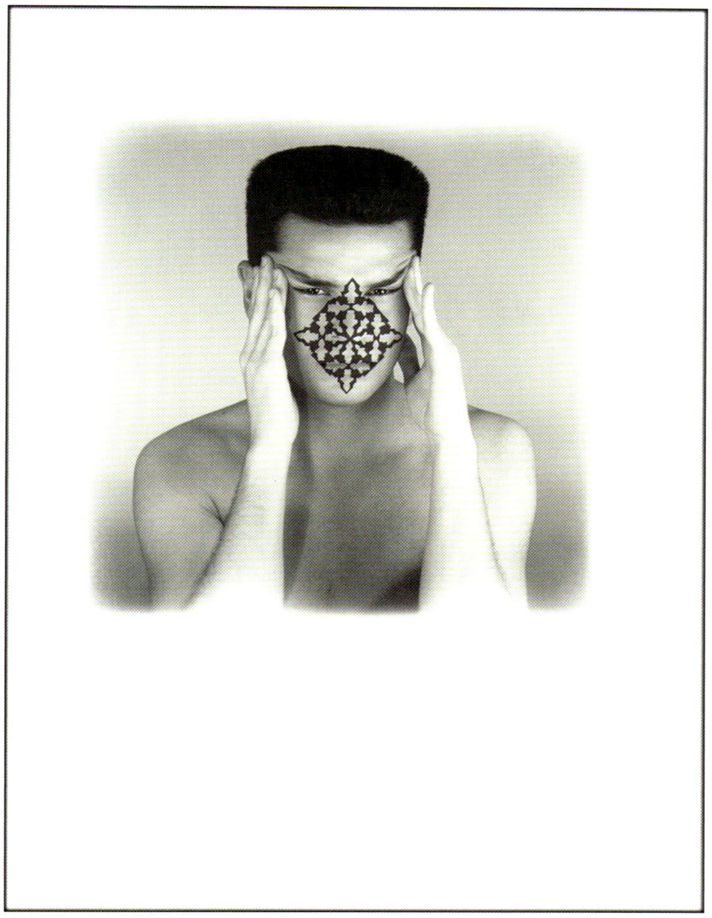

Abduction, 1994.
Silver gelatine print.
15¾ x 11¾" (40 x 30 cm).
GC 811.

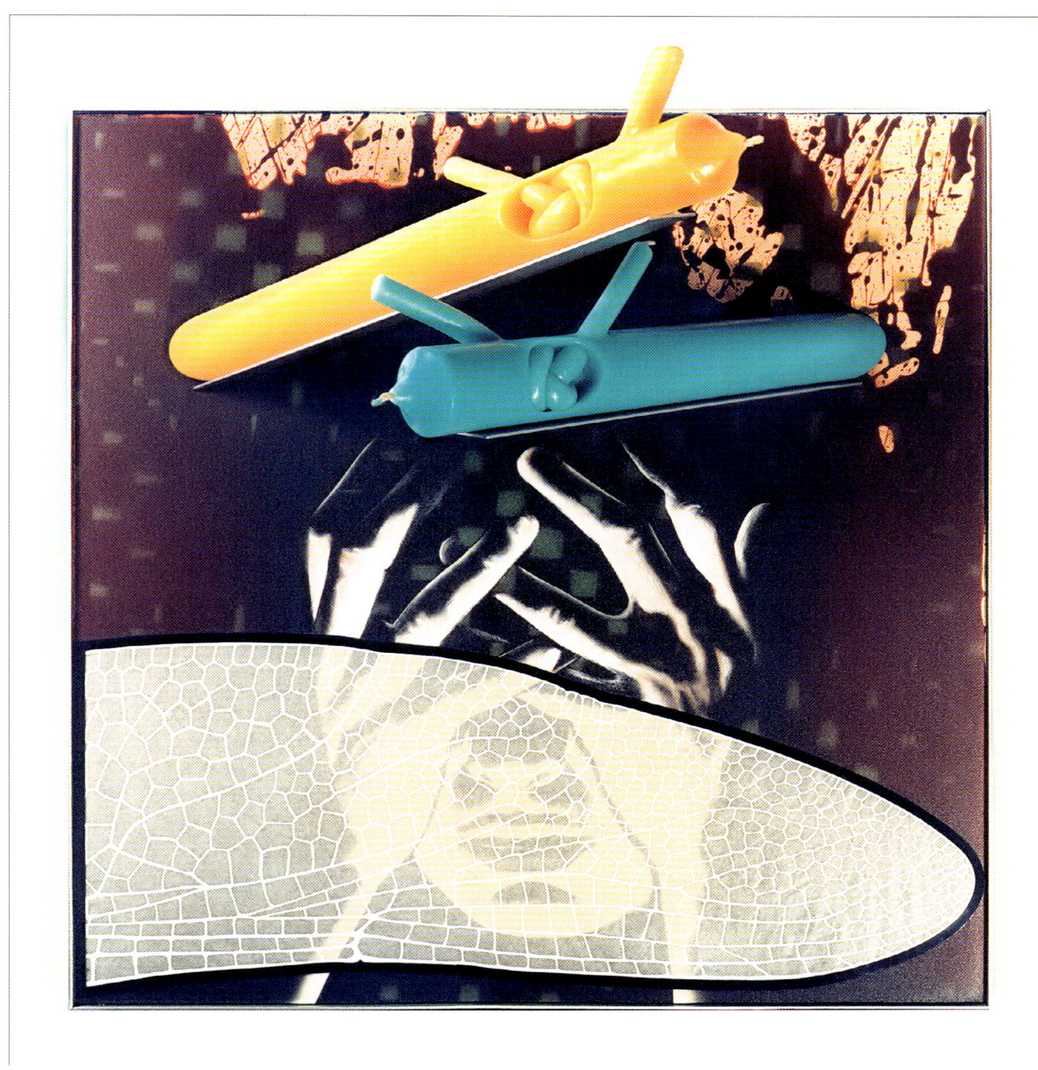

Screen-memories, 1993.
Acrylic, enamel and lacquer on wood and parchment-like paper; carved wax candles on aluminum bases; aluminum frame.
18¾ x 18¼ x 11¾" (48 x 46,5 x 29,5 cm).
GC 774.

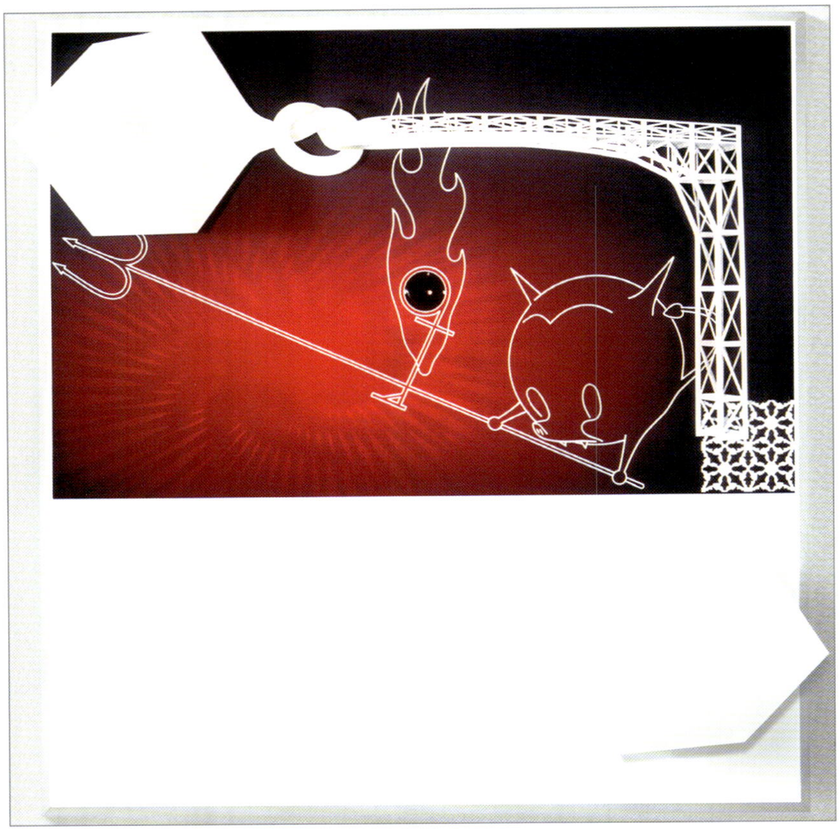

(The Abstraction of the) Cube Root, 1994.
Enamel and lacquer on fiberglass, pvc, paper cutout, concave black mirror.
89 x 87½ x 31” (226,3 x 222,5 x 79 cm).
GC 814.

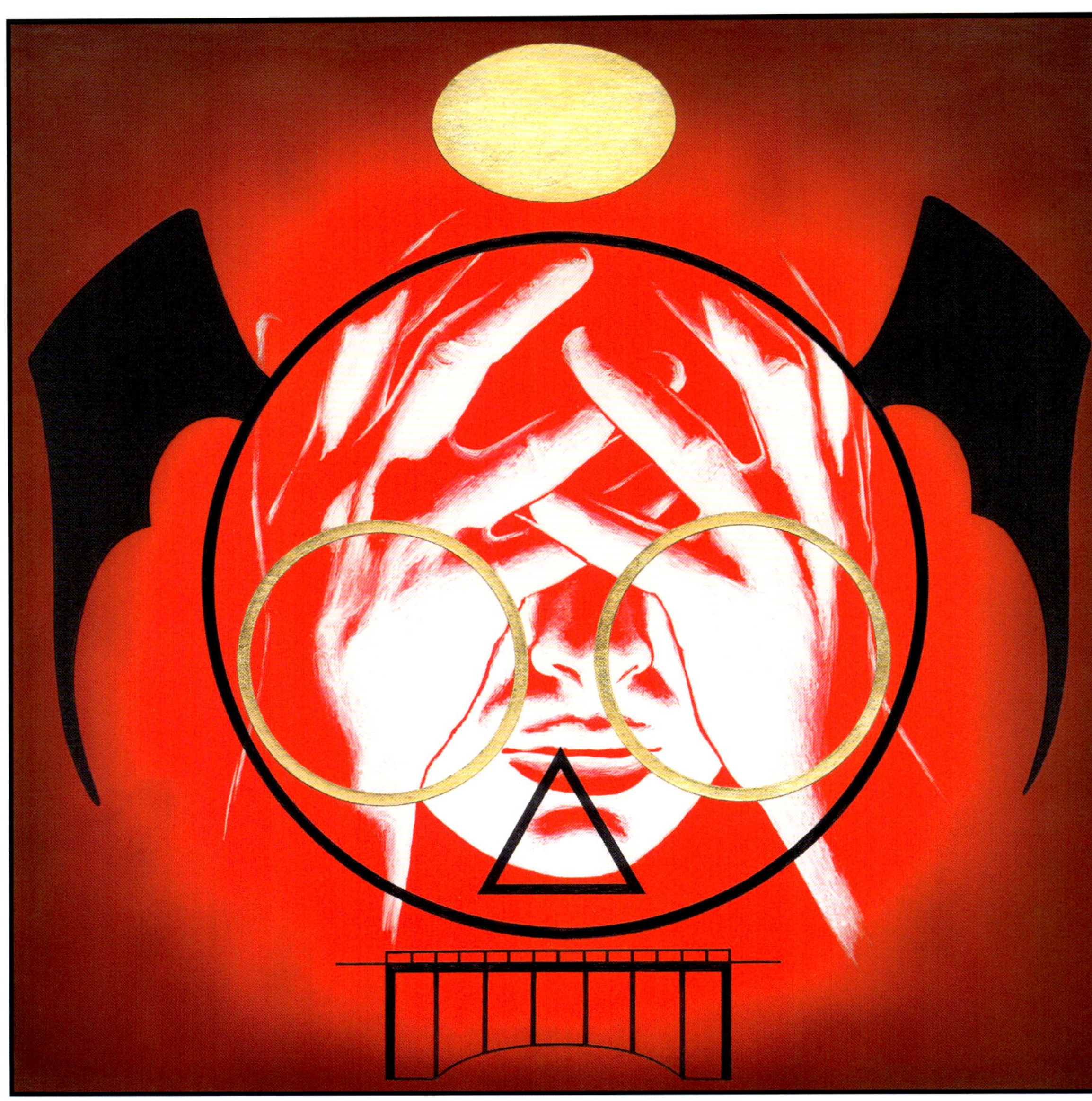

Drawing from the *Hobbyists* series, 1994-96.
Ink, enamel, tempera, gold leaf on bindakote.
13¼ x 13¼” (33,3 x 33,3 cm).
GC 837.

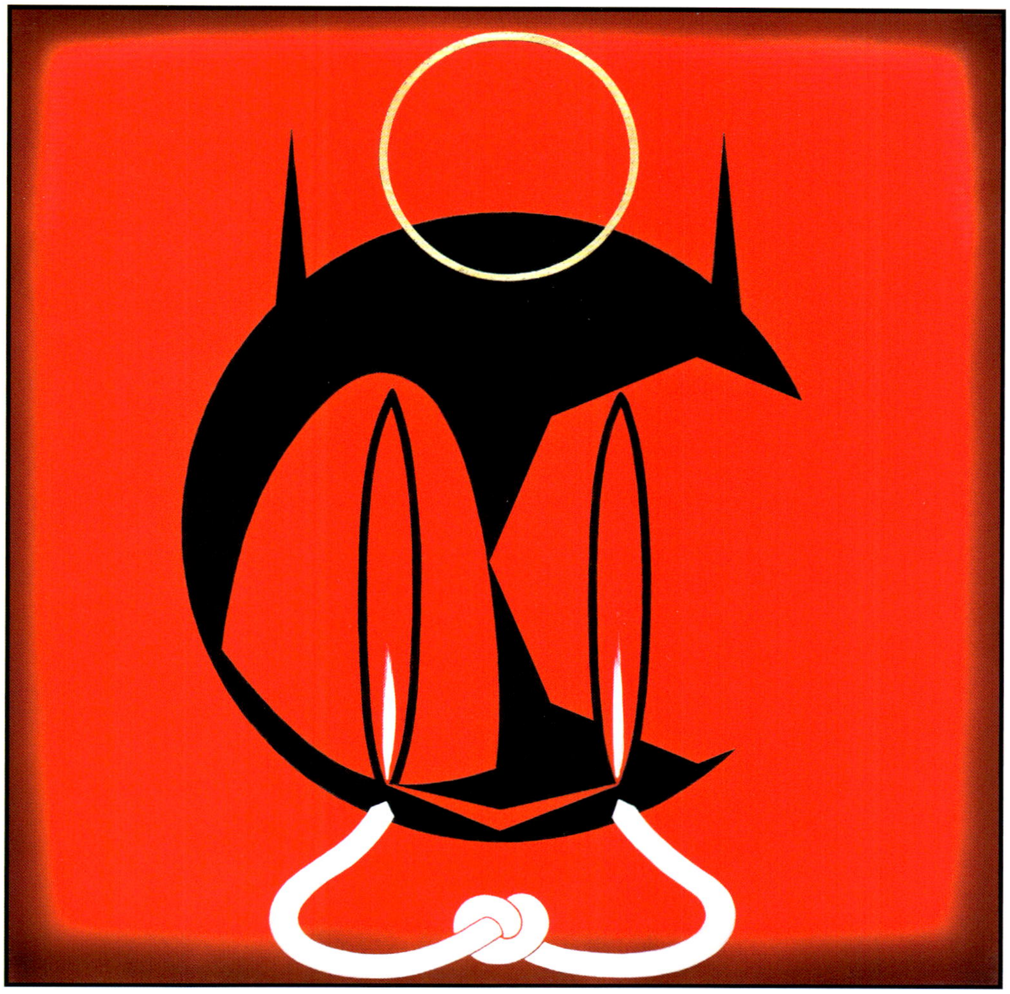

Drawing from
the *Hobbyists* series, 1994-96.
Ink, enamel, gold leaf on bindakote.
13¼ x 13¼" (33,3 x 33,3 cm).
GC 846.

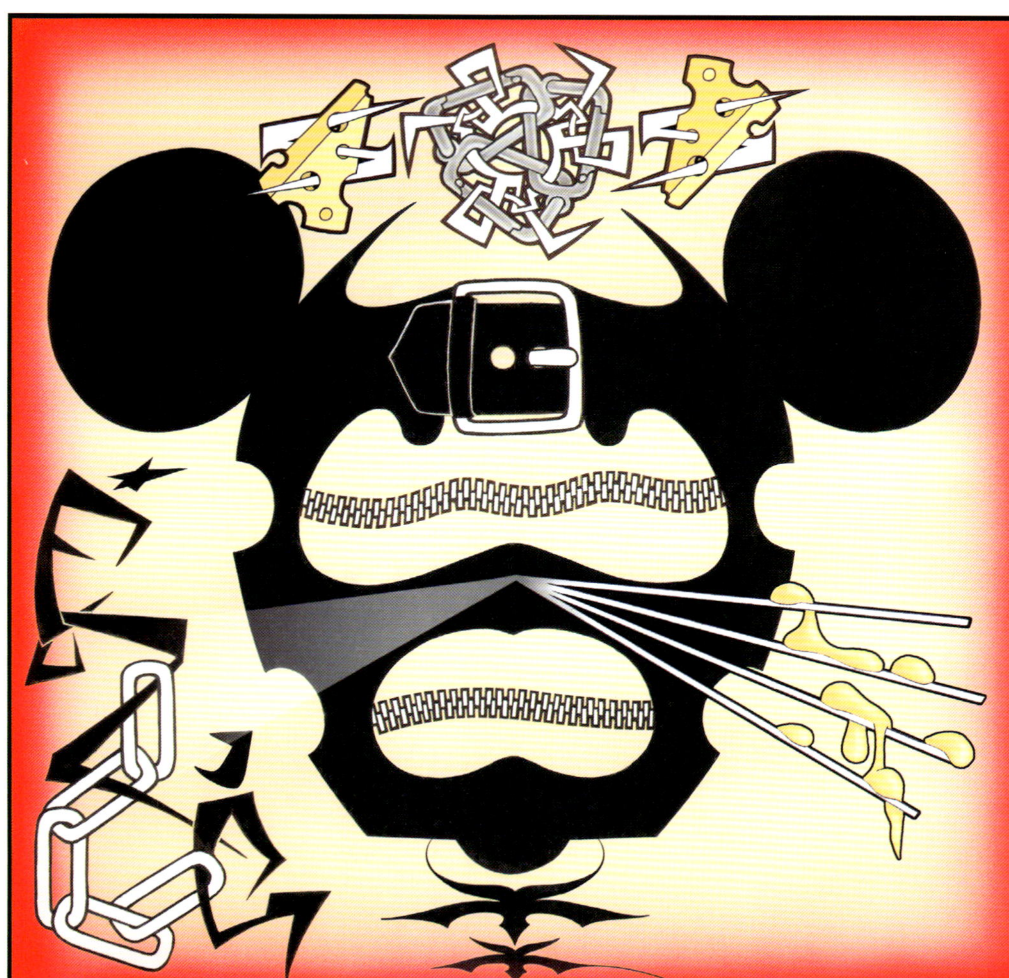

Drawing from
the *Hobbyists* series, 1994-96.
Ink, enamel, graphite, tempera,
on paper and bindakote.
13¼ x 13¼" (33,3 x 33,3 cm).
GC 842.

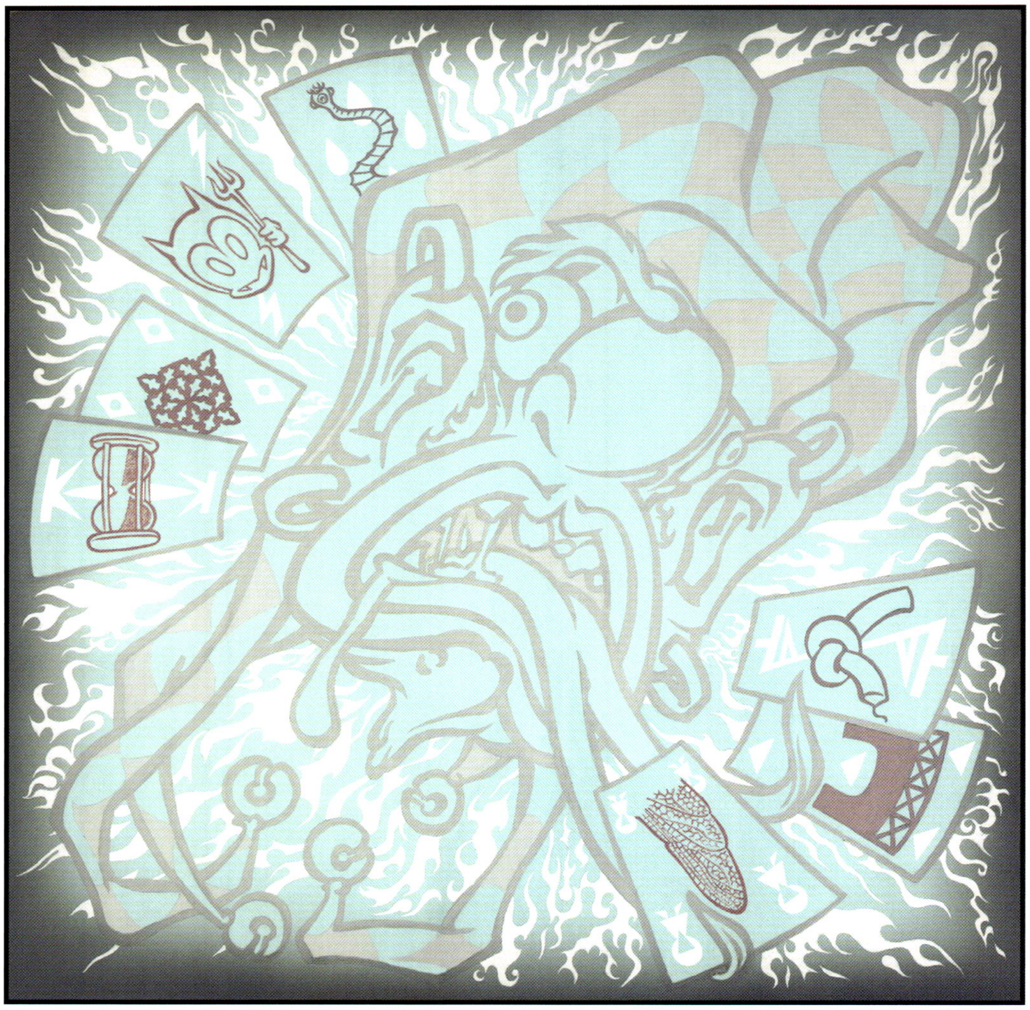

Drawing from
the *Hobbyists* series, 1994-96.
Enamel and tempera on splendorlux.
13¼ x 13¼" (33,3 x 33,3 cm).
GC 860.

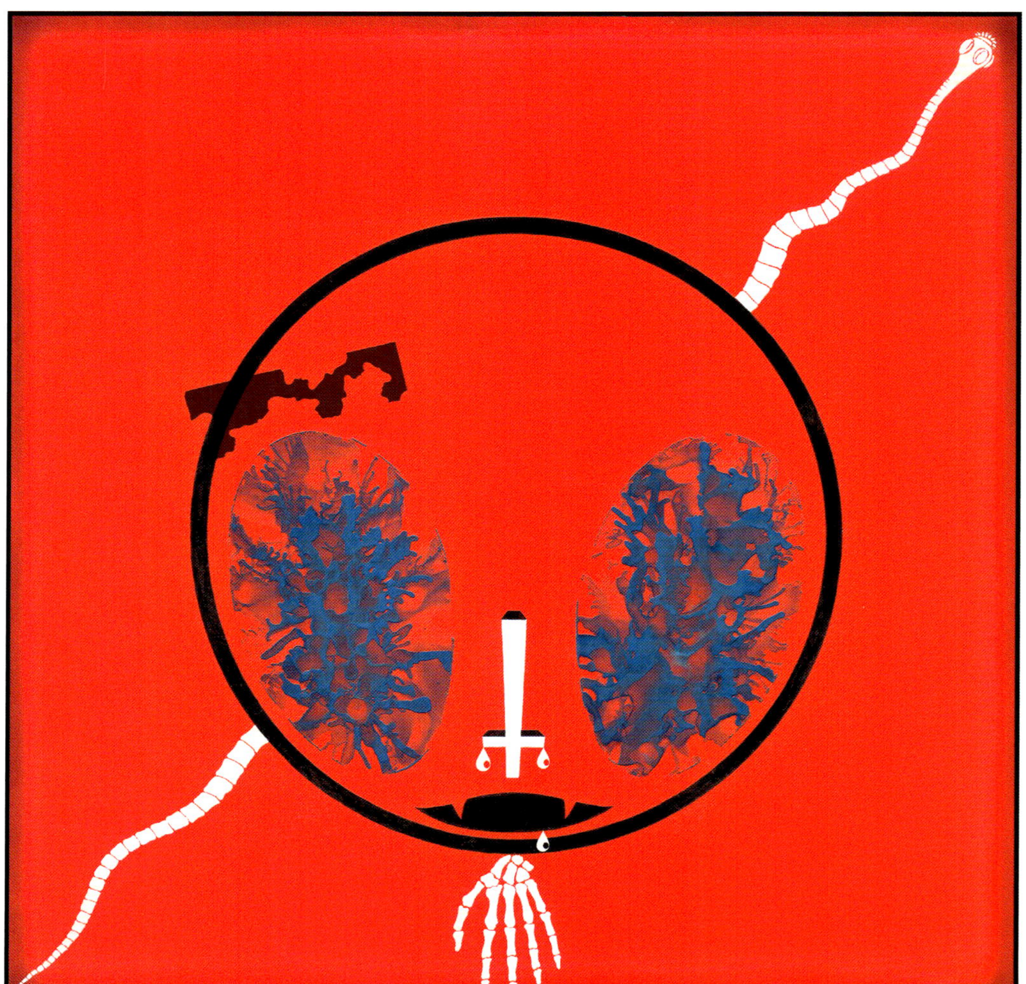

Drawing from
the *Hobbyists* series, 1994-96.
Ink, enamel and tempera on bindakote,
with fragment of black tissue paper cutout.
13¼ x 13¼" (33,3 x 33,3 cm).
GC 851.

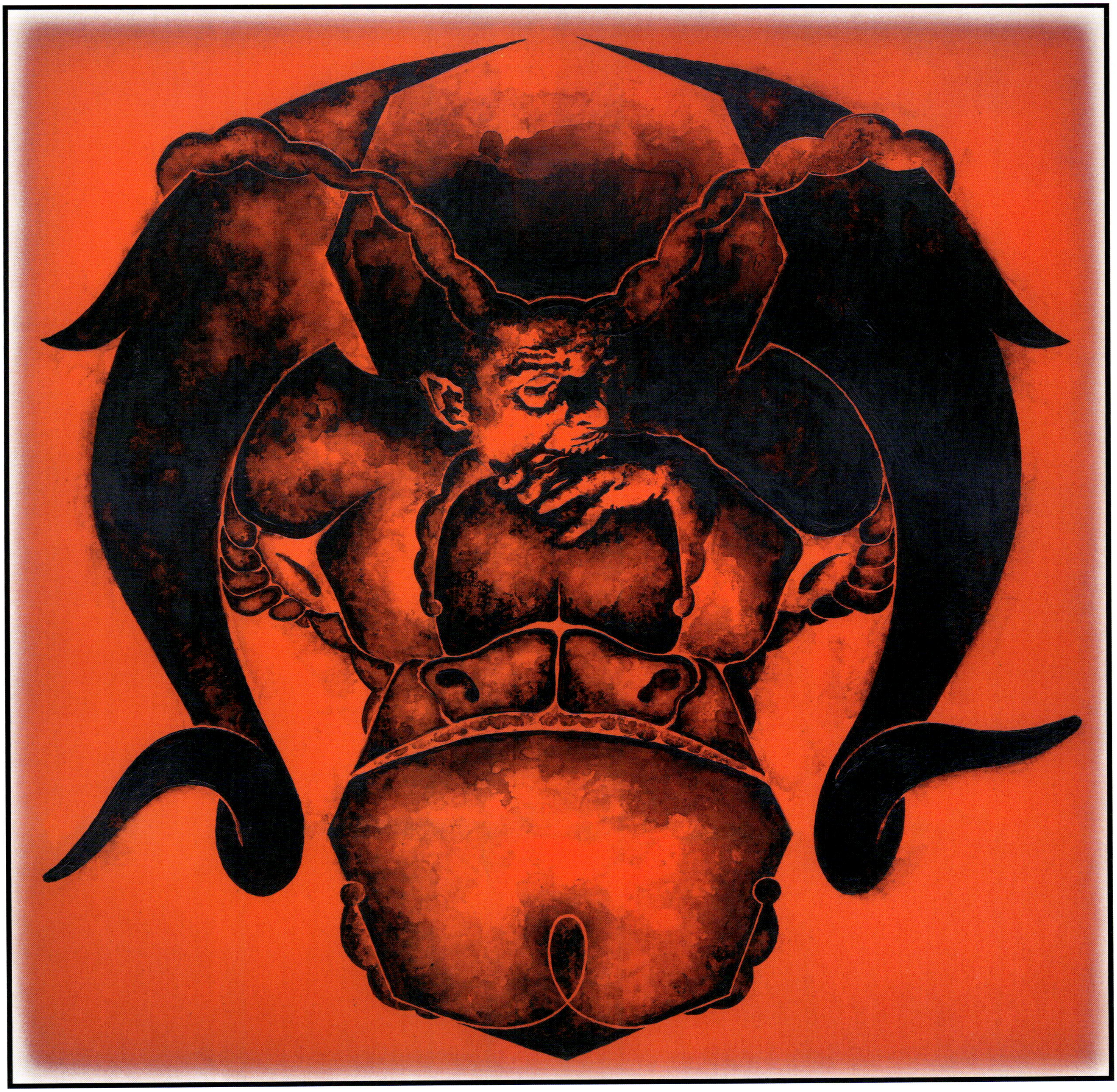

Drawing from the *Hobbyists* series, 1994-96.
Ink and enamel on bindakote.
13¼ x 13¼" (33,3 x 33,3 cm).
GC 869.

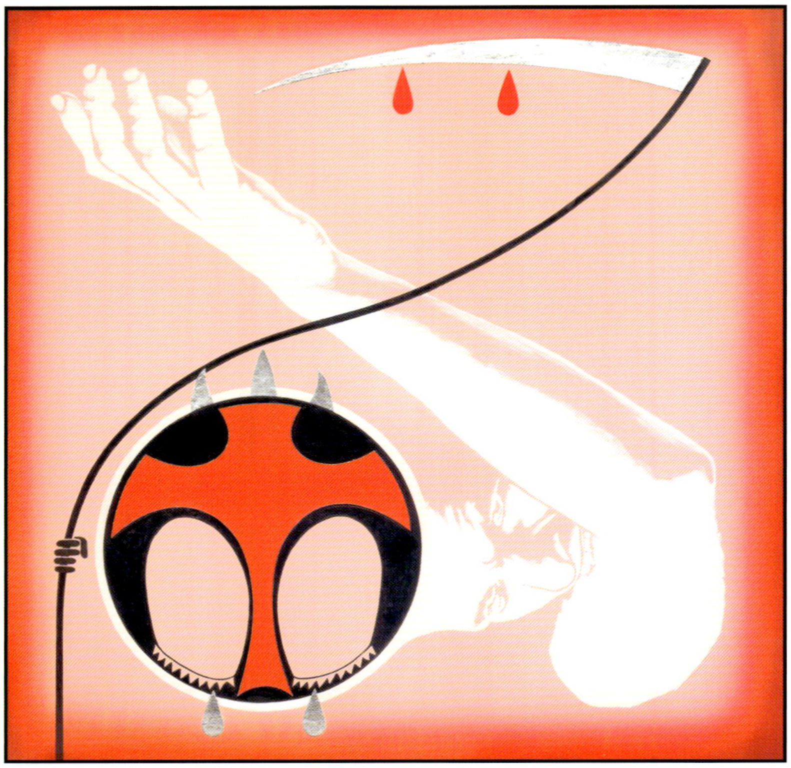

Drawing from the *Hobbyists* series, 1994-96.
Ink, enamel, tempera, silver leaf on paper and bindakote.
13¼ x 13¼" (33,3 x 33,3 cm).
GC 838.

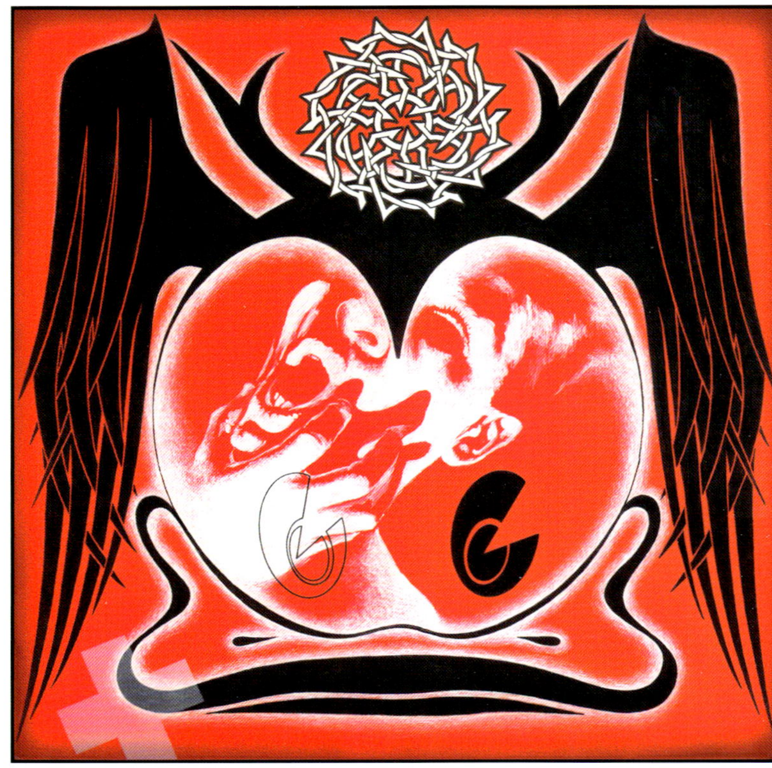

Drawing from the *Hobbyists* series, 1994-96.
Ink, enamel, tempera on paper and bindakote.
13¼ x 13¼" (33,3 x 33,3 cm).
GC 840.

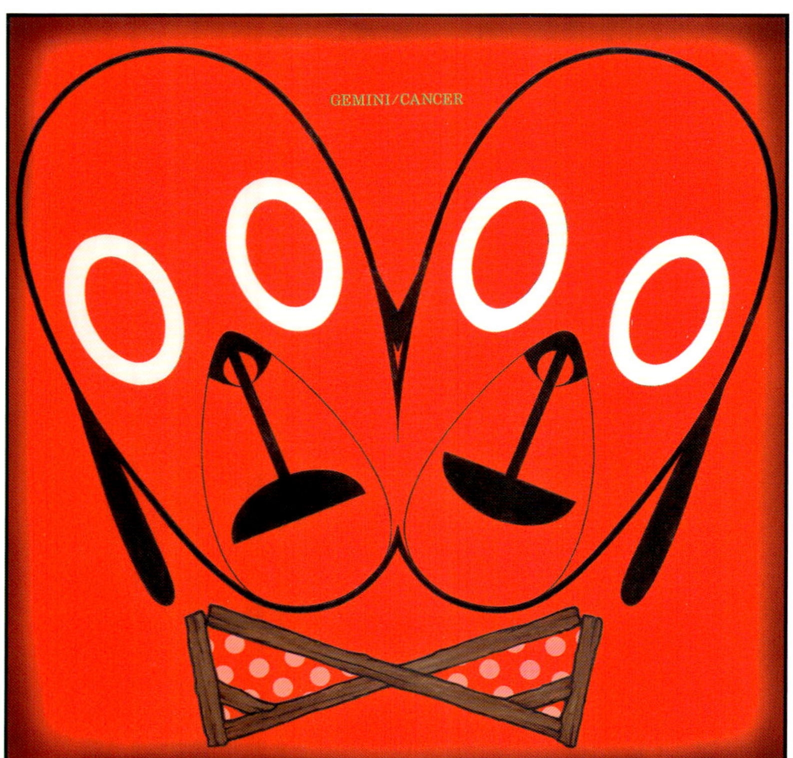

Drawing from the *Hobbyists* series, 1994-96.
Ink, enamel, tempera on paper and bindakote.
13¼ x 13¼" (33,3 x 33,3 cm).
GC 857.

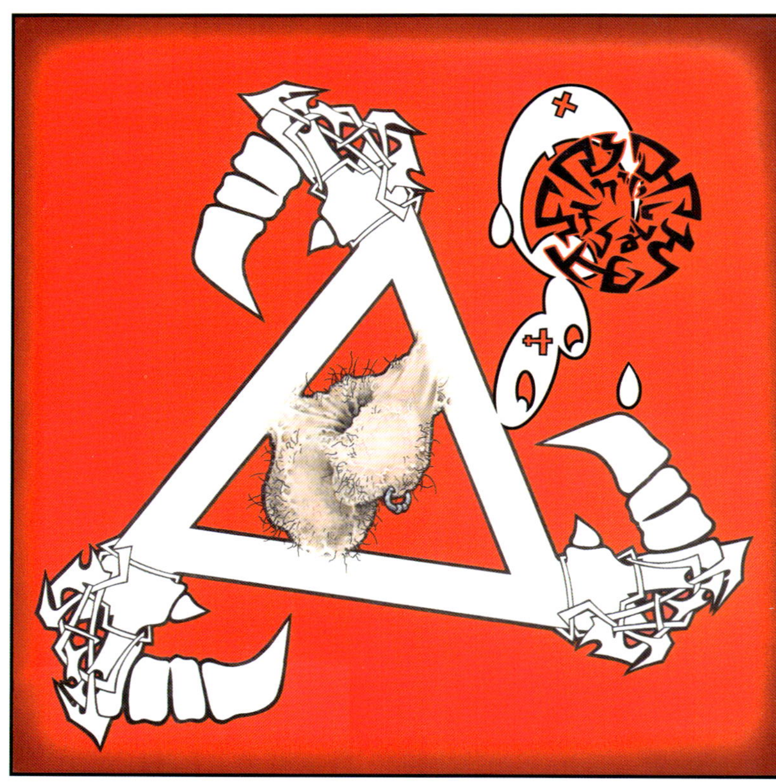

Drawing from the *Hobbyists* series, 1994-96.
Ink, enamel, tempera, silver leaf on paper and bindakote.
13¼ x 13¼" (33,3 x 33,3 cm).
GC 850.

Drawing from the *Hobbyists* series, 1994-96.
Ink, enamel, tempera on bindakote.
13¼ x 13¼" (33,3 x 33,3 cm).
GC 834.

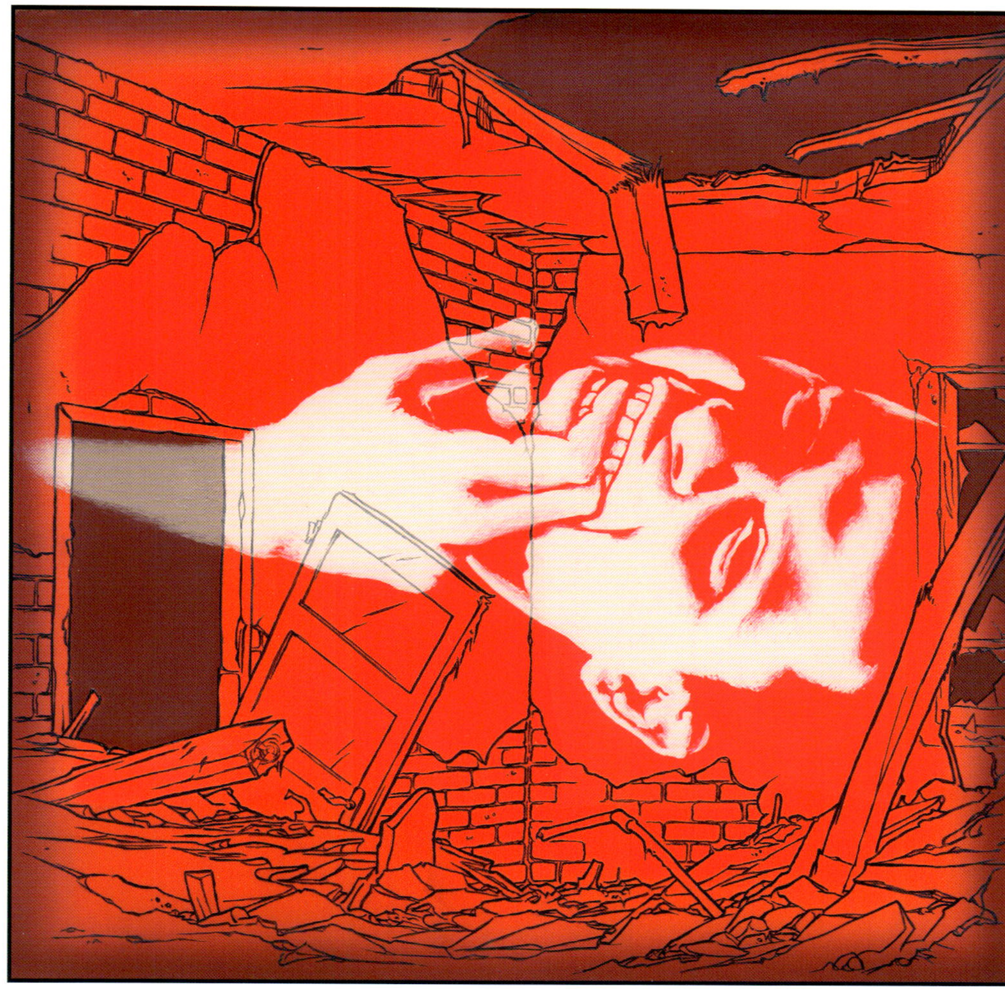

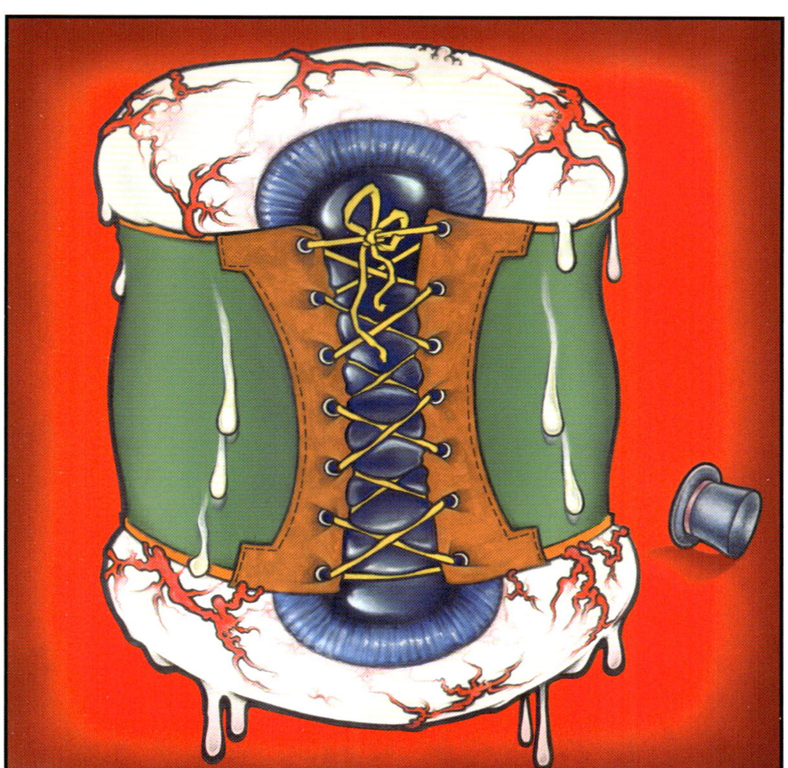

Drawing from the *Hobbyists* series, 1994-96.
Ink, enamel, pencil, pastel, tempera on paper and bindakote.
13¼ x 13¼" (33,3 x 33,3 cm).
GC 855.

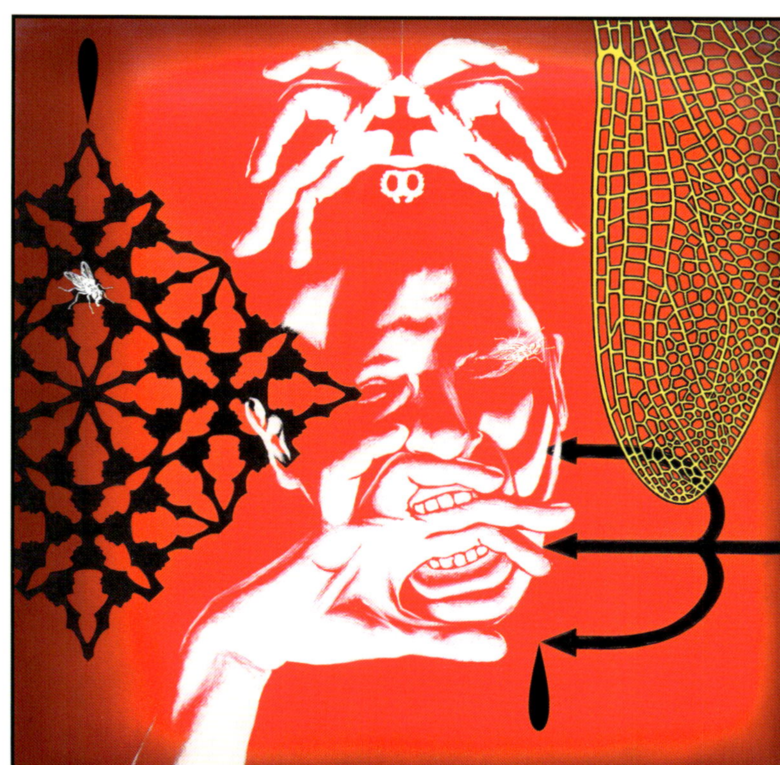

Drawing from the *Hobbyists* series, 1994-96.
Ink, enamel, tempera on bindakote.
13¼ x 13¼" (33,3 x 33,3 cm).
GC 832.

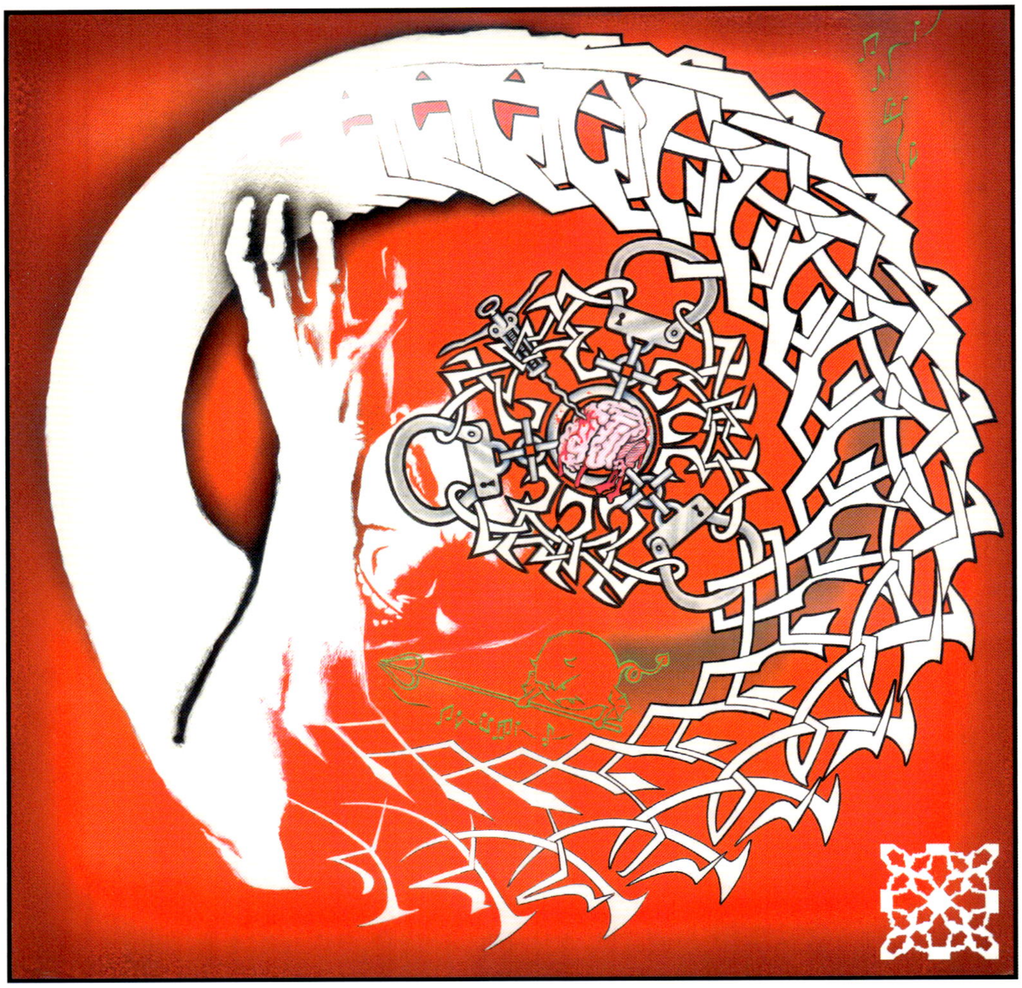

Drawing from
the *Hobbyists* series, 1994-96.
Ink, enamel, tempera, graphite
on paper and splendorlux.
13¼ x 13¼" (33,3 x 33,3 cm).
GC 833.

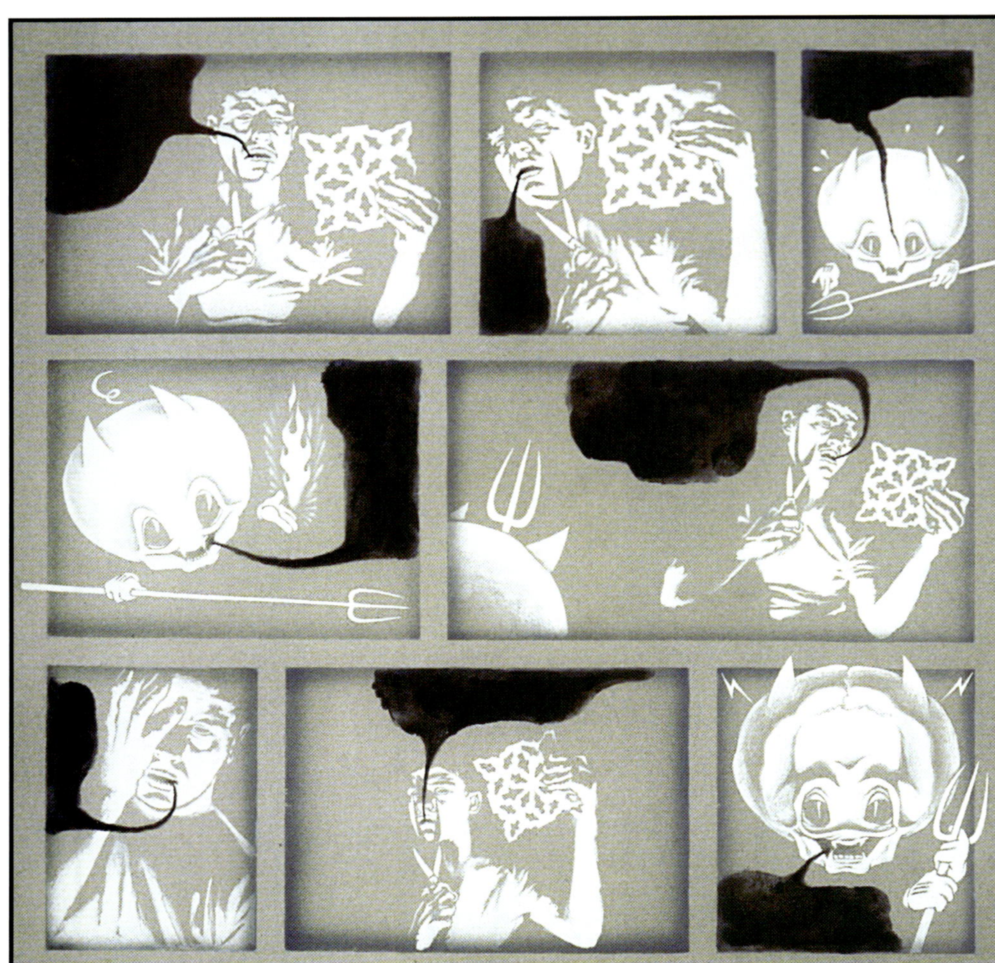

Drawing from
the *Hobbyists* series, 1994-96.
Tempera on cardboard.
13¼ x 13¼" (33,3 x 33,3 cm).
GC 868.

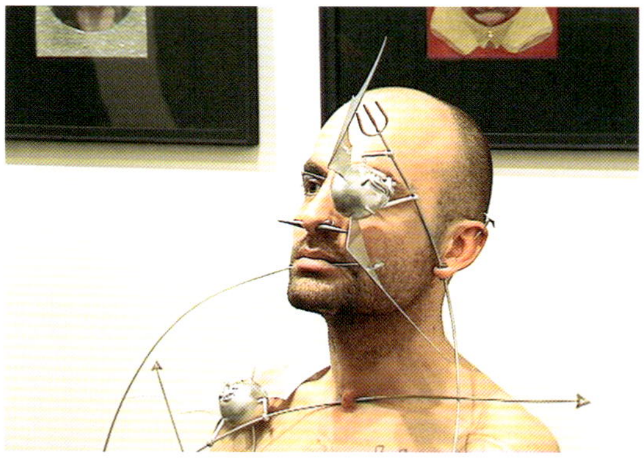
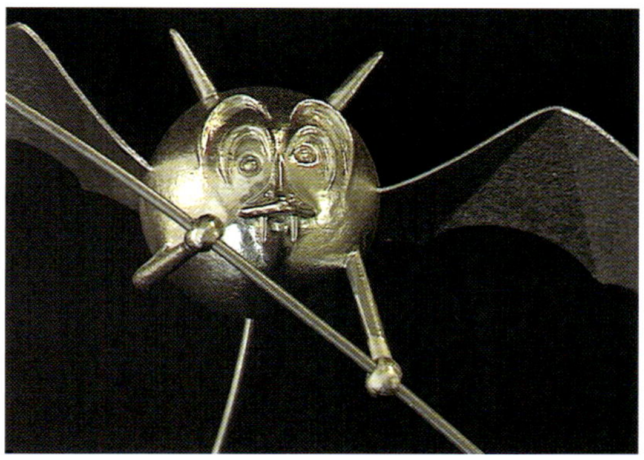
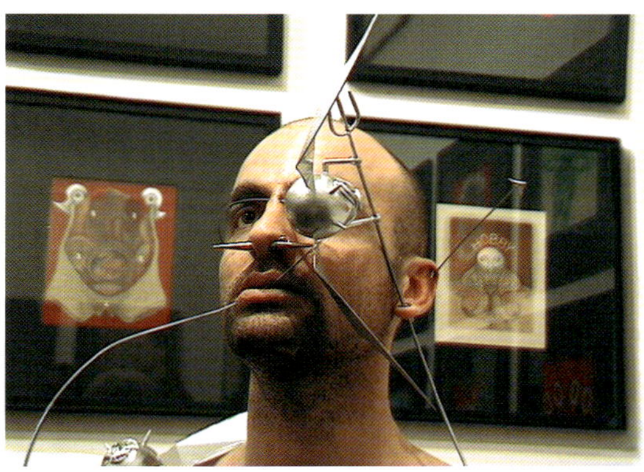
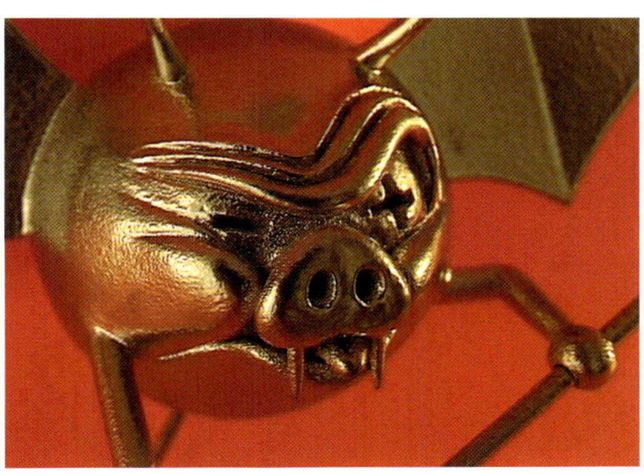
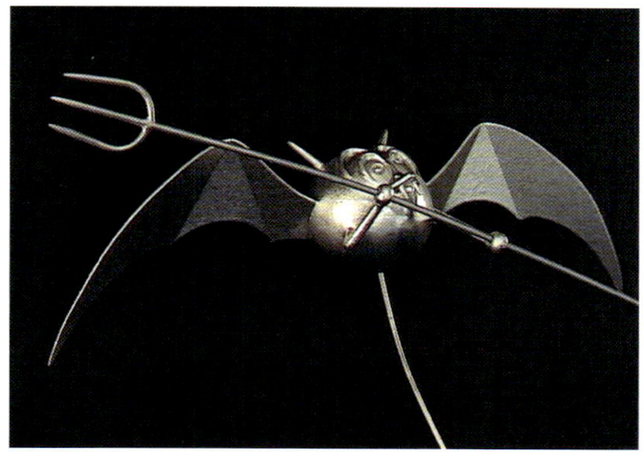
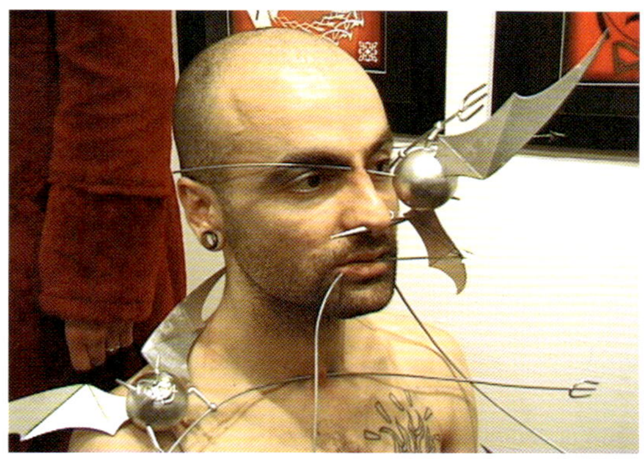
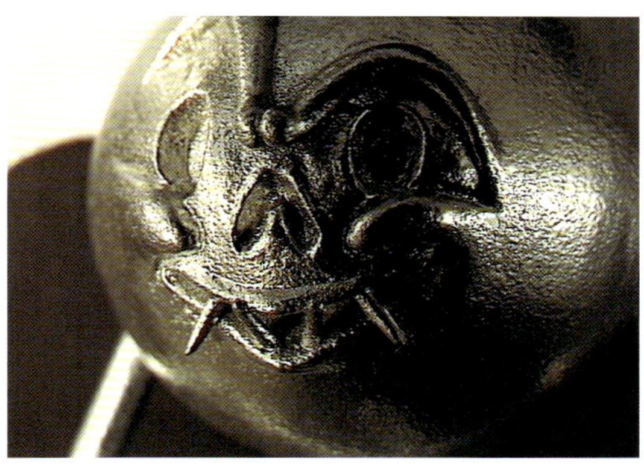
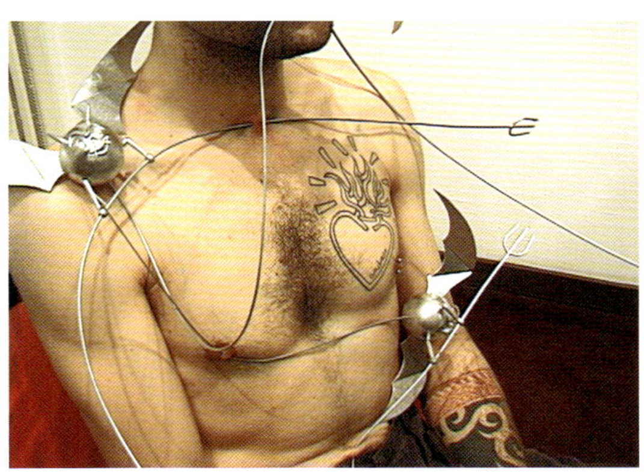
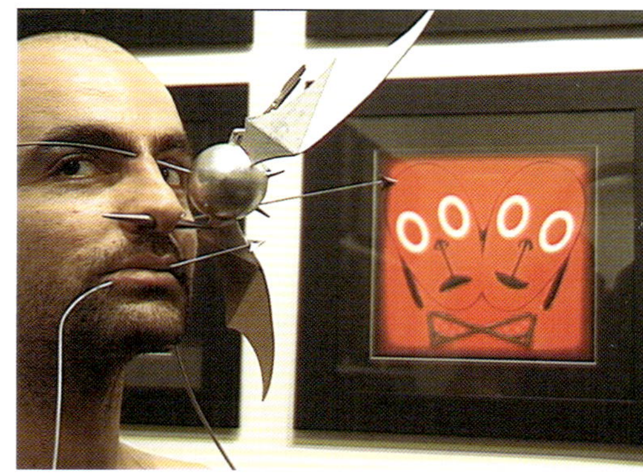
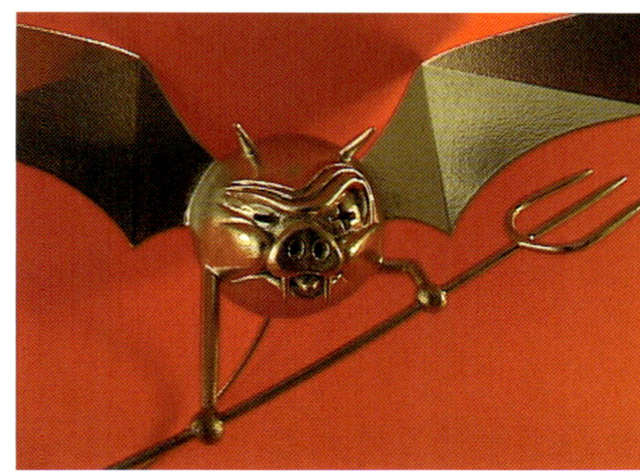
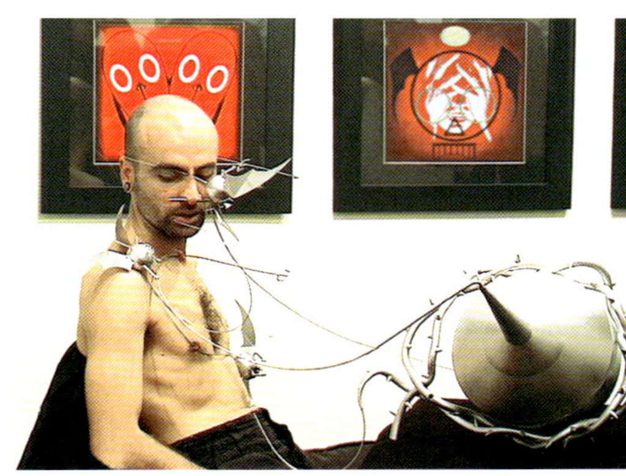
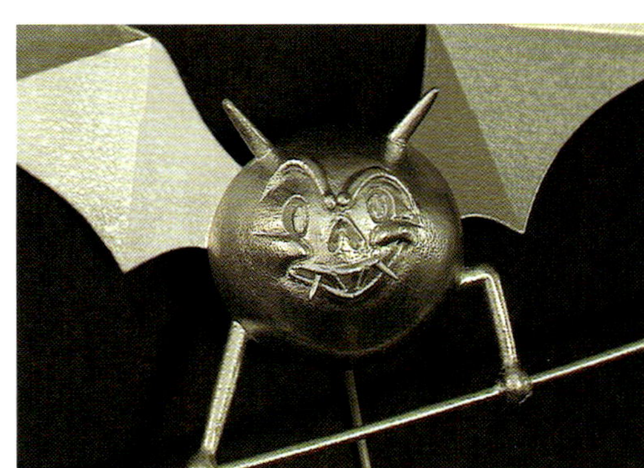

Corte & Nurcis: *Pino Piercing wears a sculpture*, 1997.
Cibachrome prints from a series of 15 video stills.
15¾ x 21¾" each (40 x 55 cm)
GC 1084-1098.

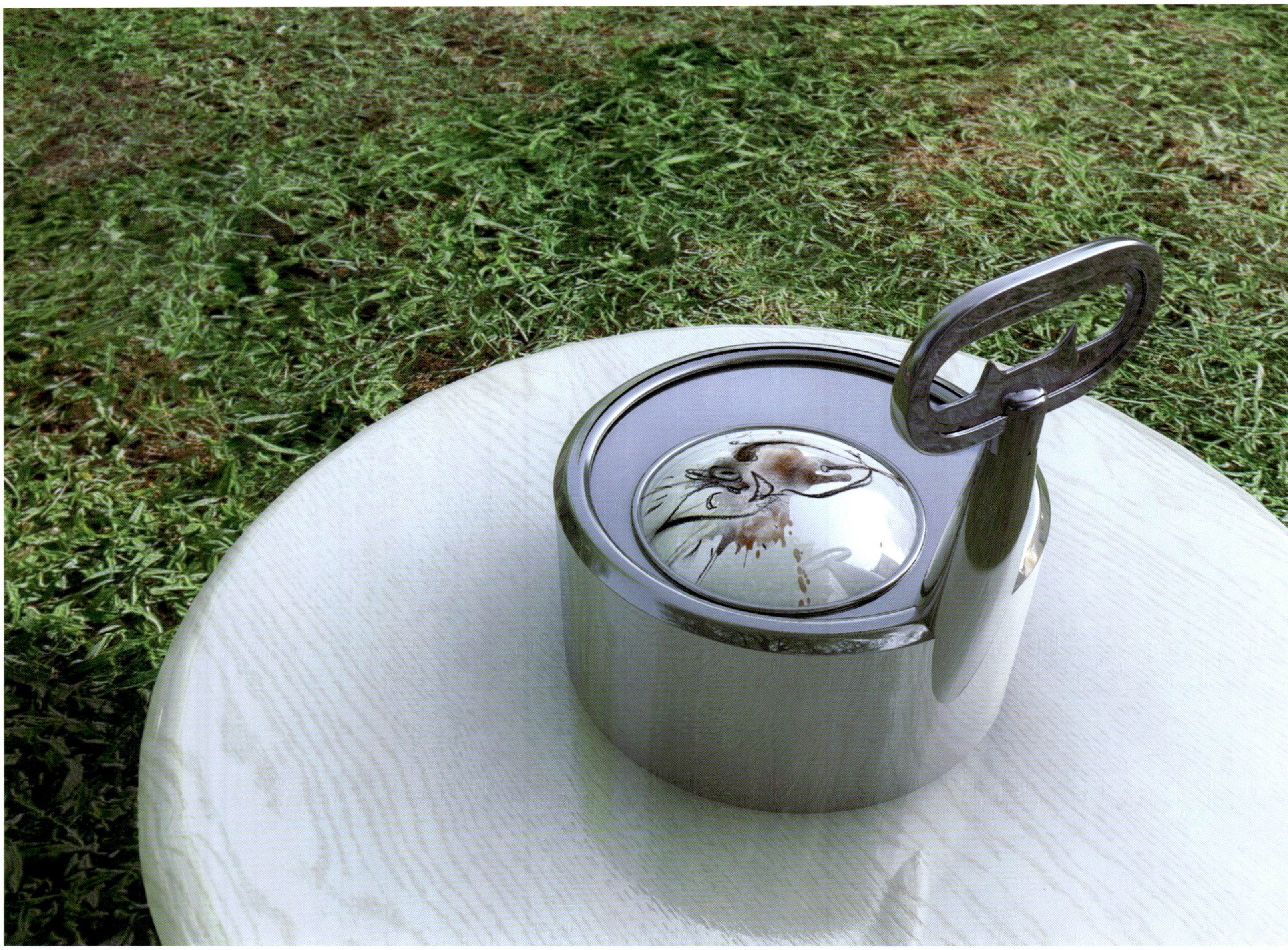

RWD (Right Wrist Disarticulation) with Bottle Opener.
Promo Picture from the *Devotees and Wannabees* series, 1994-97.
Prototype of substitutive jewelry for voluntary hand amputation.
Stainless steel, photoceramic with reproduction of a charcoal and ink drawing.
4½ x 2¾ x 2¾" (11 x 7 x 7 cm).
GC 881.

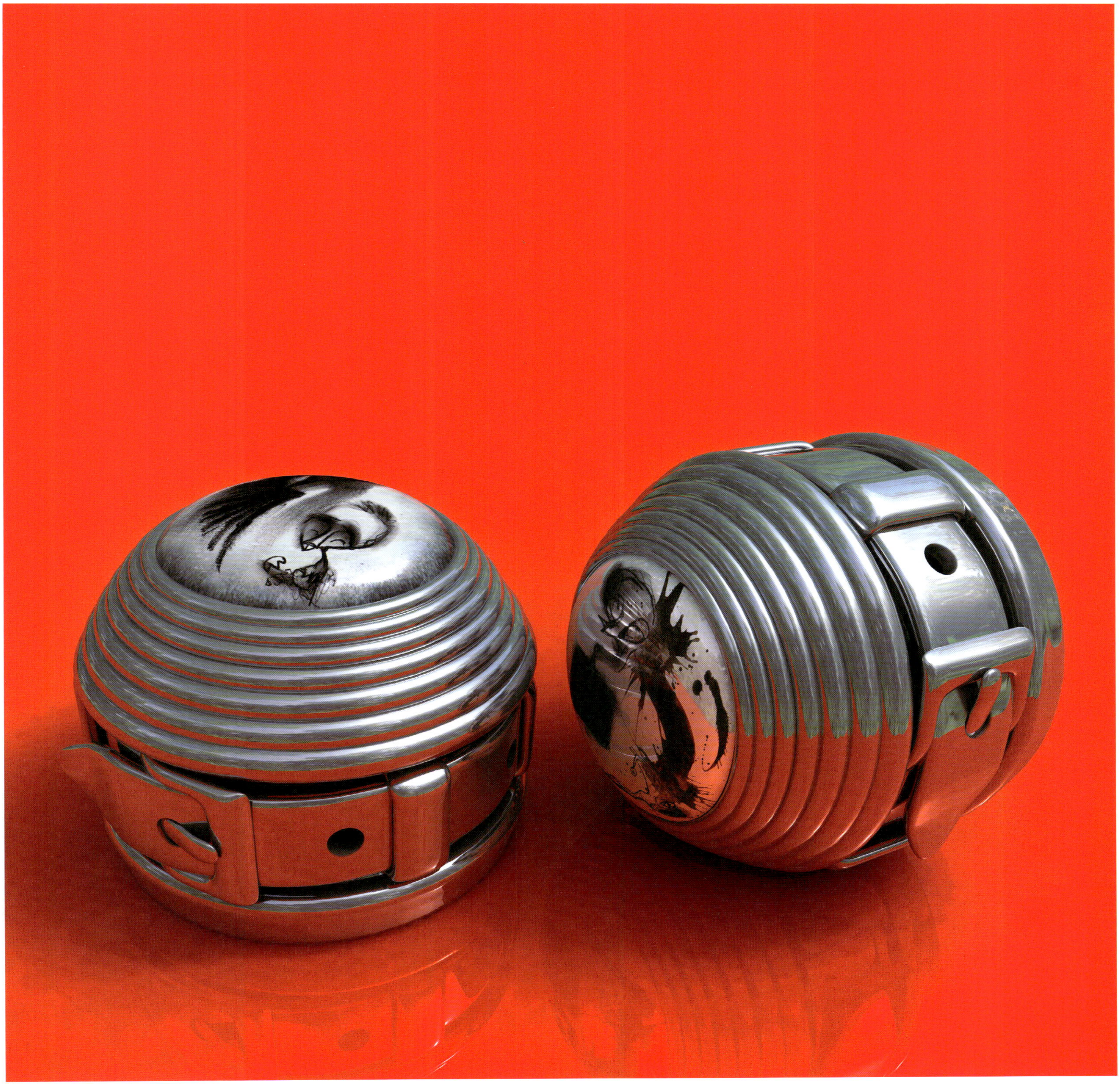

LWD - RWD (Left Wrist - Right Wrist Disarticulation).
Promo Picture from the *Devotees and Wannabees* series, 1994-97.
Two prototypes of substitutive jewelry for voluntary hands amputation.
Stainless steel, photoceramic with reproductions of charcoal and ink drawings.
3 x 2¾ x 2¾" each (7,5 x 7 x 7 cm).
GC 876, 877.

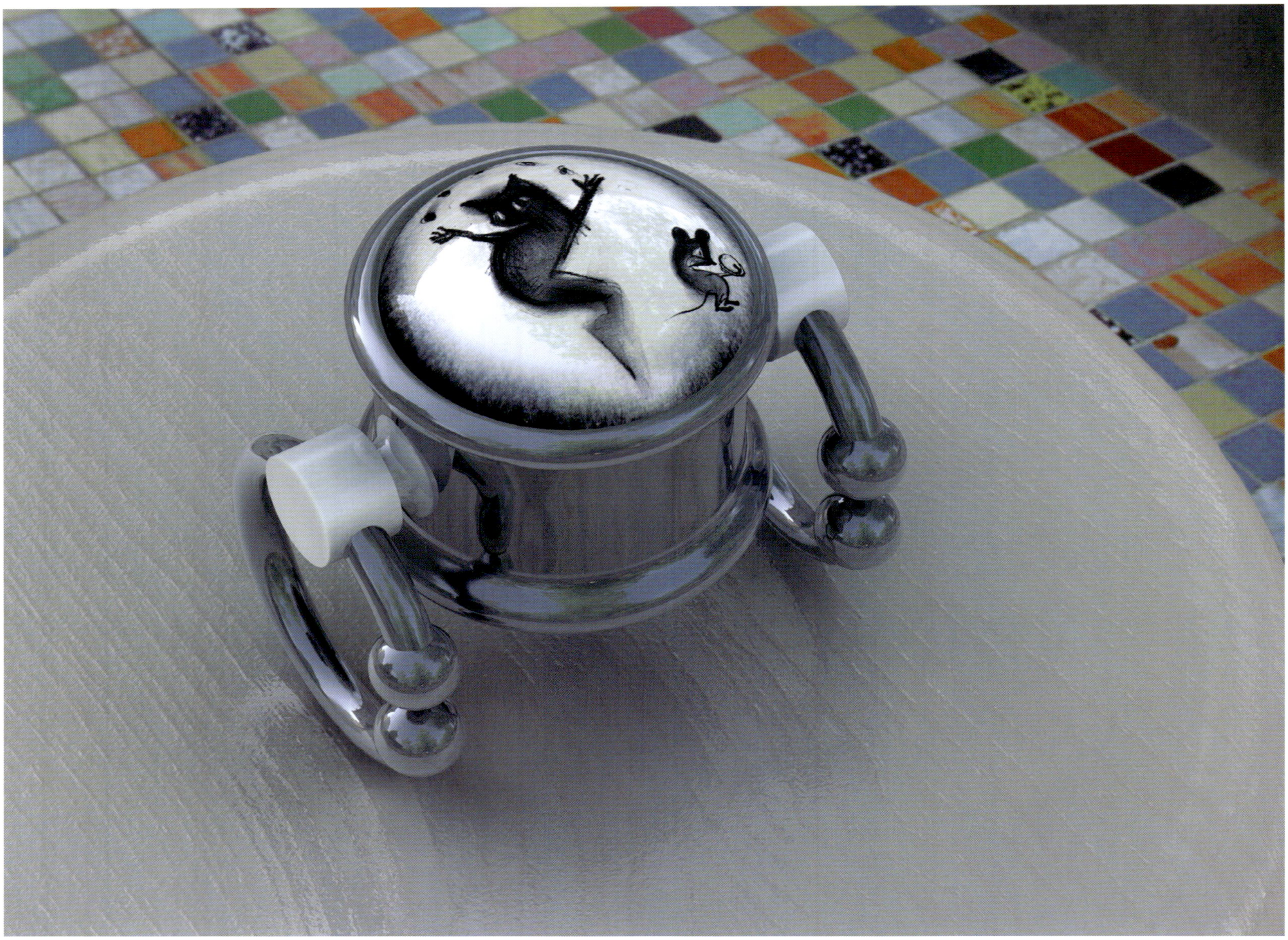

PD (Phalanges Disarticulation).
Promo Picture from the *Devotees and Wannabees* series, 1994-97.
Prototype of substitutive jewelry for voluntary finger amputation.
Stainless steel, photoceramics with reproduction of a charcoal drawing.
1½ x 1¼ x 0,9" (3,5 x 3,2 x 2,2 cm).
GC 884.

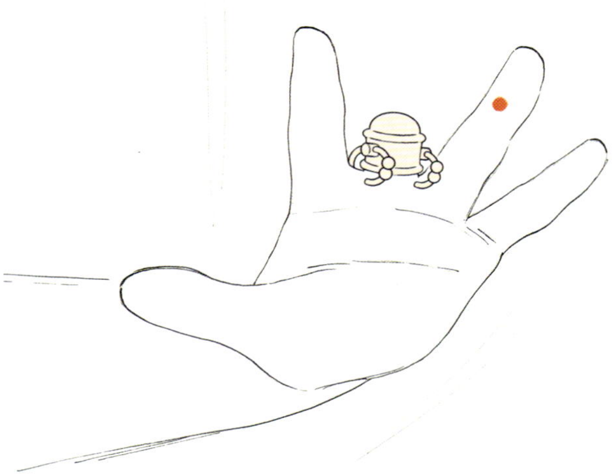

PDP (Phalanges Disarticulation Project). Detail.
Sketch for the *Devotees and Wannabees* series, circa 1994.
Graphite, ink, watercolor mixed with blood on paper.
23½ x 27½" (60 x 70 cm).
SC 657.

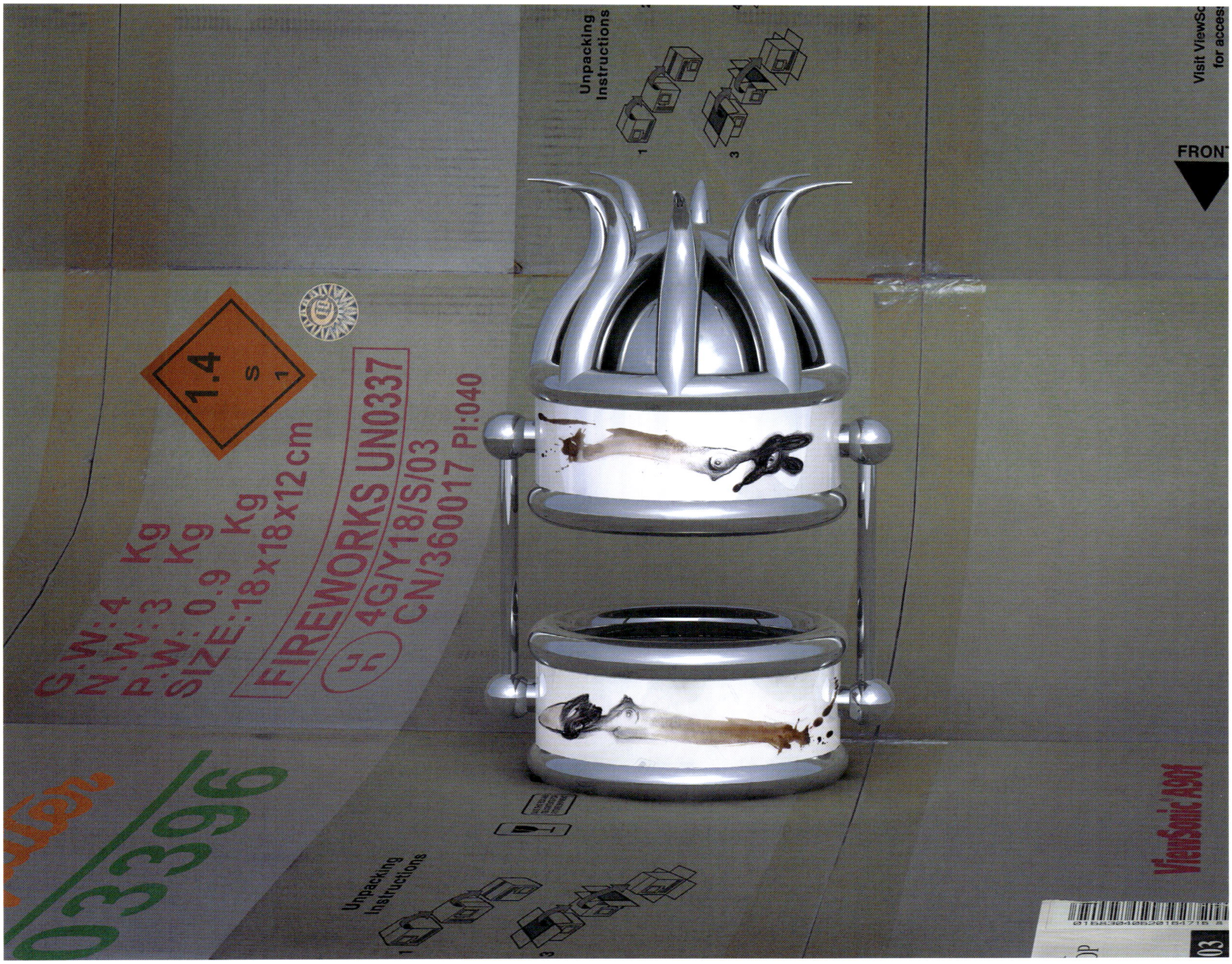

DWD (Defensive Wrist Disarticulation).
Promo Picture from the *Devotees and Wannabees* series, 1994-97.
Prototype of substitutive jewelry for voluntary hand amputation.
Stainless steel, photoceramics with reproductions of charcoal and ink drawings.
6 x 3½ x 3½" (15 x 9 x 9 cm).
GC 875.

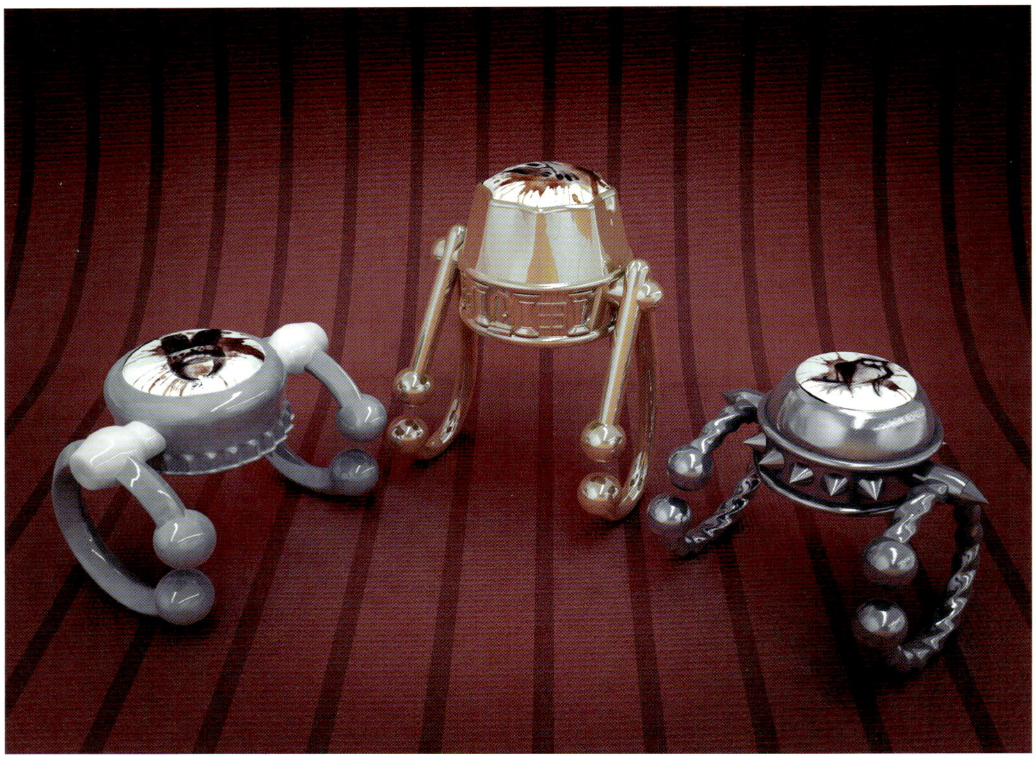

IPD - MPD - RPD (Index-finger Phalanges - Medium-finger Phalanges - Ring-finger Phalanges Disarticulation).
Promo Picture from the *Devotees and Wannabees* series, 1994-97.
Three prototypes of substitutive jewelry for voluntary fingers amputation.
Metals, photoceramics with reproductions of charcoal and ink drawings.
L to R: 1 x 1¼ x 0,8” (2,7 x 3,2 x 2 cm); 1½ x 1 x 0,7” (3,7 x 2,5 x 1,8 cm); 1 x 1¼ x 0,9” (2,7 x 3,2 x 2,4 cm).
GC 878, 879, 880.

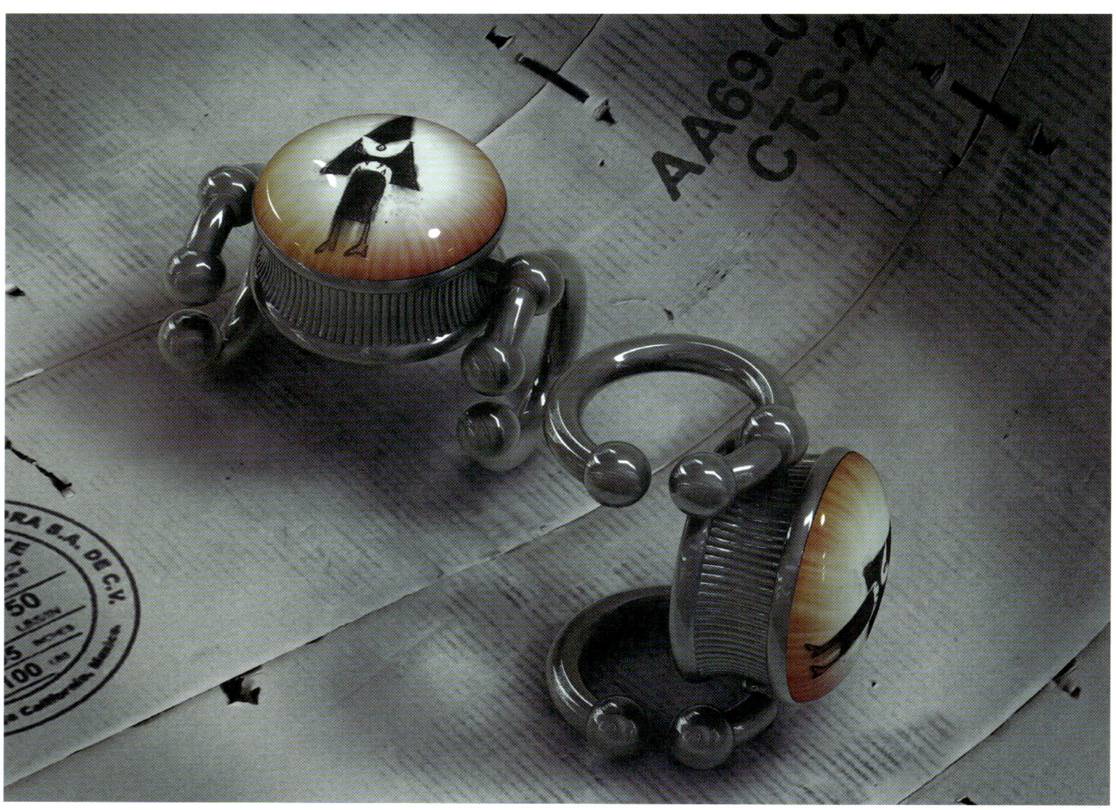

DPD (Double Phalanges Disarticulation). Promo Picture from the *Devotees and Wannabees* series, 1994-97.
Two prototypes of substitutive jewelry for voluntary fingers amputation.
Metal, photoceramics with reproductions of charcoal and ink drawings.
1 x 1½ x 0,9” each (2,7 x 3,2 x 2,2 cm).
GC 882, 883.

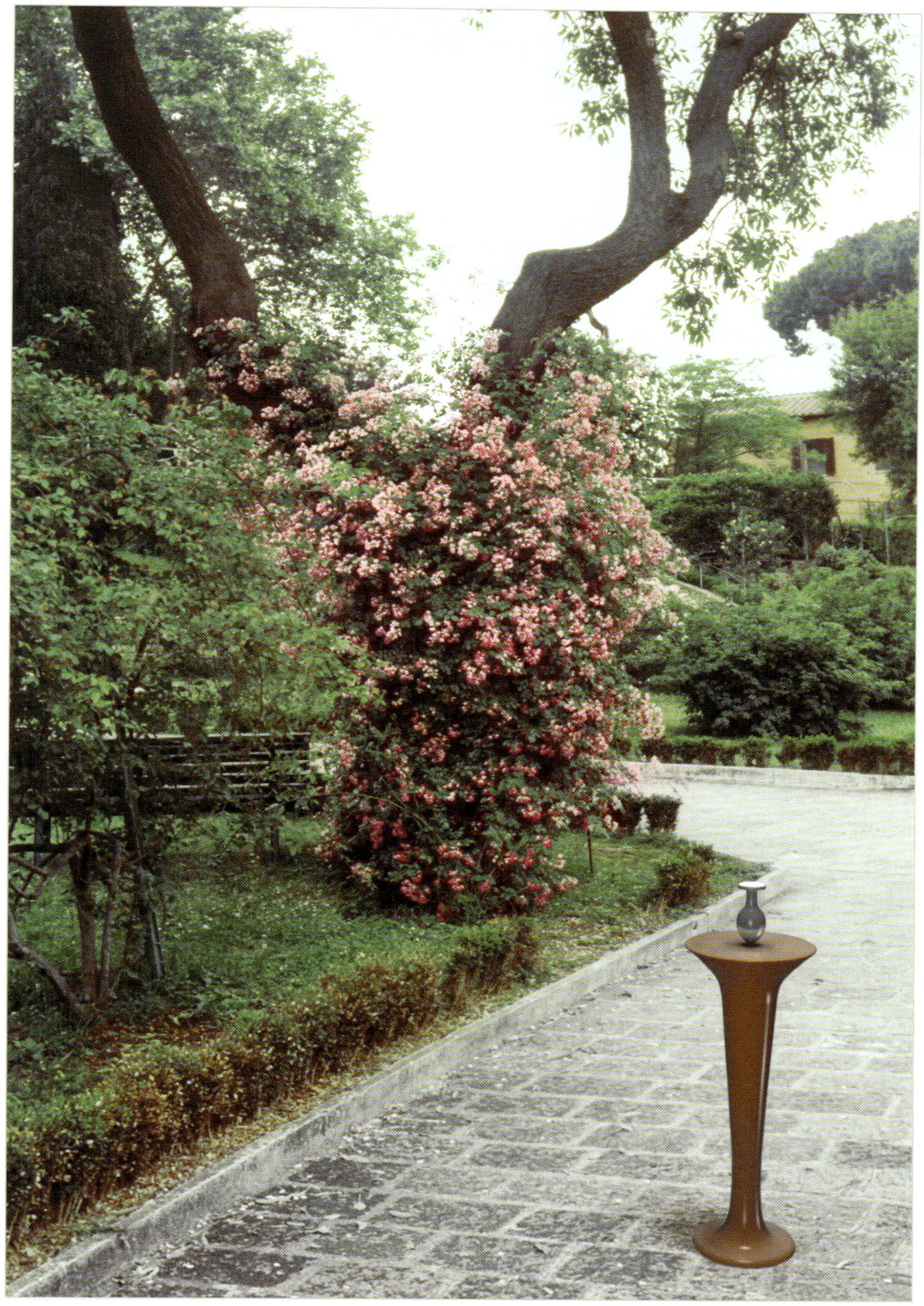

Cibachrome from the *New Botanical Rarities* series, 1998.
Installation at the City Rose Garden, Rome (detail).
Metal body-insertable sculpture with ceramic setting balanced on fiberglass pedestal.
43¼ x 11½ x 11½" (110 x 29 x 29 cm).
GC 1260.

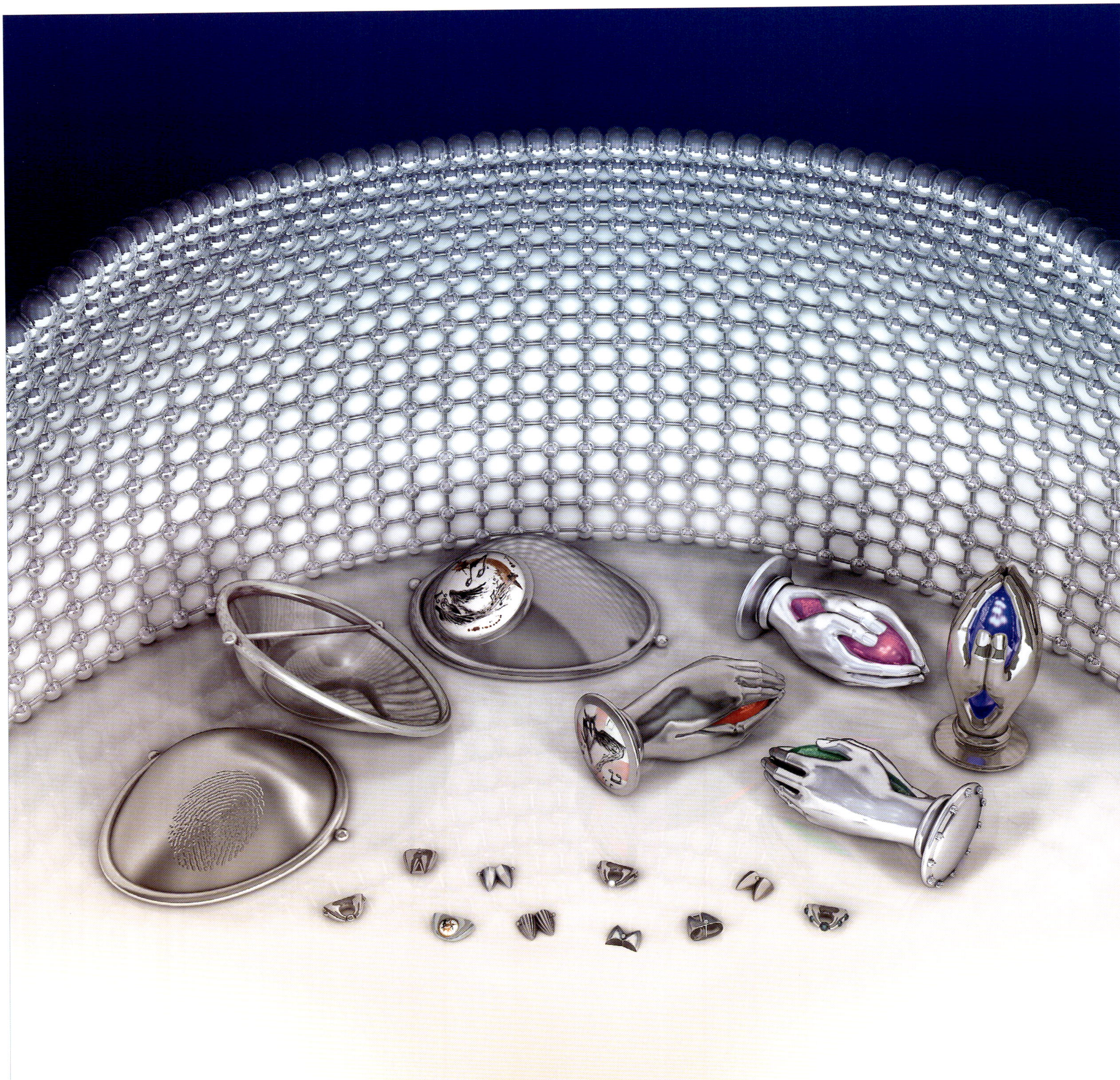

Clockwise from left:

RSD (Right Shoulder Disarticulation) front and rear; *LSD (Left Shoulder Disarticulation)*.
Two prototypes of substitutive jewelry for voluntary arms amputation, from the *Devotees and Wannabees* series, 1994-97.
Stainless steel, engraving, ceramic setting with photoreproduction of charcoal and ink drawing.
8¾ x 6½ x 4" each (22 x 16,5 x 10 cm). GC 885, 886.

Prayer; *Powder*; *Plunge*; *Plop*.
Four prototypes for body-insertable sculptures, from the *Abstraction of the Void* series, 1995-96.
Metal and glass butt plugs containing cremation ashes; ceramic setting with photoreproduction of charcoal and ink drawing.
7¼ x 4¼ x 4¼" each (18,5 x 11 x 11 cm). GC 903, 904, 905, 906.

TB (Tongue Bisection) 01-10.
Ten prototypes of substitutive jewelry for artificial tongue bisection, from the *Devotees and Wannabees* series, 1994-97.
Silver, pearl, obsidian, ceramic, photoreproduction of charcoal and ink drawing.
Circa 1 x 1½ x 0½" each (2,6 x 3,8 x 1,5 cm). GC 887, 888, 889, 890, 891, 892, 893, 894, 895, 896.

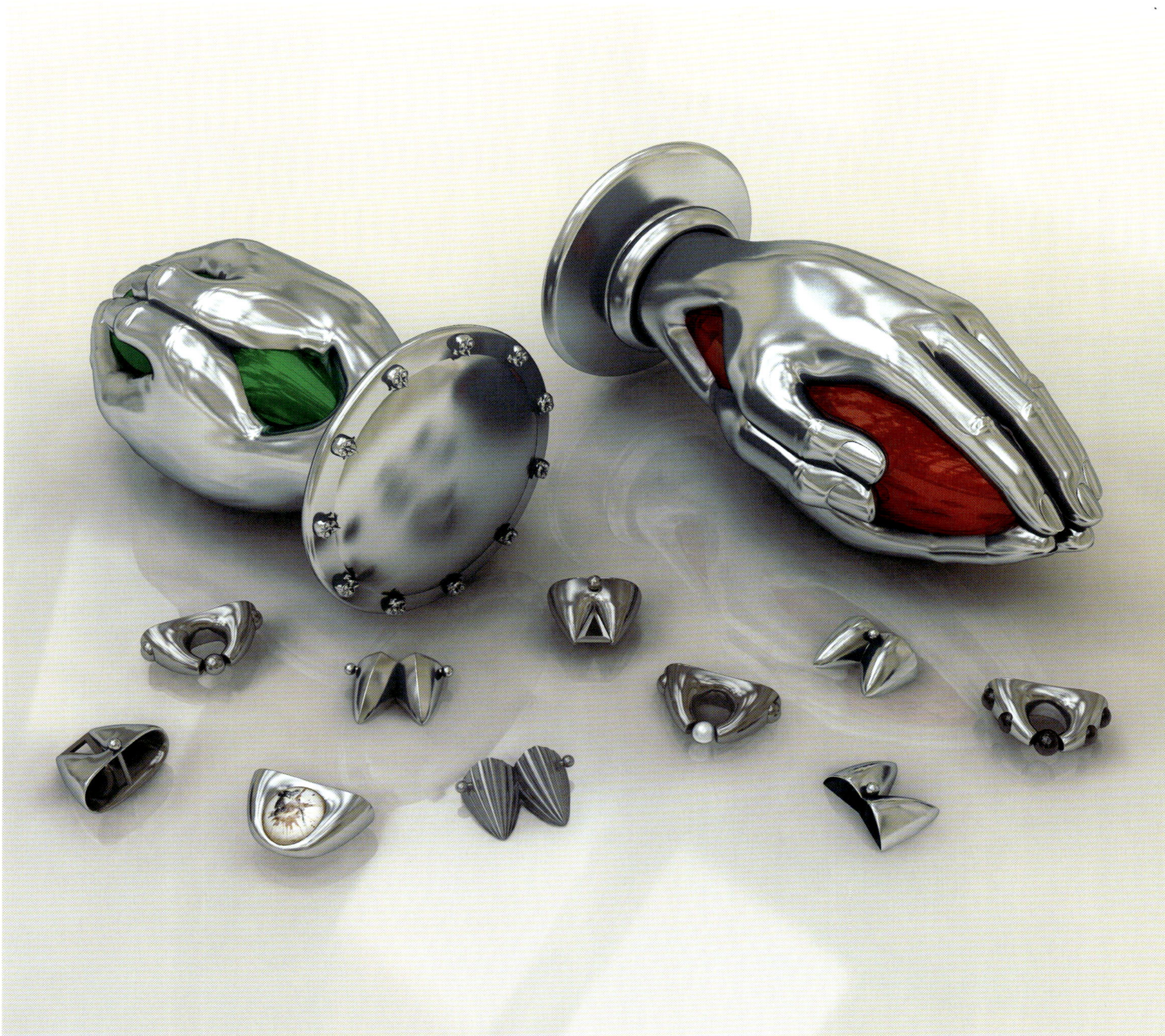

Plunge; metal, glass, cremation ashes.
Plop; metal, glass, photoceramic, cremation ashes.
TB 01-10; silver, pearl, obsidian, photoceramic.
Cf. opposite.

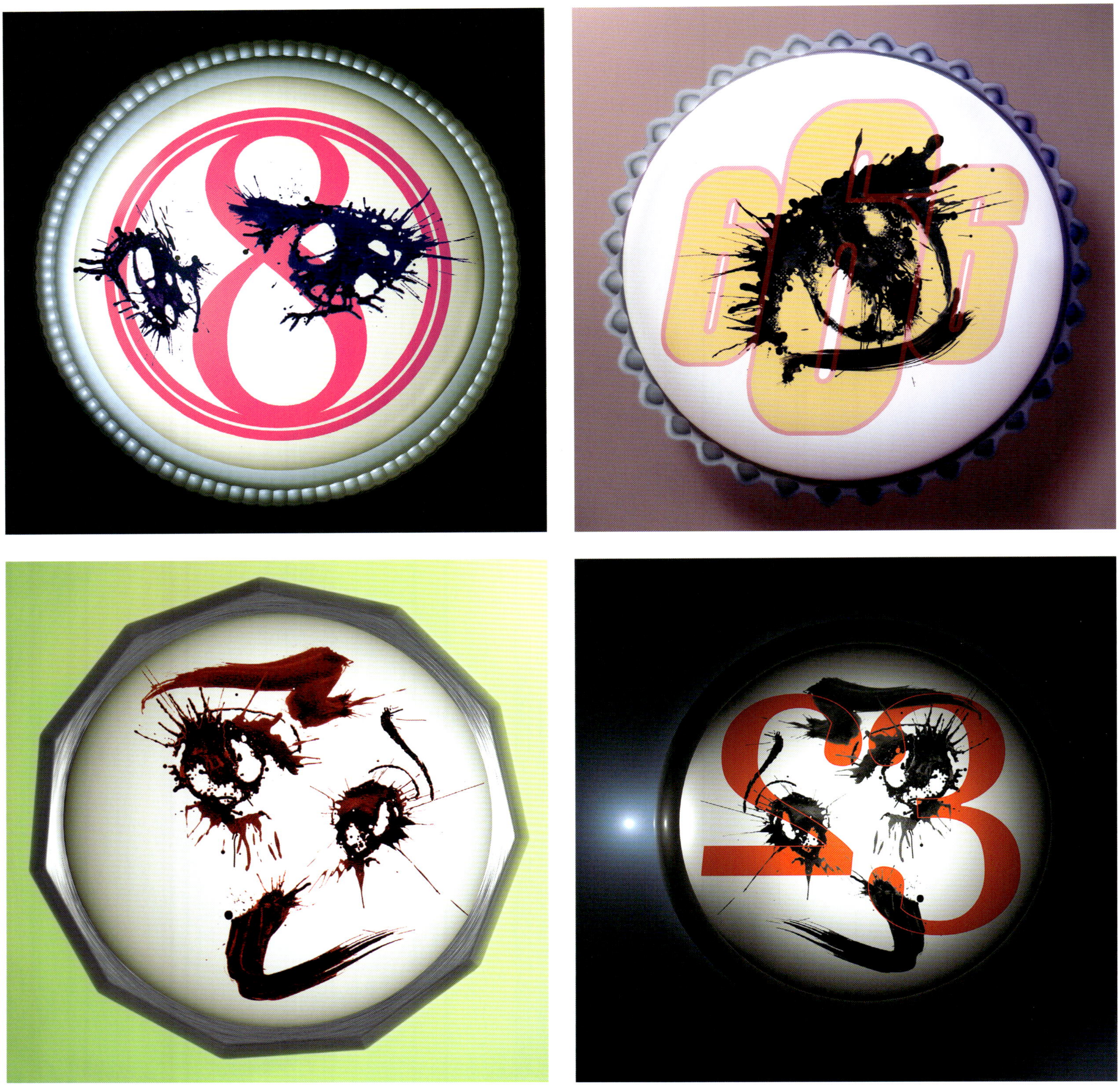

Introspectives.
Four settings for body-insertable sculptures from the *Abstraction of the Void* series, 1995-96.
Photoceramics with reproductions of ink drawings; metal frames.
Each setting: diam. 4” (10 cm).
GC 936, 937, 938, 939.

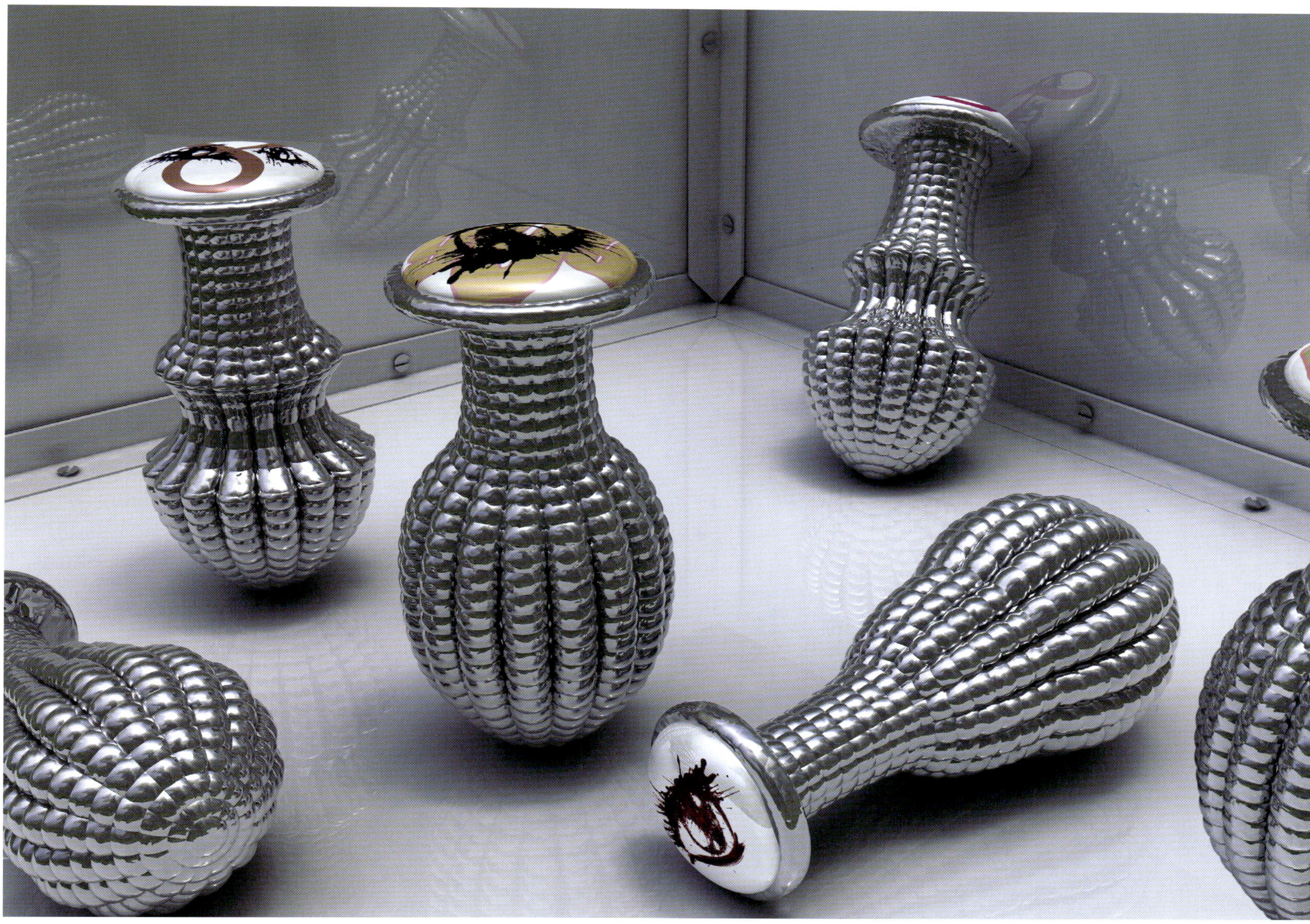

Eyes.
Promo Picture from the *Abstraction of the Void* series, 1995-96.
Six prototypes for body-insertable sculptures. Stainless steel, photoceramics with reproductions of ink drawings.
Ht. circa 6¼" each sculpture (15,5 cm).
GC 940, 941, 942, 943, 944, 945.

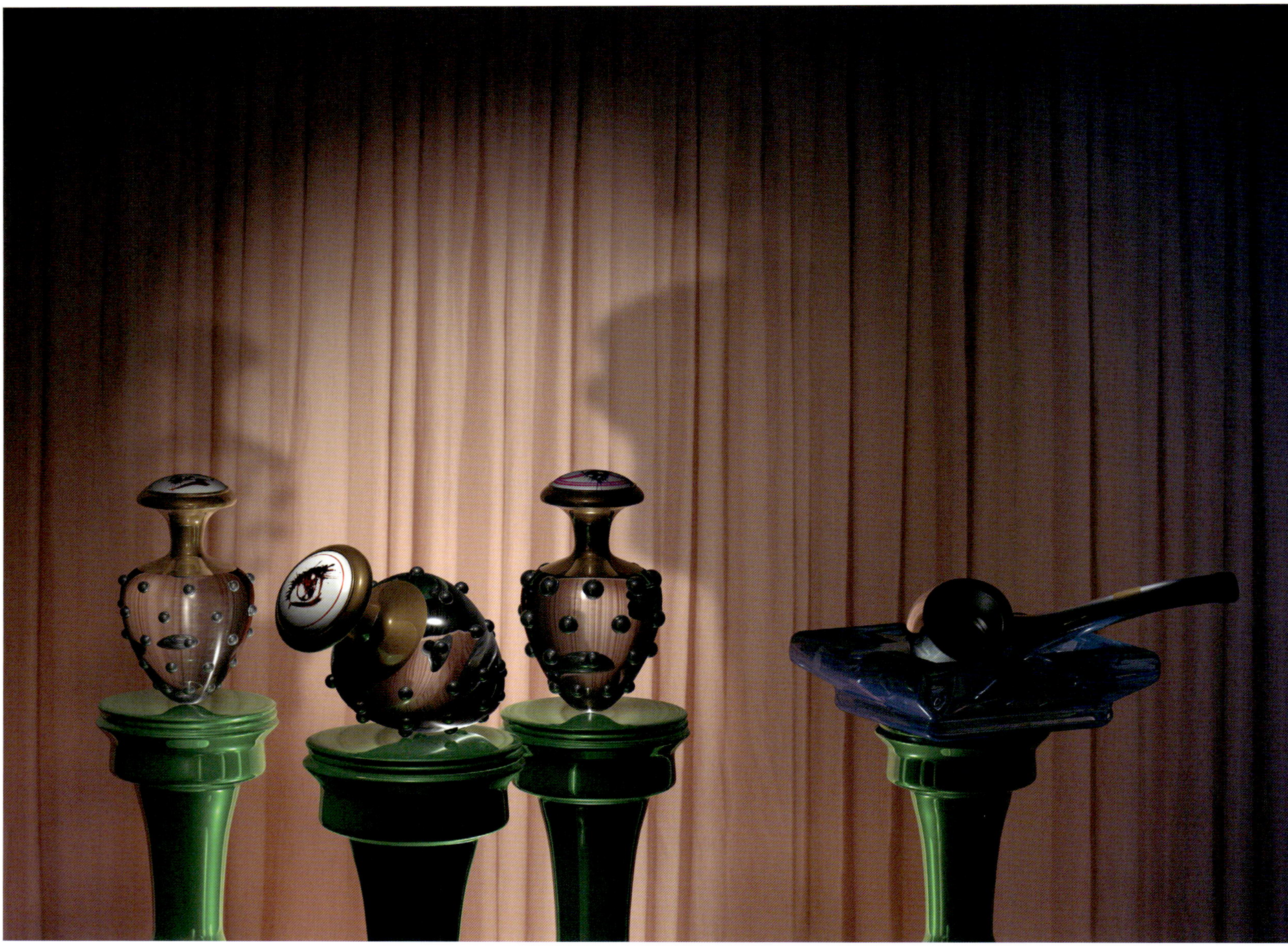

Smoke.
Promo Picture from the *Abstraction of the Void* series, 1995-96.
Three prototypes for body-insertable sculptures.
Gold, silver, glass, photoceramics with reproductions of ink drawings.
6¼ x 3½ x 3½" each sculpture (16 x 9 x 9 cm).
GC 946, 947, 948.

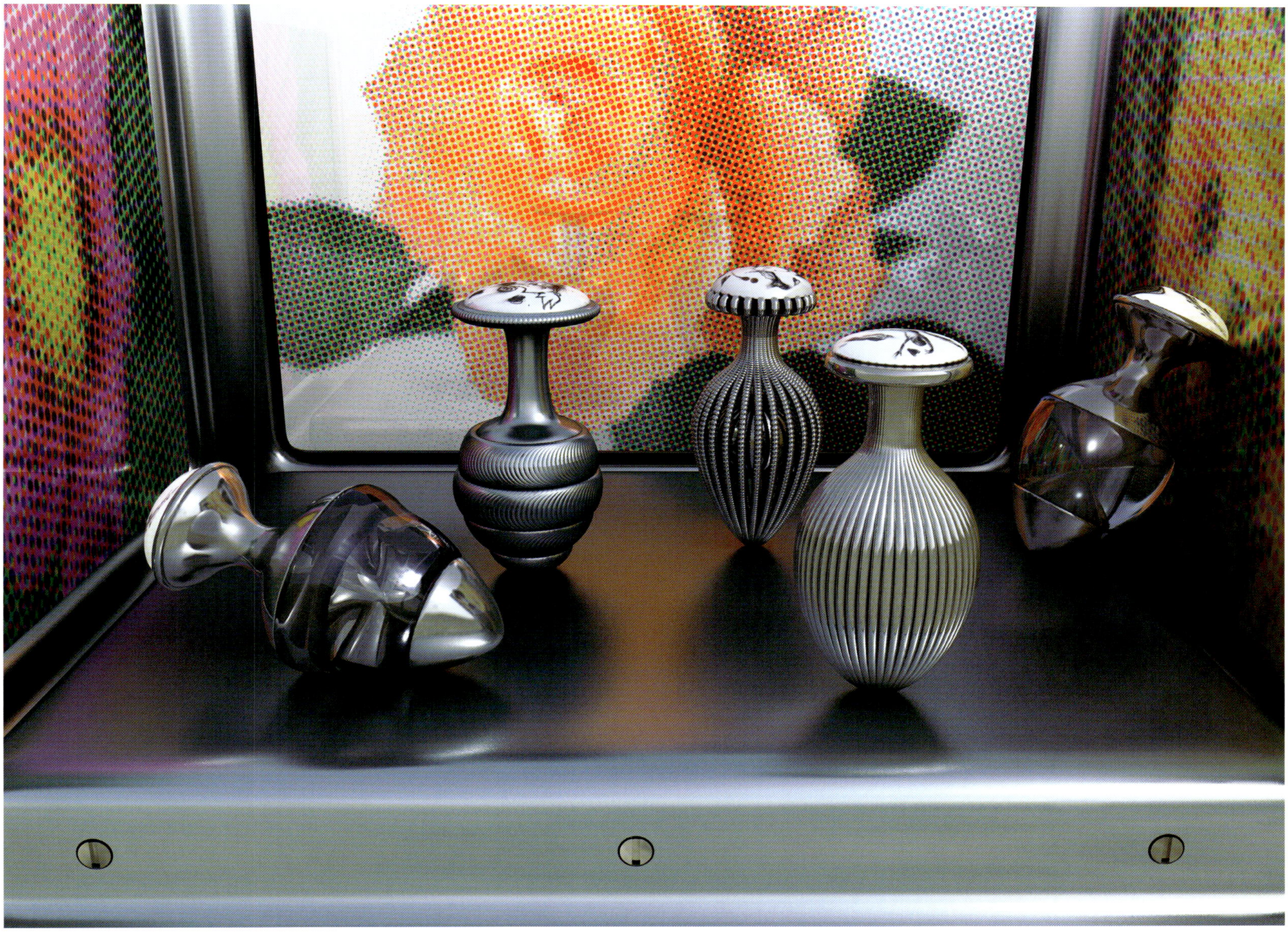

Flowers Five.
Promo Picture from the *Abstraction of the Void* series, 1995-96.
Five prototypes for body-insertable sculptures.
Metals, glass, photoceramics with reproductions of charcoal and ink drawings;
aluminum box with lambda prints on plexiglas.
Ht. circa 5” each sculpture (12,5 cm).
GC 954, 955, 956, 957, 958.

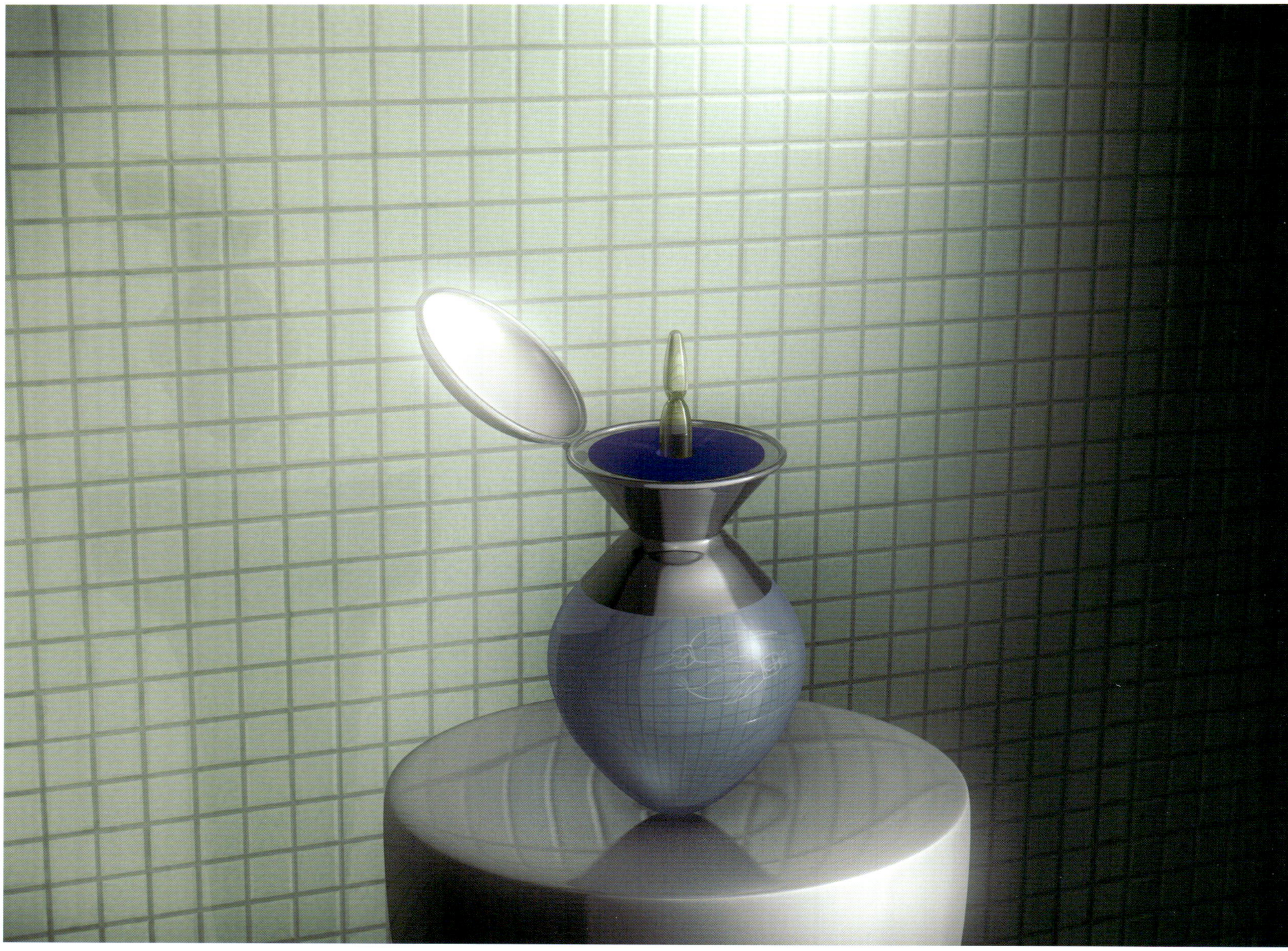

Pop.
Promo picture from the *Abstraction of the Void* series, 1995-96.
Prototype for body-insertable sculpture.
Metal, engraved glass, velvet, openable ceramic setting, little glass vial containing amyl nitrate. Ambient: wet fog.
5 x 3 x 3" (12,5 x 7,5 x 7,5 cm).
GC 959.

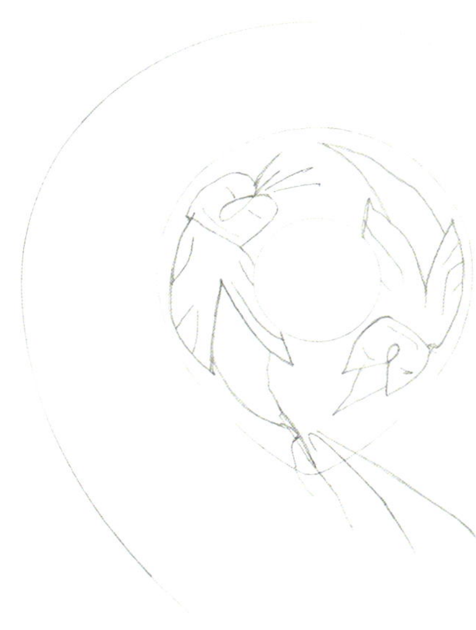

Sketch for the engraved glass of the 'Pop' Butt Plug, 1995.
Graphite on paper.
13 x 9½" (33 x 24 cm).
SC 699.

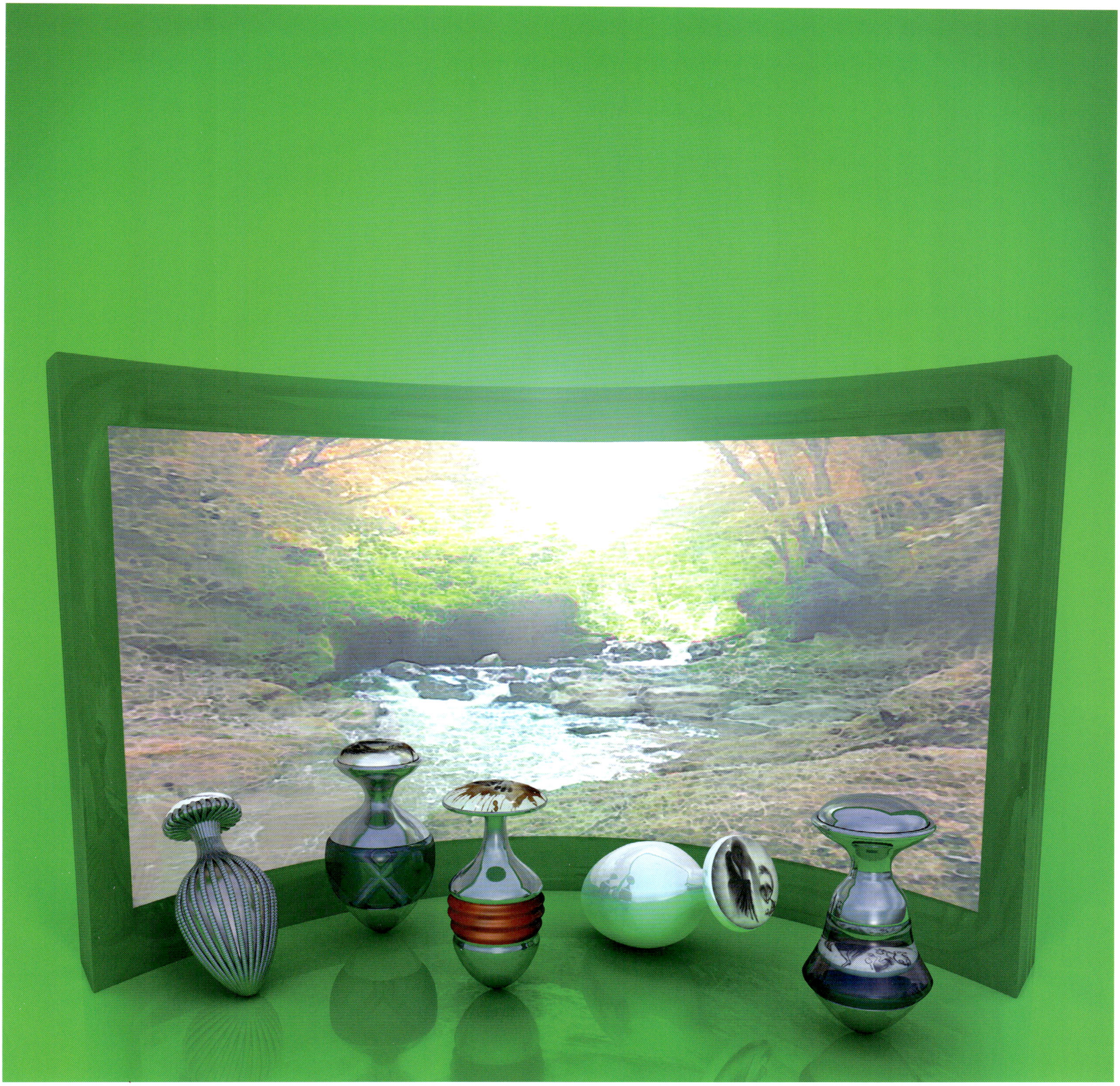

River Five.
Promo Picture from the *Abstraction of the Void* series, 1995-96.
Five prototypes for body-insertable sculptures.
Metals, glass, resin, photoceramics with reproductions of charcoal and ink drawings.
Lambda print on pvc framed in a plexiglas lightbox.
Ht. circa 5" each sculpture (12,5 cm).
GC 949, 950, 951, 952, 953.

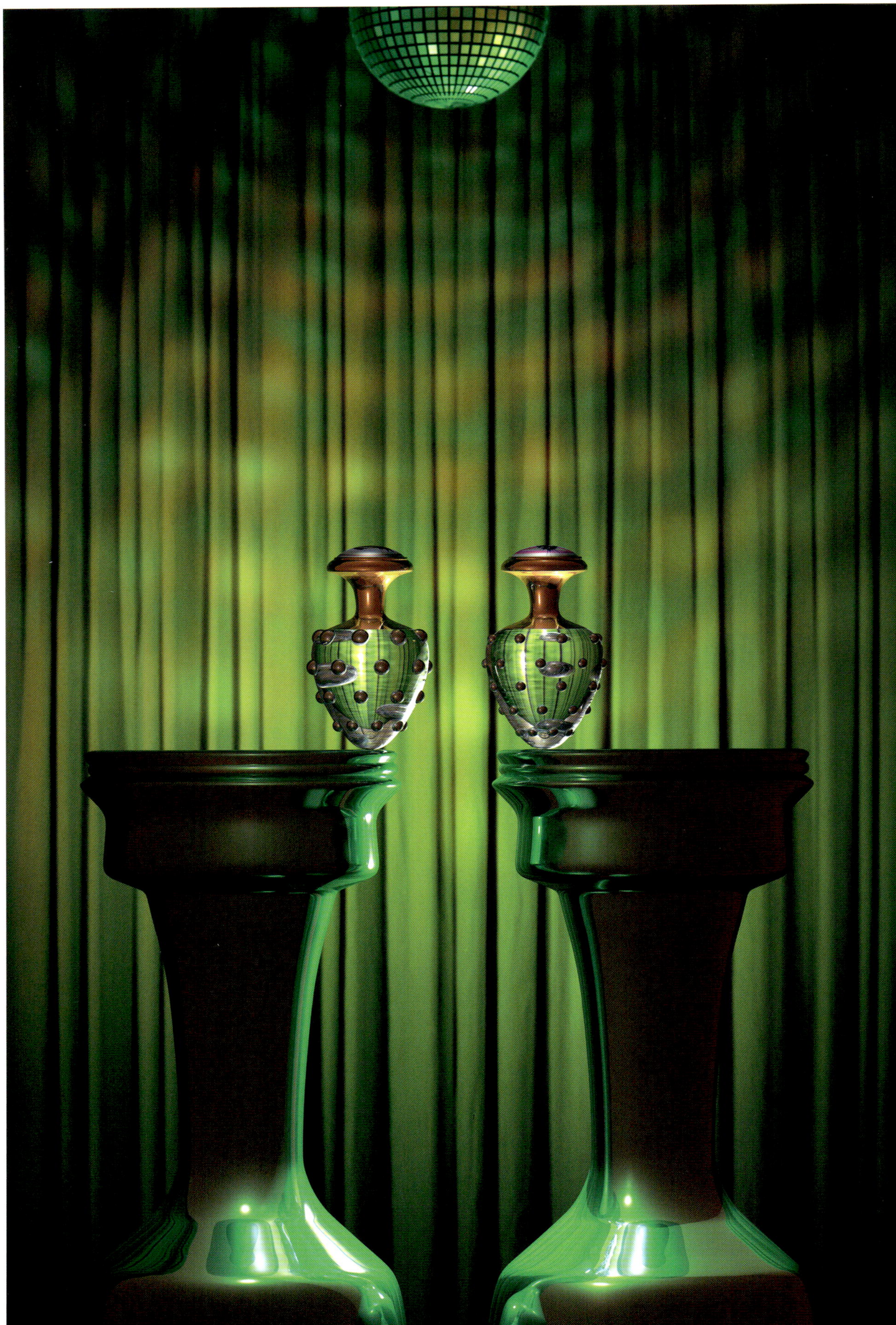

Disco.
Promo Picture from the *Abstraction of the Void* series, 1995-96.
Two prototypes for body-insertable sculptures. Gold, silver, glass, photoceramics with reproductions of ink drawings.
6¼ x 3½ x 3½” each sculpture (16 x 9 x 9 cm).
GC 946, 947.

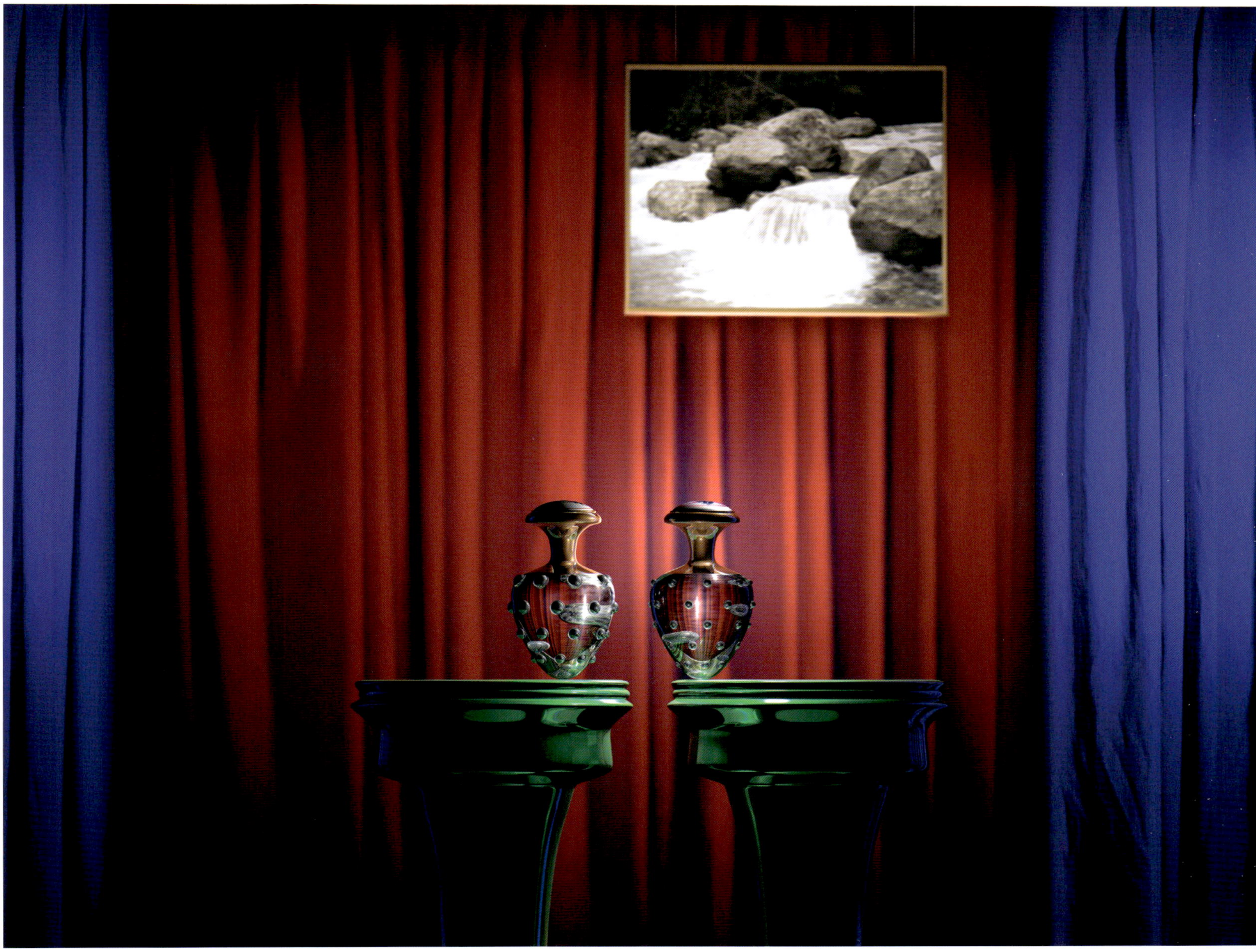

Symplegades.
Promo Picture from the *Abstraction of the Void* series, 1995-96.
Two prototypes for body-insertable sculptures.
Gold, silver, glass, photoceramics with reproductions of ink drawings.
6¼ x 3½ x 3½" each sculpture (16 x 9 x 9 cm).
GC 947, 948.

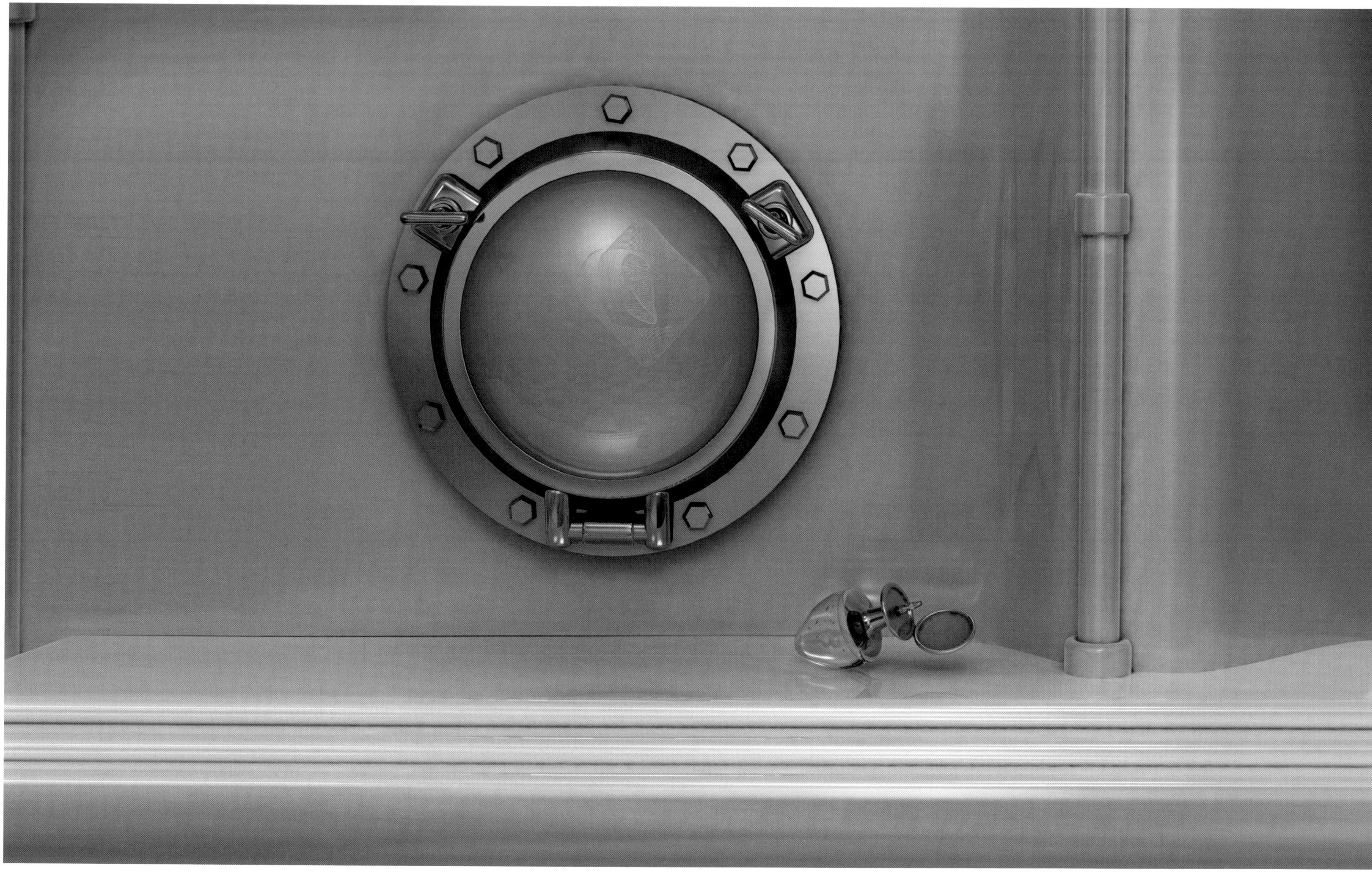

Marine.
Promo Picture from the *Abstraction of the Void* series, 1995-96. Prototype for body-insertable sculpture.
Metal and glass butt plug containing water and a group of sea-monkeys,
with openable ceramic setting and glass vial of amyl nitrate;
metal porthole with engraved glass.
Butt plug: 4¾ x 2½ x 2½” (12 x 6 x 6 cm).
Porthole: 23¾ x 23¾ x 4¼” (60 x 60 x 10,5 cm).
GC 962.

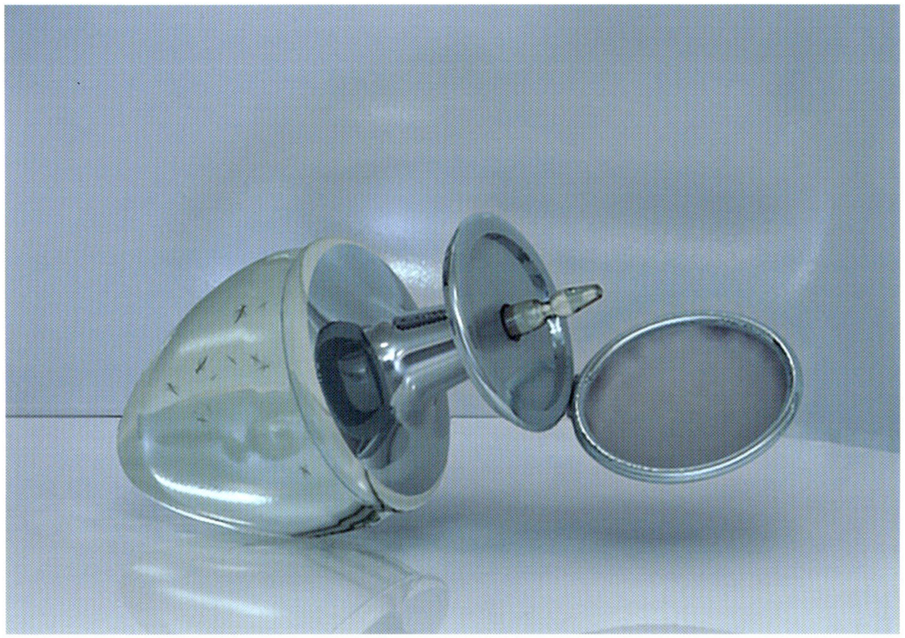

Marine (detail). Prototype for body-insertable sculpture.
Metal and glass butt plug containing water,
sea-monkeys and glass vial of amyl nitrate.
Cf. opposite.

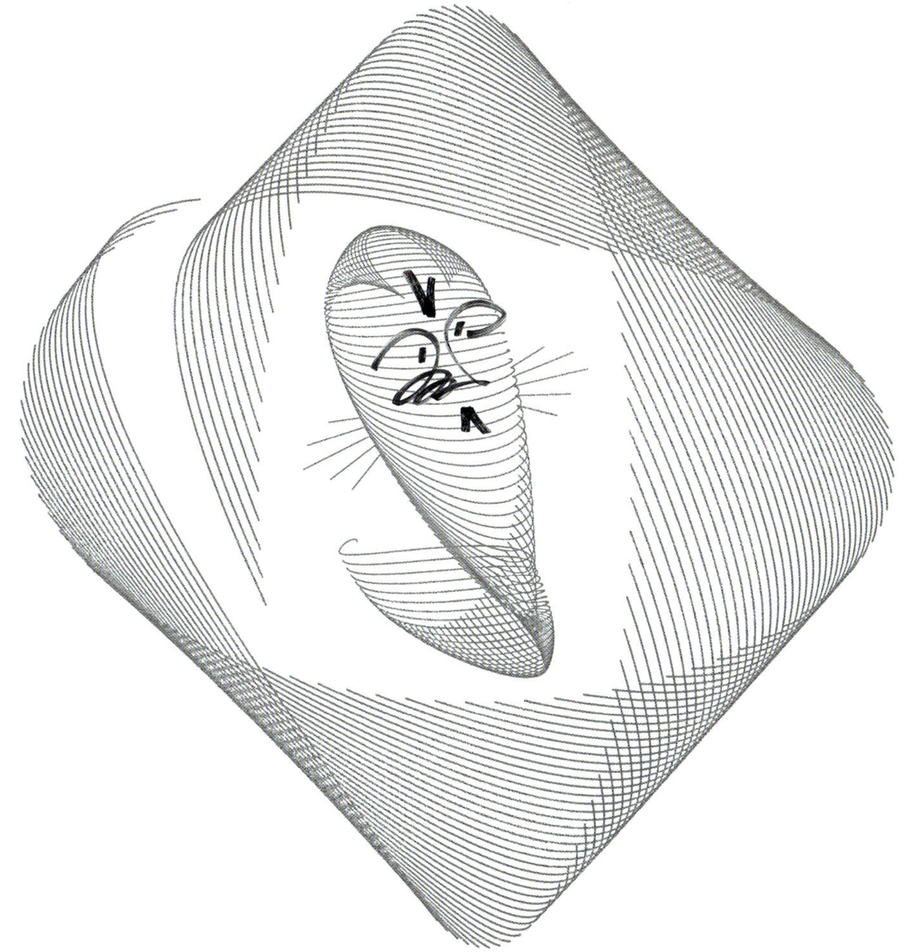

Sea Monkey, 1996.
Sketch for the engraved glass of the *Marine* porthole, from the *Abstraction of the Void* series.
Printer ink and marker on paper.
12½ x 8¼" (31 x 21 cm).
SC 726.

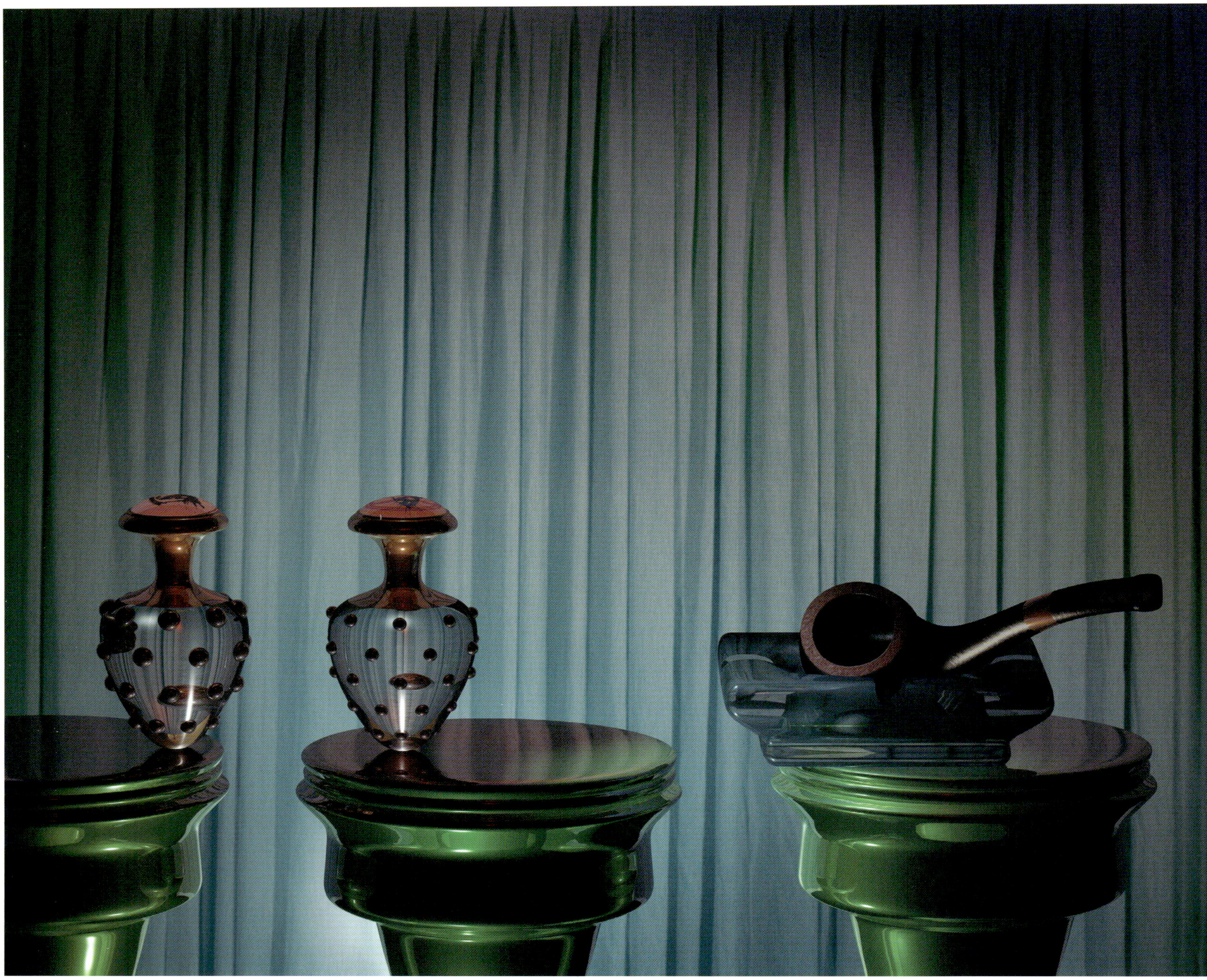

Pipe.
Promo Picture from the *Abstraction of the Void* series, 1995-96.
Two prototypes for body-insertable sculptures.
Gold, silver, glass, photoceramics with reproductions of ink drawings.
6¼ x 3½ x 3½" each sculpture (16 x 9 x 9 cm).
GC 946, 947.

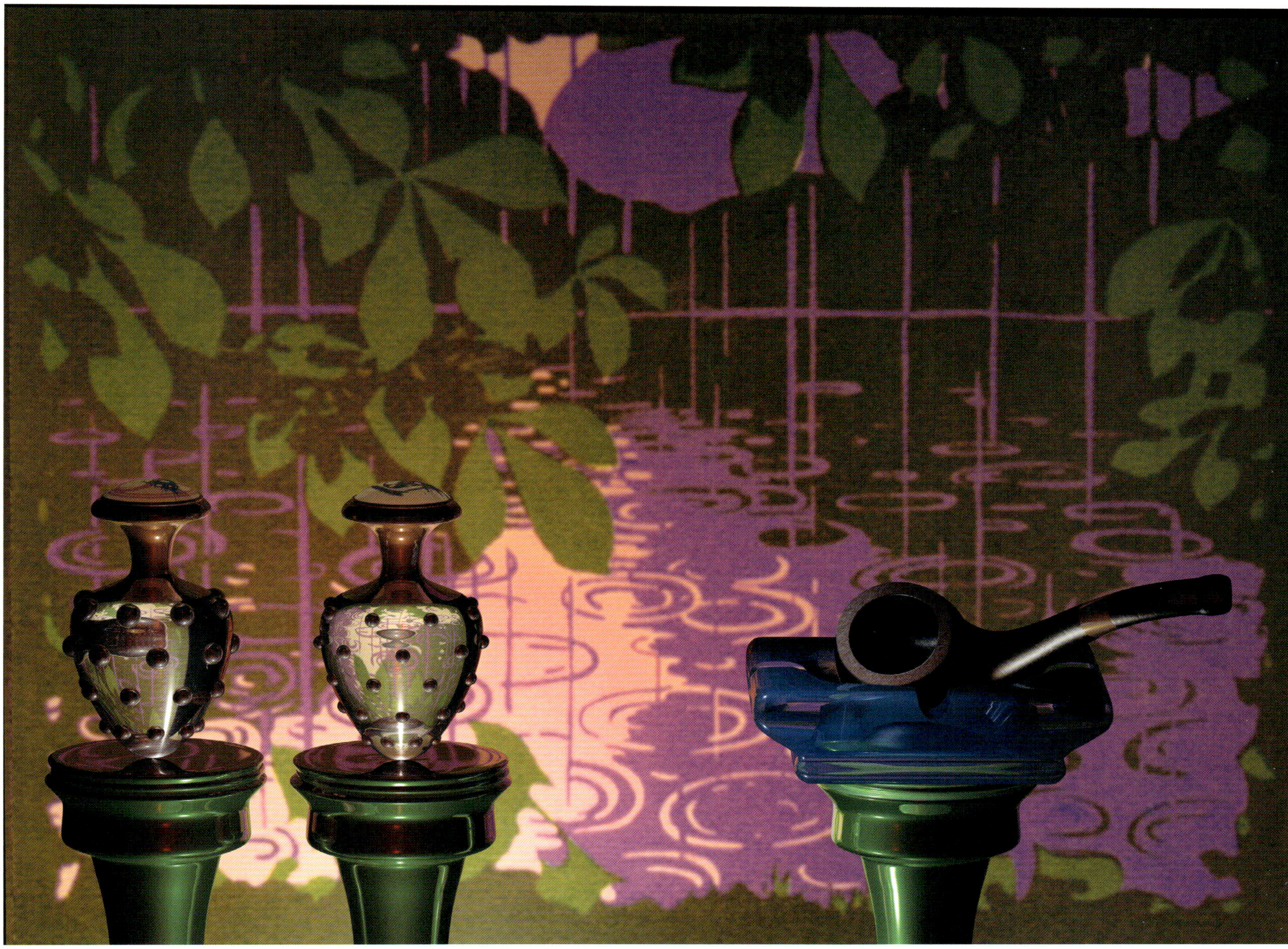

River Arras.
Promo Picture from the *Abstraction of the Void* series, 1995-96.
Two prototypes for body-insertable sculptures.
Gold, silver, glass, photoceramics with reproductions of ink drawings.
6¼ x 3½ x 3½" each sculpture (16 x 9 x 9 cm).
GC 946, 947.

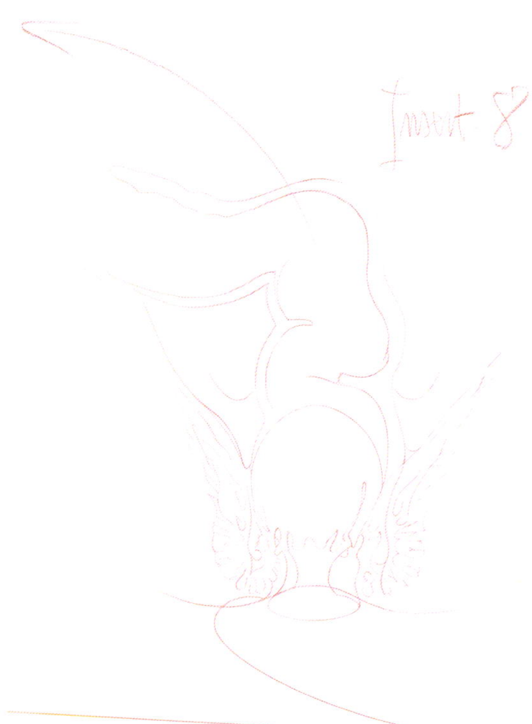

Sketch for a Butt Plug, 1996.
Watercolored pencil and tempera on paper.
13¾ x 9½" (35 x 24,2 cm).
SC 729.

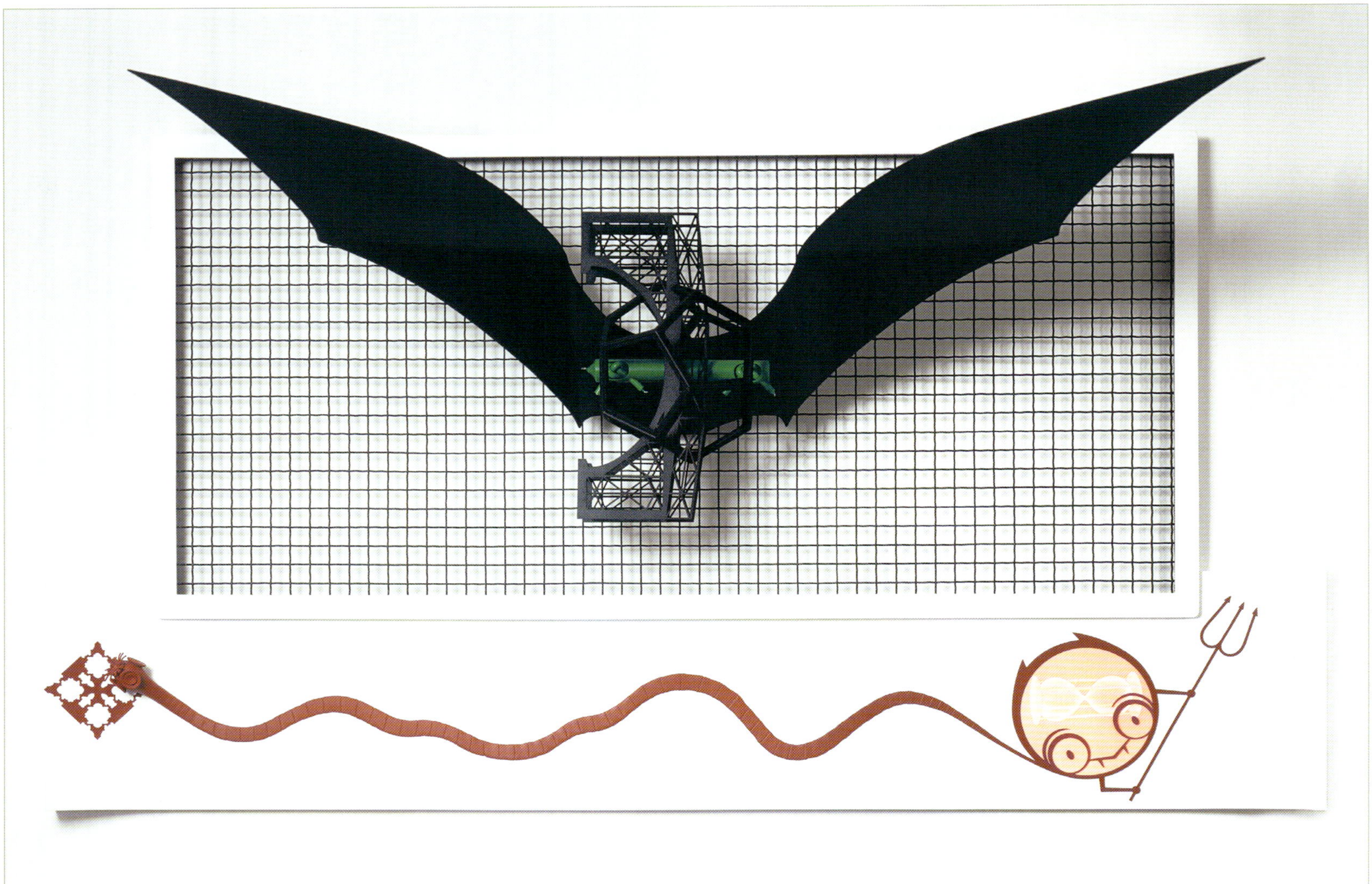

N.E.O. (*Near Earth Objects*), 1994.
Enamel on forex and iron; lacquer on wood; enamel and fluorescine on clear pvc;
enamel on paper cutout; carved green wax candles.
56¾ x 101½ x 32¼" (144 x 258 x 82 cm).
GC 813.

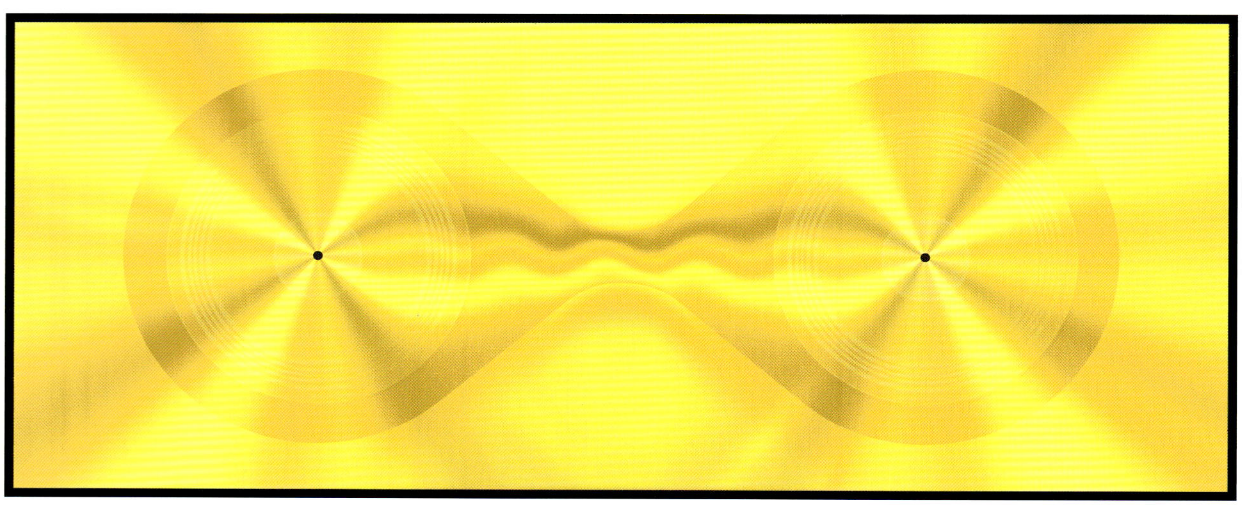

Golden Hits Sand-glass, 1995.
Nitrocellulose lacquer on plastic laminate, with two clear vinyl records.
16¼ x 47¼ x 2" (40,9 x 120 x 5 cm).
GC 910.

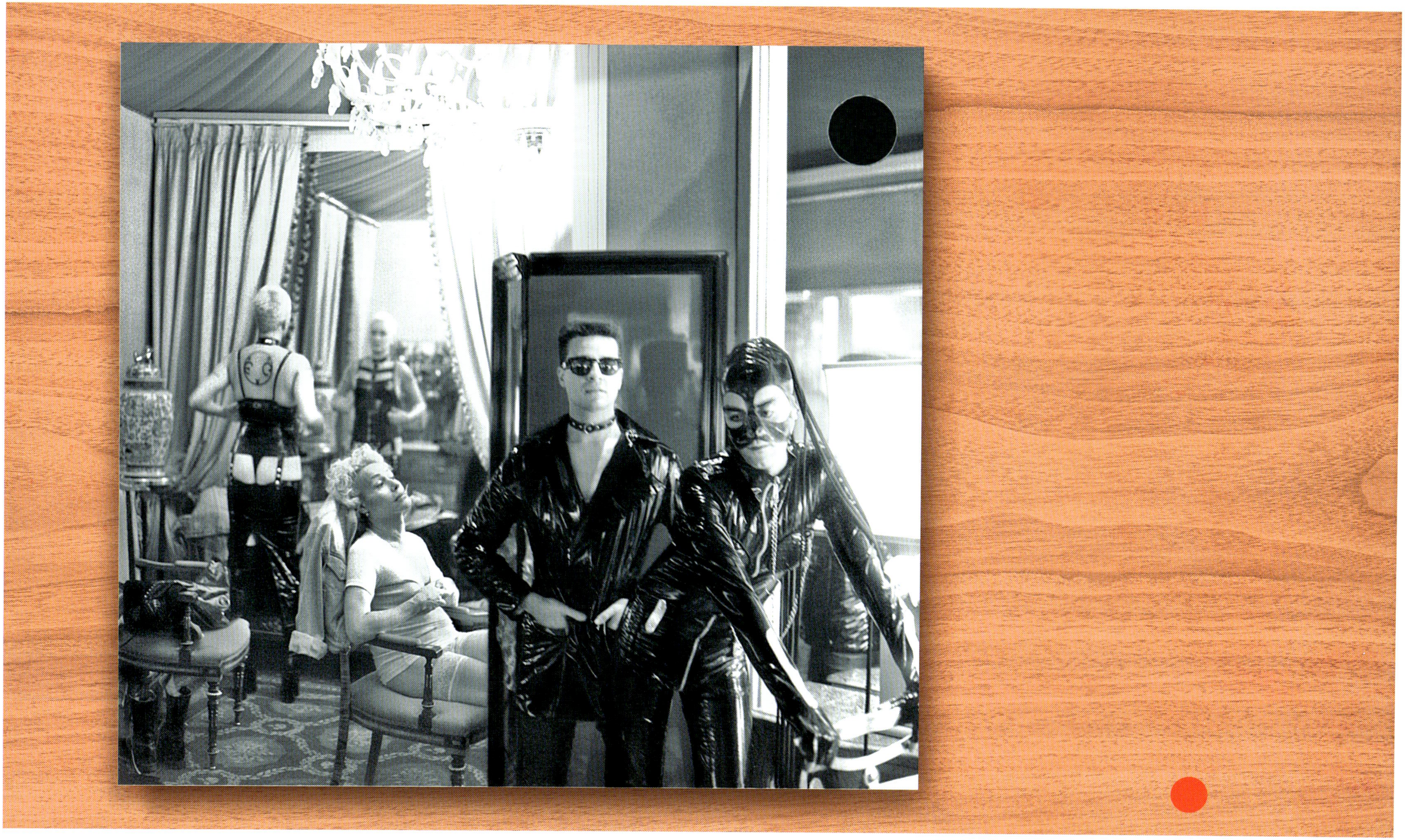

D'où Venons-nous? Que Sommes-nous? Où Allons-nous, Ce Soir? 1995 (detail). From the *Art Brothel* series.
Silver gelatine print, from a 35mm motion picture film, on aluminum;
red enamel; fake-wood plastic laminate panel deformed by heat.
Photograph: 19¾ x 22" (50 x 55,7 cm).
Panel: 37½ x 70¾ x 1½" (95 x 180 x 4 cm).
GC 915.

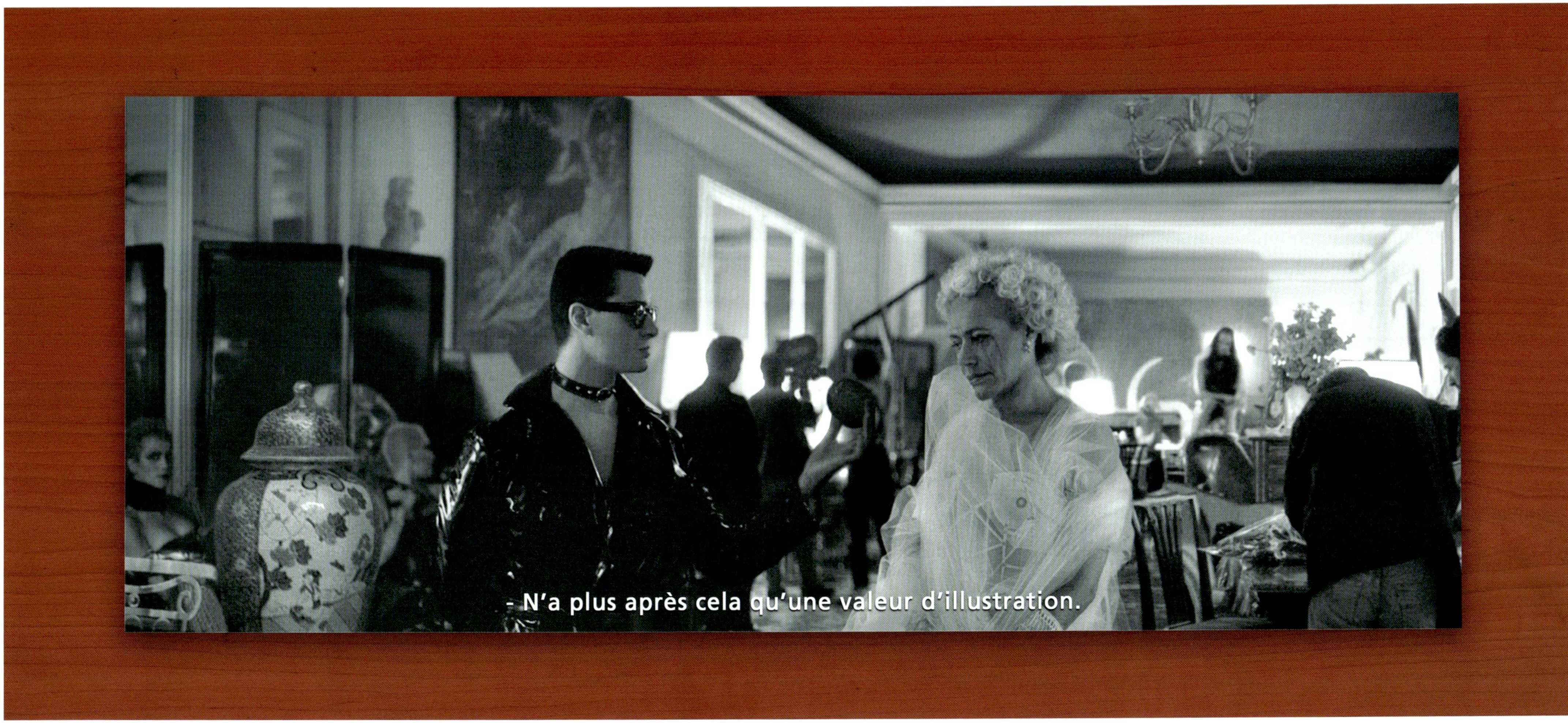

Dripping, 1995 (detail). From the *Art Brothel* series.
Silver gelatine print, from a 35mm motion picture film, on aluminum;
fake-wood plastic laminate panel deformed by heat.
Photograph: 13¾ x 35½" (35 x 90 cm).
Panel: 37½ x 70¾ x 1½" (95 x 180 x 4 cm).
GC 916.

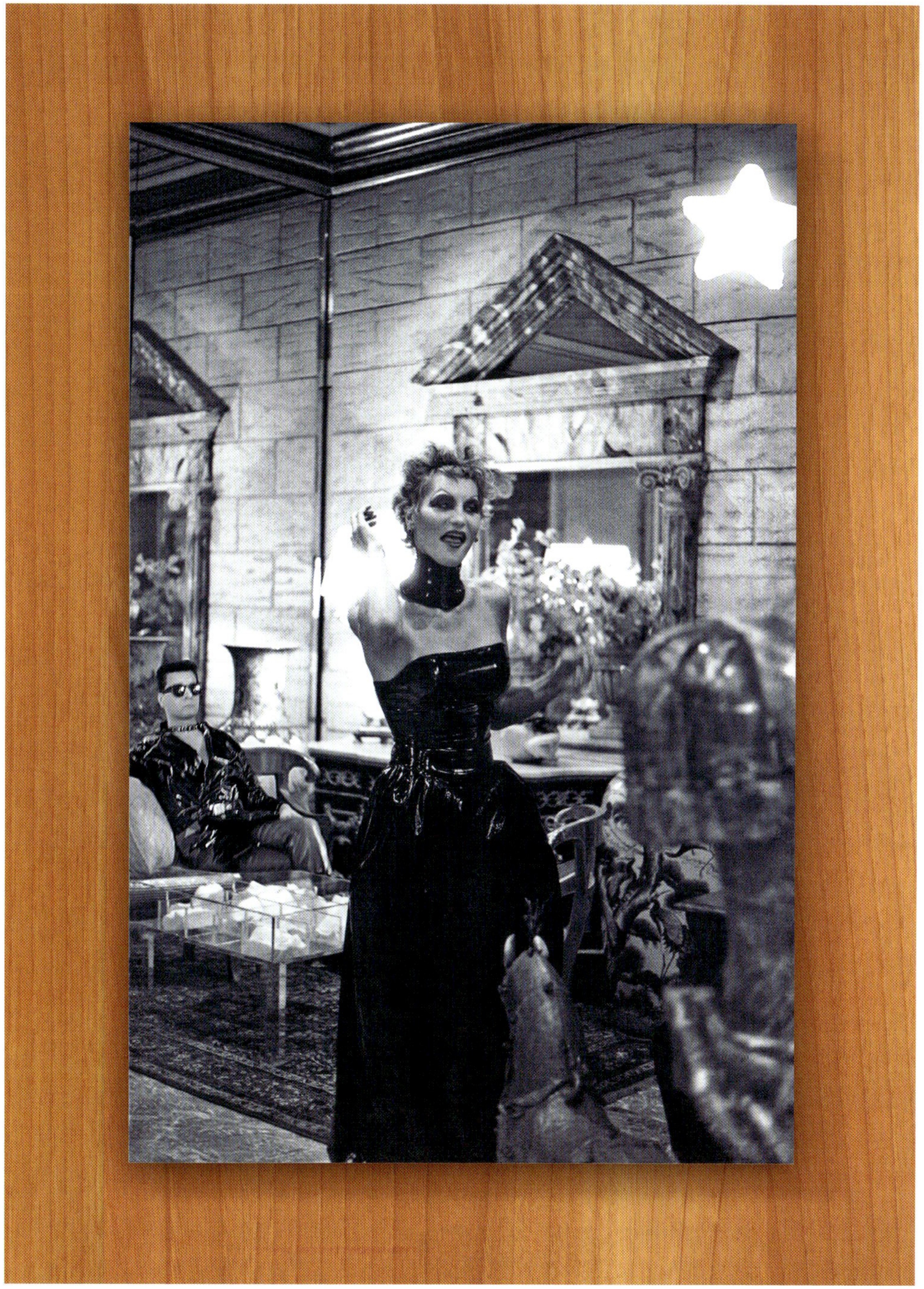

The Disquieting Muse, 1995 (detail). From the *Art Brothel* series.
Silver gelatine print on aluminum;
fake-wood plastic laminate panel deformed by heat.
Photograph: 21¾ x 14½" (55 x 36,2 cm).
Panel: 70¾ x 37½ x 1½" (180 x 95 x 4 cm).
GC 917.

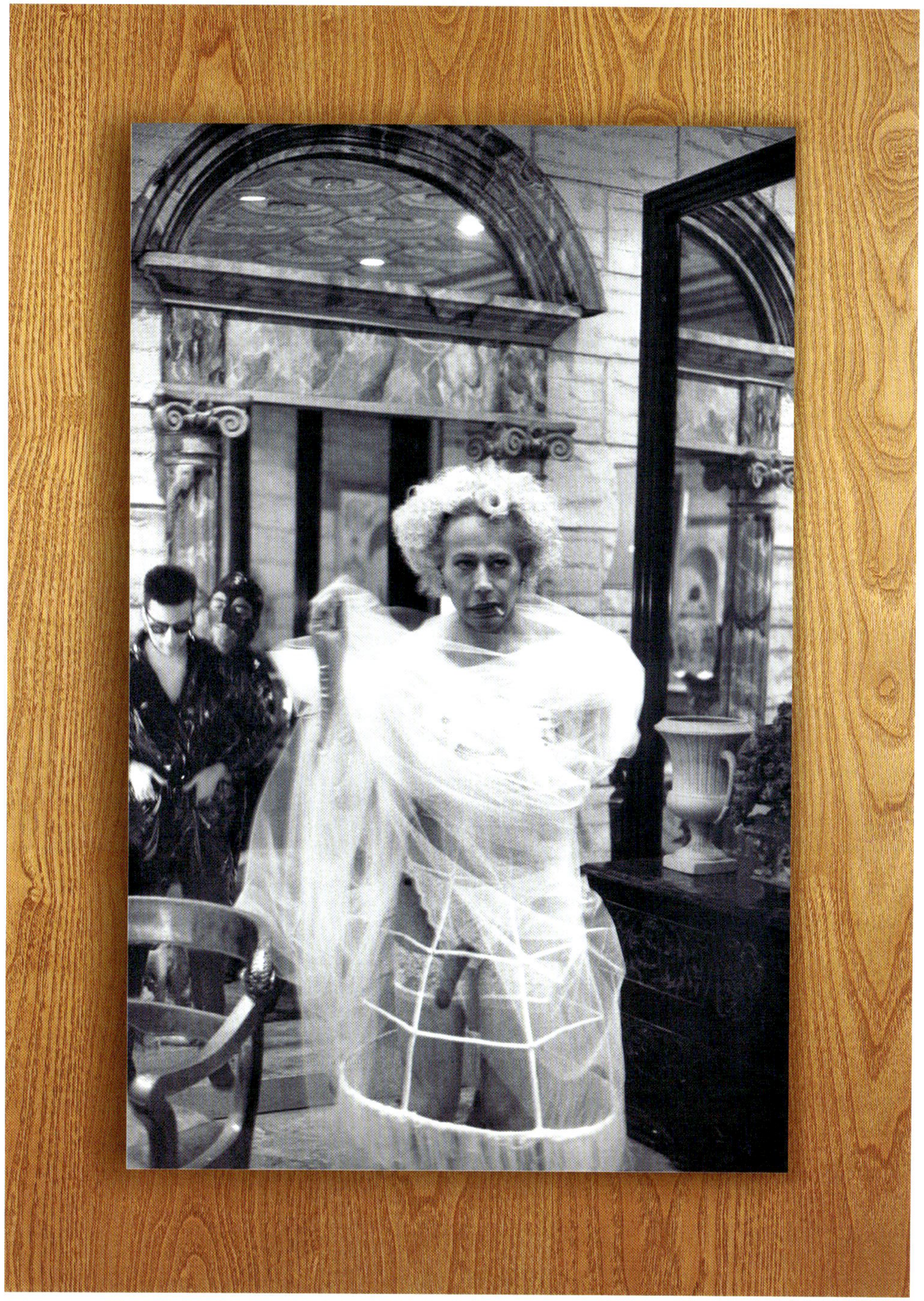

La Craquelure, 1995 (detail). From the *Art Brothel* series.
Silver gelatine print on aluminum;
fake-wood plastic laminate panel deformed by heat.
Photograph: 21¾ x 14½" (55 x 36,2 cm).
Panel: 70¾ x 37½ x 1½" (180 x 95 x 4 cm).
GC 918.

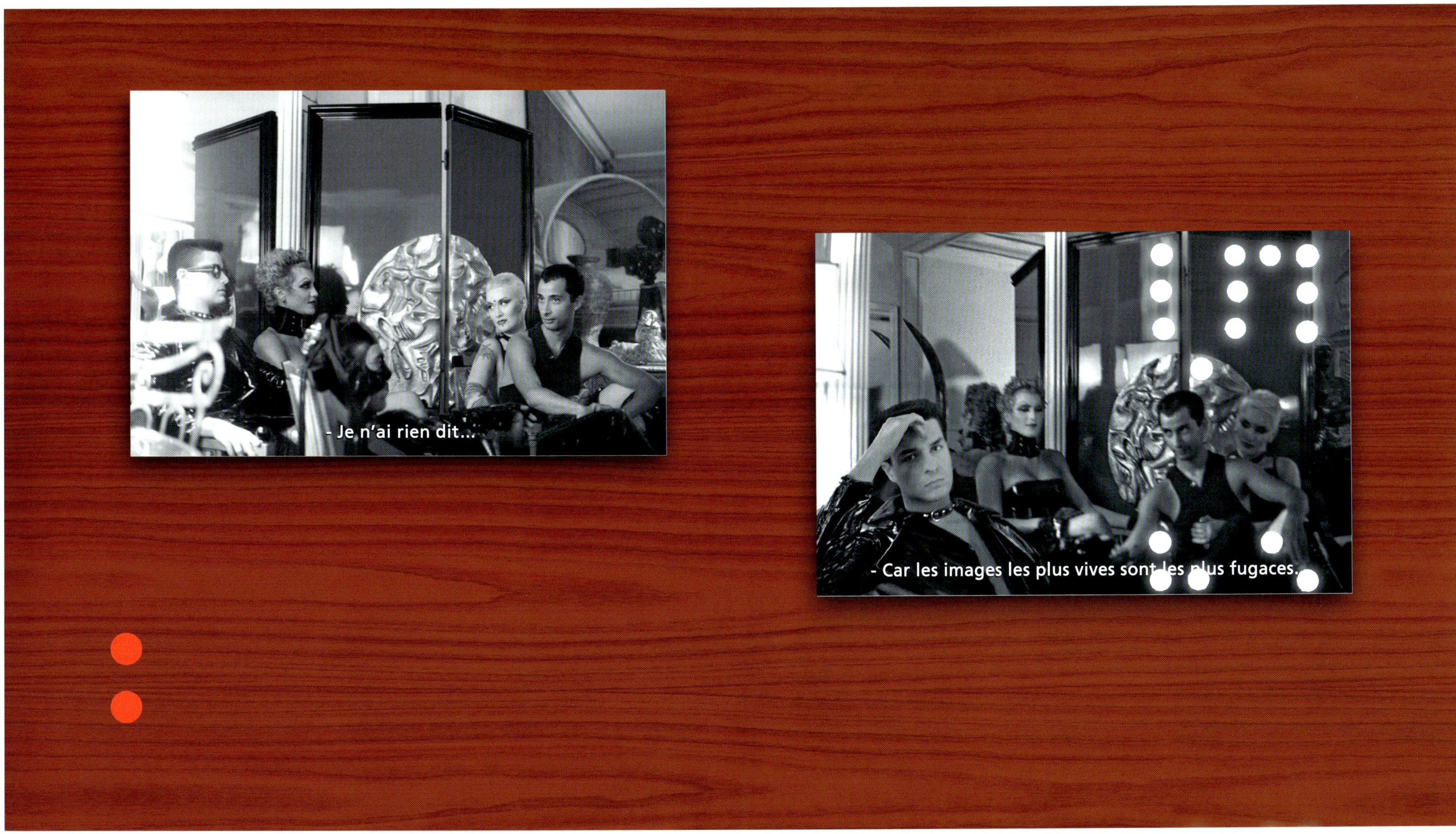

Art Forum, 1995 (detail). From the *Art Brothel* series.
Silver gelatine prints, from a 35mm motion picture film, on aluminum; red enamel; fake-wood plastic laminate panel deformed by heat.
Photographs: 14½ x 21¾" each (36,4 x 55 cm).
Panel: 37½ x 70¾ x 1½" (95 x 180 x 4 cm).
GC 920.

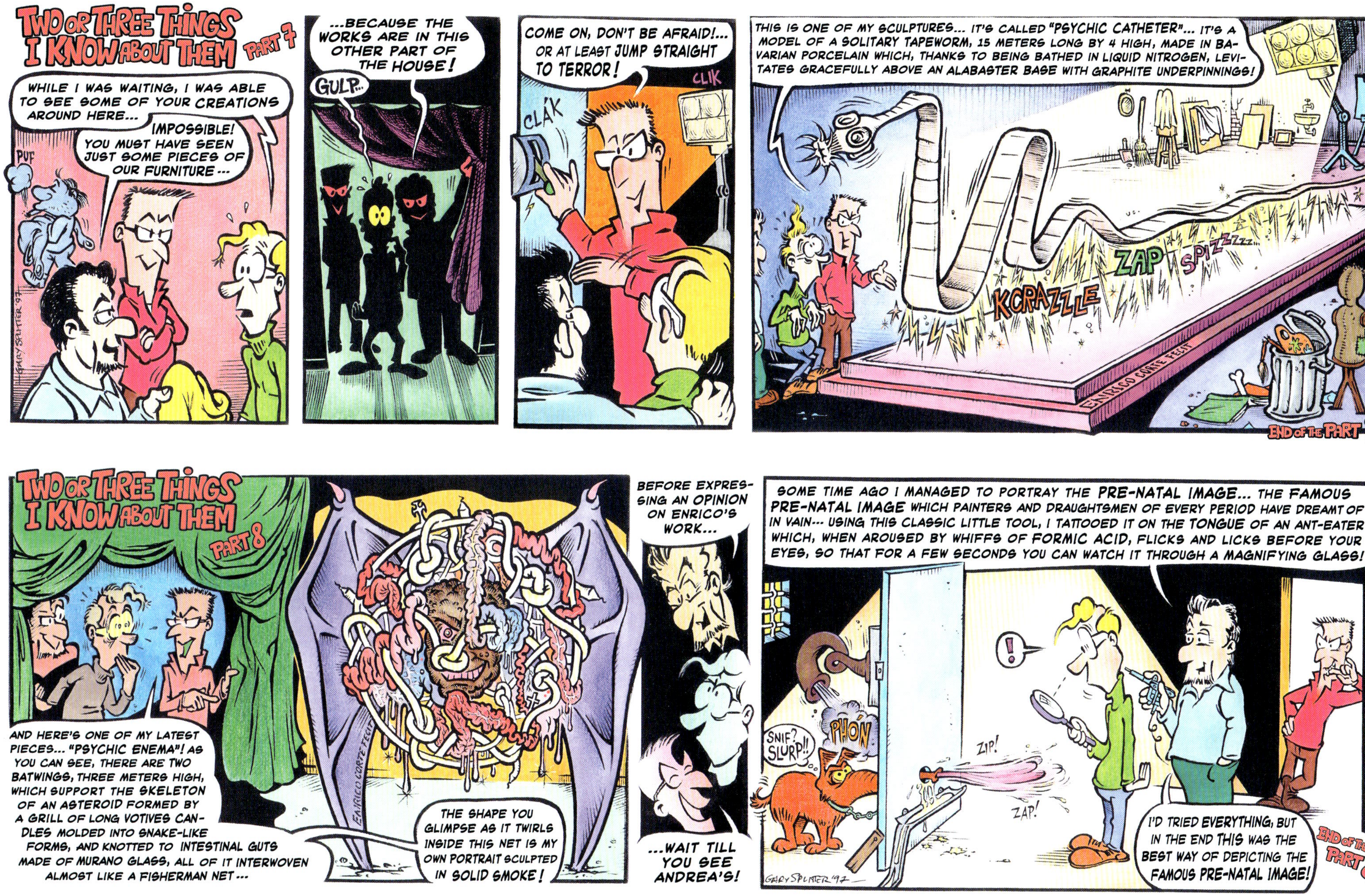

Corte & Nurcis with Gary Splitter:
Two or three things I know about them (part 7 and 8), 1997.
Series of 20 comic strips.
Inks on paper.
5¼ x 15¾" each strip (13,3 x 40 cm).
GC 1082.

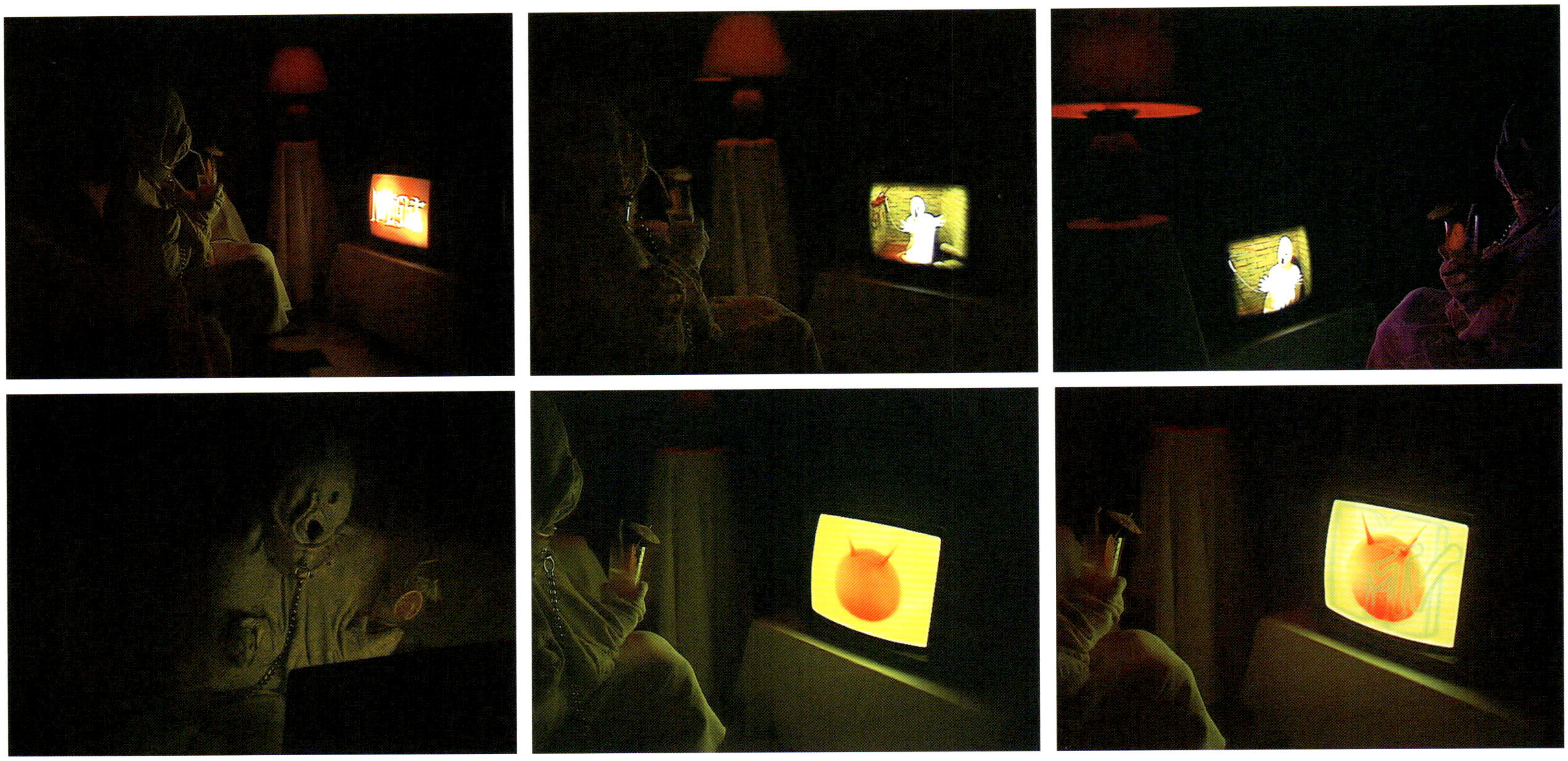

Corte & Nurcis: video stills from *Drinkin' No Light*, 1995. Cibachrome prints from a digital video for the television channel Mtv. Double video version (full: 3 minutes - short: 30 seconds). 14½ x 19¾" each still (36,9 x 50 cm). GC 966-971.

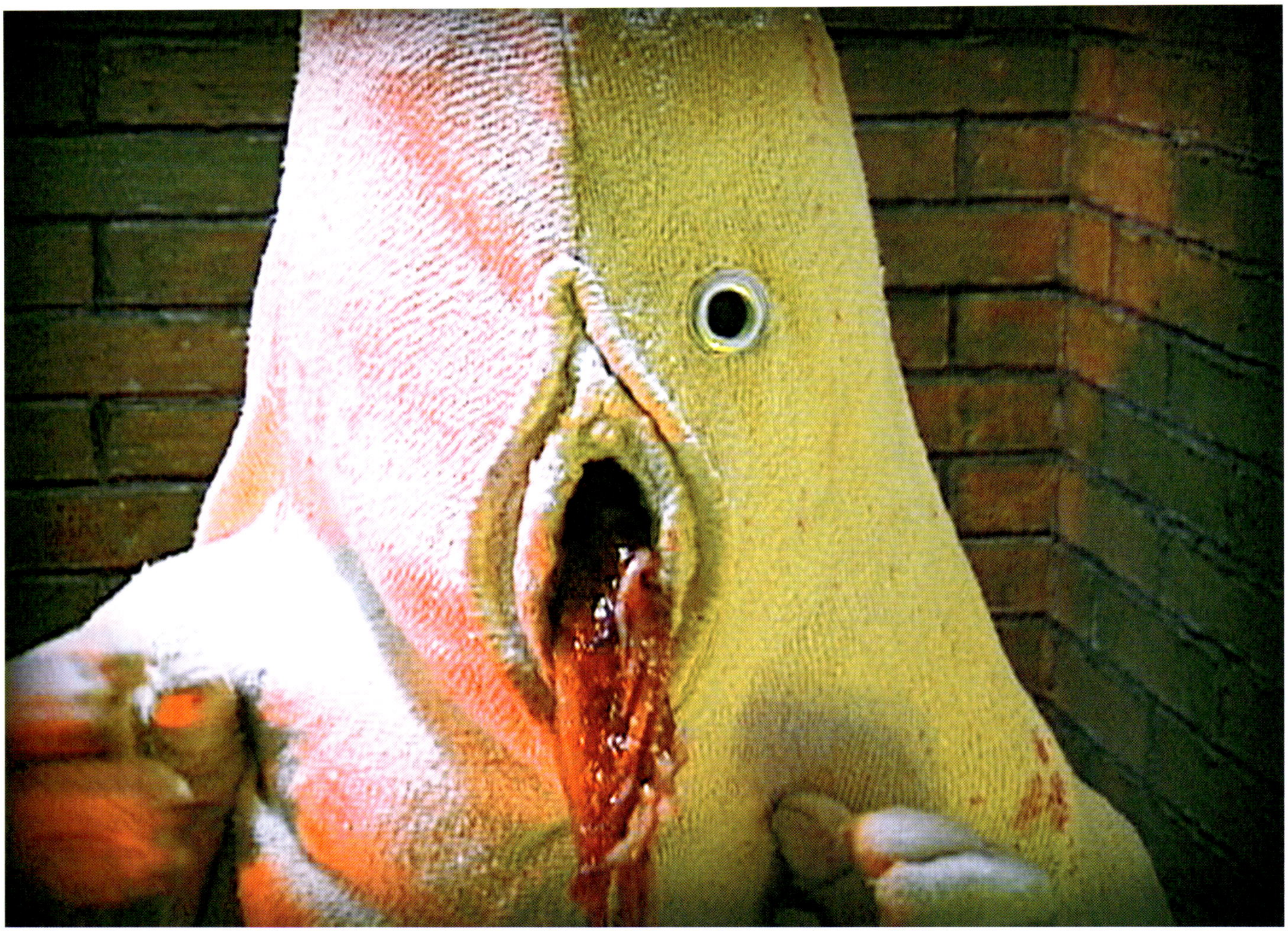

Corte & Nurcis: video still from *No Light* (digital video, 30'), 1996-97.
From a series of 450 stills on canvas and cibachrome. Variable dimensions. GC 982-1081, and 1630-1979.

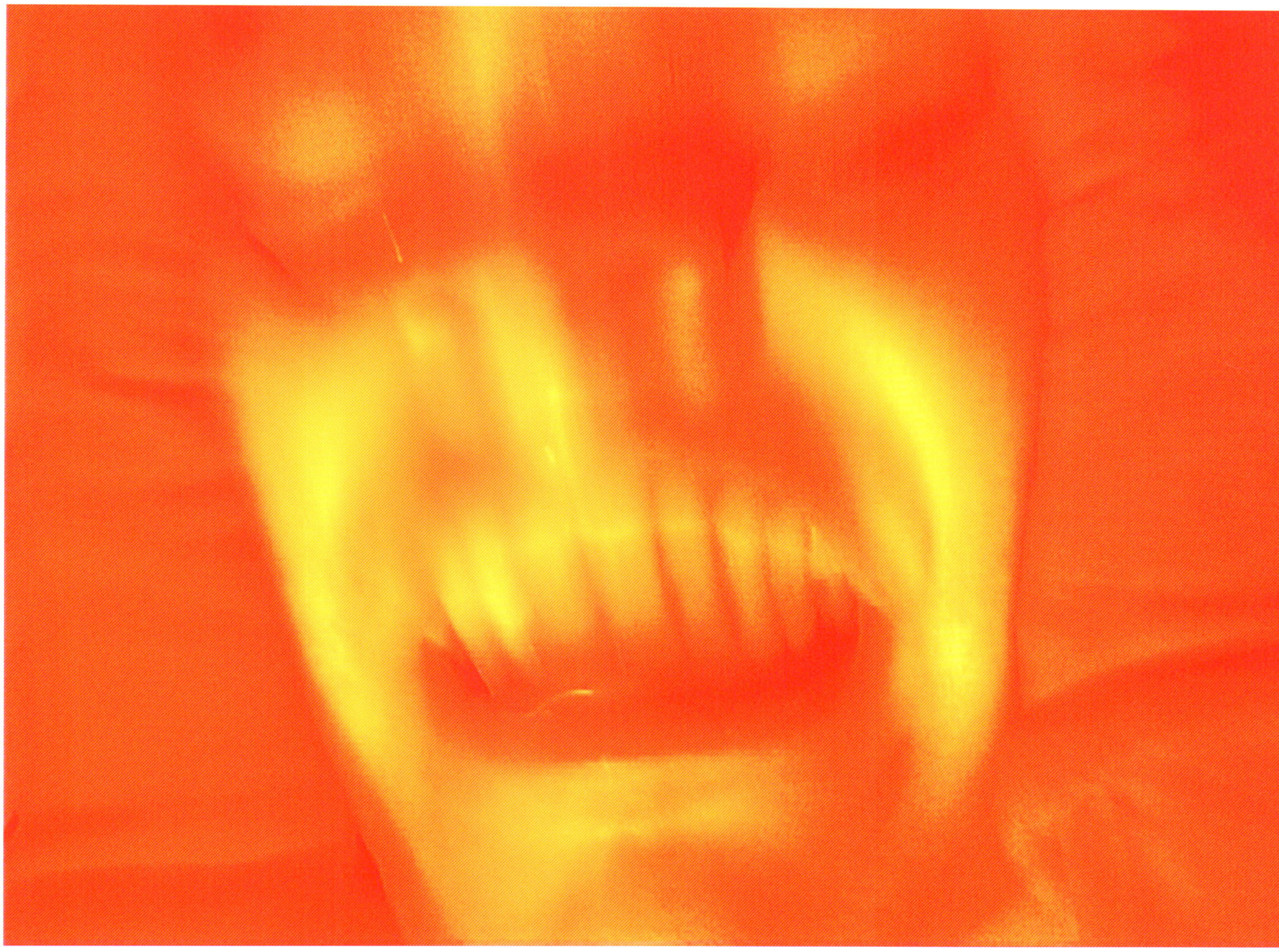

Corte & Nurcis: video stills from *No Light*, 1996-97. Lambda prints on canvas and cibachrome. Variable dimensions.

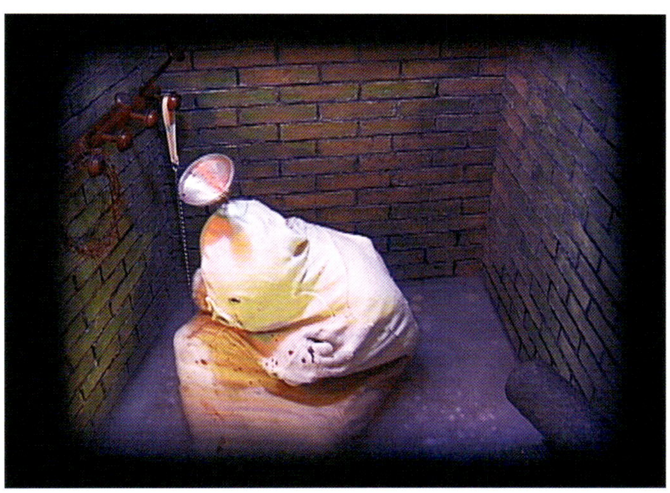

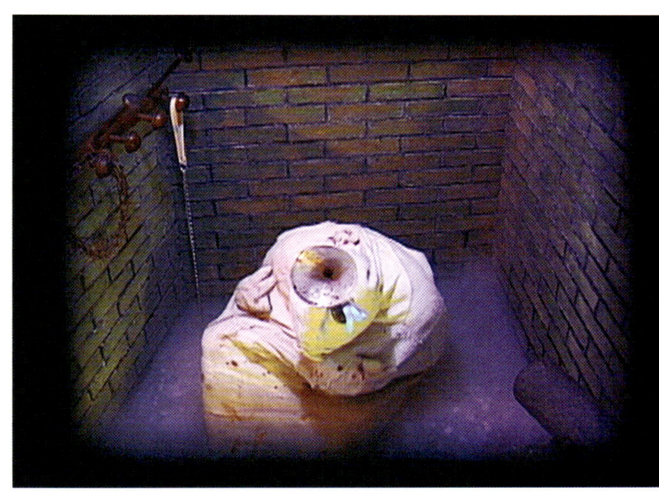

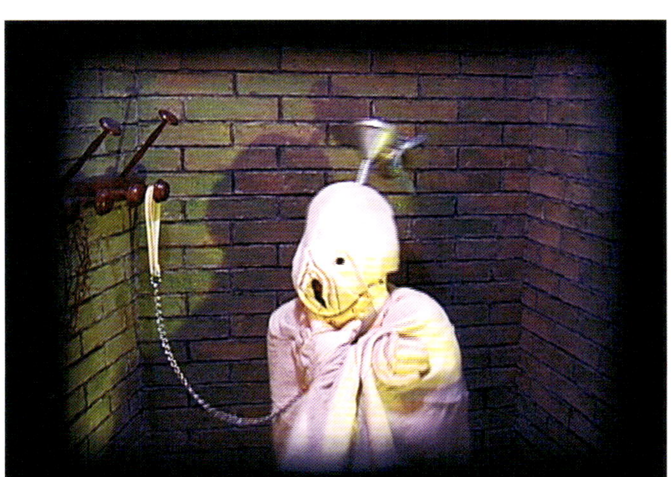

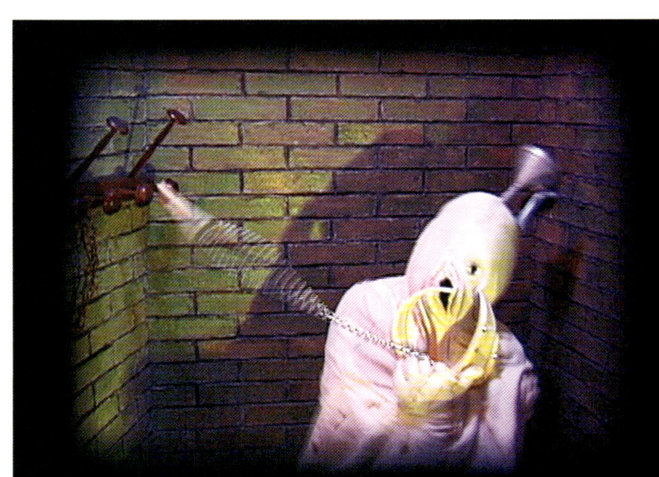

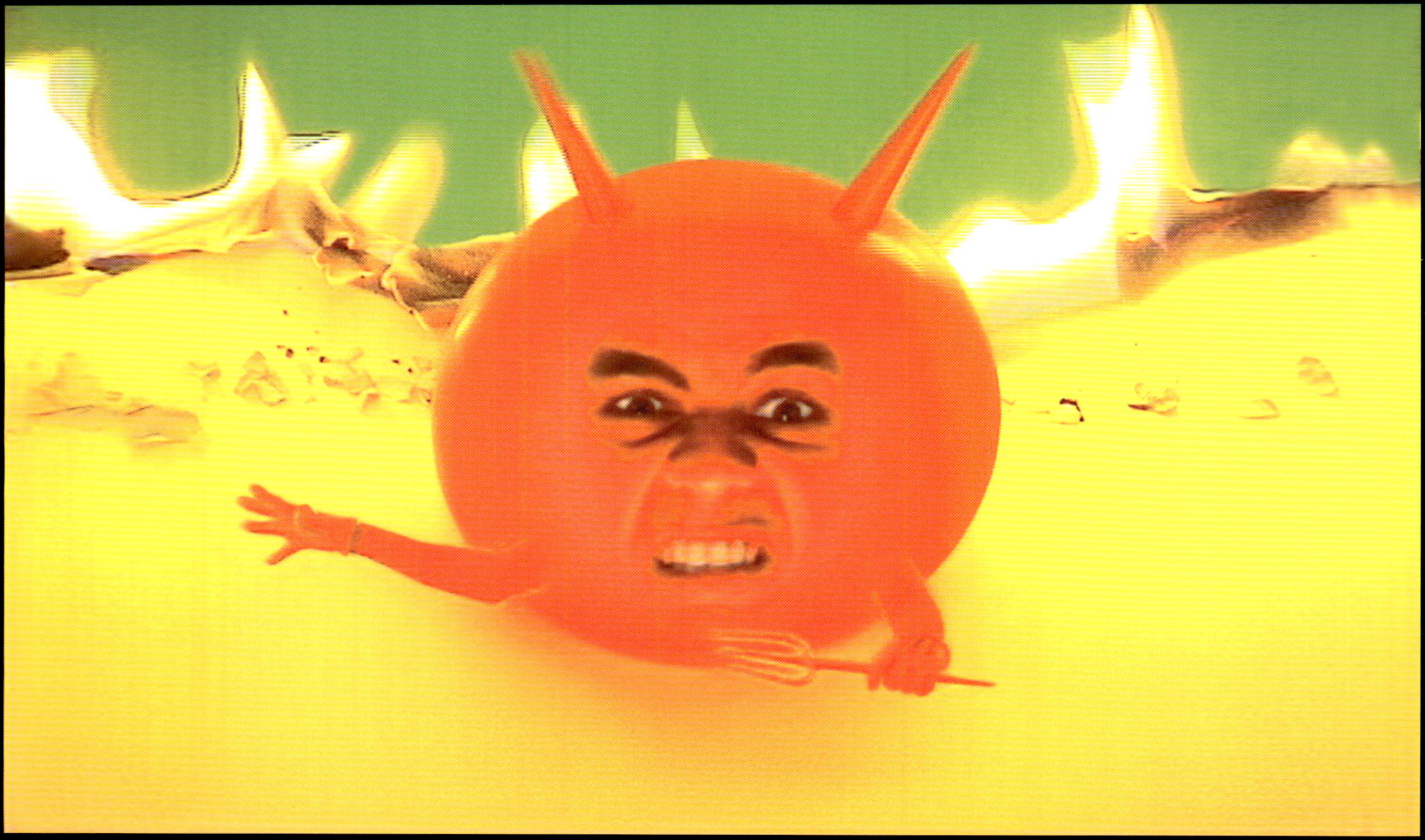

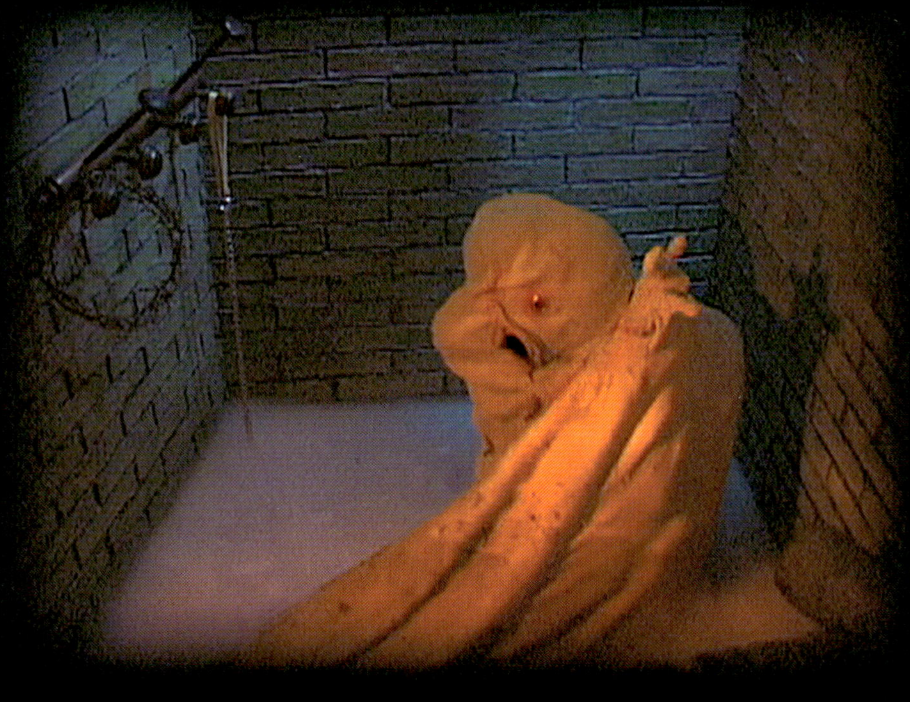

This page and opposite:
video stills from *No Light*, 1996-97.
Lambda prints on canvas and cibachrome.
Variable dimensions.

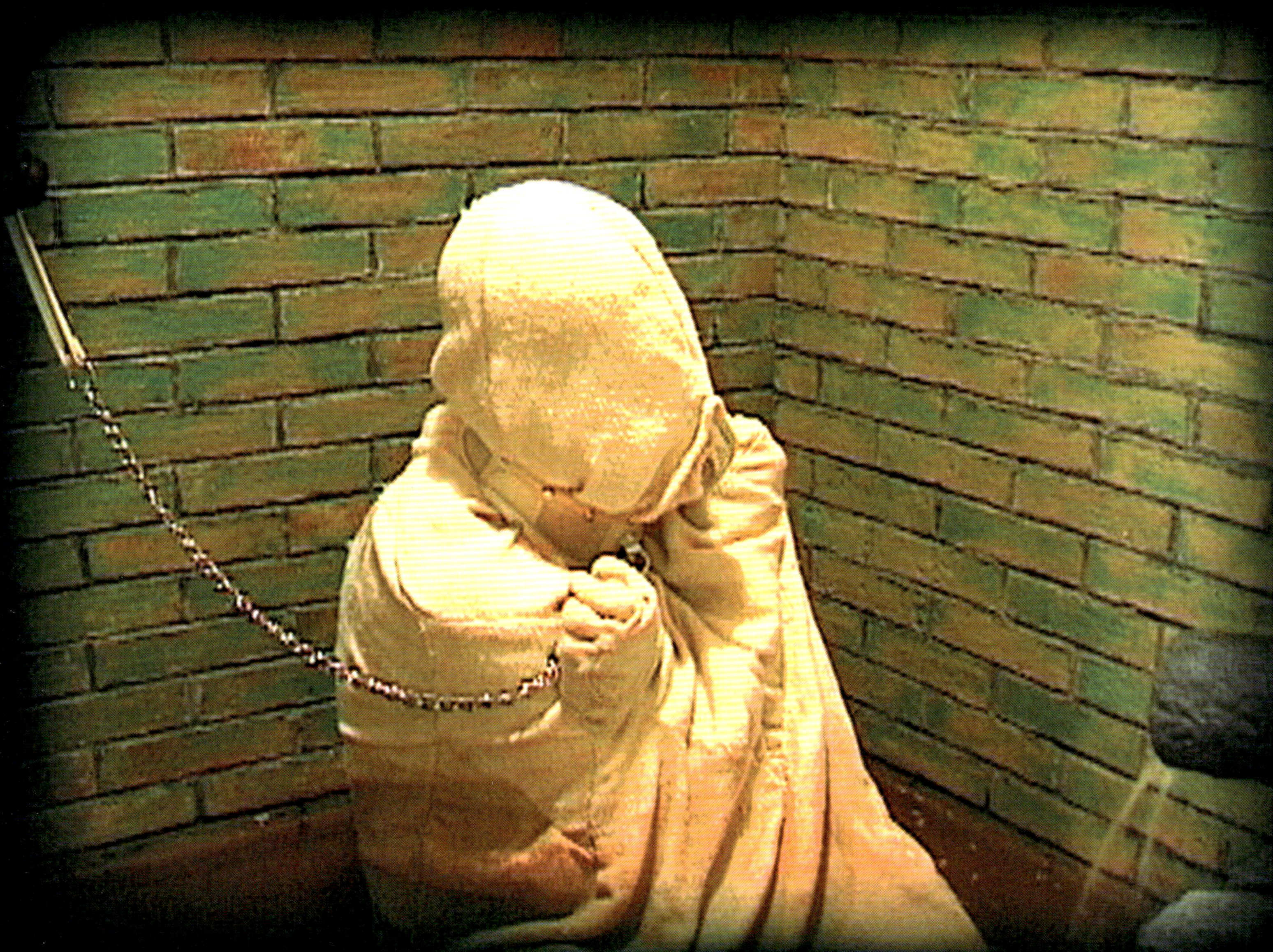

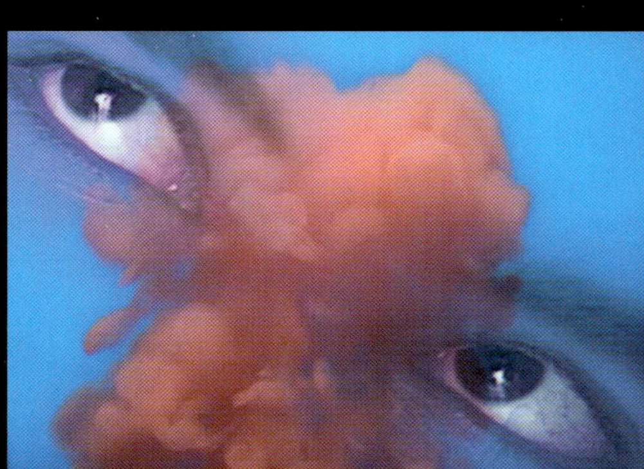

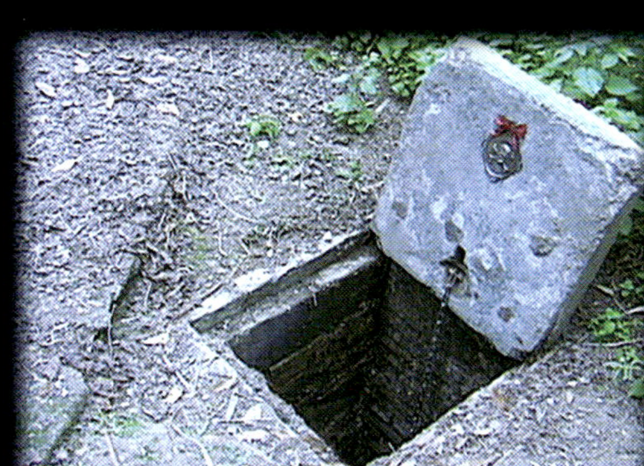

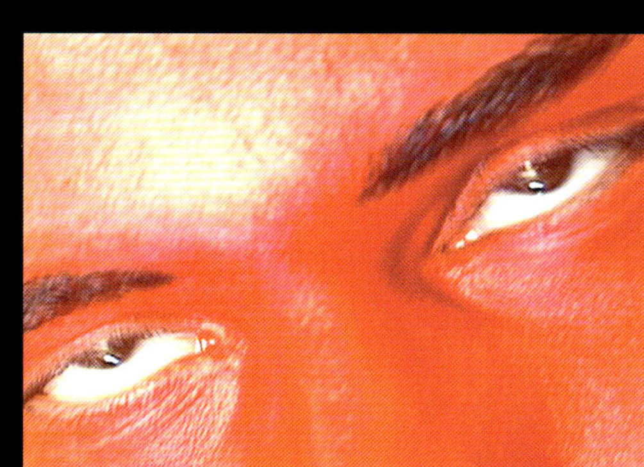

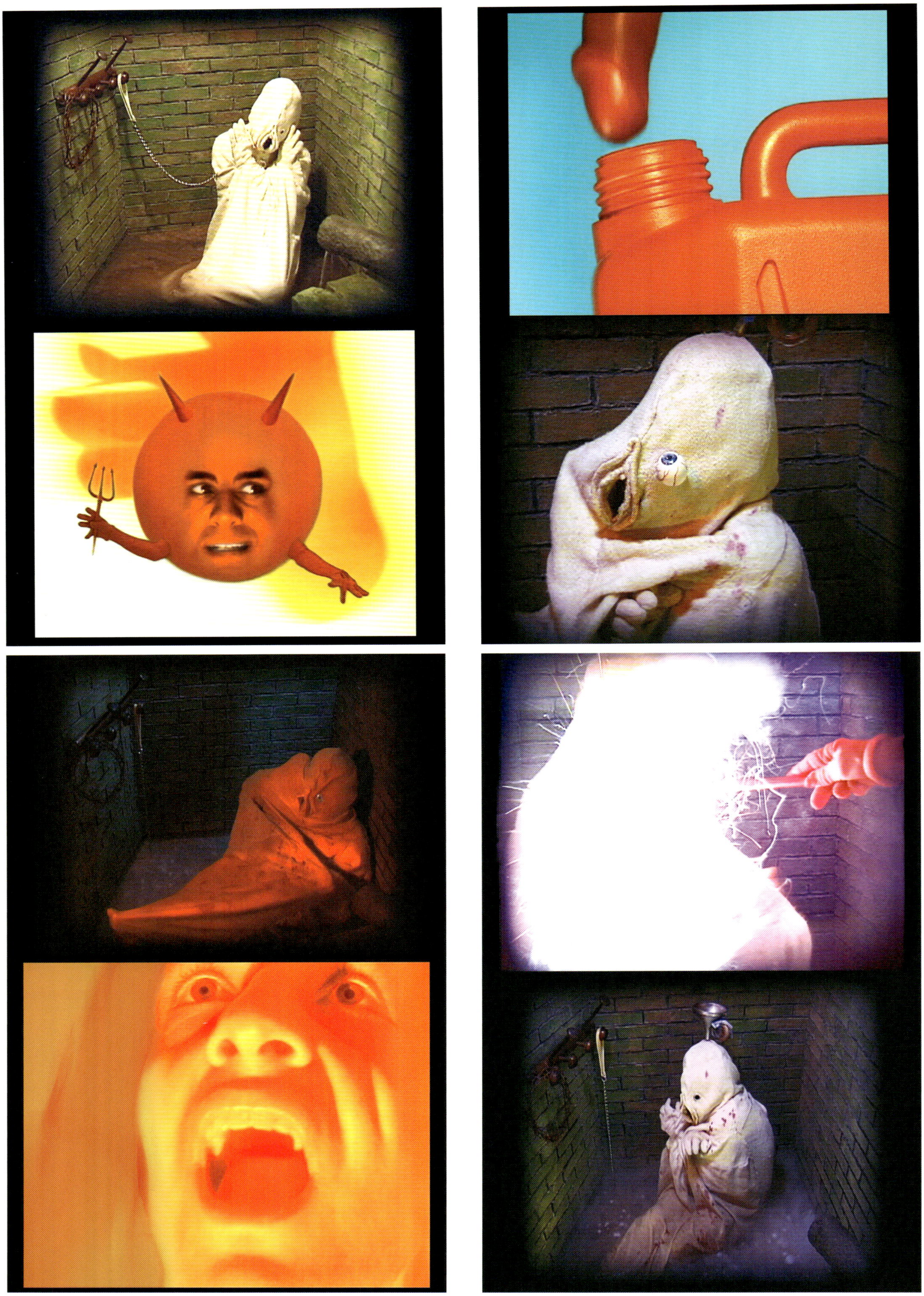

Corte & Nurcis: video stills from *No Light*, 1996-97. Lambda prints on canvas and cibachrome. Variable dimensions.

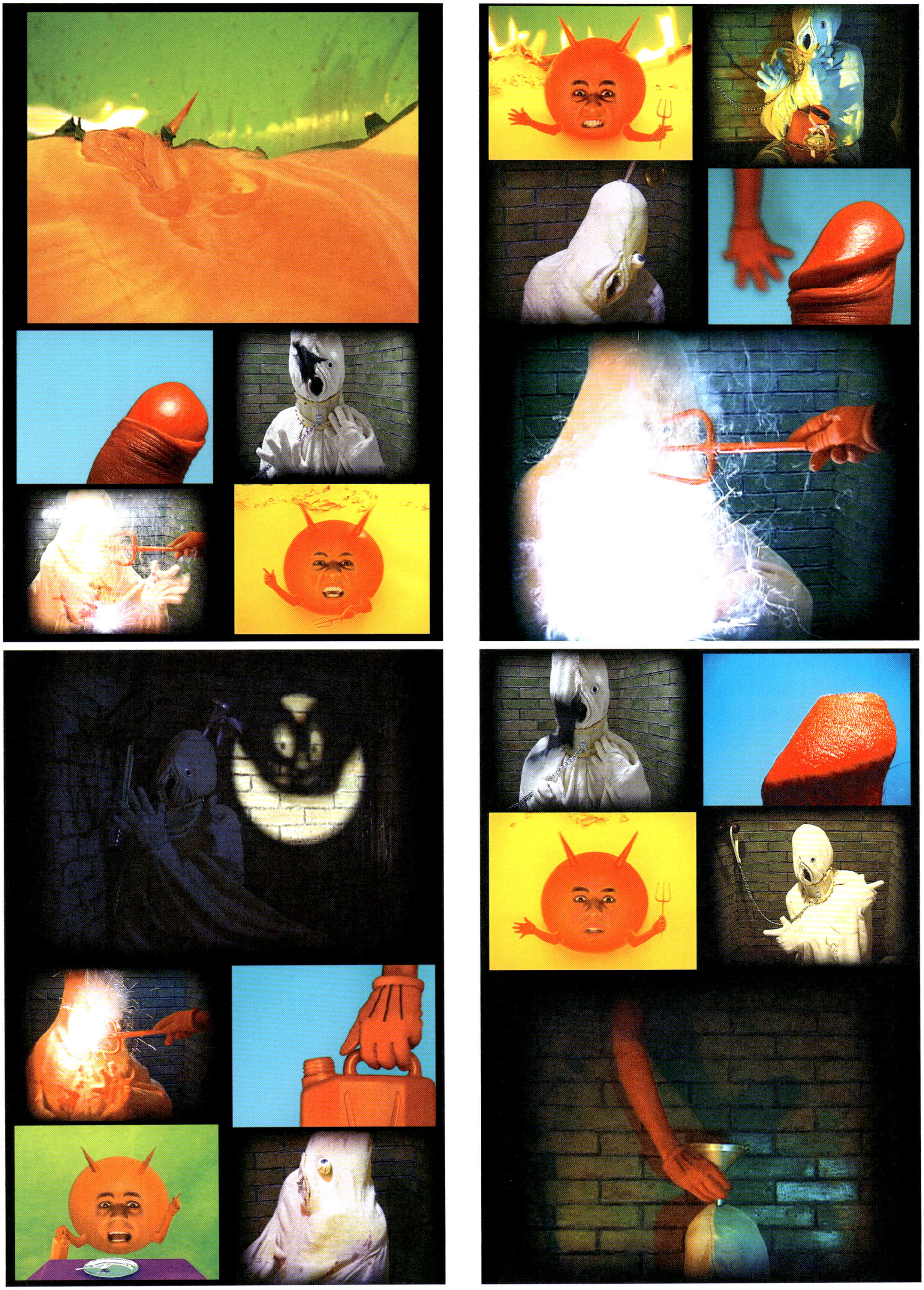

Corte & Nurcis: video stills from *No Light*, 1996-97. Lambda prints on canvas and cibachrome. Variable dimensions.

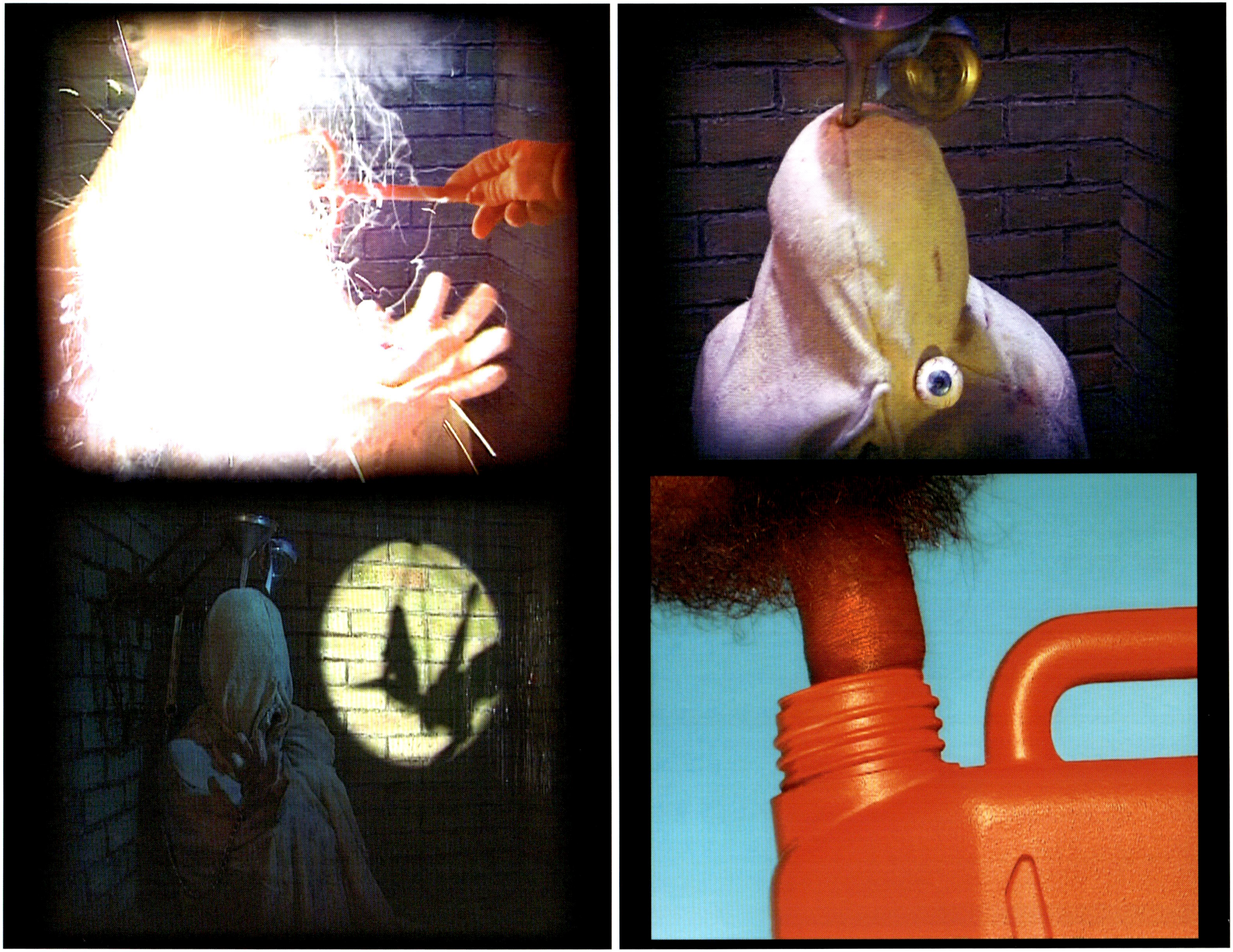

Corte & Nurcis: video stills from *No Light*, 1996-97. Lambda prints on canvas and cibachrome. Variable dimensions.

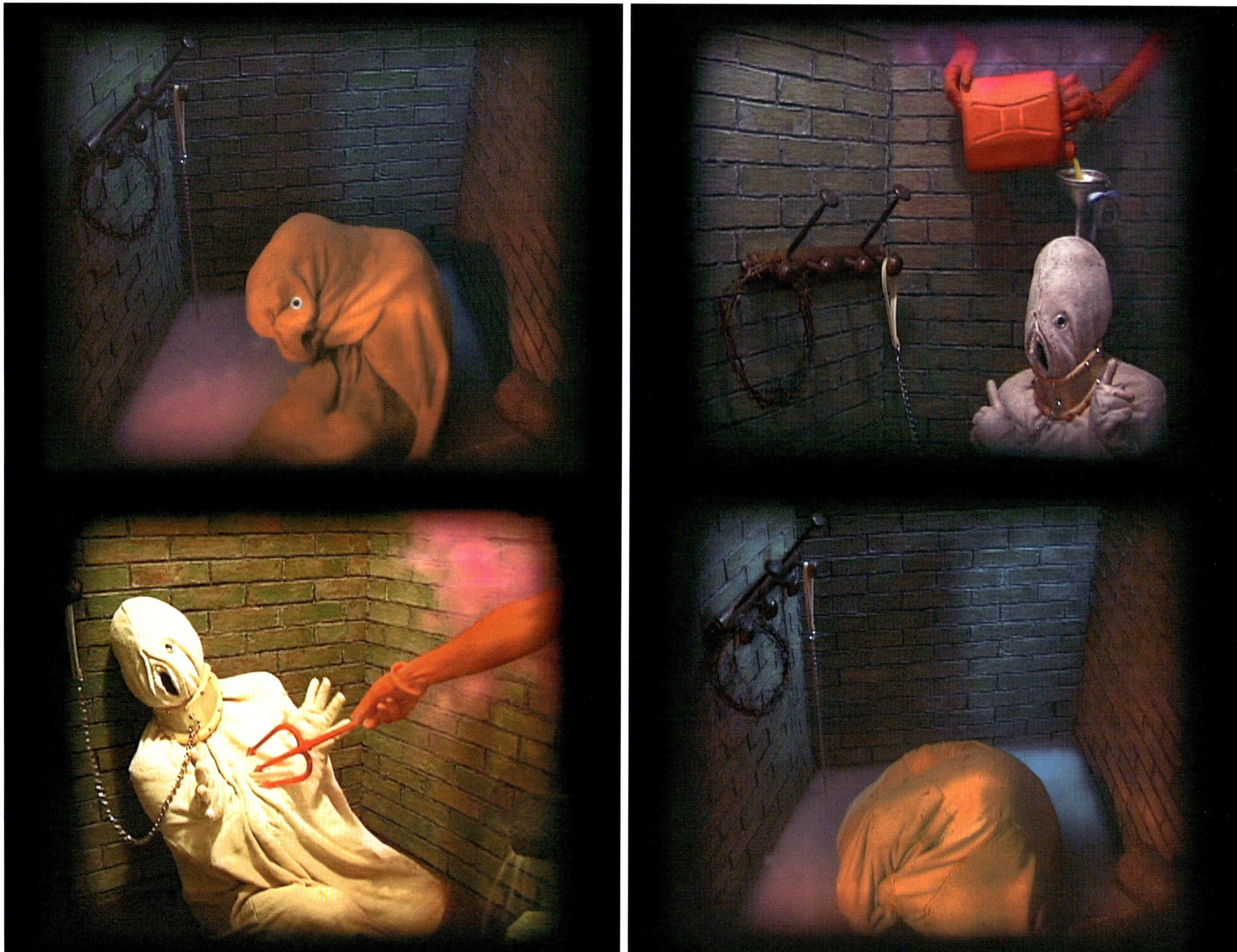

Corte & Nurcis: video stills from *No Light*, 1996-97. Lambda prints on canvas and cibachrome. Variable dimensions.

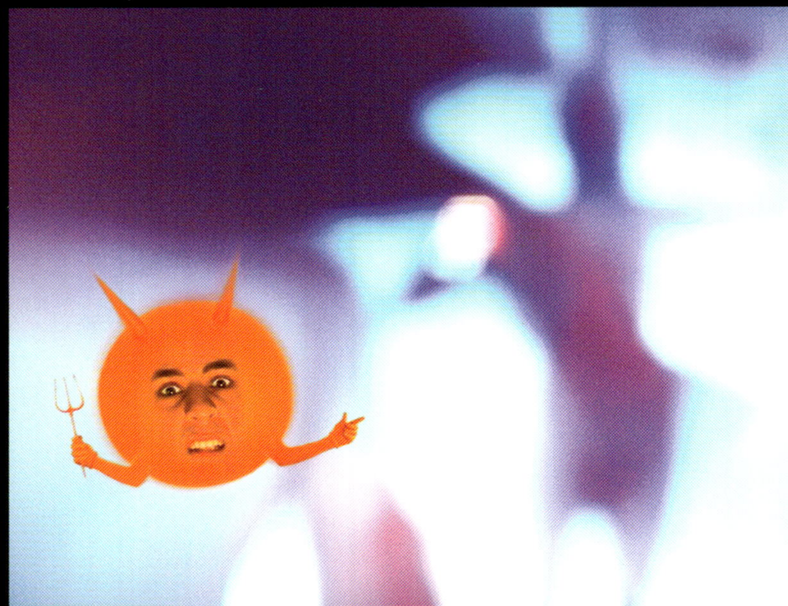

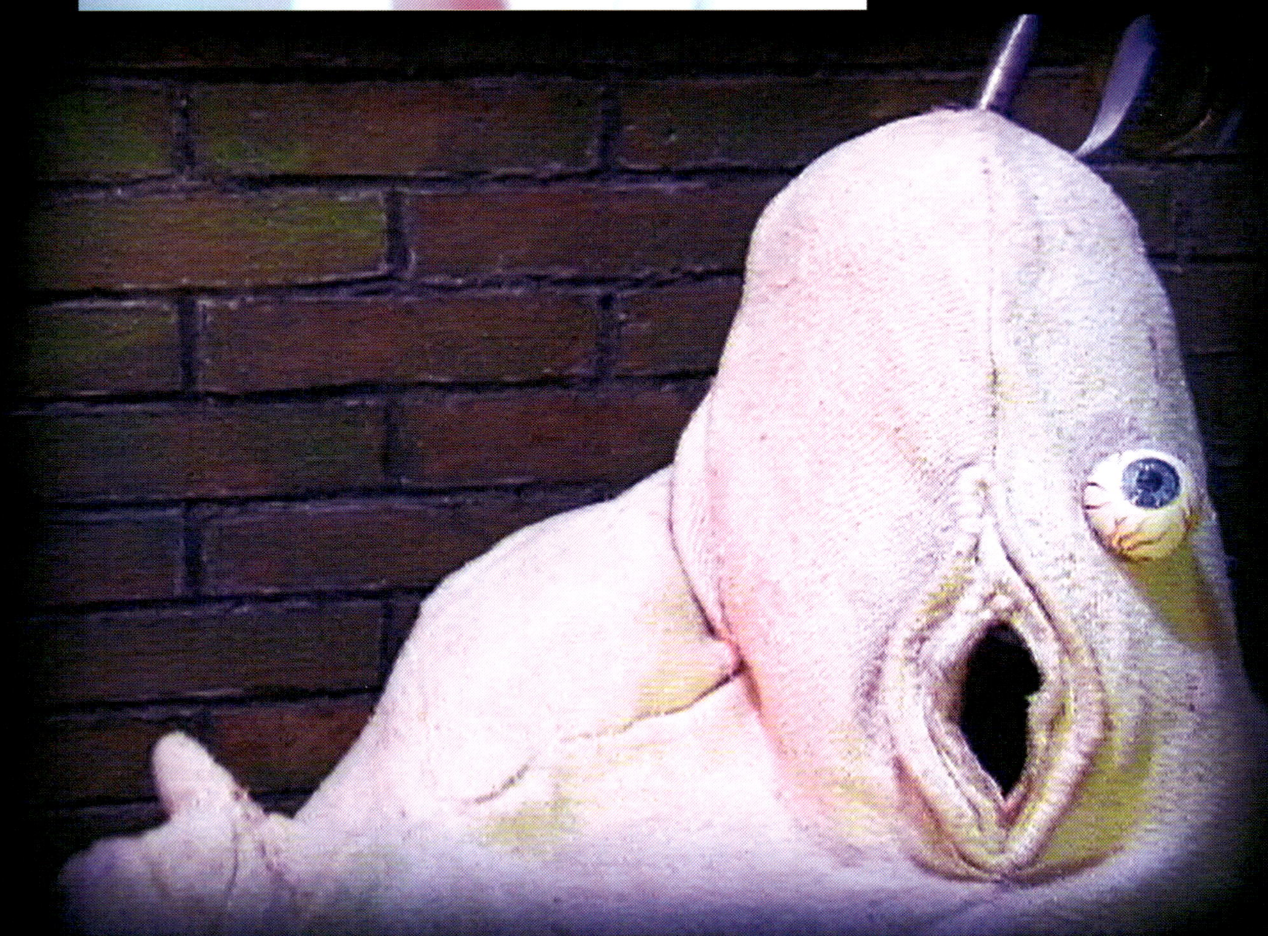

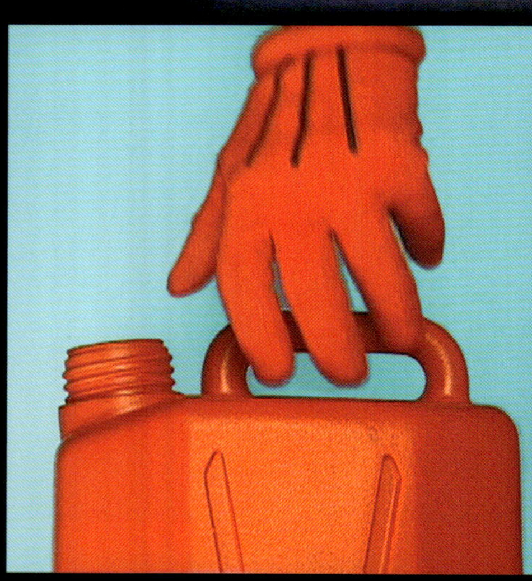

This page and opposite:
video stills from *No Light*, 1996-97.
Lambda prints on canvas and cibachrome.
Variable dimensions.

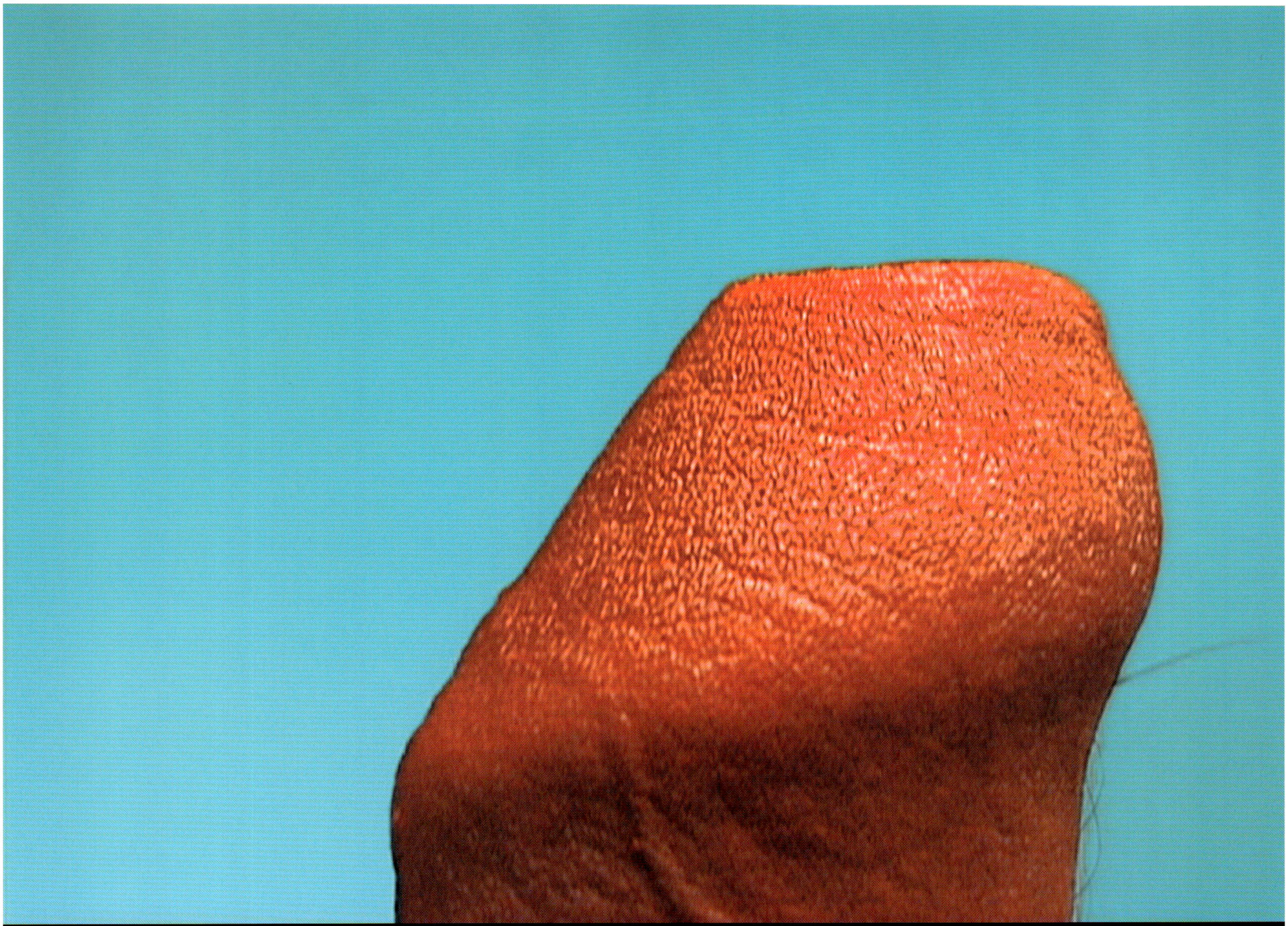

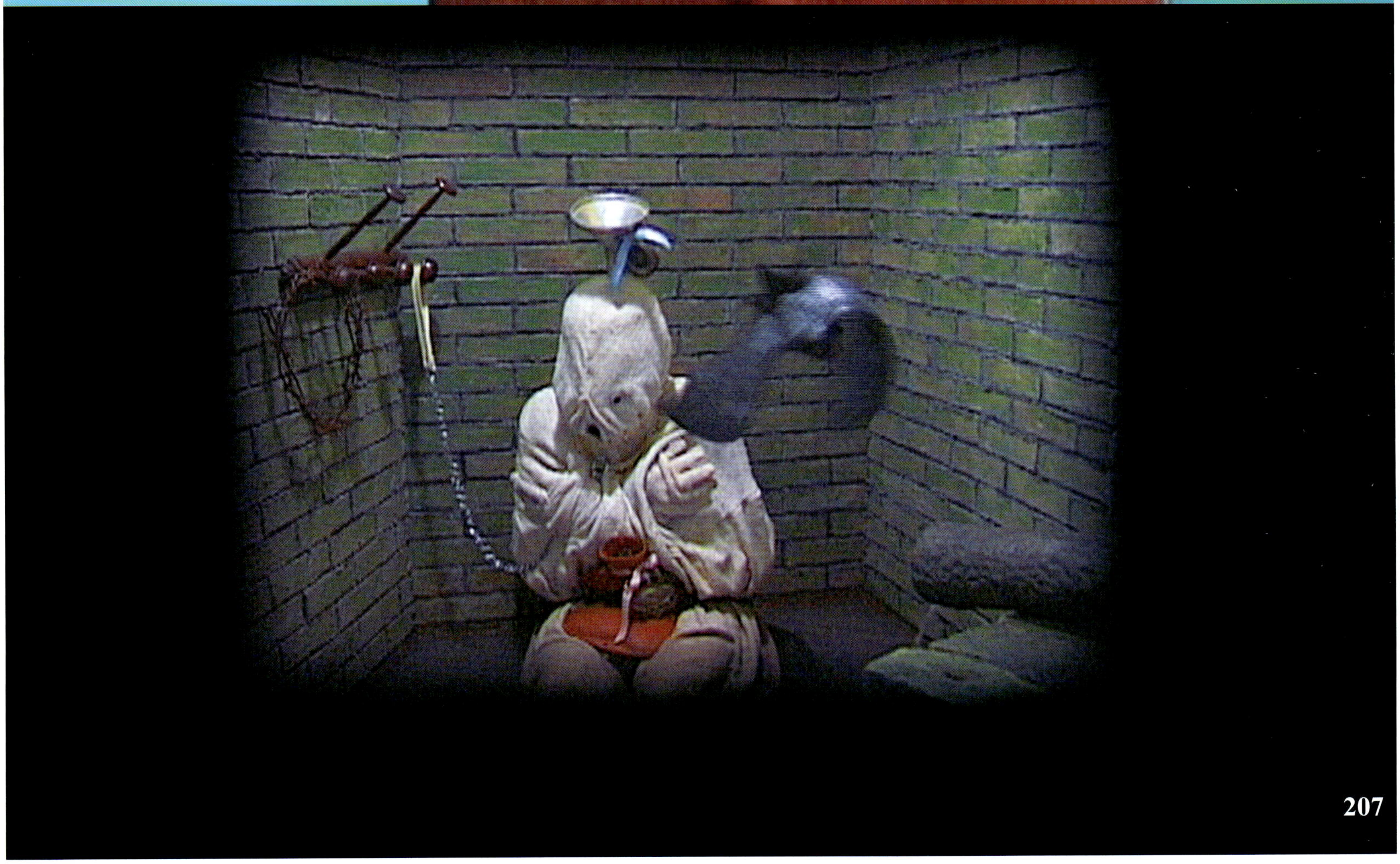

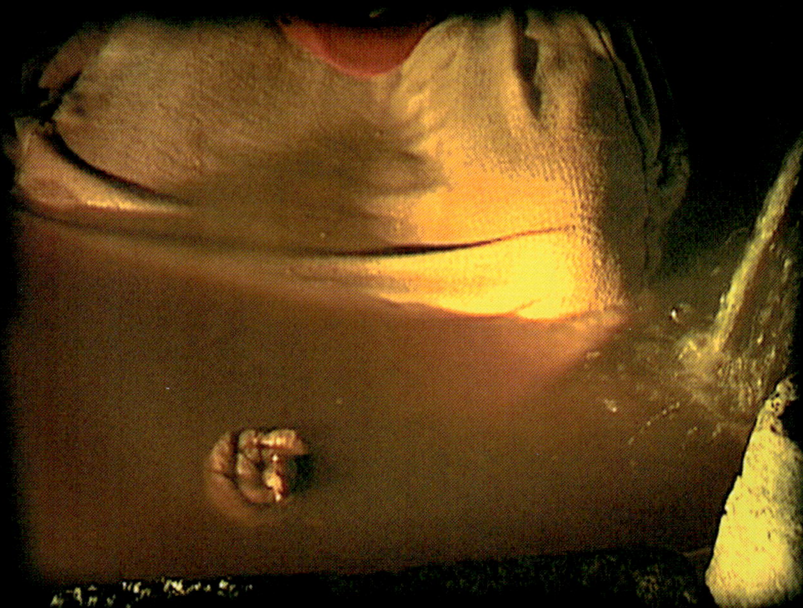

This page and opposite:
video stills from *No Light*, 1996-97.
Lambda prints on canvas and cibachrome.
Variable dimensions.

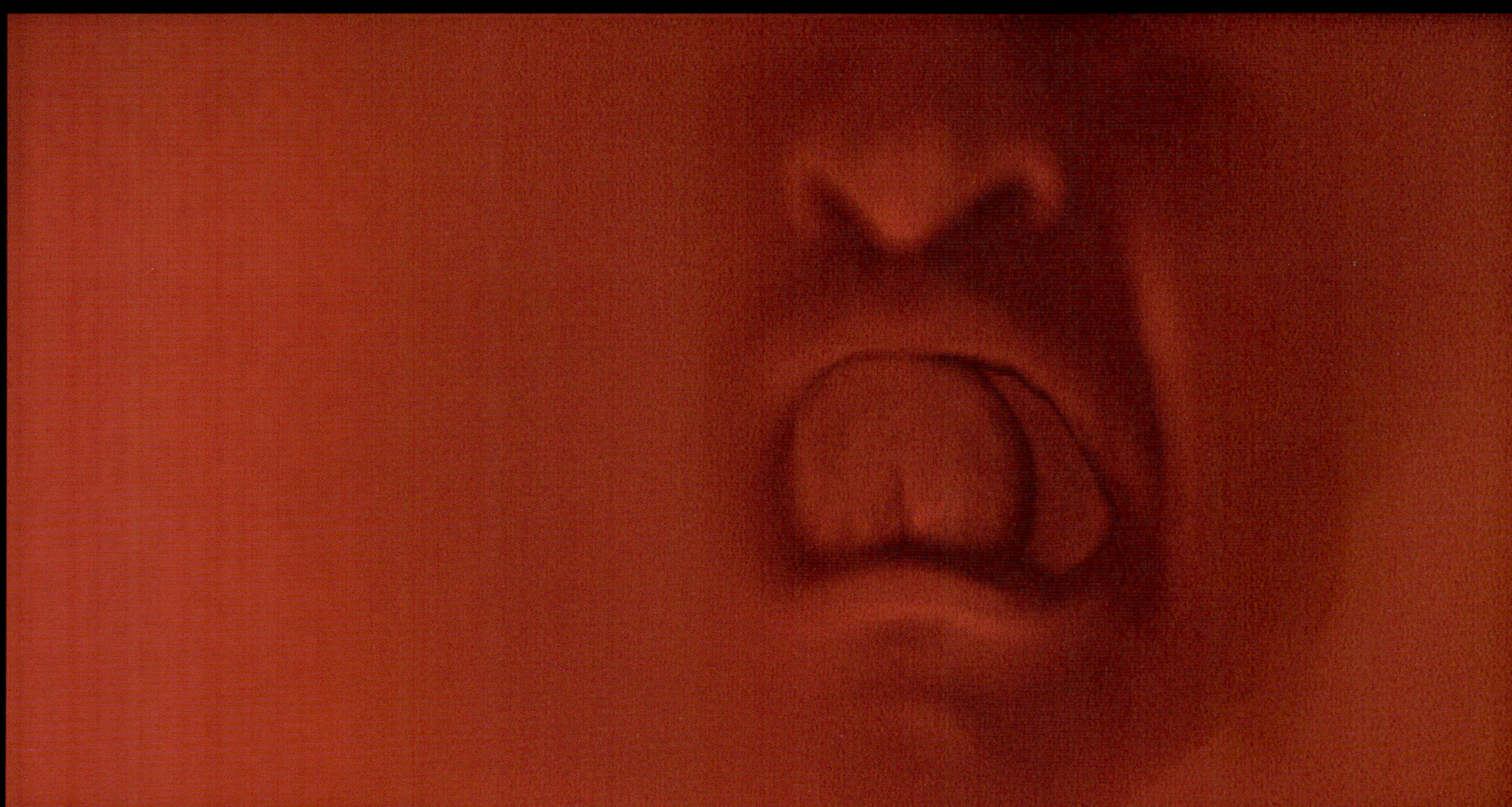

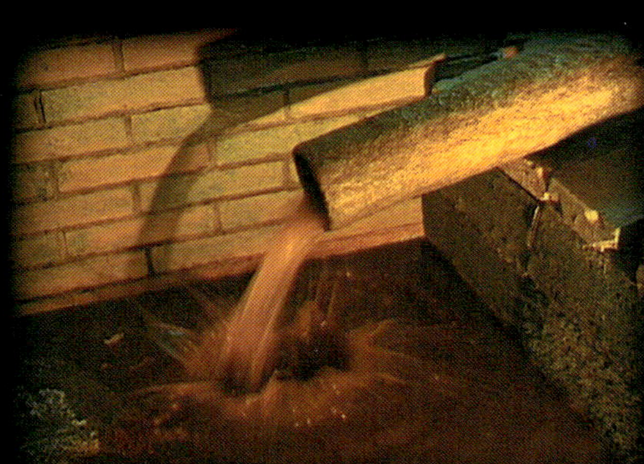

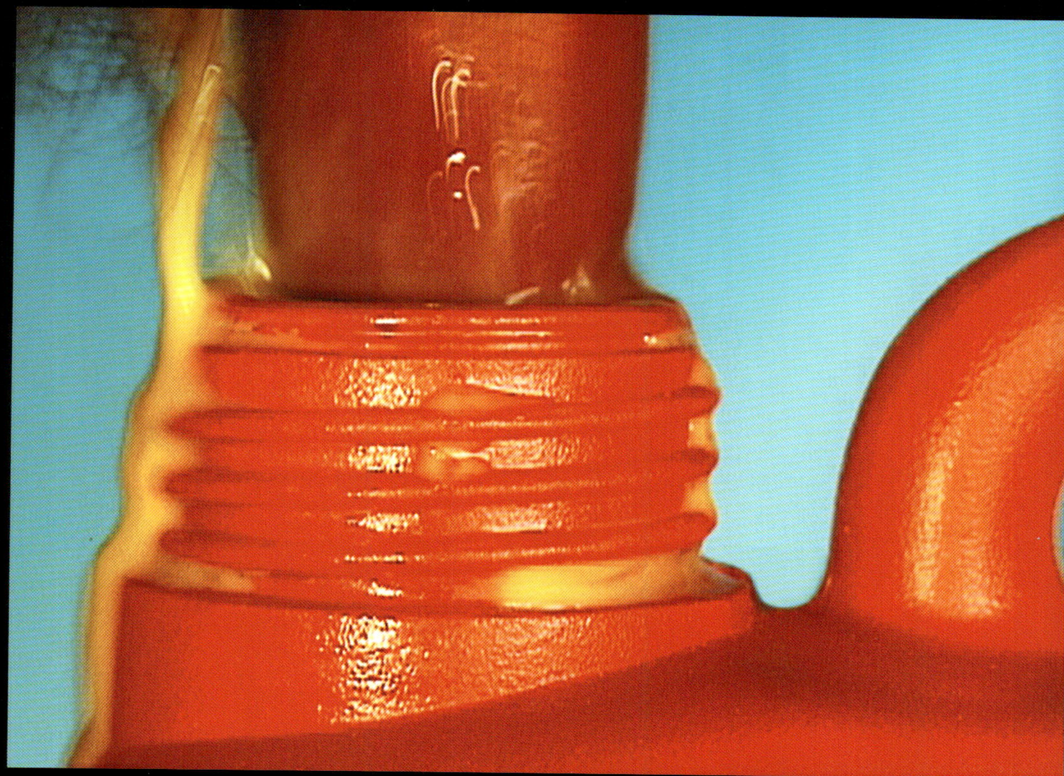

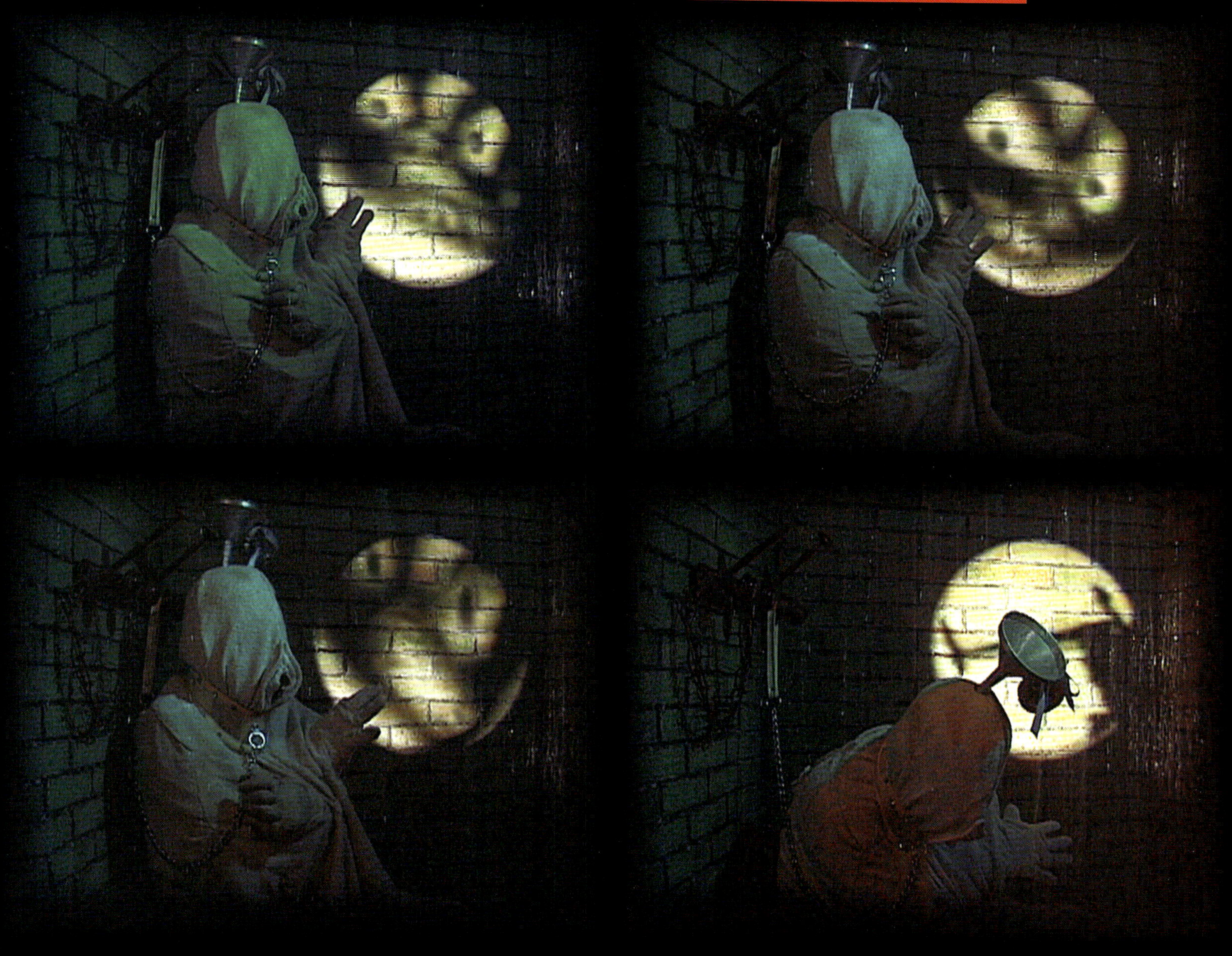

Corte & Nurcis:
video stills from *No Light*, 1996-97.
Lambda prints on canvas and cibachrome.
Variable dimensions.

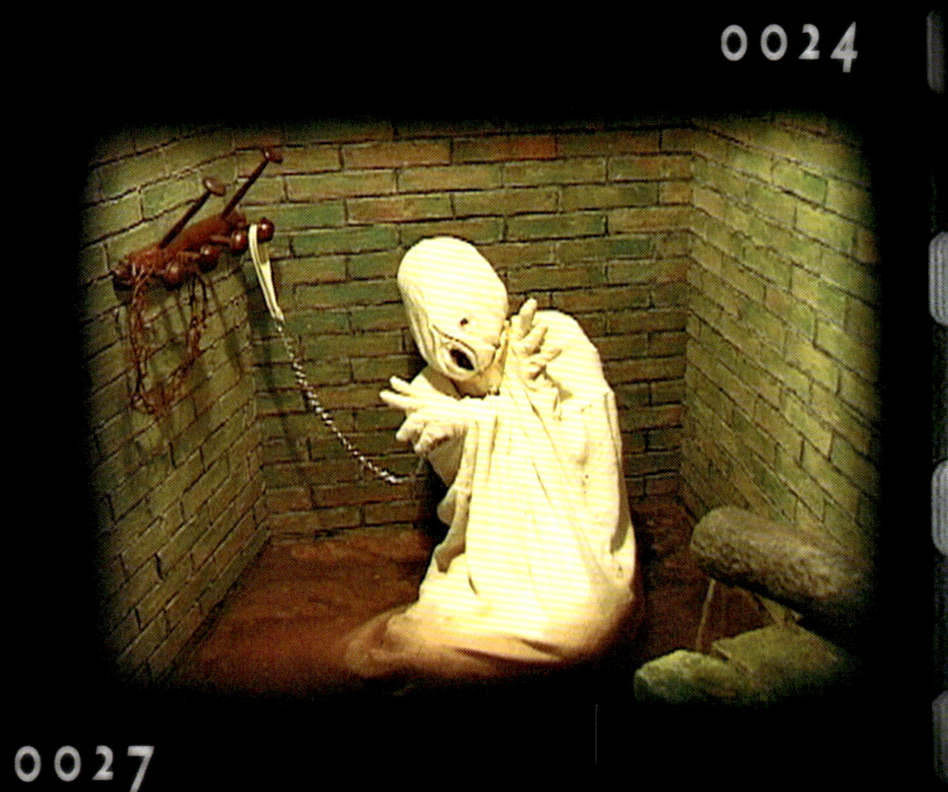

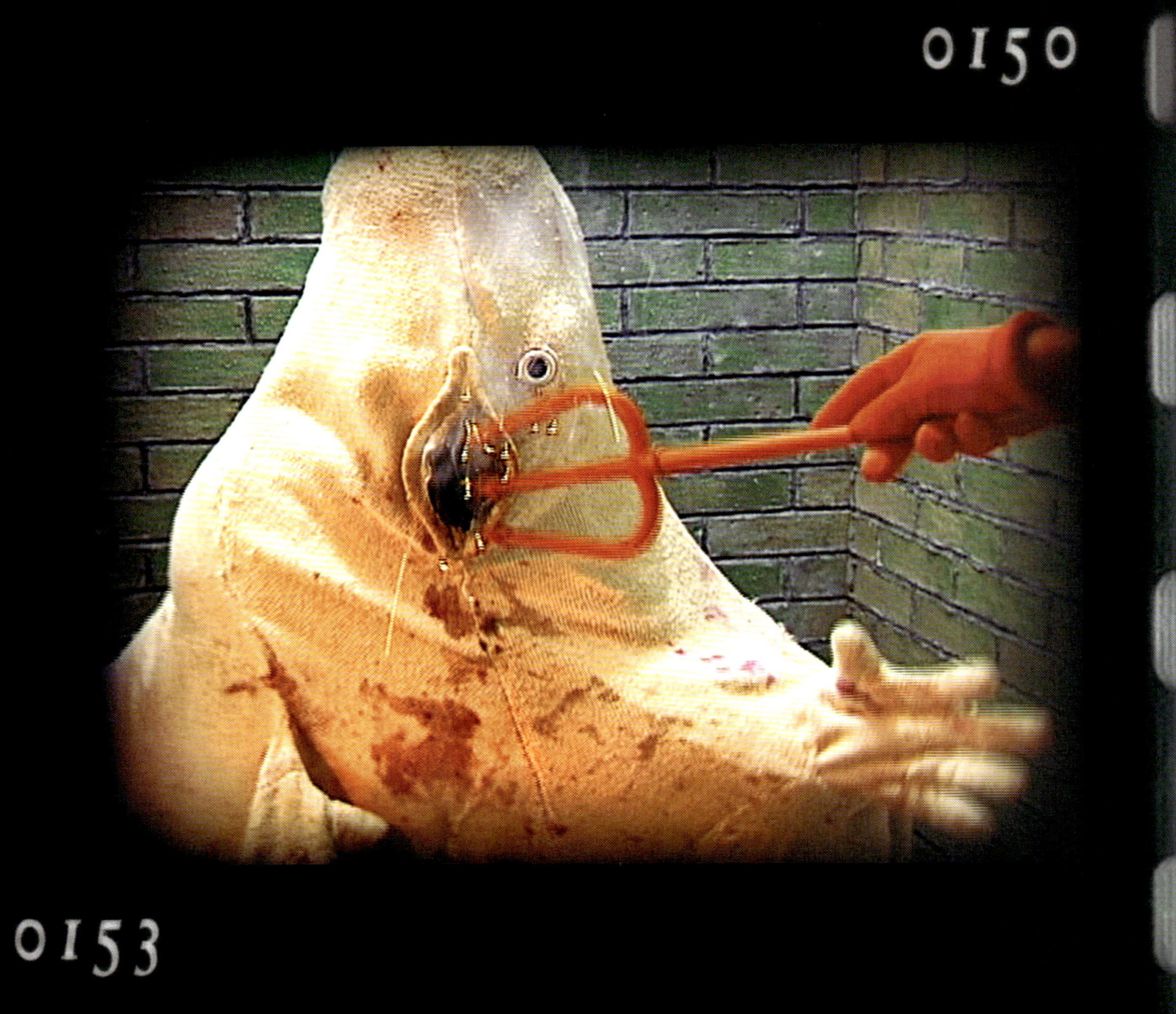

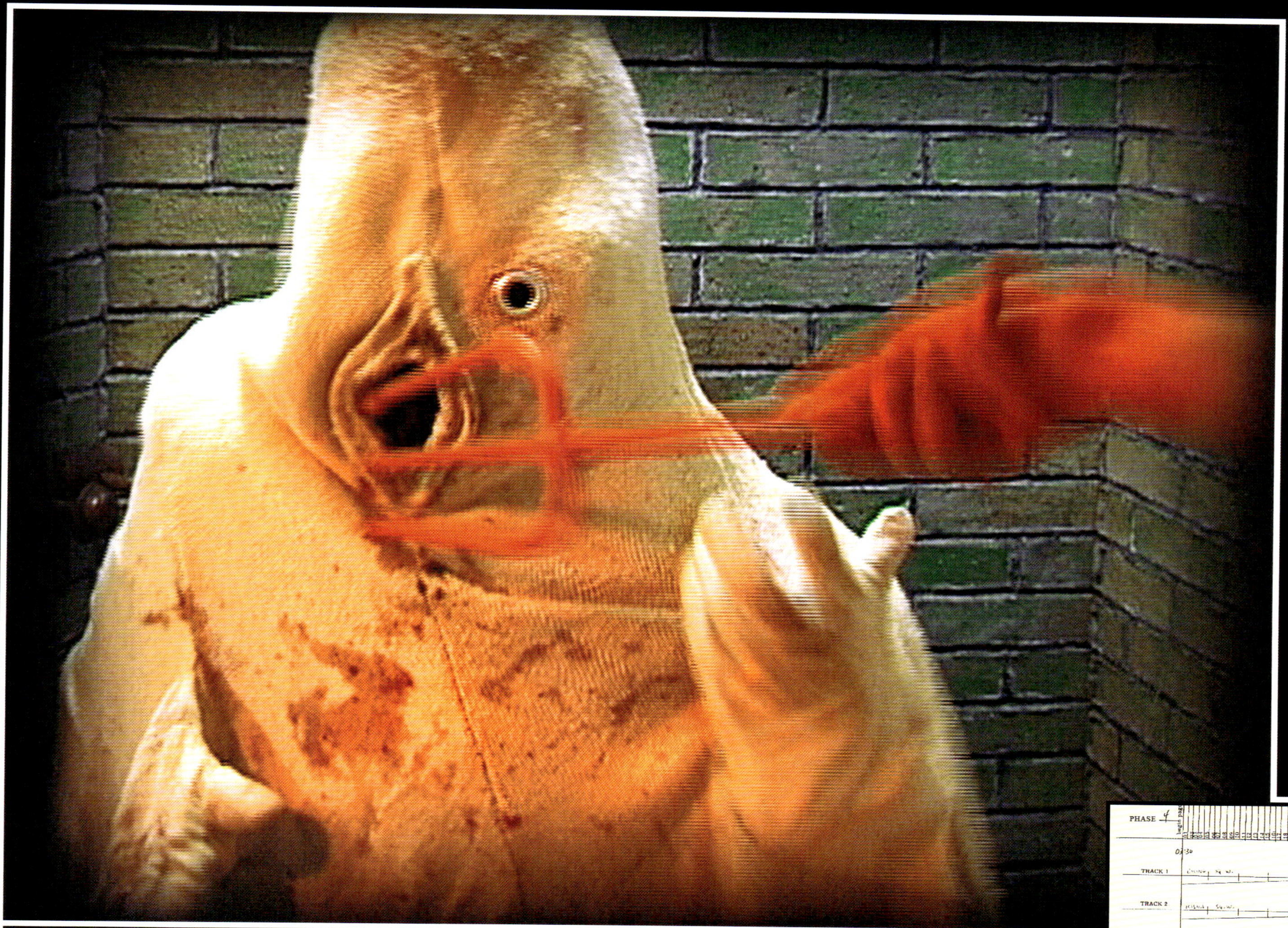

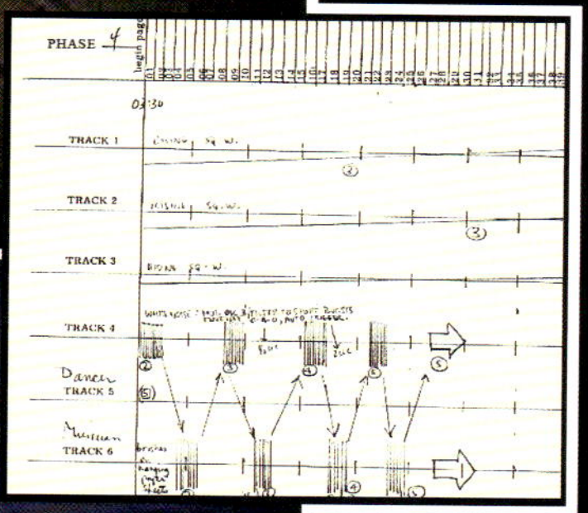

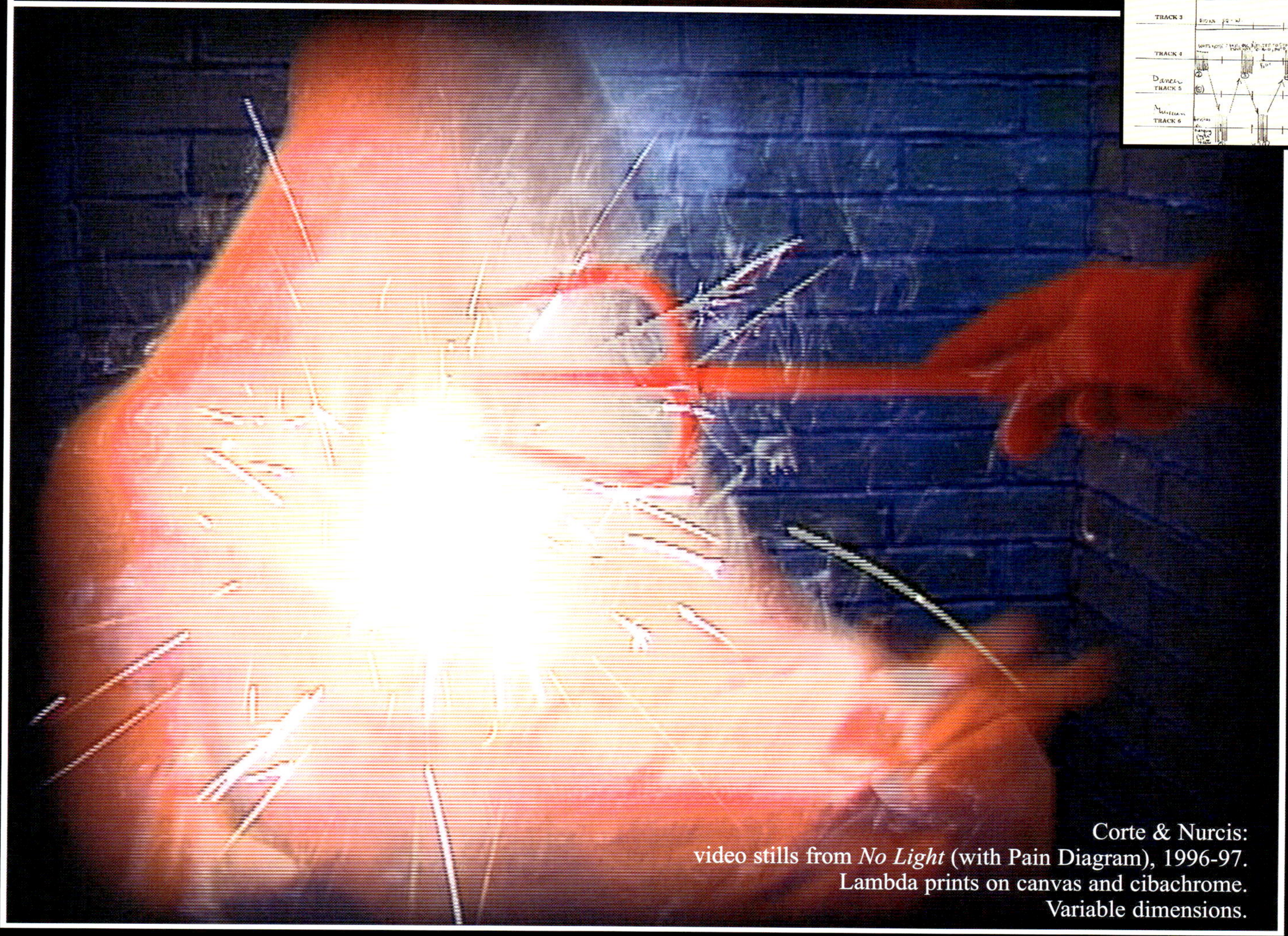

Corte & Nurcis:
video stills from *No Light* (with Pain Diagram), 1996-97.
Lambda prints on canvas and cibachrome.
Variable dimensions.

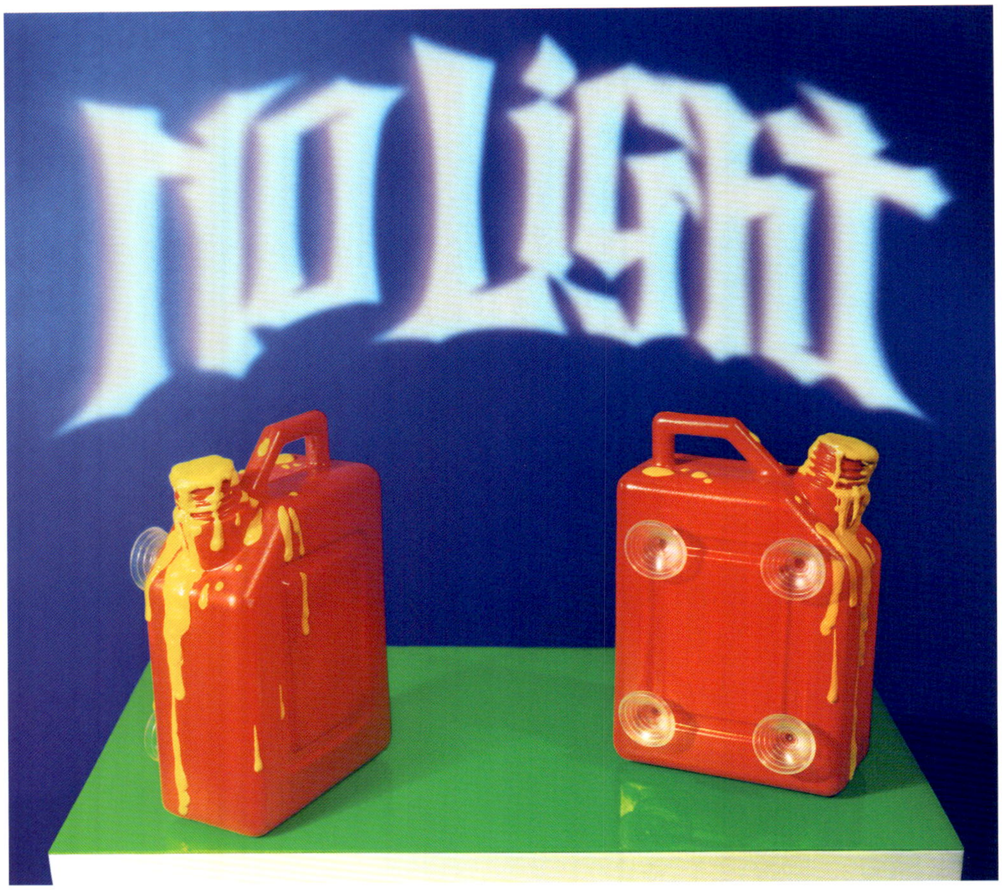

No Light: the Evil Tank, 1997.
Gadget for car windows.
Pvc and acrylic. Edition of 20.
5¾ x 3¾ x 2¼" each piece (14,5 x 9,5 x 5,7 cm).
Background: *No Light* logo. GC 981.

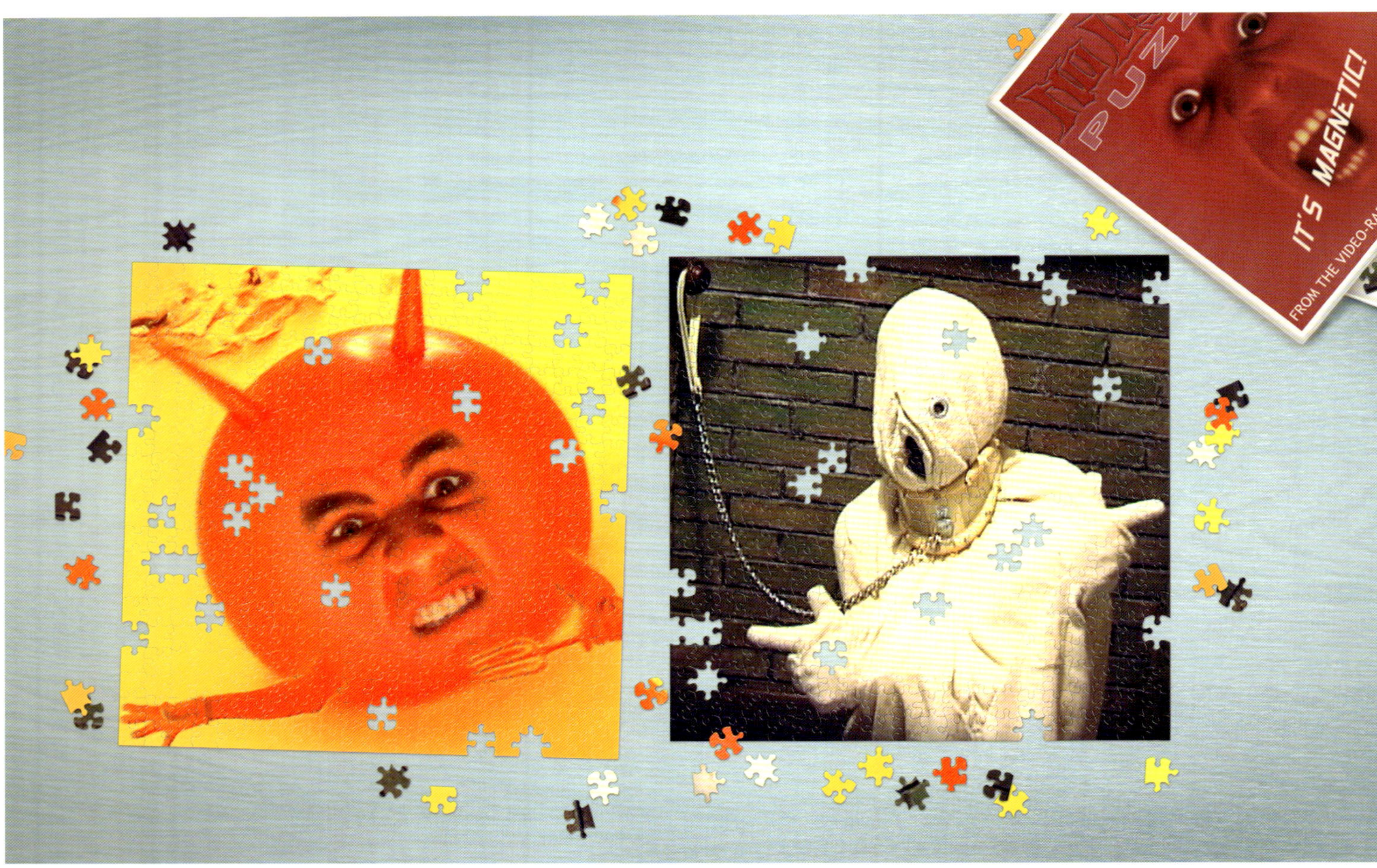

No Light Puzzle (side A and B), 1997-98.
Puzzle pieces in magnetized metallic foil covered on both sides with printed cardboard.
19¾ x 19¾" (50 x 50 cm).
GC 1226.

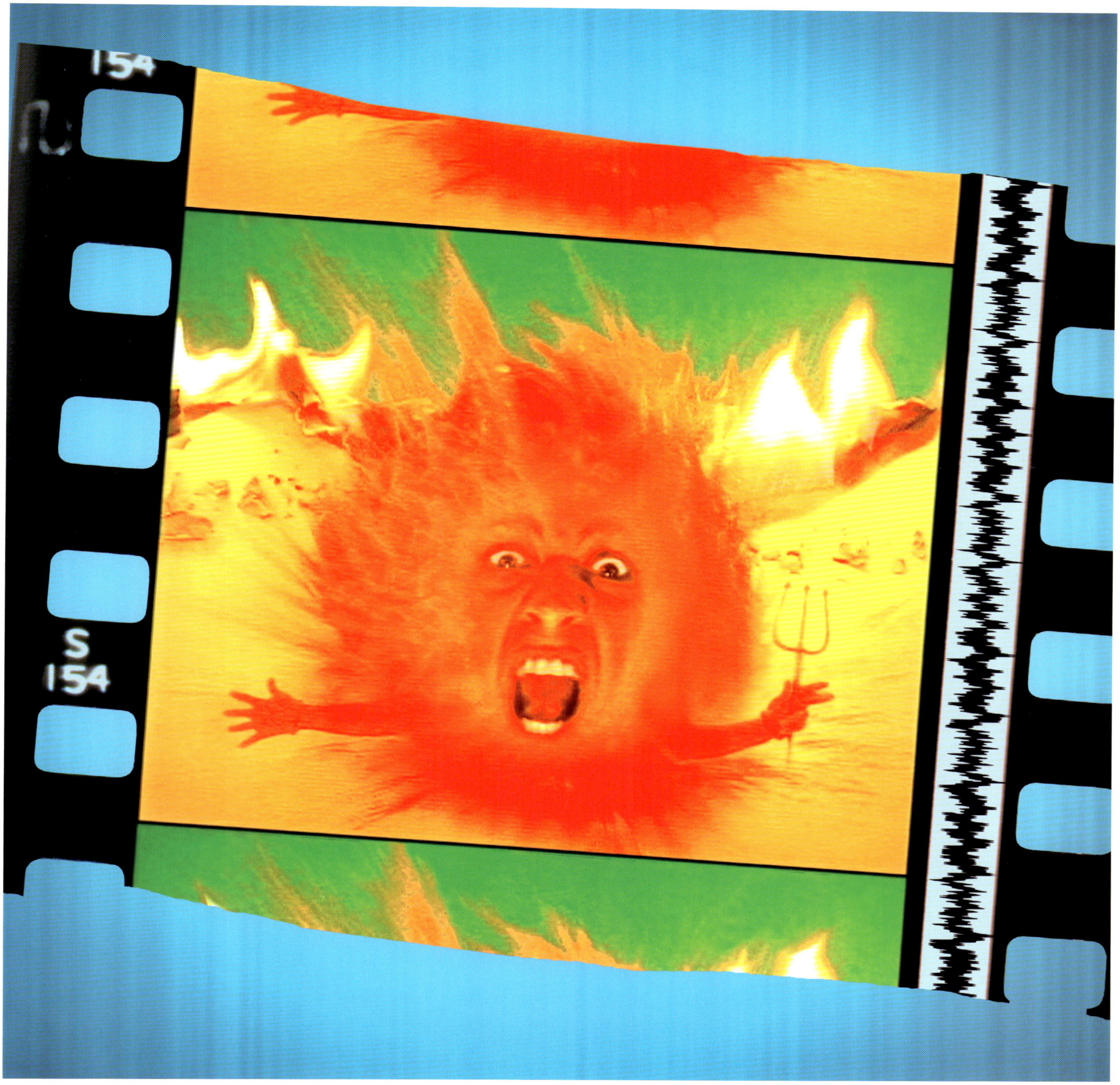

I.R.A.Q., or also *The War Bubo*, 2003.
Cibachrome print on aluminum.
47¼ x 47¼" (120 x 120 cm).
GC 1546.

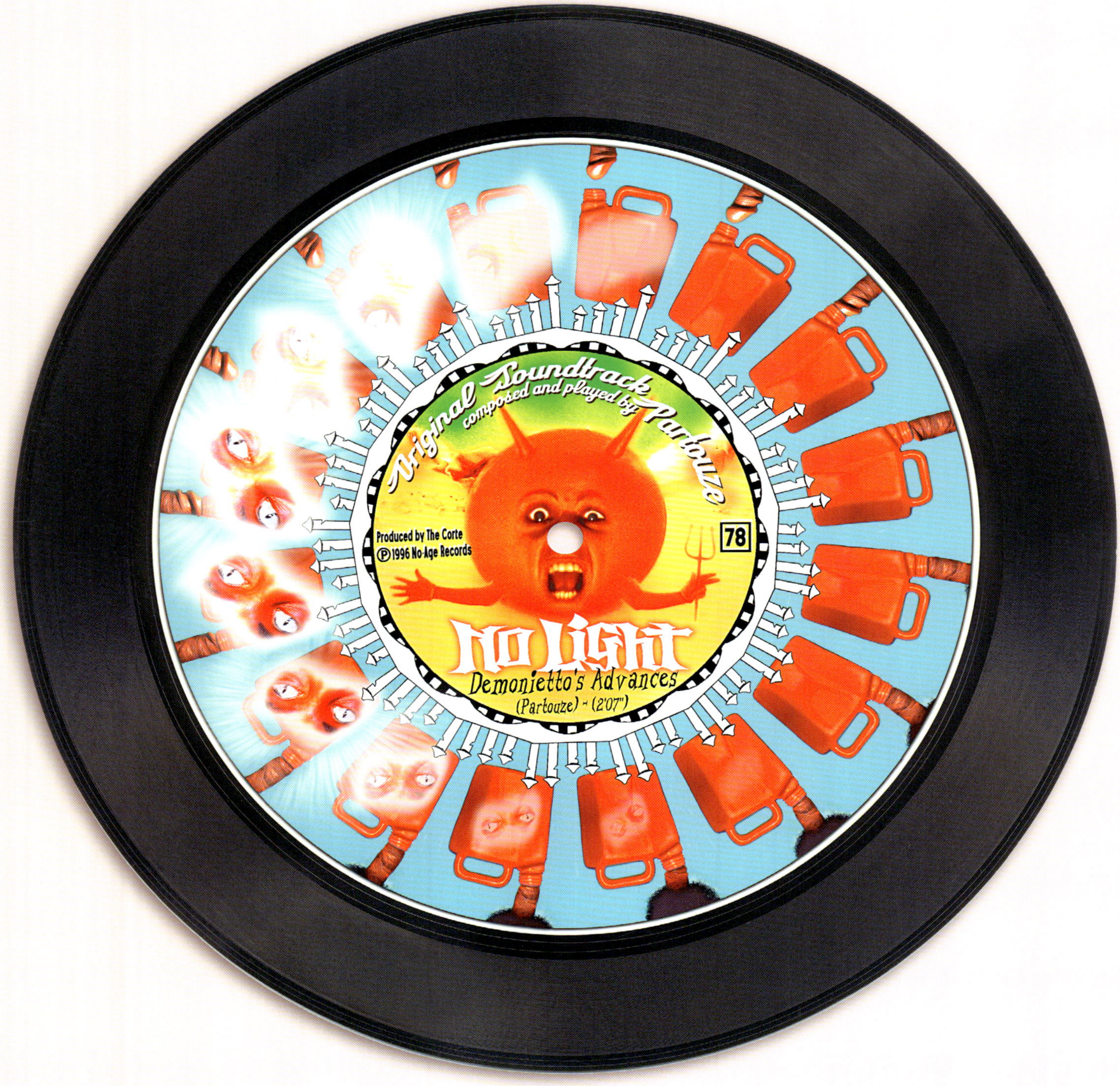

La Partouze's Sexy Vinyl Single (side A), 1997.
78rpm "movie record", containing two excerpts
from the original soundtrack of the digi-film *No Light*.
Vinyl, lambda prints. Edition of 9.
Diam. 7¾" (20 cm).
GC 1210.

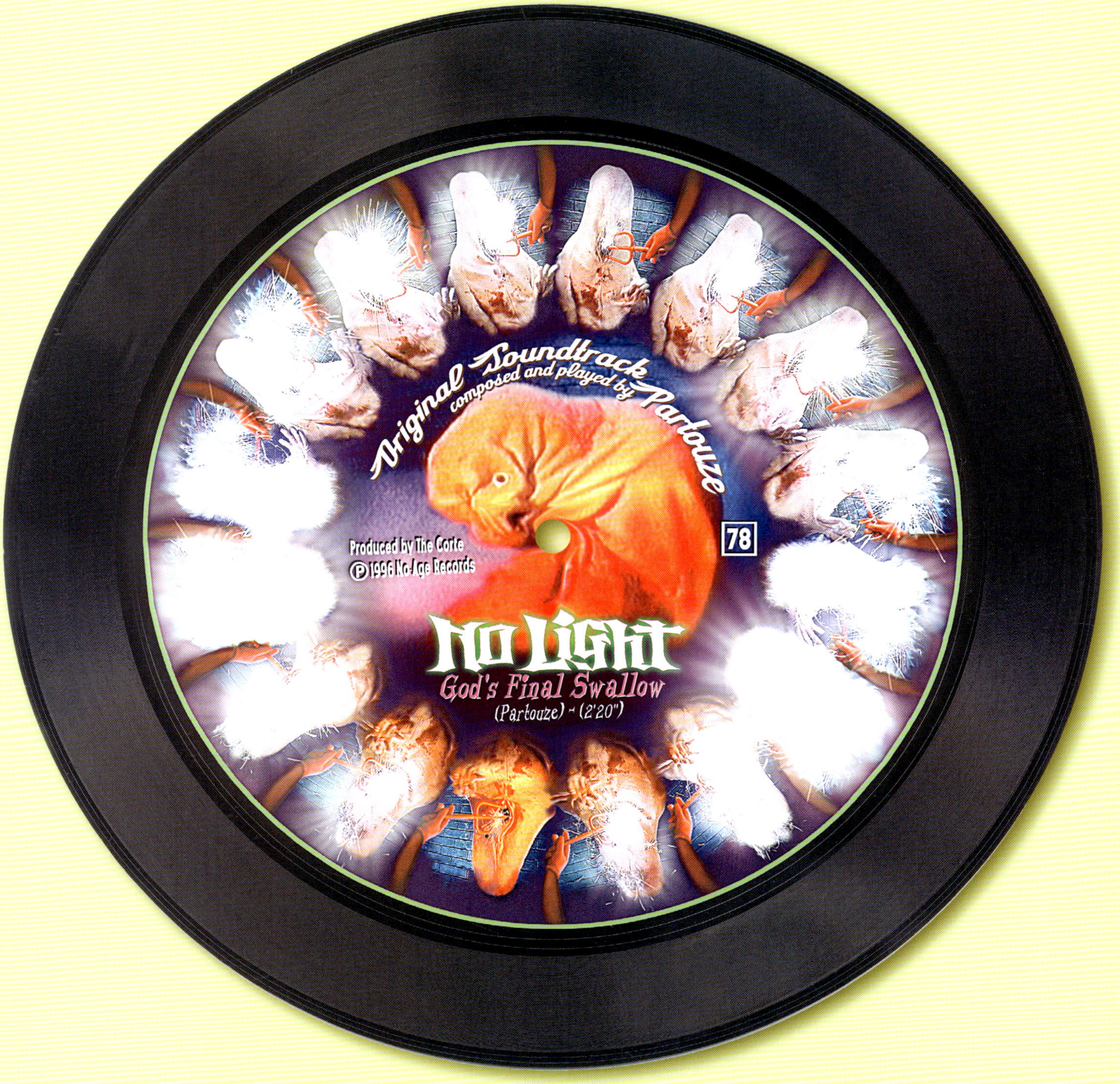

La Partouze's Sexy Vinyl Single (side B), 1997.

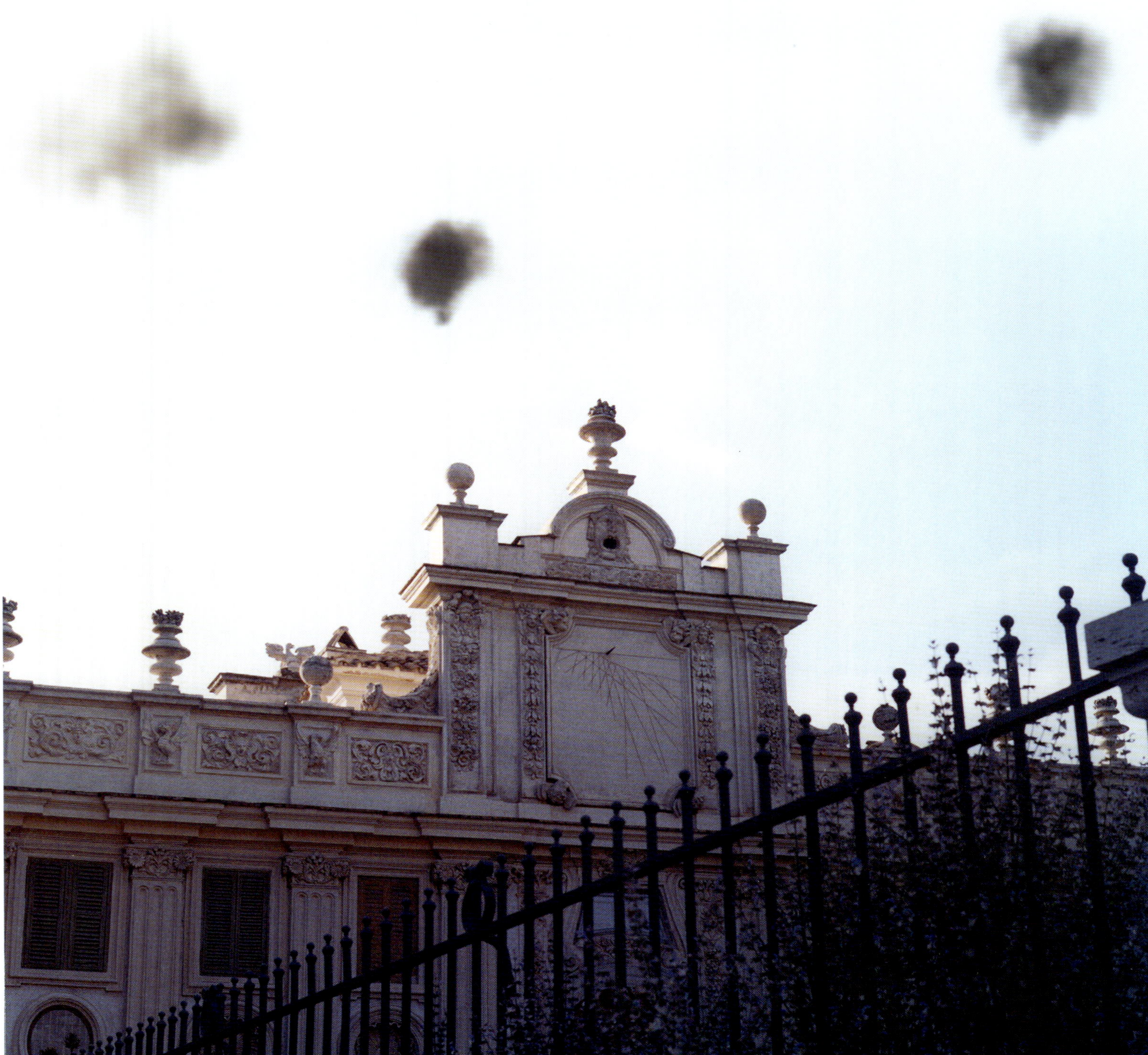

Triple Day-rip Firework, 2002.
Launch of dark fireworks celebrating the *No Light*'s 5th Anniversary.
Cibachrome print.
47¼ x 43¾" (120 x 111,6 cm).
GC 1445.

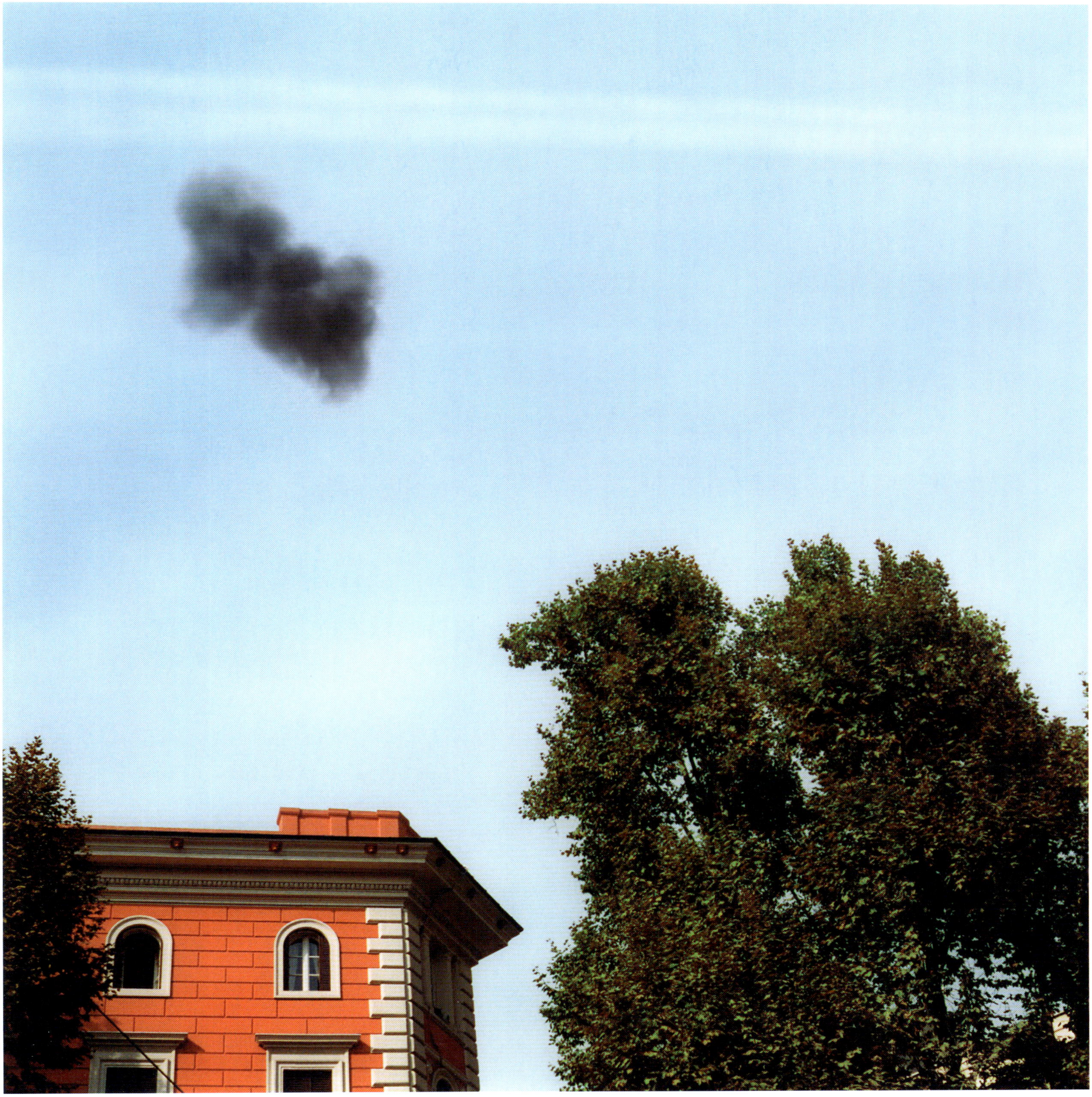

Day-rip Firework and Chemtrail, 2002.
Launch of dark fireworks celebrating the *No Light*'s 5th Anniversary.
Cibachrome print.
47¼ x 47¼" (120 x 120 cm).
GC 1448.

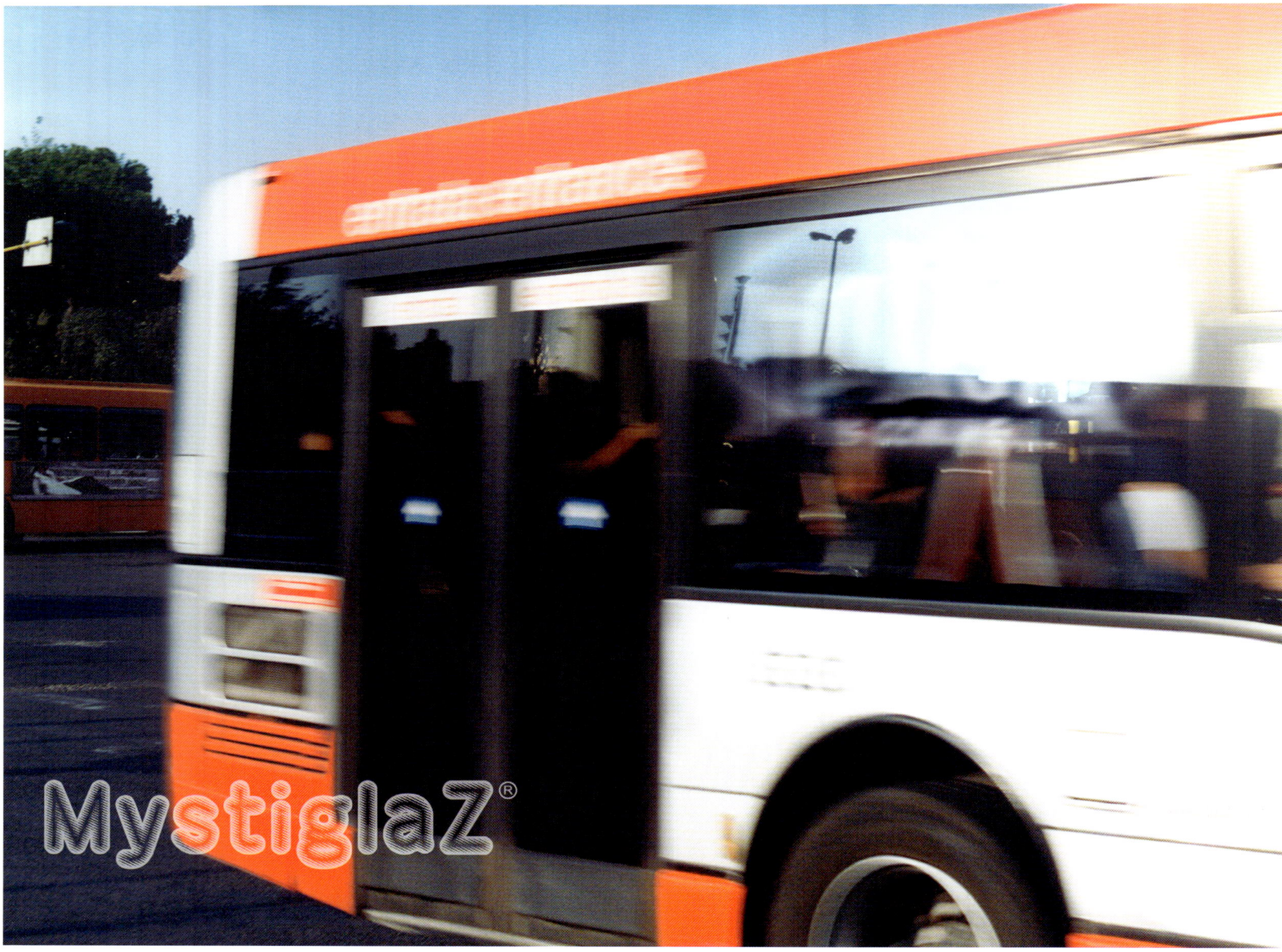

Mystiglaz Promo Picture, 1997.
Cibachrome print.
40¼ x 53¼” (102 x 135 cm).
GC 1219.

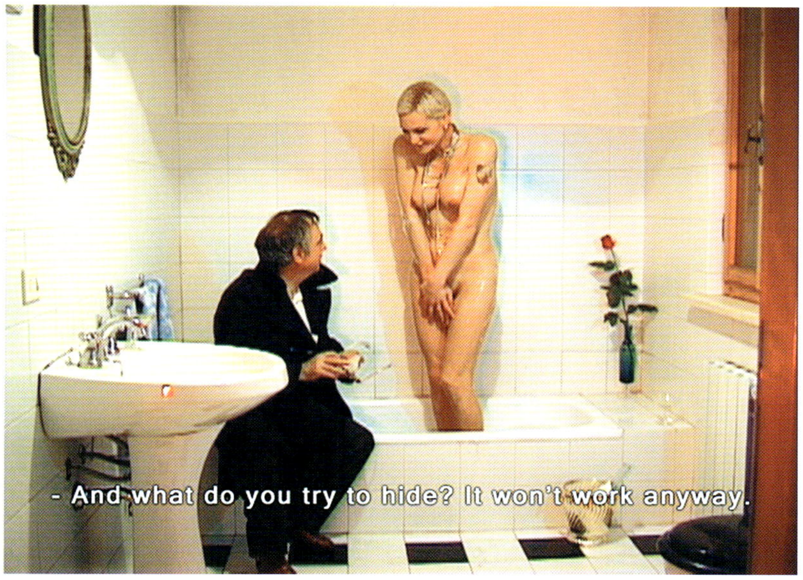

Corte & Nurcis:
video stills from *Homevideo* (digital video, 33'), 1997.
Cibachrome prints from a series of 100 stills.
Variable dimensions.
GC 1108-1207.

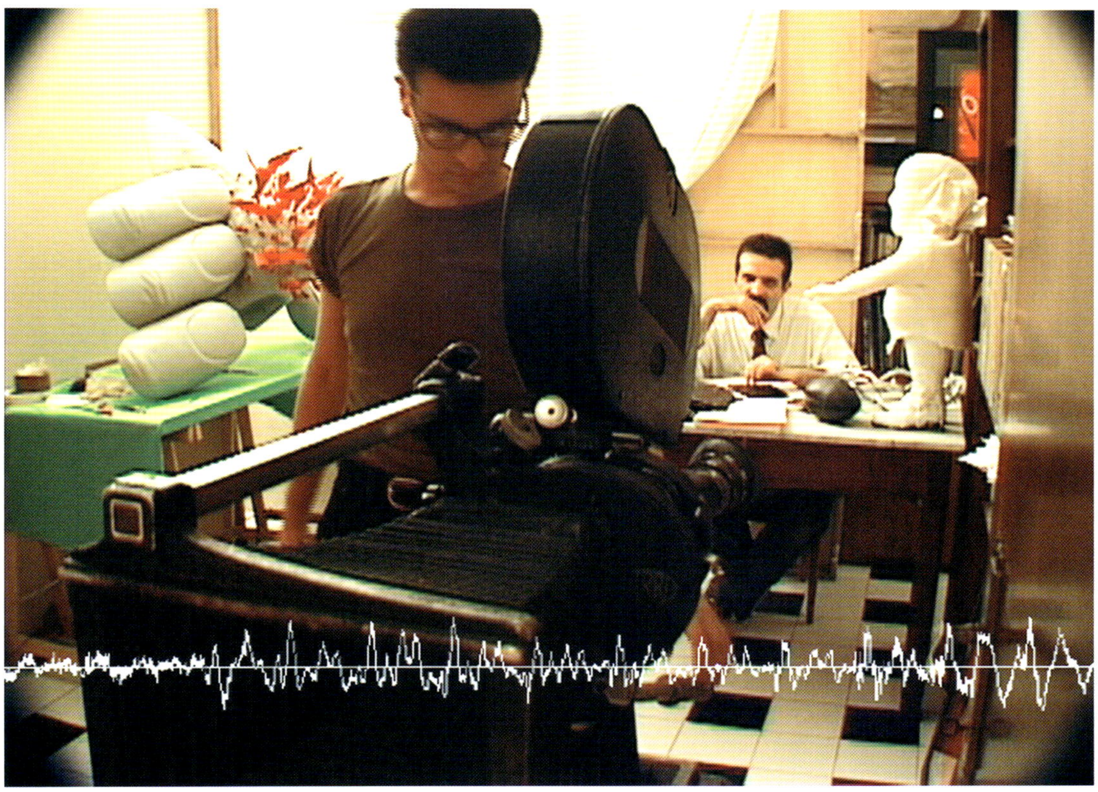

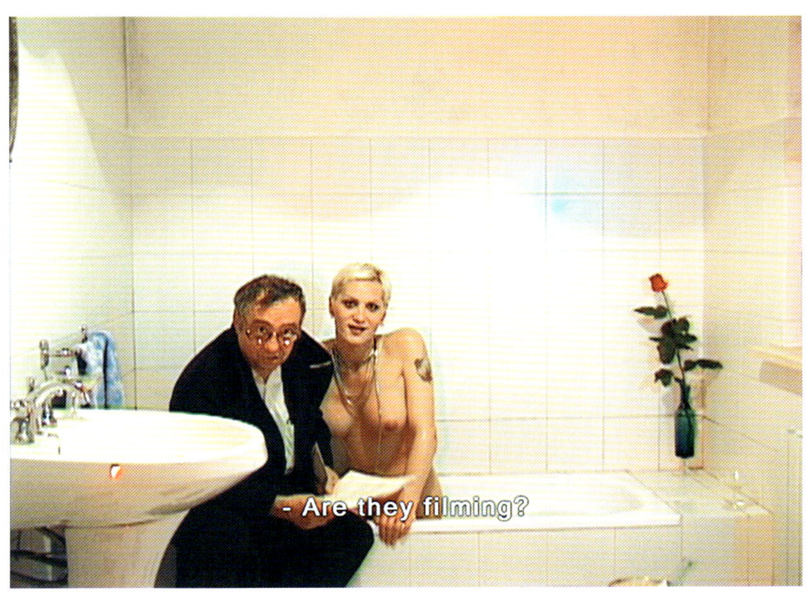

Corte & Nurcis:
video stills from *Homevideo*, 1997.
Cibachrome prints.
Variable dimensions.

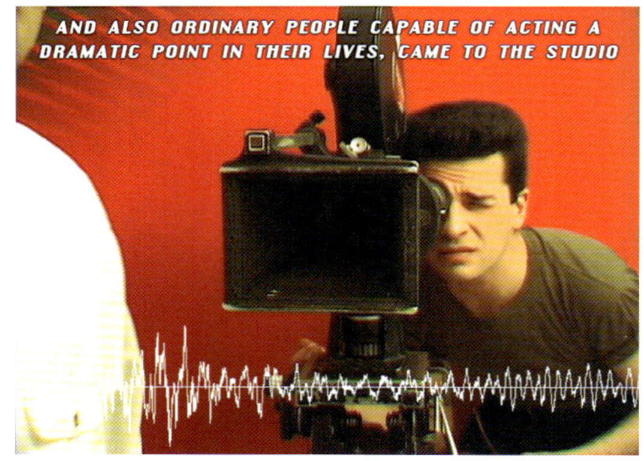

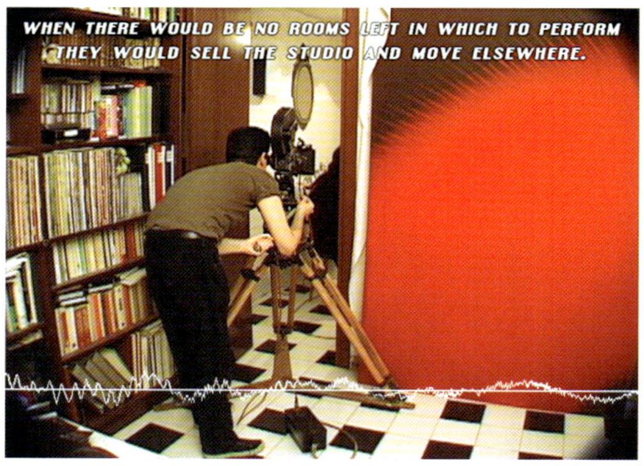

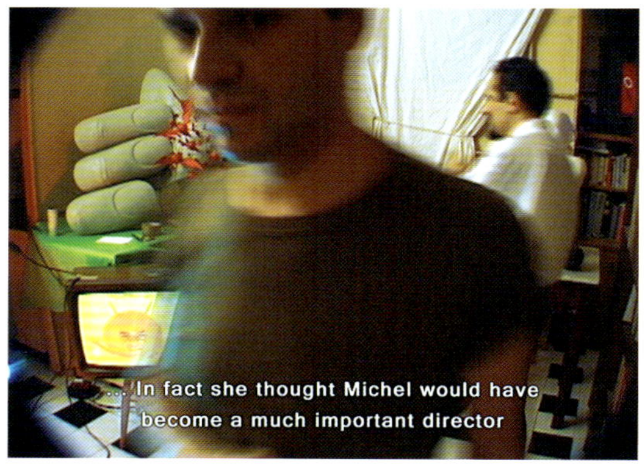

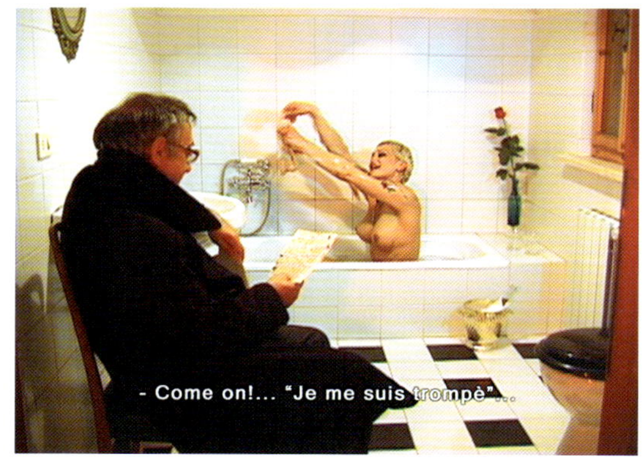

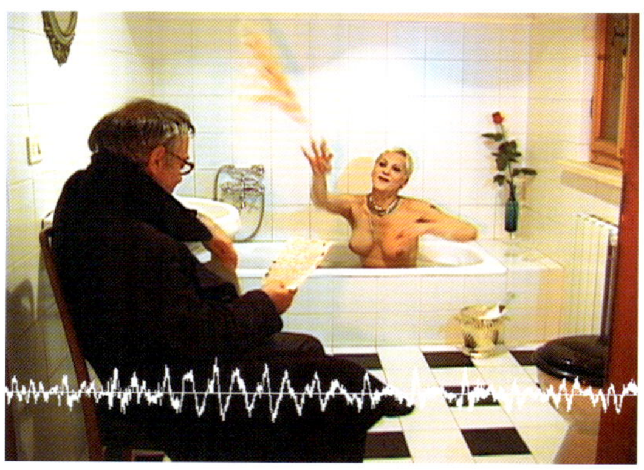

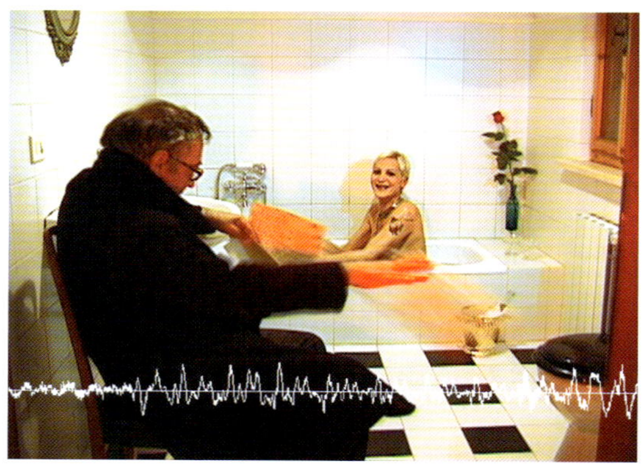

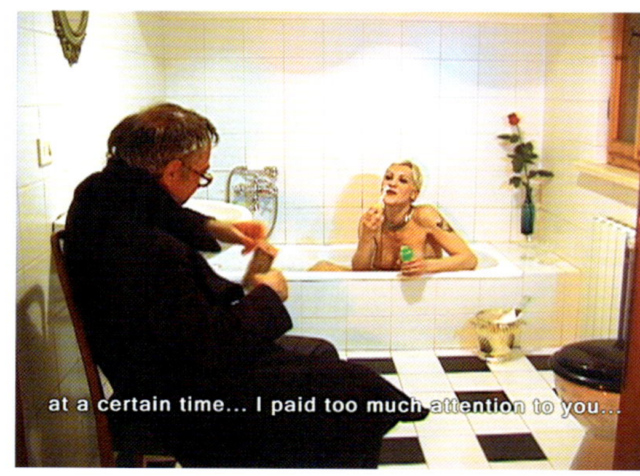

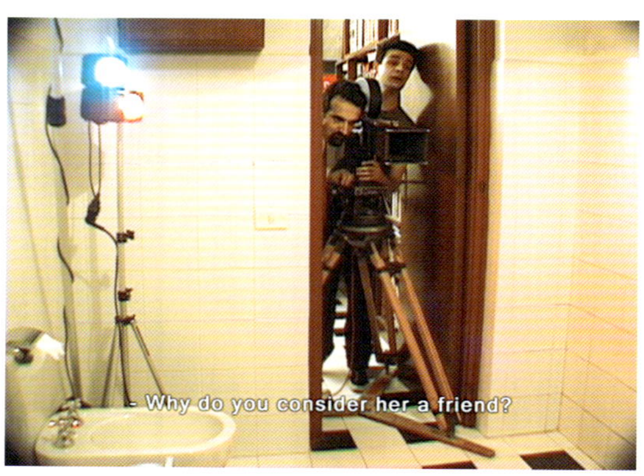

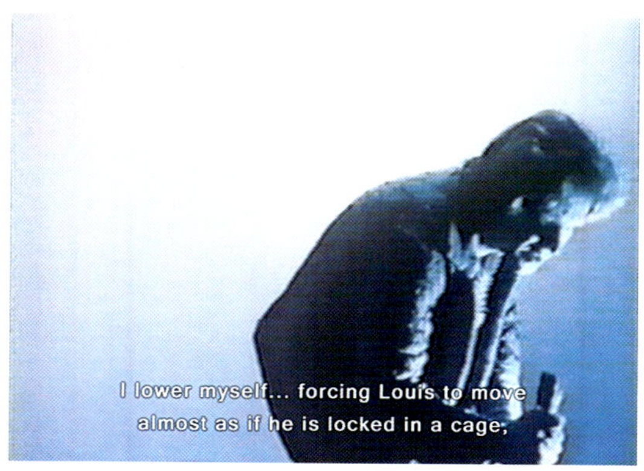

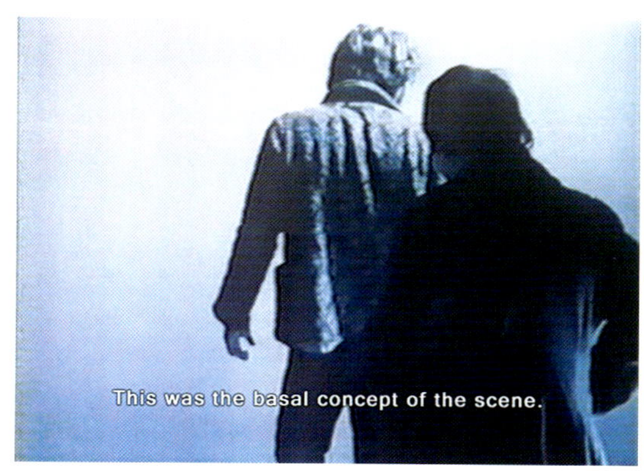

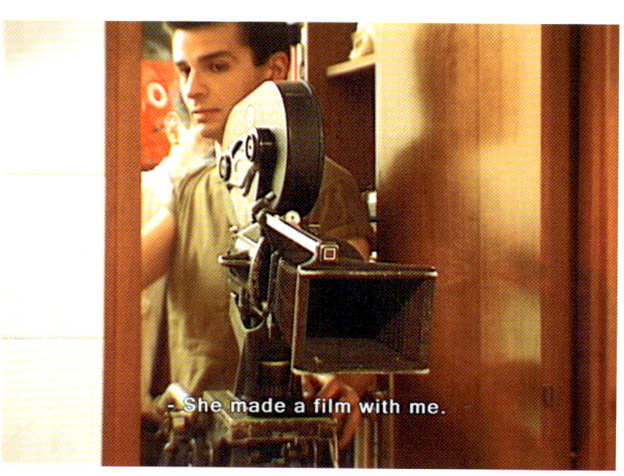

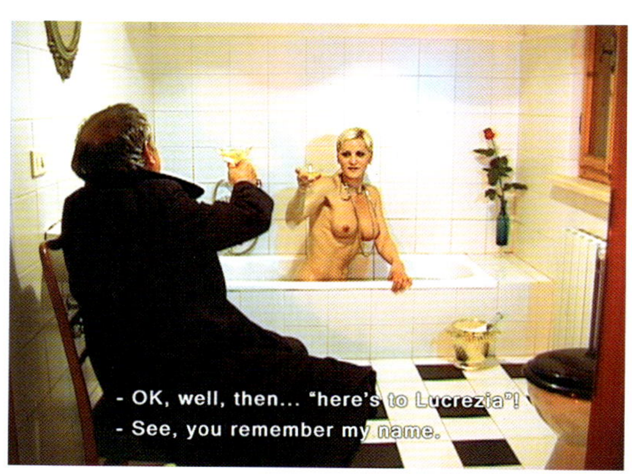

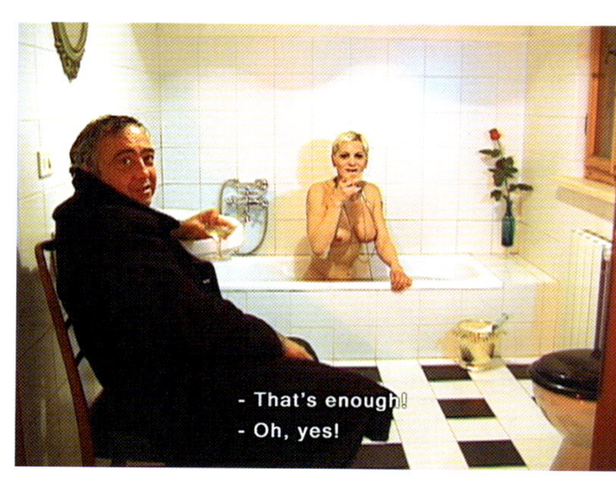

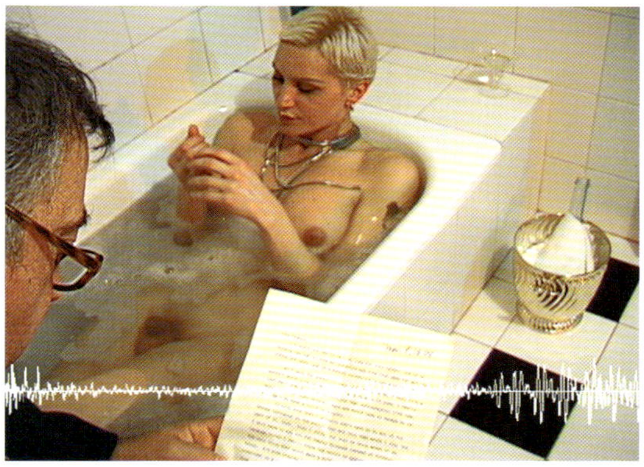

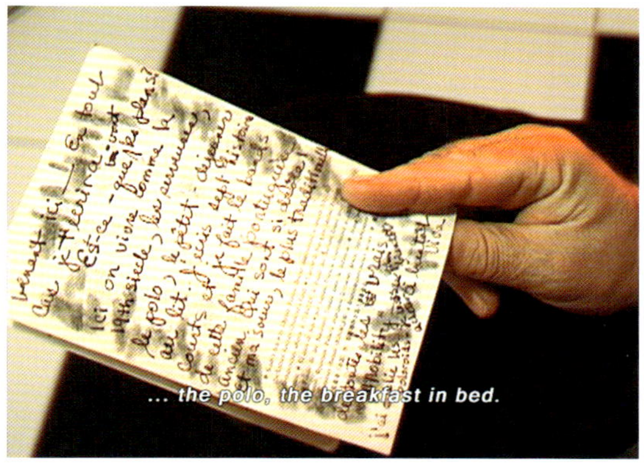

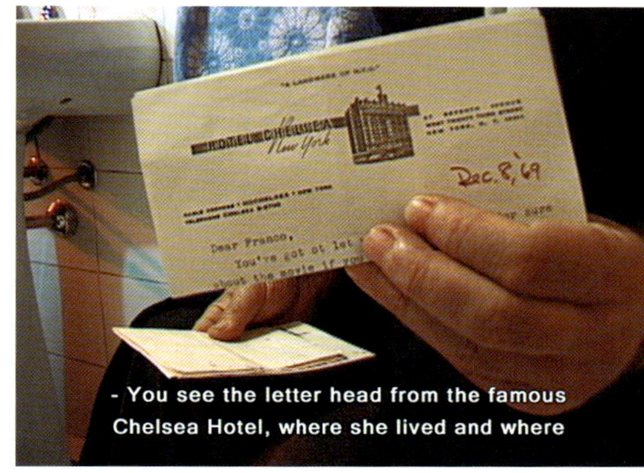

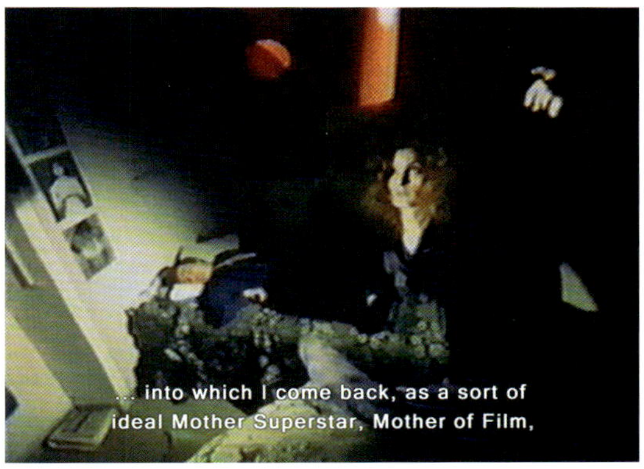

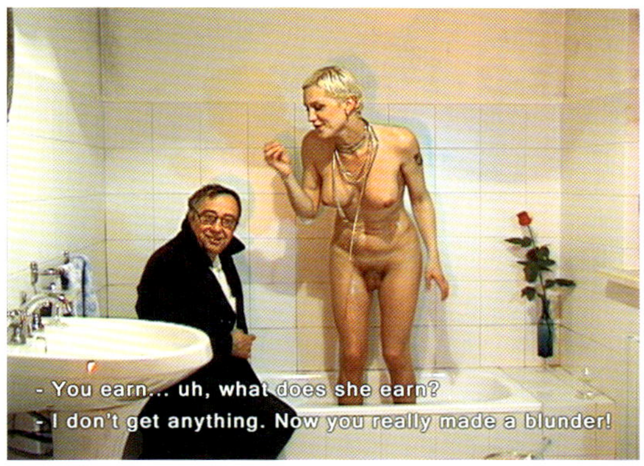

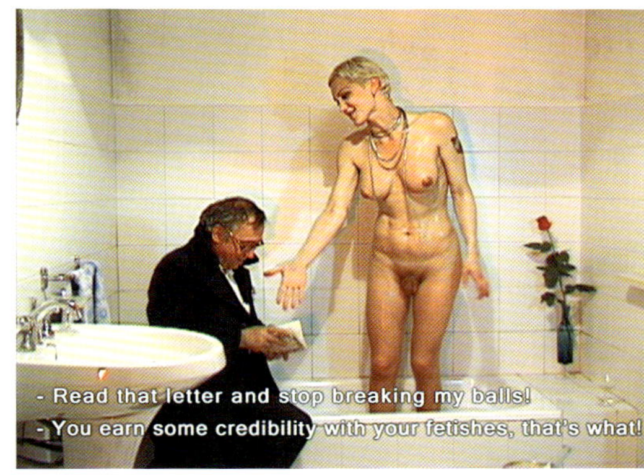

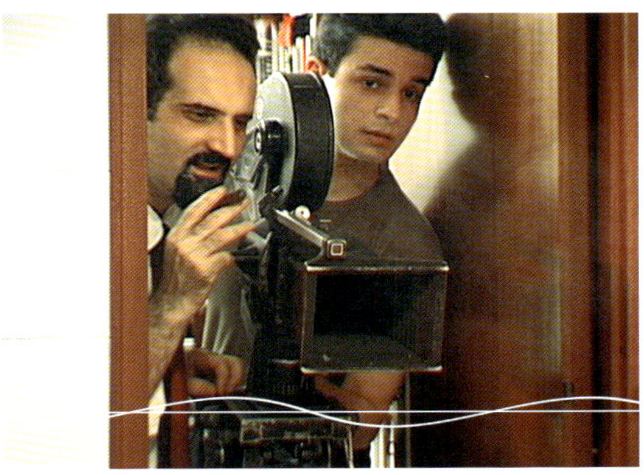

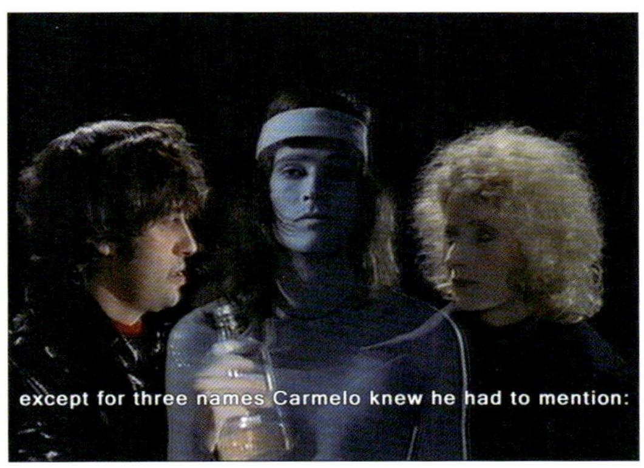

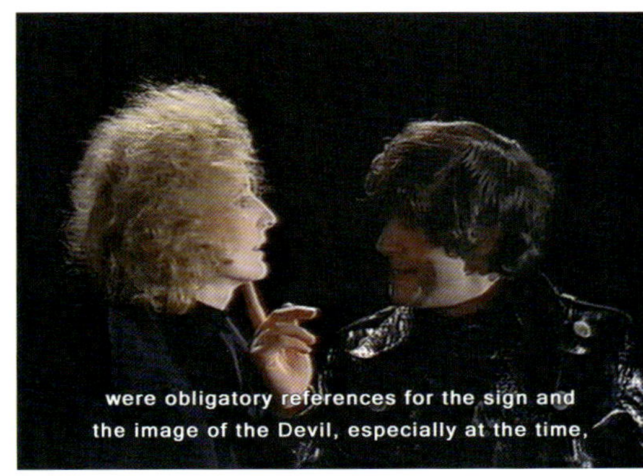

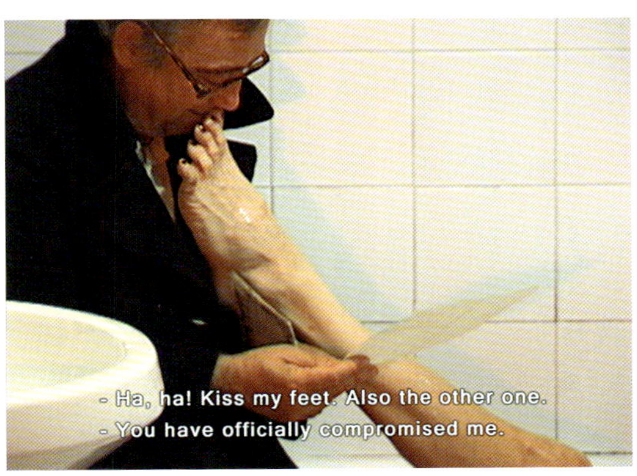

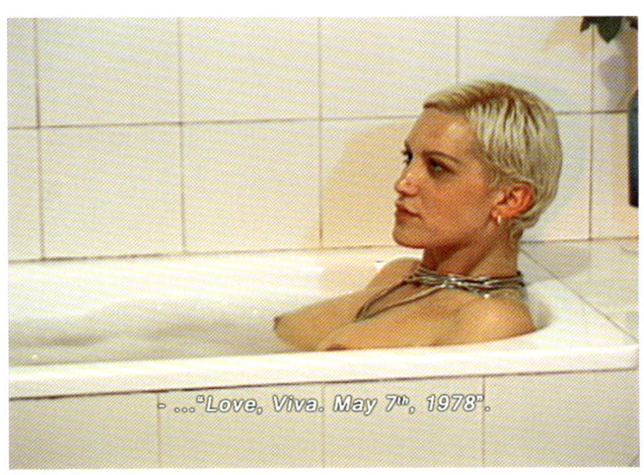

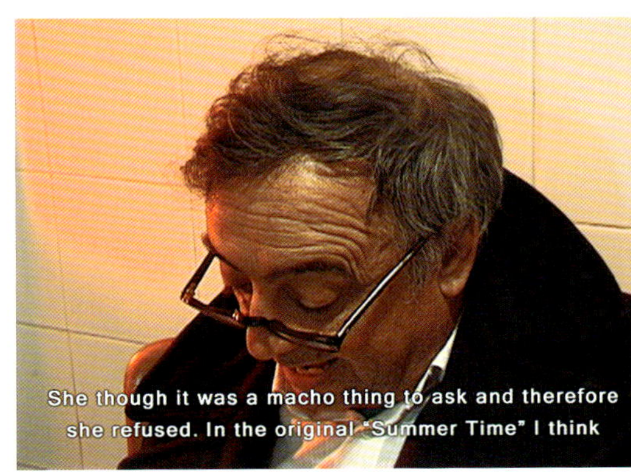

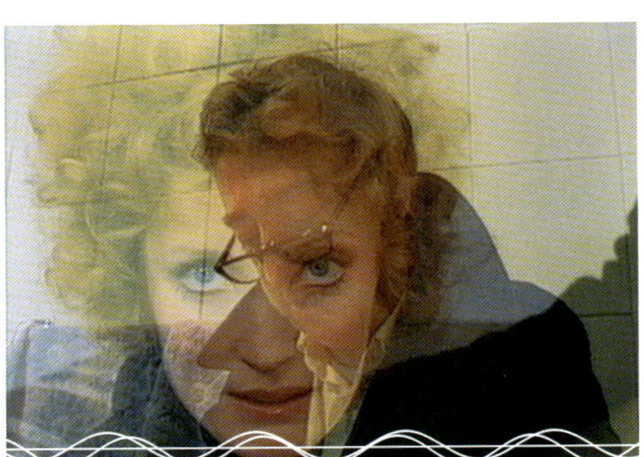

Corte & Nurcis:
video stills from *Homevideo*, 1997.
Cibachrome prints.
Variable dimensions.

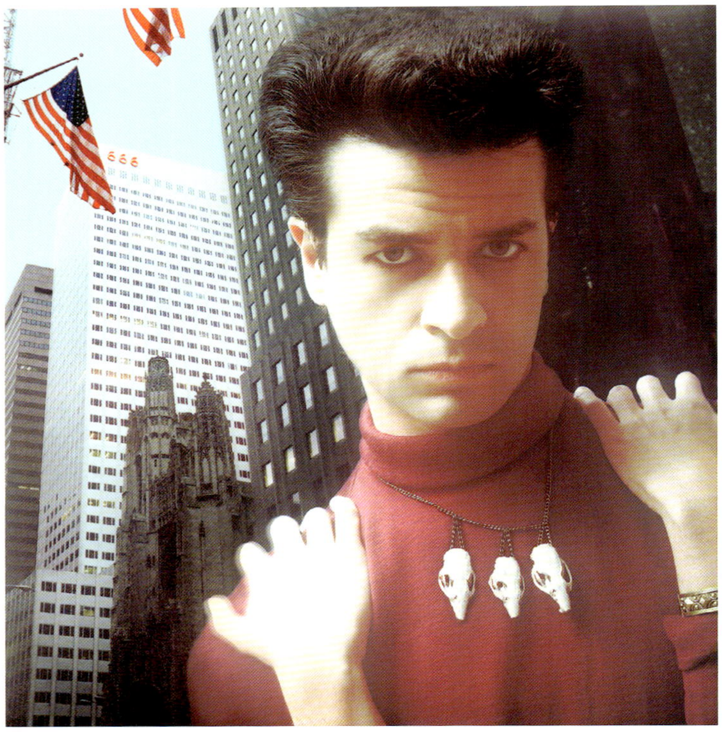

Corte & Gong: *Princeps Hujus Mundi (666)*, 1999.
Lambda print from a fashion photo in collaboration with photographer Syla Gong (from the *Buildings of NYC* series).
39½ x 31½" (100 x 80 cm).
GC 1264.

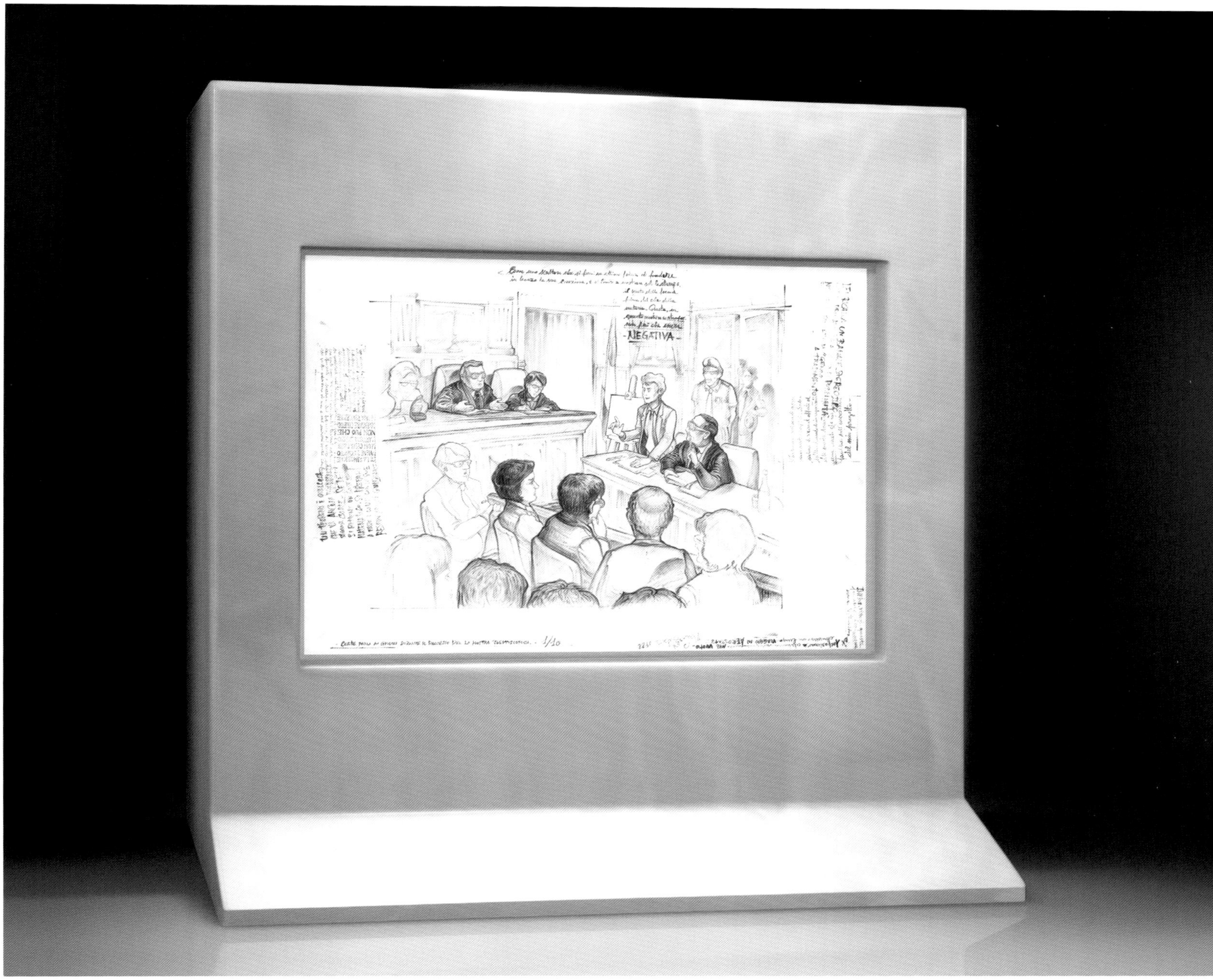

Corte & Dubois: *Corte speaks to Judges during his trial for the 'Cleptoscopica' exhibition*, 1988.
From a series of 10 *Courtroom Drawings* in collaboration with illustrator Diana Dubois;
this series was given in payment for trial costs.
Graphite and charcoal on paper; marble frame.
57 x 51¼ x 11¾" (145 x 130 x 30 cm).
GC 548.

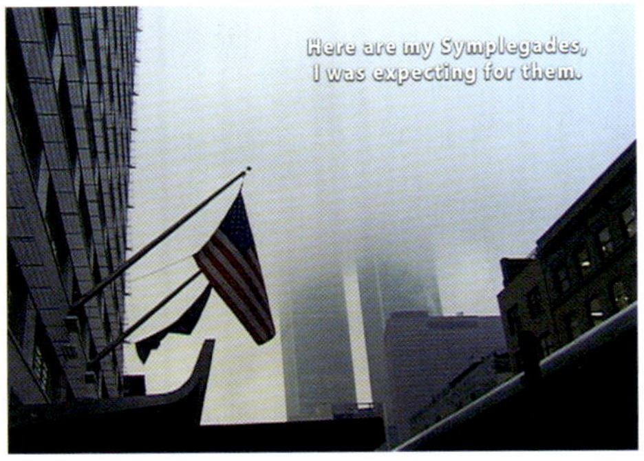

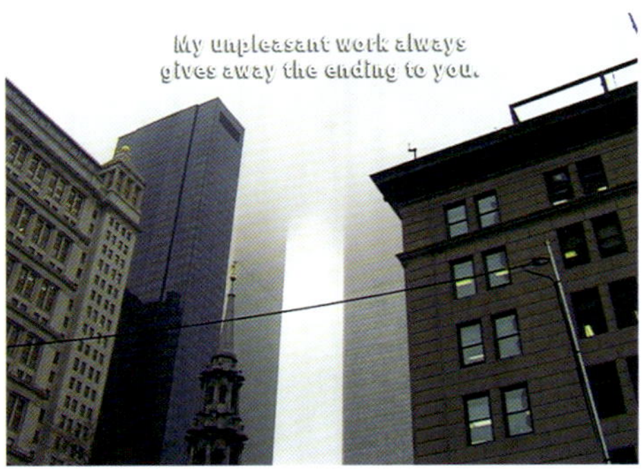

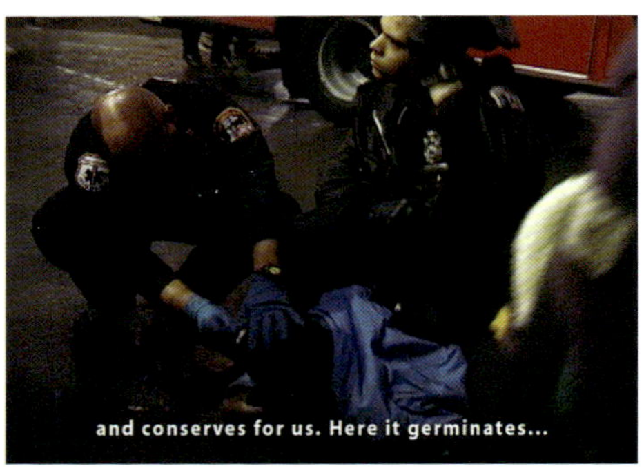

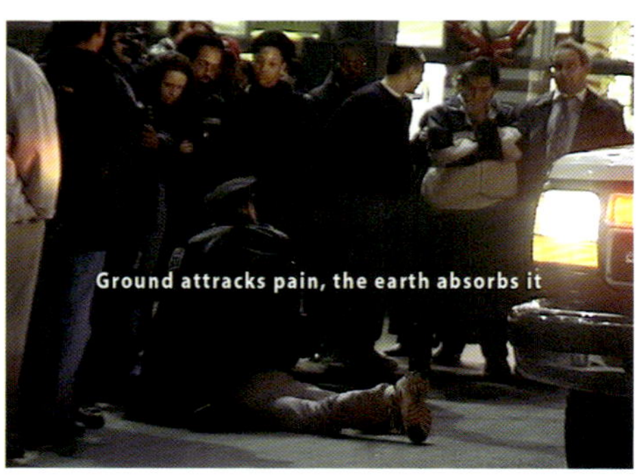

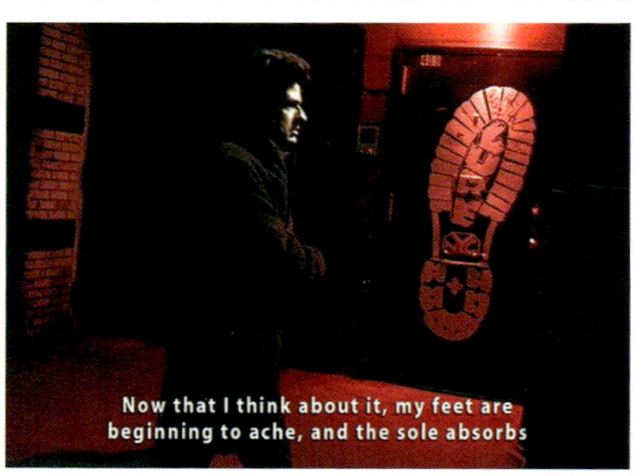

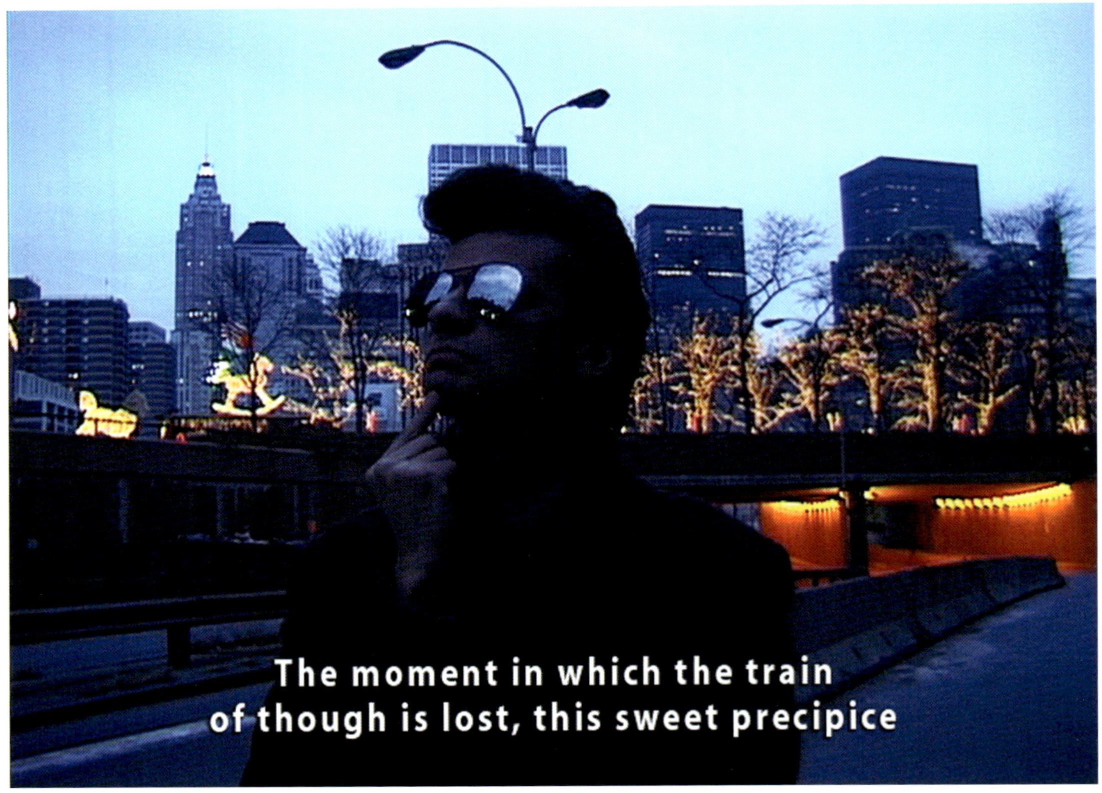

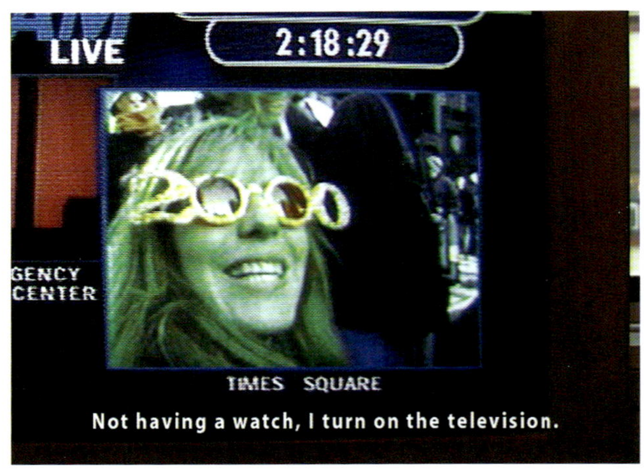

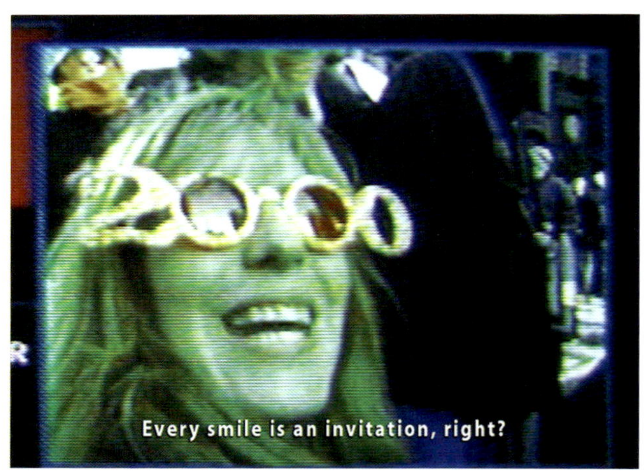

This page and opposite:
(The Making of) Videoache, 1999-2000.
Cibachrome prints from a series of 70 video stills.
14½ x 19¾" each print (37 x 50 cm).
GC 1270-1304, and 1325-1359.

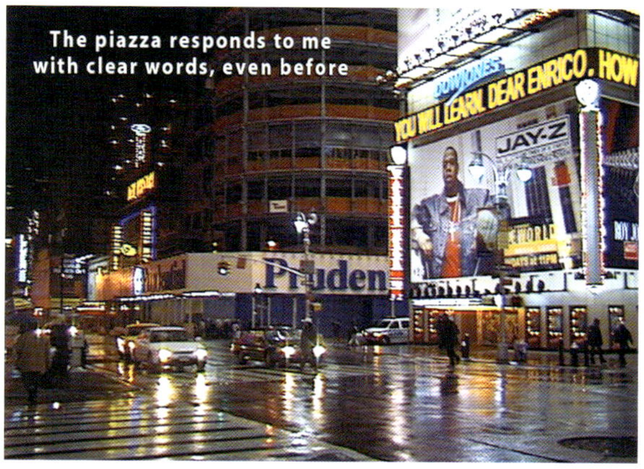
The piazza responds to me
with clear words, even before

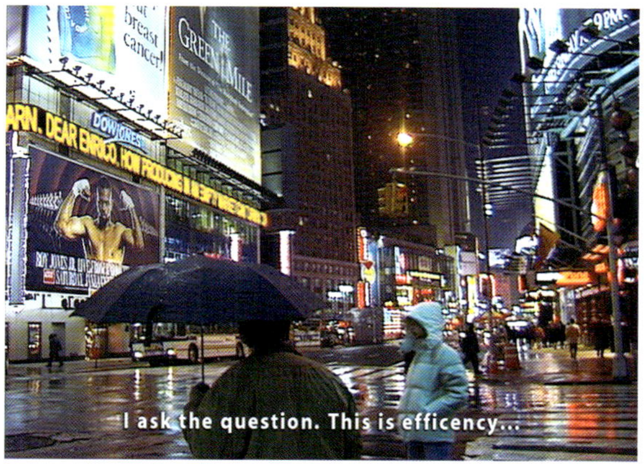
I ask the question. This is efficency...

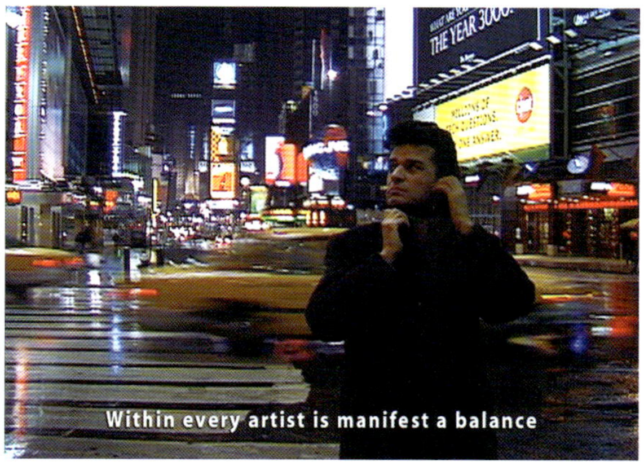
Within every artist is manifest a balance

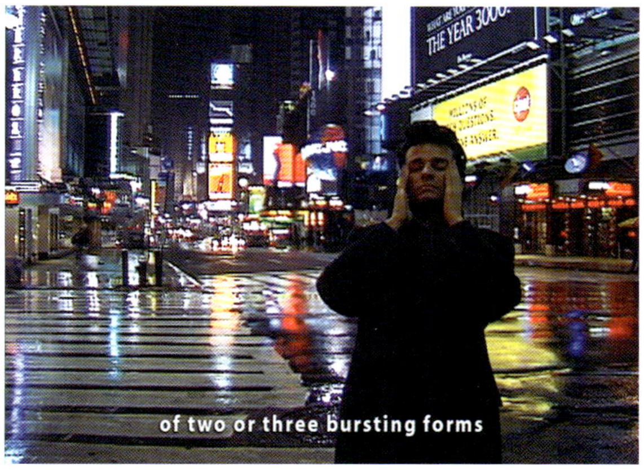
of two or three bursting forms

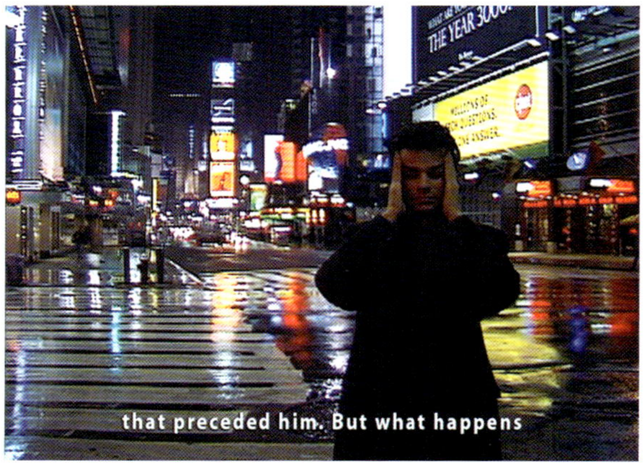
that preceded him. But what happens

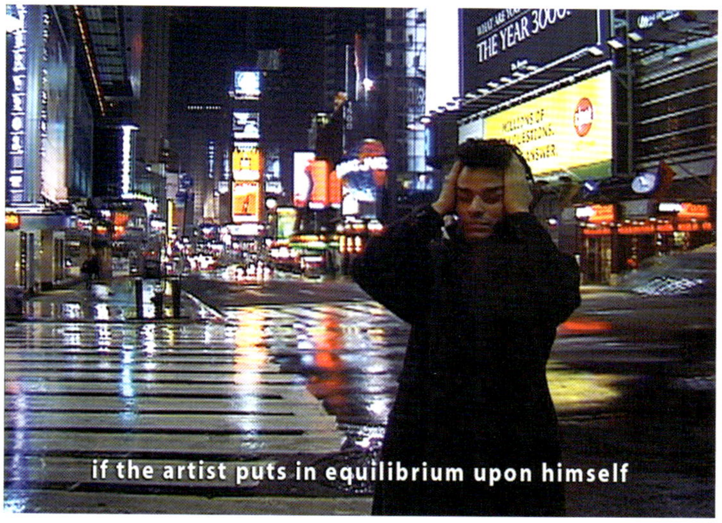
if the artist puts in equilibrium upon himself

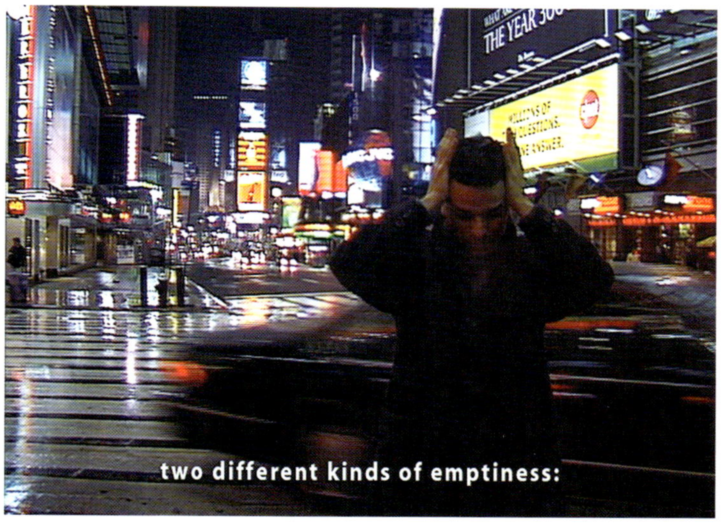
two different kinds of emptiness:

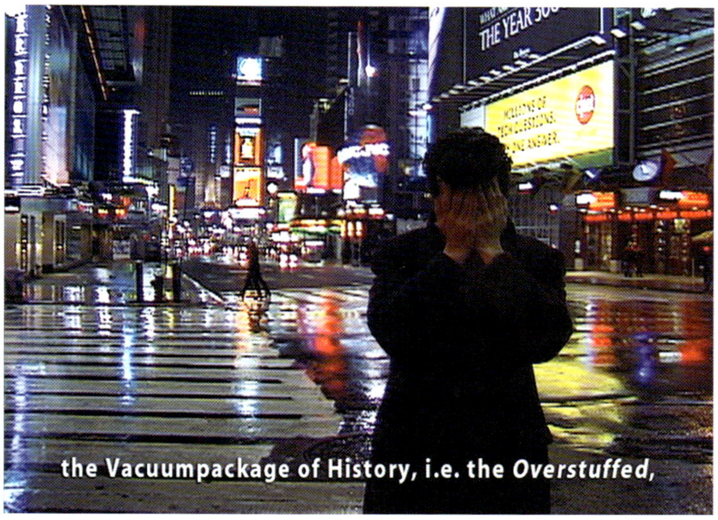
the Vacuumpackage of History, i.e. the *Overstuffed*,

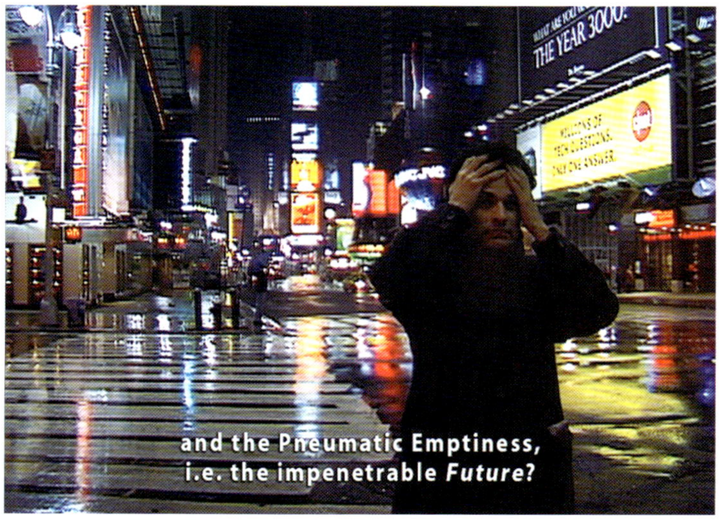
and the Pneumatic Emptiness,
i.e. the impenetrable *Future*?

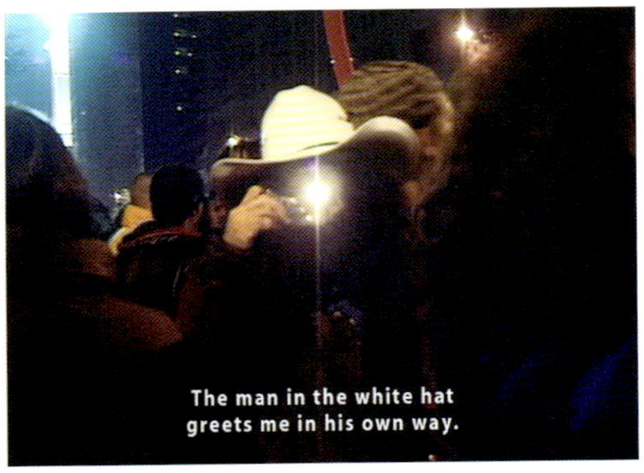
The man in the white hat
greets me in his own way.
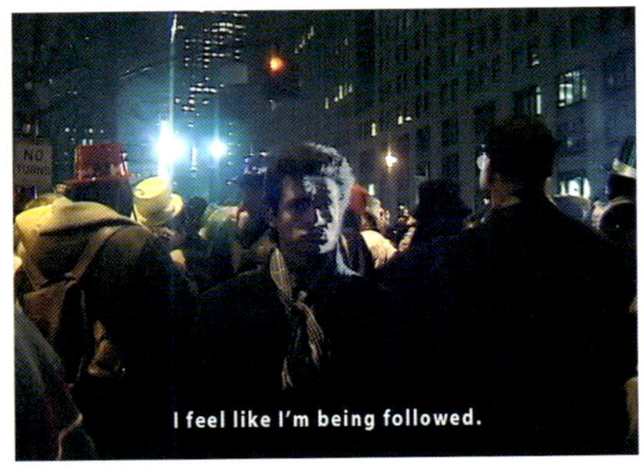
I feel like I'm being followed.
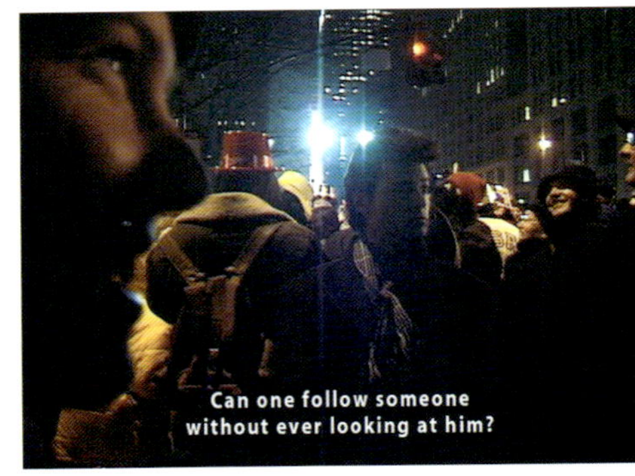
Can one follow someone
without ever looking at him?
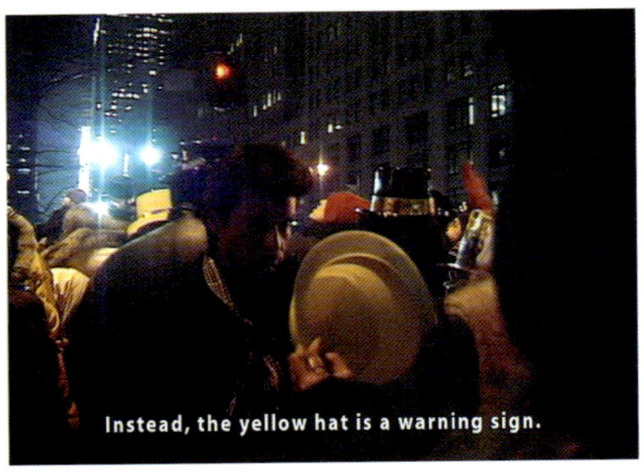
Instead, the yellow hat is a warning sign.
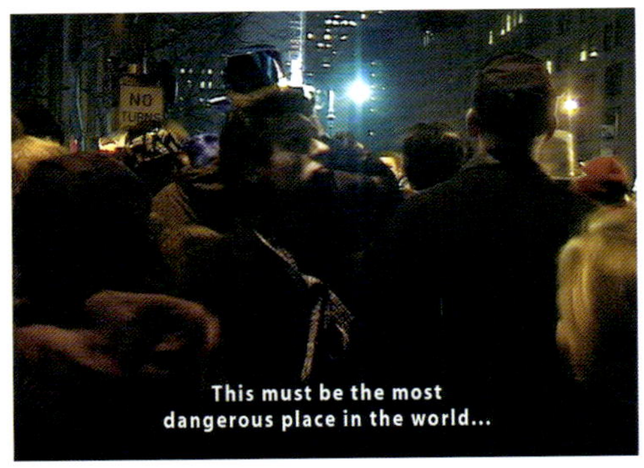
This must be the most
dangerous place in the world...
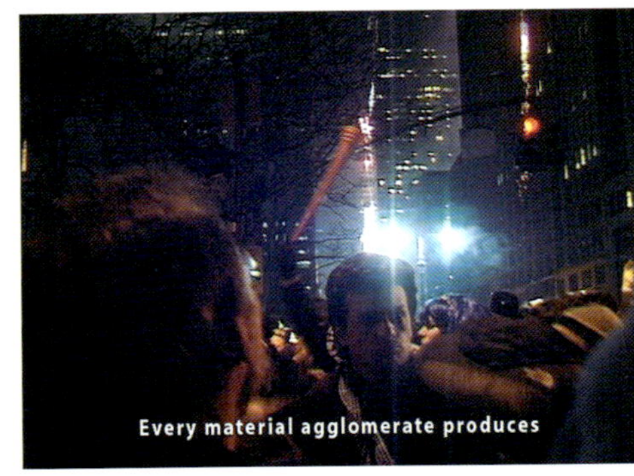
Every material agglomerate produces
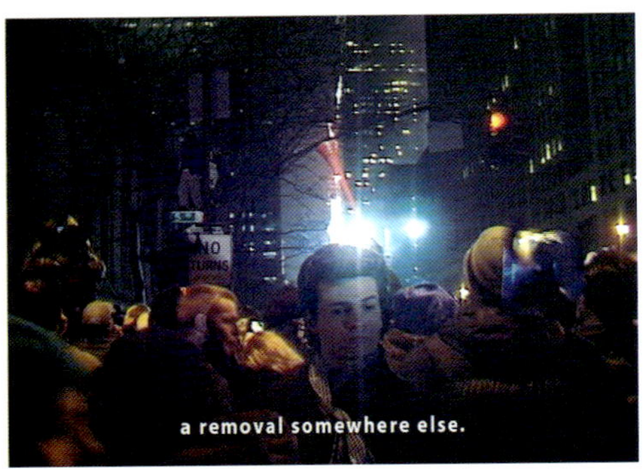
a removal somewhere else.
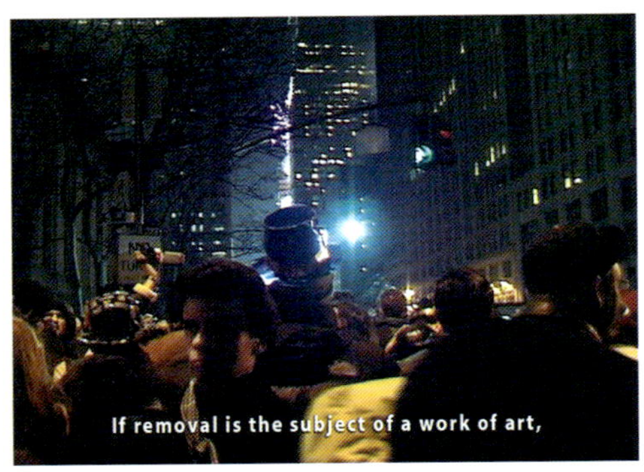
If removal is the subject of a work of art,
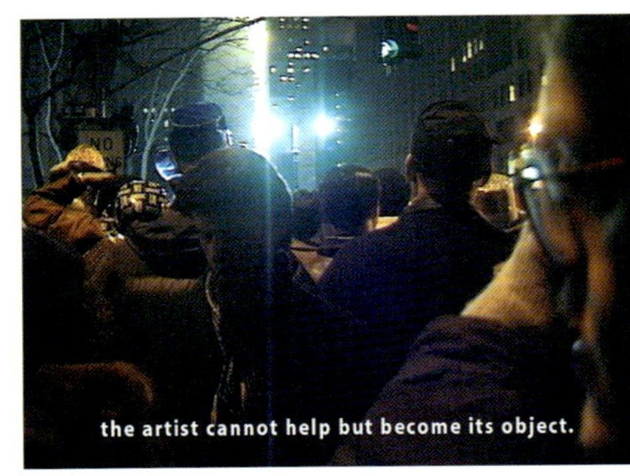
the artist cannot help but become its object.
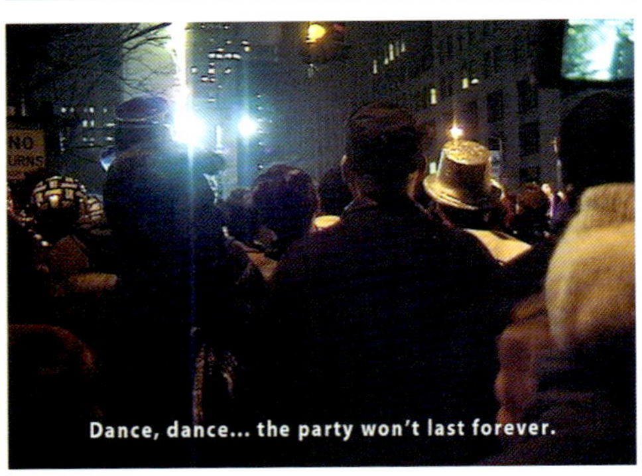
Dance, dance... the party won't last forever.
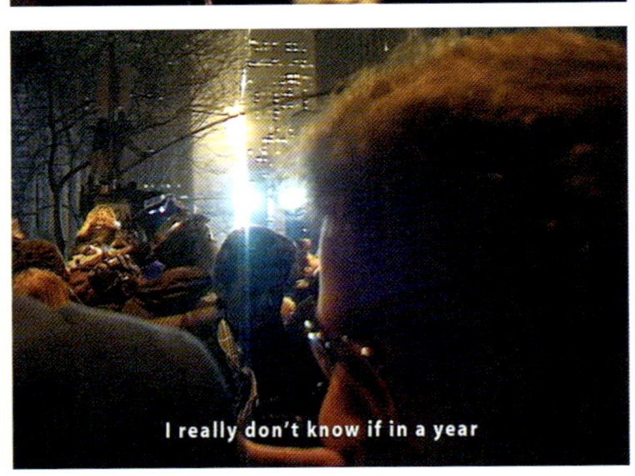
I really don't know if in a year
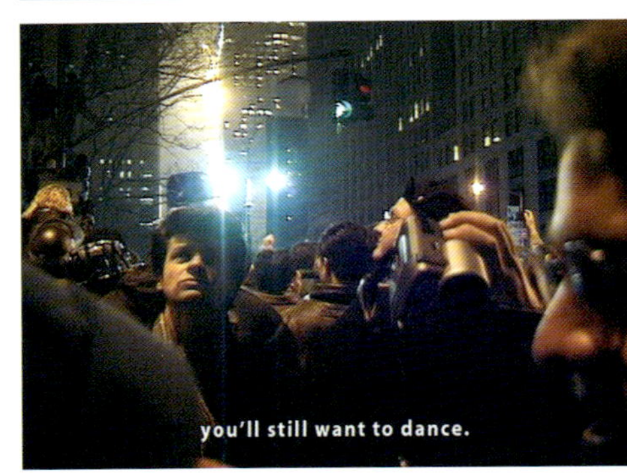
you'll still want to dance.
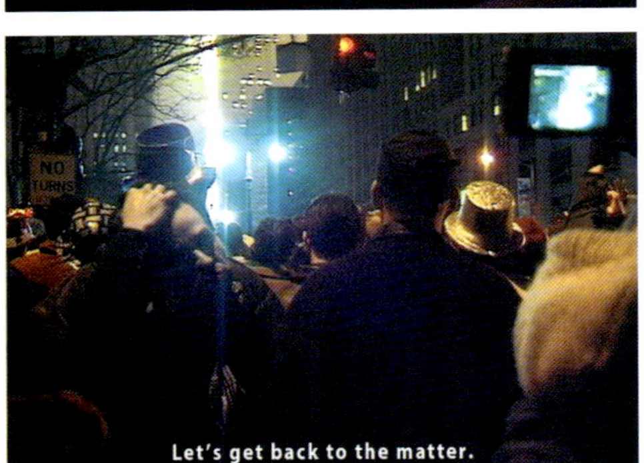
Let's get back to the matter.
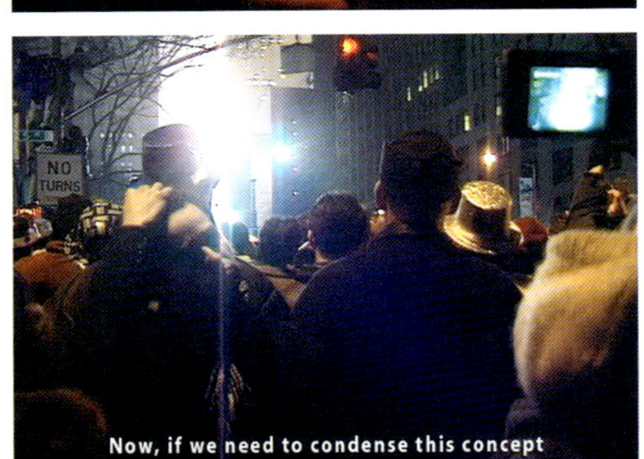
Now, if we need to condense this concept
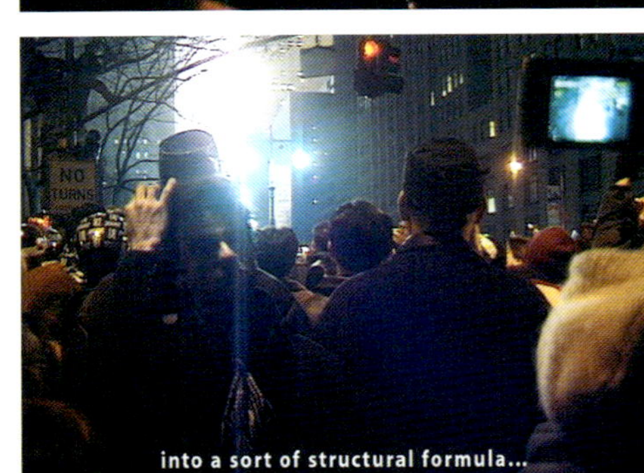
into a sort of structural formula...
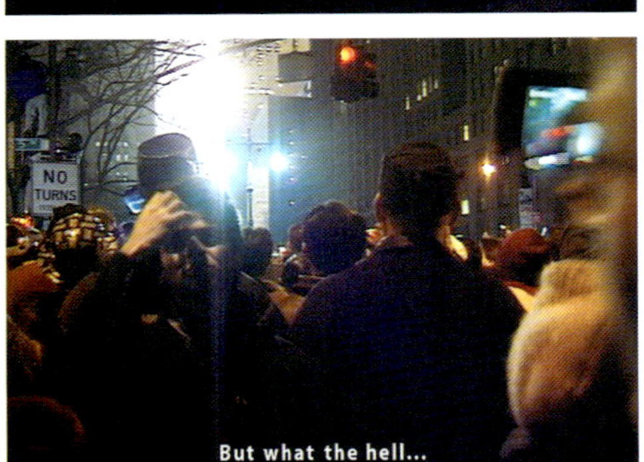
But what the hell...
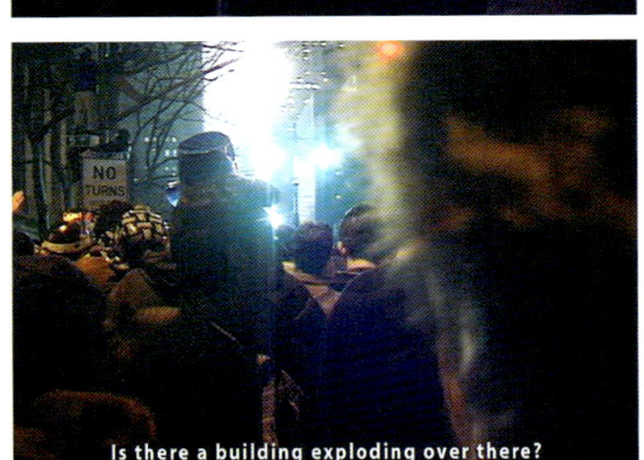
Is there a building exploding over there?
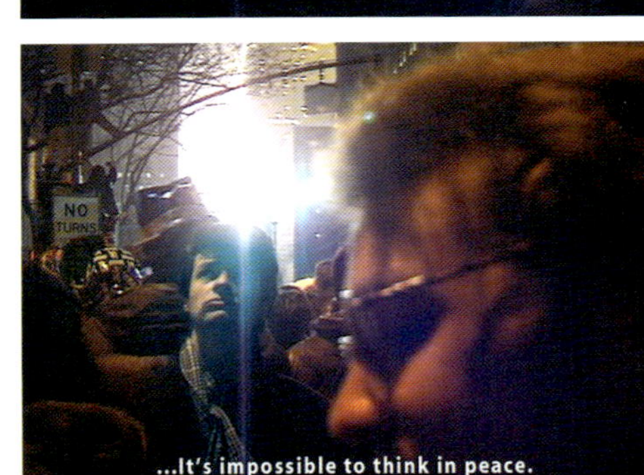
...It's impossible to think in peace.

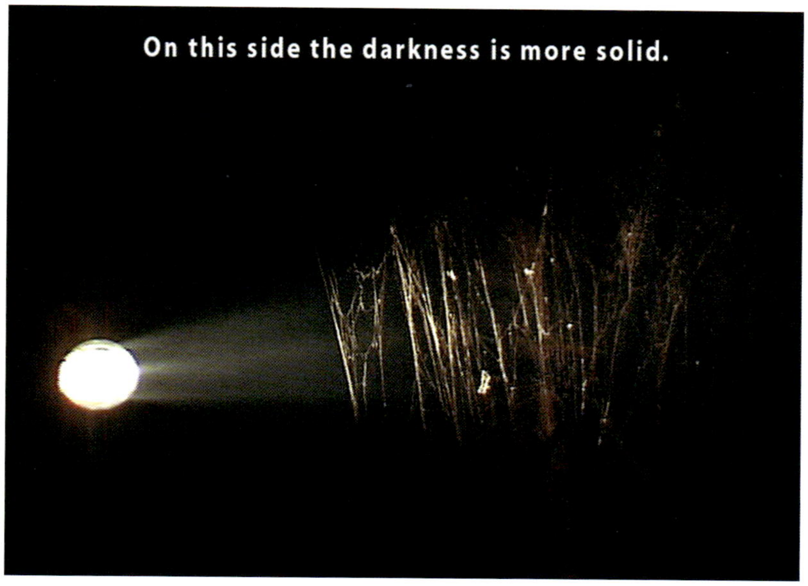

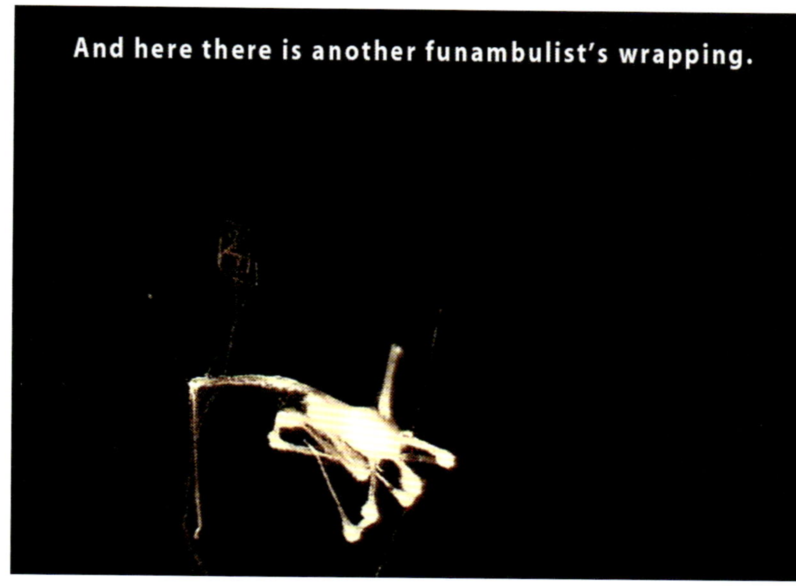

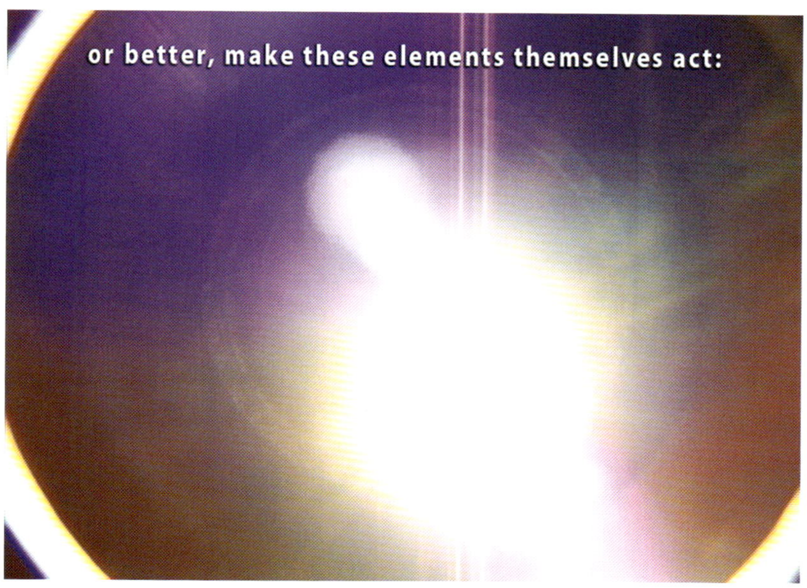

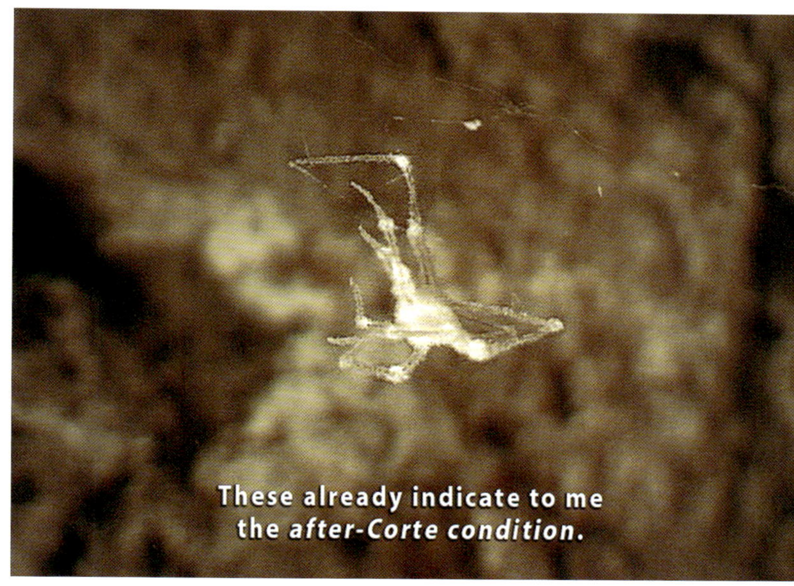

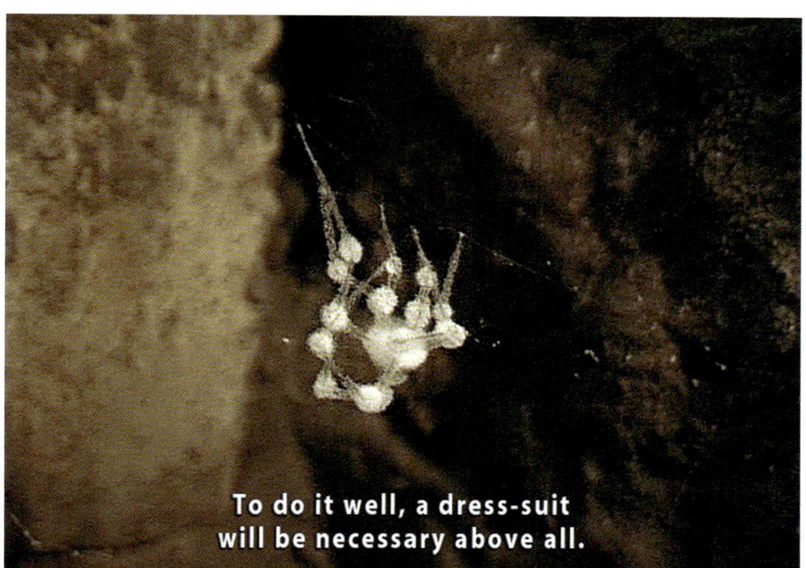

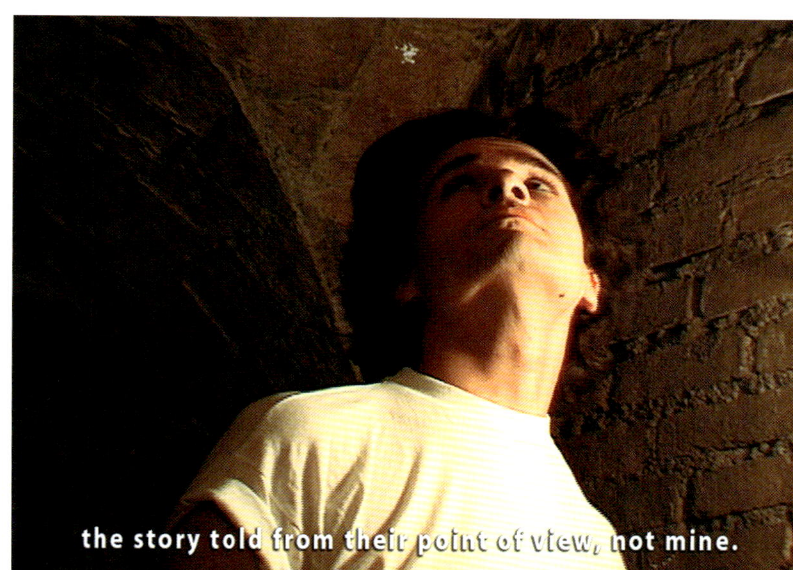

This page and opposite:
(The Making of) Videoache, 1999-2000. Cibachrome prints. 14½ x 19¾" each (37 x 50 cm).

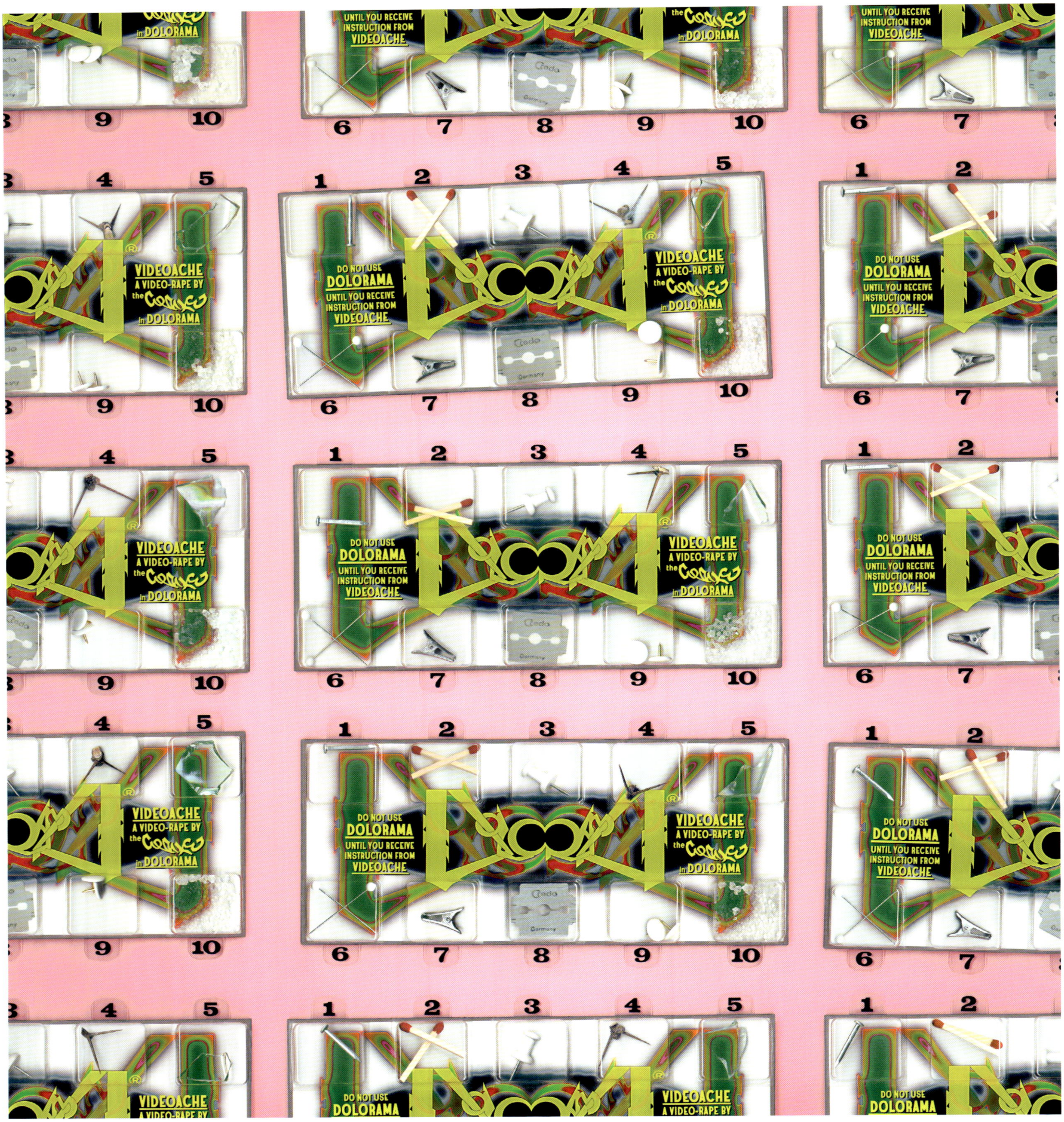

Dolorama, 2000.
Multiple gadget containing throw-away objects to be used on command during the seeing of the digi-film *Videoache*.
Lambda prints on pvc; blisters with pins, nails, thorns, razor-blades, metal clips, glass fragments, salt granules.
4½ x 7¾ x 0,5” each piece (11 x 19,4 x 1,2 cm).
GC 1320.

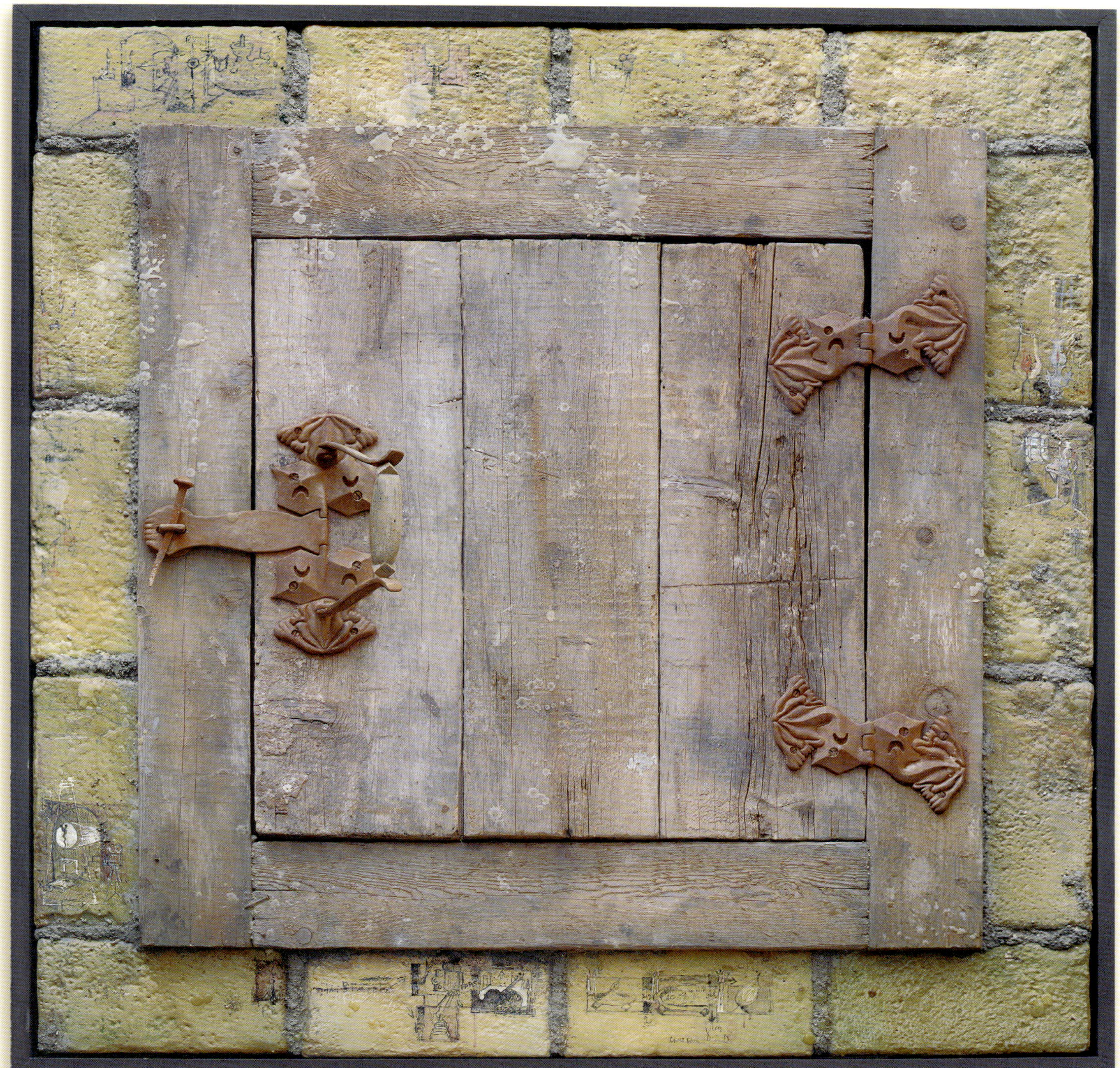

Storyboard, 2000.
Oil, graphite, pastel, mould, grease, artificial rust,
spurts of melted wax on wood, iron, plaster bricks.
47¼ x 47½ x 6" (119,7 x 120,5 x 15 cm).
GC 1306.

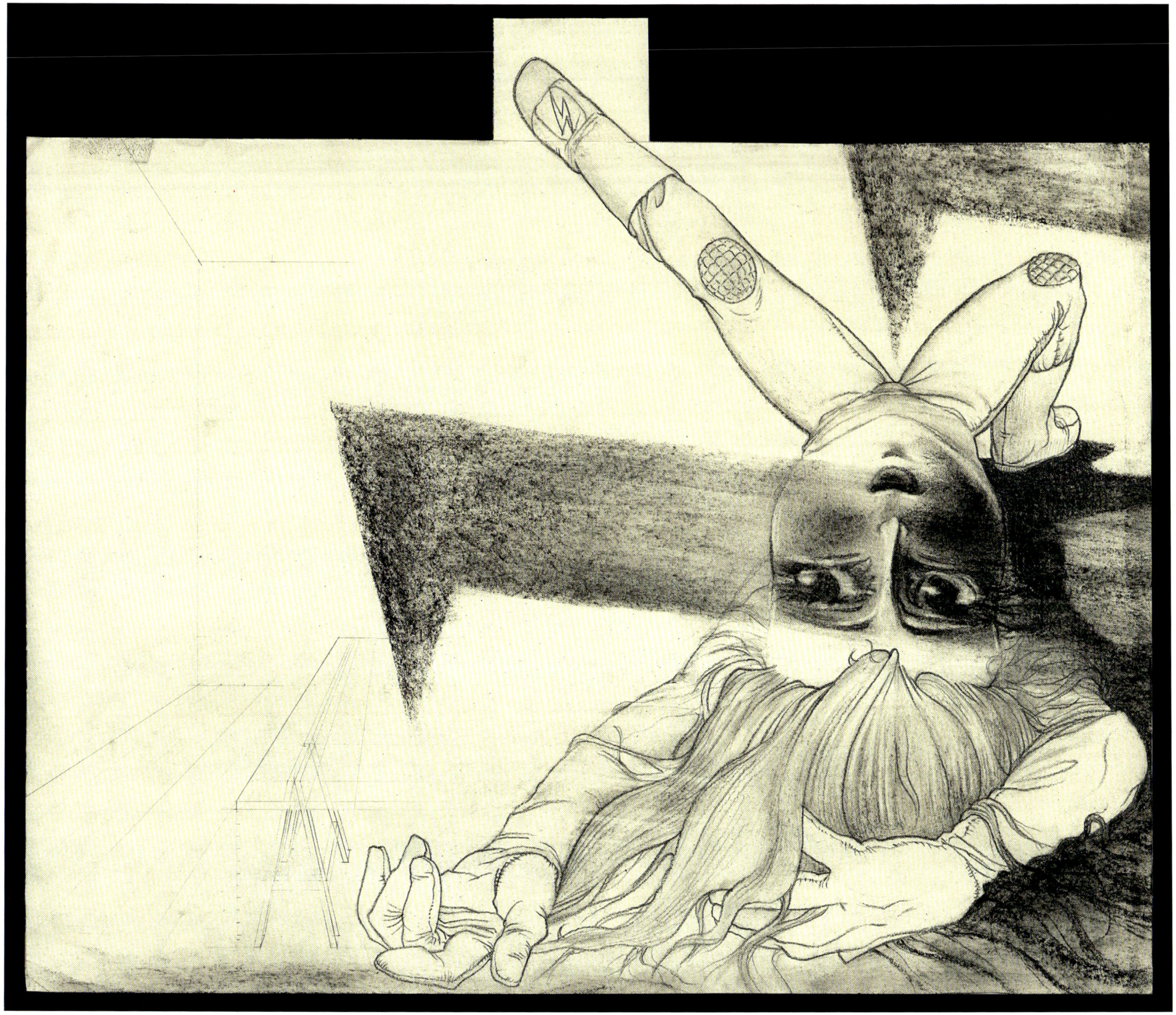

Maskon Boy, 1997 (detail). Drawing from the *Maskon* series.
Charcoal, stump and graphite on paper; metal drawing-pins; rubber backing with traces of dirt, glue blot, scratches.
31½ x 43¼" (80 x 110 cm).
GC 1231.

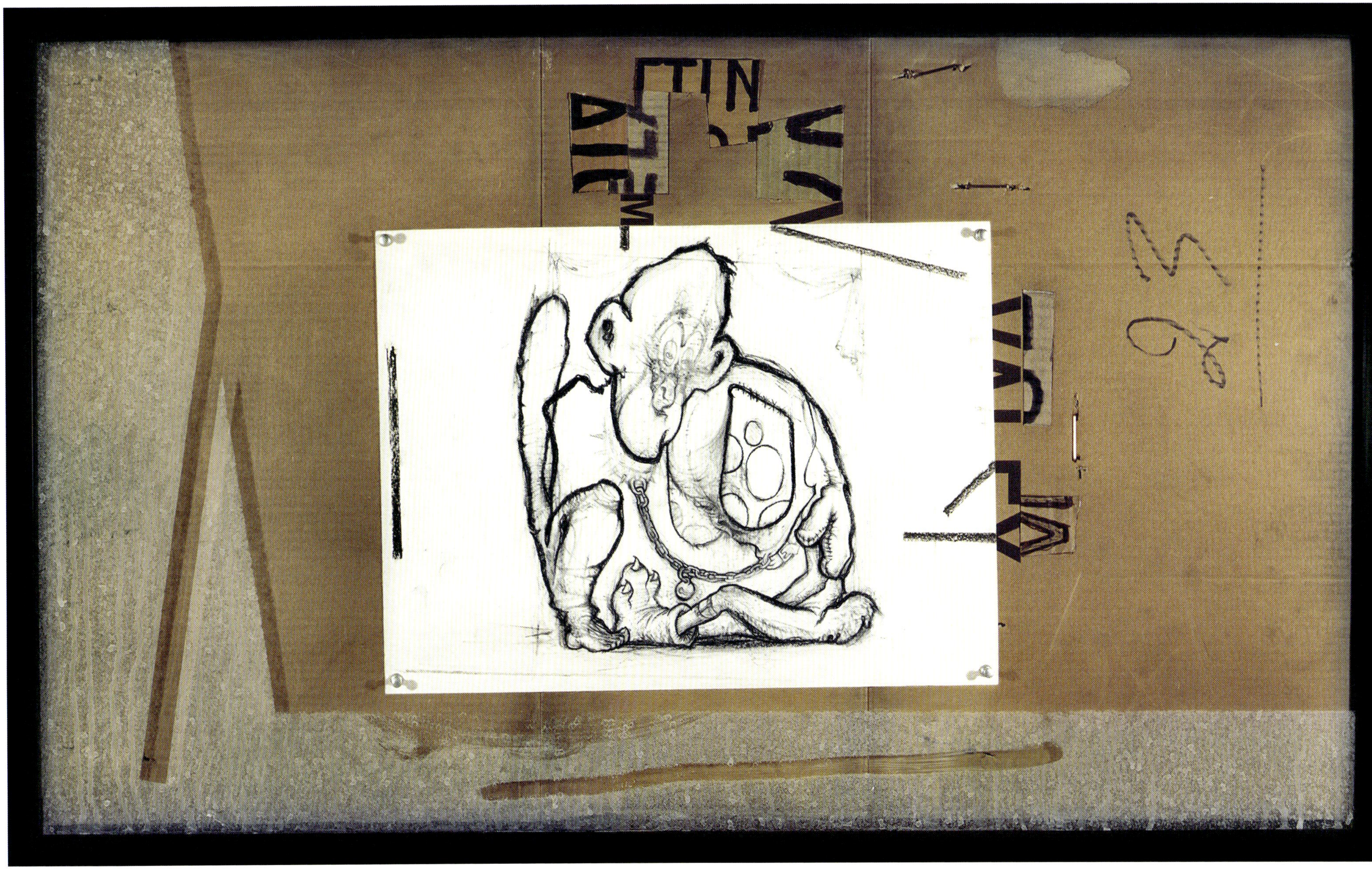

Anthrocon Marriage, 2002. Drawing from the *Anthrocon* series.
Charcoal and stump on paper; layer of dirt and grease, partially erased by the artist, on cardboard sheet belonged to a homeless person, with factory branding and notes; metal drawing-pins; metal staples; cuttings from cardboard bills written by beggars; rain smudges and finger streaks on glass.
24½ x 42¼" (62,5 x 107 cm).
GC 1460.

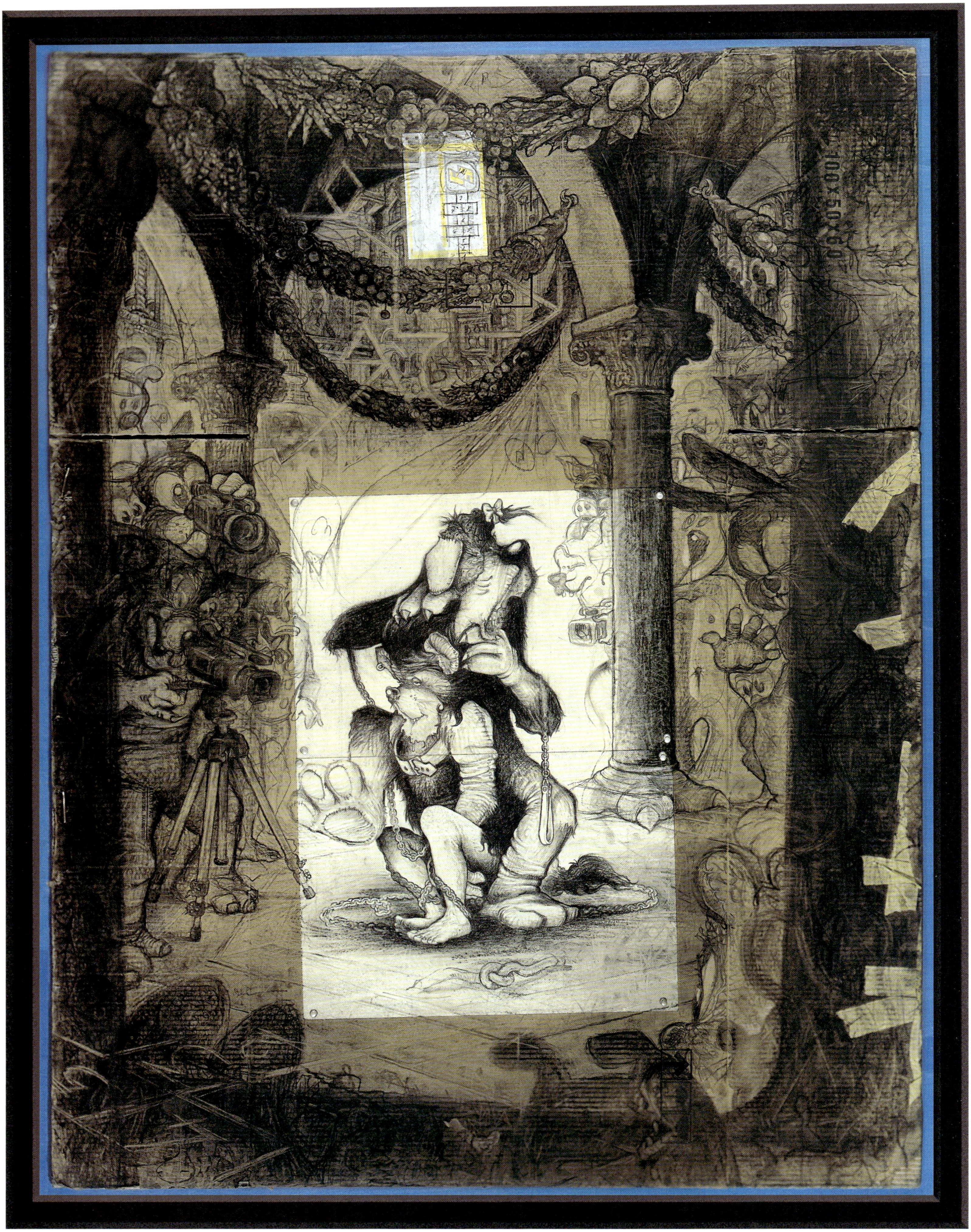

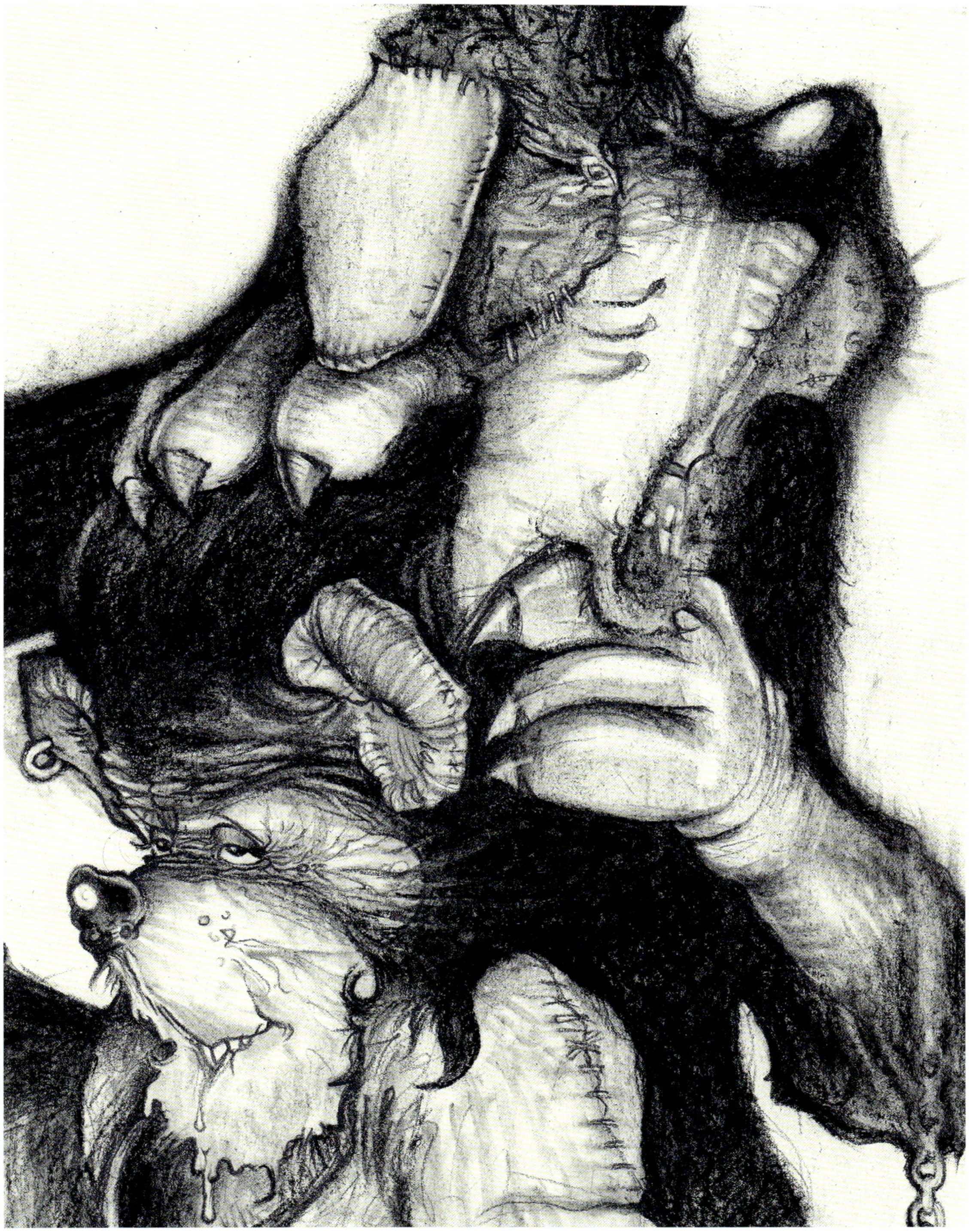

This page and opposite:
The Initiatory Symbolism of Anthrocon, 2004.
Drawing from the *Anthrocon* series. Total and detail.
Charcoal and stump on paper and cardboard sheet belonged to a homeless person,
with tears, stains and layer of dirt partially erased by the artist;
label, factory branding and notes; metal drawing-pins; metal staples;
strips of paper tape; acrylic on wooden backboard.
70¾ x 51¼" (180 x 130 cm).
GC 1577.

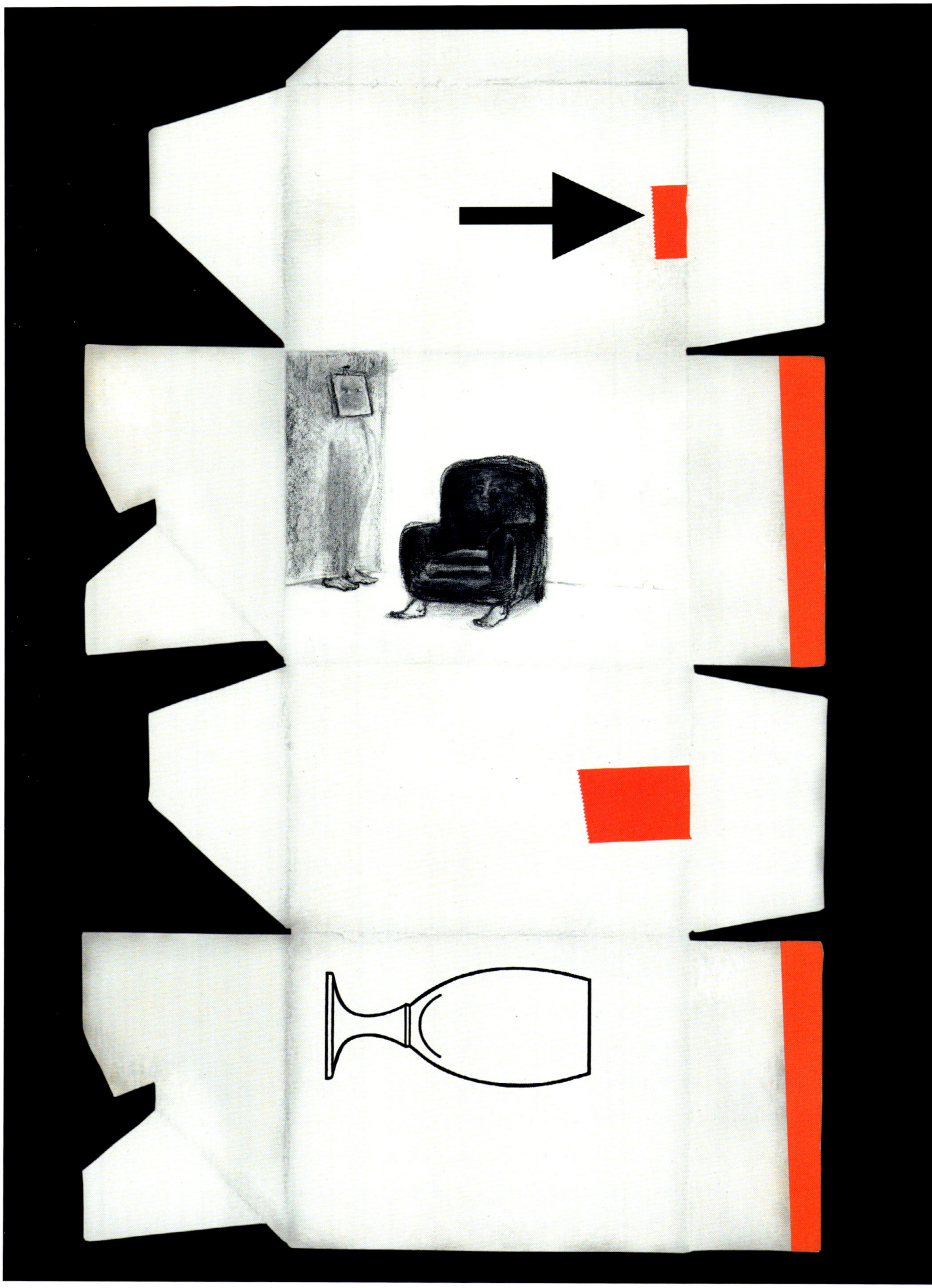

Intericon People with rat's hole, 2003 (detail). Drawing from the *Intericon* series.
Charcoal and dirt on cardboard sheet, with factory branding
and strips of red plastic tape; acrylic on cardboard backing.
39½ x 39½" (100 x 100 cm).
GC 1541.

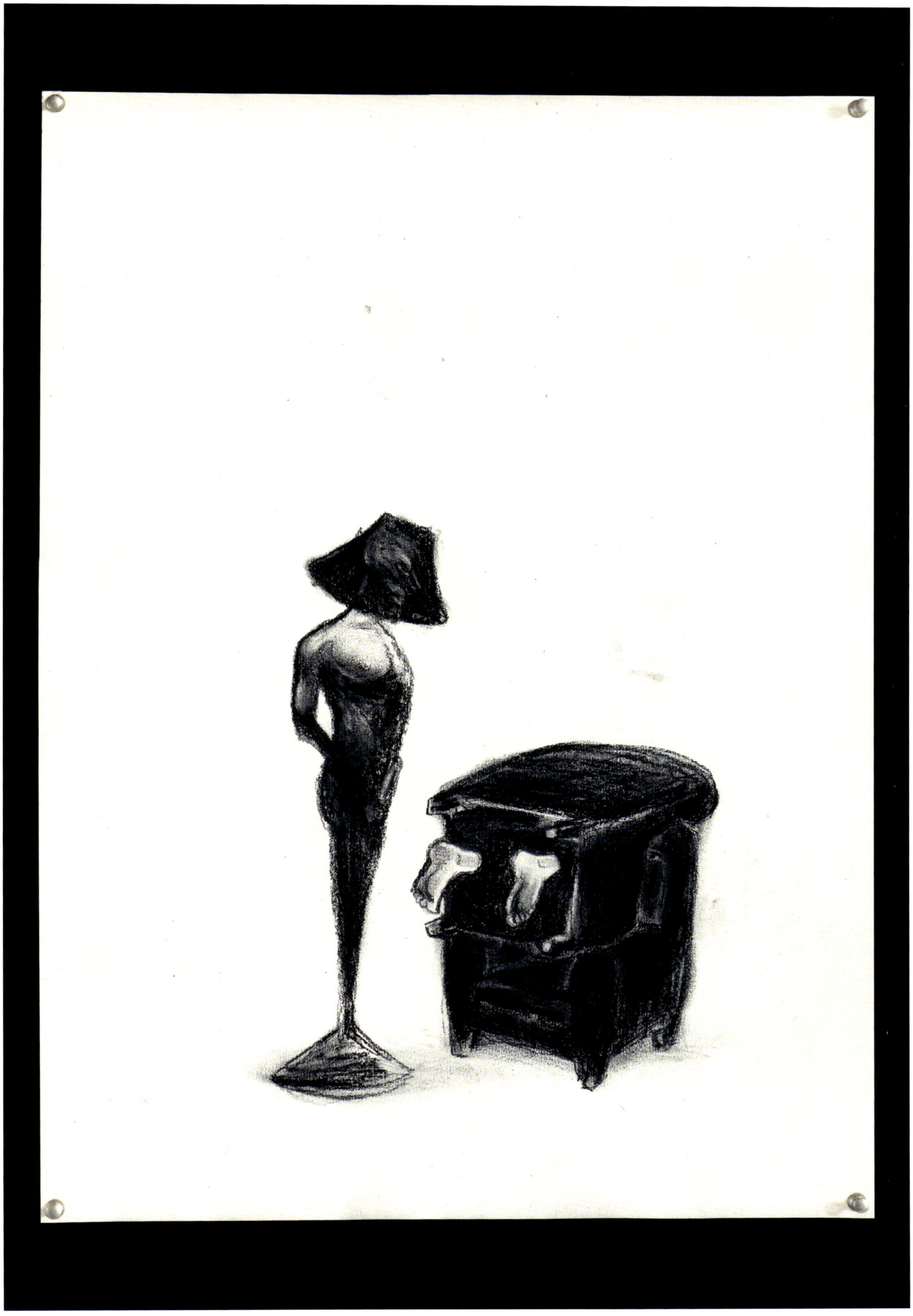

Intericon Trio, 2004. Drawing from the *Intericon* series.
Charcoal on paper; metal drawing-pins; folded black rubber backing.
33¾ x 21¾" (86 x 55 cm).
GC 1565.

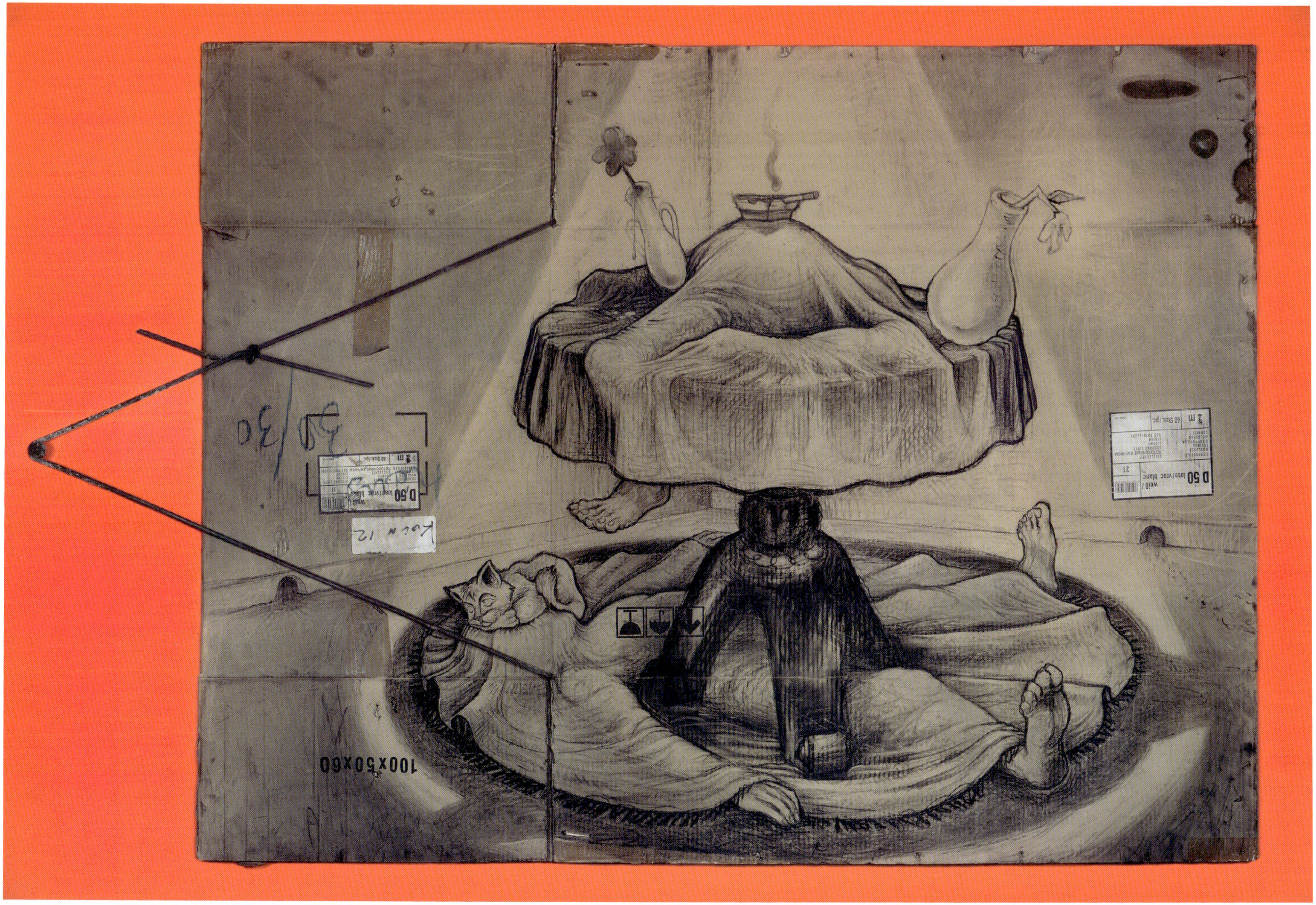

Intericon Rendezvous, 2003. Drawing from the *Intericon* series.
Charcoal and stump on cardboard sheet belonged to a homeless person, with layer of dirt partially erased by the artist; grease, tears, stains, factory branding, notes and labels; metal staples; strips of plastic tape; rusty iron rod and nail; acrylic on wooden backboard.
49¼ x 73¼" (125 x 186 cm).
GC 1576.

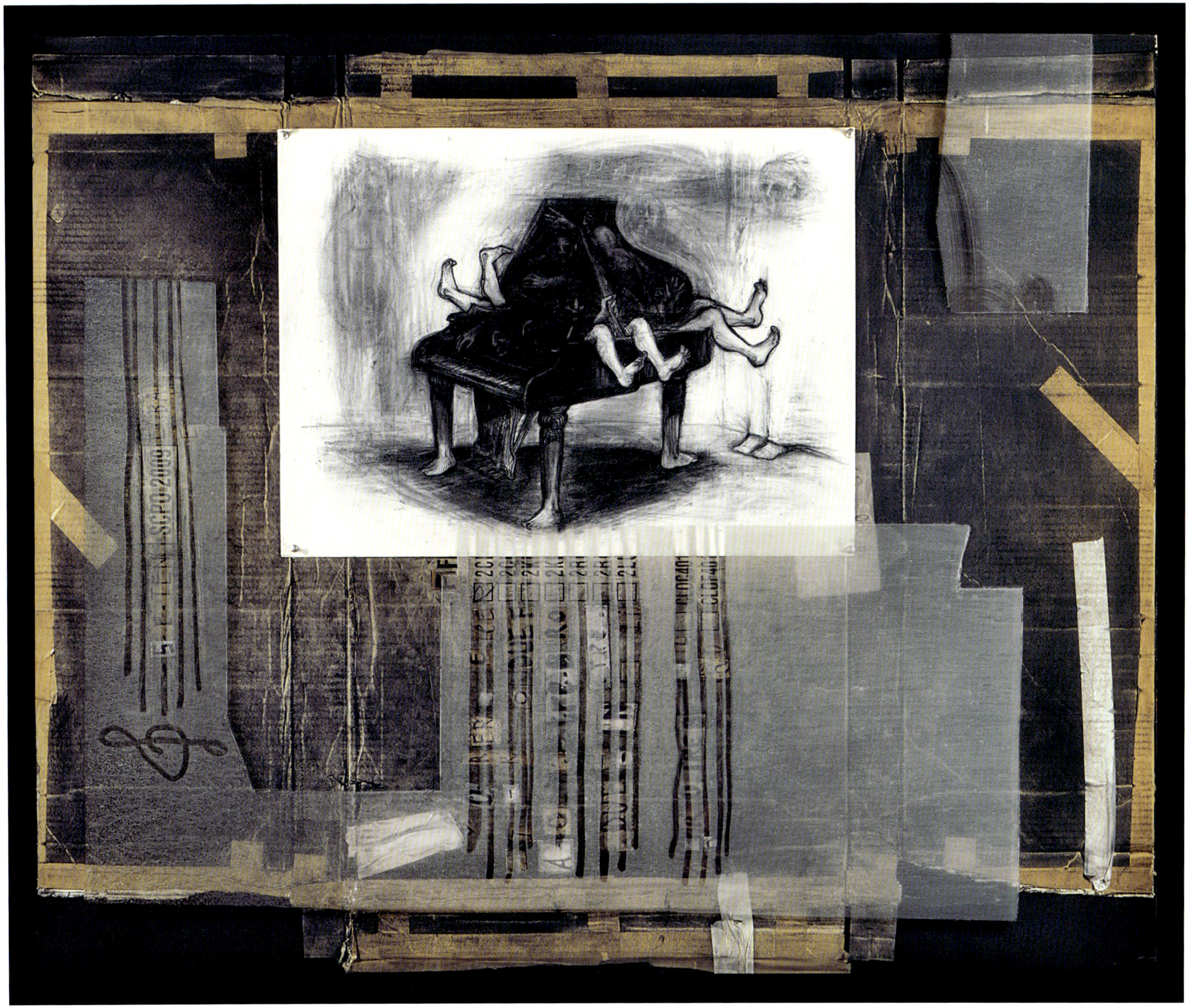

Intericon Music, 2004. Drawing from the *Intericon* series.
Charcoal and stump on paper and cardboard sheet belonged to a homeless person; metal drawing-pins; metal staples; strips of plastic tape; factory branding, notes and label; cuttings of cardboard bills written by beggars; rain smudges and finger streaks on glass; acrylic on wooden backboard.
43¼ x 55¼" (111,5 x 140 cm).
GC 1582.

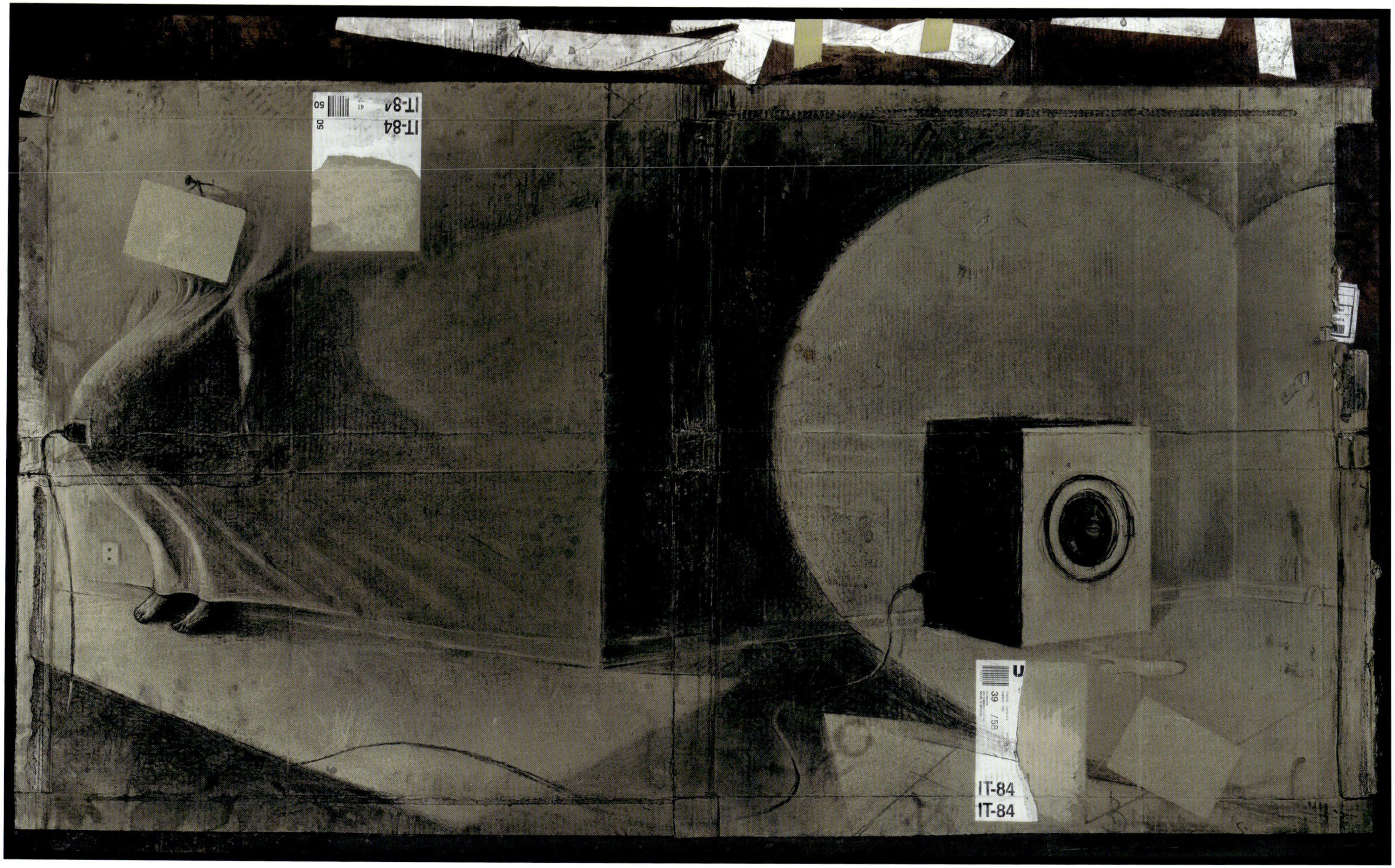

Intericon Love, 2003. Drawing from the *Intericon* series.
Charcoal on cardboard sheet belonged to a homeless person, with layer of dirt partially erased by the artist; grease, stains, tears, notes and labels; strips of plastic and paper tape; charcoal on cardboard backing.
43¼ x 75" (110 x 190,5 cm).
GC 1566.

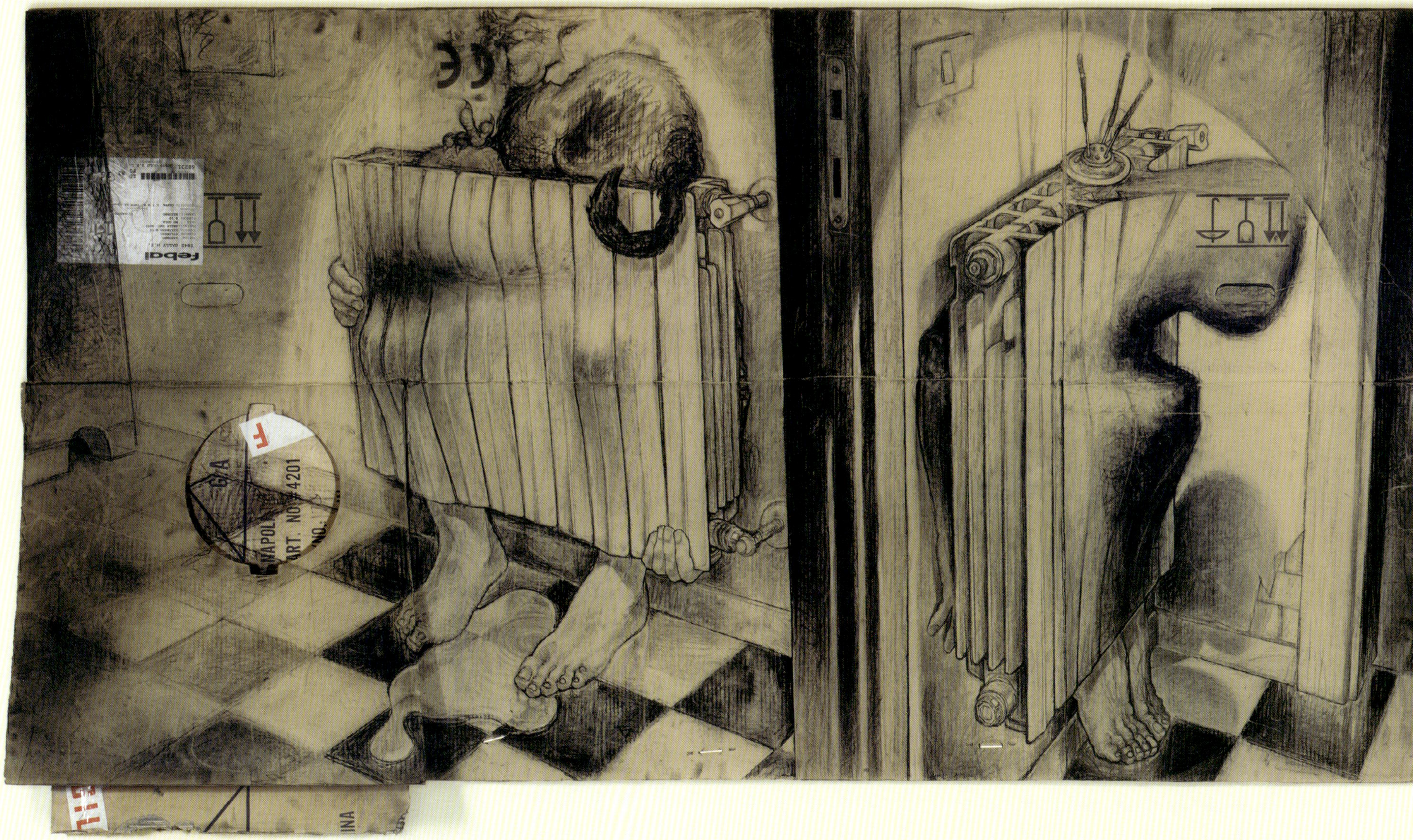

Intericon Warmth, 2004. Drawing from the *Intericon* series.
Charcoal and stump on two layers of cardboard sheet belonged to homeless persons, with stains of dirt partially erased by the artist; grease, tears, factory branding and label; metal staples; strips of plastic tape; lacquer on wooden backboard.
44½ x 81¼ x 6” (113 x 206 x 15 cm).
GC 1581.

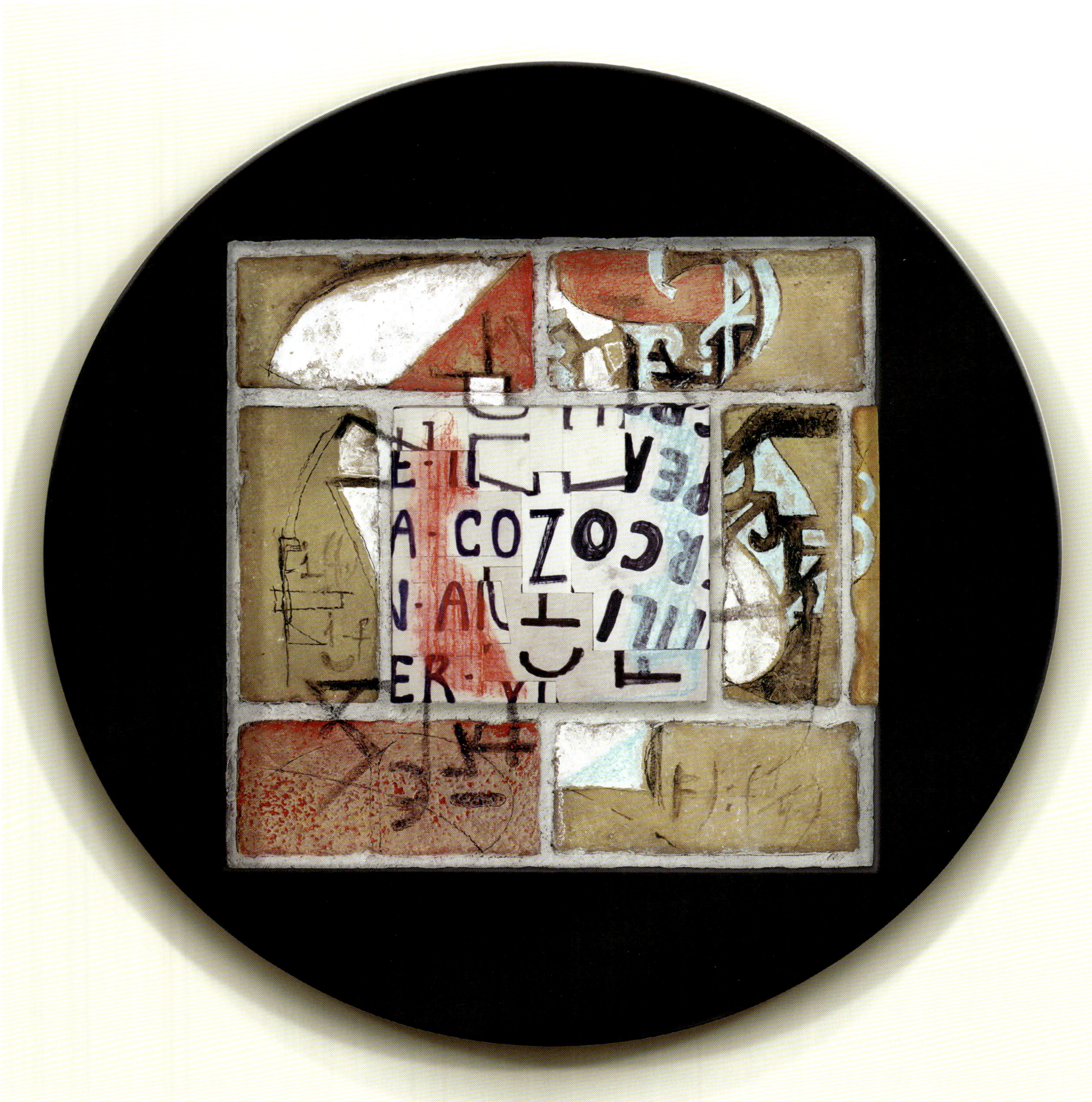

The Enigma of Destiny 1 (Self-portrait), 2005.
Charcoal and chalk on beggars' cardboard signs written with markers, cut and reassembled, and on polyurethane bricks painted with oil; mortar inserts; bakelite frame.
40¼ x 40¼ x 4" (102 x 102 x 10 cm).
GC 1980.

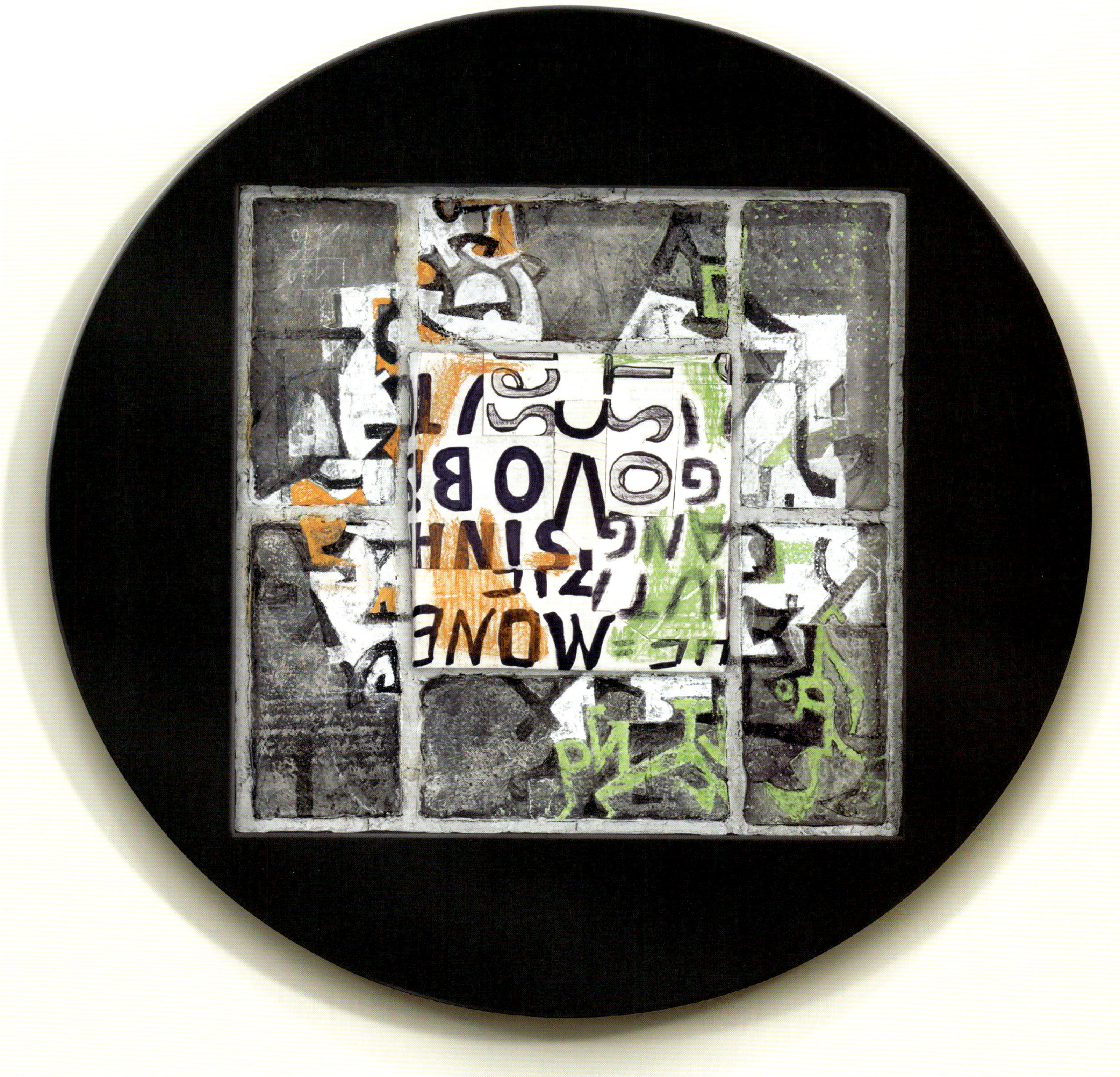

The Enigma of Destiny 2 (Andrea), 2005.
Charcoal and chalk on beggars' cardboard signs written with markers, cut and reassembled, and on polyurethane bricks painted with oil; mortar inserts; bakelite frame.
40¼ x 40¼ x 4" (102 x 102 x 10 cm).
GC 1981.

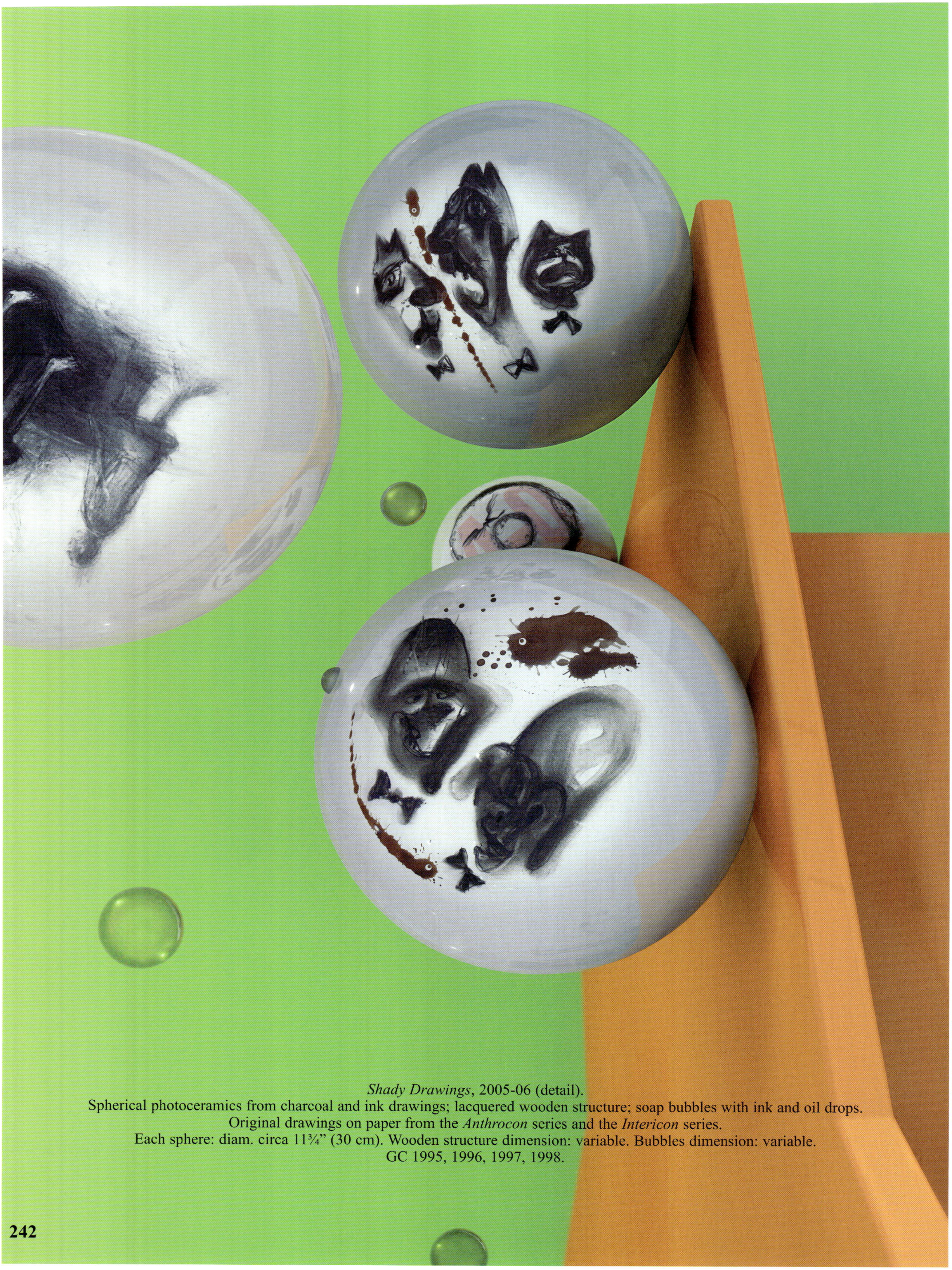

Shady Drawings, 2005-06 (detail).
Spherical photoceramics from charcoal and ink drawings; lacquered wooden structure; soap bubbles with ink and oil drops.
Original drawings on paper from the *Anthrocon* series and the *Intericon* series.
Each sphere: diam. circa 11¾" (30 cm). Wooden structure dimension: variable. Bubbles dimension: variable.
GC 1995, 1996, 1997, 1998.

Shadow of a Drawing 1, 2006.
Graphite on paper.
78¾ x 59" (200 x 150 cm).
GC 1990.

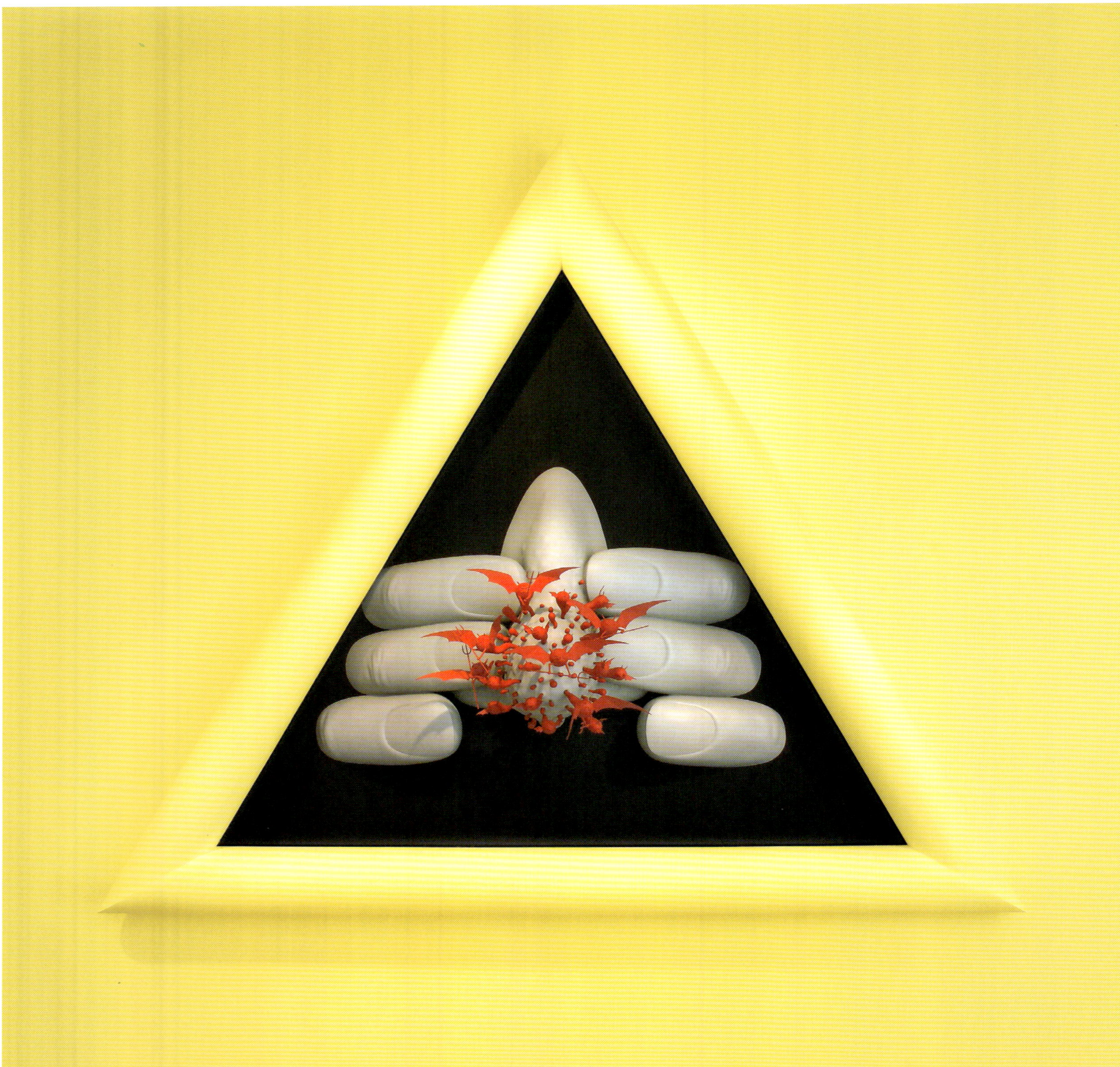

Three Cylinders, 1998.
Nitrocellulose lacquer and acrylic on fiberglass and blastoplast.
157½ x 157½ x 22" (400 x 400 x 56 cm).
GC 1230.

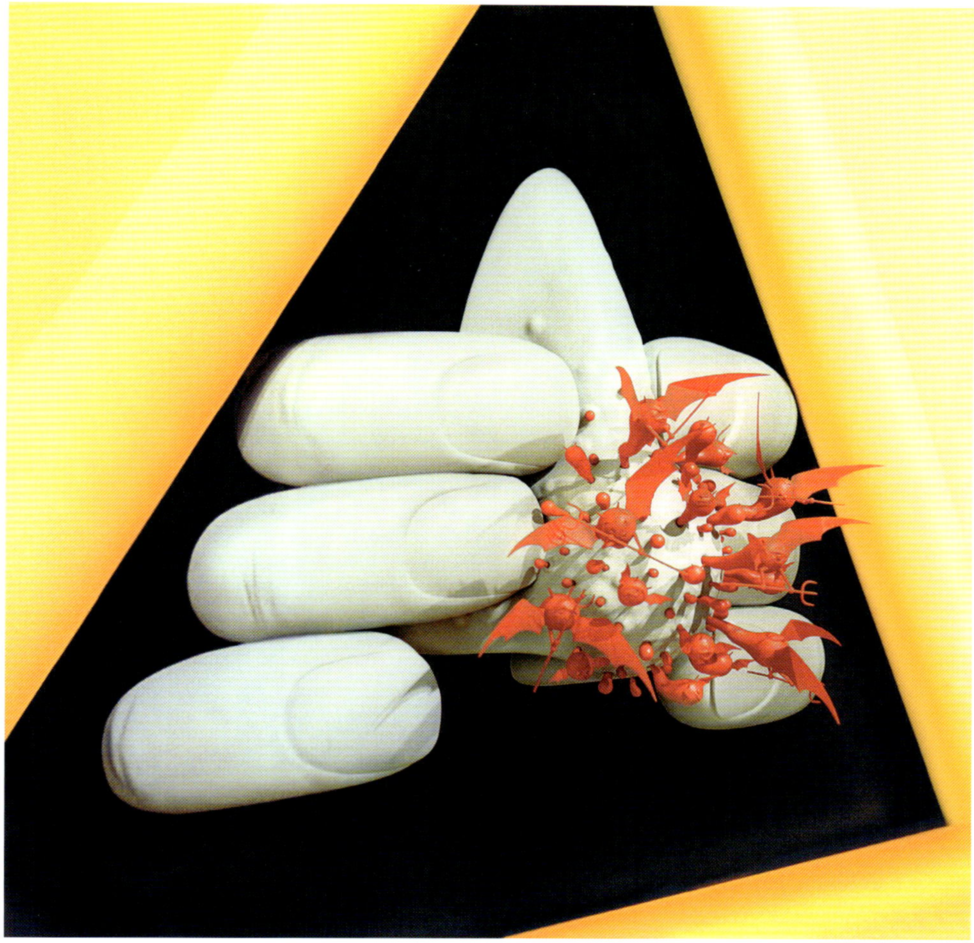

Three Cylinders, 1998. Details.

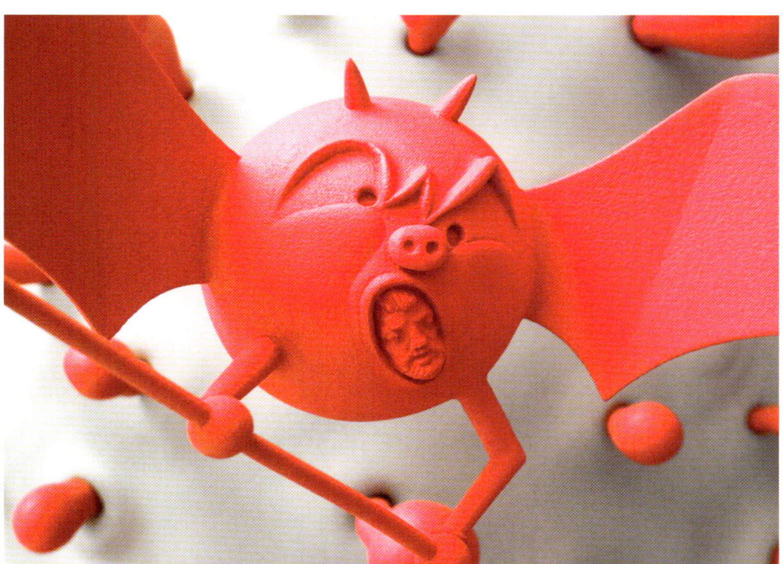

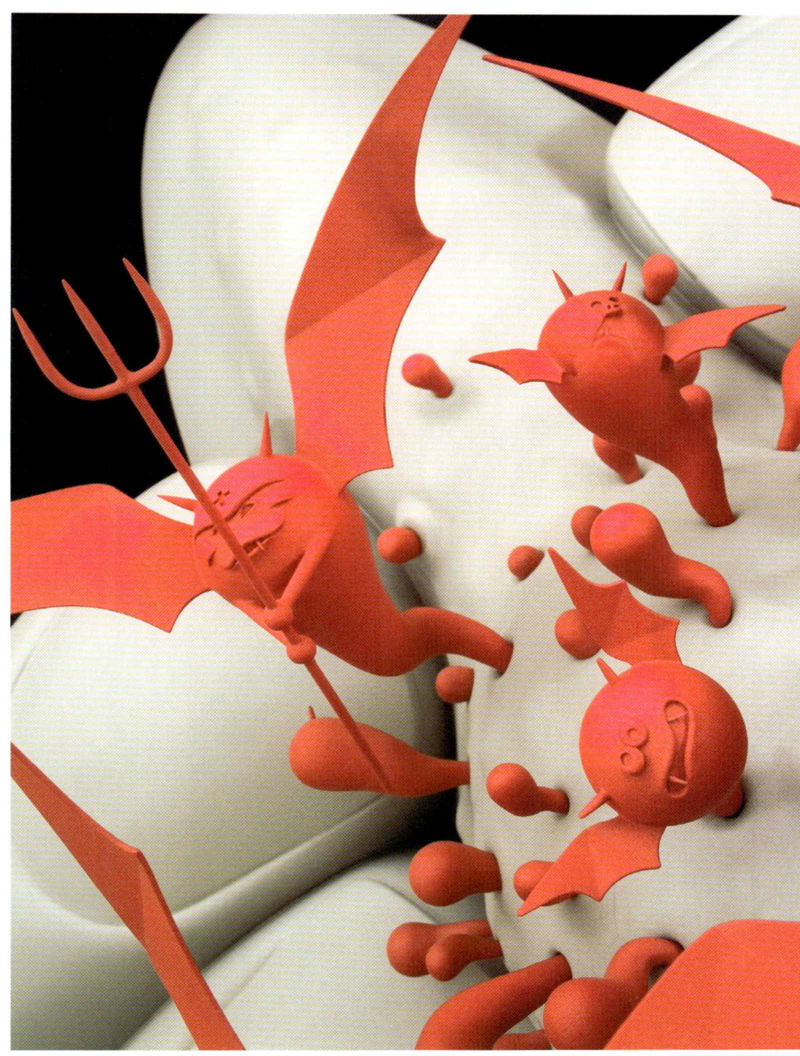

Three Cylinders, 1998. Details.

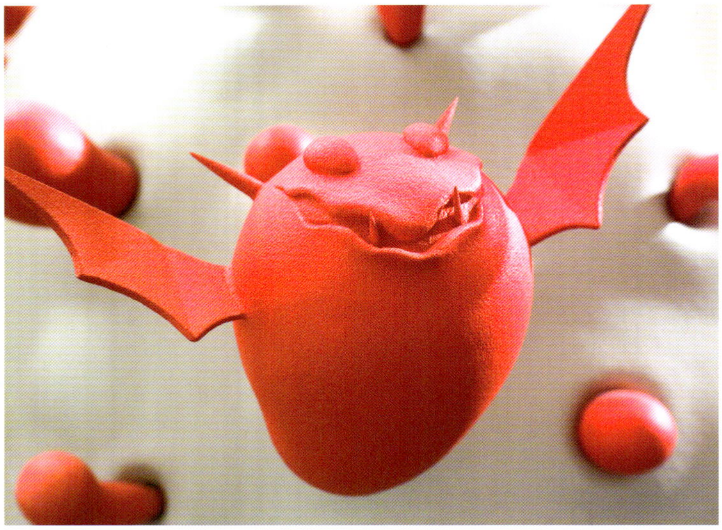

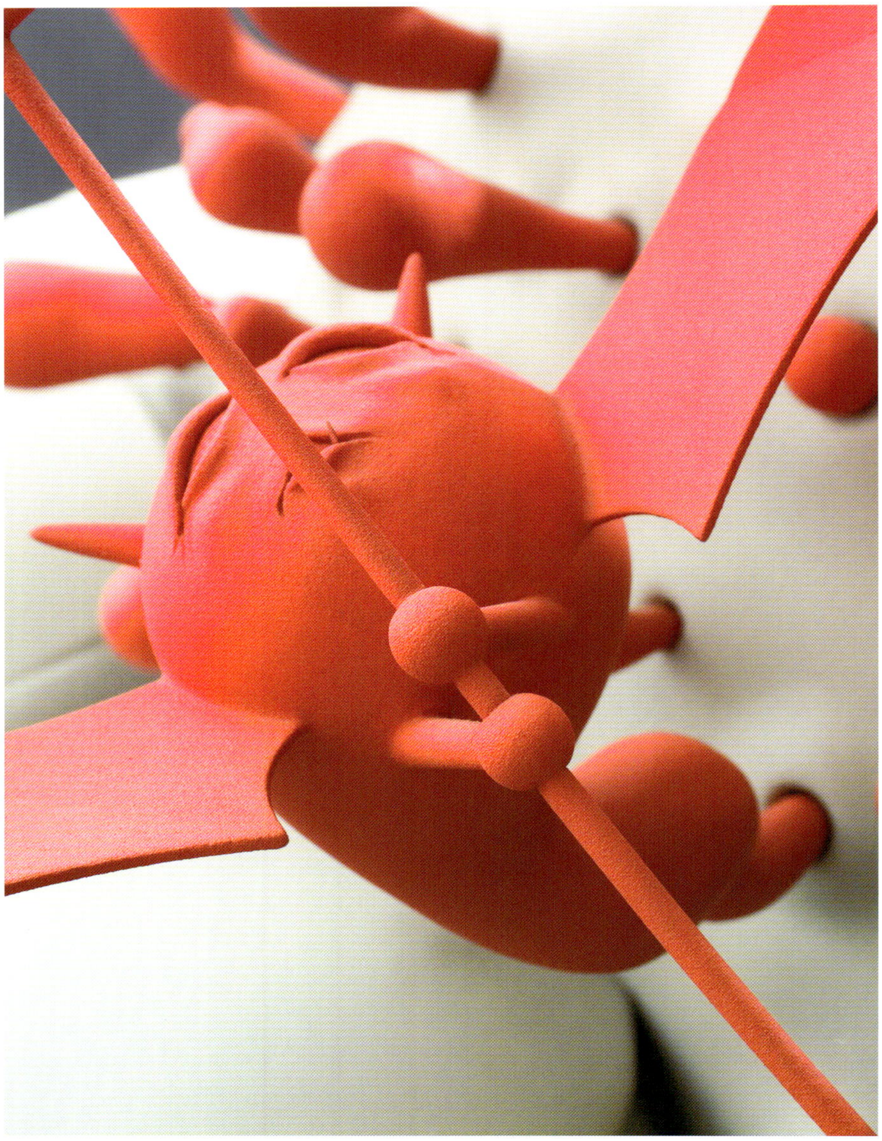

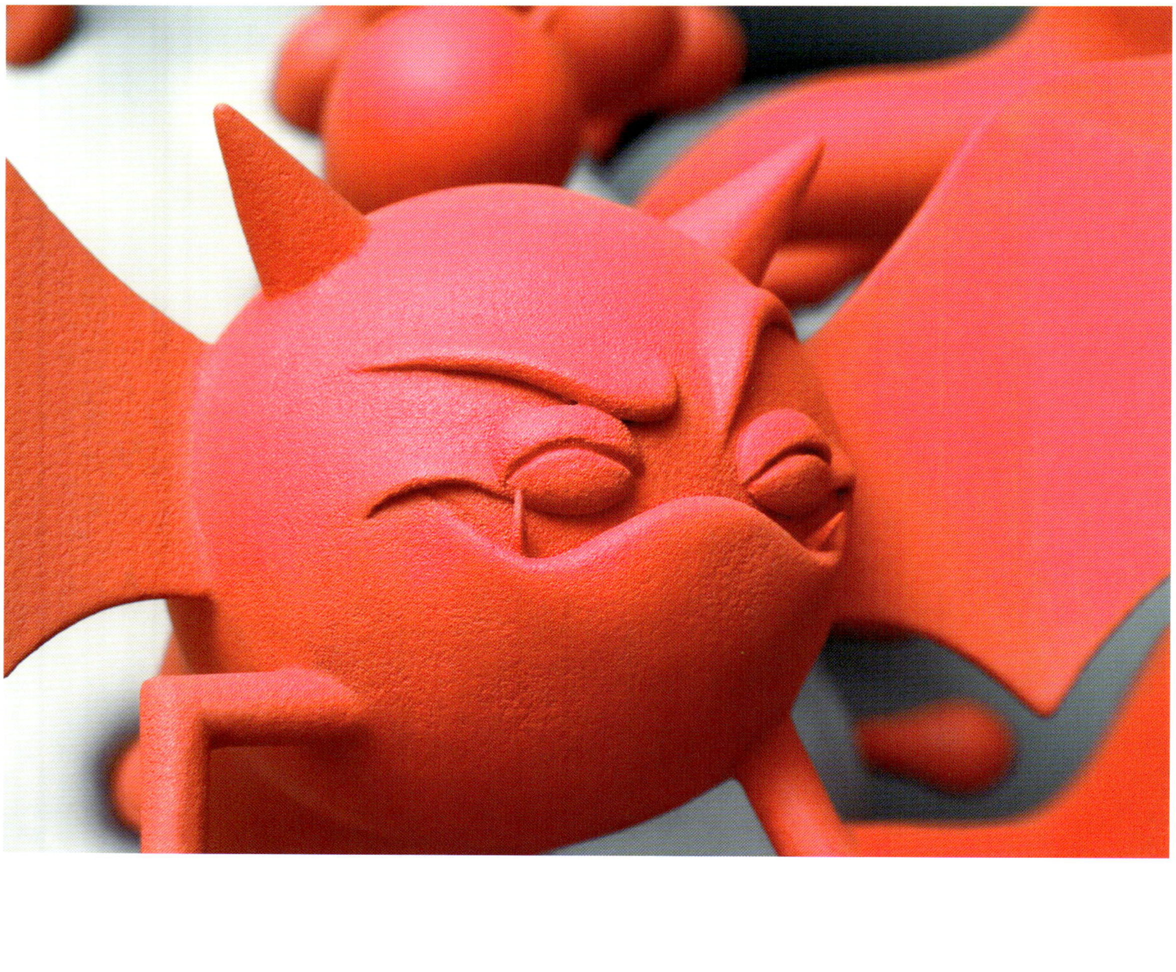

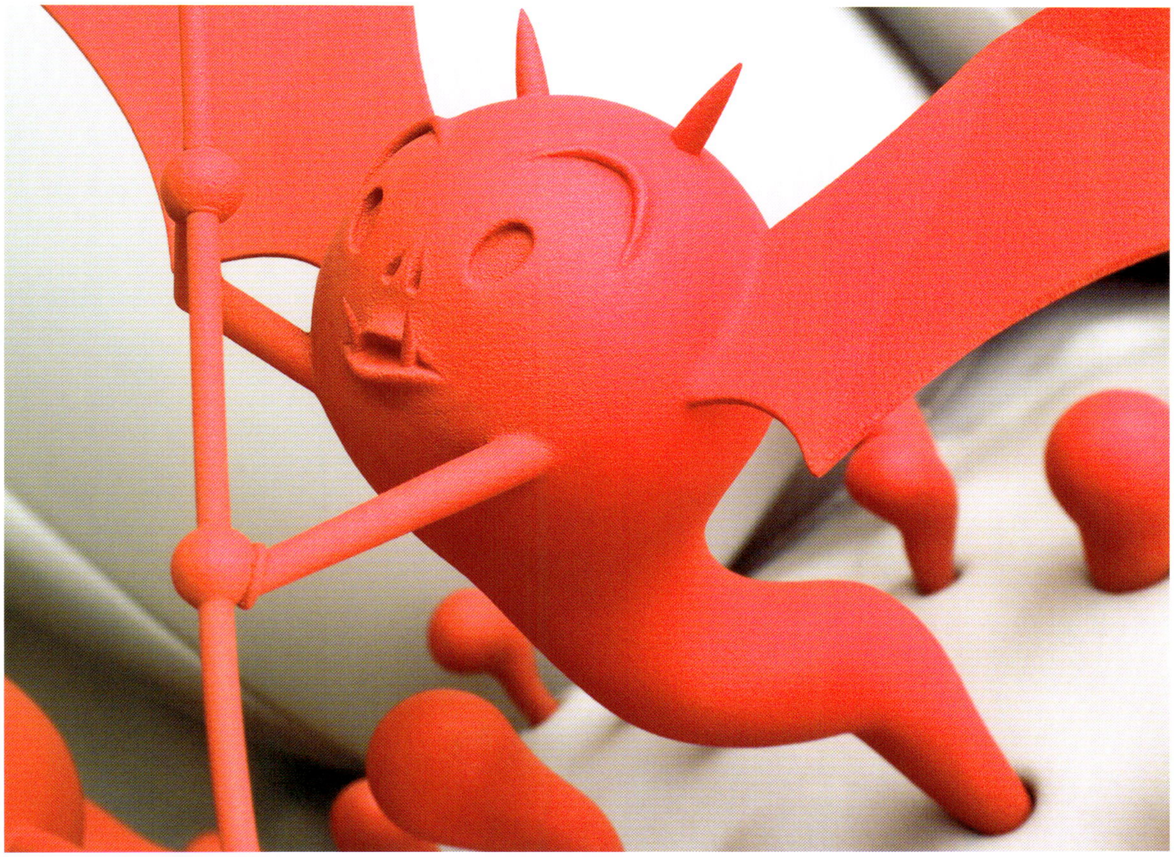

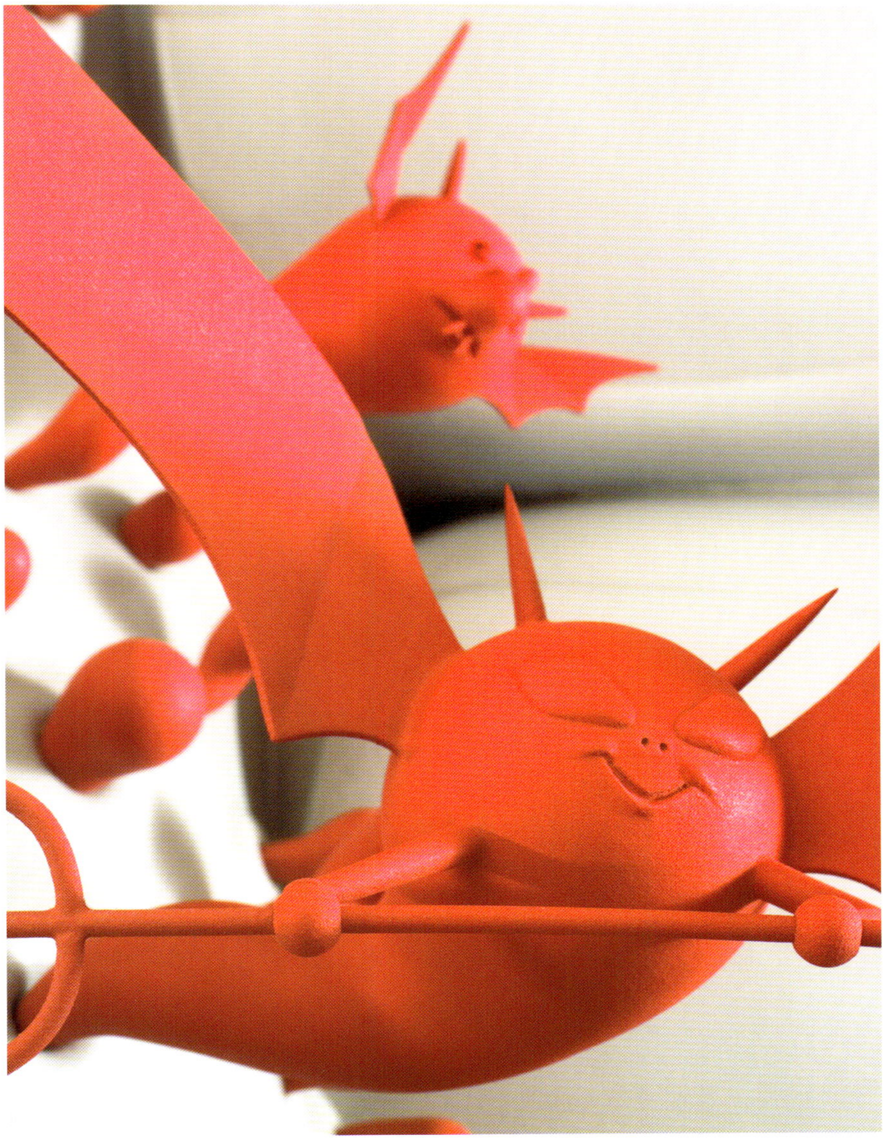

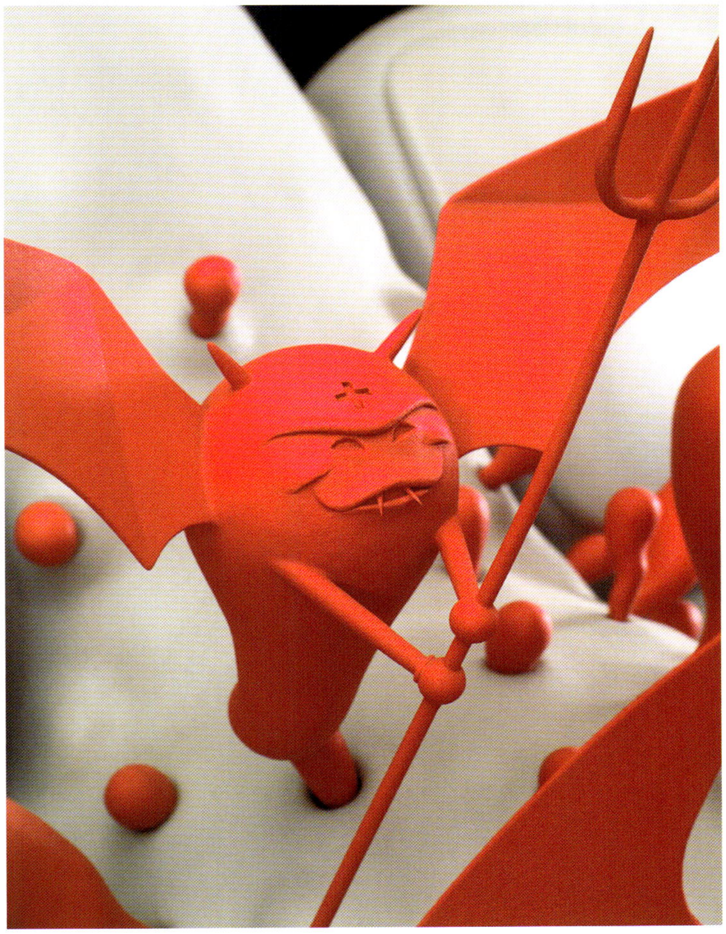

Three Cylinders, 1998. Details.

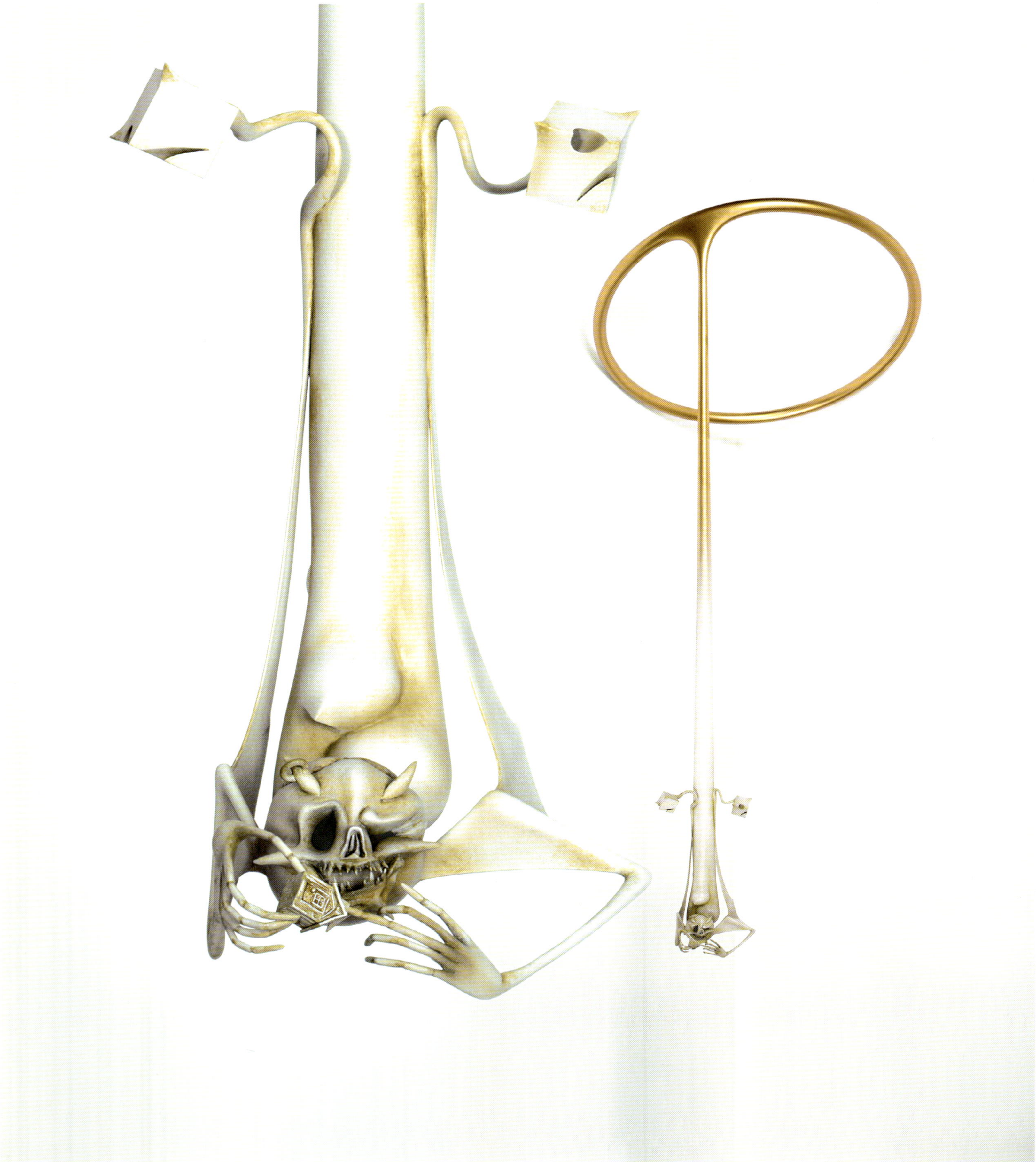

Three Little Cubes, 1999. Front view, detail and total.
Mould, grease, fly shit, gold plating on synthoceramic.
60¼ x 28 x 28¾” (153 x 71 x 73 cm).
GC 1263.

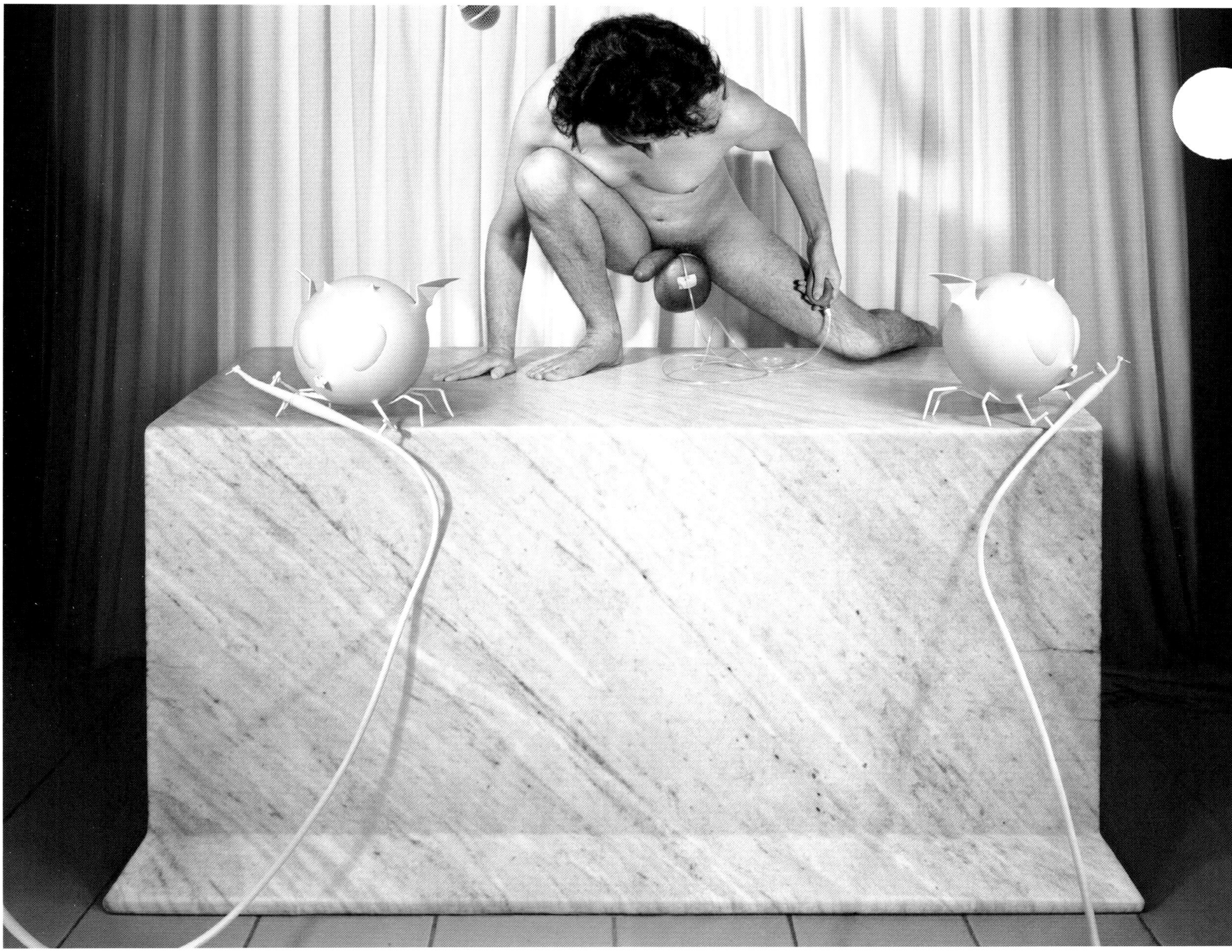

Three Little Spheres, 2001.
Toned silver gelatine print from a 16mm motion picture film.
20 x 25½" (51 x 65 cm).
GC 1405.

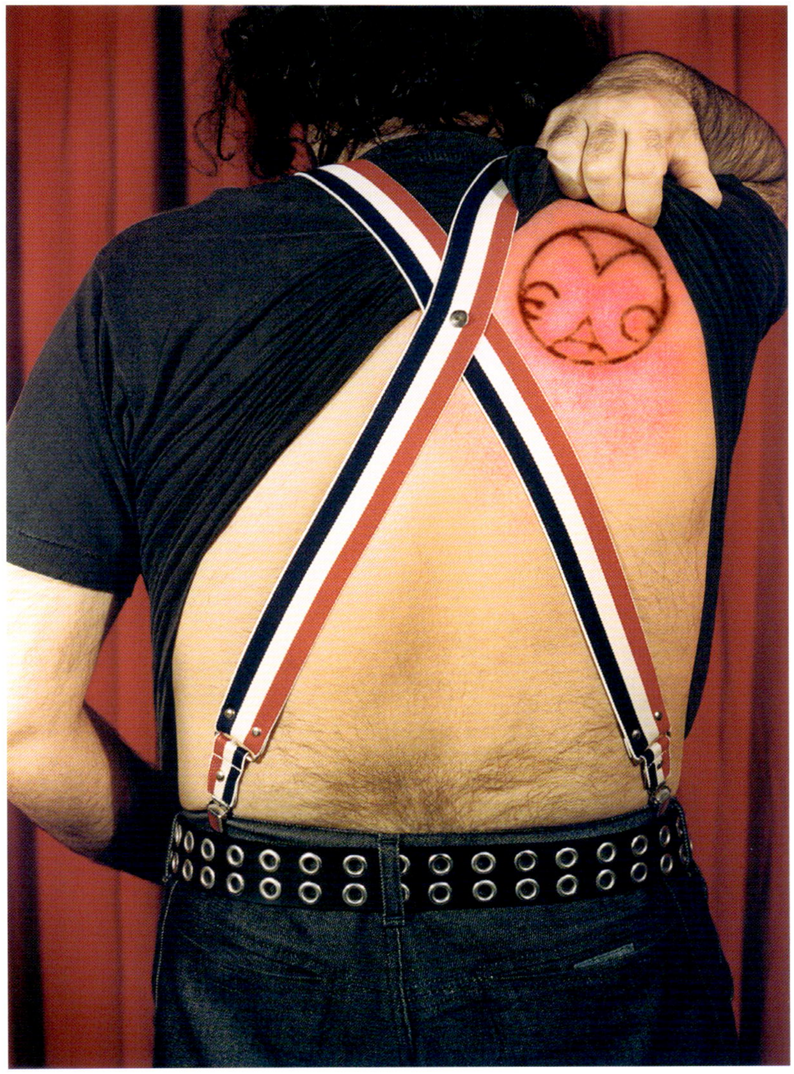

Branding Demonietto. Snapshot from a friend, n.d.

Ho *tolto* la prima pietra.

EC

Non mi era ancora capitata un'estenuante esperienza meditativa attorno alla redazione di un testo. Ho sempre dedicato tempo al metabolizzare le idee ma mai così a lungo come con Enrico Corte. Da oltre un anno ci incontriamo, vedo i lavori dal vivo, lascio fermentare le note oggettive, prendo appunti, rimastico le opere attraverso foto e files digitali, continuando a scaldare le sensazioni con il tempo lento, le aggiunte più o meno repentine, le ulteriori intuizioni, l'eliminazione di ingombranti memorie. Rifletto sugli oltre vent'anni del suo percorso creativo e giungo alla regolare conclusione che Corte rappresenta un caso esemplare di frammentazione radicale (nelle modalità) ma unitaria (negli scopi e nei risultati). Ne deduco, tra sani eccessi e insane seppur strepitose bellezze, che la sua arte nasconde chiare percezioni del sé più profondo, rapporti perfezionati tra coscienza e realtà, connessioni rigorose con le proprie sinapsi. Semplicemente: l'autoritratto di un cervello, un'interiorità che dilaga...

La consistente mole di opere si allaccia ad un principio fondativo: un gigantesco *autoritrarsi* secondo modalità diversificate nei modi, negli stili, nei riferimenti esterni. Il corpo dell'artista torna diverse volte ma per dettagli stranianti, altre volte non lo vediamo ma sta lì tra personaggi reali, assurdi o appena plausibili. Tutto indica uno scandaglio crudele del proprio universo interiore, degli artigli e tentacoli che la mente distribuisce verso l'esterno. Si sgretola un pragmatismo di stampo occidentale, colpevole di aver sviluppato autoritrattismi che si limitano tra volto e corpo, come se la fantasia e la lucida follia non fossero parte attiva del raccontarsi attraverso l'esterno e la psiche. Al contrario, alcuni modelli orientali o alternativi rafforzano il potere della duttile immaginazione, del narrare deformazioni liberatorie, strutture impossibili, visioni tra l'assurdo e l'improbabile. L'autoritratto diventa quindi, per la prima volta, una panoramica "in soggettiva" che parte dal nervo ottico per ruotare attorno alle cellule neurali dell'artista, alla loro dispersione labirintica interna, più che alla piatta immagine della realtà circostante.

Nelle seguenti pagine percorreremo le fasi creative in un misto di situazioni e tematiche, analizzando le membrane di un organismo visivo dai complicati meccanismi interiori. Mi sembrava giusto calibrare gli esempi pratici con i temi dominanti. Davanti alla disomogeneità estetica e alla stratificazione concettuale, il filo della chiarezza si snoda attraverso sintesi ed ordine, rispetto ed empatia, passione e coraggio. Artisti così risultano una sincera rarità nel panorama internazionale: e non parlo solo di qualità asciutta ma di profondo legame con le opere e le loro radici, di continua necessità del produrre per respirare.

Citando un neologismo totalizzante di Corte, considererei l'intero volume una *Spettrospettiva*. Una strana parola che attraversa il passato e il futuro nel più ampio spettro di temi e soluzioni estetiche. La Spettrospettiva confonde qualsiasi certezza acquisita: sul rapporto tra vecchio e nuovo, giovane e adulto, contenuto e contenitore, evidenza e nascondimento. Si tratta di una complessità utile e necessaria, la stessa che appartiene alla visione profonda del mondo, al senso radicale dello sguardo, ai confini aperti del pensiero coraggioso.

La Spettrospettiva è una sorta di retrospettiva, e come tale abbraccia l'intero *spettro* delle tecniche e dei temi dell'artista. Così facendo se ne dà una panoramica *spettrale* anche perché spettrali sono spesso le tematiche, i riferimenti e suggestioni che le opere emanano. La figura del "Giovane Artista" viene ad essere ridefinita (forse Corte non è mai stato propriamente giovane, almeno come artista): la Spettrospettiva è una parabola ellittica che affianca le opere del ragazzo con quelle dell'artista "affermato" annullando concetti convenzionali legati al "Tempo" e alla "Maturità" in arte (nonché quello di "Valore", anche economico, ad essi strettamente legato).

Diciamo subito che diviene impossibile racchiudere Corte dentro singole categorie: è evidente la sua autonomia da quei movimenti o gruppi sorti in Italia dopo l'affermarsi della Transavanguardia sulla scena internazionale (nonostante egli inizi ad esporre, a partire dai diciotto anni, in spazi pubblici e gallerie private di ottimo livello). Facilissimo, invece, lasciarsi coinvolgere dai suoi brani visivi, dalla grammatica disomogenea, dalla sintassi sfrenata e talentosa. Perché le sue ipotesi sviluppano una miriade di extravisioni sopra ogni forma: sempre oltre l'apparenza, oltre la comune morale, oltre noi stessi come entità univoca. Le riflessioni si inseguono, sovrappongono senso al senso, incitano a concatenare domande. La Spettrospettiva è così: garantisce rielaborazioni della forma, sgretola ogni certezza metodologica, segue un talento divagante che abiura il manierismo del metodo. Corte racconta i propri processi interiori, i codici cerebrali, le serie leggi della perversione, la geografia dello sguardo radicale: e lo fa con un miscuglio di eccesso e grazia poetica, potenza shakesperiana e ironia formale. Un progetto di specchi spettrali: dove il passato e il futuro scorrono nel corridoio di superfici deformanti, tra feticci necessari e riferimenti attuali, controculture che sono le nuove culture ed eccessi che compiono la propria catarsi.

La materia fisica delle cose è il primo elemento con cui l'artista ribalta l'evidenza del reale. Quel che captiamo dell'opera non si limita alla sua apparenza, al primo livello cognitivo della figurazione. Ogni materia simula altre materie, ogni gioco ironico nasconde percorsi di stratificata densità etica, ogni dettaglio rimanda a qualcosa di opposto o lontano dal suo uso d'origine, ogni titolo circumnaviga la retorica del linguaggio per completare il senso del progetto. Su tali ribaltamenti si plasma un modello linguistico che mescola memoria culturale, temi individuali e contemporaneità, usando una potenza che preme sulla capacità impressiva tramite formidabili archetipi del presente. Tutto è relativo e molto dipende dalla conformazione dello sguardo: una clessidra appare rovesciata e rompe la logica temporale, così come una candela in orizzontale crea equilibrio ma anche devianza; un gancio si trova dove non può sostenere il peso del quadro; lo specchio diviene concavo, riflettendo le immagini capovolte; alcuni quadri apribili si chiudono nel momento in cui valichi la porta. Come orientarsi? La ragione risiede nel terreno del dubbio e dell'anomalia, della differenza che diviene normalità. Il tema del capovolgimento e del rovesciamento riassume gli oltre vent'anni di creazioni firmate EC. Ribaltare forma e sostanza, idee e contenuti, apparenza e stratificazione. Ribaltare ogni ingrediente nel suo contrario, ogni semplificazione nella sua complessità, ogni certezza nel suo necessario dubbio. Il tema del "capovolto" ci riporta addirittura ad una delle prime raffigurazioni preistoriche del Mondo dei Morti, una Spettrospettiva ante litteram, agli albori dell'iconografia dell'Uomo lungo una ramificazione in cui scorre la memoria dell'Artista.

La Spettrospettiva trasforma questo libro in un luogo mentale, una grande opera fatta di tante opere, un centro di gravità temporanea in cui l'evidenza e il nascondimento respirano la stessa aria: seguitene il ritmo ferocemente meccanico che intreccia opere e riflessioni. E ricordate: il flusso testuale che state leggendo ricalcherà il dinamismo di una Spettrospettiva eccitabile, contaminata, mai definitiva, dove un forte ruolo hanno anche la vita e le parole dell'artista. Controllate le date per logica documentazione ma non crediate che la cronologia indichi precisi passaggi sequenziali. In realtà Corte rappresenta un flusso unitario in cui gli ingredienti sono moltissimi e tutto varia a seconda delle combinazioni istantanee. La sequenzialità del suo iter non mostra mai il segno di una maturazione rispetto al pezzo precedente. Al contrario, ogni lavoro vive di luce propria per alimentarsi di passato e futuro, citazione e archetipo, dettagli e totalità. Dando così alla singola opera un'autonomia che la svincola dalla deferenza a un preciso frangente, sia storico che spaziale. Prendendo sempre spunto da ciò che la vita offre all'artista, ogni progetto è sempre *qui e ora*: dalla nascita in poi percorre una continua attualità rispetto al singolo attimo, proprio come ogni "classico" che si rispetti. Tipicamente, nei classici, lo scorrere del tempo non altera la forza del lavoro ma modifica la sua lettura da parte nostra. E' lo sguardo esterno che si plasma in forme sempre più elastiche e tolleranti, abilitandosi alle molteplici ipotesi dell'apparenza momentanea. E qui abbiamo centinaia di pezzi per un unico, gigantesco, disomogeneo, radiciforme excursus dai molti residui riamalgamabili. Tutto si ricicla, nulla resta inutile scarto. Ogni opera si alimenta del passato delle altre, ne prende qualcosa per mantenere l'integrità di un pensiero coerente dai tentacoli vivissimi.

Enrico Corte nasce nel 1963 a Cagliari, in Sardegna, nel pieno centro del Mediterraneo. Qui compie i suoi studi d'arte e letterari e tiene le prime mostre. In seguito si trasferisce a Roma, la città in cui tuttora vive, pensa e agisce. New York, Berlino e Londra, come in misura minore altre capitali europee, rimangono luoghi di contenuto ma fondamentale passaggio. Altri territori completano una storia che ci restituisce la forma psichicamente matura di Corte: i posti geografici, involontari o prescelti, come il flusso stesso della vita, significano moltissimo nella genesi delle opere, entrano dentro i progetti influenzandoli e plasmandoli. Ma non mostrano alcuna evidenza localistica e si tramutano in pura geografia creativa. Nell'opera fotografica *Spettrospettiva dell'Umano Destino* (ill. pag. 110) l'artista si autorappresenta nell'atto di osservare una foresta devastata e inscheletrita da un recente incendio, evento frequente e caratteristico di alcune zone della Sardegna, la sua terra d'origine, ma l'episodio assume subito, grazie al suo titolo, un carattere riflessivo universalistico. Le città stesse diventano un pretesto di esperienze, così come Roma simboleggia una spinta che definisce ogni progetto senza mai disvelarsi allo sguardo turistico.

Roma, somma epocale dell'umanesimo in un passaggio secolare delle iconografie, stimola la propulsione scardinante di Corte. Un accumulo di responsabilità massima del passato che, entrando nelle opere, evita la citazione ma sopravvive solo dissolvendo la memoria forte del singolo luogo. Roma come mancata conciliazione del passato col presente... Nel lavoro dell'artista la lenta pratica della *stratificazione*, come nel tessuto urbano di Roma, fa sì che alla fine i vari, differenti apporti culturali passati/presenti/futuri generino non una semplice somma di questi fattori bensì, fondendosi tra di loro e ossificandosi, accorpino un tale peso specifico da produrre un oggetto *nuovo*, tutto da scoprire, analizzare e classificare.

Roma, quindi, come senso definitivo di catastrofe della Storia: una tale dispersione, pressione e stratificazione di Storia da opacizzarne il metabolismo e collassare nel buco nero della cultura contemporanea dove le leggi della creatività sono invertite. Ecco perché in Corte vengono spesso affiancate, nonché stravolte, varie tecniche artistiche (fotografia, pittura, video, scultura ecc.) ma soprattutto, in senso più generico, si fanno coincidere manualità e produzione industriale, cultura da strada e accademismi, vizi decadenti e fascinazioni dell'infanzia, creazione e autodistruzione.

Laddove coincidano leggerezza e immanente pesantezza, slancio e forza di gravità, si è sempre in un equilibrio di sopravvivenza a un passo dalla catastrofe, dal precipizio, dal collasso psichico. Vedremo ora come tutti questi elementi vengono a concretizzarsi nel corso del tempo e nei singoli lavori, perché solo sul piano materiale si misura ciò che è sterile e ciò che è ancora fertile per noi contemporanei.

Tra le prime opere che definiscono la figura di Corte ormai all'interno di una coscienza delle pratiche dell'arte contemporanea, va citata la serie di disegni *250 Mele Marce* (ill. pp. 69-73): vi scopriamo infatti tutta una serie di elementi che troveremo nell'analisi dei lavori futuri. Si tratta di 250 autoritratti eseguiti a gessetto e carboncino su carta grezza, rozzamente tagliata, del tipo usato nelle macellerie per incartare la carne cruda. L'artista, allora adolescente, sceglie di operare in base ad una logica quasi "impiegatizia" che svilisce il mito della "ispirazione". Egli realizza dunque metodicamente un autoritratto al giorno per la durata di un anno a partire dal 10/5/78 per finire al 9/5/79 tenendosi però liberi i weekend, le feste comandate e il giorno del suo compleanno (in tutto: 250 giorni "lavorativi" per altrettanti autoritratti appunto). Non sempre l'artista aveva sottomano la carta grezza che caratterizza questa serie di disegni, per cui certi giorni ha eseguito gli autoritratti su oggetti in ferro arrugginito o pannelli di legno in stato d'invecchiamento, trovati per strada. Allo scadere del fatidico "anno di lavoro", l'ultimo autoritratto ci mostra l'artista con i capelli cortissimi, tagliati il giorno stesso, laddove nei precedenti disegni appariva con le chiome fluenti fino alle spalle.

La serie *250 Mele Marce* è importante perché vi sono presenti alcune chiavi di lettura: la metodologia perversa, ossessiva e sarcastica nei confronti del fare artistico; la sessualità acerba dell'adolescente che si offre al pubblico (si immola, come molti esempi del Punk rock del tempo), il cui fremito è evidenziato dallo stile espressionista-gestuale, il cui senso di colpa si manifesta nelle sporcature del tratto e la cui ambiguità della sessualità acerba è sottolineata dalla presenza in alcuni disegni di scenari di latrine o gabinetti pubblici. La stessa lunghezza dei capelli dell'adolescente è indicativa della doppiezza della tematica "gender": l'artista-ragazzo dai capelli lunghi e dai tratti indeterminati è chiaramente molto simile a una ragazza, mostra lineamenti quasi alternabili, ma il taglio radicale di capelli dell'ultimo disegno può ribaltare tutto, significando sia una acquistata virilità dell'adolescente (più simile a un maschio) come anche il suo contrario: la definitiva perdita di forza virile (vedi il mito di Sansone e Dalila), o forse è un precoce invecchiamento in base ad una acquisita "esperienza".

L'artista adolescente parla di ciò che conosce meglio: le contraddizioni e le tensioni della propria età. E il materiale fisico con cui si compongono le opere delinea l'autoritrattismo psichico di Corte. Ogni oggetto, superficie, patina, rifinitura, colore, rivestimento o dettaglio indica una precisa relazione tra l'idea e la sua attuabilità formale. Il singolo pezzo prevede sempre una stratificazione funzionale, direttamente connessa alla visione interiore: la carta da macellaio indica visceralità, come in altri disegni il supporto di carta velina suggerisce l'idea di evanescenza e fragilità. L'opera diventa una superficie organica, un frammento, denso ma rigoroso, che rispecchia il pensiero modulabile dell'autore. Qualsiasi elemento si tinge di una lavorazione meticolosa e maniacale, però a tratti, come nel simbolo Yin/Yang, contiene anche un po' del suo contrario: il gesto nervoso che "sporca" il risultato o addirittura lo distrugge. E' questo il caso delle coeve serie di disegni adolescenziali intitolati *Flussi & Riflussi Stoici* e *Succhi & Risucchi Gastrici* (ill. pp. 74-83). Il primo è un gruppo di disegni realizzati mescolando matite sanguigne, sangue umano (dell'artista) e di animali (di macelleria) più altri coloranti nelle varianti del rosso tratti da materiali commestibili e quindi "viscerali" (pomodoro, vino ecc.) usati per disegnare immagini. In un disegno in particolare le tracce di sperma dell'artista rientrano forse nella categoria dei "materiali commestibili". L'altra serie di disegni, *Succhi & Risucchi Gastrici,* sempre a matita e tempera, è eseguita su carte veline colorate, sovrapposte e in seguito parzialmente disgregate dall'uso di vari tipo di acidi corrosivi stesi col pennello (creazione e distruzione coincidono) più alcune gocce di vero succo di bile umana usate come pittura. Ad alimentare il "quoziente di acidità" di queste pitture, si aggiungono anche gocce di acido lisergico (LSD) mescolate al colore a tempera.

Corte usa le materie crude del rimosso corporeo e le manipola come forma e colore, riabilitando un loro imprinting originario e liberatorio. I liquidi si sciolgono come materia plasmabile, ormai una vera astrazione rispetto allo status sociale con cui li si vorrebbe racchiudere. L'autoritratto psichico esprime la propria conformazione attraverso le materie che sostengono il corpo e la vita. Le tematiche suggerite dalle immagini, affioranti tra gli impasti di materie organiche e i brandelli di carte spappolate di entrambe le serie di disegni, suggeriscono visioni da incubo infantile e da rapimento alieno in cui figure non meglio precisate, spesso in gruppi di quattro, circondano nottetempo il letto o la culla del bambino, pronti a rapirlo: maschere geometrizzanti, zanzare fuori misura, gatti dagli occhi spiritati, ombre incappucciate o addirittura quattro nani di Biancaneve sono i molti sostituti visivi della rimossa immagine dell'Alieno, la personificazione della minaccia suprema. Occorre dire che in quegli anni l'argomento dei rapimenti alieni e della loro rimozione psichica era assai poco diffuso nelle arti visive; cinema e letteratura se ne occupavano in un'ottica di fantascienza ma l'analisi scientifica del fenomeno (mediante ipnosi regressiva delle presunte vittime ecc.) muoveva ancora i primi passi. L'interesse di Corte pare comunque rivolgersi al fenomeno psichico in sé, mantenendosi in un più generale contesto di sogno o di incubo ossessivo, come variante di una opprimente inquietudine che troverà altre incarnazioni in lavori successivi.

Altre presenze disposte in circolo, dalla fisionomia indefinibile, sono i globi oculari in frac, cravatta a farfalla e cilindro che appaiono nelle tre sculture identiche del 1979-80 intitolate *Penta-Portraits* (ill. p. 84). Si tratta dei misteriosi componenti della band californiana The Residents, quattro (ma saranno quattro?) geniali sperimentatori senza volto, età o nome proprio, anticipatori di sonorità contemporanee, amatissimi in quegli anni dal ragazzo Enrico Corte che entra in contatto diretto con loro e realizza varie opere citando la loro oscura immagine-shock fissata in maniera definitiva con la pubblicazione dell'album *Eskimo*, capolavoro del 1979. Corte è interessato alla convivenza di forme visive e modalità sonore. Ma al di là del semplice omaggio del fan, che non si addice all'artista, i Residents assurgono qui a un ruolo specifico: l'artista sostiene che il particolare approccio alla materia musicale della band di San Francisco, di difficilissima catalogazione secondo i canoni sia del rock che dell'elettronica o della musica extra-colta, rappresenti non uno *stile* musicale, come nel caso di tante altre band, ma un *genere* a sé, a sua volta suddiviso in differenti stili distribuiti nei loro vari progetti e dischi. Oltre al senso del mistero, è l'idea di autonomia creativa che affascina Corte, il fatto che si possa operare con coerenza non identificandosi in nessuna etichetta stilistica (New Wave? Contaminazione? Musica Contemporanea?) ma attraversandole tutte e anzi anticipandole in maniera sorprendente, riuscendo pure a suscitare, nella sperimentazione estrema, un forte appeal nei confronti del pubblico generico del rock. E' il tipo di modalità che Corte ha ormai scelto anche per la sua attività artistica, ed è per questo che *Penta-Portraits* rappresenta la band di quattro elementi allargata con l'inserimento di un quinto membro indistinguibile (un quinto globo oculare in tuxedo), quasi a suggerire una identificazione dell'artista come membro ulteriore, oppure spingere chiunque ad identificarvisi e incrementare di volta in volta le fila del misterioso ensemble mascherato (abbandono di qualsiasi identità prestabilita, geografica, sociale, sessuale ecc.). Inseriti in un tubo di plexiglas trasparente e dondolante, da appendere al soffitto, questi cinque ritratti di Residents ci appaiono proprio provenienti da una "quinta dimensione", teletrasportati qui da un luminoso raggio al plasma.

Nello stesso periodo EC, che ricordiamo ha tra i sedici e i diciassette anni, inizia a produrre anche opere fotografiche. Il motivo sembra lo stesso di altri artisti: «non costava niente farle». Se poi è l'artista stesso a posare come modello, i problemi diminuiscono ancora. In realtà Corte da subito sceglie di affidare tecnicamente ad altri lo scatto manuale della fotografia, per esempio fotografi dilettanti, limitandosi a curare inquadratura, posa e ambientazione. Anche quando si è rivolto a fotografi professionisti ha preteso da loro un approccio dilettantesco ed evitato di produrre immagini troppo patinate. Solo poche volte ha preferito usare l'autoscatto. *Pelle & Ossa*, del 1980 (ill. p. 85), è un esempio di riutilizzo fotografico delle sculture tubolari *Penta-Portraits* collocate come sfondo per una immagine dell'artista: Corte, dopo essersi sottoposto a un volontario razionamento del cibo fino a raggiungere il peso di circa 40 Kg, appare, smagrito, nell'atto di suonare un rullante di batteria usando due reali costole umane come bacchette. Pelli e ossa, appunto.

L'uso della manipolazione e costrizione corporea rimanda alle correnti della Body Art del decennio precedente, oppure anticipa quelle che si imporranno negli anni Novanta; il riferimento al suonare uno strumento in maniera allucinata o necrofila ha rapporti con un filone della Rock music dissonante, abrasivo e compiaciutamente degenerativo (No Wave e affini). Pare inoltre che l'uso di digiunare fino al deperimento fosse comune tra i ragazzi che, attorno a quell'età, volessero evitare il servizio militare. Un effetto di dimagrimento rapido è tra l'altro comune in un ragazzo che faccia abuso di sostanze come speed o amfetamine. In ogni caso l'opera si pone in un contesto che situa l'adolescenza come momento emblematico di crisi e sperimentazione di esperienze in cui si rispecchiano molte contraddizioni sociali.

E' ancora la carta velina colorata e ritagliata a caratterizzare una serie di lavori che Corte inizia a produrre nel 1980 e che continuerà a realizzare, a volte inserendoli in opere polimateriche più complesse, in pratica fino a oggi. Sono ritratti di persone, amici, conoscenti o occasionali presenze di passaggio, tutti rigorosamente reali e riconoscibili, ottenuti ritagliando la silhouette del loro volto visto di profilo sulla carta velina, piegata più volte su se stessa: dispiegandola, si ottiene il caratteristico arabesco traforato che in questo caso è composto da profili di persone. L'immagine figurativa è quindi presente attraverso un *vuoto* formale e vive una condizione di forte ambiguità, al limite del non percepibile, del fuoco fatuo, del fosfene, all'interno della struttura visiva del quadro. Le opere di questo tipo, centinaia nel corso degli anni, paiono situarsi in un contesto di decorazione leggera e di gioco infantile, il cui risultato visivo è simile a un mandala ipnotico. E' invece uno dei primi mascheramenti che Corte usa come espediente per far passare ben altri intendimenti. Quali sono i reali processi psicologici che portano un ragazzo, un *pittore*, a rapportarsi coi suoi modelli da ritrarre proprio attraverso questa modalità? Lo abbiamo chiesto all'artista stesso, ed ecco cosa ci ha risposto:

[Registrato: 12 Agosto 2002 – estratto]

Nel 1980 ero lì a guardarmi intorno ponendomi le solite domande dei ragazzini, ossia: come posso rappresentare la totale degenerazione mentale, lo spaesamento in una vita senza punti di riferimento, la vertigine dell'ipocrisia sociale, l'annichilimento della dignità dell'uomo e dell'artista, la catastrofe dell'arte e l'implosione della civiltà che mi circonda? E come farlo senza cadere in alcun luogo comune figurativo, in velleitarie immagini di denuncia o in quadretti di pittura selvaggia o espressionista tanto di moda all'epoca? Occorreva essere più aguzzi e più sottili. Dovevo in primis usare delle *maschere*, depistare, inventarmi un paradosso visivo in apparenza molto lontano dall'incubo che volevo rappresentare. Così decisi che mi serviva un elemento figurativo mimetico che camuffasse ma al tempo stesso concentrasse sinteticamente tutto quanto in un unico semplice stilema: questo sarebbe stato pregnante ed efficace proprio in virtù dell'assenza di dispersioni, di sovraccarico visuale, di coinvolgimento, di passione.

Con tutta la grazia e l'eleganza dei miei verdi anni ho senza il minimo sforzo subito trovato quel che cercavo. Se mi interessava la fragilità, l'inevitabilità della frattura, lo sbriciolamento della realtà, il crollo psichico: dovevo usare la carta velina. E dovrà essere in vivaci colori. Se mi affascinava la vertigine dell'abisso, il brivido dello smarrimento, la mancanza di qualsiasi appiglio e riferimento: dovevo creare sulla carta un arabesco vorticoso di buchi e piccole voragini senza fondo. Una decorazione che io vorrò ordinata, graziosa. Inoltre, osservavo la gente: il fluire, ancor più disorientante di fronte ai miei occhi, di masse di persone giovani e adulte. Prendendo atto di una distanza, avvertendoli come inafferrabili, cercavo di decifrare il perché della loro presenza, di trovare una collocazione, una logica dell'interscambiabilità dei loro ruoli. Occorreva abbozzare dei tratti, descrivere in modo fugace il profilo di ciascuna di queste personalità altrimenti impenetrabili, opache, distanti: i buchi sulla carta dovevano essere ritagli coi profili di persone. Piegando la carta velina su se stessa un profilo ritagliato diverrà senza sforzo mille profili, non m'importa se uguali o diversi, purché vengano dispersi nei frammenti dello specchio della vita.

Poteva venirne fuori persino una sorta di mappa del codice genetico umano manipolato da Alieni, un teorema algebrico della riproduzione basato sull'appiattimento e sull'indifferenziazione, su multipli, cloni, automi biologici. Visioni di questo tipo. Tutte nate dalla semplice linea di un profilo.

Persone amiche o semplici passanti nella via, utilizzavo le fattezze di tutti… i primi soggetti dei ritagli-ritratti sono stati i compagnucci dei miei quindici anni. Il più delle volte utilizzavo i profili di chi mi era d'aiuto nel realizzare un'opera – per esempio il fotografo utilizzato per un quadro fotografico – o di chi mi stava intorno mentre la realizzavo. Era un modo come un altro, in fondo, attraverso cui il pittore esegue i suoi ritratti, si rapporta al mondo. E rapportandomi in tale maniera, con mezzi così semplici, con un gioco di ritagli sulla carta ripetuti all'infinito che forse si accetta in un bambino ma è sconveniente e idiota in un adulto, io toccavo alfine il vero punto nevralgico della questione. Quale? Ovviamente, decantare l'elegia variopinta della regressione all'infanzia e della coazione a ripetere – gesti ripetuti che producono una maggiore ripetizione di figure – come deflagrazione inarrestabile di una pulsione di morte grandiosa, nerissima: io tutto questo lo trovo meraviglioso. Tutto coincide, tutto viene dunque espresso con facilità e sintesi espressiva, mascherato al punto giusto e pronto per iniziare il suo gioco di persuasione occulta in giro per il mondo. Avevo sedici anni; ho *tolto* la prima pietra.

Nascevano varie considerazioni di ordine morale. Per esempio: dal momento che questi quadri con i ritagli-ritratti di carta velina non presentavano nessun fattore all'interno della loro figurazione che potesse fungere da punto d'orientamento se non minime variazioni formali negli sfondi, li si poteva appendere indifferentemente diritti o capovolti senza mutare troppo il risultato. Così si ha una preoccupazione in meno... La mossa successiva è stata evidenziare ancora di più questa caratteristica inserendo i gancetti della cornice in punti improbabili, dando anche al futuro acquirente del pezzo una possibilità in più di scelta nell'appendere il quadro. I risultati migliori si hanno quando si riesce ad appendere al muro il quadro diritto ma con il gancetto e il chiodo collocati nella parte inferiore della cornice, così che l'opera sembri contraddire la forza di gravità, e appaia nell'atto di volarsene via, trattenuta in basso solo dal chiodino nel muro.

Mi si dice che ho una sensibilità un po' cupa e in effetti in un quadro io sono subito attratto dal lato oscuro. Nel senso che l'occhio mi cade sempre sulla parte in ombra, quella che l'illuminazione della galleria, del museo o della casa del collezionista getta sul muro, al lato della cornice. I quadri secondo me devono gettare un'ombra. Quando sei un oggetto, un'ombra forte è indice di personalità. In questo senso capisco i critici e gli intenditori d'arte che cercano nelle opere lo spessore, la consistenza: con più "spessore" si avrà più ombra sulla parete, logico. Già pensare dei quadri che potessero avere il gancetto e chiodino in basso invece che in alto, e che tendessero a volarsene in su, implica che il quadro dovesse staccarsi dal muro e gettarvi sopra una bella ombra netta.

Molteplici sono i processi psicologici che portano un artista a praticare una particolare modalità nello strutturare i propri quadri. Al di là delle sue esplicite dichiarazioni, possiamo aggiungere che la tipologia del Ritaglio-Ritratto su carta velina è un tentativo, non completamente riuscito, di mantenere una *costante* nell'infinito variare delle forme da opera a opera: un "centro di gravità", una sorta di "bussola". Parimenti, questi ritratti di vere persone possono indicare una volontà di conservare un contatto reale col mondo, anche se in un'ottica di regressione, all'interno di un flusso di opere ridondanti di figurazioni schizoidi. La stessa idea di regressione può essere letta secondo la vecchia chiave della psicanalisi "classica" (regressione-negazione), ma interpretazioni più recenti (Cooper, Deleuze-Guattari) la mostrano invece come potente deflagrazione rivoluzionaria. Infine, come sempre, ognuno è libero di vedere in questi *Ritagli-Ritratti* ciò che vuole (ill. pp. 87-89 e 91).

Per Strada e *Youthanasia 1* sono due opere fotografiche che ancora ritraggono l'artista. La prima (ill. p. 92) è una foto a colori scattata da un fotografo professionista su precise indicazioni di Corte che in seguito ha ricolorato l'immagine all'acquarello perché il fotografo ne rivendicava la paternità artistica. Il ragazzo vi appare in uno scenario urbano notturno umido e incombente, in ambigua attesa su una panchina circondato da due cuscini di seta macchiati del suo sangue, come fosse seduto dentro un salottino grottesco. E' la prima opera che suggerisce il tema della devianza minorile, della prostituzione, dell'angosciante incontro con l'*Altro* sulla "strada della vita" in un buio con pochi e vaghi punti di riferimento. *Quadrangoli Luminosi* è il titolo alternativo di quest'opera, con riferimento sia alle finestre illuminate sullo sfondo sia ai cuscini quadrati di seta riflettenti la luce di un lampione.

Youthanasia 1 (ill. p. 93) pare ambientata in un gabinetto pubblico in disuso e forse allude, in modo meno opprimente, alla stessa tematica di prima. Corte vi si raffigura come un ragazzino New Wave – qual'era – mentre indossa una T-shirt a righe (un capo molto usato dai giovani in quegli anni in Italia) con sopra tre badges di bands musicali realizzati a mano da lui, più uno strappo nella stoffa all'altezza del capezzolo (il capezzolo come quarto badge). Alle sue spalle, una serie di sculturine informi in cera, peli, spine e oggetti vari, a somiglianza di fatture da malocchio, sono montate su piedistalli fissi alla parete. Se andiamo ad analizzare quali siano le bands rappresentate dai badges, precisi riferimenti generazionali, geografici e di gusto personale, vediamo che nulla è casuale ma tutto contribuisce a svelare l'intento e la personalità dell'artista. Tre bands inglesi seminali come The Pop Group, Throbbing Gristle e Public Image Limited rappresentano casi di approccio estremo alla materia musicale in cui anche la ricerca di una violenta immagine visiva ha la sua rilevanza. Tra l'altro almeno due di queste bands hanno affrontato con efficacia il tema della prostituzione in chiave fisica e morale: il Pop Group con il loro noto singolo *We Are All Prostitutes*, e i TG, ancora sotto la fisionomia di gruppo d'artisti COUM Transmission, nella loro mostra *Prostitution* all'ICA Gallery di Londra nel 1976. I PIL, erano più o meno essi stessi prostitute. (Scendo in particolari così cavillosi per far capire come fin dalle prime opere il lavoro di Corte sarà sempre saturo di riferimenti nascosti o semi-invisibili al mondo che lo circonda in quel momento culturale e ai riflessi che ciò proietta sulle sue personali passioni o interessi).

Va detto che Corte ha sempre citato come propri riferimenti ispiratori non tanto altri artisti visivi del passato o del presente quanto i rappresentanti di alcune correnti musicali e i loro dischi, per esempio l'LP *No New York* del 1978, prodotto da Brian Eno come instant-manifesto collettivo della No Wave newyorkese attraverso quattro bands fondamentali e freneticamente autodistruttive: i Contortions di James Chance, i Teenage Jesus & Jerks di Lydia Lunch, i Mars di Mark Cunningham e i DNA di Arto Lindsay. Le tendenze e i progetti musicali che Corte ha visto nascere e crescere con lui (ne sono validi esempi *No New York*, ma anche bands di fine anni Settanta ascoltate all'età di 15 anni come Pere Ubu e, ovviamente, Suicide) hanno di certo coinvolto e influenzato Corte quanto se non più di altri artisti visivi del passato o a lui contemporanei (per esempio gli Azionisti viennesi).

La musica sarà sempre il "sub-plot" su cui l'artista svilupperà i suoi progetti visuali. Il badge, oggetto di tipico uso giovanile divenuto di largo consumo dopo l'esplosione del Punk, è anche il soggetto di altre opere del 1982, *Bad-ge* e *Nipping Nipple* (ill. pp. 100, 101): si tratta di veri badges con relativa spilla, in un caso con escrescenze maligne, bubboniche e tumorali al posto del nome della band (il gioco di parole del titolo *Bad-ge* evidenzia la radice "cattiva" dell'oggetto) e nell'altro caso con un capezzolo iperrealistico in cera che l'artista volle sostituire al proprio reale capezzolo tramite l'invenzione di un nuovo tipo di piercing.

L'attitudine estetica di Corte privilegia il contrasto tra apparenza formale e contenuto. Un universo che si relaziona con il colore, la musica, l'immaginario figurativo, la composizione stratificata, la cultura popolare nei suoi meandri meno didascalici. La risultanza è come la piccola spilla da indossare: brillante ed ironica a debita distanza, cattiva e deviante non appena ti avvicini, coinvolgente e dolorosa quando la tocchi e indossi.

Il decantare la pulsione autodistruttiva sembra essere il tema portante delle opere prodotte da Corte nel suo passaggio dai diciassette ai diciotto anni. Oltre ai *Ritagli-Ritratti*, lavori come *Cheese*, *Youthanasia 2* e *3*, *Der Weg Zum Kubismus* e i vari *Balconi* ne sono le infinite varianti. Ognuna porta con sé una storia complessa che rivela molto della particolare modalità operativa di Corte. Ho chiesto all'artista di parlare in prima persona di una di esse, *Cheese* (ill. p. 94), e lui mi ha mostrato un articolo di cronaca su un giornale della sua città ritenendolo il miglior commento possibile per una descrizione dell'ambiente di provincia in cui operava. Proprio come estremo contrattacco alla situazione sociale e culturale circostante, Corte ha effettuato già in gioventù certe scelte in campo artistico, piuttosto che altre. Per non esserne ostaggio, egli esaspera la realtà circostante, la porta a una crisi pubblica, la rende incandescente e se ne libera facendola esplodere. Mi affido alle sue dirette e colorate parole affinché vi spieghi come. Vi si trovano, *in nuce*, diversi motivi e atteggiamenti che ritorneranno nelle opere future, in quella cosiddetta – presunta – maturità. Notate come, mediante il suo sguardo, l'artista, partendo dall'oggi, tipicamente navighi verso il passato attraverso un tempo rallentato, pitonesco, con una descrizione estenuante dei minimi particolari, per poi effettuare un improvviso balzo in avanti di anni, di decenni, ma sempre conservando una posizione di distacco nell'eterno presente della mente.

[Registrato: 30 Gennaio 2003]
Una strana concezione dell'arte è il titolo di questo articoletto apparso su *Tutto*, un quotidiano di provincia pubblicato quando ero ragazzino. Nello specifico, sul numero del 2/4/1981 a pagina tre. Un'amica che conservava da vent'anni questa vecchia copia del giornale me la ha spedita di recente a Roma, pensando di farmi piacere. L'articolo è siglato *C. De.* e mi sembra di ricordare che si corrisponda al nome di un tale Carlo Devoto – o forse Corrado, e forse Devoti – un corsivista che ho conosciuto di persona, che non vedo più da allora e che comunque già al tempo mi appariva non più giovanissimo. Il testo è corredato da una piccola foto, sgranata nel suo grossolano retino tipografico e dopo vent'anni ancor più grigita dal tempo. La didascalia afferma: «Lo studente Enrico Corte». In quella foto io appaio in primo piano mentre un movimento della mia mano mi nasconde parzialmente il viso; l'immagine è stata scattata di sfuggita, a mia insaputa, e per questo non ricordo il momento preciso. Ricordo invece molto bene tutto il resto della storia vissuta e descritta in questo articolo di giornale, che adesso mi accingo a rileggere per voi.

> *«Cagliari – Il pomeriggio del giorno 30 marzo scorso un gruppo di passanti che attraversava la piazza Costituzione nel pieno centro cittadino ha adocchiato, dal basso in alto, un individuo che, avendo scavalcato il parapetto delimitante la terrazza panoramica del bastione S. Remy, pareva passeggiare reggendosi in bilico sull'orlo del cornicione sul lato esterno che prospetta il viale Regina Elena. Il gruppo di persone, allarmate da una situazione ritenuta logicamente di estremo pericolo, ha avvisato una pattuglia dei Carabinieri che si è recata sul luogo dell'avvistamento per dirigersi subito, di conseguenza, sulla sommità del bastione monumentale dove sembrava svolgersi la preoccupante scena.*
>
> *L'artefice della equilibristica esibizione è così risultato essere lo studente Enrico Corte di Cagliari, di diciassette anni, frequentante l'ultimo anno del Liceo Artistico cittadino; il giovane aveva organizzato, con il sostegno pratico di un gruppo di amici tra cui G. F., di ventisei anni, di professione fotografo e assistente di cattedra nel medesimo liceo del Corte, una sorta di sessione fotografica che avrebbe dovuto ritrarlo in varie pose tra cui appunto quella, particolarmente rischiosa, sull'orlo del cornicione di marmo del bastione, largo appena 50 centimetri».*

E' così strano avere un "passato", è come sognare. Eravamo in otto quel pomeriggio sulla terrazza. Io e altri sette volonterosi amici il cui scopo era in parte quello di ficcare il naso in questa faccenda – da me proposta loro giorni prima – ma anche quello di tenere sotto controllo tanti piccoli particolari tra i quali occuparsi della sorveglianza dell'ampio e frequentato luogo in cui ci trovavamo, per proteggere l'evento dagli occhi indiscreti degli inevitabili passanti rompicoglioni.

Vecchi compagni e amici della mia adolescenza i quali erano di fatto già *vecchi* ai miei occhi, coi loro ventiquattro, venticinque, ventisei anni, perché visti con lo sguardo di un diciassettenne che presumeva in loro una maggiore maturità e esperienza di vita. Forse l'avevano pure, l'esperienza: quella di una generazione alla totale deriva dopo aver attraversato il cosiddetto "Movimento del '77" italiano e per la quale qualsiasi gesto o evento avesse una minima parvenza di illegalità / clandestinità / sfida / rischio / alterazione della coscienza / perversione psichica / necrofilia, incontrava la loro adesione e il loro entusiasmo pure già infiacchito dall'abuso di eroina. Adoro tutto questo! In quella loro condizione, in quella loro breve stagione io li trovavo, a loro modo, grandiosi.

Difatti, si poteva fare qualsiasi cosa con quella gente; io, che ero un ragazzino ma ne conoscevo bene le debolezze "storiche", potevo sedurli e manipolarli proprio facendo leva sulle loro peggiori frustrazioni, proprio contando sul fatto che la mia irruenza e il mio delirio per la devianza rappresentavano per loro una delle pochissime alternative alla monotonia della vita di provincia. E *li ho* manipolati assai bene... almeno per un paio d'anni, prima che le loro velleità di rivolta fossero spazzate via nel corso degli '80. Chi si perse nei gironi della tossicodipendenza, chi – peggio – in quelli del matrimonio, chi si è abbonato al *Corriere dello Sport*, chi è diventato calvo, e chi – ancora peggio – si è fatto crescere i baffi. E chi tutte queste cose assieme.

Ma quel giorno erano ancora un gruppo di Cani Sciolti casualmente riunito in uno spiazzo vuoto sotto l'umida brezza di marzo. In quel pomeriggio io ero il collante della loro noia, della loro insofferenza e angoscia. Non sono sicuro che non fosse assente una certa attrazione non confessata da parte di quei ragazzotti nei miei confronti, di tipo più morboso, chiamiamolo pure erotico, che dava origine a una loro mollezza di carattere e a una disponibilità direi servile verso di me, verso le mie grazie acerbe.

Li rivedo ancora mentre mi ronzano attorno e mi osservano come per dirmi: "cioè, ma tu questo lo vuoi fare sul serio? Ma cos'è che vuoi fare, esattamente?"

Per fare ciò che dovevo fare occorreva aspettare il momento propizio, il primo dopopranzo in cui la circolazione di persone per la strada si dirada al massimo. «Ragazzi», dico ai miei amici, «da bravo artista, nell'attesa farò i vostri ritratti, o meglio: i ritratti dei vostri profili. Le silhouette dei vostri volti saranno i veri profili caratteriali che appariranno come buchi sulla carta moltiplicati in tutte le sfaccettature labirintiche della mente». Mostro loro il procedimento tramite cui traccio un piccolo e schematico disegno a matita del profilo del loro viso su un foglio quadrato di carta velina che in seguito ripiego varie volte su se stesso; poi con le forbicine per le unghie ritaglio con cura i contorni del profilo fino a ottenere un foro sulla carta, e quando dispiego il foglio ecco apparire un merletto di buchi seriali, di piccole voragini vuote il cui arabesco è formato dal profilo della persona ritratta moltiplicato all'infinito attraverso tutta la superficie.

I miei amici fissano mesmerizzati il foglio di carta velina vivacemente colorata e sono all'apice della loro cedevolezza, annegati in un'incantata ebetudine. Conoscevano di certo il giochino fin dal tempo dell'infanzia, ma io ho sfiorato le corde nascoste della loro regressione, titillato la loro assopita pulsione di morte. Ma è tempo di mettersi al lavoro.

«... cornicione di marmo del bastione, largo appena 50 centimetri. Ricordiamo che in quel punto l'altezza da terra equivale a quella di un palazzo di sei piani. Com'è inoltre noto, il bastione S. Remy è da tempo il luogo tristemente privilegiato dal punto di vista dei suicidi cittadini, con una cospicua casistica di tragici salti nel vuoto che purtroppo non sembra arrestarsi. Da qui la necessità dell'ausilio di un fotografo professionista per eternare l'attimo da brivido, un "complice" dal ruolo in apparenza innocente e passivo. Ma il cosiddetto progetto artistico di Enrico Corte non aveva fatto i conti con l'occhio indiscreto di un pubblico casuale di passanti allarmati che potesse intralciarne lo svolgimento, nonostante l'artista fosse stato attento a scegliere l'orario pomeridiano in cui attuare le pericolose pose fotografiche proprio a causa della minore frequenza di passaggio di persone nel centro storico rispetto ad altri momenti della giornata. Il ruolo del G. F. in tutta la faccenda all'inizio non era perfettamente chiaro; il fotografo, che tra l'altro sembrerebbe fosse già conosciuto dalle forze dell'ordine per un suo passato di tossicodipendenza e piccolo spaccio, appariva munito della sua attrezzatura fotografica completa ed è stato comunque trattenuto dai Carabinieri e interrogato assieme al Corte proprio per risolvere i molti lati oscuri».

Discrezione giornalistica e cautele legali fanno qui apparire con le sole iniziali GF l'amico fotografo Gismondo, aka "Mondo Gehenna", visionario di talento, almeno a quel tempo; bravissimo nel mascherare la sua identità segreta sotto le anonime spoglie di un assistente in un liceo, altrettanto bravo qualche anno dopo nell'incarnare sulla propria pelle il fatto che non esisteva per niente una sua *seconda identità*... magistrale nel produrre un'opera che magnificasse nient'altro che la propria stessa improduttività. Era la vera personificazione di ciò che allora veniva chiamato il "riflusso nel Privato", ma privato nel senso di sfornito, mancante, carente, vuoto.

Ce l'avrà ancora su con me, G. F., per non aver mai beccato una lira dalle foto da lui scattate mentre io ci ho fatto i milioni? Non li ho cercati io, i soldi... nessuno ci pensava, allora ero solo un ragazzino e nemmeno tanto ambizioso. E poi io quelle foto le ho progettate nei dettagli, ho posato, in seguito le ho confezionate come manufatti artistici e ho trovato l'occasione di esporle. Mica poco. Lui ha solo premuto un bottoncino, però poi mi ha querelato quando ho venduto la fotografia. Ma allora aveva già cambiato l'impostazione della sua vita, era già abbonato al *Corriere dello Sport*.

(In effetti le immagini ottenute da quella sessione fotografica sono state esposte nel 1982 durante la mia prima mostra personale e subito vendute per un milione di lire; ristampate nel corso dei vent'anni successivi, sono state acquistate di volta in volta per cifre assai superiori. Il fotografo fu pagato unicamente con un Ritaglio-Ritratto su carta velina di cm 15 x 15). Ma continuiamo a leggere:

«... molti lati oscuri. Il Corte, sedicente artista visivo con, di fatto, alcune esposizioni pubbliche di propri quadri alle spalle, si è subito dichiarato unico ideatore e responsabile di tutto: in pratica si sarebbe trattato del progetto di realizzazione di un "quadro fotografico" ritraente il giovane artista in giacca a vento e coi capelli tagliati a spazzola nell'atto di passeggiare con tranquillità, addirittura fischiettando un motivetto che veniva anche da lui registrato in diretta mediante un registratore portatile, sul bordo estremo del cornicione più alto del bastione S. Remy sfidando implicitamente le vertigini e il pericolo di scivolare di sotto (nonché, si potrebbe aggiungere, il buon gusto nei confronti dell'arte)».

Mi piace quell'accenno alla mia giacca a vento (in realtà era un giaccone) e soprattutto al taglio di capelli. In fondo l'abbigliamento aveva un ruolo preciso nell'economia generale della fotografia. Apposta avevo scelto di apparire in abiti da bravo ragazzo, con indosso persino i calzoni con la riga ben stirata; ritenevo invece che una cravatta mi invecchiasse troppo facendomi magari sembrare un *ventenne* e non più il bocciolo adolescente che ero. I capelli s'era cercato di comporli in una forma regolare ma un'improvvisa folata di vento al momento dello scatto, oltre a contribuire all'aumento repentino delle mie pulsazioni cardiache, ha finito per vanificare del tutto i tentativi di plasmare la consistente chioma.

Il registratore lo portavo con me anche se non è visibile nella foto. Durante il mio stazionare sul cornicione, e mente mi spostavo cercando il punto giusto per posare rispetto all'inquadratura, registravo infatti su nastro magnetico un motivetto insensato, blaterato e fischiettato improvvisando lì per lì, tra i rumori del traffico sottostante, il crocchiare delle siringhe sotto le suole delle Clark's (tipiche scarpe sportive del "giovane"), il cinguettio degli uccelli e il brusio del vento sopra al microfono. L'impressione di folle irresponsabilità totale e di fascinazione per gli abissi della mente era ciò che si voleva evidenziare correlando l'immagine fotografica con questo soundtrack colto dal vivo.

Cheese è il titolo dell'immagine fotografica stampata e confezionata come quadro, e *Cheese Sinfonia* verrà chiamata la registrazione montata in loop (7' per complessivi 20') e riprodotta su audiocassetta in 50 esemplari confezionati a mano come piccole sculture, numerati e firmati nonché esposti e venduti come multipli indipendenti dall'opera fotografica. Tre anni dopo, nel 1984, riesco a ristampare la fotografia *Cheese* in formato 36 x 36 cm rivestita da una pellicola vinilica trasparente su cui è incorporata una facciata di un disco a 45 giri *extended play*, sempre trasparente, con incisi i 7' di suoni tratti dal nastro originale. L'oggetto è suonabile sul piatto dello stereo come un normale disco in vinile.

«... il buon gusto nei confronti dell'arte). L'irresponsabilità apparente del gesto nascondeva a ben vedere una certa "logica" di ferro».

L'opera intitolata *Cheese* – dalla parola che si pronuncia quando si posa per una foto atteggiando la bocca in un sorriso in apparenza non forzato – in definitiva raffigura un ampio scorcio angolare della parte superiore del cosiddetto bastione Saint Remy, un monumentale complesso architettonico-celebrativo in marmo, rimaneggiato nel corso dei secoli dall'800 fino all'epoca fascista, collocato nel centro urbano della città in cui sono nato e ho passato la mia adolescenza, Cagliari.

L'edificio comprendeva all'origine sale da concerto, locali espositivi, spazi per il ristoro, terrazze, cripte sotterranee, giardini, scenografiche scalinate e, sulla sua sommità, una elegante passeggiata con vista panoramica e panchine all'ombra delle palme. Dal dopoguerra in poi questo elefantiaco complesso ha subito un rapido declino nonostante gli sporadici restauri e i tentativi di rilancio, per consegnarsi oggi alla nostra memoria come territorio privilegiato del bighellonamento, dello spaccio cittadino e dei suicidi. Ad uno di quei non rari suicidi assistetti anch'io da ragazzino.

L'immagine della foto è riprodotta in un bianco/nero leggermente sovresposto e tagliata in forma quadrata. Viene mostrata, oltre alla parte laterale destra del bastione, anche una prospettiva dall'alto del viale alberato sottostante con alcune auto parcheggiate e la facciata di un palazzo ottocentesco in cui si proietta la contrastata ombra del bastione stesso. In alto, la foto mostra anche una larga porzione di cielo. Al centro dell'immagine, nel punto in cui la prospettiva inquadra proprio lo spigolo della facciata del bastione, con il suo piatto cornicione che si proietta nel vuoto, l'occhio cade subito su una lontana figuretta un poco sfocata per la scarsa gettata della focale dell'obbiettivo fotografico. Col sorriso sbarazzino e con le mani in tasca, sono io diciassettenne quella figurina; sono proprio dritto in piedi sull'estremità del cornicione prospiciente l'abisso, oltre il parapetto che perimetra la terrazza, proprio sul limite. Non mi reggo a niente e non avrei la possibilità di farlo: mi circonda solo il vuoto. Dietro di me, la prospettiva dei tetti delle case sbiadisce in lontananza nella nebbiolina primaverile. Nel momento dello scatto, concordato a voce col distante fotografo, tento pure di atteggiare la gamba in un accenno di passo verso il nulla, cercando beninteso di mantenere saldo l'equilibrio; purtroppo una rapida folata di vento giusto in quell'attimo mi coglie alla sprovvista e mi irrigidisco sotto l'effetto di una scarica fortissima di adrenalina.

Veleno possente e acidognolo, l'adrenalina nasce in te, pasce in te, ti rafforza i muscoli, tempera i tuoi nervi, rinvigorisce il senso dell'equilibrio, dilata le pupille, focalizza la vertigine, rischiara la mente. E provoca dipendenza. Il mio orrore per lo strapiombo sottostante si è fatto via via più sopportabile, meno paralizzante, mentre brancolavo sul cornicione fischiettando istericamente e cercando la giusta posa per la foto, e in quell'attimo dello scatto, sempre grazie alla magia dell'adrenalina, s'è fatto lieve, mi ha reso evanescente e inamovibile al tempo stesso. Che strano. Solo dopo, scavalcando nuovamente il parapetto per tornare sulla solida terrazza, mi sono sentito svenire. Ricomponendomi con grande stile, proruppi subito in una squillante risata adolescenziale di fronte alle facce dagli occhi sgranati del gruppo d'amici. Rimesso piede "sulla terraferma" e specchiandomi nei loro occhi, ebbi per la prima volta la lucida sensazione del pericolo appena scampato. Prima, avevo la testa avvolta in una nebbia. Di conseguenza, presi pure coscienza che, da quel momento in poi, tutto il tempo che avrei avuto ancora da vivere mi sarebbe stato regalato. E in quanto regalo, potevo sprecarlo come meglio avrei voluto, in piena libertà, sconsideratamente e senza badare a conseguenze, come di fatto è stato fino a oggi. L'idea del Successo, nella vita e nell'arte, anche oggi è unicamente questa per me: riuscire a fermarsi ad appena un passo dallo schianto finale.

Un minuto dopo, scorgemmo sulla terrazza due carabinieri che ci si avvicinavano.

«... l'irresponsabilità apparente del gesto nascondeva a ben vedere una certa "logica" di ferro. "Ho sempre spinto me stesso a pensare e ad agire in modo differente da come ci si aspetta che faccia. Ci si aspetta che un artista faccia quadri, pittura, 'Transavanguardia' (un nuovo movimento pittorico, n.d.r.) oggi nel 1981. Oppure si pretende che l'arte mostri solo l'aspetto più allettante della realtà, quello della piacevolezza del colore e della riconoscibilità del soggetto" ha detto Corte interrogato sulla vicenda e sui suoi effettivi scopi e propositi, e ha aggiunto: "senza togliere niente a chi ha scelto altri tipi di ricerche espressive, l'arte può e deve però anche mostrare ciò che si tende a eliminare dal proprio orizzonte visivo, ciò che ci si rifiuta di vedere: di fatto c'è stata una esplosione dei suicidi tra gli adolescenti in Italia da due anni a questa parte, io documento questa situazione sociale illustrando a mio modo la pulsione di morte in un'ottica da adolescente. Il rock e il cinema contemporaneo rappresentano meglio queste problematiche, in modo diretto e senza censure; l'arte visiva non può restare indietro"».

«Lo scopo del mio lavoro è distruggere la famiglia», affermava un giovane Fassbinder rispondendo ad una falsa intervista nel film "Deutschland Im Herbst" che vidi quando avevo, credo, quindici anni (se ricordo bene, ero uscito con degli amici per andare al cinema ma poi ci separammo: loro preferirono "Grease"). «Grande!» pensavo io, «se ti preme di rifondare la Società dovrai azzerare la sua prima cellula costitutiva, è chiaro!» Ma come potevo farlo io, che la famiglia l'avevo già avuta distrutta dal destino? Ho trovato! Il punto centrale della famiglia non è la bipolarità padre-madre, come sembrava intendere RWF, bensì il terzo polo, il figlio, la prole. E' solo in presenza di un figlio che si può parlare veramente di famiglia. Laonde, occorreva mettere in scena la distruzione del *ragazzo*, la mia propria autodistruzione, il suicidio adolescenziale, lo spappolamento della discendenza. Beh, è poco ma sicuro: in quegli anni ero in buona compagnia, con tanti coetanei molto più determinati di me.

Da allora, la mia attività nell'arte è stata il lungo immobile funerale dell'adolescente suicida. Tutti invecchiano e passano, solo io sto ancora là in bilico sospeso sulla vacuità sottostante. La domanda è: se un artista inizia da giovanissimo a passeggiare fischiettando sugli strapiombi e a farsi pisciare in faccia, e finisce infilandosi un tubo nei testicoli e gonfiandoseli come una palla, *è andato avanti*? No, naturalmente. Non c'è mai stato bisogno di un avanzamento nel lungo immobile funerale dell'adolescente suicida. Vivo un equilibrio senza drastiche fluttuazioni. Da anni io non invecchio; è per questo che sono affascinato e attratto da personaggi rappresentativi di un certo settore – che so, attori, musicisti, scrittori, registi – che si possano dire anzianotti o almeno in una fase avanzata della loro maturità. Che siano in evidente decadenza non solo fisica ma anche in un momento di declino della loro parabola creativa. Rappresentano tutto quello che io non riesco a essere.

Nel corso degli anni mi sono così intossicato di adrenalina, le cui scariche mi procuravo nel rincorrere le situazioni più impossibili per immortalarle fotograficamente, al punto che un medico, visitandomi attorno ai ventun anni, mi diagnosticò una ipertrofia della ghiandola surrenale e un anomalo inspessimento del muscolo cardiaco. Disse con chiarezza che si era instaurata una forma di dipendenza chimica dall'adrenalina come di solito avviene in chi pratica sport estremi o chi si sottoponga a frequenti stress fisici o psichici. Ciò poteva causarmi problemi gastrointestinali, cardiaci, piastrinosi, danni al sistema nervoso centrale e persino glaucoma. Futuri sintomi di invecchiamento precoce e decadenza fisica accelerata.

In realtà, quel medico aveva toppato. Infatti io da allora in pratica non sono mai invecchiato nel fisico. Questo potrebbe essere il mio vero contributo alla Medicina. E' particolarmente chiaro confrontando alcune fotografie delle mie fattezze di oggi con quelle di allora. I miei capelli sono sempre neri, non ho una ruga in volto e la struttura del mio corpo è ancora identica a quella di vent'anni fa. Tutto senza palestra, diete, tinture, lifting, liposuzioni. Credo che dipenda proprio da quelle grosse dosi di adrenalina assunte in gioventù che hanno funzionato come una sorta di cura omeopatica contro l'invecchiamento. Il cervello è la fonte. Per questo io oggi consiglio a tutti i giovani di seguire questa mia prescrizione: iniziate prima che potete a cacciarvi nelle situazioni più pericolose e complicate possibili, inventatene di nuove, cercatevi guai, storiacce sessuali, passeggiate in equilibrio sulla ringhiera del balcone della vostra cameretta… e all'occasione, sfasciate molte vetrine di banche. Farete incetta di adre-nalina per i vostri anni peggiori.

«La vicenda si è infine conclusa senza conseguenze particolari per tutti coloro che vi erano coinvolti. A noialtri profani non resta da augurarci che le "sentenze" del giovane Enrico Corte, forse venate da un pizzico di protervia, stemperino col tempo la loro ansia di esprimere tensioni e problemi più grandi di loro; purtroppo infatti il confine tra la posizione intellettuale di uno studente e la classica fatale "ragazzata" lo abbiamo visto assai spesso oltrepassare sulle pagine della cronaca nera.

C. De.»

Termina così la polaroid di Carlo, o Corrado, Devoto, o Devoti. Con un'istanza un poco paternalistica da parte di un signore che potrebbe in teoria, essere ancora vivo, pur se anziano. Non avrò mai più sue notizie: il suo giornale è fallito poco tempo dopo la pubblicazione dell'articolo su di me, e di lui si son perse le tracce. Con un ricordo confuso ma nel complesso non sgradevole che conservo di quest'uomo conosciuto di sfuggita, devo dire una cosa a suo favore: malgrado le acide conclusioni finali, il suo articolino rimane a distanza di due decenni la cosa meglio scritta su di me e il mio lavoro. Nessun testo di critica d'arte che mi riguarda ha mai avuto quella attenzione al dettaglio, quell'amore nel descrivere tappa dopo tappa lo sviluppo cronologico di un'azione, quella cura nel puntualizzare il pensiero che all'azione artistica sottende, e soprattutto quel rispetto profondo per le parole e le dichiarazioni di un artista. La mia condizione di ragazzino, allora, avrebbe forse richiesto un tono di maggiore sufficienza o di rimprovero, meno spazio e più rapidità nel condannare e archiviare il caso.

No, gli articoli di cronaca nera che prevedeva C. De. non ne ho mai avuti, solo qualcuno nelle assai meno interessanti pagine della cultura. A parte quello relativo all'episodio di una controversa mostra da me ideata nel 1987, intitolata *Cleptoscopica*, chiusa dopo il giorno dell'inaugurazione e che ebbe come conseguenza una mia breve detenzione nonché decisione coatta di abbandonare la mia città natale. E' pur vero che il 18 novembre 1994 chissacome la Polizia scopre in via Bertola a Roma una certa quantità di materiale esplosivo nel cortile abbandonato di un edificio in rovina attiguo al mio studio, insieme ad abbozzi di progetti grafici e una pagina di giornale con articolo e foto del Presidente del Consiglio Italiano Silvio Berlusconi, tutto contenuto in una cartella rossa con sopra scritto col pennarello *1994*. Era proprio il cortile, tutt'ora disabitato, che ancora potete vedere al di là del muro del mio giardino. Tutti i ritrovamenti vennero sequestrati, portati via da un robottino degli artificieri. Effettivamente ciò ha fatto scrivere diversi articoli di cronaca a livello nazionale in cui però non mi si nomina.

Si trattava in realtà dei bozzetti e dei materiali costitutivi una scultura alla quale stavo lavorando, sul tema del terrorismo di Stato e della presa del potere da parte della Destra in Italia, e che si sarebbe dovuta appunto intitolare *1994*. Nasceva dall'interessante idea di modellare dell'esplosivo al plastico così come lo scultore plasma la creta, e dunque mi ero rivolto ad alcuni rappresentanti dei nascenti gruppi Black Blocks romani perché me ne procurassero un po'. Purtroppo tutto quello che potei fortunosamente acquistare fu del tritolo, una miccia e dei detonatori, visto che al momento sul mercato nero il plastico proprio non si trovava. Io ho comprato i materiali per così dire sfusi, con l'intento di manipolare e montare gli esplosivi da me in modo piuttosto intuitivo, fantasioso, ma anche con l'ausilio di un manuale militare. Tenevo tutto quanto nello studio, e in quei giorni ci stavo lavorando sopra.

Dopodiché qualcuno diede una informazione ai poliziotti e questi fecero il loro blitz in via Bertola, perquisendo con cura, com'è ovvio, anche la mia abitazione e lo studio confinante col cortile del ritrovamento. Ma sapete… loro avranno i propri informatori – anche se non ho ben chiaro chi possa aver fatto la soffiata – però anche io ho i miei, che sono abbastanza puntuali per permettermi un seppur tempestivo intervento in extremis. Infatti quella mattina ricevo una improvvisa telefonata da parte di un conoscente il quale in modo molto congestionato mi avvisa che la Polizia è al corrente del contrabbando di esplosivi e che sanno che vi è coinvolto un non meglio precisato residente in via Bertola, nel quartiere di Torpignattara. Il conoscente mi consiglia di agire subito perché la Polizia sta arrivando. Appena riagganciata la cornetta, filo subito a lanciare tutto il materiale compromettente che tenevo in una cartella rossa – gli esplosivi, i detonatori, i bozzetti grafici dell'opera in corso di realizzazione, il foglio di giornale con la foto di Berlusconi che usavo come immagine di riferimento per la scultura – in quella limitrofa proprietà abbandonata oltre il muretto del mio giardino, giusto venti secondi prima dell'irruzione delle Forze dell'Ordine nel mio studio. Così facendo mi sono scrollato di dosso ogni responsabilità agli occhi della legge: nel mio studio non vi era più alcunché di sospetto. L'esplosivo atterra senza deflagrare tra i rifiuti e le macerie del cortile abbandonato che ne attenuano la caduta: l'idea del Successo, nella vita e nell'arte, è sempre quella di riuscire a fermarsi ad appena un pelo dallo schianto finale.

Qualche dubbio nei miei confronti è rimasto, agli occhi dei rappresentanti della Legge… infatti, vista la mia poco classificabile condizione di "artista", per due anni sono stato indagato per sospetto coinvolgimento in attentato nei confronti di Berlusconi, e le perquisizioni nel mio studio si sono susseguite negli anni, con una scusa o con l'altra, da parte di Polizia e Finanza. Poi l'inchiesta fu chiusa in un nulla di fatto. Chissà in quale archivio delle Forze dell'Ordine sarà conservato ciò che resta di quella mia scultura rimasta incompiuta, di quei bozzetti disegnati a mano con tanta cura e poi scambiati per schemi di montaggio di una bomba… Certo, perdendo un'opera ho salvato il culo dalla Polizia; purtroppo in quel frangente non c'era tempo per caricare un rullino e immortalarne il velocissimo lancio oltre il muretto, in un'ulteriore opera d'arte fotografica, ma… ragazzi, che flash d'adrenalina che è stato…

Riprendo la parola e sottolineo che, nel corso degli anni, Corte ha dovuto risolvere qualche problema legale dovuto al carattere del suo lavoro. Ma il suo progetto intacca la moralità diffusa senza nulla di gratuito, stridente o giovanilistico. Gli echi della ribellione generazionale non stanno qui e non riguardano il rigore silenzioso della sua necessità espressiva. Non vi è ricerca dello "scandalo" a tutti i costi, quel tipo di scandalo spesso perseguito per scopi meramente pubblicitari. Per l'artista l'operazione attraversa i riferimenti culturali di un periodo storico, le zone del privilegio creativo, i poli delle migliori evidenze comunicative. Non poteva, quindi, che manipolare e filtrare i linguaggi influenti del nostro frangente storico. Come la musica, il cinema, il fumetto, il design, il videoclip, la pubblicità… mondi che si metabolizzano dentro le opere in forme autonome e inaspettate, seguendo un formidabile disincanto che si amalgama col cinismo del talento.

Corte non appartiene a gruppi o storie collettive, non si esprime con un singolo linguaggio, viaggia su formule di ricercata e onesta originalità. Quando manipola costumi sociali, retorica cattolica, poltiglia medioborghese, non fa mai sconti al populismo d'accatto, ai comunismi inficianti, alle strumentalizzazioni. Se ancora esiste un terreno anarchico su cui edificare una costruzione tra istinto e cultura, Corte ne rappresenta un baluardo prezioso. Impossibile confinarlo o catalogarlo in una corsia, così come la singola opera chiede una lettura aperta su livelli paralleli: da un primo gradino di evidente impatto formale ai successivi step che affondano, strato su strato, nel cuore dei significati reconditi. A noi scovarli nel tempo, assorbendo fluidi di memoria individuale e collettiva, pezzi di rimosso, membrane di libertà pagana. A noi la libertà di scegliere livelli e ordini di lettura, sacrificando o incensando ciò che percepiamo e sentiamo.

L'ansia di "distruzione della famiglia", di cui parlava l'artista adolescente, significa questo: Corte di fatto non si è mai "sposato" (finora) con un unico stile artistico ma ha scelto la promiscuità di interessi. La *stratificazione*, non solo la semplice contaminazione, è un altro aspetto connotativo del percorso. Non esistono opere di Corte che prendano una strada in modo unilaterale. Al contrario, qualsiasi progetto agisce su un molteplice parallelismo: quello di una struttura progettuale che supera qualsiasi apparenza della superficie e agisce su sensi molteplici; e poi di un modello estetico in cui l'opera aggiunge materiali e dettagli lungo un organizzato e complesso organismo. La struttura progettuale implica una speculare dialettica con la ramificazione prismatica del cervello. Corte rappresenta un raro caso in cui l'opera registra e sintetizza le pulsioni complesse del mondo cerebrale, comportandosi come farebbe un cervello con braccia e mani creative. Il modello formale nasce come diretta conseguenza del progetto, stratificando gli elementi necessari alla definizione di uno sguardo liminale tra psiche ed esterno.

Continuiamo. *Youthanasia 2* e *Youthanasia 3* (ill. pp. 97-99), quest'ultima in due pannelli, sono varianti dell'opera *Cheese* a qualche mese di distanza (ma senza la registrazione di suoni). La città è la stessa, la location è differente, la posa è da seduto ma l'equilibrio è altrettanto precario. Queste immagini furono all'inizio scambiate per errore, da alcuni critici disattenti, per abili fotomontaggi. Qualcuno le classificò come esempi di Performance Art, cosa altrettanto inesatta poiché vennero realizzate in segreto, fugacemente e senza alcun pubblico, a parte le persone coinvolte nella loro realizzazione pratica. *Youthanasia 2* mostra l'artista seduto sulla sedia in equilibrio sul parapetto di una terrazza panoramica con 25 metri di strapiombo, inquadrato in campo lungo, e potrebbe sembrare una semplice cartolina da "belvedere" cittadino, se non fosse per la piccola figuretta dell'artista seduto sul cornicione e per la presenza di un Ritaglio-Ritratto sovrapposta su un lato; *Youthanasia 3* è invece uno scatto della stessa posa fatto da una postazione più ravvicinata, diviso in due segmenti panoramici in cui il brivido dell'azione quasi si stempera nella convenzionale prospettiva da cartolina.

Presupponendo un rigore assoluto nel selezionare i propri riferimenti, ecco qualcuno che rischia mentalmente e fisicamente, che si sottopone alle elastiche contrazioni del vuoto, che guarda in basso e in alto, che definisce le nostre paure attraverso le sue paure. Solo chi ha davvero paura, d'altronde, tocca i vertici del coraggio. E crea alcuni segnali visivi con cui captare e metabolizzare la nostra vertigine sotterranea. Corte dimostra i confini fisici del coraggio, sviluppando opere che dilatano la percezione sensoriale e mettono il corpo davanti al pericolo reale della morte. Sviluppa il volo situazionista di Yves Klein in una dimensione immobile e solo fotografica. Diversamente da Klein, non sceglie il salto poiché confinerebbe con la definitiva coscienza della fine: Corte cerca il gesto scultoreo in una ipnotica coscienza del rischio. E il ricordo va alla poesia aerea di Philippe Petit, l'uomo in maglia nera che nel 1974 camminò per 45 minuti su un filo tra le Twin Towers di New York. Un gesto assoluto e definitivo, immobile nel cielo come la memoria iconografica dell'utopia.

Anche Corte cammina sul filo della vita, e non sceglie di morire. Perché l'artista sperimenta la morte nel proprio lavoro, usandola dentro le sintomatiche tensioni della vita più radicale. La materia organica e la sfida con la morte appartengono alla volontà di un artista lucidamente allucinato più che "semplice" visionario: una partita adulta dello sguardo immortale, logico eppure folle secondo la natura divinatoria di chi crea archetipi visivi con gli ingredienti stessi del corpo. Corte usa la fisicità essenziale, il legame tra mente e corporalità, il coraggio come principio interiore. Non dimenticando il codice stilistico dell'ironia, vero bilanciatore di un progetto serio e mai faceto, universale nella grammatica, inclassificabile nelle soluzioni espressive.

A volte, in questa tipologia di opere che stiamo analizzando, un Ritaglio-Ritratto su carta si sovrappone alla stampa fotografica, come avviene in *Youthanasia 2* o in altre opere del periodo come la serie *Der Weg Zum Kubismus* oppure in *Idolatrina*, in cui l'artista si rappresenta nell'atto di farsi pisciare in faccia. In questi casi si tratta di ritratti di profili delle persone che hanno aiutato tecnicamente l'artista a realizzare i lavori (per esempio il fotografo, o forse l'ignoto "pisciatore"…). In particolare, *Idolatrina* (ill. p. 96) ci mostra un'immagine dai contenuti assai forti che ha pochi raffronti nell'arte del periodo a livello internazionale, e nessuno in ambito italiano. Impostata sulla base di abili giochi di luce/ombra, vagamente asimmetrica, rivela in realtà una struttura rigorosa che sfrutta il dinamismo del modulo geometrico, in questo caso triangolare, che troveremo in molte opere successive. *Idolatrina* sviluppa ancor di più l'ossessione visiva per il volto come spazio vuoto, da riempire, da sporcare: metafora per inedite gioie/dolori da sperimentare solo attraverso la ridefinizione dei concetti convenzionali di "identità" e persino di "dignità".

Der Weg Zum Kubismus (ill. pp. 102-104) è un ciclo di opere fotografiche nato ancora da una storia particolare e contorta, il che ci fa capire come il flusso degli eventi della vita e l'invenzione del momento siano le cose che maggiormente alimentano lo sviluppo del lavoro di

Enrico Corte, al di là dell'approfondire una tecnica artistica o uno stile riconoscibile. Una lettera anonima e vagamente ricattatoria giunta a casa della famiglia Corte nel 1981 segnalava la presenza del giovane artista in strade o viali cittadini ove si esercita la prostituzione maschile. La lettera, sgrammaticata forse in modo artificioso per renderne meno riconoscibile l'autore, era firmata "un amico di famiglia" ed era corredata di fotografie che avrebbero dovuto raffigurare Corte nell'atto di adescare i clienti per strada, direttamente dalle loro automobili. L'autore della lettera lascia intendere di essere in possesso di altre fotografie e si dichiara disponibile a giungere ad un "accordo" per la loro consegna. Al di là del fatto che l'azione del prostituirsi sia stata vera o presunta («Ero il tipo di ragazzo che le figlie non vorrebbero veder frequentare i loro genitori», ci dice con malizia Corte), è interessante la reazione dell'artista: realizza per conto proprio altre fotografie sullo stesso tema, posando in prima persona, e poi le presenta assieme alle prime come fossero tutte una sua opera. In queste immagini va notato l'uso accorto della solita maglietta a righe, ricorrente anche nelle opere fotografiche precedenti, indossata quale "divisa" tipica dell'adolescente medio.

Inoltre Corte aveva presenti alcune trasmissioni televisive in cui venisse oscurata la fisionomia facciale di individui che, per esempio durante interviste o riprese compromettenti, necessitassero di conservare l'anonimato; la tecnologia del tempo permetteva, per la prima volta, una pixelazione quadrangolare del volto o di altre parti dell'immagine televisiva, così da rendere irriconoscibile il soggetto. Negli anni precedenti si usava sovrapporre all'immagine una sorta di rozza sfocatura o un bollo nero nei punti compromettenti. Corte coglie subito l'analogia visiva di una tale pixelazione con la pittura cubista, o con una idea semplificata che si ha del Cubismo. Usando l'aerografo e le mascherine, sovrappone sui volti dei suoi presunti "clienti" e sulle targhe delle loro automobili, presenti nelle fotografie, alcune griglie di pixel che ne impediscono del tutto l'identificazione, e poi intitola l'intera serie di immagini fotografiche *Der Weg Zum Kubismus*, *La Via Del Cubismo*, ricalcando il titolo di un libro scritto nel 1920 da Daniel-Henry Kahnweiler, primo mercante di Pablo Picasso. Sotto un gioco di parole, come da consuetudine, torna il tema del mettere in gioco il corpo. Un ritmo folle per dilatarlo e comprimerlo, distruggerlo per recuperarlo, cambiarlo e ribaltarlo… assumendo nell'azione tutti i caratteri di cui abbiamo finora parlato. Il corpo costruisce l'opera nel suo districato groviglio individuale, sociale, culturale. E attraverso le relazioni con l'esterno moltiplica la lettura del mondo stesso.

Queste opere furono proposte da Corte per un mostra celebrativa del centenario della nascita di Picasso (1981) organizzata da una rivista d'arte italiana, ma vennero rifiutate. Furono acquistate in blocco l'anno successivo, alla prima personale di Corte, diciannovenne, in un museo. "L'amico di famiglia" non ha potuto in quel caso fare rivendicazioni di sorta.

Già presente nelle fotografie del gruppo *Der Weg Zum Kubismus*, con i loro scenari di viali e giardinetti oscuri in cui si esercitano morbose pratiche sessuali, circondati da palazzi dai cento occhi, l'elemento del giardino urbano e della "natura inurbata" viene espresso al meglio nell'installazione multimediale che Corte realizza nel 1981 con Andrea Nurcis, la *Grande Esposizione di Rarità Botaniche*. Da questo momento inizia il sodalizio tra EC e AN: Nurcis è nato nella stessa città di Corte e non formerà mai con lui una "coppia d'artisti", ma sarà comunque per i vent'anni successivi il partner privilegiato di molti impegnativi progetti "a quattro mani" (o a sei, quando i due decidono di "giocare al rialzo" includendo un terzo collaboratore nel loro sodalizio). L'idea che sta alla base delle occasionali ma ripetute collaborazioni tra Corte e Nurcis è proprio quella di creare una "terza via" in un mercato dell'arte che riconosce come operatori canonici sia l'artista singolo e individualista, chiuso nel suo mondo, sia la coppia d'artisti, spesso unita anche nella vita. Corte e Nurcis rappresentano, negli anni, una situazione che sfugge a queste convenzioni per proporre un'attività più aperta alle collaborazioni e ai vari incontri della vita in cui, comunque, si privilegia sempre in partenza il rapporto tra loro due.

Le *Rarità Botaniche* di Corte e Nurcis (ill. pp. 105-109) sono piante, germogli, rizomi, funghi, arbusti e infiorescenze realizzati in cera colorata, paraffina, vaselina, sostanze viniliche e sintetiche unite a lembi di reali vegetali come spine e foglie secche. La loro realizzazione è fantasiosa ma precisa e accurata, direi illusionistica, e ha richiesto mesi di lavoro, con un evidente riferimento alle ceroplastiche anatomiche ottocentesche dei maestri italiani. Il loro aspetto è abnorme, deforme, traboccante bubboni ed escrescenze maligne: bave filamentose intrappolano insetti (veri), radici aeree si nutrono di liquami sanguinolenti dentro provette da scienziato pazzo, muffe e funghi corrodono tronchi carnosi, innesti improbabili come amplessi devianti trasudano succhi gastrici. I vari esemplari botanici sono stati inseriti come aborti in apposite teche di vetro, a loro volta collocate sopra piedistalli in laminato finto-marmo con tarsie colorate che ricordano il mobilio kitsch anni '60. Le teche e i piedistalli furono collocati in vari angoli strategici di un orto botanico cittadino, e mostrati al pubblico. Sotto il sole estivo, le cere e le varie sostanze di cui eran costituite le piante iniziarono lentamente a stillare e autodistruggersi, creando un effetto di palpitante sofferenza che rendeva ancora più vivi gli esemplari biologici. L'installazione era completata da alcuni altoparlanti nascosti tra il fogliame che diffondevano le registrazioni di versi d'uccelli tropicali, distorte da vari filtri elettronici (eco, riverbero, tremolo ecc.) fino all'irriconoscibile.

Un testo esplicativo affisso all'ingresso dell'orto botanico presentava l'installazione attraverso una storia di pura fantasia, ma credibile e precisa fin nei dettagli e riferimenti storici, secondo la quale le mostruose piante furono create in laboratorio da alcuni botanici tedeschi alla fine dell'ottocento quasi come un preannuncio delle teorie lombrosiane o dei deliri nazisti sulle "razze degenerate", e i pochi esemplari di quella serie di esperimenti originali, sopravvissuti negli anni, furono in seguito esposti in una serie di mostre itineranti per varie città della Germania. Il calendario di queste mostre fittizie di vegetali improbabili veniva fatto iniziare il 26 febbraio 1962 a Monaco di Baviera per terminare il 21 giugno 1963 a Berlino (rispettivamente le date di nascita di Nurcis e di Corte). E così come gli anni '60 venivano citati nella fattura kitsch dei piedistalli, una serie di dipinti a imitazione di manifesti, di chiara impostazione grafica Jugendstil, erano affissi all'interno dell'orto botanico come altrettanti reperti delle fasulle mostre itineranti. Bisogna aggiungere che alcune frasi scritte in una lingua tedesca in parte "maccheronica" rendevano chiaro, ad uno sguardo attento, il carattere parodistico dei manifesti. L'affiorare di una vaga sensibilità goliardica aiuta a situare l'intero lavoro all'interno della tematica "adolescenziale" già presente nelle opere precedenti (l'artista adolescente parla di ciò che conosce meglio).

Quest'opera ambientale di carattere effimero e autodistruttivo venne realizzata da Corte e Nurcis dopo un periodo di permanenza in Germania e intendeva essere un omaggio alla cultura tedesca in generale, molto amata dai due artisti, e al nuovo cinema tedesco del periodo (in particolare alla figura di Rainer Werner Fassbinder, da loro incontrato di persona a Venezia nel 1980, puntualmente destinato ad autodistruggersi un anno esatto dopo la realizzazione delle *Rarità Botaniche.* Preveggenza? In un'ottica spettrospettiva Corte parlerebbe di "celebrazione commemorativa anticipata").

In questo Giardino del Bene e del Male, dove la morbosità vegeta naturalmente e la natura si sviluppa logicamente in aborti, convivono in equilibrio (sul vuoto?) innocenza ed esperienza, come una tragica commedia dell'età adolescenziale. L'installazione nel suo complesso vive una dimensione a sé stante lontana dal forte interesse per la pittura neoespressionista che caratterizza l'inizio degli anni '80 in Italia e all'estero, ma anticipa il gusto anni '90 per l'aberrazione genetica, l'innesto biologico e la protesi "Post-human" (in questo caso, *Post-vegetal*). Al suo interno vigono le peculiarissime, contaminate e contorte (spettrospettive) leggi della storia e della biologia che caratterizzano l'universo labirintico di riferimenti e invenzioni formali su cui si svilupperà tutta l'arte di Enrico Corte. Occorre anche evidenziare un ulteriore aspetto, pienamente spettrospettivo, che si manifesta attraverso le *Rarità Botaniche* per poi svilupparsi nel corso del tempo attraverso altre operazioni analoghe o differenti: il gusto parodistico per la *celebrazione*, per l'*anniversario*, per la *ricorrenza*. Questo elemento concettuale era già presente nell'anno lavorativo rappresentato dagli autoritratti *250 Mele Marce*, come anche in *Der Weg Zum Kubismus* (il centenario di Picasso) e diverrà sempre più evidente nelle opere a venire sia come modalità per demistificare la *parata* della cultura ufficiale, sia come possibilità di re-interpretare una medesima opera a distanza di tempo sotto ottiche dissimili. Infatti le ceree *Rarità Botaniche*, che già contengono l'elemento della ricorrenza celebrativa attraverso il calendario fittizio delle mostre negli anni '60, verranno in parte recuperate e utilizzate da Corte in seguito (contraddicendo così il loro carattere effimero) in alcune opere commemorative dei loro 15 anni (1981-1996, ill. p. 109) e del ventennale (1981-2001, ill. p. 267).

La citazione del kitsch multicolore dei primi anni '60 è di alcuni caratteristici tipi di decorazione d'interni o di edifici architettonici, ricorre in molti lavori di Corte dell'inizio degli anni '80, ed ha anch'esso un significato di ambigua celebrazione della sua nascita, ma in chiave allucinatoria e necrotica. Un'opera come *Il Balcone: è il mio strumento di suicidio preferito* e le serie di *Balconi* susseguitisi nel giro di cinque anni (ill. pp. 111-115) chiariscono bene il concetto. Affascinato fin da bambino da una tipologia di decorazione edilizia popolare italiana che prevedeva, nelle facciate dei palazzi, inserti di mosaici a tassellini quadrati multicolori in corrispondenza di balconi o altre parti strutturali analoghe, l'artista ricrea quel dato tipo di mosaico usando materiali originali dell'epoca e lo applica su pannelli di dimensioni simili al prospetto di un balcone di condominio popolare. Ne risultano dei quadri a mosaico di carattere astratto, con una gamma di colori mediamente più vivace e dagli accostamenti più stridenti e fastidiosi per l'occhio rispetto ai reali mosaici degli anni '60. Su questi mosaici Corte incolla, ancora una volta, alcuni dei suoi Ritagli-Ritratti di carta piegata e tagliuzzata (ignoriamo se vi sia un rapporto diretto tra la singola opera e la persona ritratta nel foglio applicato sopra, ma è probabile che si tratti solo di conoscenze o incontri del momento).

Il balcone è ancora un luogo da Belvedere ma è in effetti anche un adattissimo strumento di suicidio. La decorazione anni '60 ci parla della nascita dell'artista, il Ritaglio-Ritratto suggerisce ancora la compresenza ineliminabile della pulsione di morte. Il lavoro manuale che sta dietro ai mosaici questi *Balconi* contiene già in sé un tale sforzo per la mano e per l'occhio da implicare un rapporto sadomasochista col proprio corpo. Corte afferma di aver subito un calo della vista permanente in seguito all'aver lavorato così a lungo su tassellini dai contrasti ipnotici e stridenti. E vedremo svilupparsi in varie opere future il concetto *percezione dell'immagine = dolore*. Dal punto di vista tecnico, l'artista ha anche ampliato la gamma di colori standard delle piastrelline di ceramica dei mosaici, gamma limitata alle esigenze dell'edilizia del tempo, usando velature di smalti per vetro stese su alcuni tassellini in modo da creare opere più variopinte. Perfezionismo.

I *Balconi* sono anche le opere che più di tutte le altre hanno richiesto una preparazione in base a bozzetti e prove di colore, per la implicita precisione della loro fattura; di solito Corte non esegue bozzetti preparatori dei suoi lavori, ma passa subito dall'idea alla realizzazione senza ripensamenti di rilievo. Gli ultimi *Balconi* hanno un carattere differente rispetto ai primi, e il loro mosaico mostra immagini di tipo figurativo: *Bal-coma 1* e *Bal-coma 2* (ill. pp. 113-115) già dal gioco di parole del titolo rendono esplicito il riferimento alla morte attraverso il tema del ricovero ospedaliero e del grafico da encefalogramma piatto. L'artista stesso ritrae le sue fattezze a mosaico mentre giace, in presumibile equilibrio tra vita e morte, sul letto della clinica.

La connivenza tra immagine e suono, o musica, non visibile nei *Balconi*, ritorna in una opera composita, con quattro fotografie che ritraggono l'artista di fronte a una sua pittura, inglobate in una struttura plastica assieme a due frammenti di nastro magnetico. *Marble Fever, Marble Junkie, Marble Hustler, Marblefucker* (ill. p. 116) è il titolo di quest'opera realizzata nel 1983 durante un soggiorno a Londra. Il quadro che appare alle spalle dell'artista nelle quattro fotografie, orientato e illuminato in modi diversi, è una pittura a smalto su vetro imitante le venature del marmo, e si rapporta quindi alla decorazione kitsch dei piedistalli delle *Rarità Botaniche* e di altre opere a venire. I frammenti di nastro magnetico, inseriti nella struttura portante dell'opera, rimandano a una registrazione di un dialogo in inglese tra Corte e un non meglio precisato individuo, frammenti di una contrattazione sul prezzo di qualcosa che potrebbe essere sia il quadro del finto-marmo come anche una prestazione sessuale fornita dall'artista. L'opera implica ancora una dimensione di sospensione ambigua tra devianza e immolazione in un contesto di raggelata freddezza di pittura e materiali; la bassa qualità visiva delle fotografie e le allampanate espressioni del ventenne Corte parlano di una opacità torbida, di una problematica scelta di vita, di un rito di passaggio obbligato nel percorso della propria esperienza.

Un rapporto tra immagine e suono è chiaramente presente nella piccola opera del 1984 *Tra i Solchi* (ill. p. 117), rielaborazione di un quadro fotografico di due anni precedente, *Il Bacio* (ill. p. 116). *Tra i Solchi* è assai simile a una "cartolina sonora" come le si produceva negli anni '50 e '60 e di fatto Corte, per realizzarla, si è affidato a una vecchia ditta in disuso specializzata in souvenir del genere: cartoline postali sulla cui superficie, oltre all'immagine della città, si trovava un rivestimento in vinile trasparente con incisi dei solchi musicali da suonare sul giradischi (di solito si trattava di musica folcloristica o canzonette popolari del luogo). L'immagine di *Tra i Solchi*, come quella de *Il Bacio* da cui deriva, è un anomalo amplesso tra lontane parti del corpo; la musica incisa sulla sua superficie è un brano elettronico di Corte dal titolo *Razzi che non si preoccupano di esplodere*.

Ancora il finto marmo campeggia in un opera del 1982, *Marmo Malato*: una pittura a smalto su formica rossa che non imita il marmo ma i laminati che imitano il marmo. E' un simulacro di un simulacro, e porta con sé i segnali della sua menzogna: due piccoli altoparlanti rotti, come nere escrescenze tumorali. Vi è ancora un rapporto con la diffusione del suono, ma in un'ottica di inefficacia e impotenza. La freddezza tombale dell'opera, al confine dell'inespressivo, la doppiezza della rappresentazione, l'handicap tecnico che suggerisce, tutto parla di una sfiducia nelle regole dell'Arte. Ma l'irrompere del flusso degli eventi ancora una volta surriscalda l'atmosfera. Durante la sua prima mostra personale in un museo d'arte contemporanea, Corte preleva un cospicuo gruppo di handicappati fisici da una vicina clinica ortopedica e li fotografa nell'atto di osservare l'opera *Marmo Malato*. Ottenendo così una ulteriore opera composta da dieci fotografie di altrettanti disabili, intitola la serie *Il Sistema dell'Arte* (ill. p. 118): lo scetticismo, il distacco, la critica e la contrapposizione altrettanto aggressiva nei confronti di quei meccanismi dell'establishment artistico che all'inizio degli anni '80 iniziavano ad apparire nella loro ferocia.

Anche un'opera fotografica come *Disegno (Schizzo)* ci parla dei primissimi anni '80 (ill. p. 119). L'immagine mostra affinità con la precedente *Idolatrina*, ma vi sono alcune rilevanti differenze. Il volto dell'artista diciannovenne è schizzato da alcune tracce di sperma che compongono una sorta di "disegno" astratto sui suoi lineamenti. L'unico altro elemento che vi appare è un lembo di corpo villoso, presumibilmente maschile, fuori fuoco, che entra di sguincio nell'obliqua inquadratura. Lo schizzo di sperma potrebbe essere il risultato di una auto-masturbazione dell'artista, ma la presenza di un altro corpo che si intuisce incombere oltre il taglio dell'inquadratura colloca forse l'azione in un ambito di raffronto omoerotico.

L'intento di Corte era quello di creare un'opera col minor numero di elementi possibile, unicamente col *vuoto* attorno al proprio volto (lui direbbe che il suo vero scopo era essere «l'artista più bello sulla piazza»… intendendo che gli anni '80 mostrano un grande *vuoto* dell'ideologia. La forma è sempre contenuto *precipitato*). L'acconciatura dei capelli, l'espressione, l'inquadratura, il bianco/nero e il taglio delle luci rimandano a un certo gusto revivalistico della posa fotografica anni '50 e '60 che ritroviamo nelle copertine di dischi di molto Techno-pop degli anni '80. Ma oltre l'aspetto visivo, l'opera ci parla di un momento dei primi anni '80 in cui prevale la disinibizione sessuale e l'AIDS non è ancora diventato l'incubo di una generazione (anzi, le informazioni sul morbo erano ancora limitatissime).

Incredibilmente quest'opera, più di tutte le altre, sarà destinata a creare molti problemi all'artista nei suoi rapporti con le gallerie d'arte. Non era solo impossibile esporla, ma ha provocato, all'epoca, reazioni di grande aggressività da parte di diversi (praticamente tutti) galleristi in Italia e la giovane età dell'artista creava un ulteriore elemento di disturbo. Ciò si spiega col fatto che fino a quel momento nell'arte italiana non sono presenti altre opere, almeno di chiaro ambito contemporaneo, che trattino esplicitamente l'omosessualità. Forse a riguardo si può risalire ad alcuni disegni di De Pisis degli anni '30, prodotti però per un mercato sotterraneo e non per i circuiti espositivi ufficiali dell'epoca. Nel dopoguerra, Informale, Pop Art, Arte Povera, Transavanguardia e il Concettuale in Italia evitano di affrontare una tematica che invece è ben presente in altri ambiti della cultura come cinema, musica o letteratura. Così un artista ci rivela quanto a volte l'arte visiva possa essere indietro rispetto al proprio tempo.

Corte non ha comunque mai inteso includersi in un contesto di "arte omosessuale", come spesso si è visto fare da altri artisti nel corso degli anni. Esistono diverse sue opere con tematiche eterosessuali seppur venate di paranoia e necrofilia, come il doppio ritratto fotografico suo e della giovane fidanzata truccata da un professionista di maquillage per cadaveri, intitolato *La mia metà, il suo doppio* (1984). In fin dei conti Corte può dire di sé: «Ho il tipo di fisico che può interessare maschi, femmine, e varie categorie intermedie. E per un certo periodo non ho trovato necessario dire no ai loro vari approcci». E di recente lo si è sentito affermare in modo categorico: «Mi sono rotto il cazzo della gente che vuole scopare».

In realtà pochi artisti affrontano i risvolti del sesso con raffinata e capillare trasversalità come Corte. Qui non si tratta di scherzare sul feticismo, sui temi della dominanza e sottomissione, sui limiti fattibili di corpo e dolore. Per Corte sesso e sessualità non appaiono in forme facili o pornograficamente didascaliche. Tornano liquidi organici, culture della sofferenza, relazioni estreme, forme di coraggio, e diventano il percorso mai scontato nella sessualità, prima psichica e poi fisica, di un artista senza inibizioni. L'inibizione è il segno motivato di un limite autoinflitto. La liberazione dal limite segna la rottura completa del moralismo a favore della moralità soggettiva.

Le opere fotografiche di Corte sono intervallate da pitture e sculture che vivono la dimensione spettrospettiva, riprendono e sviluppano temi precedenti e creano nuove simbiosi di materiali, elementi, personaggi, in una strategia di coerenza e non di eclettismo: è lo sguardo a 360° dell'artista in cima a un cornicione, su un'altura nel centro del Mare Mediterraneo. *I Demonietti Psichici* (ill. p. 120), scultura del 1983, ha rapporti con le domestiche mostruosità attorno ai letti e alle culle che abbiamo visto nei *Risucchi Gastrici* e nei *Riflussi Stoici*, ricorda i bulbi oculari di *Penta-Portraits* e ricicla uno dei cuscini di seta e sangue di *Per Strada*.

Ma appare per la prima volta il ricorrente personaggio chiamato *Demonietto Psichico*, che qui si mostra nella variante dell'atomino-marzianetto; lo vedremo apparire saltuariamente, anche come elemento incluso in opere più complesse al pari del *Ritaglio-Ritratto*, sotto varie fattezze, metamorfosi, mascheramenti. Il Demonietto Psichico è il pupazzetto – diavoletto – misirizzi – palloncino – feto – gnomo – frocio – mimo – alieno – brufolo – herpes – testicolo – ernia – nodulo – macchiolina di sangue infetto ecc. ecc., ma può manifestarsi anche come ferro forgiato per marchiare a fuoco (lasciando sulla carne il monogramma antropomorfico EC, cf. ill. pp. 122, 123), come bollino rosso da apporre sul quadro appena venduto (…«il vero Demone Personale di ogni artista», E.C. 1985), come Palla N° 8 (il popolare ed economico *fortune-teller* americano), come gettone per il gioco d'azzardo, e altro ancora. Come precisa lo stesso artista:

[Registrato: 7 Febbraio 2000 – estratto]
Il Demonietto Psichico è anche una citazione simbolica della leggenda urbana della "Luna Rossa" – o della sua variante "Occhio Rosso" – che apparirebbe agli artisti persi nella Notte del Dubbio, nel momento cruciale del loro percorso creativo, quando occorre compiere una scelta da cui dipende la possibilità di lasciare un'impronta nella Storia.

In breve, il Demonietto è la sintesi corporea di un'intera tensione creativa, dell'*azzardo* della creazione. E' una formula visiva che ritorna nel tempo e nelle opere, di certo come un'ossessione, e dunque un simbolo unificato del freudiano *Perturbante* (Unheimliche) nelle sue varie incarnazioni attraverso le età dell'uomo. In quanto elemento visivo riconoscibile con facilità, persino simpatico e "accattivante", il Demonietto strutturalmente assolve al compito di catturare l'attenzione dello spettatore più distratto e guidarlo, diciamo pure "iniziarlo", attraverso i perigliosi percorsi dell'opera d'arte. Un po' psicopompo, un po' specchietto per le allodole.

Protagonisti di un quadro dall'aspetto puerile, dalle forme sintetizzate, compiono il loro girotondo dentro una illustrazione da testo didattico per l'infanzia: sono *I Fantastici Demonietti Psichici* (ill. p. 35), sospesi tra microcosmo e macrocosmo a spiegarci le leggi della Vita come reali esseri ultraterreni. Ma attenzione: come in molti Ritagli-Ritratti, questo quadro si appende in base a un bizzarro sistema di gancetti che non si trovano dove dovrebbero e che collocano l'ingenua e fanciullesca pittura in una prospettiva di devianza totale: *Le Catastrofi ai Testicoli* è il secondo titolo dell'opera (il "doppio titolo" è una caratteristica frequente in Corte), che gioca sia sull'allitterazione fonica che sul riferimento alle forme sferiche e all'idea di regressione infantile come pulsione di morte. L'opera è una maschera della castrazione, un'altra Minaccia Suprema. Il quadro di un bambino dipinto da un adulto parla dell'impossibilità di crescere, così come i Ritagli-Ritratti sono giochi da bambini sconvenienti nell'età matura.

Nel frattempo Corte continua a sfidare le leggi dell'equilibrio sul vuoto in opere fotografiche come *Abisspettiva* e soprattutto *Il Faro*, che risulterà essere l'ultima di questo tipo. In confronto agli scatti precedenti, *Il Faro* (ill. p. 121) ha come scenario uno spazio non pubblico ma privato: la terrazza di un condominio. L'intento dell'artista era quello di farsi illuminare su un cornicione da un largo fascio luminoso sul tipo dei riflettori della Polizia, ma poi, una volta sul luogo, ci si rese conto che il faretto autoalimentato collocato sulla terrazza di fronte non era abbastanza potente e riusciva a illuminare a malapena la figura dell'artista. Il fotografo, sulla terrazza di fronte, controllava sia lo scatto della fotografia che il fascio luminoso, e davanti a lui l'artista in posa diventa egli stesso un Faro (un Faro per l'umanità?), collocato così in alto proprio nelle vicinanze del porto. Tutto questo nella miracolistica insaputa dei residenti del palazzo, uno dei quali in quel momento stava riassestando la stanza da letto a pochi metri di distanza dall'azione (come appare nella finestra illuminata). Dal punto di vista tecnico, l'immagine fotografica de *Il Faro* è più professionale delle altre, come anche l'opera nel suo insieme appare riuscita al punto da dubitare di poter fare di meglio; per questo motivo Corte ha smesso di produrre immagini simili.

Ma non sono quasi mai interessi di tipo tecnicistico a far nascere il progetto di un'opera d'arte. L'opera origina dalle occasioni imprevedibili che la vita offre giorno per giorno, dagli incontri fortuiti che permettono a una idea vaga e indefinibile di realizzarsi. E l'apertura alla vita controbilancia così la pulsione di morte tante volte proposta da Corte come modello estetico. Un esempio tipico è *Il Film Della Vita* (ill. pp. 124-127), la prima opera che ingloba direttamente e stabilmente un cadavere umano. Un reale cadavere che con la sua lenta decomposizione fa parte integrante dell'opera fin dal suo concepimento, seppur occultato alla vista da una lapide in marmo. E' il risultato di una storia particolarissima svoltasi per un lungo arco di tempo in cui convivono i principali, contrastanti ingredienti dell'arte: lucidità e allucinazione, furbizia e devozione, nonché una buona dose di "stupefacente" cinismo.

Ne *Il Film Della Vita* il "sogno degli anni '80" espresso nel 1982 da *Disegno (Schizzo)* come epoca di disinibizione, edonismo e piacere, mostra a soli due anni di distanza il suo volto di pietra. Non può che essere l'artista a parlarne in prima persona. Ancora una volta emerge dalle sue parole il singolare rapporto con la realtà del proprio tempo, certi aspetti della quale si preferisce non vedere. Una realtà afferrata giusto un secondo prima che sfugga sotto i piedi, anche se non ci si trova in bilico su un cornicione, e poi vissuta in modo intenso e ossessivo dall'artista fino al punto di modellarla come morbida creta.

[Registrato: 12 Giugno 2003]
Più o meno attorno al 1983 iniziai a chiedermi se il cosiddetto "film della vita" – come ci piace chiamare quel rapido susseguirsi delle immagini di tutti gli istanti della propria esistenza condensati in un attimo solo, che pare si verifichi nel momento supremo del nostro decesso – si svolgesse in modo lineare secondo uno schema cronologico e narrativo del tipo inizio-svolgimento-fine che coerentemente vada dalla nascita alla morte appunto, oppure, cosa secondo me assai probabile, seguisse l'andamento contrario "riavvolgendosi" su sé stesso e partendo non dalla prima immagine della vita bensì proprio dall'attimo della morte, vissuto dal soggetto in quell'esatto momento, per andare via via supersonicamente indietro fino all'atto della nascita, fino al buio della pre-nascita, lo schermo bianco in cui si parificano Vita e Morte.

La problematica a questo riguardo mi sembrava affascinante e, prima di affrontare la complicata questione della possibilità che una successione visiva così ampia da coprire l'arco temporale di un'esistenza umana si potesse sintetizzare in un unico attimo (mantenendo al tempo stesso una "leggibilità" percettiva senza fondersi in un caos indeterminato e inconcludentemente poco espressivo), iniziai a pensare a come attuare una verifica sullo sviluppo sequenziale di un fenomeno di tal fatta, da alcuni considerato inoltre niente più che una diceria o una leggenda. Io non potevo di certo, direttamente in prima persona, sottopormi all'esperienza. Occorreva trovare almeno un soggetto che si trovasse a vivere quella situazione al tempo stesso particolare e consuetissima di "stare per morire", e che soprattutto avesse la disponibilità d'animo, nonché l'energia fisica residua, per comunicarmi *in un baleno*, prima di spirare, i dettagli a proposito del senso orario o antiorario delle immagini della propria passata esistenza.

Si poteva pensare per esempio a un aspirante suicida. Venire a conoscenza delle aspirazioni autodistruttive di un qualche conoscente, di un amico di un amico. Parlarci, convincerlo, coinvolgerlo in una collaborazione con me. Sedurlo con l'idea della doppia utilità del suo progettato gesto definitivo: nel caso che egli assecondi la mia ansia di conoscenza, il suo suicidio diventerebbe certo più utile per l'Uomo, per il disvelamento dei misteri dell'Insondabile, o di quelli della chimica fisiologica e neurale, oltre a quel tipo di utilità del tutto individuale la cui convinzione nasce nell'aspirante suicida nel momento in cui decide di compiere il gesto stesso, in base a considerazioni di natura variabile, soggettive appunto e in questo frangente del tutto secondarie. Il fatto è che oggettivamente trovavo non poche difficoltà nell'imbattermi in personaggi in possesso di queste caratteristiche della personalità e di questa progettualità d'azioni. Non è che non ci fosse in giro gente con sufficienti pulsioni autodistruttive, anzi: ho sempre incontrato persone aventi *solo e unicamente* aspirazioni autodistruttive. Com'è giusto che sia. Ciò che mancava loro era una *metodologia* che portasse ad un'organizzazione pratica e puntuale del gesto estremo, una prassi e persino una coreografia stabilita col giusto anticipo in cui inserirmi con il mio progetto di registrazione di una testimonianza dall'orlo dell'Abisso. L'emarginazione psicologica di questi freaks li conduceva ad altrettanta emarginazione dagli Altri, affrontata però in modo naif, poco professionale, inaffidabile.

Badate che, a dispetto di un certo umorismo inconsapevole presente nel mio raccontare "col senno di poi", io, ventenne, affrontavo tutta la questione con la gravosità e l'impegno che una tale situazione comporta. E non che non avessi nient'altro da fare... Che poi, la mia curiosità non era di natura del tutto oziosa: il mio scopo reale era creare un'opera d'arte, diciamo un quadro o un film o qualcosa di simile, costruito in base al procedimento di successione di immagini della sequenza del "film della vita". Il concetto era di far convivere più o meno in armonia – nel senso di una *progressione fluida* che amalgamasse insieme figure diverse tra di loro *non necessariamente* armoniche – il maggior numero di immagini possibili, portatrici di un senso e della loro intrinseca *ineluttabilità*, nel minor spazio materiale possibile. Ma prima dovevo conoscere la logica temporale, la priorità di sviluppo delle sequenze del metafisico "film della vita"! Ora che ci penso, mi sa che a tutt'oggi non mi sono allontanato molto da questo tipo di intenti, quando affronto un nuovo quadro... ma adesso non ho più quell'ansia, quella frenesia di conoscenza; adesso ho l'Esperienza, la cui mancanza in quei giorni bruciava tanto.

In teoria pare che il "film della vita" appaia più di frequente a persone che muoiano di morte violenta tipo incidente o anche suicidio, come risulta dai racconti di chi miracolosamente sia scampato da tali situazioni. Altre voci invece riferiscono che non siano eccezionali i casi in cui anche chi muoia di malattia possa esperire questo fenomeno psichico-ottico. Per cui, ho iniziato a frequentare gli ospedali e i reparti dei malati terminali. E' il periodo, questo, che ricordo con maggiore fatica; fu tuttavia una pratica del tutto inutile, e non solo per il mancato raggiungimento del mio scopo – dovuto alle restrizioni degli orari di visita a cui attenersi, alla presenza severa di familiari o infermieri, al contrasto e logica mancanza di dialogo tra l'apparente o reale futilità dei miei bisogni e il destino di tutte quelle facce sconosciute, grappoli, montagne di facce – ma anche e soprattutto inutile perché quell'immagine del dolore ospedaliero la conoscevo da prima, ne ero portatore fin da bambino, e rinfrescare l'esperienza... come dire... beh, non accresceva di certo la mia visione del mondo. Comunque il tempo passava senza che riuscissi a venire a capo del mio problema. E' da allora che ho capito quanto poco convenga affidarsi agli altri e dipendere da questi, anche solo in parte o dal punto di vista della pura manodopera, per la realizzazione di una propria opera d'arte... io i miei quadri li dipingo sempre da solo.

Poi, ad un certo punto avviene un fatto. Vengo a conoscenza che Roberto, un vecchio compagno di scuola che non vedevo da qualche tempo, si è fottuto. Mi riferiscono abbia contratto "la peste del Duemila", come si diceva nei primi anni '80. La cosa non mi stupisce più di tanto, sapendo delle abitudini sessuali promiscue di Roberto e del suo uso abbondante di eroina; essendo lui un ragazzo ancora molto giovane, rimango comunque colpito nell'apprendere la notizia.

Certo, per tutto l'arco della mia vita io ho avuto bisogno di trovare soluzioni a problemi molto particolari. Come ho fatto? Sono uscito di casa alla loro ricerca e... beh, come vedrete in un modo o nell'altro sono sempre riuscito a trovarle.

Mi faccio dunque vivo con Roberto. Parlo prima con i familiari con cui ancora abita, i quali mi dicono subito che le condizioni sono gravi. In seguito lo incontro a casa sua. E' a letto, in un palese stato critico. L'aspetto fisico è molto cambiato dall'ultima volta che mi è capitato di vederlo, circa un paio di anni prima; non è più bello, ora traspaiono le ossa e il teschio, e non ha quasi più capelli. Il carattere invece, pur nella spossatezza della devastante malattia, sembra mantenere alcuni tratti che mi piace riscoprire col passare di quei primi minuti in sua compagnia. E' come se ci fossimo visti il giorno prima; è contento di vedermi, mi tratta con affetto ma anche con una certa non-chalance ribadendo quella svagata e distante freddezza che era già una sua caratteristica fin da quando lo conobbi alla fine dei '70, lui diciottenne e io quindicenne. In parte il suo atteggiamento conserva ancora tutto il cinismo affettato della prima generazione New Wave. Com'è comprensibile, mostra pure un leggero appannamento del suo gusto estetizzante per un'idea di decadenza che adesso non è più vagheggiata ma vissuta da lui in modo tragico.

Non occorre molto tempo perché si ristabilisca la vecchia complicità tra adolescenti di un tempo. Anche in un momento particolare e per lui disperante come quello, Roberto rimane ancora legato alle sue velleità artistiche di una volta per capire le strane ragioni della mia ricerca e assecondare il mio intento. Gli spiego nei dettagli di aver bisogno che lui, morendo, mi renda edotto sulle modalità di scorrimento delle sequenze di immagini della sua non troppo lunga vita, nel caso che riesca a percepirle così come si sente dire tra leggenda e realtà. Occorre inoltre organizzarsi perché ciò avvenga malgrado i molti prevedibili intoppi; innanzitutto dovrò trasferirmi al suo capezzale e accudirlo in attesa del momento della sua dipartita, un po' come un avvoltoio. E da parte sua dovrà esserci l'impegno a conservare anche nello spasimo finale l'energia e la lucidità sufficiente per riferirmi, come ultimo sussulto di vita, la risposta al mio problema. Mi procuro anche un registratore a cassette nell'eventualità assai probabile di aver bisogno di riascoltare o decriptare le parole esalate con l'ultimo respiro.

Il *bello* è che l'intera situazione non appariva così melodrammatica come potrebbe sembrare. Mi accampo piuttosto bene nella loro grande casa da ricchi, con il malato costantemente sotto morfina in uno stato di attonito stupore in cui sopravviveva sempre la distaccata dignità New Wave, e con la quasi perenne assenza dei genitori e fratelli di Roberto impegnati col lavoro, forse anche esausti e rassegnati dopo troppi mesi di malattia del proprio caro. In realtà ho come l'idea che, non conoscendosi ancora molto bene in quegli anni le modalità di trasmissione del nuovo virus, i parenti e gli altri amici preferissero stare il più possibile lontani da Roberto.

Io intrattengo Roberto durante il giorno mettendogli sullo stereo tutti i suoi dischi preferiti e per il resto del tempo, avendo la terapia musicale una presumibile efficacia psicologica sul malato ma non potendone contrastare il deperimento fisico, lo guardo disfacersi nel suo letto. Inoltre, vista la disponibilità di morfina circolante in quella casa, di soppiatto ne approfitto anch'io. In un impeto di riconoscenza per la mia "affettuosa compagnia" Roberto mi regala tutta la serie di nastri con le registrazioni delle musiche composte da lui ed eseguite al synth; io formalmente accetto il dono ben sapendo che tutto quel materiale avrebbe quanto prima trovato alloggio sul fondo della mia pattumiera.

La mia condizione era senza dubbio bislacca e nella mia memoria mi sembra occupi un tempo indefinito, di cui oggi devo rintracciare le date esatte su un vecchio calendario per farmi un quadro preciso di quei giorni: in fin dei conti io quel tipo manco lo conoscevo bene, e d'improvviso mi ci ritrovo in una situazione di tragica intimità resa ancora più complicata dalle incognite riguardo al fattore contagio di un morbo su cui nessuno ancora sapeva nulla. Roberto, da bravo new-waver, ha sempre amato gli iniziatori delle nuove mode e tendenze generazionali nel vestiario, musica, comportamenti sociali, e d'altra parte si ritrova adesso tra i primi a inaugurarne una: la tendenza a crepare di Aids.

Passa qualche giorno e guarda caso la situazione precipita. La malattia peggiora, la febbre è perenne, i dolori costanti, la morfa inefficace. Una mattina siamo soli, io, Roberto e una giovane infermiera. E' evidente a tutti e tre che il sipario sta calando, e sta calando proprio *ora*. Roberto, grondante sudore, mi sussurra: «non mi sono mai sentito così. Sono sull'orlo, adesso non torno indietro». OK, mi preparo; mi avvicino con una sedia al suo capezzale, avvio il registratore e cerco di tenere sveglia la sua attenzione con vaghe frasi e discorsi, per evitare che gli ultimi rimasugli di lucidità gli si offuschino o che perda conoscenza prima di morire. Emette un rantolo, un tremolio, gli occhi gli si chiudono sui bianchi globi spiritati; gli metto i palmi delle mani sulla faccia per bloccare il fremito e con entrambi i pollici cerco di sollevargli delicatamente le palpebre per monitorare il suo sguardo vitreo, accertarmi che sia ancora cosciente... cristo, mi sembra di palpeggiare della carta velina umida, le palpebre si scostano come le pellicine sulle fave bollite, lo sguardo del mio amico si volge verso di me... è ancora qui, è lucido.

Gli dico, sotto la sorveglianza un po' disgustata dell'infermiera: «Robi, stai attento. Sai che devi dirmi ciò che ti ho chiesto. Stiamo per lasciarci e tu andandotene potrai avere probabilmente un'ultima visione riassuntiva in cui in un lampo tutta la tua vita ti passerà davanti». Roberto annuisce con un rantolo. «Come d'accordo, tieniti pronto», aggiungo, «e appena questo avverrà cerca di riferirmi nel modo più chiaro che puoi, ma anche con rapidità perché sarà il tuo ultimo istante di vita, la risposta a ciò che mi è indispensabile sapere». Tutto quello che avverrà tra me e Roberto da questo momento in poi, oltre ad essere del tutto veritiero, è anche verificabile tramite la testimonianza diretta della signorina Sandra Martino, infermiera a domicilio tutt'oggi operante. La sequenza dei fatti da me vissuti, nel loro svolgimento secondo dopo secondo, viene riportata così come è stampata nel mio ricordo indelebile, lucido e chiaro, anche se qualcuno ha insinuato una possibile distorsione delle mie percezioni dovuta in quei giorni alla alterazione dei miei periodi di sonno o all'assunzione ripetuta di morfina, cosa tutta da dimostrare... ma andiamo avanti.

Io continuo a tenere le mie mani sul suo volto. «Dimmi, Roberto, amico mio, è dunque giusta la supposizione che ho avuto, che la sequenza delle immagini della propria vita, nell'istante della morte, non si svolge linearmente dall'inizio alla fine come un vero film ma va a ritroso come un nastro che si riavvolge in modo meccanico ritornando al momento della nascita e magari anche oltre?» A questo punto sento la temperatura del teschio di Roberto, che morbidamente bloccavo tra le palme delle mie mani e che sentivo scottare di febbre, scendere in un botto di almeno venti gradi... i suoi globi oculari, nel mentre, subiscono un fulmineo risucchio di tutto il sangue che iniettava le miriadi di venuzze e ora mi appaiono bianchissimi, vuoti di tracce... persino le sue iridi risentono di questa repentina mutazione, e da castane divengono quasi verdi, è inspiegabile, non ho mai più visto niente di simile! Ma la pupilla... dio, le sue pupille!... Nel tempo di un secondo le vedo restringersi e dilatarsi, restringersi e dilatarsi almeno mille volte, come in un crepitio elettrico impazzito. Le sue pupille *stanno vedendo qualcosa ad una velocità straordinaria*... In un secondo si susseguono mille mutamenti di forma delle sue minuscole pupille, le vedo diventare capocchie di spillo, poi grossi cerchi neri atti a raccogliere più luce possibile, poi ancora capocchie invisibili di spillo, e ancora e ancora, e in mezzo centinaia di disordinate varianti intermedie di grandezza, di apertura, di contrazione... e tutto questo *in un secondo*!

Ebbene, in *quel secondo* il viso di Roberto non tremava più di febbre; come ho detto l'ho sentito gelare e poi, *nel secondo successivo*, la sua bocca si apre per fare uscire il fiato più pestilenziale che potessi immaginare, il vero lezzo dell'Inferno come non ho trovato uguale in tutto il corso della mia vita, insieme al suono di una frase che è il suo lascito per me, ossia la mia *risposta*. Il registratore stava andando già da qualche minuto, così ho potuto riascoltare più volte nel tempo quell'ultima frase, già all'origine comunque nitida per le mie orecchie, nella sua brevità e concisione, malgrado la voce rotta dallo spasimo di Roberto e il mio zompare indietro per il mefitico alito.

«E' vero il contrario», questa è la frase. *E' vero il contrario*, e Robi spira. E' di certo una risposta, e più di tanto non si poteva fare, morendo. Ma ancora non so come interpretarla. Se è vero *il contrario* di quello che chiedevo a Roberto in quel frangente, cioè se la sequenza di immagini vada essa stessa all'incontrario come io supponevo, vuol dire dunque che le immagini scorrono *non al contrario*, bensì vadano dalla nascita alla morte così come la vita è stata cronologicamente vissuta dal morituro. Ma *è vero il contrario* può anche voler dire che le immagini viste in punto di morte *veramente* descrivano la storia della propria vita riavvolgendosi all'incontrario, sul tipo del rewind in una videocassetta, com'era la mia brillante nonché inedita intuizione iniziale... infine, il mio modesto contributo alla Conoscenza dell'Uomo.

Questa seconda ipotesi mi sembra la più gratificante, è ovvio. Ad ogni modo ho suggerito ai familiari di Roberto di incidere sulla sua lapide tombale, in quanto lui ne sarebbe stato contento (mentivo), le sue ultime parole rese così ancora più sibilline dalla loro decontestualizzazione. Mi sono pure offerto di progettare io la lapide su un mio preciso disegno e di seguire con cura le fasi della sua realizzazione nella bottega dello scalpellino. I genitori accettano la mia proposta senza problemi: sono stato uno dei migliori amici di Roberto e l'ho assistito fino all'ultimo, e inoltre io sono Enrico Corte, un artista giovane ma già attivo e promettente che ha avuto molta stampa a livello locale. La mia offerta appare loro generosa e per di più quella lapide ai loro occhi potrebbe un giorno avere un certo valore; d'altra parte loro sono agiati, colti e raffinati e quindi senza problemi per "scucire". Li osservo mentre li imbonisco e sogghigno tra me e me pensando: non mi hanno mai fatto tanta pena, i ricchi.

I genitori di Roberto acquistano così un'ampia porzione di una suggestiva struttura, edificata da poco all'interno del cimitero, atta a contenere in una infinita teoria di nicchie le nuove bare dei futuri cari estinti cittadini. La struttura, alta sei metri e lunga trenta, in muratura rivestita di varie file di lastre di marmo chiaro che verranno di volta in volta rimosse e sostituite dalle lapidi tombali vere e proprie, aveva in origine un aspetto ancora più imponente e metafisico perché era del tutto vergine: essendo stata terminata da poco, nessuno prima del cadavere di Roberto vi aveva ancora trovato collocazione e non vi erano altre lapidi oltre quella progettata da me apposta per lui. Eravamo, per così dire, arrivati primi. Nel lucore impenetrabile di quell'enorme e immacolato muro magico tassellato di marmo, almeno in quel momento del 1984, il nero lucido specchiante della "mia" lapide tombale con sopra una bianca tarsia e l'iscrizione ambigua risaltava e attirava lo sguardo al punto da rendere superfluo il minimo fiorellino commemorativo. Tutt'oggi la tomba di Roberto con la lapide originale del 1984, ormai circondata e confusa tra le altre accumulatesi nel tempo, è visibile nell'area C / lotto 45 del Cimitero S. Michele di Cagliari, piazza Castellani, 1.

Ma c'era ancora un problema da risolvere, meno pressante del primo ma che pur sempre m'intrigava, soprattutto per un eventuale utilizzo nella realizzazione di un'opera d'arte. Come possono dunque stare tutte le immagini di una vita in un secondo? Una vita, per quanto breve, è pur sempre lunga. Forse è possibile condensando il tempo mediante un sistema di doppia o tripla esposizione che sovrapponga più sequenze alla volta, come nelle pellicole sperimentali degli anni '60. Oppure eliminando i tempi morti sulla base di una selezione dei dati meno significativi e della loro cancellazione, cioè *l'opposto* delle pellicole degli anni '60. E se così, in base a quale criterio viene stabilita la priorità d'importanza di un'immagine rispetto ad un'altra? E chi è, poi, a stabilirla...?

Per tutto l'arco della vita ho avuto bisogno di trovare soluzioni a problemi molto particolari. Come ho fatto? Sono uscito di casa alla loro ricerca e... beh, sono sempre riuscito a trovarle.

Il problema del *pittore* Enrico Corte è, a ventuno anni, una volta lasciatasi alle spalle l'esperienza delle pose in equilibrio sul vuoto e la morbosa ma irripetibile avventura di inglobare un cadavere nell'opera (un'opera che, appunto, non è solo "la lapide"), quello di continuare a produrre lavori più convenzionali ma che non si allontanino da quei presupposti. Portare lo stesso senso di precario equilibrio tra una doppia possibilità (saltare nel vuoto o restare), tra l'alternarsi di una visione del davanti e del dietro (abisso e terraferma; il cadavere in decomposizione dietro la lapide inalterabile). Rappresentare ancora il punto immobile nello spazio sospeso tra due contraddizioni ma sotto forma di quadro, di opera d'arte inseribile in un circuito commerciale, di *un lavoro come un altro*. Ecco nascere dunque una serie di quadri double-face, grandi pannelli da sospendere tramite cavi d'acciaio al soffitto o tra due pareti, e dipinti su entrambi i lati. Dal 1984 al 1987 si succedono diverse opere strutturate a questo modo: *Demone Psichico*, *Tenie Psichiche*, *Larve Psichiche*, *Lemuri Psichici* (ill. p. 136), e altre ancora, presuppongono il fatto che lo spettatore ruoti attorno al quadro, e il quadro diventi elemento plastico nello spazio al pari di una scultura, a volte inglobando elementi tridimensionali su una o su entrambe le facciate.

Le tematiche figurative sono scelte in base a contrasti visivi di forma e colore tra facciata e facciata. Vi troviamo immagini già incontrate in precedenza: gli onnipresenti Ritagli-Ritratti, le venature dipinte del finto-marmo (a cui però si aggiungono dei quasi indistinguibili profili capovolti di persone), le raffigurazioni didattiche di strutture atomiche (ma modificate, come in *Equi-lirium*, opera del 1984, in cui i protoni e i neutroni di un atomo sono allineati in un impossibile equilibrio formale; ill. p. 128). Vi incontriamo anche nuove forme: le clessidre rovesciate (altri "equilibri d'immobilità temporale" che troveremo in molte opere future, per esempio nell'ipnotica e quasi fastidiosa allo sguardo *C(L)ep(S)y(D)ra*, la quale ricorda il volto di un insetto, la libellula chiamata Aeshna Clepsydra; ill. p. 135) e le immagini favolistiche estrapolate da un libro di fiabe per bambini (si tratta di una inquietante immagine di disfacimento tratta da "Il Soldatino di Piombo" di Andersen: Soldatino e Ballerina come patetici amanti sterili che bruciano e si squagliano nello stesso Inferno popolato dai Demonietti Psichici... un'altra distruzione della Famiglia?). In più vi compaiono come sfondi strane strutture quadrangolari vuote e sghembe le quali definiscono un decorativismo che è quasi un cancro di sé stesso: il riferimento può essere alle decorazioni d'interni anni '50 o '60, cioè il momento della pre-nascita di Corte, come anche a una sorta di "spirale del DNA" distorta e corrotta da una manipolazione aliena; si può anche pensare alle schiere di loculi vuoti de *Il Film Della Vita* in un'interpretazione multicolore e alterata dall'LSD, oppure alle schiere di finestre scrutatrici nell'opera *Per Strada*... ma forse il senso di quelle strutture sta in tutte queste cose assieme.

L'uso di un certo repertorio iconografico insiste su alcune personali ossessioni visive, ricorrenti fantasmi di disfacimento emersi dall'infanzia, che l'artista riesce infine a trasformare in ossessioni *sociali*, e non solo nel senso dell'inconscio collettivo: l'opera *Era della Natalità Zero*, del 1985, con le sue due facciate in cui si confrontano due opposti (il caldo del fuoco che fonde la coppia Soldatino-Ballerina e, sull'altro lato, la sterile glacialità mortuaria della superficie marmorizzata, con un profilo capovolto accennato tra le venature; ill. p. 41) ci parla di un cruciale problema demografico in un anno, il 1985 appunto, in cui in Italia, seguendo una parabola discendente che parte dal 1970, le morti anagrafiche superarono le nuove nascite. Il problema del basso quoziente di natalità suscita tutt'oggi grandi dibattiti in Italia.

L'approccio stilistico di Corte in queste opere è quasi sempre freddo e distaccato, ottenuto spesso mediante impeccabili verniciature a spruzzo su materiali industriali che ci forniscono un lavoro sull'Immagine in versione raggelata, da "morgue", affiancabile a ciò che facevano in quel momento i graffiti-artists americani di pochi anni più anziani di lui... però trasposto in una sala di autopsia cerebrale. In parallelo con la realizzazione di questi quadri da appendere al soffitto, Corte, non a caso, inizia a collezionare corde da impiccato usate (vedi ill. p. 156, 157).

Esposte in varie mostre in Italia, le opere a due facce trovano nella installazione di gruppo il compimento della loro disorientante funzione. Collocate come fossero le pareti di un labirinto, un multipolare percorso obbligato attraverso il quale i visitatori devono passare per poi ritrovarsi al punto di partenza senza aver capito niente, oppure raggruppate quasi in un blocco unico al centro della stanza con gli spettatori costretti a passare radenti alle pareti per la mancanza di spazio, le opere double-face fanno tutto tranne che ingraziarsi i favori del pubblico o entrare nelle convenzionali strutture del mercato dell'arte. Il caso-limite si ha durante una mostra personale di Corte a Napoli nel 1986 (cf. ill. p. 129). E' l'artista che ce la racconta:

[Registrato: 19 Giugno 2003 – estratto]
La situazione si presentava così: un bel gruppo di opere a doppia faccia appese al soffitto e pendenti all'altezza del punto di vista occupava quasi per intero il centro del locale espositivo, come un coloratissimo fecaloma nell'intestino. Gli spiragli tra i quadri erano stretti e la gente poteva al massimo scrutarci dentro ma non entrare all'interno del blocco, nel "labirinto". Anzi, il pubblico quasi non poteva transitare nella stanza perché lo spazio al centro era stipato di quadri appesi al soffitto: si poteva giusto entrare dalla porta e poi strisciare lungo le pareti, a malapena sbirciando tra i cunicoli dell'ammasso di pannelli sospesi nel vuoto. Dal momento che avevo avuto l'accortezza di piantare nelle pareti una serie di chiodini quasi invisibili, la gente strisciandoci sopra per mancanza di spazio restava agganciata al muro con la giacca, il maglione o la camicetta di seta. Ed ecco quello che volevo ottenere: le persone del pubblico appese al muro al rango di oggetti, con i quadri al centro della stanza che li osservano.

I quadri a doppia faccia non rappresentano l'unica tipologia di opera sviluppata da Corte verso la metà degli anni '80. *Resident in Venice* (ill. p. 131), in collaborazione con Andrea Nurcis, è una piccola, preziosa sculturina in vetro di Murano fatta realizzare su indicazione degli artisti da un artigiano del vetro della cittadina veneta famosa per le sue pregiate fonderie. Collocata sulla Laguna di Venezia l'opera acquista un carattere "psicogeografico" giocando sul fatto che Venice è anche una località della California, lo stato americano da cui la band The Residents proviene. Lo sguardo si confonde mostrando minuscola la scultura che appare in primo piano mentre sullo sfondo troneggiano i monumenti del passato, e la spettrospettiva diviene quasi una controspettiva, una *antipodi-spettiva,* confondendo le acque, è il caso di dirlo, tra la Laguna e Venice Beach.

E sempre la musica è il leitmotiv di *N.I.C.O. Rejected Record Cover* (ill. p. 130), cioè, appunto, una copertina di LP progettata da Corte per la rockstar Nico ma rifiutata dalla casa discografica. Corte incontra Nico, suo mito musicale da sempre, nel 1984 durante un concerto e si accorda con lei per la realizzazione della copertina del suo prossimo disco. Ancora una volta non si tratta dell'omaggio di un fan: Nico, come The Residents, incarna un personaggio assolutamente a sé stante nel contesto degli stili e dei generi musicali del suo tempo, ed è questa la metodologia d'azione in cui anche Corte si riconosce. La casa discografica comunque impone di includere una immagine in primo piano del volto della cantante, cosa che Corte fa utilizzando una foto di Nico scattata da lui. Nell'interpretazione di Corte, Nico più che una "Star" appare come un "Buco Nero". E il contesto grafico della copertina punta l'accento sull'aspetto più autodistruttivo della figura di Nico, ossia il "buco", l'eroina, la sostanza che per anni ne ha governato la vita. Tutto sommato, realizzare un'opera sull'eroina era doveroso da parte di un artista appartenente a una generazione che ha vent'anni nel 1984, e l'obbiettivo di Corte diviene il dare una interpretazione del problema attraverso l'attitudine, l'approccio e lo sguardo della sua generazione: l'eroina come presenza di grande *appeal*, alle cui onnipresenti lusinghe è impossibile resistere. Infatti, nella front-cover campeggia la foto di una gigantesca siringa; il pistone è realizzato in cartoncino sagomato, movibile, e può essere spinto col dito dentro il corpo della siringa. La siringa viene proposta come un oggetto consumistico, virato in una luce oscura ma non privo di un senso ludico, accattivante. Sul retro, un nerastro Ritaglio-Ritratto col profilo di Nico (e due o tre grammi di eroina nel mezzo). Dopo la morte della cantante, avvenuta nel 1987 (non per eroina), Corte venne comunque informato dalla casa discografica che la sua copertina non era adatta.

Questo gioco di contrasto/attrazione nei confronti delle le esigenze del mercato culturale ha permeato tutta l'attività di Enrico Corte. Le opere a due facce degli anni '80, ad esempio, rappresentavano al tempo una sfida a certe regole d'allestimento di una mostra più di quanto oggi possa sembrare. Ad un certo punto Corte fu costretto a "dividere" le due facce, cioè creare una serie di pitture su supporti più convenzionali come carta o tela in cui i medesimi temi visivi delle opere double-face venivano sviluppati in normali quadri da parete, tutt'al più da affiancare tra di loro (ill. p. 134). Questo per contrastare alcuni mercanti senza scrupoli che intendevano tagliare in due i quadri a doppia faccia e vendere separatamente le due metà. E' stato, per l'artista, un momento di intelligente concessione alle esigenze del mercato e dunque tali opere acquistano un significato culturale specifico più per questo aspetto, per il disvelamento di una contraddizione, che per i temi e le immagini che vi appaiono. Però subito dopo l'artista si prende una rivincita con lavori come *Neural Marmo,* la cui installazione spiraliforme addirittura impedisce al pubblico di entrare nella stanza per vedere l'opera da vicino.

Una via di mezzo tra la double-face e il quadro appeso al muro è rappresentata dalle opere apribili prodotte dal 1986 al 1988, chiamate genericamente *Cross Fades*. Tra queste, *L'Astrazione del Petrolio* del 1987 (ill. p. 138) è un esempio tipico: due pannelli quadrati rivestiti di formica nera lucida sono uniti da cerniere invisibili e possono essere chiusi l'uno sull'altro o riaperti a piacimento. Il pannello di sinistra è fissato sul retro alla parete, quello di destra è completamente scorrevole e su di lui si esercita l'atto di chiusura o apertura, come un libro (o meglio, al contrario di un libro, che andrebbe aperto o chiuso da sinistra: il particolare non è casuale perché l'artista intendeva sottolineare la divergenza tra Arte e comunicazione letteraria).

Abbiamo così due "specchi" lucidi neri sulle cui facciate interne l'artista interviene con smalti industriali e materiali vari: carta velina ritagliata, sabbia, uno specchio concavo incastonato riflettente le immagini capovolte, ecc. Quando le due facciate vengono chiuse l'una sull'altra, alla parete è visibile solo un quadrato di laminato nero, vuoto, specchiante, dall'aspetto glaciale. Vi è poi un preciso *Progetto di installazione* dei cosiddetti *Cross Fades* (ill. p. 140), che prevede un rudimentale sistema di tiranti i quali partono dal quadro e terminano sulla porta d'ingresso al locale espositivo per cui, quando un visitatore apre la porta, il quadro nella parete di fronte gli si chiude in faccia...

Vi sono inoltre molte varianti del tema dello sportello scorrevole, come *Dismisurazione Dello Spazio* (ill. p. 140), in cui uno sportellino è inglobato sul corpo di un pannello dipinto e appeso regolarmente alla parete. L'idea fissa dell'artista, che lui usa come sibillina metafora psicologica, è che i quadri debbano "gettare un'ombra". Ecco perché i quadri sono sospesi nello spazio oppure presentano parti mobili e aggettanti: «per gettare una bella ombra netta sulle pareti». Ma l'esibizione di una conflittualità, di una vertigine, di uno smarrimento o persino di una castrazione dello sguardo porterà Corte a realizzare non solo opere che si chiudono in faccia al pubblico, ma addirittura quadri che si abbattono come ponti levatoi davanti allo spettatore (rischiando di sfondargli il cranio) che inavvertitamente azioni, camminando, un sistema di molle collegato al pavimento antistante. Quando gli viene rimproverata questa sua attitudine a realizzare opere semoventi o aggettanti, "che gettano ombra", Corte asseconderà le esigenze del pubblico arrivando ad eccessi come fare una mostra con i quadri murati dentro le pareti della galleria. "Sepolti" all'interno di profonde nicchie coperte di intonaco, i quadri sono inamovibili ma anche invisibili...e senza ombra alcuna (a distanza di anni, sono ancora lì, all'insaputa del nuovo proprietario del locale).

E ancora: nel 1986 realizza una installazione composta da una grande stanza prefabbricata, in plastica gonfiabile come un canotto, ma perfettamente abitabile e dotata di ogni comfort, che si affloscia a terra dopo il tentativo di appendere un quadro sulla parete tramite un chiodo (*L'Errore nel Quadro*). Tutto questo, ricordiamo, paradossalmente avviene nel contesto storico del boom della pittura degli anni '80. Ma in questa fase della sua attività l'artista non fa riferimento al mainstream, alle strategie del grosso mercato dell'arte, bensì a una "onda" più sotterranea, assimilabile a quella che, a partire proprio dalla metà degli anni '80, verrà chiamata *Industrial Culture*. O meglio, egli tenta di "infettare", con alcune tensioni derivanti dall'underground, il corpo dell'arte contemporanea propriamente detto.

Corte usa, in arte, il *paradosso* come strumento di analisi culturale, qualcosa di simile a quello che, nel pensiero della Scuola di Francoforte, viene chiamato "Critica dell'Ideologia". Con la differenza che l'artista non si mostra più schizzinoso nell'utilizzare cinicamente per i propri scopi gli elementi provenienti dall'industria culturale e costitutivi della "cultura di massa". Per lui sono solo congegni da smontare e rimontare secondo una logica più sadica che sprezzante o apocalittica. E tramite il paradosso, ancora una volta egli si ferma ad «appena un passo dallo schianto finale», cioè dall'apocalittismo francofortese. D'altra parte, alcune successive frange del Pensiero sul Contemporaneo (come gli scritti di Frederic Jameson negli Stati Uniti, o di Stuart Hall in Gran Bretagna, in parte debitori di molte idee di un conterraneo di Corte, Antonio Gramsci) danno un'interessante lettura della cultura di massa non in chiave di dominazione ideologica ma come campo di riarticolazione di identità, ruoli e differenze in perenne mutazione e quindi sfuggevoli dalle logiche del potere, in cui elementi utopici sopravvivono alla griglia reificante. Tra le maglie della convergenza tra le due scuole di pensiero Corte attua la sua idea del paradosso.

L'opera *Rimozione*, datata 1986 (ill. p. 154), è un esempio di come l'anomala collocazione del gancetto di un quadro sia un espediente che Corte usa nel tempo e in vari lavori. In tal caso l'impostazione del disegno (un triplo autoritratto dell'artista ventitreenne, in sequenza, che è quasi un rapido bozzetto) sembra a prima vista indulgere a un certo accademismo figurativo, ma solo quel tanto per evidenziare il contrasto con la fuorviante posizione del gancetto e del rispettivo chiodino. Invece di nascondere questo elemento antiestetico, l'artista preferisce evidenziarlo, donargli un suo personale spazio in un punto improbabile, integrarlo nella struttura dell'opera fino a fargli ricalcare il modulo triangolare su cui è basato il disegno stesso. E il quadro diventa uno strumento atto a decostruire un parametro culturale: la struttura del "perimetro" dell'opera d'arte, il suo bordo-limite (come il cornicione su cui l'artista da giovane stava in equilibrio), più che il suo contenuto figurativo.

Ecco perché ombre, psichismi, inversioni e rimozioni non distolgono Corte dall'osservazione della realtà circostante esterna. L'artista, quando può, cerca sempre di evitare ogni forma di escapismo, di autocompiacenza introspettiva, di fuga dalla realtà. E non di rado rivela, dietro la maschera dell'opera, una denuncia sociale. Il *Fluororama*, del 1988, ne è un esempio (ill. pp. 141-149): appartiene una tipologia di opere, ricorrenti nel tempo, che ripropongono oggetti di consumo popolare o per bambini. Questi oggetti riveduti e corretti, di solito risalenti agli anni '50 o '60 (il momento della pre-nascita dell'artista), hanno precisi riferimenti ai problemi della vista (i problemi della percezione visiva come metafore della fruizione artistica, e non siamo lontani dalle questioni che ossessionavano l'artista al tempo del "Film della Vita") e coinvolgono quindi l'atto del vedere in rapporto con situazioni di persuasione occulta, allucinazione, intossicazione e dolore.

Il *Fluororama* è la ricostruzione nei minimi dettagli di un dischetto visivo con una serie di diapositive in 3D da osservare sull'apposito visore binoculare. E' completo di logo, marchio registrato, grafiche e confezione ad hoc, tutto assemblato secondo la logica dell'artista. Il riferimento alla realtà, di cui dicevamo, dipende dal fatto che l'opera si ispira, pur senza illustrare pedissequamente, alle ricerche del giornalista australiano Ian E. Stephens sulla fluoridazione come sistema di controllo cerebrale di massa, espresse nel suo libro del 1987 *The Dickenson Statement – A Mind-Boggling Thesis*. Gli accurati studi di Stephens sull'uso indotto del fluoro come inibente della volontà e sull'intreccio industria/politica che vi è alla base hanno fatto molto discutere verso la seconda metà degli anni '80 e, una volta ripubblicati, anche nel decennio successivo. Corte con prontezza li prende a pretesto per un'opera di impostazione "didattica" che perversamente si rivolge alle giovani generazioni con un linguaggio visivo suggestivo e accattivante per persuadere ad un'assunzione quotidiana di fluoro attraverso il dentifricio. Le sette immagini fotografiche create secondo una tecnica stereoscopica, e presentate all'interno del dischetto come altrettante piccole diapositive, illustrano come dei diorami i precetti "educativi" del *Fluororama* e sono realizzate unendo pittura, scultura, modellini, sovrapposizioni, fotoritocchi e altri "trucchi" fotografici in un lavoro dettagliatissimo che ha richiesto mesi di applicazione. Ognuna delle sette immagini fotografiche è da considerarsi una singola opera d'arte presentabile anche sotto forma di stampa di grandi dimensioni; nel 1996 l'artista le rielabora in versione digitale (ill. pp. 12 e 144-149). Sono questi gli unici casi in cui Corte dimostra di tenere in gran conto la qualità dell'immagine fotografica; quasi sempre infatti il suo approccio alla fotografia rimane fedele non tanto al dilettantismo (nulla è casuale nel suo lavoro) quanto all'*improvvisazione* dello scatto: come viene, viene. Per questo si affida ad apparecchi fotografici di poco valore, con obbiettivi standard da 50 mm e pellicole ben lontane dall'offrire un'alta risoluzione dell'immagine. Addirittura Corte arriverà a lasciar formare della muffa sulle lenti all'interno dell'obbiettivo fotografico, per rendere l'immagine ancora più "deficiente". Una maggiore cura viene impiegata nell'effettuare, a posteriori, un taglio panoramico o esageratamente verticale in alcune foto.

Scattare una fotografia è per Corte l'espediente per fissare un determinato momento del flusso della vita. Egli può assumere il ruolo del voyeur, come nel caso di *Der Weg Zum Kubismus*, ma più che altro sceglie un atteggiamento da "turista dell'esistenza" i cui *souvenir* possono essere contaminati da elementi di "distrazione" quali la muffa o la polvere sull'obbiettivo. (Notate che per Corte l'assunzione del ruolo da turista significa la disincantata denuncia dell'impossibilità del "Tragico" e dell'"Eroico" dentro al sistema dell'arte contemporanea. L'impossibilità del Tragico è un tema che attraversa in modo sotterraneo gran parte dei suoi lavori a partire da *Cheese*, fino al *Dolorama*). Le fotografie ad effetto tridimensionale del *Fluororama* hanno questo di diverso: si amalgamano con pittura e scultura nel rappresentare non un mondo reale (al quale comunque rimandano tramite il pamphlet di Stephens) ma un universo di pura intossicazione, un Limbo caleidoscopico popolato da simpatici lemuri di pasta dentifricia che vagolano tra mucillaggini cerebrali o in anfratti sottomarini dalla spazialità organica e vischiosa. E' interessante notare come Corte concretizzi questo scenario da allucinazione attraverso una costruzione puntigliosa, iperrealistica, con un "tocco" e una sensibilità per la forma plastica affinato durante gli anni. Nel *Fluororama*, infine, Corte realizza un magico *equilibrio*: il massimo della complessità e della stratificazione dentro dimensioni contenutissime (il dischetto del *Fluororama* con le relative diapositive stereoscopiche misura appena 9 cm di diametro), in netto contrasto col gusto per il sovradimensionamento dell'arte degli anni '80.

Connessa col *Fluororama*, per la tematica allusiva all'apparato dentale e alla cavità orale come luogo di loschi processi bio-psichici, è *Clean-o-rama* (1988-89). Si tratta di una "scultura" dalle dimensioni altrettanto paradossali di 10 metri di altezza per 4 millimetri di spessore, composta da un lungo filo interdentale sul quale si abbarbicano microscopici rimasugli antropomorfi, nuove ammiccanti incarnazioni dei "Demonietti". Da osservare con la lente d'ingrandimento, realizzati in modo perfetto, appaiono come "caccolette" psichiche equilibristiche, funambolici "tarli" da rimuovere.

L'intreccio di pittura e scultura in una serialità ipnotica entra nel lavoro di Corte con un'installazione di opere come *25 Secondi*, *25 Secondi ¼*, *25 Secondi ½*, *25 Secondi ¾* e *26 Secondi* (ill. pp. 150, 151). Si tratta di cinque pezzi quasi simili che inglobano calchi del volto dell'artista, vere candele distorte e i Ritagli-Ritratti, mentre sullo sfondo trascolorano paesaggi tridimensionali e fosfeni in un'allucinata controluce. Nel contesto di deprivazione sensoriale in cui occhi bocca e orecchie sono occluse dalle ceree protuberanze delle candele, il tempo si distorce: per realizzare l'intera serie di cinque quadri Corte si dovette impegnare per un anno di lavoro (il 1989, in cui egli passa dai 25 ai 26 anni), ma nei loro titoli un anno di lavoro – il ventiseiesimo della sua vita – equivale a un secondo (ovvero: il passaggio da 25 a 26 secondi, in cinque microfrazioni di tempo, o in altrettanti *microintervalli di tono*; incidentalmente, ricordiamo che l'uso dei microintervalli è un punto cruciale della musica del XX e del XXI secolo). A questo punto ci chiediamo: perché l'artista si concentra, distorcendolo, proprio sul passaggio dai 25 ai 26 anni? Ma perché il 25simo anno di vita è il momento in cui i biologi situano mediamente la massima efficienza, nell'uomo, del proprio organismo, la perfetta esultanza del metabolismo, della fertilità ecc. Dai 25 anni in avanti si può dire che per l'uomo inizi il lungo, impercettibile processo dell'invecchiamento.

Per contro, nell'opera *Sveltospettiva* (ill. p. 132) l'esecuzione di un piccolo e semplice disegno a matita può coprire un arco di vent'anni senza apparente distinzione (notate il non casuale riferimento, nel disegno, al gioco infantile della "Campana": vent'anni si contraggono in un salto di bambino, o nel rapido passo di un uomo sui trampoli. Secondo Mircea Eliade, inoltre, la "Campana" è il gioco che nasconde gli archetipi più profondi della vita e della morte, una allegoria del "labirinto", una iniziatica "discesa agli Inferi" e conseguente ritorno sulla terra da parte del bambino). Fa coppia con *Sveltospettiva* il disegno *Bruciospettiva*, la cui esecuzione è durata anch'essa un ventennio (1984-2004; ill. p. 133). Qui una mascheratura è stata apposta su alcuni punti della carta, permettendo alla luce del sole di ingiallire gli spazi scoperti e produrre così un "disegno" col passare del tempo: rimuovendo la mascheratura, appare un autoritratto dell'artista – del suo sorriso – la cui fisionomia da adolescente rimane inalterata per vent'anni mentre il suo supporto cartaceo si deteriora e invecchia. *Sveltospettiva*, *Bruciospettiva* e la già citata *Antipodispettiva* sono lavori che ribaltano le coordinate materiali, spaziali e temporali della percezione visiva.

Tornando a opere come *25 Secondi*, *25 Secondi ¼*, *25 Secondi ½*, *25 Secondi ¾* e *26 Secondi*, vediamo che questo tipo di quadri, a metà tra pittura, scultura e inserimento di oggetti "deviati" (soprattutto candele in posizione orizzontale, distorte o addirittura annodate, che sono il sostituto della precedente immagine della clessidra rovesciata), acquisterà con gli anni un senso sempre maggiore di pesantezza e immanenza. Gli sfondi dai colori squillanti, gli ipnotici fosfeni e i Demonietti Psichici che vi danzano dentro convivono con simbologie complesse e oscure, con ibridazioni pastose di oggetti quotidiani la cui forma e funzione trasmutano in qualcos'altro di non facilmente definibile, qualcosa di *nuovo*. L'osservatore viene costretto a mutare in continuazione il suo punto di vista, ad allontanarsi e riavvicinarsi, ad infilare la testa tra i piani prospettici sovrapposti nell'opera, dentro il rito cannibalistico dei volumi, per scoprire particolari nascosti. La realizzazione plastica delle opere è impeccabile; manualità virtuosistica fino all'ossessione e produzione industriale non solo convivono, ma creano un paradosso visivo per cui, nella fredda perfezione della forma, l'una è indistinguibile dall'altra (come lo erano le parti vegetali vere e quelle fittizie nelle *Rarità Botaniche* del 1981).

Alla fine si arriva al monumento funebre di *Skullaby* (chiamata anche *Circonvolutarli & Circonvolutarme*, ill. p. 155), dove la metafora del *salto del livello di coscienza* è espressa dal calco del corpo dell'artista risucchiato nell'auto-obnubilazione, sprofondante nell'indefinibile, nell'afasia, *nella propria merda*. Opere come questa, come *Enuresi Psichica Notturna* (ill. p. 162), *N.E.O.* (p. 192), *Radice Cubica* (p. 164), *Brainscan* (p. 153) e altre ancora, presentano calcolatissimi equilibri interni, rapporti di pieno/vuoto, spinte e controspinte, in un dialogo tra forma e contenuto che quasi imita il labirinto di influenze reciproche della rete neurale. Già al tempo del "Film della Vita" l'artista cercava il modo di "comprimere" ed equilibrare il maggior numero di elementi in origine non armonici. Forse non a caso, questi sono lavori contemporanei alle scoperte, da parte di una équipe di giovani neurobiologi milanesi, sul ruolo delle singole sinapsi nella comunicazione cerebrale, con conseguente individuazione, e addirittura fotoriproduzione, della "unità elementare di attività" che vi viene sviluppata.

Certamente nelle opere dell'artista il delirio equilibristico delle forme sembra svilupparsi in base a una logica più parascientifica che esoterica. Una logica parascientifica e paratecnologica – si badi bene – che rimanda a una critica di tanti neo-positivismi di oggi, rivelando squarci su territori neri della mente, ingovernabili dal corpo. E così molte opere degli anni '80 già dai titoli si riferiscono a terminologie medico-scientifiche come quelle relative, ad esempio, ai presunti danni fisici e psichici dovuti alla sovrapproduzione di adrenalina (titolazioni beffarde: sono danni da cui Corte, come abbiamo visto, è immune).

Le opere di Corte possono spesso dare un'idea di pesantezza mortuaria, di una gravità di linguaggio che diventa eco catacombale di indecriptabili simbologie, e di fatto, in una rassegna di interviste tra circa 80 artisti italiani di tre generazioni pubblicata dalla rivista Flash Art nel 1988-89 (*La Parola agli Artisti*, Flash Art Italia 147-150) Corte è l'unico fra i suoi colleghi che relaziona l'arte al senso di colpa, addirittura all'espiazione, e soprattutto a quello che sarà uno dei principali temi sulla scena internazionale dell'arte degli anni '90: la Morte.

Questa idea di "pesantezza" è però contraddetta da un lavoro come *RitagliOntani* (ill. p. 152) in cui Corte e Luigi Ontani, affermato artista italiano della generazione precedente, si scambiano un reciproco ritratto. Abbiamo visto come alcuni personaggi della cultura contemporanea entrino nel lavoro di Corte. Accade sempre dopo lunghi percorsi intellettuali, dopo una scelta che privilegia la sinergia tra visioni lontane che si incastrano oltre il paradosso. Il mutuo omaggio nasce qui in base all'equilibrio del reciproco rispetto. Ontani è un artista che ha fatto di una attitudine ludica e leggera il suo stile di vita e di lavoro. Corte, relazionandosi a Ontani, rende manifesto il fatto che nelle proprie opere pesantezza e leggerezza convivono (come in una visione a 360° dalla cima del cornicione). Ma in che modo riescono a convivere? Da un certo punto di vista, l'atteggiamento caratteristico di gran parte dell'attività di Corte risulta chiaramente essere il bazzicare il "lato oscuro", l'ansia di attraversare o di cimentarsi fin da ragazzino in tutte le esperienze più devastanti della vita: fascinazioni suicide, prostituzione minorile, gusto dell'intossicazione, celebrazione delle ossessioni psicotiche, derive sessuali, modificazioni anatomiche, vagabondaggio, contrabbando, denunce, carcere. E, non ultima, l'esperienza più devastante di tutte: "cavarsela" per vent'anni di seguito producendo opere d'arte senza compromessi né concessioni alle facili letture o commerci. Ma, come un eroe delle favole, l'artista attraversa queste esperienze restandone incontaminato, un eterno, distaccato, algido adolescente nell'anima e persino, incredibilmente, *nel corpo*.

Col passaggio agli anni '90 la produzione di opere fotografiche si dirada a favore della tridimensionalità, e nelle poche foto che l'artista produce vi è una spazialità e sintesi formale libera dai sovraccarichi dei quadri-scultura, dai quali intende differenziarsi. Ne sono esempi *Collezione Dell'Artista*, che rivela un irrinunciabile aspetto necrofeticista (con l'artista in posa davanti alla sua personale collezione di rudimentali ma autentici cappi, corde e lacci da impiccato, *usati*, raccolti nel corso di svariati anni e corredati da documenti medico-legali e articoli di cronaca; ill. pp. 156, 157) e *Abduction* (ill. p. 163), in cui è ripresa ancora una volta l'ossessione latente per i rapimenti alieni che Corte, avendone parlato già dal 1980, ritiene essere diventato «il basilare fenomeno psicologico degli anni '90».

Un caso a parte è invece *Naftorama* e la correlata *Sigh-seeing* (ill. p. 158), ossia due immagini del 1991 tratte da una particolare "scultura" effimera: palline di naftalina con piccoli nodi scolpiti al loro interno. In un certo senso le palline di naftalina sono nuove, sintetiche incarnazioni dei Demonietti Psichici. Essendo la naftalina "evaporata" nel corso del tempo, ciò che rimane oggi è la stampa cibachrome *Naftorama*, in cui l'intero gruppo di palline appare installato dall'artista dentro un costoso apparecchio per la rilevazione spettrografica delle particelle olfattive esalate dagli oggetti. L'apparecchio viene usato in medicina per visualizzare i processi di decomposizione delle sostanze organiche, e quindi la susseguente *Sigh-seeing* è una cibachrome analoga all'opera *Naftorama*, ma ottenuta attraverso l'elaborazione fotografica prodotta dal rilevatore spettrografico di particelle olfattive (tempo di esposizione: 48 ore circa). E' così che la Chimica e la Fisica, oltre alla Botanica, aggiungono necessarie tessere al puzzle psichico. Entrano in alcuni progetti, agiscono sui volumi scultorei, non mancando di incidere segnali sul corpo umano. E talvolta scatenano reazioni dalle potenti conseguenze concettuali.

Il paradosso autodistruttivo della "scultura" in naftalina viene reso ancora più aspro dall'accurato lavoro manuale che è occorso per scavare al loro interno delle forme "a nodo" piccole e precise. A questo si aggiunge il fatto che l'artista, nel corso di quell'anno 1991, *sceglie di non produrre alcuna altra opera d'arte*, a parte *Naftorama/Sigh-seeing*. Corte ha voluto inaugurare gli anni '90 all'insegna della *cupio dissolvi*, con un'unica scultura autodistruttiva in cui un considerevole – e sconsiderato – lavoro manuale (la realizzazione dei vari "nodi") si sovrappone a un prodotto dell'industria (le palline di naftalina) per lasciare di sé solo il simulacro fotografico ottenuto mediante una apparecchiatura da ospedale. La vera opera d'arte, quindi, è il fatto che *non c'è più alcuna opera d'arte nel 1991*. Svuotamento totale.

Lo studio del *vuoto* è una delle tematiche classiche dell'arte scultorea. Partendo dalla cima di un cornicione, Corte ha finito per estendere l'ossessione del vuoto ad una gamma di problemi che invadono la sfera psicologica e l'ambito sociale su scala globale. In questo senso va interpretata la "collaborazione" in progress con un gruppo di giovani ladri romani – a modo loro "produttori di vuoto" nelle abitazioni private – iniziata da Corte nel 2002, e che a causa della complessità dei suoi contenuti ho scelto di tenere fuori da questa prima monografia sull'artista. Voglio parlarvi invece di altri esempi di "vuoto" che trovo nelle opere pittoriche e plastiche della metà degli anni '90 dedicate agli *Hobbyists*, ai *Devotees* e ai *Wannabees*, ossia gruppi di individui che condividono la passione, anche erotica, per la pratica dell'autoamputazione totale di parti del proprio corpo come dita, mani, orecchie, arti e ovviamente organi genitali.

La sensibilità verso questi fenomeni è l'ennesima esplicazione di un dialogo maturo con controculture reali e realizzate. Non conosco progetti di Corte che nascano quando mode e tendenze "pompano" sui media un dato fenomeno. Al contrario, l'intuito psichico dell'artista gioca un ruolo decisivo e mai preclusivo, una sorta di radar emotivo che percepisce il momento più *onesto* di una tensione culturale. La serie di opere *Hobbyists* (ill. pp. 164-170) consta di quaranta quadri realizzati combinando disegno e tecniche pittoriche, dagli svariati riferimenti visivi che riconducono sempre al mondo dell'autoamputazione o alle pratiche del piercing, del branding o del tatuaggio ad esso connesse. Corte evita di affrontare queste tematiche in modo illustrativo ma ci gira attorno "infestandole" con ciò che gli viene in mente sul momento, lasciandosi trasportare dalla propria abilità grafica. L'esecuzione è fredda e precisa, i colori squillanti catturano l'attenzione come fossero dei "segnali stradali". Ma sotto a tutto questo, come al solito l'artista nasconde un sostrato di riferimenti occulti, un percorso di simboli iniziatici da decodificare con fatica.

La convinzione di Corte è che, laddove tra gli anni '80 e i '90 alcune "avanguardie" della modificazione corporale si sono orientate su un abbellimento e una decorazione fisica di tipo accrescitivo (piercing e tatuaggi come sovrapposizioni "in più" sul proprio corpo, ormai entrati nel gusto popolare), nel futuro si andrà verso una idea di sottrazione radicale (amputazione come decorazione "in negativo" e alla portata di tutti). Nel presente le due possibilità ancora convivono e si contaminano; a dimostrazione di ciò Corte espone nel 1997 a Roma i suoi quadri *Hobbyists* assieme a una ingombrante scultura in metallo realizzata con Andrea Nurcis. La scultura è stata progettata dai due artisti per essere "indossata" da un terzo collaboratore, Pino Piercing – fachiro metropolitano e piercer di professione – che porta sul proprio corpo vari "nuovi buchi" in cui inserire il suo campionario di anelli e gioielli. Partendo da un grosso blocco centrale, le molteplici protuberanze metalliche filiformi della scultura di Corte e Nurcis vanno a inserirsi nei molteplici buchi artificiali di Pino, per terminare nelle classiche forme a forcone, appendici di altrettanti piccoli Demonietti Psichici in metallo.

Per la verità, pochi minuti prima dell'inaugurazione della mostra romana ci si accorse, nonostante i calcoli fatti in precedenza, che la scultura aveva una protuberanza in più rispetto al numero di buchi di Pino. E così lo stoico "indossatore" si praticò seduta stante un nuovo foro di 5 mm di diametro, senza anestesia, trapassandosi da parte a parte la carne all'altezza del pomo d'Adamo, usando uno dei filamenti metallici della scultura. Gli artisti hanno così dimostrato che certe pratiche della Body Art estrema sono state superate dalle realtà comportamentali delle giovani generazioni che si collocano fuori dall'arte. L'esibizione è documentata dal video *Pino Piercing indossa una scultura di Enrico Corte e Andrea Nurcis* (ill. p. 171).

Oltre a questo, Corte progetta una cospicua serie di "gioielli" sostitutivi di parti del corpo mutilate (la serie *Devotees and Wannabees*; ill. pp. 172-179). Moncherini, dita amputate, lingue e organi genitali sezionati vengono inglobati e rivestiti da piccoli, preziosi oggetti-scultura. A volte questi gioielli, che sono la celebrazione del vuoto e dell'assenza, presentano castoni in ceramica con fotoriproduzioni di disegni a inchiostro e carboncino la cui fattura contrasta con la freddezza metallica degli oggetti. Concepiti secondo una logica del cattivo gusto spinto fino al paradosso, questi gioielli si riferiscono al mondo appariscente del Rock, dei Bikers, di tutte quelle controculture che spettacolarizzano la loro diversità fino all'eccesso. Su tale logica è concepita anche un'altra serie di oggetti assimilabili ai precedenti nella ricerca di una concettuale *Astrazione del Vuoto*: si tratta di sculture in metallo chirurgico e vetro, con castoni in ceramica, ispirate ai butt plugs, "tappi" decorativi da inserire nell'orifizio anale soprattutto durante giochi erotici di natura scatologica (la serie *Abstraction of the Void*; ill. pp. 177-191). Anzi, le sculture di Corte *sono* butt plugs, sono pensate e realizzate *per essere introdotte in quello spazio vuoto*... anche se le loro dimensioni leggermente oversize farebbero pensare a una certa difficoltà di "collocazione". Si potrebbe forse dire, giocando con le parole, che Corte è passato dalla *escatologia* delle grandi sculture alla *scatologia* delle piccole, ma in realtà orina, sperma, sangue, bile e fluidi vari sono presenti fin dal 1979-80 («Se l'Arte non può cambiare la Società può perlomeno cambiarne i pannolini», E.C. 1983).

E ora il cattivo gusto raggiunge livelli di estrema compiacenza, con tappi che includono una lampadina e possono essere utilizzati come torce elettriche anali nel buio delle dark-rooms, o tappi contenenti ceneri funerarie, oppure tappi dentro ai quali addirittura nuotano le misteriose "scimmie di mare" (questi sono adatti a situazioni e abbigliamenti "rubber" che ricordino le mute da sub e conseguenti orpelli sottomarini), oppure ancora tappi dal castone ribaltabile che contengono una fialetta di nitrato di amile, il cosiddetto popper, un vasodilatatore molto adatto alla bisogna. Nel complesso questi butt plugs appaiono curati nella forma, accattivanti nelle loro sinuosità, sorprendenti nelle soluzioni formali che accorpano cromature, vetro, gomma, ceramica, immagini pittoriche stampate, incisioni e fregi.

Le immagini promozionali e le animazioni digitali che Corte realizza, per pubblicizzarne la produzione in serie, ci mostrano questi tappi metallici ovulari posti in "impossibile" equilibrio verticale, come "uova di Colombo", all'interno di ambientazioni varie, spesso tra asettici lavacri o sanitari igienici in cui comunque scorra l'acqua. Così Corte si spinge fino a citare, con questi tappi in verticale, la pratica del cosiddetto "rock balancing", l'arte di posizionare in equilibrio i sassi sui greti dei torrenti... una "disciplina" stravolta dallo sguardo caustico dell'artista che ne azzera l'originario spirito New Age "canadese".

Di ambiente licenzioso, vizioso, quasi decadente, sono anche le opere del ciclo *Il Bordello dell'Arte* (ill. pp. 193-196): 10 stampe fotografiche tratte da pellicola cinematografica 35 mm collocate su pannelli di laminato finto-legno deformati a fuoco. Nel 1995 Corte rifletteva sulla realizzazione di un'opera celebrativa del centenario della Biennale di Venezia (ancora il tema della celebrazione, ovviamente in chiave parodistica) e la giusta occasione arrivò quando un regista si rivolse a Corte e Nurcis per la costruzione di scenografie nonché reclutamento di attori e comparse da utilizzare nella scena di un film. Ancora una volta la vera opera d'arte sta nella capacità di mescolare gli elementi sulla "tavolozza della vita". Corte ha l'idea di reclutare un cast interamente di reali prostitute e prostituti, includendo con naturalezza sé stesso nel gruppo (per via della sua presenza scenica, più volte Corte è stato utilizzato dai registi come attore). Nel film Corte recita poche battute dentro una scenografia in apparenza sfarzosa da bordello filosofico, nella quale ha avuto cura di lasciare molti *vuoti* – scaffali privi di libri, pareti prive di quadri o con strani accostamenti tra arazzi antichi e riproduzioni delle sue stesse opere – e una certa vaga incoerenza "cubista" nella suddivisione degli spazi (gli arredi e gli orpelli della scenografia sono un indiretto riferimento al Cinema: Corte li preleva dall'arredatore italiano delle ville di Sylvester Stallone). Durante le pause di lavoro, chiede alla produzione di permettere a Nurcis di effettuare, come operatore, alcune riprese del backstage utilizzando rimasugli di pellicola nella coda delle bobine. In seguito Corte seleziona una serie di fotogrammi dalla pellicola impressionata da Nurcis e li fa stampare, sfruttando anche le scritte di lavorazione sulla celluloide, le impronte digitali involontarie e le punzonature di montaggio.

Le immagini fotografiche che compongono la serie ritraggono l'artista tra un indolente gruppo di prostitute (femmine, maschi e transgender) che si attardano nel backstage di un film (si nota la troupe e le attrezzature, ma la "scena" resta volutamente fuori campo) e altro non fanno se non parlottare e truccarsi, mentre occasionalmente ma in modo esplicito qualcuno di loro si masturba. I costumi di attori e comparse stanno a metà tra abbigliamento sadomasochista e Haute Couture, con "costrizioni" fisiche come collari metallici, tute in gomma e corsetti. Quasi ricalcando l'assunto baudelariano dell'arte come prostituzione, ogni singola fotografia porta un titolo specifico che mette in rapporto, in modo allusivo, l'immagine con la Storia dell'Arte parafrasando titoli di quadri famosi, nomi di riviste d'arte, di tecniche pittoriche ecc. Un esempio è *Dripping*, che cita la tecnica pittorica di Jackson Pollock riferendola al particolare dello sgocciolamento di mascara sulla faccia di una attempata attrice/prostituta transex con la congiuntivite. O ancora: *D'ou Venons-nous? Que Sommes-nous? Ou Allons-nous, Ce Soir?*, in cui l'interrogativo cosmico del noto dipinto di Paul Gauguin viene riproporzionato sui travestimenti e maquillage di personaggi dall'identità incerta che si preparano per il consueto, licenzioso nightclubbing. Costoro, desiderosi più di *perdersi* che di trovare sé stessi, rappresentano forse dei modelli a cui Corte fa riferimento in questa fase della sua attività. Lo sterile *Bordello dell'Arte* ha idealmente una certa affinità con la serie fotografica del 1982 *Il Sistema dell'Arte*, e può essere in effetti un ottimo commento commemorativo dei cent'anni di una istituzione come la Biennale. Le 10 stampe fotografiche del *Bordello* sono collocate su pannelli sintetici in finto-legno, su cui la fiamma ha creato bubboni e cicatrici, rivelando la falsità del materiale sintetico ma al tempo stesso, con ambiguità, trasformandolo in materia carnosa, quasi palpitante e organica.

Una collaborazione più stretta tra Enrico Corte e Andrea Nurcis si ha a partire dal 1996, con le riprese del loro digital-film *No Light* e col successivo *Homevideo*. E Nurcis si conferma come una figura-chiave per una ridefinizione dell'arte italiana degli ultimi vent'anni nel senso del "lato oscuro". *No Light*, editato nel '97, vede i due artisti assumere le fattezze dei "personaggi" ricorrenti nei loro reciproci quadri, sculture, installazioni: per Corte è un Demonietto Psichico, per Nurcis un Eremita che vive in una fogna. Corte costruisce il suo alter-ego tramite la computer graphic, col proprio volto e braccia sovrapposti ad un palpitante palloncino di gomma rossa pieno di sangue, mentre Nurcis recita il ruolo dell'Eremita in costume, con un saio di tela grezza che ne maschera le fattezze facciali. E così i personaggi prendono il sopravvento sui loro creatori. Nel corso di 30 minuti, in dodici scene più epilogo, si dipana una narrazione attraverso il lungo dialogo tra i due personaggi, una sorta di *Tentazione di S. Antonio* con un finale oscuro e senza speranza. Il trattamento della lingua italiana viene sviluppato dai due artisti tramite l'imposizione ironica di uno stilema di parlata assai inconsueto, per quartine rimate, a somiglianza delle filastrocche dei libri per l'infanzia. Ma a livello dell'immagine vi è anche un dialogo tra linguaggi visuali (pittura, scultura, animazione digitale, cinema espressionista, cartoon, porno, videoclip ecc.). Effetti speciali "fatti in casa" convivono con l'uso di più sofisticate tecnologie di compositing, similmente all'interscambio che si verifica, nei quadri e sculture di Corte, tra la manualità e l'industria.

Grande importanza ha la musica, sotto forma di composizioni originali che "citano" le pianole usate per sonorizzare i film dell'epoca del muto, il cui suono è poi rielaborato dalle strumentazioni digitali. Ma ad un orecchio esperto risulta evidente che l'artista ha assimilato bene l'uso del pianoforte preparato da parte di John Cage negli anni 1942-54. Sotto il punto di vista tecnico, i vari brani vivono in una situazione ambigua tra musica tonale e atonalità (uno psicanalista li definirebbe come riflessi della ambivalenza sessuale dell'artista) con un uso anche di studiati elementi cacofonici. In apparenza la struttura compositiva sembra tonale, ma manca un *centro tonale*, o se vi è, risulta un centro promiscuo, vagabondo, che si muove per spostamenti spastici. Le scene "di sesso" di *No Light*, poi, non hanno eguali in tutta la storia del cinema d'artista.

No Light ci propone una *imagerie* che anticipa di alcuni anni la scandalosa sequela di fotografie di segregazione, scatologia e umiliazione del carcere di Guantanamo, ma come filtrate attraverso gli occhi di un bambino che ne abbia avuto una visione casuale in televisione e la rigurgiti, in seguito, tramite coloratissimi incubi notturni. E già dal titolo "No Light" il progetto si propone come "pesante", con l'intento di mettere a dura prova l'attenzione dello spettatore. La materia tragica della narrazione viene affrontata in un'ottica parodistica in base a un preciso assioma: in un sistema culturale amministrato dalle regole del mercato, si verifica "l'impossibilità del *Tragico*". Qualsiasi approccio al *Tragico* si trasforma in una sua parodia. Quindi l'unico modo di parlare del *Tragico* è farne la parodia in partenza. Ed è quest'ultima a divenire il vero "aspetto tragico" dell'infinito sistema dei segni che ogni giorno consumiamo. In diverse altre opere Corte ci farà prender atto di questa impossibilità o irraggiungibilità del *Tragico*. Nel caso di *No Light*, l'artista non attua una denuncia, piuttosto una disincantata constatazione.

No Light, tra i più complessi progetti multilinguistici realizzati in Italia, ha uno sviluppo composito e onnidirezionale che ha dato origine a ulteriori opere d'arte, idee culturali, proposte estetiche e varie iniziative, tra le quali ricordiamo:

A) gadgets e merchandise (i *No Light Screensavers* per computers; gli *Evil Tanks*, piccoli bidoncini di sperma da collocare sui vetri dell'automobile tramite ventose; ill. p. 212);

B) quadri (il grande *No Light Storyboard* che ricicla parte della scenografia in chiave pittorica; una cospicua serie di stills su cibachrome; ill. pp. 198-211);

C) costumi-scultura (*Sacco e Rosso*, il grottesco sacco-saio dell'Eremita; ill. p. 51);

D) oggetti d'uso quotidiano (Demonietto & Eremita come Saliera & Pepiera; Demonietto & Eremita come Bambole Gonfiabili);

E) giochi da tavolo (il *No Light Puzzle*, un frustrante puzzle metallico double-face – una per il Demonietto e l'altra per l'Eremita – il cui montaggio è complicato dal fatto che alcuni dei pezzi che compongono le immagini sono calamitati in modo da respingersi l'un l'altro e dunque finiscono per saltar via da tutte le parti invece di rimanere assieme; ill. p. 212);

F) operazioni di marketing del video attraverso l'invenzione di nuovi materiali (ossia il *Mystiglaz*, un particolare sistema di advertising – brevettato da Corte dopo un anno di lavoro in una fabbrica di cristalli – che si basa su particelle riflettenti la luce, fuse invisibilmente all'interno dei vetri degli autobus urbani, le quali proiettano scritte e immagini come barbagli improvvisi di luce accecante sfruttando l'incidenza dei raggi solari durante il movimento del bus; ill. p. 218);

G) celebrazioni pubbliche (col lancio in cielo dei *Day-rip Fireworks*, brevettati fuochi d'artificio "oscuri" – come squarci di notte in pieno giorno – che sono costati all'artista sei mesi di sperimentazioni in una fabbrica di razzi pirotecnici; ill. pp. 10, 216 e 217);

H) "omaggi" da parte di altri artisti (il concerto del compositore americano John Duncan, eseguito in *totale oscurità* nel settembre 1999 all'Aula Magna della Facoltà di Architettura di Venezia, nell'ambito delle manifestazioni della 48ª Biennale d'Arte e in contemporanea con la proiezione pubblica di *No Light* su schermo gigante nel Padiglione Italia ai Giardini di Castello).

...Notate come l'artista si sposti lungo i binari della propria attività secondo un ritmo tachicardico, macinando e bruciando continuamente le idee e andando oltre la capacità di fruizione e assimilazione dello stesso pubblico dell'arte (ulteriore strategia autodistruttiva).

Soprattutto da *No Light* deriva l'opera *Partouze's Sexy Vinyl Single*, la fedele riproposizione di un disco a 78 giri per bambini del tipo "animato" (ill. pp. 214, 215). Il disco presenta sull'etichetta una sequenza di fotogrammi del film che, visti attraverso un prisma specchiante da collocare sopra il disco stesso quando gira sul piatto, formano una breve animazione in loop, come in un antico praxinoscopio. I due brani musicali del disco sono tratti dalla colonna sonora di *No Light* (composta e eseguita da *La Partouze* e prodotta da Corte). Da notare che in alcune sequenze di *No Light*, che si propone come "progetto propedeutico per l'infanzia", gli autori ci mostrano quei caratteristici e veloci flash di luce che, è accertato dal punto di vista medico, possono scatenare attacchi epilettici in soggetti infantili "a basso tasso di tolleranza". Ebbene, vediamo che le stesse sequenze sono riproposte nei fotogrammi sull'etichetta del disco, la cui animazione in loop dovrebbe idealmente creare i famigerati flash luminosi. Infatti il loro scintillante sfarfallio, come Corte ha scoperto, ha una frequenza intermittente analoga alla velocità di un disco a 78 giri. Con questo cinico riferimento all'epilessia infantile, ancora una volta l'artista esibisce la sua attenzione per l'aspetto "neurale" dell'opera.

Esiste poi un mini-video interpretato da Eremita e Demonietto che è un vero e proprio short pubblicitario per l'emittente Mtv (*Drinkin' No Light*; ill. p. 198). Qui torna il principio fondativo di Corte, ovvero, agire dentro meccanismi diffusi tramite una stratificazione alterna di apparenza e zone complesse. Si può dire che l'approccio di Corte al video pubblicitario metta a frutto una precisa strategia da *adbuster* che ritroveremo ogni qual volta l'artista confronti le proprie immagini con le pratiche del marketing. Un progetto per Mtv senz'altro significa comunicazione veloce, popolo giovane, ricezioni di pochi secondi. E lo short sembra proprio così, un miniclip dalle apparenze ironiche. Ma è una strategia per penetrare in ambiti imprevisti. E tutto si tramuta nel dubbio, il tarlo scava nel profondo. Come accade nel magistrale romanzo "Sabbath's Theater" (1995) di Philip Roth, dove il burattinaio di strada Mickey Sabbath stuzzica il bigottismo newyorkese attraverso il palpeggiamento erotico della sua marionetta sul seno di una giovane spettatrice. Qui e altrove il protagonista detiene il pretesto per dire altro rispetto alle apparenze.

No Light, infine, contraddice le "regole" strutturali ormai codificate della stessa videoarte, creando una stratificazione dove gli elementi (costumi, foto, sculture, installazioni, gadgets, short, soundtrack con relative partiture musicali "grafiche") ricreano la geografia multisegnica della mente. A partire dalla polivalenza del titolo "No Light" si è in piena antinomia rispetto a tanti discorsi su leggerezza, ironia, gioco, decorazione: quei tipici, duttili e riconoscibili caratteri fondativi dell'arte italiana, una sorta di DNA che scorre silenziosamente tra abitudini sociali e pieghe culturali. Corte e Nurcis prendono distanza da ciò e tentano un ribaltamento analitico di quelle posizioni. *No Light* è un lavoro che mette alla prova la pazienza, l'attenzione, l'esasperazione dello spettatore, a partire dalla manipolazione effettuata sui tempi narrativi, a volte dilatati ossessivamente e a volte contratti come spasmi epilettici. Così i loro segnali figurativi nascondono una distanza anarchica dai localismi di tanta arte contemporanea. EC/AN non puoi collocarli in un luogo poiché l'esperienza diretta viene filtrata dentro il loro cervello. Il mondo passa dentro al cervello; il cervello ricostituisce il mondo con le modalità di un istinto sotto precise ragioni; il cervello espelle la forma ulteriore che diventa opera finale ma mai definitiva. La totalità delle opere conforma un autoritratto psichico con le sue molteplici dinamiche.

Differisce per ambientazione e impianto narrativo, ma non per impostazione "cerebrale", il successivo progetto *Homevideo* (ill. pp. 219-221), un'opera "aperta", dai molti contributi e dalla durata indefinita ma che finora gli autori hanno preferito lasciare in una fase di montaggio provvisoria di 33 minuti. La premessa del digi-film *Homevideo*, che scorre sullo schermo dopo il titolo di testa, è questa: a partire dal 1997 Enrico Corte e Andrea Nurcis hanno deciso di aprire la loro comune casa-studio, a Roma, ad amici, conoscenti, visitatori occasionali. Ad ognuno di loro è stato chiesto di scegliersi una stanza della casa all'interno della quale "mettere in mostra sé stessi" attraverso dialoghi e narrazioni, fino all'inserimento di contributi come lettere, foto, musiche, brani da video o film. In particolare questi contributi vengono inseriti nel montaggio con un accorto gioco di regia sui tempi narrativi, ma per il resto i protagonisti di *Homevideo* agiscono nella totale improvvisazione e le riprese mostrano tutta la loro incertezza, la timidezza e i "tempi morti" del caso, con effetti a tratti esilaranti.

Le persone invitate non sono "artisti" ma operatori di altri settori culturali (cinema, musica, ecc.) oppure personaggi che vivono la creatività sulla propria pelle, giorno per giorno, fuori da una logica professionale. In ogni stanza Corte e Nurcis hanno collocato varie videocamere, microfoni, "giraffe" e cineprese per riprendere l'azione, lasciando il tutto acceso indifferentemente attorno agli ospiti che agiscono per conto loro, mentre i due artisti continuano il lavoro sulle proprie opere. In conclusione del progetto, quando ogni stanza sarà stata occupata, nel tempo, dai vari ospiti, la casa-studio verrà venduta e gli artisti Corte e Nurcis si trasferiranno altrove.

(Bisogna spendere almeno un accenno alla stravagante struttura architettonica della periferia romana in cui Corte e Nurcis hanno installato il loro Quartier Generale: un antico casolare semidiroccato e solo in parte ristrutturato, piuttosto isolato nel contesto urbano circostante e con un giardino selvaggio che lo nasconde alla vista, composto da un insieme di locali dove gli spazi abitativi si compenetrano con quelli lavorativi, più altri ambienti come una "cripta" e una torretta che si eleva sopra le cime degli alberi… attorniato da un nugolo di lugubri, cadenti casupole illuminate da fioche lucine che costituiscono il cuore del quartiere di Torpignattara, risalente agli anni '10 – ma guarda, un'altra *spettrospettiva*! – è una costruzione ormai quasi leggendaria che i vari ospiti di *Homevideo* ancora non sono riusciti ad invadere del tutto).

Ciò che Corte vuole evidenziare, tramite i suoi ospiti, è il paradossale aspetto della creatività che possa sconfinare nel suo opposto, ovvero, ancora una volta, nell'autodistruzione. In tal senso si può leggere la compresenza, nella stanza da bagno, di un regista cinematografico dell'avanguardia anni '60 (Franco Brocani) e di una ragazza trans (Lucrezia Valia Medici): il primo ha scelto la perigliosa via della "ricerca" voltando le spalle a un cinema di tipo commerciale che gli avrebbe garantito guadagni e vita migliore, la seconda ha dovuto distruggere la sua parte maschile per ricreare una nuova personalità. Tra i due pare debba scoccare una scintilla erotica da un momento all'altro ma alla fine tutto resterà in uno stato di sospensione sterile. Attraverso spezzoni di films, lettere e dialoghi tra gli improvvisati "attori" di *Homevideo*, emergono aneddoti e curiose informazioni legate a fatti e personaggi della cultura, del cinema e dell'arte. Le battute improvvisate si dipanano attorno alla figura di Viva, la superstar di Andy Warhol, e al suo rapporto di lavoro col regista Brocani in Italia nel 1970. Tutta la sequenza sembra essere un velato riferimento a uno dei films "scomparsi" di Warhol, *Tub Girls*, del 1967 (trent'anni prima di *Homevideo*: ancora un "anniversario"). Emerge un po' il ritratto di un'epoca attraverso figure come Sharon Tate, Mick Jagger, Louis Waldon, Kenneth Anger, Michel Auder, Carmelo Bene e Mario Schifano. Corte e Nurcis intendevano con *Homevideo* realizzare un prodotto *ipertestuale* che non solo intrattenesse, come un normale video d'arte, ma desse informazioni culturali curiose e inedite, avesse cioè un *livello di utilità* in più.

Un ulteriore progetto comune tra Corte e Nurcis si ha con le comic-strips *Due o tre cose che so di loro* (ill. p. 197). Qui la collaborazione viene estesa a un terzo collaboratore, il disegnatore e graphic artist italoinglese Gary Splitter, che è l'autore materiale delle strips in questione. Gary descrive in una serie di 20 tavole a colori il suo incontro coi due artisti durante una travagliata visita al loro (mitico) studio. Col suo linguaggio grafico accattivante, che rivela all'occhio esperto uno stile del segno da fumetto italiano, il disegnatore descrive in modo parodistico l'habitat degli artisti, l'arredamento dello studio, le persone e le abitudini che popolano la loro giornata, le loro fobie e soprattutto le loro opere, ricostruite con fantasia "perversa", esagerandone fino all'assurdo le caratteristiche formali.

Dopo aver assunto su di sé il ruolo da cartone animato di uno dei suoi personaggi ricorrenti, il Demonietto Psichico, ed essersi visto utilizzare nel ruolo di sé stesso come prostituto all'interno di un film, la normale conseguenza per Corte era quella di farsi disegnare come protagonista di un fumetto. La logica è sempre quella di uno "smarrimento", di uno sdoppiamento di ruolo nello sguardo dell'Altro, di una diversa chiave di lettura della propria figura d'artista mediante il filtro di altri media culturali. E attraverso il pretesto di un fumetto "divertente" si riesce a far passare, di straforo, alcuni concetti-cardine del lavoro sia di Corte che di Nurcis, raggiungendo, più di molti testi critici, strati sociali anche esterni al mondo dell'arte. Le strips di Gary Splitter su Corte e Nurcis sono state anche stampate su supporti autoadesivi e distribuite in giro per la gioia di grandi e piccini. A distanza di qualche anno è ancora facile trovarle attaccate sui muri della città.

Un ritratto di Corte sotto forma di fumetto si trova anche nel buffo quadro "manga-kitsch" di un altro comic-artist, il giapponese Yapponaro Sato (*Enrico Corte European Painter*, ill. p. 54). Le varie e produttive collaborazioni manifestano, in Corte, l'esigenza di uscire dall'individualismo autocompiacente dell'artista in cui è facile essere imprigionati se si fanno scelte estetiche simili alle sue. Nel corso degli anni '90 la sua attività artistica e sociale ha avuto il perenne supporto di un piccolo entourage di amici e collaboratori fedeli che qualcuno, ironizzando sull'aspetto spesso bizzarro di tali compagnie, ha definito, con un gioco di parole, una "Corte dei Miracoli".

Rinomato per questa sua volontà di ficcare il naso in ambienti marginali o persino malavitosi, nel 1996 troviamo Corte tra i bassifondi notturni di Roma mentre accompagna il fotografo Joel-Peter Witkin aiutandolo nella ricerca di modelli da immortalare (*freaks* e abnormità assortite, è ovvio). Durante una di queste perlustrazioni, chiedendo di fotografare una prostituta ermafrodita, Corte fa scoppiare una rissa e si prende di striscio una coltellata al fianco (diretta al torace) da un lenone ubriaco.

Il culmine dell'atteggiamento sopradescritto, mirante a uscire dall'individualismo, si verificherà quando Corte si propone come artista-curatore di una serie di incontri culturali all'interno del Padiglione Italiano della 48ª Biennale di Venezia nel 1999, diretta da Harald Szeemann (così come il gramsciano "intellettuale" deve essere pronto a "fare" oltre che pensare, anche la figura intellettuale dell'artista deve "organizzare" oltre che creare). Qui Corte annulla i suoi prodotti artistici preferendo riconoscersi in quelli di operatori provenienti da altri settori (cinema, musica, teatro, informazione e controinformazione), da lui scelti sul panorama internazionale e invitati a Venezia, il cui insieme costituisce infine una sorta di suo ideale autoritratto multiscopico. Tra le molte presenze selezionate e chiamate a dibattere col pubblico della Biennale, molto interesse riscosse un gruppo di registi provenienti dalla allora martoriata ex-Jugoslavia, figure basilari all'interno della storica Radio B-92, struttura dichiarata fuorilegge dal regime di Milošević. Corte contatta i registi a Belgrado, sotto i bombardamenti Nato della primavera '99. La controversa e quasi impossibile trasferta veneziana di tali personaggi in un momento storico così difficile è da considerarsi uno dei capolavori di diplomazia e d'astuzia dell'artista, attuato mediante fantasiosi stratagemmi burocratici semilegali, col sostegno dell'ambasciatore italiano a Belgrado e della Soros Foundation.

Attraverso tale esperienza, Corte attua ancora una volta, ma non più sotto la maschera della parodia, la sua verifica della possibilità o impossibilità del *Tragico* dentro al sistema dell'arte contemporanea. In questo caso si tratta del *Tragico* vissuto da una intera nazione a soli pochi chilometri di distanza dalle luci della ribalta della Biennale di Venezia (che verrà definita da Corte, in una intervista, come "escapista" ["Culture & Culture", RadioTre Rai, sett. 1999]).

L'incrociarsi degli incontri e lo scambio di vedute entra dentro le opere di Corte, influenzando la struttura stessa del pensiero e della successiva formulazione materiale. Un altro esempio si ebbe quando una fotografa cinese gli chiese di scegliere un edificio di New York per rappresentarsi (e il nostro autore optò per un civico 666, numero della Bestia; ill. p. 222). Anni prima, nel 1988, una serie di opere in collaborazione con l'illustratrice Diana Dubois ritrae l'artista durante un processo in seguito alla controversa mostra *Cleptoscopica* (chiusa il giorno dopo l'inaugurazione) con un chiaro riferimento ai classici e popolari "courtroom drawings", realizzati da artisti commerciali per documentare i dibattimenti nelle aule di Giustizia in cui è proibito scattare fotografie (ill. p. 223). Il risultato, qui come altrove, è sempre lo stesso: parlare del corpo anche senza il corpo e le sue protuberanze, cercando segnali sparsi che siano la forma mentale delle scelte interiori. La stessa realtà esterna può formulare uno spicchio del gigantesco autoritratto psichico.

La cultura contemporanea è per Corte un gioco di spinte e controspinte. Entrando e uscendo dal suo ruolo d'artista, fa comunque in tempo a produrre una serie di opere dai compatti meccanismi formali. Tenendo a mente la lezione formalistica di artisti come Cézanne o Picasso, o forse facendone una tragica parodia, Corte realizza negli anni alcune sculture basate su moduli come il cilindro, il cono, la sfera, il cubo. Questi elementi vengono però "annegati" in un contesto pullulante di simboli e riferimenti vari realizzati con attenzione maniacale, arrivando fino al delirio della cruenta manipolazione corporea e sviando l'attenzione dai presupposti costruttivi formalistici. In *Tre Cilindri* (ill. pp. 244-247) il modulo del cilindro viene utilizzato per costruire un grande triangolo che rimanda alla classica figurazione del biblico "Occhio di Dio". Ma ora al posto dell'occhio scrutatore vi è un enorme naso purulento spremuto da dita dal quale schizza via un nugolo di Demonietti Psichici come altrettanti zampilli di pus. E' una sorta di Dio Negativo, il Signore che governa il tormentato universo in cui vagolano le creazioni di Enrico Corte. E i Demonietti che sprizzano con allegria dalla sua epidermide hanno ali da pipistrello e forcone appuntito. Ognuno di loro ci mostra una propria fisionomia e una espressione individuale, diversa dall'uno all'altro ma sempre beffarda, come fossero dei Pokemon perversi.

Questo genere di opere tridimensionali appare particolarmente impeccabile nel trattamento della forma plastica e dei volumi; solo i presupposti teorico-formalistici del cilindro-cono-sfera-cubo divengono paradossali. Come in *Tre Cubetti* (ill. p. 248), una stupenda scultura sospesa in precario equilibrio verticale tra due angoli di parete. Qui abbiamo una dorata aureola da cui "sgocciola" una struttura allungata, dalla terminazione scrotale, che si plasma come per metamorfosi in una malefica tenia/teschio, con un piercing su un corno, che ci fa l'occhiolino. Questo ennesimo Demonietto compie un gesto osceno su un piccolo modello di casetta infilando il dito medio attraverso lo stretto camino. Ai suoi lati, il Demonietto sviluppa due ali da pipistrello che a loro volta si trasmutano in due filamenti spermatozoici cubici e "cornuti". Si tratta di due ulteriori Demonietti Psichici, ma "cubizzati", cioè resi ancora più inumani. Muniti di un foro a mo' di occhio e di una bocca tagliata di netto, questi due cubetti cornuti assumono una espressione sofferente, come due maschere greche della Tragedia e della Commedia… ma qui anche la Commedia piange. Il terzo cubetto, citato nel titolo dell'opera, è la piccola casetta, simbolo del Focolare Domestico, manipolata e violentata dalle dita ossute del Demonietto centrale. Tra l'altro, per realizzare l'opera *Tre Cubetti* Corte sperimenta la synthoceramica, una tecnica di sua invenzione che gli ha richiesto anni di ricerche e tentativi, ma subito dopo indulge nello sporcare e corrompere la superficie levigata dell'opera con tracce di grasso, grumi di muffa, addirittura cacche di mosca bene in evidenza.

E ancora, in *Tre Sferette* (ill. p. 249) abbiamo un altro riferimento formalistico che è solo un pretesto, un modo per rendere manifesto l'atteggiamento paradossale con cui Corte stravolge e la forma e la materia. *Tre Sferette* è un'opera fotografica che include l'immagine di due sculture, due marmorei Demonietti molto simili a palloncini gonfi e sferici, ma con occhi da alieno, ali da pipistrello e zampette da ragno. Ambedue tengono tra le zampette degli strani attrezzi a metà tra il trapano del dentista e la falce per mietere il fieno. I Demonietti sono collocati su un largo piedistallo di marmo e tra di loro campeggia la figura dell'artista, nudo, che mostra una particolare modificazione dello scroto.

Occorre dire che nel corso degli anni '80, e in modo più consistente nei '90, soprattutto in Nord America, si è assistito a un crescente interesse di alcune frange di persone nella modifica dei propri organi genitali, o di altre parti del corpo, per scopi erotici e ornamentali. L'artista ha bisogno di sentirsi in contatto non solo con gli stili della moda, ma con le "avanguardie" del comportamento umano che saranno le consuetudini di domani. Crescenti gruppi di persone, di solito nell'area gay ma non solo, amano modificarsi i genitali attraverso diverse modalità, più o meno definitive, più o meno "pesanti". Le dimensioni del pene e dei testicoli possono essere consistentemente accresciute per esempio tramite iniezioni di silicone (modalità permanente) oppure di soluzione salina (modalità provvisoria). Inoltre si possono inserire i genitali in apposite campane pneumatiche all'interno delle quali si crea il vuoto estraendo l'aria con una pompetta (vacuum pumping) e provocando così un allargamento delle parti carnose, o ancora si può immettere dell'aria a livello sottocutaneo in una precisa area dello scroto tramite un tubicino, pompandola lentamente come si fa con un pallone. Corte adotta quest'ultimo sistema: una modificazione provvisoria e meno invasiva di altre ma non priva di gravi rischi (embolia fulminante, in caso di penetrazione d'aria in una vena). L'operazione viene effettuata dopo test e prove scrupolose effettuate sotto la supervisione di un professionista della modificazione genitale. In *Tre Sferette*, lo scroto diventa così un modulo sferico, la terza *sferetta* insieme agli altri due Demonietti che gli stanno ai lati. Più che un lavoro sulla forma piena, quest'opera ci parla di strutture gonfiabili e quindi è ancora una ulteriore variante sul tema del *vuoto*.

Il palloncino pieno d'aria o di sangue, l'oggetto gonfiabile, il corpo gonfiabile (come anche la stanza/habitat gonfiabile del già citato *L'Errore nel Quadro*) tutto ciò non manca di rapportarsi alla scena *rubber* o a quella *baloon-fetish* – assai attrattive per l'artista – popolata di feticisti che amano inguainarsi in abiti di gomma e tute aderenti, a volte gonfiate con l'aria o dalle quali si può estrarre l'aria rendendole ancora più coercitive. Da qui, da vent'anni di frequentazioni degli ambienti della sperimentazione corporale/sensuale, nasce un'opera che poco ha a che fare con le più recenti mode delle "mutazioni" corporee. Per le sue caratteristiche, l'opera *Tre Sferette* è centrale nella produzione di Corte, e ne esistono alcune varianti in cui l'immagine fotografica viene confezionata in vari modi, ad esempio "incorniciata" plasticamente da un salvagente in apparenza gonfio e soffice ma in realtà realizzato in durissimo *blastoplast* (cf. ill. p. 59). Questo sottolinea ancor più la tematica del *vuoto*, uno dei problemi classici della scultura di cui Corte dà una sua peculiare interpretazione.

Per il tema scrotale/genitale, confrontate *Tre Sferette* con l'opera del 1982 *Scrotospettiva* (ill. p. 110), assai più sintetica e "sbarazzina", in cui un semplice foglio accartocciato pronto per essere gettato via è diventato un'opera d'arte.

E' noto che alcune correnti del Pensiero contemporaneo hanno analizzato e propugnato la frantumazione dell'Io, lo sparpagliamento molteplice della coscienza: dal "soggetto scisso" di Lacan alla sua totale dissoluzione, con Deleuze. Certo, qui parliamo di arte visiva e non di filosofia, ma è su questi crinali che Corte si è formato. Di fatto, la "schizofrenia" creativa è ormai una sua pratica abituale. Ricordate? Già dal suo esordio con le *250 Mele Marce* egli inscena la parodia del pittore "impiegato del pennello", che non si mette mai in discussione, specializzato in un unico, riconoscibile tipo di quadro proposto con minime variazioni per un mercato dell'arte che cerca rassicurazioni. Corte non dà rassicurazioni. Ma in lui, nonostante la molteplicità delle forme, l'ispirazione proveniente dal "lato oscuro" resta invariata nel tempo e quindi non si può parlare di semplice eclettismo; non è nemmeno esatto suggerire, come è stato fatto, che questa caratteristica origini da fattori generazionali comuni ad artisti nati negli anni '60 e cresciuti con lo zapping televisivo. Nel caso di Corte si tratta di cortocircuiti neurali prodotti dal flusso della vita che travolge l'artista. C'è, di certo, la spinta a sperimentare tutto, a rischiare tutto; peraltro, ciò non implica affatto una sopravvivenza dell'antiquato concetto Arte = Vita.

Affermando con una certa semplificazione che vi sia una analogia di funzionamento tra le cellule cerebrali e i chip del computer, si potrebbe dire che Corte preavverta, già dai primi anni '80, quel tipo di cultura estetica tentacolare, ipertestuale (vedi *Homevideo*), basata sui rapidi spostamenti nel sistema ramificato e imprevedibile dei link: una cultura che chiede al pubblico un rapporto interattivo (molte opere di Corte sollecitano l'intervento fisico e mentale del pubblico) e non solo di ricezione passiva di programmi "per il grosso pubblico" (come invece avviene nella fruizione televisiva), e che diverrà il patrimonio linguistico della "Generazione Internet".

Di fatto Corte attraversa, in modo onnivoro e frenetico, stili e tecniche senza soffermarsi e senza ripetersi. Ma al tempo stesso dimostrando da subito, magicamente, perfetta padronanza di ogni mezzo adottato, re-inventato, stravolto, nuovo o vecchio, artigianale o tecnologico che sia. Corte la ritiene una strategia vitale in una società culturale dominata da un continuo bombardamento di informazioni, suggestioni, stimoli, segnali. E la sua attitudine al rifiuto di ogni inquadramento, di ogni definizione, di ogni catalogazione conclusiva, di ogni "sistemazione" anche economica («Scommetto che stai per chiedermi come faccio a campare» dice il personaggio-Corte a un perplesso Gary Splitter in visita al suo studio nel già citato fumetto) fa in modo che l'artista sia sempre portatore di uno sguardo critico nei confronti di tale sistema culturale. Le sue opere non sono mai compiacenti di esistere ma si presentano come diagnosi di una malattia («Ogni *riempimento* dello spazio da parte dell'opera d'arte rivela un *vuoto* vertiginoso altrove, in qualche altro settore della Società», E.C. 1990).

Dalla schizofrenia estetica alla metafora della catastrofe antropologica e comunicativa, il passo è breve: in tale chiave va visto l'interesse dell'artista, a partire dal 1996, per *Maskon* e *Anthrocon*, in cui atomizzazione della personalità, condizionamenti culturali, rimozione e mascheramento vanno a braccetto. Questo interesse si concretizza, negli anni, attraverso un cospicuo numero di disegni. La parola "Maskon" (dall'unione di mask + convention) designa l'attitudine di folti gruppi di persone a riunirsi e travestirsi fin nei minimi particolari da Lolite dei fumetti manga giapponesi.

Questa "moda" nasce e si incrementa ovviamente in Giappone ed è il culmine di una situazione psicologica in cui si sono sviluppati anche i cosiddetti *Otaku* (giovani "intossicati" da un'unica passione consumistica che governa le loro vite) e che porta ad un totale mescolamento tra la realtà e il mondo illusorio degli oggetti di consumo. Le romantiche o fantascientifiche eroine dei manga assurgono a vita propria spingendo i loro fans e seguaci, soprattutto maschili, a impersonarle nel corpo, tramite la maschera, e nell'anima. Queste maschere sono costosi feticci prodotti da ditte specializzate o fatti in casa dagli stessi appassionati, e sono corredate da adeguati costumi sempre precisi nei minimi dettagli, che non lasciano scoperto un solo punto del corpo. Non è un fenomeno epidermico o relativo unicamente all'ambito degli svaghi o passatempi, ma nasconde un aspetto più ossessivo, una identificazione schizoide, un annullamento della propria persona.

Si potrebbe accusare lo sguardo dell'artista, ancora troppo "occidentale", di un caricamento di aspetti morbosi che comunque egli non giudica deteriori bensì fecondi per la propria arte. Però ci sembra che Corte non esprima drastici giudizi, prende solo atto del fenomeno in sé. Rifiuto di crescere, transessualità sublimata, feticismo, recupero di un erotismo rimosso… ma l'interesse dell'artista, se ben stimolato, passa sempre dal fenomeno psicologico al fenomeno sociale, non rimane mai preso nelle maglie del compiacimento introspettivo. Occorre ricordare che già nei primi anni '90 Corte aveva prodotto alcune serie di opere pittoriche, in formato medio-piccolo, dedicate alle "fissazioni" mediatiche caratteristiche di una cultura giapponese contemporanea che da sempre esercita un fascino sull'artista, abituato ad uno sguardo a 360° sui fenomeni estetici della sua epoca. Questi tre gruppi di opere si intitolano *Aidoru*, *Onapetto* e *Bishonen*, ossia tre tipologie dei personaggi dei manga da cui dipendono manifestazioni di scissione patologica tra realtà concreta e fantasia adolescenziale. Prefigurano una mutazione antropologica e neurale delle generazioni di giovani degli anni '90, i cosiddetti *Shinjinrui* ("Nuova Razza Umana").

"Anthrocon" (anthropomorphs-convention) è invece un appuntamento annuale in alcune città americane (Albany, Philadelphia, ecc.) da cui è nata una situazione e un gusto analogo al Maskon, diffusosi in tutto il mondo. Si tratta di incontri tra individui che condividono la passione, dai latenti risvolti erotici, di travestirsi da animali pelosi antropomorfi. In questo caso c'è un transfert di personalità forse minore rispetto al Maskon, mentre è più ampia la gamma di possibilità dei camuffamenti (svariate tipologie di animali che possono nascondere/rivelare altrettanti aspetti della personalità di chi le impersona). Corte dà una lettura di Anthrocon come fosse una setta iniziatica portatrice di rituali simbolici in cui inserire elementi del proprio universo visivo.

Dunque Corte prontamente realizza una serie di disegni e pitture intitolate a *Maskon* e *Anthrocon* (ill. pp. 230-233), e non si ferma lì, decidendo di inventare lui stesso un nuovo *fenomeno sociale*, una modalità di travestimento come sublimazione erotica da promuovere e caldeggiare. Nasce così nel 1998 *Intericon* (interiors + convention), la pratica di travestirsi da mobili e oggetti d'arredamento d'interni e consumare i propri sterili incontri sensuali nell'immobilità più assoluta. Decantata da Corte in vari disegni (ill. pp. 234-239) e video, e già consistente di molti adepti e amateur, Intericon ha Roma come centro di diffusione. Capitare nel mezzo di un meeting di Intericon vuol dire aggirarsi nella penombra di quelli che a prima vista possono sembrare anonimi appartamenti ammobiliati, per poi rendersi conto – con un capovolgimento del concetto di "nonluogo" coniato da Marc Augè – che mobili e suppellettili sono ancora una volta *maschere*, sofisticati costumi che nascondono gli statici e appartati partecipanti, percepibili solo dall'ansimare rauco per la fatica da immobilità forzata e per la crescente eccitazione… ecco una interessante variazione sul tema gramsciano dell'artista che deve "organizzare" oltre che creare.

I disegni realizzati da Corte per la serie *Intericon* vanno dal 1998 al 2006 e sono eseguiti in prevalenza a carboncino su carta, o su cartone tratto da scatoloni da imballaggio. Corte tende a evitare il realismo o l'illustrazione pedissequa della realtà, e il disegno spesso segue schemi che includono elementi figurativi, anche fumettistici, ma li contamina con varianti grafiche astratte e informali fino a giungere, nel tempo, a una sintesi di rappresentazione non facile da classificare in cui comunque l'occhio si smarrisce. Ciò nonostante è possibile riconoscere tutti i soggetti che rappresentano Intericon: corpi anonimi, immobili, come paralizzati dallo sforzo di mimetizzarsi tra i canonici oggetti d'arredamento di una casa: tavoli, lampadari, elettrodomestici, tappeti, divani, specchiere, quadri, strumenti musicali (non sono disdegnati i modi più improbabili, come quello che diventa il simbolo stesso dell'intera iniziativa: travestirsi da parete della stanza facendosi rivestire di carta da parati e "mummificandosi" al muro). Osservando con cura le loro fattezze è anche possibile individuare le singole persone che Corte ritrae nell'atto di praticare gli immoti riti di Intericon: a volte si tratta di facce note dell'ambiente artistico e culturale italiano, frequentatori o sostenitori del lavoro dell'artista.

Il cartone da imballaggio su cui i disegni vengono realizzati non è nuovo di zecca ma in molti casi è appartenuto a homeless o clochard che lo utilizzavano per proteggersi dal freddo, oppure si tratta di fogli di cartone adoperati da extracomunitari, venditori di minutaglia per la strada, come tappeto per la loro mercanzia. L'homeless o il lavoratore immigrato, e quindi apolide, appaiono paradossi viventi nel momento in cui creano un cortocircuito – nel senso che evidenziano uno *squilibrio* sociale – con l'idea di travestirsi da arredamento d'interni come pratica di piacere libidinale; d'altronde anche il cartone degli scatoloni è vagolante e nomade. Questo cartone dall'aspetto "vissuto", oltre ad essere stampato con indicazioni tecniche di fabbricazione e a mostrare scritte manuali da parte di chi l'ha adoperato quando era sotto forma di scatolone, mostra evidenti segni di sporcizia, strappi, tracce e macchie di vario tipo, e tutto viene alla fine piegato ad un uso espressivo e incorporato nell'opera. Così il disegno diventa il campo di battaglia privilegiato della vita e dell'arte. Ecco: emerge a tratti il virtuosismo grafico che è da sempre uno dei "doni naturali" dell'arte di Corte, ma è una "soddisfazione" visiva che viene subito contraddetta dal calcolato sfaldarsi dell'immagine nella lacerazione del cartone o nel grumo immondo di lordura.

Corte si procura questo cartone spiegando l'uso che ne vuole fare ai proprietari, agli homeless o ai venditori da strada, e comprandolo da loro secondo un prezzo concordato. I clochard a Roma sono spesso artisti essi stessi quindi non ha difficoltà a far capire il suo progetto, ma il cartone proviene anche da altre città europee in cui gli capita di soggiornare. In questo caso è interessante notare come l'aspetto del cartone cambi da città a città, non solo per le scritte e indicazioni tecniche che vi sono stampate sopra, ma per la tipologia di sporcizia e untume che vi viene depositato dall'uomo col tempo. E anche questi sono elementi che determinano le molte varianti dei disegni della serie *Intericon*.

A volte il disegno viene fatto emergere non col carboncino o matita ma con la gomma da cancellare tramite "ripulitura" dello strato di sporco e untume del cartone. Il disegno, più che l'atto del "dipingere", si mostra qui come una delle linee-guida del lavoro dell'artista, anche se in modo sommesso e sotterraneo. Bisognerebbe dedicare una trattazione a parte all'uso continuo seppur "deviante" che Corte fa del disegno su carta (cf. ill. pp. 90 e 240-243). Ma il disegno a mano libera rimane il modo più personale e immediato attraverso cui la mente visualizza un'idea del reale percepita attraverso lo sguardo.

Il gusto del paradosso spinto fino al collasso estetico è ben rappresentato da *Videoache*, un progetto video che dovrebbe rappresentare un mondo parallelo al nostro ma governato da un'unica legge: quella della *sofferenza*. Nel mondo di *Videoache* (che è proprio quello su cui aleggia la purulenta Divinità Nasale di *Tre Cilindri*) ogni cosa trasuda sofferenza. Si nasce nel dolore, si vive nel tormento e si muore urlando. Ma a rappresentare questa condizione non sono i corpi umani, totalmente rimossi, bensì gli oggetti, le cose d'uso quotidiano rese "viventi" e che presentano, mediante accorgimenti visivi, tratti espressivi e caratteristiche antropomorfe. Qui si è già oltre *Intericon*, in cui i corpi si camuffavano da oggetti nell'aspirazione al piacere, e giungiamo a una dimensione in cui abbiamo oggetti camuffati da corpi nell'espressione del dolore.

Il corpo umano viene rimosso del tutto perché Corte è ormai distante dalle attitudini Posthuman: egli è interessato da sempre alla dimensione *neurale* dell'arte e tutta la sua attività appare costruita sul modello delle labirintiche circonvoluzioni del cervello. In *Videoache* la minuziosa descrizione del dolore invade persino *l'atto stesso di registrare meccanicamente le immagini delle varie scene* tramite una cinepresa (ulteriore oggetto/personaggio che popola questo mondo parallelo). Infatti, l'azione della luce, che impressiona gli strati al nitrato d'argento di cui è rivestita la pellicola vergine della cinepresa, definendo la formazione dell'immagine produce corrosione, visibile strazio, urlante dolore. La sofferenza caratterizza l'attività di una psiche che combatte, crea, distrugge, altera, ristabilisce. Dipendente in modo patologico dalla facoltà della vista, dal proprio bulbo oculare (ricordiamoci *Penta-Portraits*), senza possibilità di scampo, l'artista visivo ci fornisce ancora una sommessa chiave di lettura del suo destino con l'equazione *percezione dell'immagine = dolore*.

Videoache rimane tutt'oggi un progetto ancora incompiuto e come tale metafora esso stesso della tribolazione creativa. «Ho un concetto ancora troppo sintomatico del dolore. Mi occorre tempo per sedimentare la casistica dei contrappunti», ha affermato Corte, qualsiasi cosa ciò voglia dire. Ma il vero paradosso si esprime nel fatto che non abbiamo *Videoache* come prodotto finito ma ne esiste un "Making of…", ed è tramite questo che possiamo ricostruire il progetto originario nella sua completezza. *The Making of Videoache* è un video che segue l'artista nel suo vagare tra America ed Europa e "illustra" con sottotitoli ed espedienti di montaggio i processi psicologici relativi all'ideazione del progetto ("vacu-video" è la formula con cui Corte definisce questa sorta di documentario in progress; ill. pp. 224-227), in cui egli riesce a cogliere con acutezza e spirito d'anticipazione l'opprimente inquietudine e il senso di incombenza del momento storico appena precedente l'attacco dell'11 settembre alle Torri gemelle (è ancora il concetto di "celebrazione commemorativa anticipata"). A 36 anni, l'artista affronta la sua fase più introspettiva, e tenta di proiettarla sulla realtà circostante.

Oltre a *The Making of…*, troviamo i gadgets e le opere d'arte derivate dal non finito *Videoache*. La procedura della "proposta sul mercato" è rovesciata (come le Clessidre dei quadri anni '80). L'opera *Storyboard*, per esempio (ill. p. 229), nasce in origine come un "personaggio" di *Videoache* (una botola iperrealistica collocata in una cripta, che "parla" aprendosi e chiudendosi come una bocca, i cui cardini e maniglia sono altrettanti personaggi dalla vita propria) e poi diventa quadro a sé stante su cui l'artista ha disegnato appunti e bozzetti di sequenze sceniche come in un provvisorio story-board del video stesso. E' un'opera, lo *Storyboard*, che rappresenta bene uno dei due principali "orientamenti" tecnici dei lavori di Corte, quello in cui si evidenzia l'aspetto di caducità e deterioramento temporale dei materiali costitutivi, anche artificiosamente invecchiati per esaltarne alcune caratteristiche espressive (compresi i buchi di tarlo finti). Questa tipologia convive col suo opposto, ovvero con opere caratterizzate dalla maniacale pulizia formale dove le patine risultano perfette, le verniciature meticolose, i volumi plastici privi di imperfezioni. Non vi è contraddizione tra i due aspetti, tra la materia incontaminata e quella rovinata dal tempo: lo sguardo spettrospettivo mescola e confonde i due momenti cronologici.

Il *Dolorama* poi, è un singolare gadget brevettato da Corte che consente un maggiore coinvolgimento degli spettatori durante la visione di *Videoache* (ill. p. 228). Si tratta di un rettangolino di plastica, prodotto in serie, che presenta su un lato dieci blister trasparenti dentro ai quali sono racchiusi piccoli oggetti appuntiti o taglienti come lamette, chiodi, spilli, spine, cocci di vetro o anche granuli di sale. La cosa funziona così: i vari Dolorama andrebbero distribuiti al pubblico prima della visione di *Videoache* (abbiamo detto che *Videoache* è progettato per mostrare il dolore nel suo compiersi). In pratica, durante la proiezione le scene più efficaci dovrebbero essere accompagnate dalla sovrimpressione, sulle immagini, di un numeretto progressivo da 1 a 10. Questi numeretti corrispondono alla numerazione sui blisters del Dolorama. All'apparire di un numero sullo schermo, lo spettatore dovrebbe aprire il blister del Dolorama col numero corrispondente e usare l'oggetto contenuto per provocarsi di volta in volta piccoli tagli e punture (alla fine, i granuli di sale da spargere sulle ferite completano l'opera). I differenti tipi di dolore, autoinflitto "a comando" in seguito all'apparizione dei numeretti, corrispondono alle dolorifiche scene nel video e permettono così l'immedesimazione totale nella fiction. E non possiamo che concludere questo viaggio spettrospettivo, almeno per ora, con l'immagine del variopinto Dolorama pronto ad invadere il mondo, prodotto a livello industriale come un multiplo infinito da regalare al pubblico dell'arte di Enrico Corte.

Un'ultima cosa. In questo volume abbiamo analizzato un centinaio di opere di Corte scelte a caso tra una produzione che ne conta più di millenovecento. Il che vuol dire che si potrebbero fare altri venti libri come questo, con in ognuno una selezione diversa di opere, e dunque dare venti ulteriori interpretazioni, tutte differenti, del lavoro dell'artista. Si potrebbero mescolare questi libri tutti assieme come un mazzo di carte da gioco, e iniziare una partita con la Storia. Ma il tempo dell'opera scorre simultaneamente avanti e indietro, secondo l'andamento propulsivo della mente. Il futuro diventa memoria, l'esperienza scopre il suo passato. E il presente rinasce nella perenne attualità della psiche. Ancora una volta la Storia si mostra come *autoritratto di un cervello*.

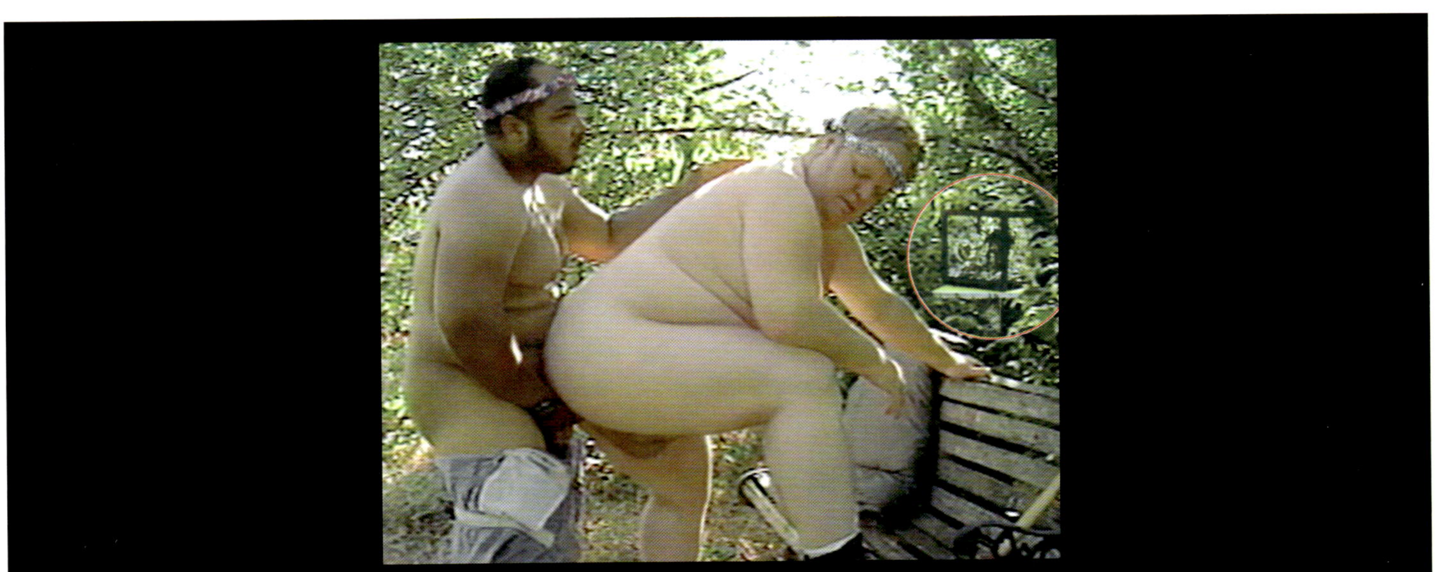

Botanical Rarities: the 20 Years After Celebration Party, 2001.
Cibachrome print from a series of 10 video stills.
31 x 39½" (78,7 x 100 cm).
GC 1403.

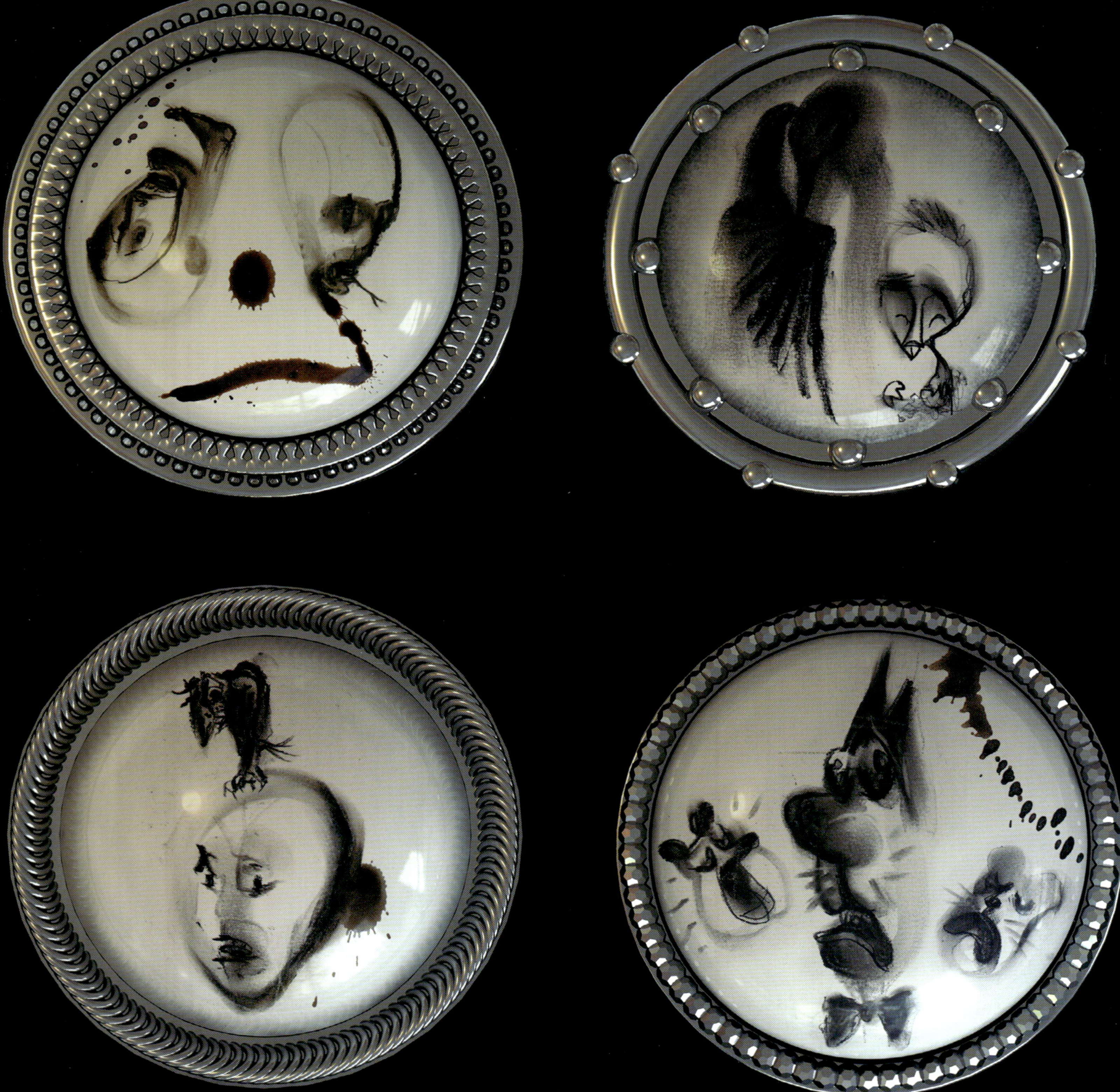

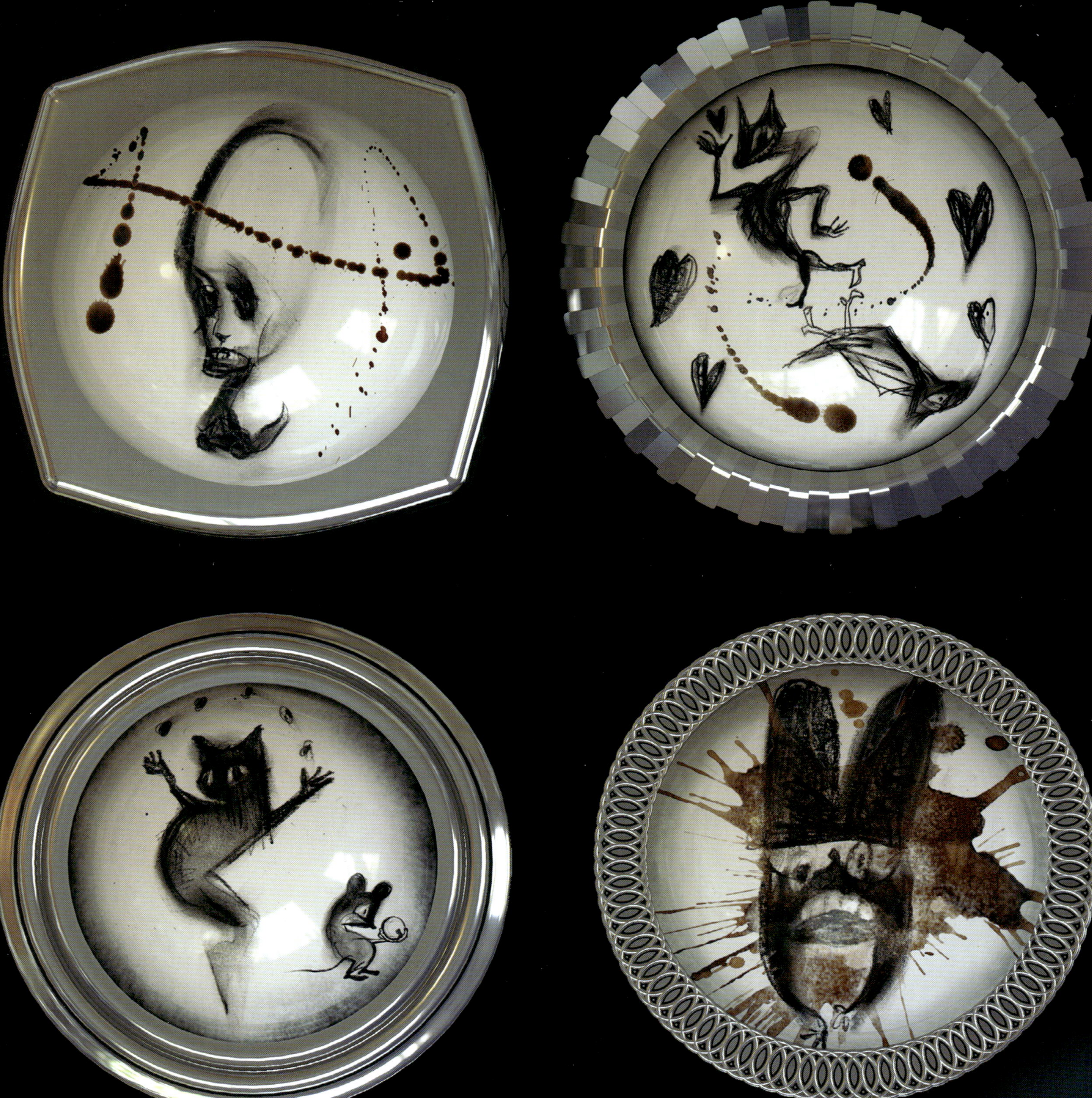

Four Settings at Dawn N°1 and *Four Settings at Dawn N° 2*, 2004. From the *Abstraction of the Void* series. Two lambda prints on cibachrome portraying 4+4 photo-ceramics from charcoal and ink drawings, with metal frames and natural light of sunrise. Cibachrome dimension: 39½ x 27½" each (100 x 70 cm); original dimension of each setting: diam. circa 2¾" (7 cm). GC 1593, 1594.